Education

The Practice and
Profession of Teaching

Education
The Practice and Profession of Teaching

Robert F. McNergney

University of Virginia

Joanne M. McNergney

University of Virginia

Upper Saddle River, New Jersey
Columbus, Ohio

Library of Congress Cataloging-in-Publication Data

McNergney, Robert F.
   Education : the practice and profession of teaching / Robert F. McNergney, Joanne M.
McNergney.—1st ed.
      p.   cm.
   Includes bibliographical references and index.
   ISBN-13: 978-0-205-60817-1 (alk. paper)
   ISBN-10: 0-205-60817-5 (alk. paper)
   1. Teaching—Vocational guidance—United States.   2. Education—United States.   I. Title.
   LB1775.2.M32   2008
   370.973—dc22
                                        2008015047

Credits appear on page 348, which constitutes an extension of the copyright page.

Acquisitions Editor: Meredith D. Fossel
Editorial Assistant: Maren Vigilante
Marketing Manager: Erica DeLuca
Production Editor: Annette Joseph
Editorial Production Service: Black Dot Group/NK Graphics
Composition Buyer: Linda Cox
Manufacturing Buyer: Megan Cochran
Electronic Composition: Black Dot Group/NK Graphics
Interior Design: Black Dot Group/NK Graphics
Cover Administrator: Elena Sidorova

This book was set in Sabon 10/12 by NK Graphics. It was printed and bound by WebCrafters. The cover was printed by
Phoenix Color Corporation/Hagerstown.

Pearson Education Ltd.
Pearson Education Singapore Pte. Ltd.
Pearson Education Canada, Ltd.
Pearson Education—Japan

Pearson Education Australia Pty. Limited
Pearson Education North Asia Ltd.
Pearson Educación de Mexico, S.A. de C.V.
Pearson Education Malaysia Pte. Ltd.

Merrill
is an imprint of

10 9 8 7 6 5 4 3 2 1
ISBN-13: 978-0-205-60817-1
ISBN-10: 0-205-60817-5

www.pearsonhighered.com

To our parents,
Quentin and Thelma McNergney,
and Elmore and Arvilla May,
and to our children,
Erin, Jonathan, Carrie, Andrew, and Mimi,
with love and respect.

Robert F. McNergney, professor in the Curry School of Education at the University of Virginia, has also been a faculty member at State University of New York, Potsdam, and University of Minnesota, Minneapolis. He has taught and coached in public schools in Iowa and Vermont. Co-author of three books and editor of four, his writing has appeared in the *Handbook of Research on Teacher Education, Educational Researcher, Journal of Teacher Education,* the *Washington Post,* and the *New York Times.* McNergney co-authored the Research Clues column for *NEA Today* for three years. He has chaired the Technology Committee for the American Association of Colleges for Teacher Education and has written the technology column for *AACTE Briefs.* He has served as secretary of Division K in the American Educational Research Association and as editor of the *Division K Newsletter.* He has chaired the Commission on Case-Method Teaching and Learning for the Association of Teacher Educators. McNergney teaches courses in foundations, evaluation, writing for publication, and research on teaching. He is co-founder and president of CaseNEX, LLC, a spin-off company from the University of Virginia that provides online professional development for teachers and school administrators.

Joanne M. McNergney is a professor in the Department of Curriculum, Instruction, and Special Education and Assistant Dean of Admissions at the Curry School of Education, University of Virginia. She teaches courses in curriculum, instruction, assessment, and educational foundations.

A former teacher in the Charlottesville Public Schools, Charlottesville, Virginia, Joanne McNergney has fifteen years' experience working with children in grades K-4. Her writings have been published in the *Journal of Personnel Evaluation in Education, Journal of Research and Development in Education, Journal of Information Technology for Teacher Education, Journal of Curriculum and Supervision,* and *Journal of Teacher Education.*

BRIEF CONTENTS

CONTENTS

The nature of classrooms and the demands on teachers are changing almost daily. Increasingly, teachers are being held accountable for results achieved by their students. Now more than ever future teachers must be able to hit the ground running as true education professionals— acquiring teaching knowledge and using it to solve real problems. The future of education in America belongs to those who can exercise their judgment intelligently and with courage to help others learn.

All professionals, regardless of their field, develop their expertise by acquiring and applying specialized knowledge. For teachers, this means mastering fundamental concepts of education in the United States and understanding the complexities of their own classrooms, schools, school districts, and communities. To do so teachers must understand the diversity of resources available to them and be able to employ these resources at appropriate times in appropriate ways.

Case Study: Scopes Revisited

"I never would've guessed that we'd be discussing the place of evolution in the school curriculum in this day and age," sighed Bill Calhoun, chairman of the science department at Pinckney High School. He was sitting the office of the district's curriculum coordinator, Lorna Kim. He put his cup of coffee on Lorna's desk. "These Intelligent Design Coalition folks have forced us to leap headlong into 1925, when William Jennings Bryan be Clarence Darrow out in the Scopes trial, and the jury decided against evolution. But what that trial really did was show everyone that evolution was *real* science, and it's been the centerpiece of our curriculum ever sin Frankly, I can't believe that we're spending time on this issue when there are so many more important issues on our agenda."

"I know what you mean, Bill," responded Lorna. "I've been so fixated on our primary-level reading scor that I didn't see this coming. But I should have—the whole creationism and intelligent design movement ha certainly been getting enough publicity lately. I guess because I don't see this community as particularly religious, I just didn't pay enough attention. But the trigger should have been when that senator from Pennsylvania, Santorum, actually sponsored an amendment to No Child Left Behind based on arguments about intelligent design. I think that lit the fire under the intelligent design proponents. The amendment did pass, but Santorum did get a statement inserted into the Conference Report.

Lorna picked up a paper from her desk and read:

The Conferees recognize that a quality science education should prepare students to distinguish the data and testable theories of science from religious or philosophical claims that are made in the name of science. Where topics are taught that may generate controversy (such as biological evolution), the curriculum should help students to understand the full range of scientific views that exist, why such topics may generate controversy, and how scientific disc

Bill sat back and folded his arms. "I can't teach somethi everything I believe. And I can't ask the other science teache

Lorna shook her head as she responded. "But I'm not s ing is, basically, you have to teach students how to analyze a need to understand other ways of thinking and be able to m creationism outright—just to acknowledge that the universe believe that some kind of intelligent force was at work in cre

Case Studies, Case Perspectives, and Questions for Reflection Research supports the notion that students of teaching can learn to apply foundational educational knowledge most readily through a case study method. Every chapter opens with a brief case or an authentic moment showing real teachers confronting important issues. And every chapter ends with Case Perspectives—comments from educators and other experts—that provide context for your own analysis of each case in Questions for Reflection. How might you respond to the situations that these teachers are facing?

Case Perspectives

Think back to the case that opened this chapter. Here are Janeeta's thoughts, as well as those of a second candidate faced with the same questions. These comments are designed to provide some context for your own thoughts about these questions.

CANDIDATE JANEETA MORRIS SHARES HER GREATEST FEARS AND HOPES. I have always been terrified of public speaking. How can a teacher be afraid to speak in front of others? I don't have the slightest idea. It makes no sense. I remind myself of the country-western star Mel Tillis. He sings like an angel, but he stutters so badly when he tries to talk that he is nearly unable to communicate.

I was fine during student teaching. But if I have to stand and deliver even brief comments to an audience of adults, I freeze. When I told my husband about it, he tried to help me imagine the worst-case scenario. "Even if things go badly," he asked, "how bad could it be?"

That prompted me to imagine myself in the auditorium on Parents' Night, jaw locking, eyes rolling back in my head as I fainted while falling sideways cracking the superintendent on top of his head with my jaw, knocking him senseless. How bad could it be, indeed!

I thanked my husband—and then enrolled in a public speak-

does not pay very much, but it seems like a lot to me to the kinds of jobs I have always had.

It is difficult to say what frightens me most. I hav afraid of hard work. My fiancé says that is what worr most—not the hard work but the fact that I do not s from it. I have a tendency to overdo things—work to too hard. My mother says that the definition of a per a person who takes pains . . . and gives them to oth like her in that regard. We both find it difficult to let end of the day.

When I think about what the new job will require really am concerned about the demands. I must thin students, the curriculum, parents, and so forth and still have time in the day to have a life of my own? I great teacher, but I want to get married, have my ow and spend time with them. I don't want to be so tire sumed by teaching that I have no energy to be a goo Maybe the fact that I will have the same schedule as will help.

I would like to be remembered as someone who and who helped others do the same. The old adage ing the world better than you found it really works fo want to be remembered as a fun-loving person, not

Cultural Awareness: Lessons Learned

The Golden Apple Awards: The Way It Spozed to Be
James Herndon Memorial Award goes to Bill Cosby, Barack Obama, and Henry Louis Gates, Jr. Cosby started it, Obama legitimized it, and Gates expanded on it—it being a dialogue within the African American community about the causes of the black/white achievement gap. Cosby's comments caused a stir. Some thought them the demeaning remarks of a rich man—and maybe an old man—who had forgotten what it was like to be young, black, and poor. Aaron McGruder appeared to mock these famous African Americans in his comic strip *The Boondocks*. Others thanked Cosby for injecting honest commentary into a bad situation. Gates asked, "Why the huge flack over Bill Cosby's insistence that black teenagers do their homework, stay in school, master standard English, and stop having babies? Any black person who frequents a barber shop or beauty parlor in the inner city knows that Mr. Cosby was only echoing sentiments widely shared in the black community."

Obama, the Democratic senator from Illinois, galvanized the Democratic National Convention with a speech of remarkable beauty and eloquence. About education he said, "Go into any inner-city neighborhood, and folks will tell you that government alone can't teach kids to learn. They know that parents have to parent, that children can't achieve unless we raise expectations and eradicate the slander that says a black youth with a book is acting white."

Gates, quoting his father, averred that too many black youths now think it is easier to become a professional athlete than a doctor or lawyer: "If our people studied calculus like we studied basketball, we'd be running M.I.T." Gates admired the "marvelously rich and inventive tongue" that is black vernacular, but he observed that "there's a language of the marketplace, too, and learning to speak that language has generally been a precondition of success, whoever you are. . . . These issues can be ticklish, no question, but they're badly served by silence and squeamishness."

Question for Reflection: Cosby, Gates, and Obama have learned that being quiet about the difficult challenges of educating and evaluating inner-city youth does not help. Why are people, regardless of their race or position, wary of discussing these issues?

Source: Bracey, G. W. (2004, October). The 14th Bracey report on the conditions of public education. *Phi Delta Kappan, 86*(2), 149–168.

Cultural Awareness: Lessons Learned
Every classroom is different from every other classroom in one way or another. Listen to stories from real teachers about what they have encountered—and what they have learned.

There is no one best way to help students learn. *Education: The Practice and Profession of Teaching* reinforces this important idea by introducing a wealth of knowledge via **case studies** and **case-based analyses.** These tools will help you apply what you learn to real life.

In addition to authentic classroom experiences in cases and case-based analyses, this text provides practical examples of technology use in the classroom, lessons teachers have learned about dealing with the influences of diversity and culture, and numerous parameters defining the legal context of teaching. Here's what you will find.

REFLECTIVE PRACTICE. A mini-case at the end of each chapter integrates the foregoing content and relates the issues raised to INTASC principles. You have opportunities to think critically about what you have learned. This capstone activity helps you apply professional knowledge to classroom contexts.

And, at the end of each Part,

- **Timelines** provide a snapshot of important educational events.
- **Online Activities** encourage you to investigate questions using the Internet.
- **Developing a Professional Portfolio** helps you plan and document your professional development.

Voices Pro and Con

ILLEGAL IMMIGRANTS

It is a mistake to assume that one person's thoughts and feelings apply to a whole group of people. Nonetheless, Jim, who works on the Iron Range in Minnesota, shares the sentiments of many others who fear the loss of jobs to cheap labor from outside the United States. On the other hand, Bruce, who works for the University of Minnesota, considers himself one of the "last liberals left standing." Both men have children in the public schools.

Jim:
This is the best nation on earth, and it is being overrun with illegal immigrants. Aliens come here from third-world countries and take our jobs and take advantage of educational and social services. They don't contribute—they only take.

Bruce:
Illegal immigrants work here and pay taxes here. That is good for everyone.

Jim:
Most aliens, legal or illegal, do not adopt the values of this nation. They come here and cling to their language and their customs. They keep to themselves; they do not fit in. They may not vote, but they are counted in the census, and politicians represent their interests. They exert unfair influence on our system of government.

Bruce:
Illegal immigrants eventually become assimilated into American culture. They work long and hard for their families. Parents sometimes may be slow to assimilate, but their children become fully integrated into society much more quickly and easily. The children speak English. They make public education richer, more diverse, and more fully representative of the work world all students will eventually enter.

Jim:
We can't afford to educate children who do not belong here. Policies of "don't ask, don't tell" with regard to determining whether children are here legally only

Voices Pro and Con
What are the hot topics, the big issues in education today? What are the arguments—then decide for yourself.

Technology in Practice

THINKING AND BEHAVING LIKE A PROFESSIONAL

Case method teaching and learning can help teachers bridge the gap between the way educational life is "supposed to be" and the way life actually plays out in schools and classrooms across the nation. A case method approach to developing one's teaching performance is similar to professional development in law, business, and medicine.

A case is a representation of real educational life that invites collaborative action. When cases are online, you can "travel" from schools in New York to schools in New Mexico with stops in between. You may not actually be able to visit a Cuban classroom in Havana, but you can go there online and build your knowledge of teaching and learning in another culture.

Researchers have shown that teachers who study cases are better able to recognize important instructional issues, design educational interventions to address them, and evaluate the results than teachers who do not.

See a video that depicts how case methods enhance teacher learning at www.casenex.com.

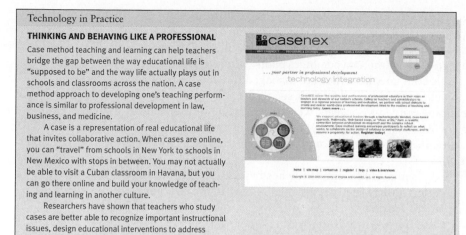

QUESTIONS FOR REFLECTION: Do you think case method teaching and learning is effective? Why or why not?

Technology in Practice
We are surrounded in almost every aspect of our lives by incredibly powerful technologies. But how can these technologies be used to enhance learning? These examples show how classroom teachers are using technology in creative ways.

How Is This Book Organized?

Education: The Practice and Profession of Teaching is organized into five parts. This organizational structure reflects a contemporary view of teaching as a profession. The demands in today's U.S. schools require future teachers both to possess foundational knowledge about education and teaching and to be able to apply it. Teachers must also understand links among fundamental topics as they are defined both locally and globally. The organization of this fifth edition will help you achieve these goals.

Part One, Teaching from the Inside Out, explains the foundations of teacher professionalism and includes an introduction to teaching as a profession, an overview of school and classroom challenges, and a discussion of the richness of classroom cultures.

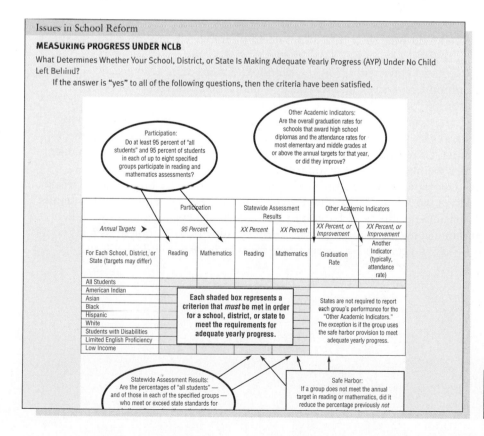

Issues in School Reform

MEASURING PROGRESS UNDER NCLB

What Determines Whether Your School, District, or State Is Making Adequate Yearly Progress (AYP) Under No Child Left Behind?

If the answer is "yes" to all of the following questions, then the criteria have been satisfied.

Issues in School Reform
Education is always changing—just like the society around it. This recurring feature highlights some major trends.

The chapters of Part Two, Our Educational Heritage, illustrate how history and philosophy have defined education in the United States and present the origins of ideas and values that make American education what it is today—and what it will be tomorrow.

Part Three, Education from the Outside In, explains why it is important for teachers to understand how schools compare, how they are managed by school leaders and governed by law, and why appropriate financing is critical to their success.

In Part Four, Helping Students Succeed, we explore the new emphasis on standards and assessment and how this affects the teaching profession, as well as how teachers integrate what they know about curriculum and instruction to increase the chances that students will succeed in their classrooms.

Finally, Part Five, A Connected Future, stretches beyond our borders to consider international and global education and anticipates an exciting future for education professionals in an increasingly interdependent world.

Throughout, the Case Studies that begin each chapter and the Case Perspectives and Reflective Activity that end them underline the goal of this book—to help you become a successful teacher in an ever more complex world.

Supplements for Instructors

- **Instructor's Resource Manual with Test Bank** is available online and includes a wealth of interesting ideas and activities designed to help instructors teach the course. Each chapter includes a chapter overview and an annotated lecture outline that provides examples, discussion questions, and student activities. The test bank includes hundreds of questions, including multiple choice questions, essay questions, case studies, and alternative assessments that are designed and correlated to reflect the content of the textbook.
- **Computerized Test Bank** is available online.

Acknowledgments

We thank the people who devoted their time and applied their expertise to this edition. The following reviewers provided suggestions along the way:

Colleen Hardy (Evangel University), Mickey Maddox (Athens State University), Anne L. Pierce (Hampton University), and Kandace Williams (The University of North Carolina at Charlotte).

We have always appreciated the support of our colleagues at Pearson. Nancy Forsyth, President, demands and gets the highest quality from everyone associated with this project. Steve Dragin, Executive Editor, has a keen sense of what readers want and need. We thank them and all the other members of the Pearson team.

We owe much to our students at the University of Virginia. They are bright, good people without whom our lives would be greatly diminished. Jane Cole helped with the gritty details on this edition. Other undergraduate and graduate students have kept us honest by challenging us to think and communicate clearly. Because they drop by unexpectedly, one of us feels compelled to clean his office on occasion—a consequence for which we are both thankful.

Education
*The Practice and
Profession of Teaching*

CHAPTER 1

A Teacher's Role

Case Study: Investigating Professionalism

"We need to split up the room. You work that side—over there where you see the National Education Association, the state department of education, and the credit union. I'll take the other side with TIAA-CREF, the teachers' insurance company, and the National Board for Professional Teaching Standards. We can pick up literature from everybody. Then let's meet back here at four o'clock and talk with the representatives from schools together," said Fatima. She and Maria were about to enter the auditorium to explore the Great American Teach-In, an annual event on campus sponsored by the university's career services.

"My advisor said that everybody who's anybody in the world of teaching and learning will be here today," noted Maria. "I want to know as soon as possible who's hiring teachers, and how much I'll make. The sooner I get some answers to those questions, the sooner I can start packing. Don't get me wrong—I love it here. It's just that I can't wait to start repaying my loans with money I make from doing something I've always wanted to do."

"I know what you mean," answered Fatima. "But the speaker in class last week sort of scared me when he talked about the great variation in beginning teachers' salaries. I want to be someplace where the money is good, but even more important, I want to be in a school where they support beginners. I'd hate to invest the next two years studying to be a teacher and then spend the first six months crying because I was lonely or couldn't get help when I needed it."

"Oh, right!" laughed Maria. "You're going to be fine. I just want to make sure I get a job—and it pays my bills. That's another thing I want to ask when we get to the schools—what kind of summer jobs look good on a résumé. I've been so focused on getting bills paid the last few summers, I've been temping for the phone company because the money is good—I can't afford to be a camp counselor like you."

"I don't think any of that makes any difference. I think they're looking more for what's on your academic record, and what you're interested in for the future. We should ask these people about professional growth opportunities—that was something the speaker mentioned too. So anyway, let's get going. Meet you back here at four!"

A double high-five, and they were on their way.

This chapter explores teaching as a profession and your place in it. As you read, think about why people teach, why they choose not to teach, how people become teachers, and what keeps them motivated.

Is Teaching a Profession?

You have spent many years as a student, but have you ever thought seriously about being a teacher, about what it means to be a *professional* in the field? Sometimes people have to "try it on for size" before they can really imagine themselves teaching. Use the short survey in Figure 1.1 to evaluate your own thoughts about being a teacher. These initial thoughts about teaching are likely to be as influential as any other information you find. **From your perspective, what does it mean to be a professional?**

Figure 1.1
What Are Your
Thoughts
about Being
a Teacher?

I want to have my summers off.

STRONGLY DISAGREE		1	2	3	4	5	STRONGLY AGREE

It is important that I have a predictable salary and health insurance.

STRONGLY DISAGREE		1	2	3	4	5	STRONGLY AGREE

I want to be respected.

STRONGLY DISAGREE		1	2	3	4	5	STRONGLY AGREE

I want the chance to be a leader.

STRONGLY DISAGREE		1	2	3	4	5	STRONGLY AGREE

I want to contribute to society.

STRONGLY DISAGREE		1	2	3	4	5	STRONGLY AGREE

I like the idea of having colleagues.

STRONGLY DISAGREE		1	2	3	4	5	STRONGLY AGREE

I want to help other people.

STRONGLY DISAGREE		1	2	3	4	5	STRONGLY AGREE

I can see myself getting higher college degrees.

STRONGLY DISAGREE		1	2	3	4	5	STRONGLY AGREE

I want to work with young people.

STRONGLY DISAGREE		1	2	3	4	5	STRONGLY AGREE

Teaching allows me to keep my career options open.

STRONGLY DISAGREE		1	2	3	4	5	STRONGLY AGREE

What is your average rating? What is most important or least important about the idea of being a teacher?

Teaching Is a Profession

Teaching, like medicine and law, can be thought of as a profession for a variety of reasons:

- *Teachers possess and can use specialized knowledge.* Teachers do not simply acquire knowledge of teaching and of one or more content areas. They apply what they know in real-life settings to improve people's lives.
- *Teachers must fulfill licensure requirements in order to practice.* They must demonstrate that they are knowledgeable and competent in order to earn a license, and they must update it periodically by staying informed of current trends in their fields. Teachers need at least a bachelor's degree, special preparation in their content areas, and a supervised internship to be licensed.
- *Teachers are decision makers.* Some people might argue that the standards and curricula with which teachers must work allow them little freedom or personal choice, but this is not true. Teachers are free to make many decisions about teaching, learning, and evaluating students.
- *Teachers get paid for their services.* Professionals get paid for what they know and what they can do. Professionals often volunteer or donate their services to worthy causes, but this is the exception, not the rule.
- *Teachers do not simply do a job; they leave a legacy.* Teachers influence people's expectations in the present, and they live on in others' memories and actions long after they have completed their work.
- *Teachers add intellectual value to an organization.* Schools staffed with accomplished professionals have greater capacity to produce desirable results—students who have been educated well—than schools short on professional talent.
- *Teachers operate according to a professional set of standards and ethics.*
- *Teachers are compelled or driven by a sense of responsibility to perform their work.*

Both the **American Federation of Teachers (AFT)** and the **National Education Association (NEA)**—professional organizations for teachers, sometimes called **teacher unions**—acknowledge in their codes of ethics teachers' responsibility to perform their work. The NEA's 1975 preamble to its Code of Ethics describes this responsibility as follows:

> The educator, believing in the worth and dignity of each human being, recognizes the supreme importance of the pursuit of truth, devotion to excellence, and the nurture of the democratic principles. Essential to these goals is the protection of freedom to learn and to teach and the guarantee of equal educational opportunity for all. The educator accepts the responsibility to adhere to the highest ethical standards.

Can you think of ways your teachers have demonstrated these standards?

Teaching Is a Semiprofession

Teaching is sometimes called a *semiprofession* because teachers do not enjoy the same privileges as some other professions. The reasons teaching might be described as a semiprofession include the following:

- *Possible lack of rigorous training.* When schools need teachers, requirements for preparation and licensure often take a back seat to filling empty slots. This can mean that inexperienced teachers are assigned to teach outside their areas of expertise with minimal or no supervision. Teacher shortages also can mean that new teachers participate in *alternative licensure* programs, which often do not expect the same length or level of professional preparation as do programs offered in colleges or universities. As a result, such programs reinforce the idea that training adds no value.

Natalia Mehlman, an investment-banking analyst who left her position to take a job as a teacher in a kindergarten through eighth grade school, quickly learned that teaching is harder than it seems. She said:

> I believed I was prepared to head a class, but a strong academic background and years in an office are not preparation for teaching. . . . As an untrained teacher, I made

my share of mistakes this year. I raised my voice at misbehaving students, trying to sound menacing, only to find that yelling was almost always ineffective. (Mehlman, 2002)

The fact that children can legally be homeschooled by their parents also reinforces the belief that teaching must not require any special ability.

- *Lack of control over entry and exit.* Unlike other professionals, teachers have little say about hiring or dismissing colleagues. School administrators and school boards—often without teacher input—make decisions about hiring. Administrators also often decide when to terminate a teacher's contract.
- *Lack of control over schedule and workload.* Teachers neither pick the students they teach nor set their work schedules. On average, full-time public school teachers are required to be at school thirty-three hours per week, but they are actually there about forty-five hours. They spend an extra twelve to thirteen hours each week on student-related activities. Generally, they teach about twenty-four students per class.

You may want to interview one or two teachers to learn more about areas in which they believe they have the greatest amount of influence or control. How much control do teachers have over selecting textbooks and other learning materials, determining content to be taught, selecting teaching techniques, evaluating and grading students, disciplining students, and determining how often and how much homework is assigned?

How Are Views of Teaching Changing?

The traditional view suggests that teachers must commit themselves to lifetime careers in classrooms to exhibit professional behavior. When college and university faculty who hold this view interview candidates for admission to teacher education programs, they often look for a commitment to the profession. They wonder whether applicants are serious about being teachers, or if they are applying because they don't know what else to do. Increasingly, however, this traditional view of teacher commitment is being challenged.

Critics of this view believe prospective teachers have been forced to make these commitments too early in their college careers, indeed too early in their lives. At age nineteen, twenty, or twenty-one, even reasonable, bright, emotionally mature people are not ready to commit themselves to a lifetime career path when so many competing career options are available. Some people may want to try teaching for a while, but then move on to another career. Or they may choose teaching as a second career. Jerry, formerly a software developer, put it this way:

I'm a career changer. I figured, why not explore a new field? . . . [I wanted to] make a difference in kids' lives and fulfill my larger mission in life, which is to bring more choices to people or to help people be more powerful in their own lives. And education is a pretty direct way of doing that. So I decided to take the plunge. (Peske, Liu, Johnson, Kauffman, & Kardos, 2001, p. 306)

Most teachers now close to retirement were committed to teaching as a lifelong career from the beginning. But the next generation of teachers includes many people like Jerry, who think of their careers and their commitment to teaching in different ways. Judging from this change, the implications for the profession seem clear:

If public education is to tap the talents and interests of this entire pool and schools are to recruit the best possible candidates into the classroom, policies must not require that all candidates conform to a single career pattern. In the end, a generic career structure is not likely to attract and retain enough good teachers. (Peske, Liu, Johnson, Kauffman, & Kardos, 2001, p. 306)

As people question the necessity of a long-term commitment, they emphasize the importance of teacher performance. That is, they are looking at what teachers do in their classrooms. In that sense teaching is becoming more like the other professions.

Traditional views of teaching are changing. Students studying to be teachers may decide to teach for only a few years, then change careers, whereas others may remain in the profession for their entire careers. What is your view?

A View of Teaching as Basic Professional Competence: INTASC

Education as a profession is often criticized for its lack of agreement about what knowledge a teacher must have and be able to apply. In recent years, however, a consensus has emerged in the form of the **Interstate New Teacher Assessment and Support Consortium Standards (INTASC)**. The **Council of Chief State School Officers**—state superintendents of public instruction—began the discussion about necessary knowledge, dispositions, and performances for all teachers, regardless of their subject areas (specialties). Representatives to INTASC from seventeen state education agencies then crafted the standard requirements for a beginning professional teacher.

Technology in Practice

THINKING AND BEHAVING LIKE A PROFESSIONAL

Case method teaching and learning can help teachers bridge the gap between the way educational life is "supposed to be" and the way life actually plays out in schools and classrooms across the nation. A case method approach to developing one's teaching performance is similar to professional development in law, business, and medicine.

A case is a representation of real educational life that invites collaborative action. When cases are online, you can "travel" from schools in New York to schools in New Mexico with stops in between. You may not actually be able to visit a Cuban classroom in Havana, but you can go there online and build your knowledge of teaching and learning in another culture.

Researchers have shown that teachers who study cases are better able to recognize important instructional issues, design educational interventions to address them, and evaluate the results than teachers who do not.

See a video that depicts how case methods enhance teacher learning at www.casenex.com.

QUESTIONS FOR REFLECTION: Do you think case method teaching and learning is effective? Why or why not?

Currently, the core standards are being translated into standards for teaching individual content areas. Underlying all the standards is the belief that children benefit from current knowledge about teaching and learning only if schools and education programs are held to the highest standards. A criticism of the standards is that they may overly regulate what and how teachers teach, preventing them from being autonomous, reflective practitioners.

For you to become more familiar with the standards, the Reflective Activity feature at the end of each chapter is correlated to an appropriate INTASC standard. (See page 19 for an example.)

What Career Issues Do Beginning Teachers Face?

Teachers at the beginning of their careers face some issues that more experienced teachers do not encounter. These include becoming licensed to teach, getting a first job, and successfully performing their responsibilities.

Teacher Licensure

Increasingly, people use the term **licensure** to mean the process of meeting basic requirements and standards for becoming a practicing teacher. A teacher, like a physician or lawyer, needs a license to practice. For years, the terms *licensure* and *certification* were used interchangeably in education. However, recently the terms **certification** and *certified* have been used to refer to experienced teachers who demonstrate teaching excellence as defined by the **National Board for Professional Teaching Standards (NBPTS)**. Created in 1987, the NBPTS is an independent, nonprofit, nonpartisan organization governed by a sixty-three-member board of directors, most of whom are teachers. Other board members include school administrators, school board leaders, and business and community members.

Teachers who meet NBPTS standards must enhance student learning and demonstrate the high level of knowledge, skills, and commitment reflected in the five core standards listed in Figure 1.2.

Being licensed does not suggest that a teacher is an expert or even exceptionally well qualified. In fact, processes of licensure are established and controlled by state governments to protect the public from harmful teaching practices backed by false claims of professional expertise. Prospective teachers have several government-approved options for obtaining teaching licenses.

APPROVED PROGRAMS Teaching licenses are typically granted in two ways: by transcript assessment and by completing an approved program. The transcript assessment process requires the candidate to submit his or her college transcript directly to the state education department. The department then compares the transcript to the state requirements and grants or denies the request for certification. The second approach requires the candidate to complete a teacher education program that has been approved or accredited by the state. (**Accreditation** is a process of review in which outside experts decide whether a program is worthy of preparing professionals.) Approved programs submit transcripts of all graduates, and the state grants licensure.

RECIPROCITY AGREEMENTS Licensure requirements for teachers differ from state to state. When a college or university student graduates from an accredited teacher education program, he or she receives licensure to teach in the state where the program is located. But many states recognize each other's licensure; that is, states have **reciprocity agreements** by which teachers licensed in one state are eligible for licensure in another state. Because states sometimes change their licensure requirements, the list of states having reciprocity agreements changes. Where reciprocity agreements do not exist, the additional requirements often can be fulfilled by taking some additional college courses.

ALTERNATIVE AND EMERGENCY LICENSURE In 2005, forty-seven states and the District of Columbia reported at least one route to **alternative licensure,** which is the approval to teach without having participated in a traditional, state-approved teacher education program. Alternative teacher licensure programs allow people with different educational backgrounds and from different walks of life, such as the military, liberal arts, or early retirement, to become teachers. Teachers licensed in this manner take education courses while they teach. On-the-job supervision, assistance, and formal instruction typically are provided for these new teachers.

Figure 1.2
NBPTS
Standards for
Accomplished
Teachers

Proposition #1: Teachers are Committed to Students and Their Learning:

(a) Teachers recognize individual differences in their students and adjust their practice accordingly.

(b) Teachers have an understanding of how students develop and learn.

(c) Teachers treat students equitably.

(d) Teachers' mission extends beyond developing the cognitive capacity of their students.

Proposition #2: Teachers Know the Subjects They Teach and How to Teach Those Subjects to Students:

(a) Teachers appreciate how knowledge in their subjects is created, organized, and linked to other disciplines.

(b) Teachers command specialized knowledge of how to convey a subject to students.

(c) Teachers generate multiple paths to knowledge.

Proposition #3: Teachers Are Responsible for Managing and Monitoring Student Learning:

(a) Teachers use multiple methods to meet their goals.

(b) Teachers orchestrate learning in group settings.

(c) Teachers place a premium on student engagement.

(d) Teachers regularly assess student progress.

(e) Teachers are mindful of their principal objectives.

Proposition #4: Teachers Think Systematically about Their Practice and Learn from Experience:

(a) Teachers are continually making difficult choices that test their judgment.

(b) Teachers seek the advice of others and draw on education research and scholarship to improve their practice.

Proposition #5: Teachers Are Members of Learning Communities:

(a) Teachers contribute to school effectiveness by collaborating with other professionals.

(b) Teachers work collaboratively with parents.

(c) Teachers take advantage of community resources.

Source: Reprinted with permission from the National Board for Professional Teaching Standards, What teachers should know and be able to do, www.nbpts.org. All rights reserved.

Since the early 1980s, more than 250,000 teachers have been licensed through alternative routes (Feistritzer, 2005).

Some states grant **emergency licensure** until requirements are met. When school superintendents are unable to find a licensed teacher to fill a position, they petition their state departments of education to hire an unlicensed person on an emergency basis. This strategy buys time for the person to become licensed or for the school district to find another teacher who possesses valid licensure.

In recent years, a philosophical war has been waged over the value of teacher education programs. In 2002, U.S. Secretary of Education Rod Paige called the traditional system "broken" (Glickman & Babyak, 2002). The secretary's report noted state-level problems with standards for teachers, existing licensure tests, burdensome requirements, and poor hiring practices. Policy advisor Rick Hess (2002) also has argued that existing systems of licensure should be "torn down" and replaced with background checks and tests of content knowledge.

Others have cautioned that the dismantling of traditional education programs may backfire. In a study of reading and mathematics gains of fourth- and fifth-grade students over a six-year period, researchers found that certified teachers who had completed approved teacher education programs consistently produced stronger achievement gains than uncertified teachers who had been recruited through Teach for America or other pathways (Darling-Hammond, Holtzman, Gatlin, & Heilig, 2005).

Do we need more or less teacher education, or is it just about right?

INTERNSHIPS FOR UNCERTIFIED TEACHERS The program Teach for America (TFA) provides college graduates who do not have teacher education backgrounds with the opportunity to become teachers. Wendy S. Kopp's senior thesis at Princeton University was the catalyst for starting this national teacher corps in 1989. The Teach for America program began with five hundred recruits from across the nation who were trained for eight weeks before assuming teaching responsibilities. In 2008, five thousand Teach for America corps members were teaching in more than twenty-six urban and rural regions across the country. Initially, funding from various foundations and corporations paid the salaries of TFA recruits. Today, their salaries are paid by the school systems where they work.

TROOPS TO TEACHERS In January 1994 the Department of Defense established the Troops to Teachers program. The program is designed to help Department of Defense and Department of Energy civilian employees affected by military reductions develop new careers in public education. Other goals are to provide positive role models for young people in schools and to help relieve teacher shortages, especially in math and science. First Lady Laura Bush helped make Troops to Teachers a visible priority during her husband's administration.

Availability of Jobs

Two factors influence the availability of teaching jobs: the number of properly qualified teachers available and the demand for these teachers. Demand for elementary and secondary teachers in any school year is determined by enrollment changes, class size policies, budget considerations, changes in methods for classifying and educating special education students, and job turnover due to retirement or attrition. Teacher attrition is the largest single factor influencing the demand for additional teachers in the nation's schools. Studies over the years indicate that about 20 percent of new teachers leave the profession within the first few years. Nonetheless, people teaching at the K–12 level are among the most stable of all employed graduates with respect to their occupations three years later (Henke & Zahn, 2001).

The supply of teachers is affected by salaries, educational and licensure requirements, interest in specific disciplines and geographical areas, the cost of living in some states, and other quality-of-life issues. The demand for teachers steadily increased through the turn of the century and is predicted to continue rising through 2014, primarily due to increases in school enrollment (U.S. Department of Education, 2005).

TEACHER SHORTAGES Why do the nation's large cities experience teacher shortages more acutely than other parts of the nation? Inner-city schools present special challenges. The working conditions often are difficult, and teaching opportunities in other settings often draw teachers away from cities. The South and West also have unmet needs for teachers because of population growth.

The need to provide bilingual education and special education services can also influence the demand for teachers. This demand varies by state and locality. The number of students with disabilities entering and leaving school systems and changes to criteria used to define specific disabilities can have a marked effect on demand for special education teachers. In some locations and in some specialties, the need for teachers is so great that school districts offer cash bonuses, higher salary ranges, and other types of pay increases to attract and keep new teachers. Needs are especially high in special education, foreign languages, mathematics, and the sciences.

About 12 percent of the nation's teachers work in private schools, including parochial (sectarian) schools affiliated with religious groups and independent (nonsectarian) schools (U.S. Department of Education, 2003). Catholic schools employ more teachers than any other type of private school because the Catholic system has the largest enrollment.

States do not require teachers in private schools to meet the same level of licensure as public school teachers. Because private schools do not receive money from the government, they are free from many state regulations governing curriculum and teaching. At the same time, because private schools are supported by private funds, average teaching salaries are far below teaching salaries in public schools. The average base salary for a teacher with a bachelor's degree in a private school is about $6,000 less than the starting salary for teachers in public schools.

PROJECTED STUDENT ENROLLMENTS AND SCHOOL BUDGETS How do enrollment trends influence the availability of jobs? In elementary schools, student numbers have been increasing steadily since the mid-1980s as a result of the "echo effect"; in other words, this is when the children of the baby-boom generation began entering school. Projections suggest that enrollment in kindergarten through eighth grade will continue to increase until 2014. In secondary schools, student numbers increased 18 percent between 1989 and 2002. Forecasters project enrollment in secondary schools to increase an additional 5 percent between 2002 and 2014 (U.S. Department of Education, 2005). Geographically, enrollment patterns will look different across regions, states, and communities. As previously mentioned, the greatest increases in public school enrollment will be in the South and West.

The federal government reports that by 2014 the student–teacher ratio in the nation's schools will be approximately 15 to 1 in public elementary and secondary schools. These figures are lower than actual class size, however, because the calculations include all the adults in schools, including many specialists, such as music, art, and physical education teachers, to mention three, who do not meet regularly with full classes. In 1993, for example, when the student–teacher ratio was a little over 17 to 1, the average class size was 24 (U.S. Department of Education, 2005).

School budgets determine the school's capacity for hiring personnel, and personnel costs require the most money in the budgets. Although considerations such as philosophy and mission drive budgets, when times are financially lean, boards of education and school administrators often fall back on pocketbook considerations. That is, when the budget is tight, positions are eliminated, most often through attrition.

Teacher Salaries

Why are direct comparisons between teachers' salaries and those of other professionals often misleading? Many educators argue that until teachers earn as much money as other professionals, they will always be relegated to subprofessional status. But these comparisons rarely account for benefits packages that may include health insurance, dental coverage, sick leave, summer breaks, workers' compensation, and retirement. Sometimes benefits for teachers are better than the benefits other professionals receive.

Another consideration that may be overlooked is that teachers typically do not invest as much money in their education as do other professionals, who must possess a graduate degree to begin practice. Someone earning a law degree, for example, will spend several extra years in school, which translates into increased schooling costs and a later start to a paying career (often referred to as *opportunity costs*). It can take many years for professionals with education beyond a bachelor's degree to recover out-of-pocket losses.

Finally, many educators do not work year-round. Many public school teachers work forty weeks per year, whereas professionals in other fields typically work fifty weeks per year, with only two weeks' vacation.

Are teachers as poorly paid as many people seem to believe? Given the importance of their work, their capacity to help society prevent problems, and the time and energy they devote to their work both during and after official business hours, the answer is clearly *yes*. In the early years of their careers, however, teachers may be better paid than some other professionals and people employed in highly skilled occupations.

The average salary in 2004 for beginning elementary and secondary teachers in public schools across the United States was $31,753 (American Federation of Teachers, 2007). Remember, this salary was earned over a period of no more than forty weeks, once vacations and summer break are counted. The average beginning teacher might be able to earn another 20 percent of his or her salary working another job during the summer—an additional $5,900 or so—thus increasing total yearly earnings to more than $35,000.

When considering salaries, it is important to keep them in perspective. For example, if you started teaching with a bachelor's degree in 2007 in Maryland's Montgomery County Public Schools, you would have earned a salary of $44,200 and benefits (Social Security, retirement, life insurance, health insurance) equivalent to 35 percent of your salary—$15,470 (Montgomery County Schools, 2008). By tacking on another 20 percent ($8,840) in the summer, you could have made the equivalent of $68,510.

Table 1.1

AVERAGE AND BEGINNING TEACHER SALARIES IN 2004–05 RANKED BY AVERAGE SALARY WITHIN REGION

State	Average Salary	Beginning Salary	State	Average Salary	Beginning Salary
NEW ENGLAND			**SOUTHEAST**		
Connecticut	$ 57,760	$ 39,259	Georgia	$ 46,437	$ 34,442
Rhode Island	$ 56,432	$ 33,815	Virginia	$ 45,377	$ 33,200
Massachusetts	$ 54,688	$ 35,421	North Carolina	$ 43,343	$ 27,944
Vermont	$ 44,346	$ 26,461	Florida	$ 43,095	$ 33,427
New Hampshire	$ 43,941	$ 28,279	South Carolina	$ 42,189	$ 28,568
Maine	$ 40,935	$ 26,643	Tennessee	$ 42,076	$ 32,369
			Arkansas	$ 41,489	$ 28,784
MID-ATLANTIC			Kentucky	$ 41,075	$ 30,619
New Jersey	$ 56,635	$ 38,408	Louisiana	$ 39,022	$ 31,298
New York	$ 55,665	$ 37,321	West Virginia	$ 38,404	$ 26,704
Pennsylvania	$ 53,281	$ 34,976	Mississippi	$ 38,212	$ 28,200
Delaware	$ 52,924	$ 35,854	Alabama	$ 38,186	$ 31,368
Maryland	$ 52,330	$ 37,125			
			ROCKY MOUNTAINS		
GREAT LAKES			Colorado	$ 43,965	$ 35,086
Illinois	$ 56,494	$ 37,500	Idaho	$ 40,864	$ 27,500
Michigan	$ 53,959	$ 35,557	Wyoming	$ 40,487	$ 31,481
Ohio	$ 49,438	$ 33,671	Montana	$ 38,485	$ 25,318
Minnesota	$ 47,411	$ 31,632	Utah	$ 37,006	$ 26,521
Indiana	$ 46,591	$ 30,844			
Wisconsin	$ 43,099	$ 25,222	**FAR WEST**		
			California	$ 57,604	$ 35,760
PLAINS			Alaska	$ 52,467	$ 38,657
Nebraska	$ 39,441	$ 29,303	Oregon	$ 48,320	$ 33,699
Kansas	$ 39,351	$ 27,840	Hawaii	$ 47,833	$ 35,816
Iowa	$ 39,284	$ 27,284	Washington	$ 45,722	$ 30,974
Missouri	$ 39,064	$ 29,281	Nevada	$ 43,212	$ 27,957
North Dakota	$ 36,449	$ 24,872			
South Dakota	$ 34,039	$ 26,111			
SOUTHWEST					
Texas	$ 41,009	$ 33,775			
New Mexico	$ 39,391	$ 33,730			
Arizona	$ 39,095	$ 30,404			
Oklahoma	$ 37,879	$ 29,174	**U.S. AVERAGE**	$ 47,602	$ 31,753

Source: Muir, E. et al. (2007). Salary and analysis of teacher salary trends, 2005. Washington, DC: American Federation of Teachers.

As illustrated in Table 1.1, beginning teachers' salaries and experienced teachers' salaries vary greatly by region of the country. Note the range of salaries and consider what the cost of living in New England states might be in comparison to the cost of living in the Plains region.

When people graduate from college with certification to teach school, they usually think more about where to live and work and less about the salary. Teachers take jobs because of the school, the teaching assignment, and colleagues. But they also consider other factors. For example, they want to get a job near family and friends on the West Coast, in a place where there is a social life, near a college or university, close to the ocean, not far from the mountains, within driving distance of the city, and so on. People consider the salary, but, interestingly, this is less important in the beginning than it is later in one's career.

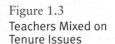

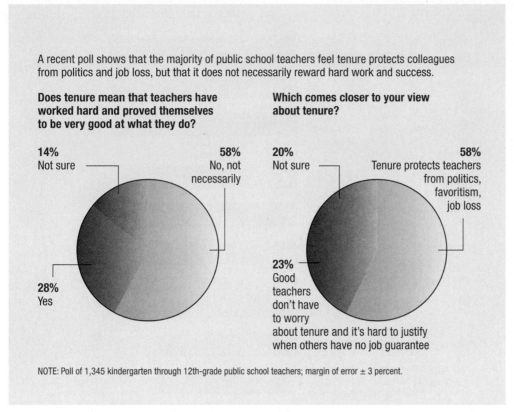

Source: Stand by me: What teachers really think about unions, merit pay and other professional matters. © Public Agenda 2003. No reproduction/distribution without permission. Available online at www.publicagenda.org.

Successfully Performing Responsibilities

Teachers at the beginning of their careers work with probationary status. If they perform to standard, they may be granted **tenure** (a continuing contract). In some school systems, tenure occurs automatically at the end of the probationary period; in other school systems, the school board determines whether tenure should be granted. Tenured teachers can be released only when "just cause," or good reason, can be demonstrated. On the other hand, most states permit nontenured teachers to be released without cause. Therefore, tenure gives a teacher some freedom from the fear of being fired. As illustrated in Figure 1.3, teachers have mixed feelings about tenure. **What is your impression of tenure?**

How Are Teachers Evaluated?

Some eight hundred survey respondents were asked to rank a number of factors they consider most important when determining the quality of a school. As illustrated in Figure 1.4, quality of the teaching force is extremely or very important, followed by information literacy rates and data on students' access to books and other curricula (Jacobson, 2002). To ensure that teachers are performing to standard, principals use two types of evaluation.

The most common type of evaluation, called **formative assessment,** is done to shape, form, and improve teachers' knowledge and behavior. Formative assessment is not concerned with making judgments about salary status or tenure. Instead, it is a helping process aimed at improving teaching techniques.

Evaluators doing a formative assessment often concentrate on teachers' in-class performance by collecting data on teacher–student interactions during instruction and by helping teachers

**Figure 1.4
Assessing the Quality
of Public Schools**
When asked what types of information they would need to gauge
school quality, poll respondents
put teacher-qualification data at
the top of the list.

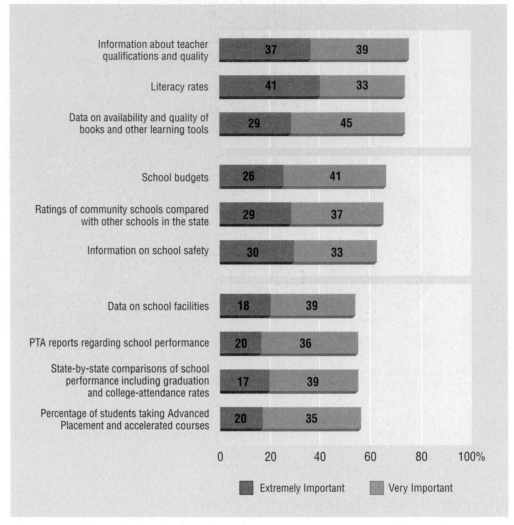

Source: Reprinted with permission from Public wants data on teacher quality, *Education Week,* vol. 21, No. 41, p. 5.
Courtesy of Public Education Network and *Education Week.*

perceive what is happening during instruction. Formative assessment is based on these philosophical beliefs:

1. Professional teachers constantly strive for continued individual excellence;
2. Given sufficient information, professional teachers can and will evaluate themselves and
   modify their performance as well as or better than others; and
3. The evaluation procedures provide feedback designed to help teachers improve their teaching
   (Barber, 1990, p. 217).

In contrast **summative assessments** collect and interpret data over a specified period of time to
evaluate such things as teachers' competence and teaching outcomes. The results of summative
assessments inform decisions about teachers' hiring, compensation, status, tenure, and termination.

Competency Testing

Why do all states require some form of competency testing for preservice teachers? States no
longer rely strictly on schools, colleges, and departments of education to provide evidence of
program quality. Competency tests are given to preservice teachers during the course of their
teaching program and are now being used to provide alternative measures of the program's
ability to prepare new teachers. Competency testing is useful because it provides perspectives on

the outcomes of teacher education beyond those offered by teacher education programs. To simplify, if prospective teachers do well on competency tests, teacher education programs can claim some of the credit for identifying and developing teaching talent. Likewise, when prospective teachers perform poorly on these tests, programs must take some of the blame.

According to their makers, competency tests simply reveal those who are minimally qualified to teach and say nothing about one's capacity to be an outstanding teacher. Nevertheless, the control of teacher education through competency tests is subtle but powerful. As preservice teachers exit their teaching programs, they must demonstrate the knowledge, skills, and dispositions that such tests claim to measure. Teacher education programs will continue to experience pressure to make sure that beginning teachers excel on these tests. In turn, teacher competency tests influence the curriculum of teacher education by focusing the program on the areas the tests measure.

Performance Evaluations of Teachers

Performance evaluations begin in field experiences, or practica, which are part of a variety of professional education courses, and they continue through **student teaching.** Student teaching involves planning, organizing, and providing instruction to students full time over a period of weeks, and it typically occurs at or near the end of a preservice teacher's program. To prepare preservice teachers for student teaching, most programs require them to engage in a variety of field experiences. The types of assignments vary, but they are generally structured to help preservice teachers become familiar with various kinds of classrooms and schools.

While they are student teaching, preservice teachers often keep journals in which they record information about students' reading levels; mathematics proficiencies; personal interests; and classroom rules, routines, and schedules. Preservice teachers also offer one-on-one tutoring sessions for students and assist teachers with classroom activities. Classroom teachers and college instructors work together to supervise student teachers' performances. **Why do you think many teachers remember their student teaching as one of the most valuable parts of their professional preparation?**

During student teaching, preservice teachers gradually assume more classroom responsibilities. They grade papers, teach parts of lessons designed by the classroom teacher (sometimes referred to as the supervising or cooperating teacher), plan for and engage in whole-class instruction for one or two class periods, and eventually assume responsibility for the whole day's instruction. Because of the demands of student teaching, preservice teachers seldom enroll in academic courses during these field placements. Many teacher education programs, however, require student teachers to attend weekly seminars held on a college or university campus or in classrooms of other student teachers. The seminars offer them opportunities to discuss problems of teaching and to share ideas about what works.

Performance evaluations use observations and evidence that attempt to provide **authentic assessments** of a teacher's knowledge and skills. Such assessments are evaluations that reflect people's true abilities to perform under real-life conditions. These assessments are concerned less with recognition and recall of facts and more with people's abilities to apply what they know. To make an authentic assessment, real information about what a teacher can do on the job must be obtained. One example of authentic assessment is videotaping teachers in the classroom for later performance analysis.

Portfolios

A **teacher portfolio,** a collection of artifacts that communicates a teacher's abilities to perform his or her job, is another example of an attempt to provide authentic assessment. A portfolio might contain tests and homework assignments the teacher gives students, samples of students' work, lesson plans, a videotape of a lesson, and so on. Teachers' portfolios provide opportunities for teachers to have input into their evaluations. They also offer excellent ways for a teacher to demonstrate his or her abilities to understand the links between educational theory and practice. What kind of material do you think would be most valuable to include in a teacher portfolio?

National Teacher Examinations: The Praxis Series

More than thirty states require candidates to take a national teacher examination as a measure of teacher competency before granting initial licensure. Most of these states use **The Praxis Series,** a series of tests developed and sold by the Educational Testing Service (ETS), the company that also prepares the common SAT and GRE tests, as well as other exams specific to professions. Praxis assesses skills and knowledge at each stage of a beginning teacher's career, from entry into teacher education to actual classroom performance. It measures teachers' basic skills in reading, writing, and mathematics, as well as their professional education and subject matter knowledge. The teaching skills measured include instructional planning, teaching, classroom management, and assessment of student learning.

How Are Teachers Supported and Rewarded?

All professionals—physicians, lawyers, teachers, and others—must demonstrate minimum competency levels to become licensed and certified to practice. But many drive themselves far beyond minimal expectations to excel in their fields, and teachers are no different. Many teachers take advantage of every possible opportunity to acquire and demonstrate increasing levels of skill and knowledge. Mentoring programs, career ladders, merit pay, national certification, and advanced college degrees offer such opportunities.

Cultural Awareness: Lessons Learned

Betsy Rogers, a twenty-year veteran from Alabama, was named National Teacher of the Year in 2003. When she returned to teaching a year later, Ms. Rogers elected to work at one of the neediest schools in Alabama. The experience was the beginning of her "metamorphosis." Believing she had the power to turn the school around, Ms. Rogers came to the school with a self-proclaimed Mighty Mouse attitude: "Here I come to save the day!" Teachers resented her attitude, and Ms. Rogers realized she knew nothing about what it means to work in a school marked by a culture of failure:

My first reality check came the day I had to attend a meeting of schools labeled Tier I. Previously this label had been High Priority School and before that Low Performing. When I was sitting in this room with the others from the area schools, I had several reactions. First, I was embarrassed to be there. I wanted to stand up and say, "This is my first year at this school, I did not do this!" Then I felt this great sense of frustration and I realized this is how the teachers in my school have felt for so long. I do not know how they have survived. I felt ashamed of what I expected from the teachers because I do not know if I could have

continued to work with this burden on me. Labeling a school as failing is devastating to one's soul and creates such a depressed climate. . . . I began to understand this negative climate takes its toll on you physically. . . .

Daily I question[ed] myself, "Am I the right person to work at this school? Can I really help and have [an] impact? Do I have what it takes? Can teachers who have been recognized for their work be accepted in hard-to-staff schools?" I do not know the answers to the questions, I just know that I want to be in this school. I want to help create a positive culture that will enable the students and teachers to overcome this label of failure. I also have learned the key to this change of climate lies within the teachers at my school, not me.

QUESTION FOR REFLECTION: What kinds of experiences have you had that might enable you to teach in an educational culture that is quite different from the one you have experienced?

Source: Rogers, B. (2005). Teacher of the Year. *Teacher Magazine.* Available online: http://blogs.edweek.org/teachers/brogers/.

Mentoring Programs

Does your state have a mentoring program for beginning teachers? Most states require mentoring or **induction programs** for new teachers for their first three years on the job. These programs support experienced teachers—mentors or coaches—to help beginning teachers adjust to full-time teaching. Mentoring programs call for high levels of collaboration between beginners and experienced teachers. Participants on both sides often share a vision of what constitutes good teaching and a commitment to continuing development. Policymakers promote such programs because of the fairly high rate of attrition during the first three years of teaching; the programs are a way of relieving pressure on beginning teachers (Little, 1990).

School leaders define mentoring in different ways. Some mentors support traditional teaching practices, and others foster change. Some mentoring programs avoid misunderstanding by clearly specifying how the program works. For instance, the Beginning Teacher Coaching Program of the Mt. Diablo School District in California and the Mt. Diablo Education Association spell out the responsibilities of the parties involved. They clearly state how and by whom full-time coaches are selected; how they are evaluated, rehired, and compensated; the eligibility of new teachers to participate in the program; how work schedules are developed; and the like (National Education Association, 1999).

Career Ladders and Merit Pay

Career ladder programs are examples of incentive programs for teachers. They offer status advancement, increased responsibility, and extra pay for exemplary teaching practice. Supporters of career ladder programs want teachers to examine their teaching, to think about alternative ways of teaching, and to focus on what students are learning. Career ladders typically acknowledge differences in beginners and master teachers. Dependent on school budgets, these programs come and go with the availability of funds to support them.

Like career ladders, **merit pay** is meant to encourage teachers to strive for excellence by rewarding outstanding performance. Merit pay plans award either bonuses (one-time cash awards) or raises (financial increases added to teachers' base salaries). Originating in the 1920s, various plans for awarding merit pay have been tried and usually abandoned.

Merit pay plans fail most often for three reasons. First, guidelines for identifying teachers of merit are difficult to design and implement. Second, until recently, teacher unions typically have opposed merit plans, because paying some teachers more might mean paying other teachers less. Third, particularly in difficult financial times, school leaders, parents, and citizens often make other demands on funds that might go to merit pay plans. Because merit plans are frequently unsuccessful, school systems often reward excellence informally through investments in professional development. In addition, public recognition of teaching excellence is provided through state and national teacher-of-the-year programs, private organizations, grant foundations, and the mass media. **Can you think of a fair way to recognize and reward teachers for being meritorious?**

National Certification

Currently, the term *certification* denotes outstanding performance. Candidates seeking NBPTS certification, or **national certification,** are evaluated on their knowledge of subjects, understanding of students and teaching, and actual classroom practice. To demonstrate their expertise, candidates complete a portfolio and then participate in a set of exercises designed to assess their knowledge of teaching and learning. The portfolio should include documentation of work both inside and outside the classroom. For example, candidates must provide videotapes of their interactions with students during instruction and samples of student work, as well as analyses of the videos and student products. Candidates also must describe their efforts to stretch beyond the classroom and involve parents and the larger community in the education of children. Teachers who successfully complete NBPTS requirements earn national certification, which is good for ten years. Depending on state and local policy, certified teachers can receive salary increases, license renewal exemptions, and public recognition.

How Do Teachers Demonstrate Professional Leadership?

Teachers demonstrate professional leadership by working with others and by modeling desirable behavior. Teachers lead students, assistants, aides, parent volunteers, and many others who have a stake in schools. Teachers chair school and community committees organized to solve problems and take advantage of opportunities. Teachers create curricula. They lead workshops for their colleagues and other members of their communities. Teachers study for advanced degrees. They blaze new technological paths in education. They run professional associations. And they do much more. The Teacher Leaders Network (www.teacherleaders.org/) provides a glimpse into how teachers across the nation exhibit and think about leadership in classrooms, schools, and communities. In her online diary, Helen Berg of St. Louis, Missouri, wonders about the meaning of "leadership" in both conventional and unconventional terms. She worries, for instance, about how important it is to "dress the part" of a leader. Does a teacher's wardrobe matter, and if so, to whom (Berg, 2004–2005)? **Do you think a teacher's personal appearance is important?**

Advanced College Degrees

Many teachers demonstrate intellectual leadership through additional schooling and advanced degrees. When they do so, teachers enhance their salaries and may assume new responsibilities in the hierarchy of school systems. Over 40 percent of teachers have master's degrees, about 5 percent have education specialist degrees, and less than 1 percent have doctorates (U.S. Department of Education, 2003).

Working with Professional Organizations

Teachers' identities are shaped in part by the associations to which they belong and by the people and organizations that publicly represent them. Professional organizations and associations educate members, lobby Congress and state legislatures on education issues, and offer a range of professional services.

Teachers, counselors, administrators, and other professionals in education often belong to professional associations based on their disciplines. These associations offer journals, conferences, and action committees designed to provide opportunities for interacting with others who have similar interests. The largest, most visible, and most powerful teachers' organizations are the National Education Association (NEA) and the American Federation of Teachers (AFT). Like labor unions, teacher unions protect members' rights to **collective bargaining** (negotiation of the professional rights and responsibilities of teachers as a group) in contract disputes and other job-related matters.

The National Education Association was founded in 1857 to advance the professionalism of teaching. It now boasts 2.6 million members, including teachers, school administrators, college and university faculty and students, guidance counselors, and librarians, as well as school secretaries, bus drivers, and custodians. Negotiating teacher salaries, reporting educational research, and supporting teachers' professional development are among the many services that the NEA provides. The NEA is one of the most effective lobbying organizations in the nation, stating views of educational matters to legislators in Washington, DC, in state capitols, and in communities across the country.

In 1916 the American Federation of Teachers was founded from a merger of twenty small teacher unions that formed after the turn of the century. More so than the NEA, the AFT has been closely allied with industrial labor unions and affiliated with the AFL–CIO (American Federation of Labor–Congress of Industrial Organizations). Like the AFL–CIO, in contract disputes the AFT has sometimes advocated withholding professional services through job actions: work slowdowns, sick-outs, and strikes. Today the AFT has more than 800,000 members, mostly in urban areas.

Teacher unions are controversial, and they are frequently criticized by outsiders for shielding their members from scrutiny and for maintaining the status quo. They are also praised, however, for exercising considerable power for the improvement of public education. Both the NEA and the AFT have helped to shape school programs to promote child welfare. Both have fought for and won increases in teachers' salaries and improvements in working conditions, have heightened public awareness about the importance of involving teachers in decision-making processes, and have helped cultivate the concept that teachers are professionals.

Meeting the Challenges of Professional Practice

Being a professional teacher means thinking on one's feet and performing in ways that support student learning. Figure 1.5 shows a model of this kind of professional practice.

A professional teacher recognizes teaching opportunities. These might be problems that need solutions, such as students' academic failure, social rejection, and emotional fragility. Or they might be opportunities to build on success, such as students' academic achievement, capacity for social inclusion, and emotional maturity. A professional perceives opportunities that increase students' chances to excel in the classroom.

A teacher–leader always considers the views of others who have a legitimate stake in a situation. For instance, parents and guardians hold strong values about what is right when it comes to their children. Other professionals can also provide objective perspectives. Thinking about issues from different points of view helps a teacher decide when and if a situation demands action.

A professional teacher must possess relevant knowledge and be able to apply it to improve a situation. Such knowledge forms the basis or rationale for teaching action. INTASC, NBPTS, Praxis, and other sources of professional knowledge exist for good reason—to guide teachers' actions and to inform their performances.

Nobody knows better than a teacher in the twenty-first century that results matter. Professionals are judged by the consequences of their actions—consequences often defined in terms of students. Did they learn? Did they enjoy the process? Were they motivated to dig deeper? Did they come back for more?

As teachers confront problems and opportunities, they rise to the occasion again and again. Many of them thrive on the challenges of professional practice, getting stronger and better over time. Teachers teach not only by sharing knowledge with their students but also by modeling what it looks like to learn.

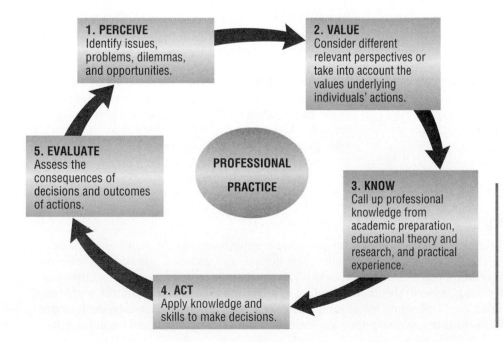

Figure 1.5
Reflective Teaching Process
It is important for teachers to be able to reflect on their work so they can develop their professional knowledge and skills over time. Why is it also important for teachers to be able to explain their methods and the reasons underlying their behaviors?

Case Perspectives

Think back to the case that opened this chapter. You are probably at about the same stage in your education as Fatima and Maria. You may have the same kind of questions: What should I look for in a first teaching position? What is most important to me? And how can I make myself a more attractive candidate to prospective employers? The following comments from two experienced educators are intended to provide some context for your thoughts on these questions.

LADONNA KENWORTH, A HIGH SCHOOL CHEMISTRY TEACHER WITH SOME TWENTY YEARS OF EXPERIENCE, OFFERS THESE WORDS OF WISDOM TO FATIMA AND MARIA: I am always impressed by job candidates who try to understand our school from our point of view. When you are seeking your first job, the tendency is to focus on factors that make a particular place desirable or undesirable from your own point of view—the salary, benefits, working conditions, and so forth. That makes sense, of course, but a little money one way or the other doesn't make that much difference once you are on the job. If you don't like the people you work with, if you don't like to go to work, all the money in the world is not going to make you happy.

I have advised beginning teachers through the years to do as much as they can before they hit the job market to test their "fit" in the profession. By that I mean, engage in as many education-related activities as possible. Volunteer to work in an after-school program. Tutor a student having difficulty in reading or math. Help a student register for college. Go to school board meetings. Sit in on a parent–teacher conference. And so on. See what if feels like to be on the other side of the desk. If you aren't excited or intrigued by these activities, you might want to rethink your career goals.

I have always really liked what I do. I think the work is important. When I started my first job, I developed a code to keep track of my feelings. At the end of every day I would mark an arrow up or down in my daily scheduler. Up meant I had a good day. Down . . . well you know. At the end of the first year I had so few down arrows that I decided to abandon the code. I knew this was the place for me. Now some twenty years later I still have the same feeling. I think a big part of my job satisfaction can be traced to the experiences I had in college that helped me make up my mind to become a teacher.

A PRINCIPAL FOR THE PAST TEN YEARS, LARRY JONQUITH THINKS BEGINNING TEACHERS SUCH AS MARIA AND FATIMA NEED TO FOCUS ON CREDENTIALS. One of my favorite maxims is "Keep your eye on your credentials." By that I mean, always be aware of what you have to offer others. It wouldn't matter if you were a doctor, a lawyer, or a fire chief, I would say the same thing. I encourage all students who are planning to become teachers to develop a résumé or a vita. If they don't know what is in a vita, I point them in the direction of their college placement office. If they don't have such an office, they can always ask a professor for help. A vita (that's the term you hear most often in education), is a record of your accomplishments—your degrees, work experience, honors, awards, special talents, and so forth.

When I read a vita from a job candidate, I am especially interested in things that set the person apart from others—a range of work and volunteer experiences, technology skills, ability to speak a foreign language, travel. Let me say a little more about work experience because that is especially important to me. If a person has been a camp counselor or a swimming instructor, that means he or she has worked with kids—a good sign. If a person has been a server at a restaurant, I'm also impressed. I was a server when I was young, and I know how challenging and rewarding it is to interact with the public. Some people might not be impressed to see that a young person has worked on a construction crew, but I know better. There is nothing quite like hard work to build character. If a person is a little older than the typical college graduate, there may be evidence of military service. I give that person special consideration. Aside from our moral obligation to veterans, I know what it means to be in the service. You train, you perform, you take orders, you give orders; in short, you grow up.

So keep your eye on your credentials. Your vita is not only a record of past accomplishments, it is also a plan for the future. Look for opportunities to make yourself a better person and better professional.

QUESTIONS FOR REFLECTION: What seems most important to you in seeking a first teaching position? Do you think these priorities might change as you continue through the program preparing you to teach? What do you think you might do to make yourself more attractive to prospective employers? ■

Summary

Teaching has been described as both a profession and a semiprofession. As views of teaching change, there is less emphasis on longevity in the profession and greater emphasis on performance in the classroom. People entering the field do so through approved programs or through transcript assessment. Some of the issues they face are getting a first job, successfully performing their responsibilities, and planning for advancement in the profession. Once established, beginning teachers demonstrate leadership through their involvement in professional organizations and by modeling desirable behavior on the job—recognizing problems and opportunities, considering values of stakeholders, calling up professional knowledge, applying this knowledge through action, and assessing the consequences of such action. The challenges of professional practice are opportunities for teachers to develop and refine their expertise so they can better meet the needs of students.

TERMS AND CONCEPTS

accreditation
alternative licensure
American Federation of Teachers (AFT)
authentic assessment
career ladder
certification
collective bargaining
Council of Chief State School Officers
emergency licensure
formative assessment
induction program
Interstate New Teacher Assessment and
    Support Consortium Standards (INTASC)

licensure
merit pay
National Board for Professional Teaching
    Standards (NBPTS)
national certification
National Education Association (NEA)
Praxis Series
reciprocity agreement
student teaching
summative assessment
teacher portfolio
teacher union
tenure

REFLECTIVE ACTIVITY: CHOOSING A TEACHING PATH

Reflective practice is an essential part of good teaching. Reflection is a process that includes making thoughtful decisions, understanding and articulating value structures, acting from knowledge, evaluating your actions and their effects, and sharing your reflections with colleagues. After reading the following scenario, respond to the questions below. The scenario reflects the INTASC Principle and Disposition at the end of this activity.

Renae Johnson was three weeks into her first teacher education course, and she was having second thoughts about her choice of secondary English as her licensure area. "I wish I could be as certain as you are about what I want to teach," she said to her friend, Nancy Hildebrand. "It's nice that there is flexibility in the teacher education program. Unfortunately, I may need more than one semester to decide on a major. The more I learn in class about the different paths teachers can take, the more confused I get!"

"Take it easy," advised Nancy. "I agree that the classroom teachers who have spoken to our group make every area of teaching sound appealing. But each speaker had different reasons for entering the profession, and at least one of them changed directions after entering the field. Remember? She was the one who started out as an elementary teacher and then became a gifted education teacher. According to her, all teachers take professional development classes, either through the school system or a university, so it is possible to add endorsements in other areas."

"You're right. I shouldn't get so worked up about this. I know I like working with teenagers, and I love English, but ever since I tutored in the after-school program, I have been thinking I might like to work with students with special needs—kids who really struggle in school. I think I'll talk to Dr. Brigham about the special education program to see if that might be the best fit for me. I should also find out how many English classes I would need to have if at some point I wanted to specialize in secondary English."

Decide 1. What areas of licensure is Renae considering? Is there demand for teachers in these areas in your own community?

Perceive and Value 2. What factors is Renae considering when trying to determine an area of licensure to pursue?

Know and Act 3. What do you know about licensure requirements in the state where you are hoping to teach? How difficult is it to add one or more areas of endorsement to your license?

Evaluate 4. What might you gain or lose by adding another teaching endorsement at this point in your program?

Discuss 5. What more does Renae need to know about teaching English and teaching special needs students that will help her make a decision?

INTASC Principle 1

The teacher understands the central concepts, tools of inquiry, and structures of the discipline(s) he or she teaches and can create learning experiences that make these aspects of the subject matter meaningful for students.

Disposition

The teacher has enthusiasm for the discipline(s) she teaches and sees connections to everyday life. (Interstate New Teacher Assessment and Support Consortium, 1992)

ADDITIONAL READINGS

Howe, R. (Ed.). (2004). *Training wheels for teachers: What I wish I had known my first 100 days on the job*. New York: Kaplan.

Intrator, S. M. (2002). *Stories of the courage to teach: Honoring the teacher's heart*. New York: J. Wiley.

National Center for Education Statistics (updated annually). *Condition of education*. Washington, DC: U.S. Department of Education. Available online: http://nces.ed.gov/.

Rogers, D. L., & Babinski, L. M. (2002). *From isolation to conversation: Supporting new teachers' development*. Albany, NY: State University of New York Press.

Stone, E. (2002). *A boy I once knew: What a teacher learned from her student*. Chapel Hill, NC: Algonquin Books.

Thompson, J. G. (2002). *First-year teacher's survival kit: Ready-to-use strategies, tools & activities for meeting the challenges of each school day*. Paramus, NJ: Center for Applied Research in Education.

WEB RESOURCES

www.aft.org/
The website for the American Federation of Teachers provides information about the organization and resources for teachers.

www.ed.gov/teachers/become/about/survivalguide/index.html
The Survival Guide for New Teachers is a resource for helping new teachers work effectively with veteran teachers, parents, principals, and teacher educators.

www.bls.gov/home.htm
This site includes an occupational handbook, developed by the U.S. Department of Labor, describing the conditions of teaching, job opportunities, and more.

www.nea.org/
The website for the National Education Association includes information about membership, services, current issues in education, and more.

www.ed.gov/pubs/FirstYear/
This website provides information about what to expect during your first year of teaching.

www.ccsso.org/
The website for the Council of Chief State School Officers houses INTASC standards.

Challenges Teachers and Schools Face

Case Study: School Violence

November 18

Kyle has been expelled for bringing a gun to school. I think it is somehow my fault.

Maria came up to me after class today and whispered that Kyle had a gun in his backpack. I thought she must be kidding, but I knew I needed to tell the administration about it no matter how unlikely it seemed.

I went to Irv's office. In the outer reception area, Jamey, Kyle's friend, was stapling papers together for the secretary. Silently, he watched me go in.

Irv sent for Kyle. Eventually there was a tentative knock at the door. Kyle came in. Irv sternly asked him to empty his bookbag: nothing. I felt huge relief. But the boy's humiliation made knots in my stomach. He didn't say a word or look at either of us.

Then, the assistant principal entered. She had searched Kyle's locker. The gun was there. It wasn't loaded, but that doesn't matter. The rumor is that Kyle bought it on the Internet using his father's credit card and that he had bullets at home.

Somehow I got through the rest of the school day. I don't know how long I had been sitting at my desk staring at my lessons plans for tomorrow when there was a knock on the door. It was Irv. He came in and folded himself down into a student desk in front of me. His voice was surprisingly gentle.

"Maggie, you should know. Maria came to my office this afternoon. Apparently last week, when they met to work on the debate project at the park, Jamey got angry with Kyle—just exploded—and beat Kyle up pretty badly. He even told Kyle he was going to kill him. Maria says Jamey has been trailing Kyle around for the past several days, even walking past his house late at night. Obviously, Kyle thought he needed the gun to protect himself. But, whatever the reason, there's nothing I can do. Automatic expulsion is district policy. The superintendent is unmoved. I've also suspended Jamey for the time being. There will be a school board hearing in two weeks."

It's late. I want to cry, but I can't. All I can think about is Kyle and Jamey and what I could have done to prevent this. Why didn't I see what was going on? What can I possibly do now?

This chapter describes some of the challenging circumstances students experience and how teachers and schools attempt to help students overcome these obstacles. Some problems students face are shaped in part by who they are—their health, attitudes, and beliefs. Other problems depend largely on the conditions in which they live—their homes, neighborhoods, and communities. To help young people succeed, teachers and schools often stretch beyond their traditional missions to involve parents, social agencies, and private businesses.

What Are Society's Expectations for Schools?

For many children, the years they spend in school are the best years of their lives. They interact with people who care about them and for them—people who help children to learn and to feel good about themselves and who nurture young people's hopes for the future.

Some critics, however, have argued that schools have taken on too many roles. Students attending school from the beginning of kindergarten to the completion of twelfth grade will have spent only about 9 percent of their lives in the classroom (Finn, 1991). Nonetheless, expectations for schools are many, as people increasingly look to schools to solve some of society's most difficult problems (see Figure 2.1). **Does society expect schools to do too much? Why or why not?**

Although many agencies address children's problems, the public supports schools with tax dollars, so people expect educators to help students succeed, regardless of the circumstances. More and more, teachers and schools are being called on to provide services far beyond the scope of the classroom. In addition to teaching students, schools also are expected to offer counseling and support services, extracurricular activities, and programs for advancing the health and welfare of students. In short, now more than ever, society expects schools to prepare children to be functioning members of society.

At the same time, the growing number of **at-risk students**—those unlikely to complete high school and likely to have a low socioeconomic status throughout life—presents unusually difficult challenges for educators. According to the U.S. Census Bureau, the following conditions suggest that students may be at varying levels of risk:

- Has at least one disability
- Retained in a grade at least once
- Speaks English less than "very well"
- Does not live with both parents
- Either parent emigrated in past five years
- Has a family income below the poverty threshold
- Neither parent/guardian employed (Kominski, Jamieson, & Martinez, 2001)

According to census data collected every ten years, at least 18 percent of all children (11 percent European Americans, 18 percent Asian and Pacific Islanders, 27 percent Hispanic Americans, and 34 percent African Americans) experience more than one of these risk factors. Among this 18 percent, young children are as likely as older ones to have multiple risk factors. In addition, the level of risk varies by the type of risk factor or factors. For example, students who have a disability or are retained (held back) are much more likely to be at risk than are students who speak English less than "very well." The children with the highest rates of multiple risks are from families with low incomes or families in which neither parent works. Over 80 percent of the children from these families have at least one other risk factor, and 56 percent of these children have three or more risk factors (Kominski, Jamieson, & Martinez, 2001).

Schools do their best, but eventually many at-risk students drop out of school altogether. In response, communities across the country have structured schools and proposed political initiatives to meet the challenge presented by school dropouts. School choice plans try to stimulate educators to make schools places where students want to stay. Some states even redraw school attendance zones (redistricting) in an attempt to prevent certain schools from becoming way stations where students pause briefly before dropping out. Efforts to equalize funding for public schools are also undertaken to help schools in poor areas reduce their dropout and failure rates. **What is society's responsibility to students at risk?**

Figure 2.1
Some Social Issues
Affecting Schools
Think of other issues that could
be added to this figure. How
might they influence teaching
and learning?

Figure 2.1
Some Social Issues
Affecting Schools
Think of other issues that could
be added to this figure. How
might they influence teaching
and learning?

How Does Poverty Place Students at Risk of School Failure?

The people who suffer most from poverty are children under the age of eighteen. Nearly 13 million children live in families that earn less than the 2006 federal poverty level of $20,650 (U.S. Census Bureau, 2007). This figure is calculated as three times the cost of a diet that meets minimum nutritional requirements for a family of two adults and two children. The figure does not include other living expenses, such as housing, transportation, and health care.

All racial and ethnic groups are represented in every socioeconomic level. Proportionately, there are more low-income children in minority families than in majority families. But in the general U.S. population (actual numbers, not percentages), many more European American than minority group children live in poverty. Most of these children live in rural areas.

Despite our wealth, living in the United States does not guarantee an escape from poverty. Our nation has a higher percentage of poor children than twelve European countries, Australia, and Canada (when poverty equals family income below half the national median). See the poverty rates in Figure 2.2. Even when using the U.S. Census definition of poverty as the minimum necessary for food, shelter, and clothing, the rate was 17.6 percent in 2003 (National School Boards Association, 2005).

A basic link exists between poverty and learning. Low-income communities often mean underfunded school districts and poorer schools in virtually every way. When child poverty and

Figure 2.2
Child Poverty Rates in 15 Countries in the 1990s
Percentage of children in poverty, defined as a family income below half the national median

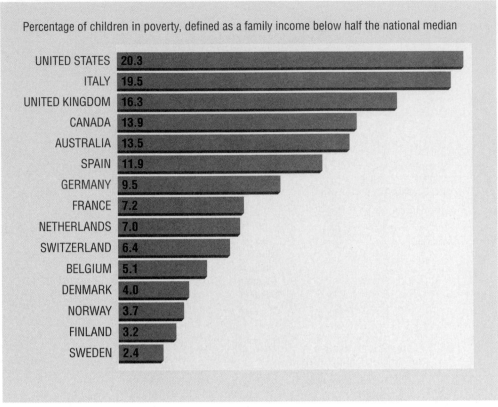

Percentage of children in poverty, defined as a family income below half the national median

Country	Percentage
UNITED STATES	20.3
ITALY	19.5
UNITED KINGDOM	16.3
CANADA	13.9
AUSTRALIA	13.5
SPAIN	11.9
GERMANY	9.5
FRANCE	7.2
NETHERLANDS	7.0
SWITZERLAND	6.4
BELGIUM	5.1
DENMARK	4.0
NORWAY	3.7
FINLAND	3.2
SWEDEN	2.4

Source: *Poor kids in a rich country* (© 2003 Russell Sage Foundation Publications), cited in *Education Vital Signs 2005* (© 2005 NSBA).

poor school funding are combined, effects on student performance can be substantial. Imagine a child who comes to school hungry and cannot concentrate in class. Now imagine that the classroom does not have computer equipment, current textbooks, and other necessary tools. **What kind of education will a student in poverty receive, when compared to a student from a wealthy family, attending a well-funded school?**

Interestingly, the effects of poverty may be moderated by the size of a school; that is, poverty does not appear to have the same negative effect on student achievement in small schools as it does in large schools. For example, Maine's smaller schools effectively reduce the negative influence of poverty on student achievement by 35 to 100 percent compared to larger schools, depending on testing grade and subject area, according to a new analysis by the Rural School and Community Trust (2005). **Although no one knows for certain why poverty may exhibit less power in small schools, can you imagine why this might be the case?**

Results of a study of migrant children indicate that socioeconomic status need not limit one's aspirations or level of achievement. The study found that when children have at least one parent who communicates high expectations for academic achievement, the children stay in school and perform well (Balli, 1996).

Although a positive family environment for learning is valuable for students, the indelible marks poverty leaves on people must not be overlooked. Some become trapped and embittered by poverty; others are resilient and motivated to defeat the circumstances in which they find themselves. In *Amazing Grace: The Lives of Children,* Jonathan Kozol (1995) described vividly what he learned in New York City about being poor.

The following day, I visit a soup kitchen where more than 200 people, about two thirds of whom are children, come to eat four times a week. The mothers of the children seem competitive, and almost frantic, to make sure their children get their share. A child I meet, a five-year-old boy named Emmanuel, tells me he's "in kiddie garden." His mother says he hasn't started yet, "He starts next year."

"You have to remember," says one of the priests with whom I share my thoughts about these meetings, "that for this little boy whom you have met, his life is just as important to him as your life is to you. No matter how insufficient or how shabby it may seem to some, it is the only one he has"—an obvious statement that upsets me deeply nonetheless. (Kozol, 1995, p. 70)

How might children in low-income neighborhoods get better schools?

How Can Schools Intervene to Help Students at Risk?

Education can foil the effects of poverty and help students at risk succeed in school and in life. The U.S. Department of Education found that the availability of free or low-cost education can lead to a reduction in welfare or public assistance programs. Furthermore, it has been found that people with more education rely less on welfare and public assistance than do people with less education.

The problems facing the young involve more than economics, however, and they are often interrelated. Many people therefore advocate comprehensive, integrated approaches to reduce the exposure of young people to high-risk settings. Such settings are characterized by poverty, substance abuse, parental neglect, and violence in many forms.

School counselors are a primary source for helping students cope with serious social and personal problems. In general, counselors try to improve self-esteem, but many also foster career awareness and offer support groups for children affected by divorce or students who need to work on study or social skills. High school counselors, in particular, focus on college or job counseling.

In 1964, funding from the National Defense Education Act (NDEA) extended counseling services beyond high schools to include elementary schools. This action acknowledged the importance of helping children succeed early in their educational careers, with the help defined increasingly in terms of preventing problems. Which of the following actions typically performed by school counselors do you believe are most important, and why?

1. Provide inservice training and consultation for teachers on preventing serious student problems;
2. Work with parents to promote understanding of child development;
3. Identify and refer children with developmental deficiencies or disabilities to others who can offer assistance; and
4. Help older children make connections between school and work.

For many children, these and other school-based interventions make a profound difference in their lives. Overall, one of the most important interventions that schools provide is caring teachers. Teachers collaborate with parents and other professionals to create the conditions necessary for student success. Can you think of a teacher who had a major influence on your life?

Providing Early Intervention Programs

Early intervention programs provide desperately needed opportunities for student success in preschool and elementary school. Such programs offer preschool children, particularly children who may be at risk, opportunities for later educational success by laying the groundwork for effective learning. In early intervention programs, young children learn speech, cognition, and other skills that are believed to make them better students once they enter school. Based on the theory that early experiences are critical to children's development and educational progress, many of these programs have focused on educating both parents and children.

Many testaments to the value of early intervention can be found across the nation. The Perry Preschool Program, begun in 1962 by David P. Weikart in Ypsilanti, Michigan, provided a preschool and home-visit program to three- and four-year-olds from economically disadvantaged families. The program captured public attention with results from a follow-up study of its students and a matched control group. A twenty-two-year follow-up study done on 95 percent of the participants revealed that, in comparison to the control group, Perry Preschool graduates had a smaller chance of being arrested, earned approximately $2,000 more per month, were more likely to own a home, and had a higher rate of graduation from secondary schools.

Many other programs help disadvantaged students enter school ready to learn. Head Start and Early Head Start—federally subsidized programs serving children from birth to age five, pregnant women, and their families—have the goal of increasing the school readiness of children from low-income families. Besides providing an individualized curriculum, the program delivers health, nutrition, and social services to families. Parents participate in program governance and parenting classes, and they have opportunities to do volunteer work or to be hired as staff members in Head Start classrooms.

On a practical level, some states and localities experiment with ways to supplement federal support for nutrition and health care to reach larger numbers of children. The intent of these intervention programs is to help all children be nutritionally ready for learning and to avoid labeling anyone as being low-income.

The younger the child, the more important it is not only to support good nutrition but also to encourage opportunities for human interaction—time to talk and listen. Project Story Boost is an early intervention program in a small New England city that targets at-risk kindergarten children and their parents in an effort to build links between homes and schools. The target schools serve low socioeconomic families from public housing along with families from more affluent neighborhoods. Most of the children in the program are from single-parent families, and many are immigrants.

At the beginning of the year, kindergarten teachers identify possible participants whom they think would benefit from read-aloud sessions. The adults who participate in the program, coordinated through the local university, report that students demonstrate a range of desirable behaviors. In particular, the students become familiar with stories, voluntarily choose to read, participate in whole-class read-aloud sessions, improve their vocabulary, and build their interest in books.

Keeping Students in School

How can we prevent students from dropping out of school? Educators cannot help young people avoid potential problems or face actual problems if they are not in school. Trying to determine who is not there and why, however, is a major challenge for school officials. Some districts count as dropouts students who have died, left school to get married, taken a job, gone to vocational school, entered the armed forces, gone to jail, or been expelled. The federal government uses three measures to calculate the national number of dropouts:

1. The proportion of students who drop out in a single academic year
2. The number of students who drop out of a specific grade level
3. The percentage of people in a certain age range who are not enrolled in school

Regardless of the confusion about who is absent and why, educators are expected to keep students in school at least through twelfth grade, ultimately turning out literate, responsible, productive citizens. **Holding power,** the ability to keep students in school until they receive a high school diploma or an equivalency certificate, has increased over the decades as youth have spent more and more years in school. When federal government officials use terms such as *on-time graduation rate, completion rate,* and *transfer rate,* they are referring to concepts of holding power. Although students may not choose to stay in school strictly because they want to learn, many students now recognize that they will need at least a high school diploma to get a decent job after they finish school.

Besides offering the possibility for a better job if students graduate from high school, teachers and schools must try to make the classroom a place students want to be. Some ways they can do this include relating the material to students' lives, offering activities that are interesting, encouraging free thinking, including all students in classroom discussion, and making school a fun place to be. To be truly effective, these methods must be in place long before students can drop out of school. Students' interest in learning must be planted early on and cultivated over time.

Providing Compensatory Education

A number of programs provide children from low-income families with additional educational opportunities beyond those offered in a school's standard program. These **compensatory education programs** attempt to provide important educational factors (e.g., teachers, curricula, time, and materials) that may be missing in young people's lives.

TITLE I Title I is the largest federally funded education program for at-risk elementary and secondary students. It began in 1965 as the first bill of President Lyndon Johnson's War on Poverty program. Today, the program meets the educational needs of millions of low-income, low-achieving students. Title I children most often receive their services in **pull-out programs** outside the regular classroom. Instruction usually lasts for thirty to thirty-five minutes and focuses mainly on reading, mathematics, and language arts. Some 65 percent of the teaching of Title I children is done for students in grades one through six by aides or para professionals. How might you decide if a Title I program was successful?

With more women working, traditional roles and responsibilities of parents have changed. What new responsibilities might fathers assume?

UPWARD BOUND Many older children also need all the help they can get. **Upward Bound,** another federally funded program, is structured to improve the academic performance and motivational levels of low-income high school students, particularly in math and science. Participants in the program receive tutoring, counseling, and basic skills instruction. The program encourages students to finish high school and win acceptance into college. At the end of the school year, students participate in a summer residential program focusing on the improvement of study skills and content knowledge. Established in the 1960s, Upward Bound programs continue to operate across the nation.

Providing Before- and After-School Programs

In the past forty years, women have entered the workforce in increasing numbers, with the sharpest increases being among married mothers of young children. With more women unable to stay at home with their children, traditional roles and responsibilities of parents have changed. In some two-parent families, fathers assume child care responsibilities. In others, parents change their work schedules so that one or the other can be home with their children during the day. Working mothers of children between the ages of five and fourteen most often hire someone to provide care in the child's home. Although most children under age four have some type of supervised care, nonrelatives typically provide this care outside the child's home.

Thousands of school-age children go home each day to empty houses. These **latchkey children,** many of whom live in low-income communities, may be without adult supervision for the several hours each day when juvenile crime is at its peak. Children who attend quality after-school programs demonstrate better behavior in school, make better grades, and spend less time watching television than those who are not enrolled in such programs. Moreover, children who participate in extracurricular activities are less likely to use drugs and less likely to become teen parents than young people who do not participate in such activities.

Schools respond to needs for child care in many different ways. Buses transport children to school in the morning and home in the afternoon. Some children arrive early enough each day to receive a hot breakfast they would not get otherwise. In the afternoon, extracurricular activities such as sports, clubs, and tutoring programs provide supervision until parents are finished with work.

In the past, children from lower socioeconomic levels in particular have had limited access to after-school programs because of transportation needs. Supplemental service provisions in the No Child Left Behind Act assure that the lowest-achieving students, regardless of income level, can enjoy the benefits of participating in high-quality programs outside regular school hours. **What kinds of before- and after-school programs might be most useful to students who are struggling academically?**

Using the Arts to Engage Children

Because of emphases on other academic areas in the No Child Left Behind Act (NCLB), people fear the diminishment and even the demise of local programs in the arts. The arts as an area of study, however, was recognized in NCLB as a core academic subject.

Unfortunately, when budgets are tight, subjects such as art and music are generally the first to be cut. This means that at-risk children and youth who live in high-poverty rural and urban areas may have less access to arts education programs than their peers in wealthier communities.

In some locales, school–community partnership programs designed to improve the educational performance of at-risk children are providing badly needed arts education services and programs. Americans for the Arts, a large nonprofit organization with offices in Washington and New York, is one of the leading supporters of such programs (see their website: www.artsusa.org/welcome.asp).

Keith Cook of one such program in Jefferson County, Kentucky, teaches Suzuki violin to children ages two to eighteen.

I have seen kids who would regularly be called to the principal's office, and now they're model students. They've had to work hard, but being involved with the arts has made all the difference for them. The program shows kids how to stick with something. They have to be disciplined and focused.

For the kids, a big reward comes when they get to perform on stage. They really look forward to it. This gets students sharing what they've been working on. The young kids especially like the opportunity to perform with the older kids, and they learn so much from them. When a young kid hears an older kid playing a song, they want to learn that song too.

The kids do great in this program. If there's a problem it's usually with the parents. . . . It's hard being a parent these days, trying to get your kids here and there, especially if both parents work. It falls on us to convince them their time, and their kid's time, is well spent on this. I tell them, "Whatever struggle you go through now will eliminate problems later on." What really works is parents talking to each other. I can talk until I'm blue in the face. What works is when parents share their stories of their child's success with other parents. (Americans for the Arts, 2004)

Providing Mentors and Tutors

Some programs try to improve the academic success and self-esteem of at-risk students through the use of tutors and **mentoring programs**—efforts to model appropriate behavior in one-on-one situations. For example, Big Brothers Big Sisters of America (BBBSA) has provided one-on-one mentoring relationships between adult volunteers and children at risk since 1904. The organization currently serves more than 100,000 children and youth in over five hundred agencies throughout the United States, and it promotes appreciation for racial, cultural, and ethnic diversity among the staff, volunteers, and children served.

Dubuque Community Schools, Iowa, have maintained a student mentoring program for years. Proponents of the program urge citizens to invest in the community by providing not just academic support but a trusted, experienced, and nonjudgmental shoulder for young people to lean on. While mentors are not expected to replace parents or guardians, they are asked to provide consistent support, guidance and help to students in need of positive role models. Many who volunteer remain with their students through high school. **What kinds of adults make good mentors?**

Other schools provide peer-tutoring programs in which students help one another with schoolwork. Some school-sponsored tutoring programs pair younger students with tutors from higher grade levels. Still other school-sponsored tutoring programs involve adults from the community, who are sometimes students from a local university.

How Can Schools Get Parents Involved in Their Children's Education?

When schools encourage parents to get involved in their children's education, the payoffs can be high. Parental involvement in children's education from birth until they leave home has a major positive effect on children's achievement at school. But how can parents become involved?

One very important way parents influence their children's lives is through the regulation of television viewing. Watching many hours of television daily has a negative effect on students' reading performances. Studies from the National Center for Education Statistics determined that students who reported watching the most television, six hours or more a day, had the lowest average reading score (2002). Those who reported watching four to five hours a day had the next lowest score. Fourth-grade students who reported watching less television—either two or three hours or an hour or less daily—had higher scores.

Implementing Parental Involvement Programs

For some parents, school involvement may seem like a luxury. Parents living in poverty worry so much about making money to support their families that they may have little emotional energy left to devote to school activities. This is neither an indictment nor an excuse; poverty, work, and worry are facts of life for many people.

Schools have always tried to involve parents in the education of their children, but school efforts seem to have increased in recent years. Common and visible examples are parent–teacher conferences, school open houses, parent–teacher associations and organizations (PTAs and PTOs), and school advisory councils. PTAs and PTOs vary in size and level of participation in schools. Their goal is to involve parents in school activities to tackle virtually every kind of problem imaginable. In many instances, the groups' fund-raising efforts allow schools to purchase classroom materials and equipment. These funds also provide educational opportunities, such as field trips and theatrical performances.

Although opportunities such as PTOs and advisory councils exist, some parents are unable or choose not to participate. Some parents may not have had positive school experiences themselves and thus are reluctant to get involved in their children's schools. Other parents may not have time to participate fully in their children's school experiences. Still other parents may not know what they can do to help their children in the classroom. Parents can participate as school volunteers in a variety of ways, such as reading stories, chaperoning field trips, helping to find a speaker, and assisting with special programs.

Beyond classroom volunteering, parental involvement figures heavily in efforts to reorganize schools. Concepts of parental choice, for example, are based on the idea that when parents can exercise some control over where their children attend school, schools become more responsive to their input as consumers. This ability to offer input may also encourage more parents to speak up about what they want in schools. In addition, parents are encouraged to participate in the governing councils that plan strategies to bring about change in school systems.

Providing Family Services through Full-Service Schools

Schools today—more than ever before—are called on to offer far more than basic education for school-age students. In recognition of this fact, **full-service schools,** or community schools, have existed around the country for about twenty years, most prominently in New York City, San Francisco, and St. Louis. The stated purpose of these schools is to offer a range of services for children and their families.

The essence of successful full-service schooling—delivering physical, intellectual, educational, and social services to students and their families—depends almost completely on building and sustaining communication between home and school (Reilly, 2008). Parent nights at school educate families about the environments in which their youngest members live and work. But as times have changed—and indeed as the definitions of "family" have changed—parents have had to learn how to be students all over again. The schools that have helped parents understand what it means to be a student in the 21st century have been most successful and stimulating and maintaining strong educational organizations dedicated to supporting families. Because two-way communication is so important, the use of email, telephones, and notes home have been integral to full-service school operation. Busy parents and guardians often find it difficult to find time for face-to-face meetings with teachers. **Why might parents be reluctant to come to school for meetings with teachers even when time permits?**

The success of these and related full-service efforts depends on many people. Teachers, families, administrators, social service providers, health care providers, and others must collaborate to maximize the benefit of their energies. When they do so, children's chances for living and learning in healthy environments are improved.

How Can Schools Reduce Risks That Threaten Children's Health and Safety?

If you were asked to describe the overall well-being of today's youngsters, what would you say? According to the Children's Defense Fund (CDF), a private nonprofit organization dedicated to educating others about the needs of children, today's children are not doing very well (2007). Each day in the United States:

- 5 children or teens commit suicide
- 4 children are killed by abuse or neglect
- 8 children or teens die from firearms
- 192 children are arrested for violent crimes
- 383 children are arrested for drug abuse
- 906 babies are born at low birthweight (less than 5 lb., 8 oz.)
- 1,839 babies are born without health insurance
- 1,153 babies are born to teen mothers
- 2,494 babies are born to mothers who are not high school graduates
- 2,261 high school students drop out
- 4,017 babies are born to unmarried mothers
- 4,032 children are arrested
- 2,383 children are reported abused or neglected
- 17,132 public school students are suspended

At every age, among all races and income groups, and in communities throughout the nation, these and other problems threaten the well-being of young people. Do you know of efforts to address these issues in your own community?

Preventing and Curing Childhood Obesity

What would happen if you ate only fast food for one month? Independent filmmaker Morgan Spurlock tried it. He documented the accretion of twenty-five pounds, accompanied by burgeoning cholesterol and triglycerides, in the movie *Super Size Me*. It was not, as they say, a pretty picture. Of course, he was thirty-three years old at the time. Imagine what might happen if he started at a younger age and stretched his diet over a longer period of time. The weights of children documented in Figure 2.3 are not linked explicitly to fast food consumption, but the figure demonstrates what has happened in the United States to children's weight over time.

U.S. policymakers have ranked childhood obesity as a critical public health threat. Since the 1970s, the percentage of those who are obese has doubled for preschool children aged two to five and adolescents aged twelve to nineteen. The obesity rate has more than tripled for children aged six to eleven. The government estimates that about 9 million children over six years of age are obese (Institute of Medicine of the National Academies, 2005).

Obesity can be detrimental in a number of ways, not the least of which is to a person's health. Type II diabetes used to be a disease that people got in their forties from being overweight. Now children who are ten, eleven, and twelve years old are overweight and at very high risk for diabetes.

The Institute of Medicine of the National Academies argues for a multipronged strategy to address the "epidemic of obesity," which threatens so many children—a strategy that includes the food industry, the media, state and local governments, and health care professionals. Most important, schools and teachers need to work with parents to institute changes in eating, drinking, and exercise habits. What is to be done?

- Improve the nutritional quality of foods and beverages served and sold in schools.
- Increase opportunities for frequent, more intensive, and engaging physical activity during and after school.

Figure 2.3
Prevalence of Overweight* among U.S. Children and Adolescents (Aged 2–19 Years) National Health and Nutrition Examination Surveys

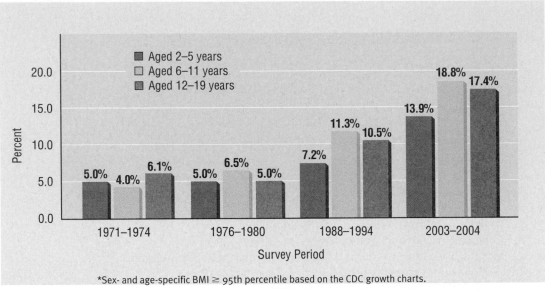

*Sex- and age-specific BMI ≥ 95th percentile based on the CDC growth charts.

Source: Centers for Disease Control and Prevention (2006). Available online (http://www.cdc.gov/nccdphp/dnpa/obesity/childhood/prevalence.htm.

- Implement school-based and home-based activities to reduce the amount of time children spend in front of television and computer screens.
- Develop and assess innovative pilot programs for both staffing and teaching about wellness, healthful eating, and physical activity.

Rod Paige, former U.S. secretary of education, put it this way:

> We must do a better job of educating our children about healthy eating habits and encourage them to increase their physical activity. Children should be encouraged to be physically active for at least 60 minutes a day. In addition to sports, simple things like taking the stairs, riding a bike and just playing outside would help prevent and combat obesity. Parents can also be role models for their children by being physically active themselves. We can't expect our children to "do as we say" if we don't act accordingly. (U.S. Department of Education, 2004)

Preventing Child Abuse and Neglect

Many youngsters suffer from physical, emotional, or sexual abuse, and many more may be the victims of neglect by their parents or guardians. Teachers are among those groups required by law to report suspected cases of child abuse. In 1974 Congress passed the **Child Abuse Prevention and Treatment Act** to provide financial support to states that implemented programs for the identification, prevention, and treatment of child abuse and neglect. Congress passed the **Adoption and Safe Families Act of 1997** to enhance the services and extend the scope of child welfare agencies.

Problems of child abuse and neglect exist in all kinds of families and across the nation. Some 906,000 children were victims of abuse and neglect in 2003. This figure translates to about twelve victims for every 1,000 children in the population. The government bases this estimate on data from all fifty states and, as Figure 2.4 demonstrates, abuse rates vary considerably by state. Educators made 16.3 percent of all child abuse and neglect reports, whereas law enforcement and legal personnel made 16 percent, and social services personnel made 11.6 percent; friends, neighbors, and relatives accounted for about 43 percent of reports (U.S. Department of Health and Human Services, 2005).

Parenting programs are one way to increase parents' involvement in their children's lives and to break cycles of abuse and neglect. The physical and mental health of parents directly affects the health and well-being of their children. Therefore many community-based parenting

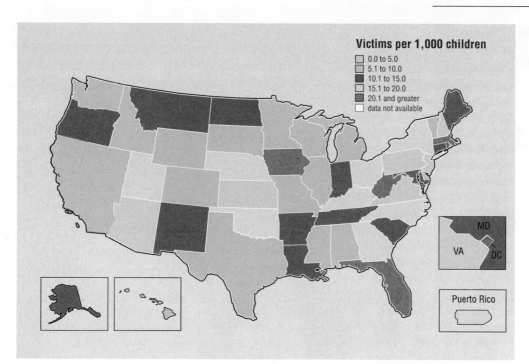

Figure 2.4
Map of Victimization
Rates, 2005

Source: U.S. Department of Health and Human Services. (2005). Map of victimization rates: 2005. Available online (http://www2.acf.hhs.gov/programs/cb/pubs/cm05/figure3_2.htm).

programs try to provide parents with the skills and knowledge they need to cope more effectively with everyday stress and to care better for their children. For particularly young, inexperienced parents, these programs offer practical knowledge for taking care of themselves and their children. To reach young parents, schools often sponsor parenting programs within their own buildings. Some schools also provide day care for infants and preschool children of high school students so that parents can complete their own high school programs and avoid the life conditions that breed abuse and neglect.

Preventing and Responding to Teen Pregnancy

The more education she has, the less likely a girl is to have a baby. For teens, having a child greatly increases the chance that a young mother and her child or children will live in poverty. Furthermore, many children of teenage parents end up as teenage parents themselves, perpetuating the cycle of poverty.

The teenage birthrate declined steadily between 1991 and 2000. In 2000 the birthrate was 48.7 per 1,000 births, 20 percent lower than the 58.9 rate in 1991. Nonetheless, the *proportion* of births to young women between the ages of fifteen and nineteen who were not married continued to increase without interruption from 13.9 percent in 1957 to 78.7 percent in 1999 and 2000 (Centers for Disease Control and Prevention, 2001).

The overwhelming majority of states encourage some type of sex education in schools, but the content and method of courses vary widely. Instruction ranges from advocating sexual abstinence to distributing condoms within the school.

Although sex education is offered in schools, the fact remains: many teenage girls will have babies while they are students. The high dropout rate among young mothers and, in many instances, the poor health of their babies have encouraged many school systems to alter their programs to meet the needs of adolescent parents and parents-to-be. In addition to their standard curricula, some schools offer home instruction to teenage mothers during their four- to six-week postpartum period. Schools may also provide teenage parents with child care, individual and group counseling, health care, parenting education, and vocational training.

Some schools offer services to young fathers and fathers-to-be. Boston schools were among the first to establish such programs. Case managers assist young fathers by helping them find

Technology in Practice

STOPPING ONLINE PREDATORS

Unscrupulous adults can and do threaten the health and well-being of children over the Internet. Predators are adept at using chat rooms, instant messaging, and e-mail to gain the confidence of young and often naïve Internet users. They prey most often on the children who are new to the Internet, who are rebellious, or who are exploring their own sexuality, and those who are isolated and lonely.

Internet protective tools can help prevent intrusion. These come in a variety of forms that (1) suggest safe websites for children, (2) monitor and track communications, (3) provide information about content when a user accesses that content, (4) warn users about content, and (5) block or filter offensive content. But there is no substitute, electronic or otherwise, for good, old-fashioned education.

Donna Rice Hughes, president of Enough Is Enough—a nonprofit organization whose mission is to make the Internet safer for children and families—has developed a set of guidelines for Internet use. Among the rules she encourages parents to emphasize with their children are the following:

1. Never give out personal information (name, address, name of school) or fill out questionnaires or other forms online.
2. Never meet in person with someone you have interacted with online without your parents' presence.
3. Never enter chat rooms without your parents' supervision. People may not be who they say they are, and they may have bad intentions.
4. Never respond to e-mails or send messages to people you meet online, unless you have first checked with your parents.
5. Never send, without parental permission, a picture to anyone you have met online.
6. Never order anything online or give out credit card information without your parents' permission.
7. Show any message or e-mail that makes you uncomfortable to your parents. If your parents aren't home, you should log off without responding and tell your parents about the message as soon as possible.
8. Any time you see something on the Internet that is upsetting, always tell your parents. (Hughes, 2001)

Remember that the old phrase "con man" is short for "confidence man"—a person who is skilled at gaining people's trust, and who abuses that trust by taking advantage of people in various ways. There are many of these unsavory characters on the Internet. As a classroom teacher, work to make certain that children can talk to you without fear or embarrassment when they are frightened, troubled, worried, or questioning any content or any person they encounter online. Also be sure to make students' parents and guardians aware of Internet safety rules. (For more information see the list of sites at this location: www.protectkids.com/links/index.htm#parentsites.)

Question for Reflection: What do you think your responsibility is as a teacher (if any) for helping your students understand the potential risks of the internet?

part-time jobs and steering them toward job-training programs. James Hall is a teenage single father in Washington, DC. He is an exceptionally rare male among some 700,000 U.S. teens who become parents every year. "There are grown men, adult men, who have the responsibility and don't do it. For him to make the attempt . . . is phenomenal," said Richard Gross, an assistant principal at Ballou Senior High School. Hall is now eighteen years old. His daughter is two years old. "He is growing up and growing old, all at once" (Fernandez, 2005). **Should states mandate that all middle and high schools provide sex education for all students?**

Preventing the Spread of AIDS and Other Communicable Diseases

As Figure 2.5 indicates, parents have definite ideas about what sex education programs should cover. No doubt statistics on the general well-being of young people have affected parents' attitudes. However parents choose to think about the subject, many students are having sex and should be taught about the health risks of their actions. Figure 2.6 lists the topics the American Academy of Pediatrics recommends that children understand.

Research indicates that students who have sex and use drugs are especially susceptible to sexually transmitted diseases, including HIV (human immunodeficiency virus), the virus that causes AIDS (acquired immunodeficiency syndrome). More than one million people in the

Issues in School Reform

NO NAME-CALLING

Name-calling is a behavior demonstrated by children of all ages. What one person perceives to be harmless fun may be viewed quite differently by others. In fact, name-calling and labeling can sometimes escalate into harassment or bullying.

January 24, 2005, marked the beginning of No Name-Calling Week in middle schools around the nation. The initiative was developed by the New York–based Gay, Lesbian & Straight Education Network (GLSEN). Some 5,100 educators from 36 states registered to participate in contrast to 4,000 in 2004. Participating schools received a resource guide, lesson plans, and a video to be shown to students. Sponsors also supported a "No Name-Calling Week Creative Expression" essay contest. The winning writer's school received a visit from James Howe, author of *The Misfits*—the book that inspired No Name-Calling Week.

According to the GLSEN, the book tells the story of four seventh-grade students who face frequent taunts based on their weight, height, intelligence, and sexual orientation or gender expression. The students, one of them homosexual, run for student council on a platform aimed at wiping out name-calling of all kinds.

A few critics characterized the special week as a thinly veiled attempt to promote homosexuality. "It appears that No Name-Calling Week may be another effort on the part of GLSEN and other event organizers to tell those who object to homosexuality on religious or philosophical grounds to 'drop dead,'" argued Warren Throckmorton, a professor at Grove City College in Pennsylvania (Jones, 2005).

James Howe, gay author of *The Misfits*, contended that "Gay students aren't the only kids targeted—this isn't about special rights for them. But the fact is that 'faggot' is probably the most common insult at schools" (Associated Press, 2005).

Questions for Reflection: Is Howe right about the most commonly used epithet? If so, is this an indication of special torment inflicted on gay students? Do you think changing students' behavior (e.g., getting them to stop calling others hurtful names) can precede changes in their attitudes, or must changes in attitudes come first?

Sources: Associated Press. (January 24, 2005). Middle schools try 'No Name-Calling.' *The Daily Progress*, p. B2; Jones, S. (January 24, 2005). No name-calling week at nation's middle schools. Available online: www.cnsnews.com/ViewCulture.asp?Page=%5CCulture%5Carchive%5C200501%5CCUL20050124a.html.

United States are living with HIV. Approximately 40,000 persons are infected each year (U.S. Department of Health and Human Services, 2008).

According to data collected by the Centers for Disease Control and Prevention (2005), 46.8 percent of high school students have had sexual intercourse; 37.2 percent did not use a condom.

When developing programs to prevent HIV transmission, educators should remember that many students experiment with drugs and sex at an early age. HIV prevention programs, therefore, must begin in elementary school and continue through high school. They must also be flexible enough to meet the needs of all children and take into account the possibility that some students are engaging in high-risk behavior.

One study of school-based HIV education programs revealed that the most effective interventions

- emphasize risk-taking behaviors that could lead to HIV infection;
- give students opportunities to practice refusal and communication skills through role playing and brainstorming;
- help students recognize social and media influences on sexual behavior;
- help students develop values regarding postponing sex, avoiding unprotected sex, using condoms, and avoiding high-risk partners; and
- use testimonials from respected peers to encourage a more conservative set of values (Landau, Pryor, & Haefli, 1995).

As for other communicable diseases, children who have not received preschool vaccinations before entering school are particularly vulnerable to typical childhood illnesses. Measles, mumps, pertussis (whooping cough), and rubella are threats to both health and learning. In recent years, drug-resistant strains of tuberculosis have developed and pose threats to children's

Figure 2.5
Sex Education: What Students Say Is Covered and What Parents Want Taught

Assuming students' perceptions are accurate, can you explain why there are such discrepancies between what parents want and what is covered in the curriculum?

	What Students Say Is Covered	What Parents Want Taught[a]
Core Elements		
HIV/AIDS	97	98
STDs other than HIV/AIDS, such as herpes	93	98
Basics of pregnancy and birth	90	90
Waiting to have sex	84	97
Other Topics		
Birth control	82	90
Abortion	61	79
Homosexuality and sexual orientation, that is, being gay, lesbian, or bisexual	41	76
Safer Sex and Negotiation Skills		
How to deal with pressure to have sex	79	94
How to deal with emotional issues and consequences of being sexually active	71	94
How to get tested for HIV/AIDS and other STDs	69	92
How to use condoms	68	85
How to talk with parents about sex and relationship issues	62	97
How to use and where to get other birth control	59	84
What to do if you or a friend has been raped or sexually assaulted	59	97
How to talk with a partner about birth control and STDs	58	88
$n =$	1,099	1,501

[a]"Very" and "somewhat" responses are used here.

Source: Hoff, T., & Greene, L. (2000). *Sex education in America: A series of national surveys of parents, teachers, and principals.* Menlo Park, CA: Henry J. Kaiser Family Foundation, p. 31. Reprinted with permission.

The American Academy of Pediatrics recommends that before they reach puberty, children have a basic understanding of the following:

• The names and functions of male and female sex organs
• What happens during puberty and what the physical changes of puberty mean—movement into young womanhood or young manhood
• The nature and purpose of the menstrual cycle
• What sexual intercourse is and how females become pregnant
• How to prevent pregnancy
• Same-sex relationships
• Masturbation
• Activities that spread sexually transmitted diseases (STDs), in particular AIDS
• Your expectations and values

The rule of thumb is to try to gear advice on sexual matters to a child's current phase of intellectual, psychosocial, and moral development. The younger the child, the simpler the advice.

Figure 2.6
Sex Education Recommended by the American Academy of Pediatrics

Source: American Academy of Pediatrics (undated). From the patient education brochures *Talking to your young child about sex* (2000) and *Talking to your teen about sex* (2004). Used with permission.

health. Public health officials have expanded outreach programs to ensure the timely immunization of children. They have also increased several immunization requirements for school-age children. To enable all children to meet these requirements, many districts offer school-based medical services including immunizations.

Preventing Suicide and Accidental Injury or Death

Adolescent suicide is a serious problem in the United States. According to the American Academy of Pediatrics (2008), suicide is the fourth leading cause of death among ten- to fourteen-year-olds. Some 60 percent of high school students have thought about it; about 9 percent have tried it.

The academy lays the blame for the shockingly high rate of suicide on society. Boys attempting suicide typically use guns, whereas girls use pills—both are easy to get. The pressures in life are many. Competition for good grades and college admission is stiff. And violence is everywhere around them; newspapers, television, movies, and music are full of it. Moreover, parents are increasingly disconnected from their children because of divorce and the demands of work.

Addressing potentially suicidal students and acquaintances of suicide victims requires special attention to young people's concepts of themselves and to signs they may be in trouble. (See Figure 2.7 for possible indicators of suicidal tendencies.) Schools also should be aware that single suicides could stimulate imitation, what some people have referred to as *cluster suicides*. Teachers and parents need to remember how acutely they felt things when they were young. Even though a problem seems small to adults, in a child's mind it can seem insurmountable.

Many of the symptoms of suicidal feelings are similar to those of depression.

Adults should be aware of the following signs of adolescents who may try to kill themselves:

- Change in eating and sleeping habits
- Withdrawal from friends, family, and regular activities
- Violent actions, rebellious behavior, or running away
- Drug and alcohol use
- Unusual neglect of personal appearance
- Marked personality change
- Persistent boredom, difficulty concentrating, or a decline in the quality of schoolwork
- Frequent complaints about physical symptoms, often related to emotions, such as stomachaches, headaches, fatigue, etc.
- Loss of interest in pleasurable activities
- Not tolerating praise or rewards

A teenager who is planning to commit suicide may also:

- Complain of being a bad person or feeling rotten inside
- Give verbal hints with statements such as: I won't be a problem for you much longer, Nothing matters, It's no use, and I won't see you again
- Put his or her affairs in order, for example, give away favorite possessions, clean his or her room, throw away important belongings, etc.
- Become suddenly cheerful after a period of depression
- Have signs of psychosis (hallucinations or bizarre thoughts)

If a child or adolescent says, I want to kill myself, or I'm going to commit suicide, always take the statement seriously and immediately seek assistance from a qualified mental health professional. People often feel uncomfortable talking about death. However, asking the child or adolescent whether he or she is depressed or thinking about suicide can be helpful. Rather than putting thoughts in the child's head, such a question will provide assurance that somebody cares and will give the young person the chance to talk about problems.

Source: American Academy of Child and Adolescent Psychiatry. (2004, July). Teen suicide. Available online: www.aacap.org/publications/factsfam/suicide.htm/. Used with permission.

Figure 2.7
Symptoms of Suicidal Tendencies

In addition, some young people have not yet developed the coping skills necessary to deal with certain life situations. School-based programs on suicide prevention and suicide curricula advocate careful training for teachers.

Another danger that students encounter is motor vehicle accidents, which are the leading cause of death among teenagers fifteen to nineteen years old. Many fatalities are alcohol-related, but an increasing number are attributed to low seatbelt use and a willingness to take risks.

To help promote safety and driver readiness, high schools offer driver education programs that precede the granting of a license to operate a motor vehicle. In addition, insurance companies often offer incentives to students who achieve high scores in driver safety and to students who do well in academic courses. In combination with health education, driver education can potentially lower the incidence of the lethal habit of drinking and driving and motivate students to buckle their seatbelts.

Preventing School Violence

The rates of assault, homicide, vandalism, and related violent acts committed by and against young people are shockingly high in the United States. Each day eight children die from gunfire. Since 1979, more children in the United States have died from gunfire than did American soldiers during the Vietnam and Gulf Wars and in U.S. engagements in Haiti, Somalia, and Bosnia combined. African American males ages fifteen to nineteen have suffered the greatest gun toll among children and teens. They are five times as likely as European American males to be gun victims.

Schools remain one of the safest places young people can be. Nonetheless, in 2005–06, 78 percent of schools experienced one or more serious violent incidents, 46 percent experienced one or more thefts, and 68 experienced some other type of crime. As might be expected, a smaller percentage of primary schools than middle or high schools reported any violent incident (National Center for Education Statistics, 2007).

Violence prevention—educating young people about the senseless, cruel nature of violence—takes many forms. Violence prevention requires healthy doses of respect for others, particularly those who are different in some way. Violence prevention programs are one way to teach students that people who appear different on the outside—ethnically, racially, religiously, and the like—have the same needs and aspirations on the inside. To teach these ideas, prevention programs offer lessons in and practice using conflict resolution, anger management, and nonviolent options for handling difficult situations. Employing a different approach, character education programs address the values that underlie civil behavior. They teach that to develop character is to prepare oneself for a successful life of contribution to the greater society. To relate to students' lives and have a hope of preventing future violence, these programs have to address everything from drug use to gang behavior, stress management, tolerance, matters of self-esteem, and community building.

Have you ever participated in a violence prevention program? If so, what was your impression of the experience?

Educators concern themselves with how to ensure children's safety. A number of efforts, many school-based, aim to change the odds for children at highest risk. To deter crime and violence on buses and at school, some localities have turned to metal detectors and video cameras. Some schools employ police officers, sometimes referred to as resource officers, to help maintain order and to prevent nonstudents from going on to school grounds. In other schools, educators are trying to eliminate teasing and bullying in the early grades by encouraging positive relationships and mutual respect among students. Using such activities as story time, meeting-time discussions, drawings, art projects, journal writing, and role playing, teachers help children explore stereotypes and behaviors that get in the way of friendship.

Increasingly, educators are recognizing bullying as a critical factor in the health of school culture. Here is how one fourth-grade student described feelings of frustration with bullying:

> I feel I always get picked on at school. I don't get included at all. People tell me I am going to hell. I get called carrot top, loser, mentally retarded. I get so mad. I tell, and no one believes me. Sometimes I really want to kill myself. (Siris & Osterman, 2004, p. 288)

Bullying, according to Peter Sheras and his colleague Sherrill Tippins (2002), occurs when a child is exposed repeatedly and over time to negative actions on the part of one or more students. These negative actions can be any physical, verbal, or socialization actions in which the bully intentionally causes injury or discomfort. Sheras believes that a chief obstacle to eliminating bullying is our inability to understand its root causes. Following are a few questions and answers from his true-or-false "Bully IQ Test" that educators can use to assess their own knowledge about the topic:

1. Most of the time what kids call bullying is simply run-of-the-mill teasing.
   FALSE. Kids are usually aware of the difference between playful teasing and deliberate bullying. Rarely will they complain to a parent if the teasing is "all in good fun." Kidding around becomes bullying when the instigator refuses to stop even after her target protests or it otherwise becomes clear that she is causing real pain.
2. It's the teacher's responsibility to make sure that bullying doesn't happen at school.
   TRUE AND FALSE. Certainly, it is the teacher's responsibility to refuse to tolerate bullying and to stop it when she sees it happening. In too many instances, teachers . . . [overlook] abusive behavior in the classroom. It must be acknowledged, however, that much school-related bullying behavior takes place outside the classroom . . . where teachers may not see it. If bullying is to be curbed, parents, teachers, school administrators, and other adults must work together, as a team, to prevent abuse wherever it happens.
3. A victim is never a bully.
   FALSE. Recent surveys report that roughly 40 percent of victims admit to having bullied others themselves. In some cases, a child's bullying and victim-like behaviors both stem from the same emotional difficulties or lack of social skills. In fact, victims who have found no one to help them may turn to bullying as a way of expressing their anger and attempting to escape their role as scapegoat. Bully-victims' deep feelings of rage and alienation make them the most likely children to turn to extreme forms of violence, including murder. (Sheras & Tippins, 2002, pp. 14–16)

Are you familiar with any programs or school policies that have been successful in reducing the level of bullying?
The American Psychological Association (APA) and Music Television (MTV) have collaborated to produce a warning-signs guide to recognizing and dealing with violence more broadly defined in schools and in society. The following signs suggest that violence is a serious possibility:

- Loss of temper on a daily basis
- Frequent physical fighting
- Significant vandalism or property damage
- Increase in the use of drugs or alcohol
- Increase in risk-taking behavior
- Detailed plans to commit acts of violence
- Announcing threats or plans for hurting others
- Enjoying hurting animals
- Carrying a weapon

When the following signs appear over a period of time, the potential for violence is real:

- A history of violent or aggressive behavior
- Serious drug or alcohol use
- Gang membership or a strong desire to be in a gang
- Access to or a fascination with weapons, especially guns
- Threatening others regularly
- Trouble controlling feelings such as anger
- Withdrawal from friends and usual activities
- Feeling rejected or alone
- Having been a victim of bullying
- Poor school performance
- History of discipline problems or frequent run-ins with authorities

- Feeling constantly disrespected
- Failing to acknowledge the feelings or rights of others (American Psychological Association & Music Television, undated)

Preventing Substance Abuse

Surveys conducted between 1975 and 2004 reveal that 48 percent of high school seniors used alcohol and 23.4 percent reported use of any illicit drug during the past thirty days (U.S. Department of Education, 2007). Why might alcohol use be so high? Why do you think adults often tend to overlook tobacco use among children? (See Figure 2.8)

Concerns about patterns of behavior that put students at risk have prompted parent groups in some school systems to band together to keep teenagers safe. They sponsor all-night prom and homecoming parties in an effort to give young people safe options for entertainment at times when alcohol and drug use typically are elevated.

School-based programs also attempt to curb substance abuse. Project ALERT, a curriculum developed by the RAND Corporation, is an example of a curriculum designed to help teens resist peer pressure to experiment with drugs and alcohol. Among program goals are helping students learn to make their own decisions, learning drug and alcohol facts, understanding peer pressure, and developing positive self-esteem. Results from a RAND study found reduced initiation of marijuana use by 30 percent and decreased current marijuana use by 60 percent (Project ALERT, 2008).

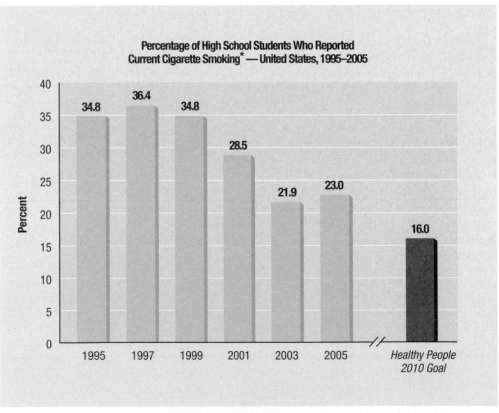

Figure 2.8
Beware of Nicotine
Adults teach children to avoid getting involved with drugs, but too often they overlook the drug most abused by adolescents–nicotine.

*Smoked cigarettes on one or more of the thirty days preceding the survey.

Source: Centers for Disease Control and Prevention (2007). Youth risk behavior surveillance system. *Youth Online: Comprehensive Results.* Available online: http://apps.nccd.cdc.gov/yrbss/QuestyearTable.asp?cat=cat=28 quest=Q30&loc=XX&year=Trend.

Case Perspectives

Think back to the case that opened this chapter. The following comments from experienced educators are designed to provide some context for this case.

A MIDDLE-SCHOOL PRINCIPAL FROM ILLINOIS DESCRIBES WHAT SHE WOULD DO IF FACED WITH MAGGIE'S SITUATION. I have two different reactions to the situation that Maggie finds herself in. First, there is no excuse for violence of any kind in the school environment. A fight between Jamey and Kyle—or any students for that matter—is unacceptable. It calls for immediate intervention. The administrators involved must be swift and clear in their actions, making certain everyone understands that violence is never tolerated. Fights must be followed quickly by consequences for those involved. And bringing a gun to school? If he were one of our students, his head would be spinning from the quick trip in the squad car on the way to juvenile authorities. Safety first. Fact-finding and educational intervention with everyone else later.

Second, too many people do not understand that schools are incredibly safe places and getting more so all the time. The media magnify the ugliness simply by telling the story. Despite what some of my colleagues say, I don't think it's some sort of self-serving conspiracy on their part. Occurrences of violence in and around schools scare the stuffing out of all of us. The press reacts much as any adult would who is not a professional educator. But the attention to horrific events erodes public faith in the tremendously positive things educators do. When this happens, our capacity for nurturing students—bending them in the right direction—and for preventing violence is diminished. At the same time I would be the first to admit that it often takes a negative story to draw attention and money to programs that help kids learn how to be good citizens. I would be working overtime to make sure that students and their parents and teachers felt safe and secure. This would mean being visible in the halls and fostering group initiatives to head off problems before they materialized.

A NEW JERSEY ENGLISH TEACHER DESCRIBES WHAT HE WOULD DO IF FACED WITH MAGGIE'S SITUATION. I can really empathize with Maggie's feelings of frustration and inadequacy. She has been racking her brain for a long time to help Jamey and Kyle and the rest of her students succeed. What could she have done to prevent these terrible circumstances?

Kids don't fight and get involved with guns for no reason. If I were in her shoes, I would try to find out a lot more about what is going on at the homes of my students. I know we aren't supposed to blame kids' problems on their home lives, but if we are going to do anything to help resolve these problems we have to know as much as we can about the students involved. I would like to know if there were some telltale signs of child abuse or neglect. If they were present, and Maggie ignored them, she would have reason to doubt herself.

I wonder too if drugs figure in here. The government reports that drug use is declining among teens, but I have also read that "huffing," or inhaling common aerosol sprays, is growing in popularity among kids. They do it to get high and to enhance their sexual experiences. Apparently the abuse may be underreported because teachers, administrators, law enforcement officials, and health care providers are often unfamiliar with the signs of inhalant abuse. I have learned through the years that if I listen carefully to my students, I can learn a great deal about who they are and what they value.

Maybe teachers can't deal with every problem that comes along, but if we don't try, who will?

Questions for Reflection: If you were Maggie, and Kyle, Jamey, and Maria were your students, is there anything you might have done differently? Do you think the outcome of this situation—Kyle's expulsion—was fair? What action, if any, do you think might be taken with Jamey? What do you think about "zero tolerance" programs that mandate expulsion for certain behaviors?

Source: CaseNEX. (2005). Up to Standard. Available online: http://casenex.com. Copyright © 2000–2005 University of Virginia and CaseNEX, LLC. All Rights Reserved. ∎

Summary

Teachers work miracles, no question about it. Every year they meet a new group of students and move them farther along the academic path, regardless of where they find students on that path. If it were only so simple as "teacher meets student, teacher teaches, student learns," the case would be closed.

But many of the challenges of professional practice are far from simple and are not easily influenced by teachers. Society expects schools and teachers to succeed, if not to work miracles, on a routine basis. This means, first, understanding the needs of students, particularly those at risk for academic and social failure, and second, intervening to improve students' chances for success. Interventions that work often involve parents as well as community agencies and reduce risks that threaten students' health, safety, and success.

TERMS AND CONCEPTS

Adoption and Safe Families Act of 1997

at-risk students

Child Abuse Prevention and Treatment Act

compensatory education programs

early intervention

full-service schools

holding power

latchkey children

mentoring programs

pull-out programs

Title I

Upward Bound

REFLECTIVE ACTIVITY: THE ACHIEVEMENT GAP

Reflective practice is an essential part of good teaching. Reflection is a process that includes making thoughtful decisions, understanding and articulating value structures, acting from knowledge, evaluating your actions and their effects, and sharing your reflections with colleagues. After reading the following scenario, respond to the questions below. The scenario reflects the INTASC Principle and Disposition at the end of this activity.

U.S. Secretary of Education Rod Paige made these remarks at a dinner sponsored by the Joint Center for Political and Economic Studies in Washington, DC, on March 26, 2002:

> *Ladies and gentlemen, we have a problem in our great country. A problem that will hurt every part of our nation every year if we fail to solve it. A problem that must become the concern of every caring American citizen. . . .*
>
> *Two-thirds of American fourth-graders cannot read at grade level. Our students rank poorly among industrialized nations on international math and science tests. Almost two-thirds of low-income eighth-graders cannot multiply or divide two-digit numbers. . . .*
>
> *Tucked inside our substandard American education performance is a subproblem that contributes to the larger problem. This problem is of special interest to the African American community, but it is a problem that affects the whole country. This problem is the stubborn academic achievement gap between the races.*
>
> *Consider the evidence.*
>
> *On the National Assessment of Educational Progress, or NAEP, fourth-grade reading test in 1992, African American scores were 15 percent below white scores. Eight years later, neither score has improved.*
>
> *On the 2000 NAEP reading assessment, 73 percent of white fourth-graders scored at or above the basic level, compared to only 37 percent of their black peers. The racial achievement gap is real, and, unfortunately, it is not shrinking.*
>
> *As the National Center for Educational Statistics put it, "While white students outperform black students in reading, the gaps decreased between the early 1970s and the late 1980s. Since then, however, the gaps have remained relatively stable or increased."*
>
> *The results in math are similar.*
>
> *Think about that. During the whole decade of the 1990s, despite all the talk about racial progress and huge increases in spending on education, the gaps remained stable or got worse. Is that good enough? Are we even going in the right direction?*
>
> *This gap is un-American and totally unacceptable. We must commit ourselves to closing it. But how?*

(The full text of Secretary Paige's talk is available online at www.ed.gov/Speeches/03-2002/20020326.html.)

Decide 1. Secretary Paige, himself an African American, described the problem as one of low academic achievement and, more specifically, differences in achievement between the races. What reasons, other than the fact that students vary in race and ethnicity, might explain why such achievement differences exist?

Perceive and Value 2. What is gained and what is lost when Secretary Paige, and indeed anyone, speaks of racial and ethnic differences in educational performance?

Know and Act   3. What do teachers say and do that communicate their belief that all students can succeed? Role play such an exchange between a teacher and a student.

Evaluate   4. How do you think an individual teacher might address Secretary Paige's concern about the lagging achievement of African American students? How might teachers' beliefs about students' capabilities affect student performance?

Discuss   5. Secretary Paige raised concerns about the achievement gap between the races. How might teachers use the kinds of knowledge suggested in this principle to try to close that gap?

INTASC Principle 3

The teacher understands how students differ in their approaches to learning and creates instructional opportunities that are adapted to diverse learners.

Disposition

The teacher understands how students' learning is influenced by individual experiences, talents, and prior learning, as well as language, culture, family, and community values. (Interstate New Teacher Assessment and Support Consortium, 1992)

ADDITIONAL READINGS

Barr, R. D., & Parrett, W. H. (2001). *Hope fulfilled for at-risk and violent youth: K–12 programs that work* (2nd ed.). Boston: Allyn & Bacon.

Jacobson, L. (2002, March 13). California charters are seen to benefit children in poverty. *Education Week, 26*(21), pp. 1–2.

Kozol, J. (1995). *Amazing grace.* New York: Random House.

Matthews, J. (2005). A new focus for teachers in training. *The Washington Post.* Available online: www.washingtonpost.com/wpdyn/content/article/2005/05/16/AR2005051601126.html.

Sheras, P., & Tippins, S. (2002). *Your child: Bully or victim. Understanding and ending school yard tyranny.* New York: Skylight Press.

Walberg, J. J. (2003). Accountability helps students at risk. *Education Week.* Available online: www.edweek.org/ew/articles/2003/04/30/33walberg.h22.html?querystring=at-risk%20students.

WEB RESOURCES

www.childrensdefense.org/
The website for the Children's Defense Fund, a private nonprofit organization, provides information about the status of at-risk students and efforts to meet their needs.

www.responsiveclassroom.org/
Responsive Classroom: A Newsletter for Teachers is an online magazine focusing on strategies for fostering safe, challenging, and joyful classrooms and schools, kindergarten through eighth grade.

www.nwrel.org/comm/topics/atrisk.html
The Northwest Regional Educational Laboratory offers a collection of resources focused on at-risk students.

http://curry.edschool.virginia.edu/curry/centers/youthvio/
The Virginia Youth Violence Project offers effective methods and policies for youth violence prevention, especially in school settings.

www.calib.com/nccanch/
The National Clearinghouse on Child Abuse and Neglect Information is a useful resource for professionals and others seeking information on child abuse and neglect and child welfare.

CHAPTER 3

The Richness of Classroom Cultures

Case Study: Are Some Curricula Discriminatory?

"Ms. Janeway, I'm sorry my parents are causing trouble for you. I love this class, and I know you just want the best for us," sobbed Rebecca Morrison. "I told them you're a good teacher, and you're not a racist. You just want us to read *Huck Finn* so we'll be ready for college, but they wouldn't listen. They're really angry. They were both so worked up that my dad was cursing. He *never* does that. He said he didn't care who you were or what you wanted, but his daughter was not going be in a class where people used the N-word. And any teacher who put me in that position should be fired."

Stephanie Janeway stood in the hall between classes feeling embarrassed and exposed while trying to comfort Rebecca. Her sympathy for Rebecca's plight surged in equal measure with her own fear. How would she ever defend having students read silently and aloud a book that was potentially offensive to others?

It had all made so much sense to her in August when she typed out her reading list. Her own American literature professor was an enthusiastic Mark Twain fan, so Stephanie had been required to study him at length. And when she had seen the actor Hal Holbrook perform his one-man Twain extravaganza on stage, Stephanie had known then and there that she would someday have her own students read *The Adventures of Huckleberry Finn* and appreciate the book for what it was—an American masterpiece. But now she felt foolish and frightened as a blur of questions raced through her mind: How could I have been so stupid? So insensitive? Why didn't I realize I would be putting students in an awkward position? And what will happen to me?

As future teachers in a culturally diverse country, you may face issues similar to the one described in the opening case study in your own classroom. This chapter explores the concepts of diversity and culture, and it speculates about their implications for education. People's view of society depends greatly on their perspectives, so we encourage you to begin thinking about cultural diversity from the different points of view you might find in the classroom. As you read this chapter, think about ways you might adapt your teaching to help students with diverse backgrounds succeed.

What Is Diversity?

What does the word *culture* mean to you? To what characteristics does one's *ethnicity* refer, and how is ethnicity different from one's national origin, if at all? Is *race* a concept with many definitions or only those limited to physical characteristics? When educators mention *minorities,* do they mean human attributes of race and ethnicity, or do they also mean gender, sexual orientation, disabilities, giftedness, and social class? What impact, if any, does economic status have on a student's aptitude for learning?

By its very nature, the language of diversity can be confusing. People speak and write about race, culture, and ethnicity as though universal agreement exists on the meaning of the terms. In some ways and in some instances such agreement does exist, but it is usually only in general terms. Often, when the issue is pressed, the agreement breaks down. For instance, when gender is defined in a physiological way, it may be easily understandable. But when the intellectual, emotional, and social characteristics of gender are thrown into the mix, not to mention, say, transgendered individuals, that easily understandable term isn't so easy. When examined, people may find that the agreement has become a stereotype that, in reality, represents no one.

In the past, public education was designed with the so-called "average" student in mind. This meant that instruction and educational materials were geared to white males from middle and upper social classes. Not surprisingly, this type of education short-changed females, people of other racial groups and cultures, and students from different economic groups. Now, instead of assuming such approaches will work for all students, researchers and curriculum developers acknowledge that differences among people can affect learning and teaching. Modern curricula takes all of these differences into account to be effective and fair to today's students.

Think back to your own experiences in school, and remember the many different kinds of students with whom you walked the halls. **What are some of the ways your teachers addressed (or did not address) diversity in the classroom? In what ways, if any, did you feel overlooked or excluded?** Chances are your feelings from back then are the same types of feelings your own students will experience.

Culture

Culture, in the larger sense of the word, refers to all of the learned characteristics of a people—language, religion, social mores, artistic expressions, beliefs, and values. In some cases a culture can be tied to a geographical region, whereas in other cases a culture exists largely independent of geography.

Culture also can be used in a *micro* sense to describe more narrowly defined groups of people, sometimes called subcultures or microcultures. These kinds of cultures may develop around a shared interest, circumstance, or condition. For instance, some people with hearing impairments choose to be part of the deaf culture. On the other hand, a subculture can be comprised of people who like the same music (punks) or the same television show (Trekkies).

In recent years, social scientists have begun to explore the influence of culture in classrooms. They have come to realize that culture is a much larger component of students' lives than previously understood. In fact, culture is now seen to influence practically every aspect of students' lives; it shapes their identities, beliefs, behaviors—it even shapes the way they learn. To ignore or misunderstand students' cultures is to risk teaching at cross-purposes with them. Educators must be informed and open to the many cultures—both macro and micro—to which their students belong.

Race and Ethnicity

One of the most often-used methods of labeling a person is by identifying his or her racial or ethnic group. People usually think about **race** in terms of physical characteristics, especially skin color, and sometimes in terms of national origin. A person of color might refer to himself or herself as black or African American or Latino and so on. Depending on appearances, however, a Latino or a person with African ancestry might self-identify as white or Caucasian (Banks & Banks, 2004). **Ethnicity** refers to membership in a group with a common cultural tradition or common national origin. Ethnic groups function as subgroups within the larger society and may share a common language or religion, customs, or other elements of culture. Although racial traits are genetically inheritable, ethnic traits are learned in social contexts such as the family.

People often find strength in their identities, and race and ethnicity are large parts of them. On a more practical level, when people complete forms for school enrollment, job applications, student loans, and the like, they are asked questions about racial or ethnic heritage. This information serves many purposes, such as monitoring equal opportunities in education and employment and tracking school desegregation.

One problem with defining diversity in racial and ethnic terms, as Table 3.1 indicates, is that numbers only hint at the richness of society. The arbitrariness of racial classification categories is evident, for example, in the changes in Census Bureau questions asked since 1790. In 1790, four categories were used to designate race: Free White Males, Free White Females, All Other Free Persons, and Slaves. In 1970, nine categories were used: white, Negro or black, Indian (American), Japanese, Chinese, Filipino, Hawaiian, Korean, and Other Race. In the 1990 census, the designation of Mixed Race was added, reflecting demographic realities and public discontent with the standard categories used by the government. Racial groups in Census 2000 included White Alone, Black Alone, Asian Alone, All Other Races Alone (Hispanic Origin, Hispanic White Alone, Non-Hispanic Origin, Non-Hispanic White Alone), and Two or More Races.

Table 3.1

PROJECTED POPULATION OF THE UNITED STATES, BY RACE AND HISPANIC ORIGIN: 2020

(In thousands except as indicated. As of July 1. Resident population.) Are figures lower, higher, or about the same as you would have estimated?

Population or percent and race or Hispanic origin	2020
Population Total	**335,805**
White Alone	260,629
Black Alone	45,365
Asian Alone	17,988
All Other Races*	11,822
Hispanic (of any race)	59,756
White Alone, not Hispanic	205,936
Percent of Total Population Total	**100.0**
White Alone	77.6
Black Alone	13.5
Asian Alone	5.4
All Other Races*	3.5
Hispanic (of any race)	17.8
White Alone, not Hispanic	61.3

*Includes American Indian and Alaska Native Alone, Native Hawaiian and Other Pacific Islander Alone, and Two or More Races.

Source: U.S. Census Bureau. 2004. U.S. interim projections by age, sex, race, and Hispanic origin. Available online: www.census.gov/ipc/www/usinterimproj/. Internet release date: March 18, 2004.

Racial and ethnic identities can be significant parts of people's perspectives and beliefs, providing a sense of history and connection. They can also be limiting factors when applied incorrectly or when taken as the full sum of a person. What we can't escape when we talk about race and ethnicity is that diversity exists. Some people believe the current vocabulary of race, often couched in terms of black and white, is losing its meaning in a world in which people are not so easily defined. Moreover, in a society such as ours, in which history has made race and ethnicity such charged topics, *black* and *white* carry connotations far beyond skin color or homeland. One researcher in particular believes that

> The problem is not simply that we have added new groups to the mix. The language of black-white differences is losing its meaning because Latinos and Asians do not fit into a world in which people are permanently and definitively marked either as insiders or outsiders. (Suro, 1998, p. C2)

What is lost and what is gained by the use of racial and ethnic designations for educational purposes?

What Other Concepts Define Diversity?

We have said that effective teachers think about teaching and learning from diverse perspectives. The viewpoints of immigrants, language minority or bilingual students, males and females, and economically disadvantaged students must be in mind when you walk into a classroom. You also need to consider the exceptionalities (special abilities or disabilities) and sexual orientations that students bring to the classroom. To be both successful and fair, teachers must be able to perceive students and situations from multiple perspectives and tailor their teaching styles and methods accordingly. **How might the experiences of immigrants differ from those of other students?**

From the Perspective of Immigrants

In 2003, 11.7 percent of the U.S. population was foreign born. As illustrated in Figure 3.1, more than half of these people were born in Latin America.

How schools deal with their changing populations is linked to society's attitudes about immigration. Reflecting these societal attitudes, throughout the past century schools have encouraged both **assimilation** (making students similar) and **pluralism** (maintaining unique characteristics). Whichever approach the school is encouraging, teachers must be aware that immigrant students likely are experiencing pressures unique to their situations. Although the student's academic progress is the prime concern, teachers should think about the reasons that might be behind a foreign-born student's setbacks in the classroom.

Immigrants' experiences vary widely and differ from those of other minorities. One difference that may affect students significantly is the reason behind their immigration. Some researchers have identified "castelike minorities," or involuntary immigrant minorities, as people who are Americans as a result of slavery, conquest, or colonization (Ogbu & Simons, 1998). They contend that, in addition to experiencing discrimination from others, involuntary minorities may also defeat themselves out of feelings of inferiority.

Immigrant students also face the complex issue of maintaining their traditional culture versus assimilating to their new one. This transition can be complicated by living in families and communities in which the native language and traditions are primary. Native values and belief systems may not encourage the same goals that the schools do.

A recent study by the Tomás Rivera Policy Institute indicated that many communities, often because of limited resources or resistance to change, have failed to meet the needs of skyrocketing immigration (Wainer, 2004). In Nebraska, for instance, the number of students speaking limited English grew from 3,714 in 1993 to 15,586 in 2003 (Zehr, 2005).

Based on studies of communities that have worked effectively with emerging Latino populations—one of the fastest growing immigrant groups—the report offers several promising education practices. One includes increasing parental involvement in their children's education

Figure 3.1
Foreign Born by World
Region of Birth: 2003
(in percent)

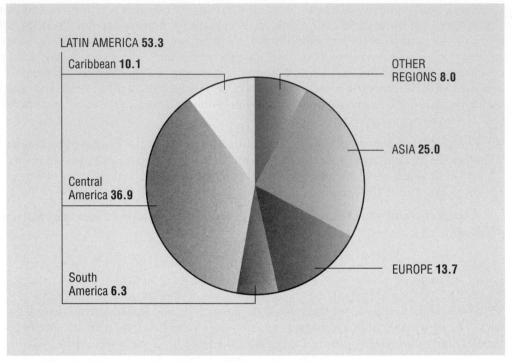

LATIN AMERICA **53.3**

Caribbean **10.1**

OTHER
REGIONS **8.0**

ASIA **25.0**

Central
America **36.9**

EUROPE **13.7**

South
America **6.3**

Source: U.S. Census Bureau. (2004). Current population survey, 2003. Annual social and economic supplement. Washington, DC: U.S.: Department of Commerce.

by making the school environment more welcoming. Some of the strategies for achieving this goal are providing a flexible schedule for parent–teacher conferences that accommodates Latino immigrants' long and varied work schedules, providing translators for immigrant parents when they register their children for school, providing programs and materials in the parents' native language, hiring parent liaisons to work in the schools, implementing family literacy programs, and integrating bilingual instructional methods into classroom instruction (Wainer, 2004).

Are you personally familiar with other strategies for making schools more welcoming to immigrant parents?

From the Perspective of Being a Language Minority or Bilingual Person

Language alone can be a formidable barrier in U.S. society. Few monolingual English speakers ever find themselves in situations in which someone else does not also speak English. But many students who are categorized as **limited English proficient (LEP)** or who qualify for instruction in **English as a Second Language (ESL)** interpret life in U.S. society from behind a language barrier.

Students with limited English proficiency receive help in the form of **bilingual education,** or instruction in both English and their native languages. Bilingual programs vary in the amount of English taught and the rapidity with which it is introduced. Definitions of bilingual programs and student success in them vary widely. Some offer instruction to students in both English and their native languages throughout their entire school career. Other programs help students move from their native languages to English by offering English as a Second Language (ESL) classes. Yet other programs remove students from regular classes to receive special help offered in their native languages. A few schools have implemented a two-way language immersion program in which children from English- and Spanish-language backgrounds study together to learn both languages.

The reason for so many types of bilingual education is that educators are divided on the best way to serve these students. Some educators believe that teaching non-English-speaking children in their native languages while easing them gradually into English is the only reasonable way to move these children into the mainstream. Others believe that bilingual programs teach neither language well and are bad for the country. **Why might some people oppose bilingual education while others advocate its use?**

How much bilingual education to offer and how long to offer it are questions open to debate. In the classroom, though, you will be dealing with actual students whose primary languages may not be English. Begin to think about what some of their unique needs might be and ways you can help these students succeed.

From the Perspective of Gender

Do you believe there is gender bias in today's schools? When they first enter school, girls' and boys' measured academic abilities are approximately equal. Studies have shown that by the age of twelve, however, girls consistently outscore boys on tests of reading and writing. At this same age, boys outperform girls on measures of higher-level mathematics and self-esteem. These differences in academic performance may be due in part to **gender bias**—discriminatory treatment, often subtle or unconscious, that unfairly favors or disfavors individuals because of their gender. Because of the fallout from comments by then Harvard University President Lawrence H. Summers in spring 2005 about the possibility of innate differences between men and women, many educators are reexamining this issue.

Critics have long charged that girls receive less attention from teachers than boys receive and that the quality of the attention boys receive is better (Sadker, 1999). Often subconsciously, some teachers tend to offer classroom activities that appeal more to boys' interests than to girls' and to use instructional methods that favor boys. Many teachers foster competition, for example, despite the fact that girls, and many boys, experience greater academic success when they work cooperatively (AAUW Educational Foundation & National Education Association, 1992). Some teachers also ask boys more challenging questions, encourage them to work to get a correct answer, offer them more praise and constructive criticism, and acknowledge their achievements more than they do for girls (Sadker & Sadker, 1993).

More recently, the fact that boys are also affected negatively by gender bias is becoming more evident. Studies indicate that teachers consider boys, in general, to be significantly more active, less attentive, less dexterous, and more prone to have behavioral, academic, and language problems than girls are. In addition, when schools identify children with learning disabilities, mental retardation, and reading disabilities, boys typically are identified more often

Cultural Awareness: Lessons Learned

You can speak with others in mind, and you can listen the same way. But you can't listen for someone else. They hear what you say and process your speech through their own set of filters. For children in Appalachia, this can spell trouble. Their accents mark them as "backward."

Dee Davis, a native of Appalachia and head of the Center for Rural Strategies, a group that fights rural stereotypes, said some of his college classmates couldn't understand his mountain dialect. He told them he wanted to study "riding." They looked at him quizzically, saying they didn't know the subject was offered. He then spelled it: W-R-I-T-I-N-G.

The Associated Press reported on a theater class in Pikeville, Kentucky, designed to rid local actors of their accents. The point was to help the actors be able to assume a diverse set of roles. The managing director said that "If you want to work professionally, you have to be able to drop the accent when it is required." They describe the accent as a kind of southern drawl heard in the movie *Coal Miner's Daughter*. "Did you eat?" becomes "Jeat?"

One lesson Davis has learned is that people can "unlearn" their accents. They can be trained to speak like people from other parts of the country. The more important and more subtle lesson, however, is that "[teachers] make sure the kids understand that their language is beautiful, that their culture is powerful, and that it's not something they should be embarrassed about." Children need to be taught, Davis argues, to hold fast to the "language you dream in" (Associated Press, 2004).

Questions for Reflection: Do you believe children should be taught to hold on to their own patterns of speech? Why or why not?

than girls. And the tendency to view gender bias in the classroom as negative only for girls has perhaps helped divert policy attention from the group at most risk for academic failure—African American boys.

An interesting case of perceived gender bias occurred when the principal of Seattle's Thurgood Marshall Elementary School split his enrollment into classes of all girls and all boys. Washington state officials said he was violating **Title IX**—the federal law that prohibits schools from discriminating on the basis of gender. Federal officials scrutinizing the schools disagreed, however, indicating that they planned to lessen the "rigid" interpretation of the gender-equity law. According to Assistant Secretary for Civil Rights Gerald A. Reynolds, a relaxing of the restriction would allow schools to provide more educational options for students and parents. The move toward flexibility stems from the No Child Left Behind Act of 2001, a law signed by President Bush that encourages innovative programs that provide more choice.

In 1995 there were two single-sex schools in the U.S.; in 2008 there were 49 (Weil, 2008). Research continues to be done on potential gender bias in the classroom and its long-term effects on students. In your own classroom, be conscious of activities and instructional methods that may exclude or be of little interest to one gender. Although culture at large is far from being free from gender bias, both female and male students deserve a classroom that promotes equality among genders.

From the Perspective of Exceptionality

Why is it important for all teachers to understand the concept of exceptionality? Nationally, about 13 percent of children have a special ability or disability that sets them apart from other children (U.S. Department of Education, 2003). In terms of education, these abilities and disabilities are called exceptionalities. More than 6 million **exceptional learners** across the United States possess one or more attributes that greatly affect the experiences they have at home, at school, and in the community. As knowledge of exceptionalities has grown, so too has public recognition of the importance of meeting the needs of exceptional learners in order to increase their chances for success.

Students with exceptionalities often are said to deviate from the "norm," or what is typically expected or desired by a society or culture. The definition of the norm, however, is as debatable and slippery as definitions of race. Although the term *norm* indicates a single shared understanding, in a culture with so many differences, a norm can mask a great deal of diversity.

In terms of education, exceptional characteristics viewed as *handicaps* only ten or twenty years ago are now characterized as *disabilities* that do not necessarily limit students' chances to advance. Also included in the category of exceptional learners are students whose skills and intellectual levels are beyond those of their peers. In practice, students with exceptionalities may possess one or both of the following characteristics.

GIFTEDNESS Because there is no federal legislation mandating special services to gifted and talented students, **giftedness** is defined in multiple ways. The Delaware definition of "gifted and talented" means a person between the ages of four and twenty who is capable of high performance and excels in one or more of the following areas: general intellectual ability, specific academic aptitude, creative or productive thinking, leadership ability, ability in the visual or performing arts, and psychomotor ability. In Colorado the term refers to a secondary school student who possesses one or more of the following attributes: intellectual giftedness, outstanding school achievement, and outstanding performance in particular areas of human endeavor, including the arts and humanities.

In most cases, definitions are determined by state legislatures or state boards of education. Four states—Massachusetts, Minnesota, New Hampshire, and South Dakota—have no mandates regarding gifted education (Education Commission of the States, 2004).

DISABILITIES The majority of students who qualify for special education services have one or more of the following disabilities: speech and language disorders, learning disabilities, emotional and behavior disorders, and severe attention problems. Each of these conditions is defined by federal special education laws and regulations.

Some disabilities occur less among young people, including cognitive disabilities, hearing and visual impairments, and orthopedic or other health impairments. But teachers often must respond to these special needs as they occur in combination with other disabilities.

As more and more children are found to have exceptionalities, teachers must be prepared to have classrooms full of students representing all levels of physical and mental abilities. **Can you think of ways you could engage all students? What special needs must you be aware of?**

From the Perspective of Sexual Orientation

Education for diversity often sparks disagreement concerning which groups are identified as subcultures, and some debate on these matters seems to be about much more than student ability levels. Such is the case with students' sexual orientation and how the subject is addressed in the classroom. Sexuality is a hot-button subject, largely unaddressed in curricula. Many people believe that sexuality is not a matter for the school to address, but this belies the fact that, especially in high school, many students are coming to terms with their homosexuality. In addition to a lack of discussion in the classroom about homosexuality, feelings of isolation and "otherness" are increased for gay and lesbian students by the prejudice and harassment they face from other students and sometimes from teachers as well.

Beyond the classroom, homosexuality raises concern and provokes ire in the community at large. For instance, when the National Education Association passed a resolution in support of Lesbian and Gay History Month, a group called the Concerned Women for America (CWA) placed advertisements in newspapers around the country condemning the NEA's action. They billed the resolution as a "threat to morality and decency." CWA's language was so strong that two newspapers in which the ads appeared later apologized for running inappropriate statements (Ponessa, 1995).

Some people believe that gays, lesbians, and other minorities press their concerns for fair and equal treatment to the detriment of the community at large. Separate dormitories, preferential admissions, campus study centers, fiscal aid policies, and faculty hiring quotas, they argue, make people concentrate on attributes such as skin color or sexual orientation first, before they assess the content of their own or others' characters.

One of the leading organizers of efforts to promote tolerance and acceptance of homosexuality in schools and the culture at large has been the Gay, Lesbian, & Straight Education Network (GLSEN). Through more than 2,500 high school clubs known as Gay–Straight Alliances, the GLSEN has provided skills and resources to students and educators focused on "the ABCs of respect"(*NEA Today,* 2005). The GLSEN also conducts an annual school climate survey. Based on that data, Kevin Jennings—executive director of the GLSEN and winner of the 2004 NEA Human and Civil Rights Award—believes teachers can be a powerful force in creating safer learning environments:

> When we polled teenagers to understand why they use homophobic language and what could get them to stop, 80 percent of girls and 68 percent of boys said that if a teacher they respected told them to stop using the language that would have a major impact on them. Teachers can make a huge difference. So, if you see something happening, do something. The worst thing to do is to say nothing because what you're doing is giving tacit permission for that behavior to continue. (*NEA Today,* 2005)

As future teachers, you will need to consider how you might deal with gay and lesbian students. How will you encourage other students to treat them? How will you balance this issue with all the other interests in your classroom and still provide a beneficial learning experience?

What Is Multicultural Education?

Teachers need more than ideas, enthusiasm, and a love of children to be successful. Great teachers do not have "a way" of behaving toward all students or "a style" of teaching that works equally well with all people. Instead, great teachers adapt their methods to help all students

Teachers adapt their methods to help all students succeed. What strategies would you use to be sensitive to the diversity of your students' needs and abilities?

succeed. They must be able to use educational strategies that can be fitted intelligently and sensitively to the diversity of their students' needs and abilities. Increasingly, educators are turning to concepts of multicultural education and inclusive education to provide such support.

Five general approaches to multicultural education are outlined here and shown in Figure 3.2 (Sleeter & Grant, 2002).

1. *Teaching the culturally different* tries to assimilate people into the cultural mainstream using transitional bridges in the regular school program.
2. *Human relations approaches* attempt to help students of differing backgrounds understand and accept each other.
3. *Single-group studies* encourage cultural pluralism by concentrating on the contributions of specific individuals and groups.
4. *Multicultural approaches* promote pluralism by reforming entire educational programs—altering curricula, integrating staffs, and affirming family languages.
5. *Education that is multicultural and social reconstructionist* actively challenges social inequalities.

Teaching the Culturally Different

Mainstreaming is an approach that attempts to assimilate students of different races, low-income students, and special education students into a single classroom, a sort of real-world approach. For years mainstreaming was the preferred approach to multicultural education. As immigrants arrived in this country, they were placed in programs designed to teach the knowledge, skills, and attitudes deemed appropriate for a successful life in the United States. Such programs often made their goals explicit. For example, students learned to read and write English, master U.S. history, and adopt prevailing social customs.

Mainstreaming programs, then and now, are also characterized by their unspoken implications. Teachers' expectations for appropriate behavior, for example, may cause students to question their backgrounds or view themselves negatively. Although teachers attempt to accommodate all skill levels and backgrounds in a single classroom community, the task of meeting the needs of every student can seem next to impossible.

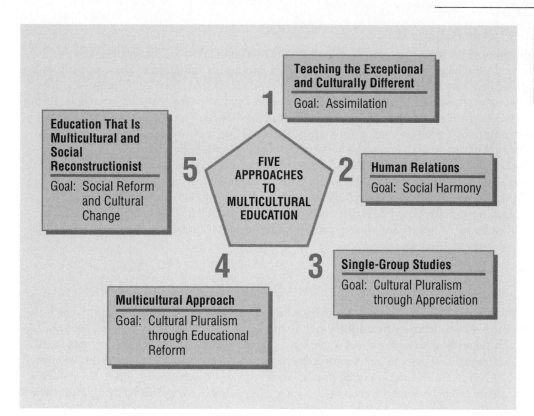

Figure 3.2
Five Approaches to
Multicultural Education
Think of one clear example of each
of the five approaches identified in
this figure.

Source: Adapted from *Making choices for multicultural education: five approaches to race, class, and gender* (4th ed.),
by C. E. Sleeter and C. A. Grant, © 2002. New York: John Wiley & Sons, Inc.

Human Relations Approaches

Human relations approaches to multicultural education try to help students from different
backgrounds understand and accept each other on a personal level. These approaches can be
as informal as teachers assigning a "friend" to a new student or forming work or play groups
to improve understanding and acceptance. Human relations approaches also include formal
procedures for accomplishing goals, such as **conflict mediation,** an approach that helps students
resolve their differences peaceably.

One mediation program, called Teaching to Be Peacemakers, enables students to solve for
themselves the daily conflicts that arise. The training helps students reject notions of winning
disputes and shows them how to apply negotiation and mediation procedures. When students
are trained to be their own peacemakers, discipline problems handled by teachers decrease by
about 60 percent (Johnson & Johnson, 2003).

Did schools you attended use conflict resolution or other human relations approaches?

Single-Group Studies

Do you remember celebrating Women's History Month when you were in school? Single-group
studies concentrate on individual and group contributions, emphasizing the importance of
learning about the lives of outstanding people in various cultures. The goal of single-group
studies is to help young people feel proud of their heritages and recognize that their accomplishments do not depend on their race, gender, or culture.

Single-group approaches often address affective objectives (objectives aimed at influencing
feelings, attitudes, or values) and promote appreciation and respect for other ways of life. In the
simplest or most traditional approaches, students participate in activities that feature the food,
dress, and customs of foreign countries. Unfortunately, single-group studies can emphasize differences among groups to the extent that diversity is celebrated over unity.

Multicultural Approaches

Multicultural approaches try to reform education by revising curricula, integrating school staffs, and acknowledging the importance of families and family languages. These approaches encourage students to consider different viewpoints, and they often draw on content developed in single-group studies. Instructors also involve students by discussing real-life situations, trying to draw connections between the curriculum and students' own experiences and backgrounds.

One example of a multicultural approach is the way Robert Moses teaches algebra to sixth-grade African American students in the Mississippi delta. A firm believer that algebra is the "gatekeeper" to the college prep math sequence, Moses uses a variety of multicultural approaches to help students succeed in the course and to see themselves as thinkers. He teaches some lessons using the contrasting rhythms of African drumbeats, while other lessons are taught by having students construct their own recipes. Moses believes these and similar methods help hold student interest and make content understandable. **What are the benefits of relating academics to students' lives?**

Education That Is Multicultural and Social Reconstructionist

A multicultural, socially reconstructive approach to diversity in education challenges social inequality and seeks to restructure educational institutions in ways that will change society. Teachers who want to achieve these goals use students' life experiences as opportunities to discuss social inequalities. They encourage students to think critically about the classism, sexism, racism, and social inequities that may be present in textbooks, newspapers, and other media sources. Students are encouraged to consider alternative points of view and to think about ways they might work constructively to achieve social justice for all people.

When studying U.S. history, for example, students might investigate how the racial category of "Other" has evolved over time. They might begin by reading passages from Christopher Columbus's diary, in which he describes his encounter with the Taíno Indians in the Caribbean. Through discussion, students could consider how his perceptions of the Taínos were influenced by European ideas and concepts (Banks, 2002). From there, students could discuss views of "others" in their extended families or in the larger society. Teachers might then encourage students to speculate about personal, social, and civic activities they could participate in that might change common attitudes about these "others." In this way, a history lesson becomes a way for students to build a more democratic and just society.

What Types of Multicultural Education Curricula Exist, and How Are They Evaluated?

National and state initiatives related to multicultural education are numerous and varied. Overall, they relate to the larger, continuing dialogue about the meaning of *e pluribus unum*—one out of many. These initiatives are often concerned with protecting the rights of cultural and ethnic minorities. Primarily, the purpose of the legislation is to ensure **equal educational opportunity.** At the federal level, this has meant focusing on providing equal educational opportunities for female students, students of different races, LEP students, students from low-income families, and students with disabilities. This legislation, however, usually does not discuss the preparation necessary for all students to function effectively in a culturally diverse society.

National educational associations, on the other hand, promote attention to multicultural education, equity, and opportunity by advocating direct intervention at all levels of the public education system. National accreditation standards for programs and national certification programs for teachers also acknowledge the importance of multicultural education. Prominent among such standards are those promoted by the National Council for the Accreditation of Teacher Education (NCATE).

With all of the multicultural approaches available to teachers, along with national and state initiatives, it can be hard to know how to judge their effectiveness and appropriateness. James Banks offered a specific model for integrating ethnic content into elementary and high school

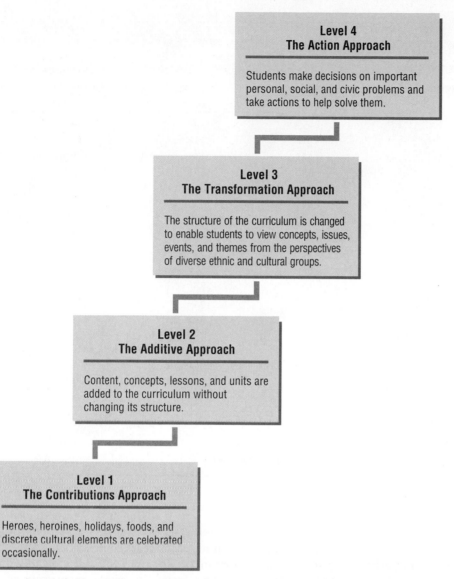

Level 4
The Action Approach

Students make decisions on important personal, social, and civic problems and take actions to help solve them.

Level 3
The Transformation Approach

The structure of the curriculum is changed to enable students to view concepts, issues, events, and themes from the perspectives of diverse ethnic and cultural groups.

Level 2
The Additive Approach

Content, concepts, lessons, and units are added to the curriculum without changing its structure.

Level 1
The Contributions Approach

Heroes, heroines, holidays, foods, and discrete cultural elements are celebrated occasionally.

Figure 3.3
Banks's Approaches to Multicultural Curricular Reform
How is Banks's model similar to and different from the five approaches to multicultural education identified by Sleeter and Grant? (see Figure 3.2.)

Source: Reprinted with permission from James A. Banks, *An introduction to multicultural education* (3rd edition). Boston: Allyn & Bacon, 2002, p. 30.

curricula (2002). As part of the model, he provided a practical guide that teachers might use to judge various multicultural approaches (see Figure 3.3). The guide envisions a four-tiered approach to multicultural curricular reform, in which the lowest tier is "The Contributions Approach" and the highest tier is "The Action Approach." Overall, how programs are accountable for results and by what criteria a program is deemed a success are issues of primary importance when deciding what multicultural approach to use.

Accountability Issues

How would you decide whether multicultural education really works? When deciding what form of multicultural education to adopt, a school has to consider several questions: What does multicultural education cost? How are educational activities affected? What are the outcomes of these efforts? The answers to these questions are judged acceptable or unacceptable by comparing them to the claims the program makes, to competing programs, or to the expected standards of any educational effort.

One common method of judging the success of educational programs is standardized test scores. Standardized tests often are accused of being unfair to certain groups of students and

Table 3.2

SAT[a] SCORES BY RACIAL/ETHNIC GROUP

Racial–ethnic background	1990–91	2004–05	Score change 1990 to 2005
1	2	4	5
SAT—Verbal All students	499	508	9
White	518	532	14
Black	427	433	6
Hispanic or Latino	**458**	**463**	5
Mexican American	454	453	−1
Puerto Rican	436	460	24
Asian American	485	511	26
American Indian	470	489	19
Other	486	495	9
SAT—Mathematical All students	500	520	20
White	513	536	23
Black	419	431	12
Hispanic or Latino	462	469	7
Mexican American	459	463	4
Puerto Rican	439	457	18
Asian American	548	580	32
American Indian	468	493	25
Other	492	513	11

[a]Formerly known as the Scholastic Aptitude Test.

Possible scores on each part of the SAT range from 200 to 800.

Source: U.S. Department of Education, National Center for Education Statistics (2006). *Digest of Education Statistics, 2005* (NCES 2005–030). Table 126. Available online (http://nces.ed.gov/fastfacts/display.asp?id=171)

inaccurate reflections of students' progress. In general, minority-group students have not scored as well on such tests as have majority-group students. But in recent years some evidence suggests the test scores of minority group students have been increasing. As Table 3.2 indicates, members of minority groups appear to be gaining advantages from educational opportunities in ways that many had not in the past.

Many other types of outcomes can be examined to judge the effectiveness of multicultural programs. These outcomes can be acquired conveniently and inexpensively, and they can be extremely useful. For example, students' written assessments of their satisfaction with programs and with school in general can be obtained and tracked over time. These can be supplemented with student, parent, and staff interviews to determine what they do and do not like about school. One also could examine records for school attendance, dropout rates, and participation in extracurricular activities to determine a program's merits. In practice, these types of outcomes can provide more truthful and relevant insight about a program's success than can a standardized test.

INSTRUCTION Sensitivity training and cultural awareness programs for both teachers and students promote understanding of cultures. For example, the Chicago Children's Museum features an exhibit called Face to Face: Dealing with Prejudice and Discrimination, which aims to help students deal with discriminatory behavior. One portion of the exhibit is a full-size board game called Race for Ubuntu that allows children to explore such issues as stereotyping, name-calling, and exclusion. The game uses photographs and information to show ways that students around the world can respond to prejudice and discrimination and move toward unity.

CURRICULA Diversity issues in education have led to the creation of new curricula. Blues in the Schools (BITS), for example, is a curriculum shaped over the past twenty-five years by a variety of individual and cooperative efforts. The goals of the program are to affirm the cultural heritage and contributions of African Americans and to promote understanding across racial and socioeconomic lines. Participating schools find that the program offers lessons in history, music, literature, and even geography.

Some people believe that efforts to promote multicultural approaches of openness and acceptance in education have themselves become closed, producing what is known as *political correctness*. Multiculturalists have been criticized for going too far in the other direction, making the differences between students more important than the similarities. They have also been accused of focusing on moral and social issues, thereby distracting people from practical problems, such as adequately funding programs and finding the time to use the new curricula. The challenge has been and continues to be one of finding ways to help all young people succeed—not just separately, but together—and to appreciate one another in the process.

THE FUTURE OF MULTICULTURAL EDUCATION As with any other part of the curriculum, both the content and processes of multicultural education are subject to scrutiny. Does multicultural education promote student interest in intellectually and socially relevant activities? Does it promote academic achievement? Does it encourage understanding and acceptance among students? Can it help forge ties between schools and homes? Answers to these and similar questions will shape and reshape multicultural education.

How Are Educational Services Adapted for Students with Exceptionalities?

Public schools in the United States are morally and legally obligated to create environments that enhance children's learning. As a result, both curricula and instructional methods are adapted to meet the needs of all students. The ultimate goal is to create an educational opportunity that best serves the particular needs of each student. When you hear the term *special education, what do you think of?*

Delivering Services to Students with Disabilities

Several laws, including the 1975 **Education for All Handicapped Children Act** and the 1990 **Individuals with Disabilities Education Act (IDEA)**, have established equal educational opportunities for students with disabilities. IDEA, the current act, changed the term *handicapped* to *with disabilities* and extended the opportunity for free and appropriate public education to every person between the ages of two and twenty-one, regardless of the nature or severity of the disability.

IDEA guarantees individuals with disabilities the right to free and appropriate education in the least restrictive environment. This means that students with disabilities must be educated in regular classrooms whenever possible. During the 2003–2004 school year, almost half of students with disabilities spent 80 percent of their days in regular classrooms. As illustrated in Figure 3.4, however, there were marked racial and ethnic differences in students' placement in this category (U.S. Department of Education, 2005).

LAWS THAT SUPPORT INCLUSION Today, many students with special needs receive **inclusive education,** which is education designed for and offered to all people, regardless of their physical, social, emotional, and intellectual characteristics. Most often, however, people use the term to refer to education provided in mainstream classrooms to students with disabilities. By design, inclusive education stands in contrast to special education offerings that occur in separate classrooms or segregated facilities.

Legal and moral grounds supporting the concept of inclusive education can be seen in the principles laid out in the 1954 Supreme Court case *Brown* v. *Board of Education*. This landmark ruling said that separating children by race in order to educate them was not only illegal but morally wrong as well. The beliefs behind that case have grown since 1954, and they are now applied to the education of students with disabilities.

PROVIDING FOR SPECIAL EDUCATION Special education services for students with disabilities range from those that fully integrate students into general education classrooms to those that

Technology in Practice

COUNTERING PREJUDICE

The Southern Institute for Education and Research provides a variety of resources for teachers to use for improving ethnic relations. Founded in 1993 at Tulane University in New Orleans, Louisiana, the institute's programs are aimed at helping young people in the Deep South understand the causes and consequences of prejudices by examining the past. In the area of tolerance and Holocaust education alone, the Southern Institute has provided training to more than 3,600 teachers from 800 schools in Alabama, Florida, Louisiana, and Texas. Visit the institute's website (www.southerninstitute.info/) for information about programs, services, and online materials available to teachers.

Questions for Reflection: For what age groups might online teaching guides from the Southern Institute be most appropriate? Who should you consult about using these and other online materials before integrating them in the curriculum?

Source: The Southern Institute for Education and Research, with permission.

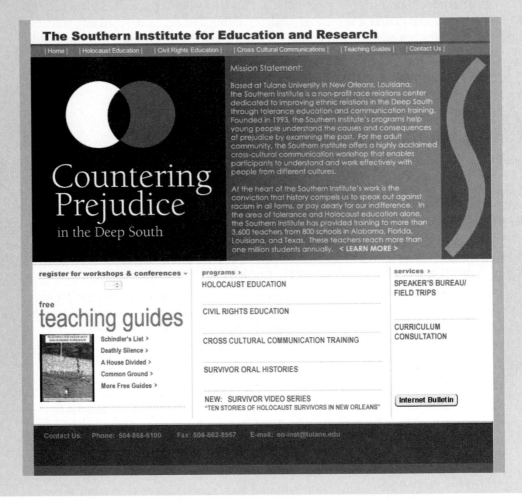

seldom integrate them. In more integrated environments, the general education teacher meets all the needs of the student. Sometimes a special educator acts as a consultant to the teacher, or a special education teacher may be within the regular classroom to offer some instruction to a student. At other times, a student goes to a resource teacher for part of the day and receives specific help. In less integrated programs, a student may spend the majority of the day in a self-contained special education class and leave only occasionally to participate in school activities. Sometimes special education students attend separate schools, or they may be in a residential setting (Hallahan & Kauffman, 2006).

Effective elementary teachers think and behave in particular ways with children who have disabilities. After observing a large number of these teachers, researchers interviewed five individual

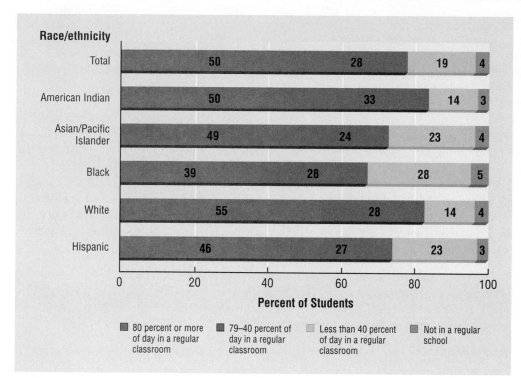

Figure 3.4
Students with Disabilities: Percentage distribution of students ages 6–21 served by the Individuals with Disabilities Education Act, by placement in educational environment and race/ethnicity: 2003–04

NOTE: Students counted as disabled are those students served under Part B of the IDEA in the United States and outlying areas. American Indian includes Alaska Native, Black includes African American, Pacific Islander includes Native Hawaiian, and Hispanic includes Latino. Race categories exclude Hispanic origin unless specified. Detail may not sum to totals because of rounding.

Source: U.S. Department of Education. (2005). Special programs: Inclusion of students with disabilities in regular classrooms, Indicator 27. *Condition of Education.* Washington, DC.

Issues in School Reform

SERVING CHILDREN WITH SPECIAL NEEDS THROUGH INCLUSION

Everybody wants to help children who need special attention because of their disabilities. The difficulty is knowing how to do so effectively and efficiently. As the following excerpt from special education professor Bruce Marlowe (Johnson State College, Vermont) suggests, the demands are outstripping the human and material resources.

Unfortunately, in the last ten years, inclusion has become an increasingly difficult ideology to sell to my students, and to myself. My home state of Vermont has been committed to "full inclusion" since long before it became a national issue. As a teacher educator in a state where virtually all students with disabilities are placed in regular education classrooms, I have a mandate to prepare prospective teachers for classes in which there will be a wide range of student abilities. And while mainstreaming is often a hot topic of debate with my students, the primary emphasis in my classes

has always been on how to plan, manage, deliver, and evaluate instruction effectively in diverse classroom settings—as this is what new teachers must do when they graduate, regardless of their politics. . . .

Perhaps the greatest threat to inclusion is the reluctance of competent special educators to work as special educators. While there are numerous openings for special educators, few want these jobs because of the enormous disincentives. These include: a staggering amount of paperwork, overwhelming caseloads, endless meetings, escalating discipline problems (with little support from agencies outside the school), and increasingly adversarial, uncivil, and litigious parents. In addition, many feel that the job requires almost daily compromising of one's integrity, as special educators often must choose between protecting the fiduciary interests of the school (on which their jobs depend), and the educational needs and civil rights of the students on the caseloads.

(Continued)

(Continued)

Questions for Reflection: How might more financial support for special education be used most effectively? Will more licensed special education teachers fix the problems? Does the system need more **paraprofessionals** (unlicensed teachers' aides)? Are there other ways to invest in children's development that might be desirable?

Source: Marlowe, B. (2001, April 18). The Special Education Conundrum. *Education Week, 20,* (31): 43.

teachers to determine why they behaved as they did toward students with special needs (McNergney & Keller, 1999). Table 3.3 shows what researchers learned about effective teachers' actions. Overall, the most effective methods to help students with disabilities in the classroom are paying attention to their progress, actively including them in learning activities, and offering guidance and praise for what they do accomplish.

Table 3.3

SOME EFFECTIVE TEACHERS' ACTIONS WITH CHILDREN WITH DISABILITIES

1. Teachers watch students as they work on tasks:
   a. to see if students need help.
   b. to keep students involved.
   c. to determine when to move on to the next activity.
2. Teachers give step-by-step directions:
   a. to help students work independently.
   b. to avoid interruptions during instructional time.
3. Teachers help learners by giving hints and clarifying misunderstandings:
   a. to make the content of a lesson more meaningful.
   b. to help students make connections between old and new material.
   c. to get students to think.
   d. to keep students from giving up.
   e. to give students more time to think.
   f. to help students succeed so they feel good about themselves.
4. Teachers recognize special needs of learners:
   a. to give students concrete examples to help them understand.
5. Teachers summarize and review throughout the lesson:
   a. to help students synthesize information.
   b. to keep students involved.
6. Teachers praise learners publicly and explain why:
   a. to encourage student involvement.
   b. to make students feel good about their achievements.
   c. to encourage students to behave like others.
   d. to enhance self-concepts of students.
7. Teachers make connections to students' interests, to the outside world, and to other subjects:
   a. to increase student attention and interest in the lesson.
   b. to make content real or meaningful to students.
   c. to help students see that there is an overlap in content areas.
   d. to help students form linkages between subjects.
   e. to reinforce what the teacher and class have just discussed.
8. Teachers urge students to answer or comment:
   a. to get and keep student involvement.
   b. to get students to think about the material.
   c. to give students a chance to answer correctly and feel good about themselves.
   d. to make students feel that what they have to say is important.
9. Teachers check understanding throughout the lesson:
   a. to see if students are "with" the teacher.
   b. to keep students involved in the lesson.
   c. to get students to think on their own.
10. Teachers question and respond—they praise, acknowledge, approve, redirect, reenter, make eye contact, check status, and so on:
    a. to keep students involved in the lesson.
    b. to check understanding.
    c. to get students to think.
    d. to review concepts.
11. Teachers work to build students' self-concepts:
    a. to help students feel that what they have to say is important.
    b. to help students develop a feeling of power or control—a "can do" attitude.
    c. to increase student participation.

Source: McNergney, R., & Keller, C. (1999). *Images of mainstreaming,* Appendix: Some effective teachers' actions. New York: Garland Publishing, Inc. Reprinted by permission.

Regardless of where children with disabilities are placed in schools, general and special educators need to work with parents and other professionals to plan an **individualized education program (IEP)**. IEPs are used to make sure each student receives the best and most fitting education possible. This customized program outlines a child's current performance levels (strengths and limitations), long- and short-term goals, criteria for success, methods for assessing mastery of objectives (e.g., observation, testing), amount of time to be spent in general education classrooms, and beginning and ending dates for special services.

Delivering Services to Gifted and Talented Students

What is the best way to educate students who are gifted or talented? As with special education programs for students with disabilities, programs for gifted and talented students take many forms. In one type of program, students who qualify remain in general education classrooms but are assigned accelerated curricula. Alternatively, they may be pulled out of the general education classroom for special instruction in a resource room. Sometimes gifted and talented students attend self-contained classes for talented students. They may also skip a grade in school. In later years, some of these students will take Advanced Placement courses and college courses.

Studies of students selected to participate in gifted and talented programs suggest that economically disadvantaged students are significantly underrepresented. Looking at Table 3.4, it is easy to see a direct correlation between family income and students' test scores. This and many other studies have concluded that wealth and parental educational background combine to

Table 3.4

SCHOLASTIC ASSESSMENT TEST[a] SCORE AVERAGES BY SELECTED STUDENT CHARACTERISTICS: 2004

Selected characteristics	Verbal score	Mathematics score
All students	**508**	**518**
Family income		
Less than $10,000	422	450
$10,000 to $20,000	440	457
$20,000 to $30,000	459	467
$30,000 to $40,000	478	482
$40,000 to $50,000	493	496
$50,000 to $60,000	501	504
$60,000 to $70,000	507	510
$70,000 to $80,000	515	518
$80,000 to $100,000	527	530
More than $100,000	553	562
Highest level of parental education		
Less than high school	415	445
High school diploma	469	474
Associate degree	488	490
Bachelor's degree	523	531
Graduate degree	558	564

[a]Formerly known as the Scholastic Aptitude Test.

Possible scores on each part of the SAT range from 200 to 800.

Source: College Entrance Examination Board, National report on college-board seniors: Scholastic assessment test score averages for college-bound seniors, by Race/Ethnicity. www.collegeboard.com. Copyright © 2003 by collegeboard.com. Reproduced with permission. All rights reserved.

influence student achievement. This correlation also may help explain why children in poverty are not able to take advantage of gifted and talented programs.

Studies also indicate that disproportionately fewer limited English proficient (LEP) students are included in gifted and talented programs. Although schools provide instructional assistance to these students, many people argue that the programs do not teach the language or higher-order skills that students need to perform well on placement tests. Gifted LEP students may end up in lower-level classes and even be erroneously placed in special education classes because of language barriers.

Although the teaching of gifted students defies simple prescriptions, most educators agree on some general guidelines. First, definitions of giftedness must be expanded to include criteria other than standardized test scores. Second, competition is not always conducive to academic and personal growth. Gifted students often do better when they pursue projects of particular interest to them. They need specific feedback on their performances, not comparisons of their performances to other students.

The goal of educators and families is to enable students to have the best possible education, so gifted students would seem to be at an advantage. But we shouldn't overlook the social stigma attached to being labeled gifted or talented. The fact is, sometimes students do not want to be labeled high-achieving. Being a "brainiac" is not always conducive to making and keeping friends. In addition, some students in gifted and talented programs find the combined pressure of meeting high expectations and being like other students overwhelming. As always, teachers should not underestimate the social implications of any treatment perceived to draw "special" attention to a student.

How Can Teachers Create Culturally Relevant Classrooms?

Three factors influence positive attitudes in schools: the quality of teachers' relationships with students, the quality of education, and the social skills teachers impart to students (Louis Harris and Associates, 1996). When these factors are present, students view the school's social problems as less serious. They also express more confidence that people from different backgrounds receive equal treatment by adults in their community. To a large extent, these factors depend on teachers' knowledge of and attitudes toward their students.

Children and teachers who grow up in diverse communities have opportunities to learn about those who differ from themselves and about themselves in relation to others. These opportunities do not always result in social harmony. Nor do they necessarily lead to tension and conflict. But both outcomes are possible in culturally diverse schools.

Cultural Mismatches

What teachers expect from the mix of students they teach and how they act on those expectations are crucial. This process can be made even more complicated in a classroom in which the teacher believes she or he has nothing in common with the students. When cultural mismatches between teachers and students occur in the classroom, the effects can be hard on each. Inner-city schools with high proportions of racial and ethnic minorities, low-income students, and at-risk learners, for example, commonly have mismatches between teachers' and students' values. Such differences can be frustrating and frightening, particularly to novice teachers.

How could you prepare yourself for a classroom of students with whom you share little in terms of cultural background, experiences, and values?

Responsive Instruction

Successful teachers create "culturally relevant" classrooms—places where curriculum and instruction are "friendly" to difference (Oakes & Lipton, 1999). But how do teachers develop such settings? Researchers suggest teachers begin by getting to know their students and their

Case Perspectives

Think back to the case that opened this chapter. The following comments are intended to provide a context for your own thinking about this case.

AN ATTORNEY CONSIDERS FREEDOM OF EXPRESSION IN LITERATURE AND THE LAW. Stephanie Janeway appears to have stumbled into a thicket of social and legal issues that have grown up around curriculum development and curriculum selection. Generally speaking, schools must develop and make public their processes for defining their curricula. These processes must operate in ways that protect people equally from discriminatory material; that is, committees' procedures must be defensible and fair—not biased and discriminatory against a racial or gender group.

It is too bad Stephanie didn't think about the possibility that requiring *The Adventures of Huckleberry Finn* might cause some problems. If she had, then she might have been able to consider in a calm, collected fashion what would be best for her students. To be sure, she might still have required the book and taught it the same way, but at least she would have had the benefit of being governed by rationality instead of by emotion. Many teachers are required to clear their reading lists with school or district curriculum coordinators. Apparently Stephanie's district did not have this requirement. But next time she might want to run her reading list by her department chair or an experienced colleague, or a curriculum committee if one exists, before making a final decision.

The courts have been reluctant to weigh in on matters of curriculum development and selection, which means that the responsibility rests with state and local decision makers. They must decide what is acceptable and unacceptable for their own communities.

A HIGH SCHOOL PRINCIPAL REFLECTS ON STEPHANIE'S ASSIGNMENT OF *THE ADVENTURES OF HUCKLEBERRY FINN* IN AN ELEVENTH-GRADE ENGLISH CLASS. I believe all of our social science and humanities courses need help with their reading lists. Let me say that a different way: Our teachers need the protection that a curriculum committee can provide. So I have all of our teachers submit their reading lists at least two weeks before distributing them to students in the fall. The teachers note any books they believe may be controversial to alert the committee to be particularly mindful of these selections.

The curriculum committee's job is not to censor the lists. They simply raise questions and make suggestions. Teachers make the final decisions about what to include, what to exclude, what to require, and what to recommend. Teachers file the committee's reports and their final reading lists in my office. Only once has a teacher disagreed with the committee's recommendations. We resolved the disagreement by purchasing a PBS series on race in America for the teachers to use. She was delighted to use the series as a replacement for a book that the committee believed was outdated.

Our success has everything to do with the fact that the curriculum committee is highly respected. It is composed of seven teachers—five veterans and two young staff members. Because the committee takes its work seriously, it is a powerful force. I have felt quite confident on different occasions when curriculum issues arise in school board meetings, because we have these professional voices speaking on behalf of our school.

I would encourage Stephanie Janeway to investigate her school's policies on curriculum development and curriculum selection. She is part of the system. She is not alone in these matters.

Questions for Reflection: Do you think you would be more comfortable teaching in a district in which you were entirely responsible for your own curricular decisions, or one in which the curriculum was determined by a coordinator or committee? What would your "ideal" situation be for making these decisions? What do you think Stephanie might do at this point? What resources might she have? ■

---

communities and then transferring that knowledge into new ways of approaching a subject. They also recommend that teachers read literature describing other teachers' experiences in diverse settings.

When teachers work with students who are bilingual or who are developing English language proficiency and literacy, making content culturally relevant can be particularly challenging. For example, the recommended strategy for increasing science literacy is to have children act as scientists, asking and answering questions to understand the world (National Research Council, 1996). But how would this approach be used with students from diverse language backgrounds who may not possess the English skills necessary to participate fully? Would they just not learn what the other students learn? On a larger scale, the question is this: Should teachers serve as *knowledge transmitters,* leading students through predetermined lessons and activities, or as *facilitators,* guiding students to ask questions and to investigate their own interests? Can teachers strike a balance?

Teachers who share the languages and cultures of their students may choose instructional approaches that reflect students' native cultures. Researchers have worked to examine the effectiveness of different approaches not only in science, but in other content areas as well (Brown, 1994; Lehrer & Schauble, 1998; Metz, 1995; Rosebery & Warren, 1998; Valdes, 1999). Prospective teachers shouldn't think, however, that there are definite answers to these kinds of questions. Nor is there a "magic" moment when everything will be answered once and for all. Good teachers know these are ongoing issues; the answers change and sometimes even the questions change.

Summary

Differences among people take many forms and have many implications for teachers and schools. Such differences include culture, race, ethnicity, primary language group, gender, special needs and talents, and sexual orientation. How learners think about themselves matters, but how teachers think about learners matters too.

Teachers use a variety of instructional approaches adapted to their perceptions of students' needs. Teaching in a culturally responsive way means fitting instruction to learners, not fitting learners to instruction. Teachers accomplish such adaptations by selecting curricula, delivering instruction, and evaluating student progress.

Certainly people differ from one another in some important ways, but we are all similar too. To know what others think or feel—even people from cultures with which you are unfamiliar—it can be helpful to begin by looking deep within yourself. The phrase "trust your instincts" suggests that if you think or believe something others may too. But good teachers do not stop there. They observe, question, listen, read, and get out there among the people they serve.

TERMS AND CONCEPTS

assimilation
bilingual education
conflict mediation
culture
Education for All Handicapped
    Children Act
English as a Second Language (ESL)
e pluribus unum
equal educational opportunity
ethnicity
exceptional learners

gender bias
giftedness
inclusive education
individualized education program (IEP)
Individuals with Disabilities Education
    Act (IDEA)
limited English proficient (LEP)
paraprofessional
pluralism
race
Title IX

REFLECTIVE ACTIVITY: ONE IMMIGRANT'S SUCCESS STORY

Reflective practice is an essential part of good teaching. Reflection is a process that includes making thoughtful decisions, understanding and articulating value structures, acting from knowledge, evaluating your actions and their effects, and sharing your reflections with colleagues. After reading the following scenario, respond to the questions below. The scenario reflects the INTASC Principle and Disposition at the end of this activity.

Fairfax County Public Schools Superintendent Daniel Domenech is a Cuban refugee. He describes his transition from school in Cuba to school in the United States:

> *I started school in Cuba and went through the fifth grade. I actually started school at the age of three. I did kindergarten as a three-year-old. So when I came to the United States, I was already a fifth grader in Cuba. I was instantly placed in a second grade class here. (Seymour, 2001, p. A1)*

Nine-year-old Domenech spoke no English when he and his family arrived in the United States in 1955. He recalled, years later, the difficulty he had understanding his lessons and making himself understood while attending a Catholic boarding school in Tarrytown, New York.

Domenech soon transferred to public schools in New York City and began to excel in his studies as his English improved. His path to the head of the Fairfax schools—the twelfth largest system in the nation—is a success story of personal triumph and a testament to the power of education.

Decide 1. What factor(s) may have given Daniel Domenech an edge in obtaining educational success in the United States?

Perceive and Value 2. Why might some people such as Daniel Domenech and his family leave Cuba while others choose to stay?

Know and Act 3. What would you want to know about the strategies Domenech's teachers, both Cuban and American, used to help him succeed? What might you do to help immigrant children in your classroom succeed? Would you encourage non-English speakers to keep speaking their native language?

Evaluate 4. Should non-English-speaking students' educational performance be judged differently from that of students who speak English fluently?

Discuss 5. Ask someone you know who has learned English as a second language about his or her learning experience. Did that person experience a formal program to help in learning English? What helped the person most? What was most difficult?

INTASC Principle 3

The teacher understands how students differ in their approaches to learning and creates instructional opportunities that are adapted to diverse learners.

Disposition

The teacher knows about the process of second-language acquisition and about strategies to support the learning of students whose first language is not English. (Interstate New Teacher Assessment and Support Consortium, 1992)

ADDITIONAL READINGS

Banks, J. A. (2004). *Multicultural education: Issues and perspectives* (5th ed.). New York: Wiley.

Gollnick, D. M., & Chinn, P. C. (2004). *Multicultural education in a pluralist society* (7th ed.). Columbus, OH: Merrill.

Hernandez, H. (2001). *Multicultural education: A teacher's guide to linking context, process, and content* (2nd ed.). Upper Saddle River, NJ: Prentice Hall.

Koppelman, K., & Goodhart, L. (2005). *Understanding human differences: Multicultural education for a diverse America.* Boston: Allyn & Bacon.

Tatum, B. D. (2003). *Why are all the Black kids sitting together in the cafeteria?* New York: Basic Books.

WEB RESOURCES

http://inclusion.ngfl.gov.uk/
"Inclusion" is an online catalogue of resources to support individual learning needs. The catalogue is part of the British government's National Grid for Learning (NGfL) website.

www.tolerance.org
Visit this website for ideas on ways to alert people of all ages to problems of hate and intolerance.

www.census.gov
This website reveals racial statistics for the United States.

www.edchange.org/multicultural/
The Multicultural Pavilion includes a variety of multicultural education resources for educators.

www.ngltf.org/
The National Gay and Lesbian Task Force works to eliminate prejudice, violence, and injustice against gay, lesbian, bisexual, and transgender people at the local, state, and national levels.

www.gifted.uconn.edu/nrcgt.html
The National Research Center on the Gifted and Talented provides a variety of gifted and talented education resources for educators.

*Developing a
Professional
Portfolio*

DIGITAL PORTFOLIOS

A portfolio is a collection of materials teachers create to document their professional growth as educators. Many of you may choose to create a digital portfolio on the Web or on a CD-ROM because the technology is available, you know how to use it or want to learn, and you want to demonstrate that you possess special skills that make you an attractive candidate to employers and graduate programs.

There are some other benefits of making your portfolio digital. Kilbane and Milman (2005) suggested that a teacher with a digital portfolio demonstrates that she has the competency to affect students' abilities to use technology; that is, if she has the computer skills, then she can share them with her students. Digital portfolios are also more portable than hard-copy materials. They can be easily revised and copied, as well as shared inexpensively and widely.

Kilbane and Milman point their readers to several online samples of teachers' portfolios. For instance, see the work of Mayra Almodovar, a doctoral student at the University of Massachusetts at Amherst.[*] The primary audience for the portfolio is undergraduate student teachers in the Amherst area. Almodovar's website includes information about her educational philosophy and prior experiences; it also includes examples of teaching competencies related to INTASC standards. **What do you notice about Almodavar's efforts to increase teachers' and students' understanding of diverse cultures?**

As you explore the use of digital portfolios, ask yourself what items of professional information you might include in your own portfolio. What technologies and design features might you use to communicate your knowledge, skills, and values to others? What might you do today to begin to prepare yourself to create an electronic portfolio?

Keep in mind that the digital presentation of your portfolio is a complement to the contents of your portfolio. In the end there is no substitute for substance, so you must focus on the materials you collect for your portfolio and how they reflect your professional goals as an educator.

[*]www.digitalteachingportfolios.com/workbook/

Online Activity

The Learning Network

Teachers, students, and parents can take advantage of the Learning Network (sponsored by the *New York Times*) to make the richness and diversity of life a central part of the curriculum from grades three to twelve. The site (www.nytimes.com/learning/) offers daily News Summaries, along with News Quizzes. Learn what happened On This Day in History; boost your vocabulary with the Word of the Day. Do a Crossword Puzzle to reinforce what you know about particular subject matter (e.g., to keep the Periodic Table of Elements fresh in your mind). Wonder how to help parents help their children talk at the dinner table? Go for the Conversation Starters. Do you feel relatively uninformed about a particular cultural issue? Get up to speed by consulting Issues in Depth. Take guided Web Tours about significant topics of the day.

Visit the Lesson Plan Archive, which is linked from the homepage (www.nytimes.com/learning/teachers/lessons/archive.html). When you arrive:

1. Select a subject area of interest (e.g., current events)
2. Specify the grade levels of interest (e.g., 6 to 8)
3. Type in a key word to use for a search (e.g., war)

The documents that fit your search instructions will be displayed. Peruse the abstracts that appear with the document links and click on one of particular interest—one for which you might be able to develop your own lesson plan, but at a different grade level. Print a copy of the full plan that you selected.

1. Now try to develop your own lesson plan on the same subject, one that might complement the plan you selected. Use the categories provided (title, grade levels of interest, overview of your plan, suggested time, objectives, resources/materials, activities/procedures, evaluation/assessment).
2. Share your plan with a classmate, inviting suggestions.
3. If you are satisfied that the plan is a good one, you might choose to submit it to the *New York Times* for inclusion on its website. (You will see a link that allows you to upload your own plan.)

Education in America: The Early Years

Jack Bollinger got the call midway into third period—the time he used for planning while his kids went to phys. ed. Annie Bryant, the mother of a new student in Jack's class, wanted to set up an appointment to talk about an issue that "really concerns" her. She had heard that the school was considering the establishment of a "religious release program" like the one at McSwain Elementary in Staunton, Virginia. She could not understand how any public school could support religious education, and she wanted "some answers."

Jack knew about the McSwain program, and he knew there was talk of replicating it at Rolling Rock Elementary. After lunch on Mondays and Tuesdays at McSwain Elementary School and three other public schools in Staunton, Virginia, groups of students walk to Memorial Baptist Church to study the Bible, while other children, whose parents have declined to enroll their children in weekday religious classes, are at recess. Some 80 to 85 percent of the first-, second-, and third-graders in Staunton attend the classes—and have done so for almost seventy years.

When Jack first started hearing about the Staunton program, he had been surprised to learn that, under certain circumstances, using class time for religious study is not against the law. He also knew, however, that some parents in Staunton were beginning to challenge the practice at McSwain, citing the potential effect of this "pull-out" time on students' performances on the state achievement tests (Standards of Learning), and in turn on the district's performance under the No Child Left Behind legislation. Time, these parents argued, is the key variable in children's lives. It should not be siphoned away from academic work for the study of God or for any other well-intentioned activity.

Jack did not fully understand the historical forces that operated to make the conditions in Staunton possible. The people in Staunton were not in period costumes. They were not actors in a living history museum. Yet history seemed to have shaped educational life in their community. History had created an educational tradition that, some of Jack's colleagues contended, was markedly at odds with the constitutional separation of church and state.

Others objected, as the parents were now arguing, that the situation had less to do with church and state than it did with a need to focus the schools' full attention on helping children demonstrate traditional indicators of success. Having students out of class for almost an hour several days each week made that focus almost impossible.

All Jack knew about Staunton was what he read in the newspaper. And being a first-year teacher in a new community, he certainly didn't know much about the history of Rolling Rock Elementary School and the community of which it was a part. But Jack knew that Annie Bryant probably wanted more than "some answers." He suspected that she was looking for evidence that her son's teacher was not an extremist or, worse yet, a functional moron.

Jack didn't think he had to defend a particular point of view about the relationship of religious instruction and Rolling Rock Elementary School. He wasn't a lawyer. He wasn't a school administrator or a school board member. He was a professional educator—one with a history minor in college. And because of that, Jack felt intellectually obligated to help Mrs. Bryant understand how history can exert such a powerful influence on our present-day educational practice. But where to begin?

This chapter examines early educational life in the United States and the forces, both within and beyond people's control, that changed life between 1600 and 1865. Hold this question in your mind as you read: How do early historical forces continue to influence our educational lives today?

English philosopher
John Locke
(1632–1704)

Which Europeans Influenced Early Education?

Most early American colonists emigrated from England and Europe. Not surprisingly, European thinkers shaped the colonists' formal educational system. Who were these intellectuals, and what did they believe?

Comenius: Value of Structure

Is there a danger in thinking that education is the means for improving society? John Amos Comenius (1592–1670), a Czech theologian and philosopher, thought education could improve society. Comenius believed all children should be trained methodically by teachers using quality textbooks in schools supported by governments and the clergy. He envisioned education programs divided into four distinct grades: the nursery school (birth to age six), the elementary or national school (ages six to twelve), the Latin school or gymnasium (ages thirteen to eighteen), and the Academy (gifted youths ages nineteen to twenty-four). Comenius argued that a child's mind should be "prepared" to receive instruction and that education would be "easy and pleasant" if it began early, before a child's mind was "corrupted." He also thought instruction should move from the general to the specific, with tasks arranged from easy to difficult.

Comenius thought the number of subjects studied should be manageable for children. Teachers should present lessons at a reasonable pace, use age-appropriate instruction, keep materials constantly before children's eyes, and use a single method of instruction at all times. Comenius also advocated universal textbooks and schools and a universal language (Edwards, 1972; Ulich, 1968). Which of Comenius's ideas are relevant today in discussions about education in the United States?

Locke and Rousseau: Enlightened Views

How did formal education encourage the idea that we, and not God, were responsible for the conduct of our lives? The English philosopher John Locke (1632–1704) believed the human mind at birth was a blank state *(tabula rasa)*, not a collection of preformed ideas placed there by God. He thought children should interact with the environment by using their five senses to gather and test ideas. In his view, teachers should tailor instruction to the individual child's talents and interests. Teachers should encourage curiosity and treat children as "rational creatures" who might unlock life's mysteries. Locke also believed that children learned through imitation; an effective teacher taught by example and suggestion, not by coercion (Gay, 1964).

Locke's ideas about education were consistent with the Age of Enlightenment, a period when reason was valued as a supreme virtue. In keeping with the beliefs of that period, Locke thought people were inherently good. It followed then that children taught by benevolent educators were bound to grow intellectually and prosper.

Swiss philosopher Jean-Jacques Rousseau (1712–1778) had ideas about education that were similar to those of Locke. Most significantly, Rousseau criticized educational methods he believed were inconsistent with children's ways of thinking, seeing, and feeling. He contended that schools imposed books and abstract ideas on minds not yet ready to deal with such demands.

In his book *Emile,* Rousseau described the development of a human being from infancy to maturity, using the character of Emile. According to Rousseau's ideas about education, Emile's tutor provided experiences that matched the natural conditions of Emile's growth.

From infancy through age eleven, Emile's tutor removed obstacles that might impede development. During this time, Emile explored the environment with his senses, learning through trial and error and experiencing joy and pain from naturally occurring experiences. Between ages eleven and fourteen, Emile was introduced to geography, astronomy, and his first book, Daniel Defoe's *Robinson Crusoe*. Emile also learned carpentry, a practical skill that might serve him later in life. Abstract thought processes developed during adolescence, and Emile began to compare himself to others, think about his place in the world, and explore the mysteries of the universe. Because his tutor had respected his human nature, removing obstacles that might hinder his development, Emile's educational development happened naturally (Boyd, 1962; Ulich, 1968).

Pestalozzi: Encouraging Development

Johann Heinrich Pestalozzi (1746–1827), a Swiss educator, tested Rousseau's ideas on teachers and students at two German schools for boys. Pestalozzi (1898), like Rousseau, worried about educational conditions that stifled children's playfulness and natural curiosity. He thought young children lost their natural love of learning by being treated "like sheep" who were forced to spend their time in flocks studying boring letters and numerals.

Pestalozzi also believed that children pass through a number of stages of development. Teachers needed to be kind, and they needed to provide experiences that appealed to all the senses when teaching concepts and skills, rather than relying on verbal instruction (Gutek, 1968). In *How Gertrude Teaches Her Children,* a book written for mothers, Pestalozzi (1898) demonstrated why it was important to "always put a picture before the eye."

> It was inevitable, for instance, when [the teacher] asked, in arithmetic, How many times is seven contained in sixty-three? The child had no real background for his answer, and must, with great trouble, dig it out of his memory. Now, by the plan of putting nine times seven objects before his eyes, and letting him count them as nine sevens standing together, he has not to think any more about this question; he knows from what he has already learnt, although he is asked for the first time, that seven is contained nine times in sixty-three. (p. 97)

Have you seen or do you know of other examples of teachers helping young children visualize problems and solutions?

Froebel: Start Early

Friedrich Froebel (1782–1852) was a German philosopher who founded the first **kindergarten** in 1837 at Blankenburg, Germany. Froebel's kindergarten was not a school in the traditional sense, but a "general institution" where young children learned through the use of educational games and activities. He thought play was an important part of learning. In the kindergarten, much of the children's day was spent gardening, an activity aimed at helping them see the similarity between the growth of plants and their own development (Downs, 1978).

Froebel viewed mental life as the result of God's creativeness (Ulich, 1968, p. 287). To Froebel, a person's senses, emotions, and reason were the necessary attributes for learning. He valued quality early childhood experiences that focused on play, music, and art. Children were not "lumps of clay" to be molded; instead they were like plants and animals, needing time and space to develop according to natural law (Downs, 1978).

In 1855, Margaretta Schurtz, a German immigrant and one of Froebel's former students, established one of the first kindergartens in America in Watertown, Wisconsin. These early kindergartens were primarily meant to guarantee the preservation of the German heritage and language. The first kindergarten conducted in English was founded in Boston in 1860 by Elizabeth Peabody.

The Froebel Foundation USA, located in Grand Rapids, Michigan, was founded in 2001 to promote Friedrich Froebel's educational ideas and to preserve the history of the U.S. kindergarten

Froebel kindergartens centered on play, music, art, and activities such as gardening.

movement. Most of these ideas, now widely accepted, continue to shape kindergartens across the nation:

- Humans are creative.
- Play drives learning.
- Children can learn only what they are ready to learn.
- To educate means to lead or guide someone to knowledge.
- A teacher cannot control the child, but she can control the educational environment.
- Children's experiences in controlled environments provide valuable diagnostic information that help teachers help children. (Froebel Foundation USA, 2005) **Why do so many people believe that beginning formal education at an early age is critical?**

How Did Informal Education Develop before the Civil War?

European settlers who arrived on the shores of the New World in the 1600s adapted their European ideas to the new environment as they struggled with themselves, each other, and outside forces to survive and prosper. Education lessons and practices during this time both reflected and shaped people's values as they established their settlements along the eastern coast of America.

Students in the colonies, young men called "scholars," were educated through a tutoring system, in which the quality of education often depended on the quality of the "master." The schoolmaster typically was a member of the clergy and a prominent figure in the community. The purpose of education was to prepare young men for the ministry and for leadership. In their recollections, Meriwether Lewis, who later explored the Northwest Territories on the famous Lewis and Clark Expedition, and his younger cousin and classmate, Peachy Gilmer, complained about one of their schoolmasters and praised another. Of their schoolmaster Dr. Charles Everitt, Gilmer said he was

> afflicted with very bad health . . . peevish, capricious, and every way disagreeable. . . .
> He invented cruel punishments for the scholars. . . . His method of teaching was as bad
> as anything could be. He was imparient [sic] of interruption. We seldom applied for

European settlers who arrived on the shores of the New World in the 1600s had to adapt to the new environment. What aspects of education do you think were most important at that time?

assistance, said our lessons badly, made no proficiency, and acquired negligent and bad habits. (Ambrose, 1996, p. 27)

In 1790, Lewis transferred to a new schoolmaster, Reverend James Waddell, who was a great contrast to the ill-tempered Everitt. Lewis called Waddell "a very polite scholar," and wrote to his mother, "I expect to continue [here] for eighteen months or two years. Every civility is here paid to me and leaves me without any reason to regret the loss of a home or nearer connection. As soon as I complete my education, you shall certainly see me" (Ambrose, 1996, p. 27).

Education in the Southern Colonies

Many settlers in the southern colonies of Virginia, Maryland, Georgia, and the Carolinas lived on large plantations with rigid class distinctions. A plantation functioned as a small community where growers raised crops such as tobacco, sugar, or cotton. The owner's home often was the center of the plantation, surrounded by a kitchen, smokehouse, stable, and sometimes a school. A hired tutor usually taught the landowner's children. Education on the plantations was fairly formal, and the children were taught reading, writing, and mathematics. Learning to read was central to becoming a good Christian. If you knew how to read, you could follow the will of God as expressed in the Bible.

Slaves from Africa and indentured servants from Europe lived in cabins and barns around the property border. They were the backbone of plantation life, serving as field workers, household workers, and skilled artisans (cobblers, carpenters, tailors, blacksmiths). Slaves, servants, and their children rarely received any type of education on the plantation, and most could neither read nor write.

Small farmers in the southern colonies lived in isolated areas. Although they worked for themselves, their livelihood often was affected by plantation owners, because they had the power to purchase or sell surplus crops, rent out land, and loan money. Small farmers' decisions about where to settle were based mainly on the lay of the land, the quality of the soil, and the proximity of water. For those who struggled to make a living by working the land, there was no community of any sort, nor were there nearby schools or churches.

For the most part, education for the children of small farmers was informal. Skills that boys and girls needed to learn were taught by the family. Families also taught their children to read, and families conducted their own worship services until the middle of the eighteenth century, when traveling missionaries began to reach people in rural areas.

Education in the Middle Atlantic Colonies

Middle Atlantic colonists (in New York, New Jersey, Pennsylvania, and Delaware) were more diverse than were settlers in the Southern colonies. Most Middle Atlantic colonists spoke English, but there were also Dutch-, German-, French-, and Swedish-speaking families whose religious orientation varied greatly from one another. There were Catholics, Mennonites, Calvinists, Lutherans, Quakers, Presbyterians, and Jews, all eager to preserve their languages and beliefs.

Religious groups in this area established their own **parochial schools.** English, Irish, Welsh, Dutch, and German Quakers, for instance, who settled mainly in Pennsylvania, stressed the importance of teaching religion, mathematics, reading, and writing. They also offered some vocational training to children. In accordance with their religion, teachers viewed children as inherently good and rejected the use of corporal punishment. These parochial schools were open to everyone, including Native Americans and slaves (Bullock, 1967).

Education in the New England Colonies

In the New England colonies (Massachusetts Bay, Rhode Island, New Hampshire, and Connecticut), many people shared similar values, which made it possible to establish town schools. In particular, two laws moved New Englanders in the direction of town schools. The Massachusetts Act of 1642 required that parents and master craftsmen with apprentices be monitored to ensure that children were learning to read and understand religious principles. The Massachusetts Act of 1647, sometimes referred to as the Old Deluder Satan Act, required towns to educate youth so they might thwart Satan's trickery. To produce Scripture-literate citizens, every town of fifty households had to employ a teacher of reading and writing, and every town of one hundred households had to provide a grammar school to prepare students for continuing study at Harvard University.

Many settlers in the Northern colonies were Puritans who followed the teachings of John Calvin, a Swiss religious reformer. Calvin believed God was omnipotent and good, whereas human beings were evil and helpless, predestined for either salvation or eternal torment. Schools were to produce literate, hardworking, frugal, and respectful men and women who could resist temptation. Calvin saw children as savage and primitive creatures who needed training and discipline to achieve a life of social conformity and religious commitment.

Colonists living in northern cities experienced a lifestyle quite different from colonists in other areas of the country. Northern cities were densely populated trading centers. Merchants, who were key people in the community, offered an array of goods and services not found elsewhere. Ships brought both goods and ideas from England and Europe that seldom made their way south. Overall, city dwellers on the eastern seaboard were among the best informed and sometimes the most influential of the colonists. In addition, many schoolteachers in the North were better educated than teachers in other parts of the country (Blum et al., 1993). **How does geography continue to influence education in our nation?**

A National View of Education

For democracy to work, people had to be literate and information had to be available. By the middle of the eighteenth century, almost every colony had a printing press churning out a daily newspaper that contained not only local and international news, but also literary and political essays. These weekly newspapers, essays, and verse were popular reading material in the colonies. Technological advancements also made it easier for printers to produce almanacs, flyers, and books.

Most colonists understood how government worked, but they did not always agree on what it should do. Some argued the country should free itself from England. Others believed they should reconcile their differences with England and remain a colony. The struggle for people's loyalties, both on and off the battlefield, shaped the talk and writings of the day. Thomas Paine's book, *Common Sense,* published in 1776 was especially popular. It presented a compelling case for the country's independence and sold 100,000 copies in its first three months of publication.

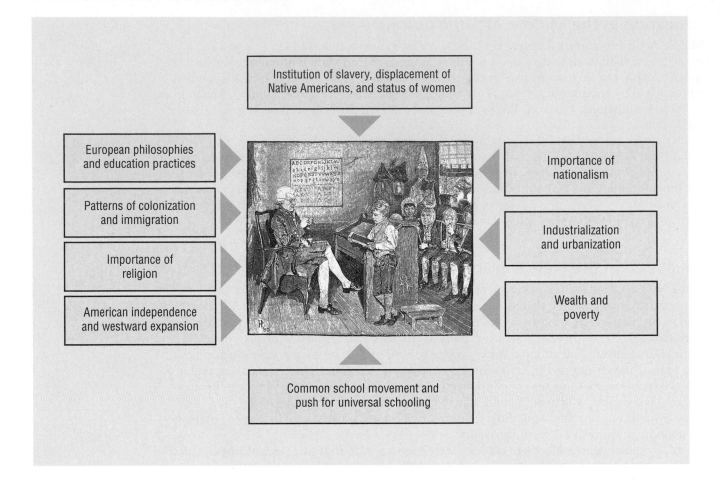

Institution of slavery, displacement of
Native Americans, and status of women

European philosophies
and education practices

Patterns of colonization
and immigration

Importance of
religion

American independence
and westward expansion

Importance of
nationalism

Industrialization
and urbanization

Wealth and
poverty

Common school movement and
push for universal schooling

Figure 4.1
Some Factors Affecting
Education before the
Civil War
Whose contributions might
you add to this figure under the
heading "Influential Early
Educators and Their Ideas?"

Paine captured the minds and hearts of the delegates to the Continental Congress and
of many others outside Philadelphia, which was the nation's capital at the time
(Cremin, 1970). As Figure 4.1 shows, national independence was one of several devel-
opments that significantly affected the American system of education. **Which of these
forces exert pressure on public education today?**

As the country grew, competing forces from within continued to shape Americans
views of themselves and others. Plantation owners in the South protected their virtually
self-sufficient communities with a permanent labor force (slaves), while abolitionists in
the North battled both covertly and openly to destroy the system of slavery that supported the plantations. The Cherokee, Creek, Iroquois, and other Native American tribes fought
to preserve their land and their physical and spiritual well-being, while European Americans took
this land by trickery and force to improve their own lives and to fulfill what they believed was
their divine destiny.

Between 1800 and 1840, the value of agricultural products grew remarkably, largely due
to westward expansion and continued immigration to the United States. The increased speed
and volume of people heading west can be seen in the following statistic: in 1810, only about
one-seventh of the total population lived west of the Appalachians, but by 1840 it was one-
third of the total population. To meet the increased demand, the number of farmers increased
from about five million to fifteen million during this time (Blum et al., 1993).

In the midst of all this conflict and expansion, the nation's founders believed that education was the best hope for the republic. Freedom had to be tempered by the need to maintain
social order, and education would prepare good citizens. The founders believed virtuous, disciplined, and intelligent citizens would know how to participate responsibly in a democracy.
National education leaders Noah Webster (Connecticut), Benjamin Rush (Pennsylvania), and
Thomas Jefferson (Virginia) argued that the ability to read, write, and compute numbers

would make the people and the nation strong. Jefferson viewed education as the key to advancing civilization.

> If a nation expects to be ignorant and free, in a state of civilization, it expects what never was and never will be . . . whenever the people are well-informed, they can be trusted with their own government; that, whenever things get so far wrong as to attract their notice, they may be relied on to set them right. (Jefferson as cited in Padover, 1939, pp. 88–89)

The Northwest Ordinance of 1785 sliced the Northwest Territories (now the states of Ohio, Indiana, Illinois, Michigan, Wisconsin, and part of Minnesota) into townships, each having thirty-six square miles. As depicted in Figure 4.2, each township had a section of land set aside for educational purposes. The Northwest Ordinance also set the precedent for financing education through **land grant schools.** Each area was given land free of charge (granted), the size of which usually depended on the population. The local government used the income from this land to fund schools, thus the phrase "land grant schools."

Most historians recognize the Northwest Ordinance as the greatest accomplishment of the government under the Articles of Confederation, the governing principles established by the Continental Congress prior to the U.S. Constitution. Fear, however, is what stimulated passage of the ordinance. Leaders in the East feared that those who moved to the Northwest would become less civilized than people on the East Coast. To protect the Union, the framers of the ordinance wanted to make sure residents of the Northwest did not undo democracy from their corner of the country. For these leaders, education meant socialization and the continuation of the democratic values of the young nation. How do public schools today socialize students toward democratic values?

Figure 4.2
A Precedent for Public Education
Under the Northwest Ordinance of 1785, the sixteenth square mile of a township's land grant was reserved for town-supported education.

What Were the Aims of Education?

In addition to the advancement of democratic ideals in an expanding country, many European Americans believed the purpose of education was to save souls. In general, during this time schooling began at home with the family, and religion was a major aspect of education. In general, Father laid down the rules, keeping an eye on the King James Bible, and Mother enforced them. Formal schooling was patterned after English schools. In New England, legislatures reminded parents of their responsibility for their children's education, but the related laws were not well enforced.

Under the Northwest Ordinance of 1785, the sixteenth square mile of a township's land grant was reserved for town-supported education.

Families and communities sometimes provided schooling for their children at inexpensive **dame schools,** or schools run by women, in the area. Dame schools taught rudimentary skills of reading, writing, and calculating. For some children, particularly girls, this was the only formal education they received. At this point, schools were private, although some received town support, and attendance was voluntary. Most wealthy Americans sent their children abroad for their education.

As the country grew both in population and land size, though, the term *educated* quickly came to mean more than learning God's law. People began to associate education with personal advancement. In addition, government leaders promoted education as a way to develop informed, wise, and honest people who would help the young democracy succeed. But education for personal advancement and civic participation was rarely extended to women and to non-European populations, such as Native Americans, Africans, and Mexicans. Later, as the nation industrialized and urbanized, education also came to mean occupational training for immigrants and low-income citizens.

The Role of Religion

Is the role of religion any more or less important in schools today than it was in colonial times, or is it merely different? Many religious groups were present in the country at this time, as

Religious freedom was one of the reasons settlers came to America. How do you think religion affected education in the 1700s?

religious freedom was one of the main reasons the settlers originally came to America. In a time long before the emergence of an American popular culture, religion occupied a central place in the lives of most citizens. Religion often was a key characteristic by which people identified themselves, and it informed many other areas of their lives, including education. For example, a majority of colonists, particularly in the South, were Protestant. They believed the Scriptures were key to self-determination and to understanding God's will. Simply put, education should help save souls. As early as 1619, Virginia law made religious study on Sunday afternoons standard practice. The textbook used was the Bible.

Except in the New England colonies, where church, state, and school were closely related, there generally was a separation of church and state. Nonetheless, church leaders greatly influenced people's thinking. Some leaders, such as Cotton Mather, were among the most prolific writers in America, and some, such as Michael Wigglesworth, enjoyed wide readership. Between 1662 and 1701, Wigglesworth's *The Day of Doom,* an account of the Last Judgment, went through five editions (Blum et al., 1993). To this day in England, religion continues to play a part in government-supported schools. What are some of the many different ways religion of all stripes might be formally intermingled in U.S. public schools? What problems and benefits might arise as a result?

In the 1740s religious experiences were brought to thousands of people as stricter Calvinism beliefs spread among the colonies. George Whitefield, a traveling English preacher, prompted the Great Awakening with his religious revivals. Whitefield combined Calvinism and showmanship as he dramatized the pain that awaited sinners, urging his audience to confess their sins and submit to God. Jonathan Edwards, a minister from Northampton, Massachusetts, was a staunch defender of the Awakening who preached an even stricter Calvinism. His theology suggested that children were inherently evil and in need of strict discipline at home and at school (Blum et al., 1993).

By the nineteenth century the rigid beliefs of orthodox Calvinism began to soften, and Americans adopted more rational and humanistic views. As strict religious beliefs lessened, so did their influence over educational methods. Many people began to challenge the traditional methods of education and demanded secular (nonreligious) curricula. Transcendentalist philosophers Henry David Thoreau, Bronson Alcott, and Ralph Waldo Emerson were among those who advocated the radical reform of education. These philosophers were concerned, in particular, with the stifling nature of education. In fact, many of their ideas about teaching methods matched those of Rousseau. According to Emerson (1884),

> Education has so cold, so hopeless a sound. A treatise on education, a convention for education, a lecture, a system, affects us with slight paralysis and a certain yawning of the jaws. . . . Education should be as broad as man. . . . The imagination must be addressed. (p. 133)

Industry Affects Education

Industrialization in the Northeast shaped the character of the nation in the late eighteenth and early nineteenth centuries. After 1830, factories grew larger and more complex. As roads and shipping improved and as transportation costs decreased, people distributed their goods to mass markets.

The Northeast had all the necessary ingredients to become a center for industry: waterpower for factories and mills, iron and coal, and entrepreneurs ready to make the region the manufacturing center of the nation. Engineering marvels, such as the Erie Canal, symbolized people's technical capabilities and passion for economic prosperity. Around this time, federal law permitted people to patent their inventions, and many people took the opportunity to invent machines and products they hoped would make them rich.

While the North propelled itself toward industrialization, the South remained rural and dependent on agriculture for its economic well-being. As more colonists migrated westward into Alabama, Mississippi, and Louisiana, King Cotton continued to dominate southern agricultural life. Once Eli Whitney's cotton gin, a machine that separated seeds from cotton fibers, was invented in 1793, cotton production jumped from about 10,000 bales per year to about 500,000 bales in the 1820s (Blum et al., 1993).

Industrialization in the early nineteenth century led to an increasing emphasis on practical rather than theoretical learning. As industrial work increased, rather than study poetry and philosophy, people wanted to learn mechanics and trade skills that would lead to jobs with a paycheck. In addition, demands for cheap, reliable labor had a direct negative effect on schools' enrollment. Instead of staying in school, women and children met the increased demands for labor in the Northeast by working long hours under extremely difficult conditions. Infant schools, a concept devised by a Welsh cotton-mill owner and social reformer named Robert Owen (1771–1858), gave child factory workers a minimal education and provided an early form of day care for young children of working women. **Can you think of examples of industrial demands that influence the form and function of education in today's schools?**

Education for Slaves

The institution of slavery that flourished in the South made the cultures in northern, mid-Atlantic, and southern colonies vastly different from one another. Many people in the northern states, especially the Quakers, fought slavery. By the early nineteenth century, antislavery groups had produced enough pressure to achieve abolition of slavery in the northern states. But the federal Constitution recognized slavery as a local institution within the jurisdiction of individual states, so it continued in the South. For plantation owners, slavery was profitable and provided an unending supply of workers.

In the 1850s nearly half the populations of both Alabama and Louisiana and more than half the population of Mississippi were African slaves. Although the number of slaves was high, actually only a few people owned most of the slaves. Three-fourths of southern European American families never owned slaves (Blum et al., 1993).

When the Civil War began in 1861, 7 million slaves were living in the southern and western states. By the time the war ended in 1865, there were about 4 million (the rest having been freed during the war), about 5 percent of whom could read and write (Blum et al., 1993). Both before and after the war, efforts were made to provide slaves with educational opportunities. In the early 1600s, when the slave trade began, English clergy wanted to provide religious training for slaves and made some progress in achieving their goal. Presbyterians went a step further, providing formal training to African Americans to prepare them for religious leadership. In 1740 Hugh Bryan opened his school for African Americans in Charleston, South Carolina. By 1755, the Presbyterian schools had extended to Virginia, where slaves were being taught to read and write.

During the 1800s, European American missionaries and free African Americans established African schools and black academies in the North and the South. In 1811, Christopher McPherson, a free African American, started an African school in Richmond, Virginia, to teach other free African Americans and slaves. From dusk until 9:30 each night, a European American teacher he had hired taught English, writing, arithmetic, geography, and astronomy for about $1.25 per month. Flush with success, McPherson ran an advertisement for his school in the newspaper. Southerners in positions of authority, however, were not quite as enthusiastic about his efforts. They closed his school as a public nuisance and sent McPherson to the Williamsburg Lunatic Asylum (Berlin, 1974).

Although some educational opportunities for slaves existed, obviously not everyone supported these efforts. In some southern colonies, laws were created that forbade teaching slaves to read and write. Teaching one or two slaves was not a serious crime, but opening schools for slaves was a different matter. Some colonists justified such laws by persuading themselves that slaves could learn only what was required to perform their menial jobs. Others believed that education would produce slaves who would lead rebellions. In fact, such leadership did evolve.

In 1829, David Walker of Wilmington, North Carolina, published his widely read *Appeal,* a bold attack on slavery (Bullock, 1967).

Just before the Civil War, well-educated, vocal freed men and escaped slaves demanded equal rights and privileges. In the 1840s fearful citizens created a list of safe books that reflected the Southern viewpoint. The South Carolina Legislature made it a misdemeanor to teach a slave to write, subject to fine and imprisonment (*The Sun,* 1833, p. 2). Later safe reading lists included a Confederate edition of the New Testament. Many European immigrants in northern cities also feared and hated Africans and non-European immigrants, perceiving them as threats to their jobs and way of life.

Occasionally, slave owners themselves were sources of education for some slaves. Some slave owners placed their slaves with master craftsmen and even helped slaves establish small businesses to help them buy their freedom. Other slaves who did not receive formal education sometimes learned informally from their associations with literate European Americans. When assigned to houses, domestic workers might learn to read from their masters' personal libraries and from studying recipes, music, and the Bible. Slave children also learned from their master's children as they played school with one another, hidden from public view.

Some owners taught their slaves because it was good for business; others educated slaves out of respect and caring. Henry Bullock (1967) called these educational activities the **hidden passage** to freedom—literacy helped slaves to escape bondage and to make lives for themselves after the Civil War. **There are clear historical precedents that suggest education can be a dangerous force. Is there any evidence that such attitudes still exist today?**

Education for Native Americans

Native Americans should be "civilized," that is, taught the ways of European Americans, or so argued many settlers in Revolutionary times. On the other hand, people such as Thomas Jefferson believed that European Americans should intermingle with Native Americans and become one people. However, he also believed that African Americans did not possess the mental capabilities to achieve equality with European Americans and should probably be resettled elsewhere. As history shows, racial and ethnic inequality and prejudice have been present in America since the first European settlers came ashore.

Assimilation of Native Americans—educating and socializing Native Americans to make them similar to the dominant culture—and their intermarriage with European Americans was rare, however. Native American tribes made every effort to protect their heritage, customs, and languages. In 1821 a Cherokee named Sequoyah devised an eighty-six character phonetic Cherokee alphabet. A printing press using Sequoyah's type churned out stories, hymns, and even a Bible in Cherokee. A newspaper, *The Cherokee Phoenix,* advanced literacy and knowledge among the tribe. Education of this sort, however, did not protect the Cherokees from the forced relocation and genocide that affected all Native American tribes during the nineteenth century.

In Native American cultures, families bore the primary responsibility for education. Educators and caregivers surrounded Native American children—father and mother, grandparents, older siblings, uncles and aunts, other adults, and specialists, such as weavers, potters, warriors, and shamans (Coleman, 1993). Elders taught children by example, explanation, and imitation (Cremin, 1980). Therefore, formal schooling for Native Americans was a continuation of their education, not a beginning (Barman, Hebert, & McCaskill, 1986).

Overall, traditional Native American education emphasized observation, practice, and self-discipline:

Close beside my mother I sat on a rug . . . with a scrap of buckskin in one hand and an awl in the other. This was the beginning of my practical observation lessons in the art of beadwork. . . . It took many trials before I learned how to knot my sinew thread on the point of my finger, as I saw her do. . . . The quietness of her oversight made me feel strongly responsible and dependent upon my own judgment. She

Sequoyah
(1770?–1843)

treated me as a dignified little individual as long as I was on good behavior; and how humiliated I was when some boldness of mine drew forth a rebuke from her! . . . Always after these confining lessons I was wild with surplus spirits, and found joyous relief in running loose in the open again. (Zitkala-Sa, 1921)

During the early nineteenth century, Protestants and Catholics established **mission schools** among the Native Americans to teach English and Christianity. Brainerd Mission in Georgia, for example, tried to prepare the Cherokees for assimilation into the dominant culture. The schoolmaster even gave each child a new English name. The mission became a self-sufficient society, producing nearly everything students needed to live. By 1830 there were eight such schools. The Brainerd Mission became the most common model for educating other eastern tribes and nations. Many believed such schools were the best answer to "the Indian problem." **What are modern examples of education used as a process of "fitting in" the dominant culture?**

Education in Spain's American Colonies

In the early seventeenth century, the Spanish were establishing colonies in the Southwest. In 1607 the English settled Jamestown in Virginia, and in 1609 the Spanish settled Santa Fe (now New Mexico). In 1790, there were about 23,000 Spanish-speaking people in what is now the southwestern United States. They had migrated north from Mexico, the center of the Spanish conquest. Most of these settlers were of mixed Native American and Spanish descent, Spanish-speaking, and Catholic.

The Church and its missionaries provided what little formal education existed for Mexican Americans in those early years (Manuel, 1965). The schooling was basic and heavily religious, conducted mainly by older men for younger men. But upper-class women, such as Juana Ines de la Cruz (1648–1695), also had access to education:

I was not yet three years old when my mother sent an older sister of mine to be taught to read at a school. . . . Moved by affection and a mischievous spirit, I followed her; and seeing her receive instruction, such a strong desire to read burned in me that I tried to deceive the teacher, telling her that my mother wanted her to give me lessons. (Hahner, 1976, pp. 22–23)

Juana Ines later studied Latin and became a nun and a writer (Flynn, 1971). Her intellectual abilities made her a favorite of the Spanish viceroy (ambassador) and his wife in Mexico City, and she served as a court poet, successfully debating teachers from the university.

Spanish colonization of the Southwest fulfilled more than one purpose. Priests established mission schools to convert Native Americans to Catholicism and thus affected peaceful conquest of the native people (Fogel, 1988). Junipero Serra, for example, was a Franciscan priest who established missions in the California territory in the 1770s. His missions taught Native Americans how to farm and ranch, while keeping them faithful to the Church. A second purpose for the Spanish missions was to capture and hold territory and resources for Spain, while making it difficult for France and Britain to do the same.

From the beginning of their interaction, the Spanish- and English-speaking peoples in the Southwest fought for control of the land. English-speaking Texans achieved their independence from Mexico in 1836. The United States, in turn, annexed Texas in 1844. In 1846, the United States and Mexico began the Mexican War. It ended two years later with Mexico's defeat and the addition of California, Utah, New Mexico, and other western territories to the United States. These struggles, like other grand events in American history, served to educate the people involved. **How are people's attitudes and beliefs about their neighbors passed from generation to generation even today?**

Over time U.S. public schools have tried various approaches to teaching Spanish-speaking children in schools that have been largely devoid of Spanish-speaking teachers. Recently, in northern Virginia, school officials have taken the unusual step of hiring teachers from Spanish-speaking countries.

How did Roman Catholic missions and a class system based on racial origins shape the educational experiences of Native Americans and Africans in Spanish colonies?

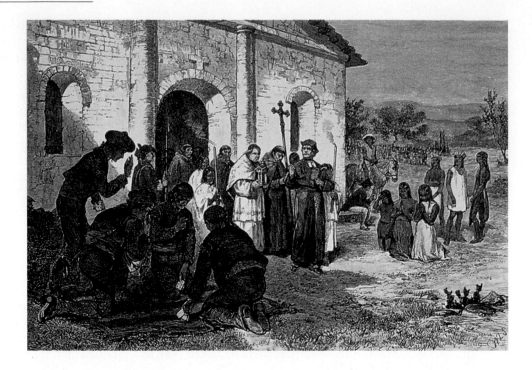

Gilmar Mejia, a native of Colombia, teaches Spanish at Stonewall Jackson High School in Manassas, Virginia, to immigrants from Honduras, Mexico, and El Salvador. Mejia is part of the Visiting International Faculty program that recruits teachers worldwide to teach in U.S. schools.

"We thought staying here was an adventure, but we never thought it was going to be this great," Mejia said. "The class was like my baby. The parents love it. . . ." Because Mejia is in the United States on a three-year visa, he must return to Colombia.

One of Mejia's students, Pedro Henriquez, eighteen, whose parents are from El Salvador, said Mejia is firm but fair and easygoing—important for students who might be adjusting to a new country. "It's easy for people's personalities to come out in class. They feel comfortable," Henriquez said. "When he told us he was leaving, everybody was like, 'For real?'" (Shapira, 2005).

Education for Women

How and why has the role of women in education changed? Women played an insignificant role in the formal education of children in colonial times. In almost every colony, however, records show one or more women being employed as teachers. These women usually taught the younger, poorer children in dame schools. Typically, women taught during the summer months (April to September), and men taught during the winter.

The Quakers in Pennsylvania did not discriminate against women to the degree that other religious sects did, so they were allowed to teach. Although they were not paid as well as Quaker schoolmasters, Quaker women comprised a large proportion of the teachers in Pennsylvania (Elsbree, 1939).

The opportunities women had to be educated and their opportunities to be educators appear to have been closely linked during this period. Benjamin Rush, for example, advanced education for women in his 1787 speech "Thoughts upon Female Education." He argued that men spent so much time outside the home working that they could not possibly assume responsibility for teaching the children—women had to do it. If this were so, then women needed to prepare for the task by becoming educated themselves.

Catherine Beecher
(1800–1878)

Efforts to open formal education to women continued during the early and mid-nineteenth century. Some of these efforts called for the creation of separate schools and programs for women only. Emma Willard was among several educators who developed academically focused programs for women. In her speech to the New York legislature in 1819, Willard advocated the formation of schools that would teach geography, science, domestic skills, music, and other courses to women. Willard opened such a school in 1821 in Troy, New York. Catherine Beecher, Zilpah Grant, Mary Lyons, and George B. Emerson also established institutions expressly for the purpose of educating women (Deighton, 1971). During the mid-1800s Catherine Beecher borrowed concepts from Swedish gymnastics to introduce young women to calisthenics to improve their health, beauty, and strength (Steinhardt, 1992).

On the other side of the argument were people who believed women should not be formally educated. Charles Bathurst, who wrote about the young British women often emulated by women in upper-class American society, believed that women's natural liveliness and feelings ought not to be encouraged. After all, "passion was passion"—one thing could lead to another.

In studies of the foundations of education, the contributions of women traditionally have been downplayed or ignored. For instance, Elizabeth Palmer Peabody, sister-in-law of Nathaniel Hawthorne and Horace Mann, was one of America's most important writers and educational reformers from the Transcendental Movement (Ronda, 1999). Major efforts to improve formal education for women did not occur, however, until the mid- to -late nineteenth century. Until then, the education that most women received, especially those who were not from wealthy families, was informal, in the home, and short-lived.

Education for People with Disabilities

Why do you think attitudes toward people with disabilities have changed so much? The object of many superstitions, people with physical or mental disabilities in the seventeenth and eighteenth centuries most often were confined and forgotten or exploited. Clergymen and physicians were among the leaders in providing care and training for people with disabilities. The first permanent, state-supported school in the United States built expressly for the mentally retarded was opened in Syracuse, New York, in 1854.

Many scholars credit Jean-Jacques Rousseau for the ideas that stimulated the development of special education. Rousseau championed the idea of encouraging children to achieve the potential they possess inherently. He wrote of the importance of sensory-motor development in young children, followed by higher intellectual development in their later years. His ideas stimulated Jean-Marc Itard (1775–1838) and Edouard Seguin (1812–1880) in France, Johann Pestalozzi (1746–1827) in Switzerland, Friedrich Froebel (1782–1852) in Germany, and Maria Montessori (1870–1952) in Italy to fit education to a child's natural development.

Samuel Gridley Howe and Thomas Gallaudet both studied abroad in the early 1800s before establishing programs in the United States to educate children with disabilities. Howe taught Laura Bridgman, a person without sight, hearing, or speech, and achieved international fame. He also taught Anne Sullivan, who later became Helen Keller's teacher. Gallaudet founded the first residential school for the deaf in Hartford, Connecticut. Named after the pioneer in education for people with hearing impairments, Gallaudet College for the Deaf in Washington, D.C., currently is the only college for the deaf in the world.

The development of education programs specially fitted to people's needs is deeply rooted in the past (Hallahan & Kauffman, 2006). Many of today's special education practices can be traced to much earlier ideas, including prescribing instruction based on the child's characteristics, carefully sequencing tasks from simple to complex, emphasizing stimulation of the child's senses, and tutoring in functional skills. See Figure 4.3 for one approved to develop curriculum for the blind.

Thomas Gallaudet
(1787–1851)

Figure 4.3
Braille: Deciphering the Code

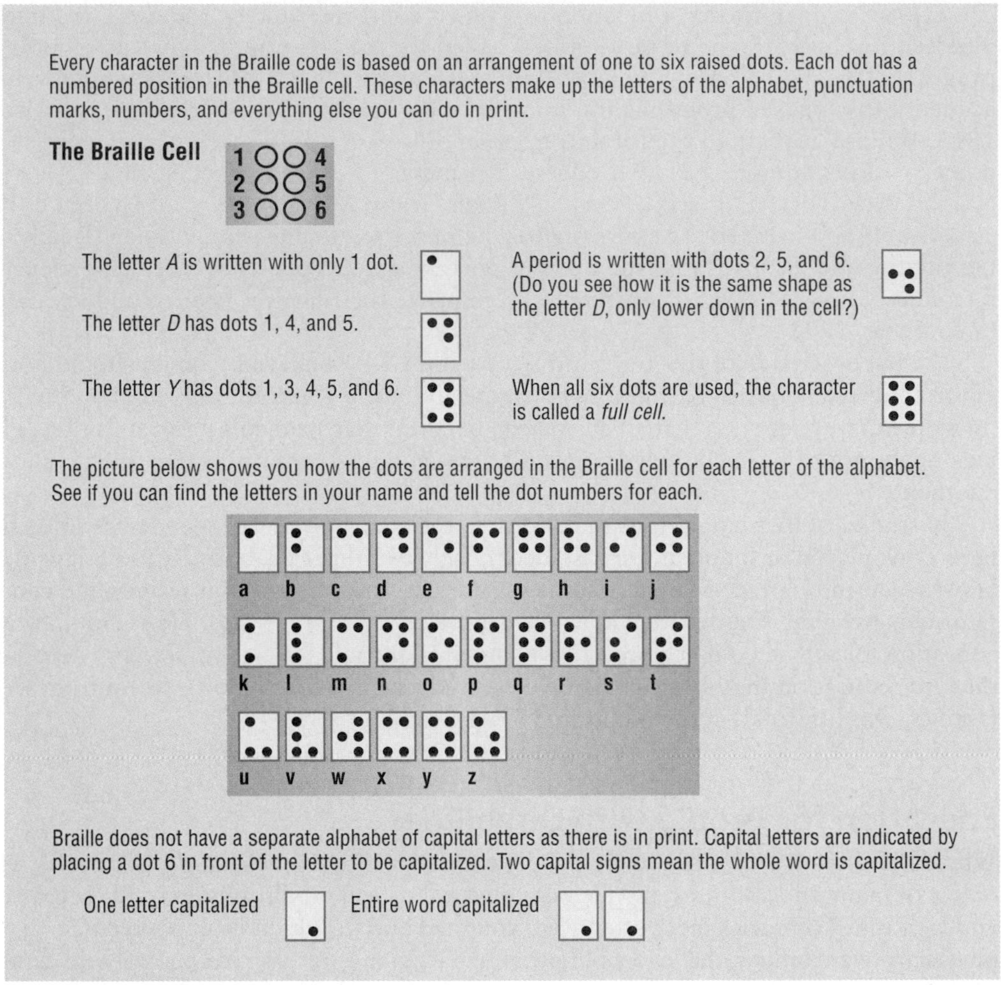
Every character in the Braille code is based on an arrangement of one to six raised dots. Each dot has a numbered position in the Braille cell. These characters make up the letters of the alphabet, punctuation marks, numbers, and everything else you can do in print.
The Braille Cell
1 4
2 5
3 6
The letter *A* is written with only 1 dot.
The letter *D* has dots 1, 4, and 5.
The letter *Y* has dots 1, 3, 4, 5, and 6.
A period is written with dots 2, 5, and 6. (Do you see how it is the same shape as the letter *D*, only lower down in the cell?)
When all six dots are used, the character is called a *full cell.*
The picture below shows you how the dots are arranged in the Braille cell for each letter of the alphabet. See if you can find the letters in your name and tell the dot numbers for each.
a b c d e f g h i j
k l m n o p q r s t
u v w x y z
Braille does not have a separate alphabet of capital letters as there is in print. Capital letters are indicated by placing a dot 6 in front of the letter to be capitalized. Two capital signs mean the whole word is capitalized.
One letter capitalized
Entire word capitalized

Source: Reprinted from http://afb.org/braillebug/braille_deciphering.asp,

How Did Formal Education Develop in America before the Civil War?

In colonial America, neither teachers nor lawyers required formal training. Academic qualifications of teachers, most of whom were men, ranged from having the ability to read and write to being a college graduate. The more rural the school, and the younger the children, the lower the teacher's qualifications usually were. For the most part, communities were not as interested in a candidate's scholastic preparation as they were in his character and religious orthodoxy.

Life in Colonial Schools

Schoolmasters had to teach and perform a variety of duties outside school. In New England, some of the more common tasks included conducting religious services, leading the church choir, sweeping out the meetinghouse, ringing the bell for public worship, and digging graves (Elsbree, 1939). Schoolmasters usually juggled teaching and extra duties with one or more other jobs, ranging from surveying to innkeeping to artisanship. Teaching often was a stepping-stone for other careers, particularly the ministry; as a result, teacher turnover often was quite high (Rury, 1989).

Schoolhouses usually were one-room cabins attended by students from the ages of three to twenty or more. All the students were in a single class, no matter their age or education level.

Most often, teaching in these large-group settings meant making students memorize facts. Students had to sit quietly for long periods of time on backless benches until called on by the teachers to recite. Teachers relied on whole-group instruction and choral responses in these mixed-ability classes. The entire system depended on repetition and drill, helped along with a more than healthy dose of punishment (Boyer et al., 2000).

> Eliphalet Nott, who grew up in Connecticut in the 1780s, said, "If I was not whipped more than three times a week, I considered myself for the time peculiarly fortunate. In 1819, six-year-old James Sims was sent to a boarding school in South Carolina where new boys were always flogged, usually until the youngster vomited or wet his breeches." (Kaestle, 1983, p. 19)

During the mid-1800s, teacher brutality toward students decreased. Historians attribute this change to the fact that graded schools came into existence. This new arrangement separated older children from younger children, so teachers who had once dealt with as many as one hundred students now dealt with smaller groups. Around this same time, women began entering the teaching profession, and they were not so cruel. In addition, educators such as Pestalozzi set out to explain to teachers the benefits of teaching students to behave in certain ways, instead of beating or coercing them into submission. Some school systems, particularly those in the cities—Syracuse, New York, for example—passed ordinances prohibiting corporal punishment (Elsbree, 1939; Kaestle, 1983). **Did you know that corporal punishment is still legal in twenty-three states? Do you know in which states most instances of corporal punishment occur? Do you know if it is legal in your state?**

Curricula

Curricula in the colonies were based on interpretations of God's preferences and the three Rs. The Old and New Testaments served as the main reading books in the late eighteenth and early nineteenth centuries. Arithmetic students learned from what was around them. Dealing with money, for example, reinforced the importance of math skills.

Students learned to read by first learning their ABCs. Next, they moved on to memorizing vowel sounds, such as *ab, eb, ib, ob, ub,* then one-syllable words, and then longer words and sentences. They practiced on slates with chalk and worked their way up to quill pens and copybooks. Many children studied whatever books their families sent to school with them—books that were jealously guarded. Sometimes teachers had to contend with as many different books as they had children in their schools (Kaestle, 1983).

HORNBOOKS, PRIMERS, AND ALMANACS The **hornbook** was the first reader for many students. It was a single piece of parchment imprinted with the alphabet, vowels, syllables, and a couple of prayers. To increase its durability, the parchment was covered with a transparent sheet of cow's horn, and the two pieces were tacked to a board. The hornbook was eventually replaced with more elaborate books of several pages.

The *New England Primer* appeared in the late seventeenth century and was the prototype for the **primers**—textbooks designed to teach rudimentary reading skills—widely used in the colonies through the eighteenth century. The *Primer* was a collection of rhymes for the letters of the alphabet, adorned with woodcut drawings. Each rhyme, an admonition or prayer, reflected the religious values of the colonies (Ford, 1899).

Benjamin Franklin left his imprint on the curriculum in the eighteenth century, as he did on so much of colonial life. His *Poor Richard's Almanack* promoted the virtues of thrift, hard work, and creativity. The *Almanack,* which was used in many classrooms, guided the self-made colonist.

GEOGRAPHIES, SPELLERS, AND DICTIONARIES Jedidiah Morse helped children think about their cultural identity as Americans when he produced his *Geography Made Easy* in 1784. The book focused on the geography of the United States, rather than on that of Europe or Britain. Much like Franklin's *Poor Richard's Almanack,* it contained patriotic and moralistic themes.

In the late 1700s and early 1800s, Noah Webster promoted a common English language. Webster's *American Spelling Book,* sometimes referred to as the ***Blue-Backed Speller,*** was first published in 1783; by 1837, 15 million copies had been sold. Webster's *An American*

Issues in School Reform

CHILDREN'S BOOKS HAVE STAYING POWER

You can still buy *McGuffey Readers* and other classic books on Amazon and elsewhere. Here is what one person said about the *McGuffey Readers*:

> I received this boxed set when I was 10 years old and I'm now in my 30s and I still read through them. I have a 5-year-old that has learned to read from the primer and we both love to take turns reading aloud from the books. I think this collection is a great way to introduce children to literature. The books are classic and timeless and there is nothing

wrong with learning some simple wholesome values from the past!
   Andrea Buschman (Rio Rancho, New Mexico, USA)

Questions for Reflection: For years, people have disagreed over the teaching of moral values in public schools. The content of instruction often ignites arguments. Do you think modern public schools still teach values? If so, how?

Source: Amazon.com. (undated). *McGuffey's Eclectic Readers*/boxed www.amazon.com/review/product/0471294284/ref=cm_cr_pr_link_/

Dictionary, first published in 1825, became the authoritative source on information about English words. Webster believed that power and prestige as a nation distinct from Britain would never come to the United States until it established its own distinctive vocabulary, spelling, and usage.

MCGUFFEY READERS William Holmes McGuffey, a clergyman and professor of philosophy, produced his legendary reader in 1836. It was the most widely used reading book in the United States in the nineteenth century. *McGuffey Readers* taught literacy skills and sought to advance the Protestant ethic through stories and essays about thrift, honesty, and diligence. By including speeches of the nation's founders, McGuffey also used his book to promote patriotic nationalism. *McGuffey Readers* are still produced and sold.

Recognizing Educational Success and Failure

School is much more a part of life today than it was in earlier times. From the arrival of the colonists until the Civil War, few people went to school. Those who did attend public schools got a dose of reading, writing, calculating, and the Protestant ethic, and then went their own ways. Most people instead acquired the knowledge necessary to survive and prosper from their families, churches, and work. Because these communities depended on family and church to teach moral values and on work to train young people for occupations, schools were believed successful if they provided rudimentary skills at low cost.

Most of the children who received the narrowly defined and severely delivered education in the young nation were white males. For young people who were Native Americans, African Americans, immigrants, and living in poor, rural places, schooling, if it existed at all, was a mixed blessing. Public schools saved some of these students from illiteracy, but also reinforced the idea that one's worth was measured in terms of race and social class.

Various types of schools and educational methods were used from colonial times to just before the Civil War. Some schools were open to everyone; others were restricted according to gender or wealth. Some were based on European concepts and institutions; others were wholly American. All of them can be seen, however, as steps taken by a new nation toward developing its own concept of successful education.

The Monitorial Method and the American Lyceum

Children started school at different ages. *Abecedarians*—beginners at school—often started as young as age three. Teachers often faced very large groups of students of varying ages who differed markedly in abilities (Kaestle, 1983). The Lancasterian or **monitorial method** of teaching provided one response to this challenge.

In the 1820s Joseph Lancaster, a Quaker, found urban classrooms to be fertile ground for the monitorial method of teaching used in Europe. In this educational pyramid scheme, the master teacher served as a "silent bystander" and "inspector." He taught the monitors, and they, in turn, taught the younger children. The older students also took attendance and kept order in the classroom. The approach made reading, writing, and arithmetic available to large numbers of children, and it was cheap.

In 1826 a wealthy Connecticut farmer, Josiah Holbrook, founded the American Lyceum, an organization devoted to the advancement of education for children and adults. Holbrook wanted to provide an economical and practical education to American youth and to encourage the application of science and education in everyday life. People belonged to a **lyceum** for $1 a year. Types of lyceums included reading circles, debating clubs, and concert bands.

The first branch of the American Lyceum was formed in Millbury, Massachusetts. By 1829 the lyceum concept had spread across the country. Ralph Waldo Emerson, a frequent lecturer on the lyceum circuit, considered the American Lyceum a new form of education and a broad cultural movement. This first formal adult and community education movement thrived in the late 1820s and 1830s, but faded in the years following the Civil War.

The Latin School and the English Academy: No Girls Allowed

The **Latin grammar school**, the first formal type of secondary school in the colonies, was established in Boston in 1635. Boys entered the grammar school at age nine or ten, if they could read and write English, and attended for four to five years. Although Latin grammar schools often taught arithmetic, geography, algebra, trigonometry, or rhetoric, their main purpose was teaching Latin, Greek, and the associated literatures. The very few students who attended college during this time went to Latin grammar schools first. Girls were not admitted.

At the other end of the spectrum was Benjamin Franklin's English-language academy in Philadelphia, which he started in 1749. Franklin recognized the need to prepare young people for highly skilled occupations and for the world of commerce. The classics were not neglected entirely, but the **English academy** emphasized the acquisition and application of practical knowledge believed most useful to the modern man.

The English academy taught practical subjects such as penmanship, arithmetic, and bookkeeping. Unlike in the Latin grammar school, English was the language of instruction, but students could study other languages as they needed them. Prospective merchants studied French, Spanish, or German, whereas prospective clergy studied Latin or Greek. Franklin's academy also taught practical skills, such as farming, carving, shipbuilding, carpentry, and printing.

Early Ideas of Public Education

Why have so many political leaders, both past and present, valued public education so highly? The idea of free public education had its roots in the early republic. Thomas Jefferson believed it was to society's benefit to educate all of its citizens so they might provide leadership and support for the country. As a member of the Virginia Assembly's Committee to Revise the Laws of the Commonwealth from 1776 to 1779, Jefferson drafted the Bill for the More General Diffusion of Knowledge, a bill he considered one of his finest pieces of work (Cremin, 1980).

The bill proposed the establishment of **common schools**—tax-supported schools for reading, writing, arithmetic, and history—that children could attend free for three years and then pay thereafter. The bill also proposed the establishment of twenty grammar schools, in which Latin, Greek, English grammar, and advanced arithmetic would be taught. The brightest students from the lower schools who could not afford to pay tuition would attend these grammar schools at public expense; children whose families could afford to pay would do so. From the grammar schools, ten scholarship students would go on to the College of William and Mary for three years at public expense. Jefferson believed this system of education would allow society to safeguard liberty. Although successful in establishing a public university, Jefferson did not live to realize his dream of publicly supported schools for Virginia's children (Cremin, 1980, pp. 440–441).

The spread of common schools led to sweeping educational reform on a national scale. In the 1830s reformers in the common school movement pressed for a variety of measures: (1) taxation for public education; (2) longer school terms; (3) a focus on getting particular groups of nonattenders enrolled in schools, particularly those living in urban slums and factory tenements and the children of free blacks; (4) hierarchical school organizations (e.g., state education agencies headed by a superintendent, schools headed by a "principal teacher," graded schools); (5) consolidation of small school districts into larger-scale school units so that per-pupil expenditures would be more uniform from district to district; (6) standardization of educational methods and curriculum; and (7) teacher training (Kaestle, 1983). **Which, if any, of these issues do you think are still being debated today?**

Primary school enrollment rates increased over time. In the late 1700s and early 1800s, school attendance was higher in rural areas than in the cities. More girls began to go to school, particularly in the Northeast (Kaestle, 1983). Signs of literacy, such as the number of people able to sign their names and the number of newspaper subscriptions, pointed to rapid social change during this period (Cremin, 1970). From the 1600s through the early 1900s, however, no more than 10 percent of eligible school-age children ever went beyond elementary school.

In the 1820s, the public high school emerged as an alternative to the Latin grammar school and the English academy. High schools did not become important in American education, however, until the late 1800s, when courts ruled that people could raise taxes to support such schools (Krug, 1964). With this funding, high schools became public institutions that provided a classical secondary education. In other words, this early high school made available to day students the kind of education previously available only to wealthy boarding school students (pp. 389–390).

Leaders in the Movement for Universal Education

The tax-supported system of free schools developed in the 1820s, thirty years before the Civil War. The Jeffersonian ideal of **universal schooling,** educating all citizens for the common good, came close to reality, but only for those who were not of African, Native American, and Hispanic descent. At the same time, women, through their own schooling and then by assuming roles as teachers, took advantage of new and socially acceptable opportunities for independence. More specifically, women benefited from the chance to fill jobs that men, for a number of reasons related to the expanding economy, no longer wanted. At least in this respect, progress toward universal education was made.

HORACE MANN The name most often associated with the development of public schools in this country is Horace Mann (1796–1859). He served as secretary to the Massachusetts State Board of Education from 1837 to 1848. Mann revolutionized education in the United States by making it the financial responsibility of the state. He established the system of grade levels by age and performance, extended the school calendar from two or three months to ten, standardized textbooks, and made attendance mandatory (Boyer et al., 2000).

HENRY BARNARD With Horace Mann, Henry Barnard (1811–1900) led the struggle for the common school. A journalist by training, Barnard served in various government positions related to education across the Northeast. He wrote about public education and European educational reformers such as Pestalozzi and Froebel in the *Connecticut Common School Journal* and the *American Journal of Education*. Barnard praised the teaching of civic values and basic skills, but he believed the most important subject was the English language. He wanted strong teacher preparation and enough pay to get good teachers and keep them, and he built public support for such actions.

Henry Barnard also promoted the concept of the public high school. He argued that primary schools were not up to the task of providing the intellectually rigorous education that students needed. He also believed that, by reaching out to students over a larger geographical area, the high school would serve the public better than private schools did. The high school "must make a good education common in the highest and best sense of the word common—common

Technology in Practice

TURN ON, TUNE IN—LEAP FOR JOY!

Historically speaking, human ingenuity combined with often only the most rudimentary technology has given those with disabilities the capacity to function fully in society. Braille, orthopedic devices, transportation mechanisms, chemical diagnostics, and on and on—the list of technological innovations that compensate for disabilities is seemingly endless. Now one of the latest "hot" products of the digital revolution is providing new levels of support to those with vision loss.

For decades, people with low vision have taken advantage of opportunities offered by audio technology. Books on Tape and other programs have transformed lives. The technology of the Apple iPod™, however, is moving support to a new level.

American Foundation for the Blind reviewer Adrianna Montague-Gray reported, "The iPod can hold an amazing amount of music as well as audio books, and any commercial CD audiobook can be converted easily to be played on the iPod." Moreover, the iPod can be completely accessible to those with vision loss. "With a few small adjustments, which wouldn't be difficult or costly to implement, all of the functions of the device could be usable by everyone—signed or visually impaired."

The capacity of the iPod and its accessibility make the device nothing short of revolutionary for people with low vision. "Having thousands of books, songs, and text documents literally at your fingertips—what not too long ago would have required a large archive, is the next step for sighted people; for people with low vision it's nothing short of a leap."

Even as we write this technology feature on last year's state-of-the-art computer keyboards, we can be confident that the competition is scrapping to give iPod a run for its money.

Question for Reflection: What other resources are available for people with visual disabilities? (Hint: What do you know about Recording for the Blind?)

Source: Montague-Gray, A. (March 4, 2005). Tuning in to the digital revolution with vision loss: American Foundation for the Blind reviews: Apple's iPod audio player. Available online: www.afb.org/Section.asp?SectionID=47&DocumentID=2719.

because it is good enough for the best, and cheap enough for the poorest family in the community" (Barnard, 1857, p. 185).

The Development of Parochial Schools

Protestants were the dominant religious group during colonial times, but there was great diversity in religious preferences. Of the 260 churches existing in 1689, 71 were Anglican, 116 Congregational, 15 Baptist, 17 Dutch Reformed, 15 Presbyterian, 12 French Reformed, 9 Roman Catholic, and 5 Lutheran. There were also loosely organized groups of Quakers, Mennonites, Huguenots, Anabaptists, and Jews (Cremin, 1970). Depending on their religious beliefs, different groups had unique ideas about the education of children, so they established parochial schools, or private schools with religious affiliations.

German Lutherans, for example, wanted to protect their language and way of life. By 1840 there were more than two hundred Lutheran parochial schools in Pennsylvania. In 1856, in return for a rent-free house, firewood, a salary of $12 per month, plus extra pay for baptisms and marriages, Lutheran minister Edmond Multanowski preached and taught members of his congregation for six hours a day, nearly eleven months a year in Carlinville, Illinois (Cremin, 1980). Groups such as the Amish and Mennonites also educated their own children and did not send them to common schools. Parents were fearful that outside influences might corrupt their sons and daughters.

In the 1840s, Catholic leaders protested the use of the King James Bible in the common schools. They also fought against the religious and ethnic slurs aimed at Irish Catholics, in particular, in the common schools. The climate was right for the establishment of their own alternative school system—one that has since grown to be the largest alternative to public education in the world. John Hughes, bishop of New York, admonished his parishioners "to build the schoolhouse first, and the church afterwards" (Lannie, 1968). By 1865, Catholic schools were teaching 16,000 students, or about one-third of the Catholic school population, in New York (Dolan, 1985).

Catholics, Lutherans, Amish, Mennonites, and others wanted to protect their children and their ways of life, as did the general public. Reformers in the common-school movement, however, viewed parochial schools as the greatest possible threat to democracy. In their minds, "the goals of a common-school system—moral training, discipline, patriotism, mutual understanding, formal equality, and cultural assimilation—could not be achieved if substantial numbers of children were in independent schools" (Kaestle, 1983, p. 116). **Why might some people view religious schools as a threat to democracy today?**

The Growth of Institutions of Higher Education

Oxford and Cambridge, the most prestigious universities in England, served as models of higher education for the colonists. Only six years after the Puritans landed in Massachusetts, they founded the college that was later named after its first benefactor, John Harvard. Harvard students studied the liberal arts and sciences: Latin, Greek, Hebrew, mathematics, logic, rhetoric, astronomy, physics, metaphysics, and philosophy. The other colonial colleges that formed also promoted the idea that higher education prepared young men for lives of leadership.

As for training teachers, most prepared on the job in schools and did not attend college. Usually, new teachers first served as apprentices to teachers who had instructed them. Occasionally, they would read a textbook or attend a teachers' institute meant to transmit some new bit of scientific knowledge about teaching and learning. The first of these institutes, established by Henry Barnard at Hartford, Connecticut, in the autumn of 1839, provided six weeks of instruction focused on instructional strategies and curriculum to twenty-six young men (Cremin, 1980; Elsbree, 1939).

Private **seminaries**—academies for girls—were the primary means for advancing the skills of future teachers. In 1823 Samuel R. Hall opened a seminary with a model school at Concord, Vermont. That same year Catherine and Mary Beecher, sisters of Harriet Beecher Stowe, opened a seminary for young women in Hartford, Connecticut, that eventually became the Hartford Female Seminary. (Elsbree, 1939).

Gradually, private and semiprivate institutions gave way to public teacher training schools called **normal schools.** Public school proponent Horace Mann opened the first normal school in Lexington, Massachusetts, in 1839 (Elsbree, 1939). Prospective teachers entered normal schools and were trained to meet high standards or "norms," hence the name. Mann borrowed the idea from the Germans, French, and English—all of whom had had such schools for over one hundred years. (Elsbree, 1939; Kaestle, 1983).

The Morrill Act (1862) provided federal assistance for the establishment of colleges of agriculture and the mechanic or industrial arts. The act granted each state thirty thousand acres of public land for each of its congressional representatives. The income from the grant went to support at least one state land grant college devoted to agricultural and mechanical instruction. The Morrill Act emphasized the importance of applied science and made higher education accessible to millions of people in the years that followed. Like the Northwest Ordinance of 1785, it foreshadowed major federal involvement in education.

Today the United States celebrates a system of higher education second to none. The opportunities for education beyond high school are legion. Just how far has higher education progressed beyond its humble beginnings at Harvard in 1636? Some would argue not far enough—pointing to the *U.S. News and World Report*'s annual ranking of American colleges and universities. Among criteria used to rank the so-called "best colleges" in the nation are acceptance rates, percentage of freshmen in the top 10% of high school classes, graduation and retention rates, and alumni giving rates. These rankings are the subject of great debate. Some people believe they serve a vital role in helping consumers judge institutional quality. Others argue that the whole idea of ranking colleges and universities on these or any other criteria is a ridiculous endeavor. The important issues, they argue, are to determine, not whether any college is good, but good for whom and for what purpose. **What do you think are the most important factors to consider when judging the quality of an institution of higher education?**

Case Perspectives

Think back to the case that opened this chapter. The following comments are intended to provide a context for your own analysis of Jack Bollinger's dilemma.

A PRINCIPAL IN NEW YORK CONSIDERS HOW HE WOULD EXPLAIN STAUNTON'S POLICY IN THE CONTEXT OF HISTORY. I don't want to disparage the efforts of the good people of Staunton, Virginia, or anyone else who wants to advance morality in our society. When I was younger, I would have bristled if anyone wanted to mix religion and public schools. I guess you could have called me a "radical" or at the very least a "liberal." Well, I still don't like the idea of people telling me or anyone else how to get to heaven, but I'm not so young anymore either.

I have watched immigrants on Manhattan's Lower East Side come here on their first stop in America with nothing to hang on to but their religion. It can be tough in New York, but the bright side is that if you make it here, you can make it anywhere—baptism by fire, baby, that's what my father called it (chuckles). Annie Bryant ought to read stories about the Irish, the Jews, the Chinese, the Russians, and all the rest who came here and worked like demons so their little angels would have a real stake in America. History is replete with examples—I can take you to the library and show you—of how public education and religion can complement each other.

I have seen the kinds of misery caused by people who don't care about themselves or anybody else. If releasing kids to attend religious instruction helps develop compassion for your fellow man or woman, I'm all for it. Many of our Jewish and Islamic students pray quietly before they eat their lunches. They celebrate religious holidays. And now with the increasing attention being placed on standardized testing, I would be shocked if 99 percent of all our students aren't out there praying like crazy before the state math exams. I mean God, Yahweh, Allah, and every supreme being with any juice in the math department is working overtime these days (laughs).

Students don't just dream up the idea of connecting religion and earthly challenges. They have generations of ancestors who worked on these ideas long before these kids came on the scene. Ideas live on in people's minds; they are passed from mothers and fathers to sons and daughters, again and again through history. People may look different, dress different, sound different from their ancestors, but they are carrying many of the same old ideas that have withstood the ravages of time.

We may have done a lot more damage to kids and to our society by downplaying religion in schools than we have by letting kids study the King James Bible, the Koran, or the Baltimore Catechism. After all, our educational roots are deep in British history. They have never prohibited the mixing of religion and education in government-supported schools. My father, God rest his soul, would never believe I'm saying these things.

A TEACHER IN NORTH CAROLINA CONSIDERS HOW SHE MIGHT HANDLE THIS SITUATION. I believe Jack Bollinger is thinking about things correctly. He appreciates the power of history, even though he has not yet formulated what he might say to Annie Bryant. And I think he is probably right about Annie's motivations too. She wants to believe her son's teacher is a good person, a good professional. At the end of the day this is probably what matters most to her. So what is Jack to do?

The first thing Jack needs to do is talk with his principal. That person is bound to have some suggestions. Indeed the principal is often the griot or "walking historian" of the building. This action should be followed by some quick study—this could mean dusting off his old history books.

I would turn first to biography. I would much rather study history by reading biographies than any other way I can imagine. I didn't really like my history courses in college. Maybe I was too young to appreciate them, but they did not engage and hold my interest. I was more interested in other things. After I left college, I discovered that I could learn so much about our institutions, our politics, and our culture when they were wrapped in the story of one person. Jack might be wise to start with a biography of a person who was deeply religious and rabidly secular at the same time. It could be a lot easier to understand the power of history on education by reading David McCullough's *John Adams* than by anything else he might do.

Adams's story is one of varying doses of disappointment and exhilaration, laced with generous amounts of old-fashioned religiously inspired guilt and heaps of enlightened optimism. If you were headed out to do a Web search on the power of educational history, this tome would probably not pop up on your screen. Certainly I would not try to "sell" it as the answer to "religious release programs" in Rolling Rock Elementary School or in McSwain Elementary School. But if Jack wanted to enrich his understanding of the educational conditions in early America vis-à-vis beliefs about right and wrong, this book would be difficult to beat. Who knows, he might even recommend it to Annie. It could just be the springboard Annie and Jack need to begin productive communications.

Questions for Reflection: What responsibility does an individual teacher have for explaining the policies of a school or district to parents? What if your district enacted a policy with which you did not agree? What do you think your responsibility would be? Do you have any other guidance for Jack before he meets with Mrs. Bryant? ■

Summary

We might think about early American education as a classic psychology exercise: Is the glass half empty or half full? Our ancestors made plenty of mistakes. All sorts of negative words and phrases leap to mind in regard to education in our nation's infancy: neglectful, boring, biased, inequitable, mean-spirited, and so on. People who received even some formal education in those early days might well have thought they were the losers, even though they were among the privileged.

There are so many stories of courage and educational success, however, that the glass also appears to be overflowing. Opportunities to "get ahead," however they were defined, became increasingly dependent on what people knew and what they were able to do, not on what their names were or where they came from. Education, previously a largely informal system, began to grow visible as a reasonably well marked path to a better life. Historical forces were converging to widen the path so many people could travel it together. Despite fits and starts, our system of universal public education was to become the envy of the world.

TERMS AND CONCEPTS

assimilation
Blue-Backed Speller
common schools
dame schools
English academy
hidden passage
hornbook
kindergarten
land grant schools
Latin grammar school

lyceum
McGuffey Readers
mission schools
monitorial method
normal schools
parochial schools
primers
seminary
universal schooling

REFLECTIVE ACTIVITY: ELIZA PINCKNEY

Reflective practice is an essential part of good teaching. Reflection is a process that includes making thoughtful decisions, understanding and articulating value structures, acting from knowledge, evaluating your actions and their effects, and sharing your reflections with colleagues. After reading the following scenario, respond to the questions below. The scenario reflects the INTASC Principle and Disposition at the end of this activity.

Elizabeth "Eliza" Lucas Pinckney was born on the British island of Antigua in the West Indies in 1722 to a British soldier and his wife. For her mother's health, she and her family later moved to South Carolina, where her father owned three plantations. When her father was recalled to Antigua to serve as a royal governor, Eliza, at age sixteen, was placed in charge of her father's plantations.

Eliza ran a school on the plantations for the family's young slaves and was close friends with others who believed in the cause of "negro" education. She also was an avid reader, scientist, and musician,

Eliza was continually experimenting to see if a particular crop would grow well in South Carolina. She experimented with flax, hemp, and silk culture. In about 1740, she grew indigo with seeds sent by her father. Indigo had been used for thousands of years to make a beautiful blue dye. Her early efforts were failures, but by 1744 she succeeded, and she shared her methods with others. The crop eventually became the main cash crop in South Carolina.

Eliza married Charles Pinckney and had two sons who fought in the Revolutionary War with the Continental army. Both of them signed the Declaration of Independence. Eliza Pinckney died at age 71 in Philadelphia where she had gone for cancer treatment. George Washington was one of her pallbearers.

Decide   1. What special challenges do you think Eliza Pinckney encountered as a female landowner during these times in this place?

Perceive and Value   2. Pinckney once told her son that the welfare of their whole family depended greatly on their moral virtue, religion, and learning. She told him he must fortify himself "against those Errors into which you are most easily led. . . . What I most fear for you is heat of temper. . . ." Moral weakness was a pervading theme in early America. Certainly, the times and prevailing religious beliefs accounted for this circumstance. Yet, guilt also had practical value. How might a wily landowner have wielded the force of guilt to advance her power over others?

Know and Act 3. Most of us do not "do science" as Pinckney did in her day. We rely on others—specialists—to do the kind of scientific investigation of which we are incapable. Eliza and others in the colonies had no choice but to be "generalists" who identified and solved their own problems in a variety of areas. What do you believe has been lost and what has been gained in the evolution of specialists in our society? How has this evolution affected the role of teachers?

Evaluate 4. Life in colonial times was uncomplicated in some ways, but difficult in many others. Do you think educational success and failure were easier or more difficult to identify than they are today?

Discuss 5. What forms of informal assessment did Eliza use on her plantations? What similar forms of assessment might you use in a classroom?

INTASC Principle 8

The teacher understands and uses formal and informal assessment strategies to evaluate and ensure the continuous intellectual, social, and physical development of the learner.

Disposition

The teacher values ongoing assessment as essential to the instructional process and recognizes that many different assessment strategies, accurately and systematically used, are necessary for monitoring and promoting student learning. (Interstate New Teacher Assessment and Support Consortium, 1992)

ADDITIONAL READINGS

Cremin, L. A. (1970). *American education: The colonial experience, 1607–1783.* New York: Harper & Row.

Handlin, O. (1991). *Boston's immigrants, 1790–1880: A study in acculturation,* Enlarged Edition. Cambridge, MA: Harvard University Press.

Hoff, D. J. (2002). History of math instruction retold through new Smithsonian exhibit. *Education Week.* Available online: http://www.edweek.org/ew.

Morgan, Harry. (1995). *Historical perspectives on the education of black children.* Westport, CT: Praeger.

Parkerson, D. H., & Parkerson, J. A (1998). *The emergence of the common school in the U.S. countryside.* Lewiston, NY: Mellen Press.

Ronda, B. A. (1999). *Elizabeth Palmer Peabody: A reformer in her own terms.* Cambridge, MA: Harvard University Press.

WEB RESOURCES

www.ilt.columbia.edu/academic/digitexts/locke/bio_JL.html
Learn more about the English philosopher John Locke.

www.nwhp.org
Here is a view of the world of women's history.

http://valley.vcdh.virginia.edu
The Valley of the Shadow explores two communities, one northern and one southern, through the American Civil War.

http://lcweb.loc.gov/homepage/lchp.html
The Library of Congress is a must for teachers in every discipline.

www.masterstech-home.com/ASLDict.html
This site contains a basic dictionary of American Sign Language terms.

www.afb.org
Information on Braille.

Education in America: Then and Now

Case Study: Where Do I Fit?

Dear Dad,

Hope you're checking e-mail tonight, because I could sure use some of that good old fatherly wisdom. I always thought I knew myself and where I was going, but something happened today that really shook me. Fact is, it still hurts so much that I have trouble telling you about it.

I was standing by the door of the school with Mrs. Jackson, my supervising teacher, saying goodbye to the kids as their parents picked them up when one woman pulled me aside. I knew her—we'd had a parent conference earlier in the year. Her daughter Sarah is a constant source of annoyance to everyone, Mrs. J. and the kids included. She's loud and pushy and just generally obnoxious. Last week I made her sit in time-out after she kicked one of the boys. I told her she had to stay there til she was ready to apologize. She just sat there and did her work for more than an hour, and then finally she came up and told me she was ready. But her apology consisted of walking up to Kenny, blurting "Sorry," and then going back to her desk. I probably shouldn't have accepted it as readily as Kenny did, but I think he and I were both just ready to put the whole thing behind us.

When Sarah's mother got me by myself, she looked angrier than I've ever seen anyone. She didn't yell, but her voice was just full of rage. What she said was, "How much do you really know about this place? This school, and this community? You aren't from here. There's no way you can really understand us and what's good for our kids. You know what? Why don't you go back to where you came from? Why don't you go student teach with your own people?"

Daddy, I was so shocked I could hardly breathe, let alone answer her. Then she grabbed Sarah and took off for the parking lot. Mrs. J. didn't hear any of this, and I was just too embarrassed to tell her.

The whole thing might have rolled off my back if this woman were a hothead or a chronic troublemaker or something, but truth is, Dad, I really don't think she's that kind of person. I know she was upset because I gave her daughter a time-out—and maybe she's as frustrated as we are with the way Sarah behaves. But I keep thinking that there's a kernel of truth in what she said. I'm *not* from here. I haven't "walked the walk," as they say here. And I never will.

You taught all of us that we should care about "social justice," and we watched you and Mom make it happen in so many ways by what you did and just being who you are. But am I supposed to pretend to be somebody I'm not? Am I supposed to turn into somebody else? Should I just admit that I don't belong here and go someplace where I'll fit in? I'm really confused.

Love, Ginny

This chapter describes education in the United States from 1865 to the present. It provides a historical overview of slavery and the reconstruction of the South after the Civil War; of calls for educational and social reform; of the influence of science, philanthropy, and the mass media on education; and of federal involvement in schooling.

How Did Educational Life Change after the Civil War?

When the Civil War ended, people had to rebuild the nation. Slavery was abolished and with it went a set of social customs that had governed people's conduct in both the North and the South. There was no blueprint for how people would live and work together. During this time of transition, leaders and ordinary citizens redefined education both inside and outside schools. Several events and reform efforts also changed the nature of education in the United States (see Figure 5.1.).

Ending Slavery and Reconstructing the South

People's passion for intellectual freedom and civil liberties grew stronger after the Civil War. The Thirteenth, Fourteenth, and Fifteenth Amendments to the U.S. Constitution ended slavery, defined citizenship, and forbade states to deny nonwhite men the right to vote. The customs of segregation and discrimination, however, remained. Northerners moved to reconstruct and reeducate the South to fit their own vision. Not surprisingly, many Southerners detested and resisted these actions.

The **Freedman's Bureau,** established one month before the end of the war, provided food, medicine, and seed to destitute southerners. The bureau secured legal rights for freed slaves and

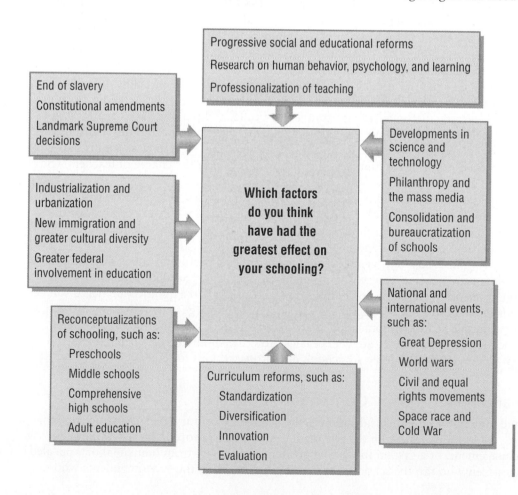

Figure 5.1
Some Factors Affecting Education in the Modern Era

created educational opportunities for them. Hundreds of northern teachers went south to teach African American children and adults. Despite opposition, the Freedman's Bureau succeeded in establishing and operating more than four thousand primary schools, seventy-four normal schools, and sixty-one industrial schools for former slaves. The bureau was another step toward strengthening the role of the federal government in education (Degler, 1959).

After the war, Southerners constructed **black codes** of conduct to keep "Negroes" in an inferior position. These codes, which were "halfway stations back to slavery," allowed African Americans to hold property, to sue and be sued, and to marry. On the other hand, the codes forbade them to carry firearms, to testify in court in cases involving European Americans, and to leave their jobs (Degler, 1959, p. 211).

So, although the Civil War was over, violence toward African Americans was not. Although precise numbers are impossible to determine, between 1865 and 1900, approximately 2,500 lynchings occurred, and the victims were mainly African Americans. Between 1900 and 1914, the start of World War I, more than 1,100 African Americans are known to have been lynched (Franklin, 1967). After the start of World War I, lynchings were more rare, but they continued into the 1950s.

In 1934 the **National Association for the Advancement of Colored People (NAACP)** was formed as the first nationwide special-interest group for African Americans. The NAACP lobbied for an antilynching bill, but the legislation failed to pass during the Roosevelt and Truman administrations of the 1940s and 1950s. In 2005 the Senate apologized for its failure to stand against lynching (Associated Press, 2005).

We Need Educational and Social Reform

Why were national development and education so closely linked in the nineteenth century? Why do they remain so closely linked today? The push for universal education that began in the 1830s gained momentum throughout the twentieth century. In 1867 Congress created a Department of Education, largely in response to pressure from the National Teachers Association. President Andrew Johnson appointed Henry Barnard to be commissioner of education and to run the department. The commissioner collected statistics and facts on education and tried to promote the cause of education throughout the country.

By the beginning of the twentieth century, critics increased pressure on public schools, particularly in the cities. Social reformers, sometimes called muckrakers, wrote about mechanical teaching and learning methods, administrative ineptitude, and parents' lack of interest in their children's welfare. Joseph Mayer Rice (1969), for instance, thought that the environment of the New York City schools was nothing short of evil: "children [are] in class-rooms the atmosphere of which is not fit for human beings to breathe, and in the charge of teachers who treat them with a degree of severity that borders on barbarism" (p. 11).

Leonard Ayres's *Laggards in Our Schools* (1909) presented what he claimed was scientific evidence that schools were filled with retarded children or children who were too old for their grade. He blamed this condition on the schools for focusing on unusually bright children and ignoring the slow or average children.

In the early twentieth century, even more problems plagued schools: an antievolution crusade, anti-immigration movements, organized campaigns against Roman Catholics, and increases in anti-Semitism, to mention but a few. In addition, people continued to exploit children as a source of cheap labor in the rapidly expanding industrial economy. To a large extent, the desire to end such abuses encouraged the development of public schools and the organization of labor. The existence of schools and mandatory attendance laws protected children by educating them and keeping them from working. In doing so, schools also protected jobs for adults.

Science and Philanthropy Combine to Educate

If science and money fueled industrialization in the nineteenth century, then the same combination of forces could fix education in the twentieth century, or so people believed. Studies on scientific management, or a system for getting greater productivity from human labor, appealed to the businessmen who ran the school boards who, in turn, hired the superintendents who ran the schools (Callahan, 1962). Encouraged by grants from private foundations, leaders in school administration encouraged educational specialization and scientific management (Tyack & Hansot, 1982).

Early scientific research on teaching and learning began to take root in schools at the turn of the century. An increase in testing for mental ability was one of the first results of the new, more scientific approach to education. Psychologist James Cattell introduced mental tests to assess people's individual differences. He then encouraged counseling agencies and schools to incorporate such tests as part of their routine procedures. The work of psychologists Alfred Binet, Lewis Terman, and, later, Edward L. Thorndike on the measurement of intelligence was hailed as a great practical advance for schools (Travers, 1983).

Other ideas about education also gained popularity. For instance, psychologist Charles Judd emphasized the importance of viewing teaching and learning as social constructs, that is, as ideas that derive meaning from their use in everyday life. In contrast, John Watson viewed behavior and learning as mechanical phenomena—elements to be manipulated continually by outside sources. His ideas prompted a revolution in the way people thought about human behavior. Although strikingly different in philosophical persuasions, these researchers all believed in the power of science to improve the human condition.

From the late nineteenth century on, society placed a premium on the value of education not only for students but for the general public as well. Several fine-art museums opened in the 1870s, including New York's Metropolitan Museum of Art and Boston's Museum of Fine Arts. The Library of Congress opened its Jefferson Building in 1897, permitting wide public access to its book collection (Cole, 1979). By 1900 more than 45 million volumes were housed in more than nine thousand public libraries across the country (Blum et al., 1993).

One reason for the increase in public works aimed at public education during this time was donations from philanthropists who profited from the industrial revolution. Andrew Carnegie and Andrew Mellon, for example, donated money for promoting public access to books and art and for establishing philanthropic foundations. Northern capitalists, such as merchant Robert Ogden, railroad man William Baldwin, and oil magnate John D. Rockefeller, also funded educational projects in the South, where industry did not have the same financial impact that it did in the North.

In 1936 the Ford Foundation, started by the Ford Motor Company, began programs intended to strengthen democratic values, reduce poverty and injustice, and advance international cooperation. Since its inception, the Ford Foundation has given some $9.3 billion in support of educational and social causes. The philanthropic spirit in education continues today. For example, the Bill and Melinda Gates Foundation gives millions to educational endeavors.

Learning from Mass Media

How do people learn from what they have around them? The press was a particularly powerful instrument of social education in the twentieth century. Newspapers and magazines catered to the masses, often by appealing to readers' love of adventure or scandal. The sensationalism of the "yellow press" of New York City—the front pages of special editions were printed on yellow paper to catch the potential reader's eye—led by William Randolph Hearst and Joseph Pulitzer shaped American opinion on education and just about every other subject.

From 1885 to 1900, the number of periodicals published in the United States increased by 2,200. By 1905 there were twenty 10¢ monthlies, with a combined circulation of 5.5 million (Blum et al., 1993). From 1920 to 1940, "newspapers and magazines continued to rival schools and churches as the chief instruments of mass education and the dissemination of ideas" (Link & Catton, 1963, p. 295).

By 1930 the United States was in an economic depression. At the same time, new communications technology was fast becoming a part of daily life. About twenty-three thousand motion picture theaters with a combined seating capacity of more than 11 million were spread across the country (Link & Catton, 1963). Especially in the midst of a national depression, movies lured people from their everyday troubles. The more subtle educational influences of the movies—their power to foster dreams of how people wanted to live—would become an enduring national issue.

Radio also captured Americans' imaginations in the 1920s, 1930s, and 1940s. The first radio broadcast was made in 1920. Just two year later, there were 220 radio stations, and by

Figure 5.2
Which Media Young
People Use

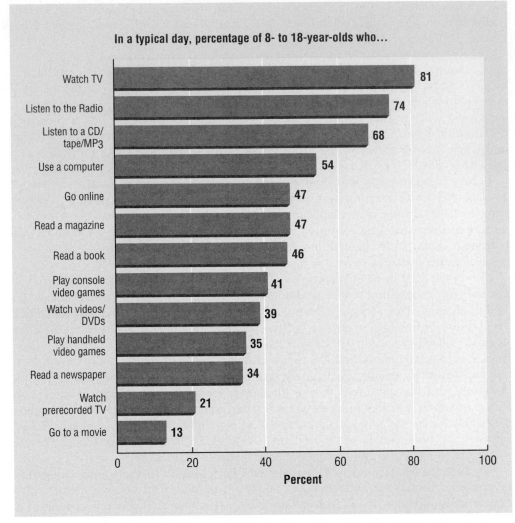

In a typical day, percentage of 8- to 18-year-olds who...

Media	Percent
Watch TV	81
Listen to the Radio	74
Listen to a CD/tape/MP3	68
Use a computer	54
Go online	47
Read a magazine	47
Read a book	46
Play console video games	41
Watch videos/DVDs	39
Play handheld video games	35
Read a newspaper	34
Watch prerecorded TV	21
Go to a movie	13

Source: Generation M: Media in the lives of 8–18 year-olds, (#7251), The Henry J. Kaiser Family Foundation, March 2005. This information was reprinted with permission from the Henry J. Kaiser Family Foundation. The Kaiser Family Foundation, based in Menlo Park, California, is a nonprofit, independent national health care philanthropy and is not associated with Kaiser Permanente or Kaiser Industries.

1923 more than 2.5 million radios were scattered around the country. Approximately 80 percent of American families had radios in their homes by 1937 (Link & Catton, 1963).

Radios educated by delivering live voices of famous people into listeners' homes; television added images to these voices. Television, like radio, also increased the speed with which people heard news from home and abroad. By January 1960, nine out of ten homes in the United States had television sets, competing with, contradicting, and complementing teachers and parents.

As illustrated in Figure 5.2, young people today live media-saturated lives. Children from age eight to eighteen spend three hours and fifty-one minutes per day watching TV and videos, forty-three minutes a day reading, and an hour and twenty-five minutes in physical activity. Two-thirds live in homes where the TV is usually on during meals, and half (51 percent) live in homes where the TV is left on most of the time, whether any one is watching it or not (Rideout, Roberts, & Foehr, 2005). **What are the pros and cons of children's increased media use?**

Federal Influence on Education

Why do people argue that the federal government must be heavily and directly involved in education, whereas others are so adamantly opposed to the idea? Although it began in the 1800s, federal involvement in education became even more direct in the late 1950s, when the

In the late nineteenth and early twentieth centuries, the children of many industrial workers often left school to work in factories.

Supreme Court ruled that racial segregation in schools was unconstitutional. Schools became front-page news once again in the 1960s as they became battlegrounds in the war on poverty and the quest for racial equality. In the twentieth century, the federal government exerted its influence in education with money, legislation, and ideology in many arenas: desegregation, aid to schools serving children of low-income families, legislation guaranteeing racial and sexual equity, new entitlements for students with disabilities, bilingual–bicultural programs, and career education.

The most dramatic example of federal involvement was the **Elementary and Secondary Education Act (ESEA) of 1965**. The ESEA made the federal government the center of policy-making power; previously, states and localities had been the center. The act also provided funds and support for poverty programs, school libraries, textbooks and other instructional materials, counseling and health services, and remedial instruction. Research centers and laboratories to advance educational practice also were established with funds provided by the ESEA.

The New Federalism of the 1980s, under Presidents Ronald Reagan and George Bush, returned power and financial responsibility for educational programs back to individual states and localities. As federal support for education shrank in terms of actual money, talk of educational reform increased. Commissions and task forces on the national, state, and local levels called for changes in everything from how public schools are organized and schoolbooks are written to how teachers and students are taught and tested.

In the twenty-first century thus far, federal involvement in public education means maintaining existing programs and trying to improve educational practice through performance standards. The No Child Left Behind Act, signed into law by President George W. Bush on January 8, 2002, requires states to close the achievement gap and ensure that all students, including those who are disadvantaged, achieve academic proficiency within twelve years. School districts and schools that fail to make adequate yearly progress (AYP) toward statewide proficiency goals will, over time, be subject to improvement, corrective action, and restructuring measures aimed at getting them back on course to meet state standards.

Who Are "We the People"?

The United States is one nation containing many people—*e pluribus unum*. If in no other way, we the people are similar because we are different: nearly one in four Americans in the United States is a member of an ethnic or racial minority group (Fuchs, 1990).

After the Civil War, the population of the United States grew rapidly in cities and other industrialized areas. In the 1890s about 30 percent of the population (63 million) lived in cities; by 2000, about 80 percent of the country's people lived in urban areas (U.S. Census, 2002). Although the population of the United States grew 200 percent between 1859 and 1914, the number of workers in manufacturing jobs increased 650 percent (U.S. Census Bureau, 1975).

The late nineteenth and early twentieth centuries were particularly hard times for industrial workers. In 1910 about one-half of the men and women in the labor force lived in poverty. They worked long hours for meager wages, and their children often left school to work in factories. Only one-third of the enrolled children finished primary school; less than one-tenth finished high school.

Social reformers, nearly all of them women, worked on behalf of low-income people in various cities and industry centers. They investigated sweatshops and tenements and established settlement houses in poor neighborhoods to help immigrants adjust to life in a new country. The first of these houses was established in 1886 in New York City; by 1910 there were four hundred such houses (Carlson, 1975). Jane Addams's Hull House in Chicago had an education program that included playgrounds, a nursery, and a library.

Life was difficult in rural areas too. The 1930 census indicated that tenant farmers and their families constituted 64 percent of the population in Alabama and 66 percent in Georgia (Dabney, 1969). *Let Us Now Praise Famous Men* was James Agee's 1960 account of the lives of three tenant farm families in Alabama. Accompanied by Walker Evans's photographs, the book created a classic documentation of the period and included the families' educational needs:

> They learn the work they will spend their lives doing, chiefly of their parents, and from their parents and from the immediate world they take their conduct, their morality, and their mental and emotional and spiritual key. One could hardly say that any further knowledge or consciousness is at all to their use or advantage, since there is nothing to read, no reason to write, and no recourse against being cheated even if one is able to do sums. (p. 268)

Poverty has been a chronic and painful condition in the United States. Even though more people go to school each year, poverty dominates the lives of millions. The rates today are the lowest they have been since the early 1970s; nonetheless, 35.9 million people live in poverty. In 2007, the official federal poverty guideline for a family of four was an annual income of $20,650 (U.S. Department of Health and Human Services, 2007).

If President Franklin Roosevelt was right when he said that a nation's compassion can be measured in how it treats its children and its elderly, what grade would you give us?

Native Americans

After the Civil War, Native Americans suffered wars with settlers and the government, the destruction of the buffalo, the expansion of railroads, confinement on reservations, and theft of their land. As Helen Hunt Jackson noted, the official abuse and neglect of Native Americans shaped *a century of dishonor*. Some 250,000 to 300,000 Native Americans lived in the United States, excluding those in Alaska.

The **Bureau of Indian Affairs (BIA),** established in 1824, was a government agency founded to "educate" Native Americans. Off-reservation boarding schools were meant to help Native Americans survive, but they also served to destroy their culture. Besides taking children away from their families, the schools used food, dress, regimented schedules, religion, and job and language training to impose on them the values and customs of the dominant European American culture. Students were compelled to learn English and to "breathe the atmosphere of a civilized instead of a barbarous or semi-barbarous community" (U.S. Bureau of Indian Affairs, 1974, p. 1756). One such school, the Carlisle Indian School, was established in 1879 and educated approximately four thousand children over a period of twenty-four years.

Even though it was teaching children a set of customs totally foreign and often at odds with their own history, many Native Americans of the time accepted as valid the white man's education. Some of them even helped the cause by offering the white man's education themselves. In the late nineteenth century, for example, Princess Sara Winnemucca founded a school in California for Piute children. She taught them to spell, read, write, and calculate in English. She also taught drawing and sewing (Peabody, 1886).

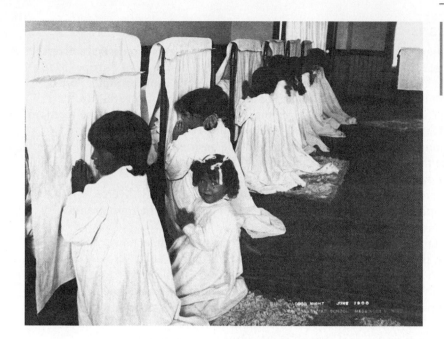

Indian boarding schools were conceived as a humanitarian way to help Native American children assimilate into the culture of the United States. Did these boarding schools do more harm than good?

The Dawes Act of 1887 further undermined tribal authority by breaking up reservation land into smaller parcels and allotting these to individual Native Americans. The land allotments—most unsuitable for farming, particularly by people who had not been farmers—were initially held in trust and were supposed to be transferred to individuals at a later date. In truth, four out of five individuals were cheated out of their property (Blum et al., 1993).

The Indian Wars, a series of bloody encounters between white settlers—sometimes with the aid of U.S. troops, sometimes without—and Native Americans continued until 1890 and the massacre at Wounded Knee. At this point, Native American resistance to subjugation and displacement from their land was crushed.

Native Americans continued to live on U.S.-mandated reservations in limbo until the Citizenship Act of 1924, which made them citizens of the United States. At about the same time, the Meriam Report, a study conducted by the Brookings Institution, revealed the poor condition of education programs provided by the Education Division of the Bureau of Indian Affairs.

The 1930s and early 1940s were a period of gain for Native Americans. John Collier, commissioner of Indian affairs for Franklin Roosevelt, encouraged preservation of Native American culture by permitting reservation schools to offer instruction in Native American languages and culture. Collier also promoted the idea of local self-government, hired Native Americans in his agency, and channeled millions of dollars into improving Native American lands. Passage of the Indian Reorganization Act of 1934 returned self-government to Native Americans. It also eliminated allotment policies that had reduced tribal land holdings and prompted the improvement of the poor economic, health, and social conditions of Native Americans.

Our involvement in World War II suspended the Native American struggle for autonomy. The National Congress of American Indians, founded during World War II, was aggressive in its efforts to improve the lot of Native Americans. The American Indian Movement of 1968, composed mostly of militant urban Native Americans, resorted to violence. As Native Americans continued to press their case, Congress reversed its decision to terminate federal reservations and in 1975 passed the **Indian Self-Determination and Educational Assistance Act.**

Today, Native American cultures are tremendously diverse. Yet, collectively, Native Americans trail others statistically in terms of income, life expectancy, and level of education. Unemployment for them is much greater than that for the total population. Poverty is rampant, particularly among widowed, divorced, and aged women. In 2000, approximately 71 percent of Native Americans ages twenty-five and older had graduated from high school, and 11.5 percent held bachelor's degrees or higher (U.S. Census Bureau, 2003). These figures are well below national averages for the general population. **Why might Native Americans as a group trail in levels of educational achievement today?**

European Americans

After the Civil War, immigration made the population of the United States increasingly diverse. From 1880 to 1924, most immigrants came from southern, central, and eastern Europe. Many settled in American cities and took jobs in industry. In Chicago in 1910, for example, 75 percent of the residents were immigrants or the children of immigrants (Cremin, 1988). In the 1930s and 1940s, Europeans fled the totalitarian regimes of Italy and Germany for the freedom and safety of the United States. Survivors of the Holocaust followed in the 1950s.

Increased immigration rates meant schools had to provide basic education to more people, and they had to socialize these new arrivals to the ways of the nation. Assimilation, once again, became a major educational goal.

As the population increased, it also grew more religiously and ethnically diverse. Differences in language and culture among the new arrivals and between the immigrants and native born made assimilation slow and difficult at best.

Many immigrants retained their ethnic identities through the years, while many others shed these identities. Certainly, the push for assimilation in schools had a great effect on how immigrants responded to American culture. Based on a carefully selected sample of 524 households, in 1991 Richard Alba found that almost no ethnic people were fluent in the language of their ancestral group. Few joined ethnic social clubs or lived in neighborhoods having concentrations of their own ethnic group. In some ways, then, assimilation seemed to work quite well. **What factors impede assimilation into the mainstream society of some cultural and ethnic groups?**

African Americans

After the Civil War, African Americans began to participate more fully in society. In 1860 less than 2 percent of all school-age African American children were enrolled in school; by 1900 the figure had risen to 31 percent. Furthermore, illiteracy dropped from 82 percent in 1870 to 45 percent in 1900 (U.S. Census Bureau, 1990).

After the Civil War, emancipated slaves and European Americans established Sunday schools and universal public education. Churches and ministers in African American communities often formed the nucleus from which educational campaigns spread. By 1868 the African

---

Technology in Practice

ACCESSING HISTORY

With the click of a computer mouse, Tina Schuster's students travel through history. Although she uses textbooks, videos, and other traditional materials, technology is a key component of Schuster's curriculum. In 2005 she was awarded the Virginia Governor's Innovative Technology Award for her dedication to integrating technology into her U.S. history and government classes at Fluvanna County High School.

Her students use technology to view and compare campaign advertisements, search a Civil War database, create a timeline of U.S. history, take virtual field trips and research and write a bill, which they electronically exchange with high school students around the nation. She teaches more than history, Schuster said. Incorporating technology into the curriculum prepares her students for the future. "Technology is already so integrated in life outside of school," Schuster said. "If we expect our students to be competitive, I feel that we have to

provide opportunities for them to see technology in use." (Mayhew, 2005)

Questions for Reflection: If you were to use technology to teach history, what student outcomes would you hope to achieve? How might you judge student progress in the short term?

Methodist Episcopal Church had already enrolled forty thousand pupils in Sabbath schools; by 1885 there were two hundred thousand. African American teachers offered almost all the instruction. In addition, thousands of "Yankee school marms" ventured south to teach in needy schools established for African Americans (Degler, 1959).

Booker Taliaferro Washington was among the many African Americans who flocked to normal schools to become effective leaders of their people. Washington attended and later taught at Hampton Normal and Agricultural Institute in Virginia. In 1881 he went to Macon County, Alabama, to become principal of Tuskegee Institute, the newly created state normal school for African Americans. At Tuskegee, Washington built programs in academics, agriculture, industrial arts, health, religion, and music. He even created a mobile school on a horse-drawn cart that delivered basic education to ex-slaves' doorsteps. Through Washington's leadership, the Tuskegee Institute became a national model for educating African American teachers, farmers, and industrial workers.

Booker T. Washington
(1856–1915)

Washington believed that vocational or industrial education was the best way for African Americans to gain financial self-sufficiency and better their lives. According to Washington (1907), "Mental development is a good thing. Gold is also a good thing, but gold is worthless without an opportunity to make itself touch the world of trade" (p. 77).

Washington's ideas about the need for practical rather than academic education are evident in his autobiography, *Up from Slavery*. He discouraged African Americans from seeking education to become lawyers, doctors, or politicians. Although the war was over, African Americans were still viewed by many as inferior, and educated African Americans were a threat to white supremacy. Washington believed that achieving respectability as a trained worker contributing to the economy, and not upsetting the social order, was the key to advancement.

An opposite view was taken by Washington's severest critic, W. E. B. DuBois, an African American sociologist with a doctorate from Harvard. DuBois (1904) argued that African Americans would never achieve civil and political equality with only industrial education. Instead, DuBois advocated a more academic approach to "train the best of the Negro youth as teachers, professional men, and leaders" (p. 240). On the difficulty of being both an American and a Negro, DuBois wrote:

W. E. B. DuBois
(1868–1963)

> The history of the American Negro is the history of this strife—this longing to attain self-conscious manhood, to merge his double self into a better and truer self. In this merging he wishes neither of the older selves to be lost. He would not Africanize America, for America has too much to teach the world and Africa. He would not bleach his Negro soul in a flood of white Americanism, for he knows that Negro blood has a message for the world. He simply wishes to make it possible for a man to be both a Negro and an American, without being cursed and spit upon by his fellows, without having the doors of Opportunity closed roughly in his face. (1903, p. 3)

DuBois encouraged political activism and challenged the ideas of both African and European Americans. He helped start the civil rights movement that continued through the 1970s (Carr, 2000). As editor of *The Crisis*, the journal of the NAACP, DuBois helped shape the educational policy of that body: All American children and youth should have an equal opportunity to pursue an education.

Mary McLeod Bethune was also instrumental in promoting education. Bethune believed, as did other African American leaders of the time, that education was the means to better lives for all children. In 1904 she founded the Daytona Normal and Industrial School for Training Negro Girls, which later became Bethune–Cookman College. During the Depression and World War II eras, she served in the administrations of Franklin Roosevelt and Harry Truman as director of the National Youth Administration and adviser to the United Nations. As an educator concerned with practical training for upward mobility and as a political activist, Bethune represents a combination of the views of Booker T. Washington and those of W. E. B. DuBois.

Mary McLeod Bethune
(1875–1955)

Cultural Awareness: Lessons Learned

The Supreme Court's decision in *Brown* v. *Board of Education* represented an important victory in the battle against segregation by overturning the decision in *Plessy* v. *Ferguson.* Despite the intent of the *Plessy* decision to establish "separate but equal" facilities for African Americans, the reality was "separate and anything but equal." Voting laws, however, restricted African Americans from exercising any political leverage on lawmakers. A small band of civil rights leaders recognized that equality would never be realized until the *Plessy* decision was overturned. The architect of this important legal effort was Charles Hamilton Houston.

Charles Houston was born in 1895, eight months before the *Plessy* decision, to a middle-class African American family in Washington, D.C. Houston's father was a lawyer and his mother was a schoolteacher turned hairdresser. After success in both all-black and predominantly white academic settings, Houston was exposed to harsh racial discrimination while serving his country in World War I. This experience, combined with his father's influence, pushed Houston toward a career in law. After entering Harvard Law School in 1919, he became the first African American elected as editor of the *Harvard Law Review.* After receiving his degree and completing an additional year of study at the University of Madrid, Houston took a faculty position at Howard University's Law School. Houston instilled in his students a sense of obligation to work for racial justice. Among his students at Howard were Oliver Hill, William Bryant, and Thurgood Marshall.

Houston concentrated on attacking the application of "separate but equal" in education. His strategy involved first arguing against the prevailing inequality of professional schools, starting with the lack of access for blacks to law schools. Houston recognized that the cost for a state to establish a separate black law school would be prohibitive and that, if they were forced by the courts to do so, some states would choose some degree of integration instead. This could establish precedent needed to chip away at *Plessy.* Houston also reasoned

that white society perceived the greatest danger in desegregation to be the social intermingling of young black males with young white females. Because there were relatively few females in law schools, racial integration there might be seen as less of a threat. In cases arising in Maryland (*Murray*) and Missouri (*Gaines*), Houston successfully presented the NAACP's case. With favorable decisions established in these law schools, he proceeded to argue for broader equal educational access in lower levels of education.

While higher-education cases were being argued before the courts, Houston's writings and actions make clear his focus on public schools and the segregation that diminished the self-esteem of young African Americans. In 1934, the year before he argued the *Murray* case, Houston began a video safari into the deep South. His goal was to document the blatant inequality of educational facilities in a manner more powerful than statistics. Hours of 16-mm film captured by Houston's camera found its way into courtroom evidence.

Charles Hamilton Houston died of a heart attack in 1950 at the age of fifty-five. Many desegregation cases were being heard by the lower courts at the time, among them the cases that would lead to the *Brown* decision. Hamilton's protégé, Thurgood Marshall, the NAACP's lead attorney in the *Brown* case, would later say in a speech at Howard University that "It all started with Charlie."

Questions for Reflection: Why did people in the early part of the twentieth century fight so hard to end institutionalized segregation? In what ways did they succeed? In what ways did they fail?

Sources: Greenberg, J. (1994). *Crusaders in the courts.* New York, BasicBooks; Jones, N. R. (1993). Civil rights after *Brown:* "The stormy road we trod." *Race in America: The struggle for equality.* H. Hill, R. Jones, Jr., James E. Madison, eds. Madison: University of Wisconsin Press; McNeil, G. R. (1999). Charles Hamilton Houston. *American national biography.* New York: Oxford University Press, 11: 273–274; Williams, J. (1987). *Eyes on the prize: America's civil rights years, 1954–1965.* New York: Viking Press.

The efforts of leaders such as DuBois and Bethune gave rise to the civil rights movement that grew over the next fifty years and beyond. Yet, for years, education did little to improve economic opportunities or to create political and social equality for African Americans. Because of segregated housing and voting districts, schools for African Americans were funded from separate tax bases and were chronically underfunded.

In 1896, in **Plessy v. Ferguson,** the Supreme Court ruled that public facilities for European and African Americans could be separate but equal. The ruling effectively legalized school segregation. By 1917 African American schools had less than one-quarter of the financial resources that European schools had. In some rural areas, schools for European Americans received fifteen times more support. In Georgia from 1928 to 1929, for example, 99 percent of the money budgeted for teaching equipment went to European American schools, even though African Americans composed 34 percent of the population (Bond, 1934).

By 1900 African Americans outnumbered European Americans in several southern cities. African Americans had few opportunities for employment, however. Jim Crow—the colloquial name for laws and customs supporting racial segregation—sharply restricted opportunities. In 1907 in Alabama, for example, European American teachers were paid roughly five times more money than were African American teachers.

In 1900 southern states spent an average of $9.72 per pupil, compared with $20.80 per pupil in the north-central states. Between 1902 and 1910 appropriations for schools in the South doubled, enrollment of European American students increased by almost a third, and school terms increased from five to six months. Illiteracy among European Americans declined from 11.8 percent in 1900 to about 5.5 percent in 1920. During the same time period, illiteracy among African Americans ten years of age or older declined from 44.5 percent to about 22.9 percent (Link & Catton, 1963).

Poverty forced many African Americans to live in squalor. As industrialization advanced in the post–Civil War period, many African Americans migrated north, hoping to find work. After the Civil War, approximately six thousand freed slaves left Louisiana, Mississippi, and Texas for Kansas in what was called the Kansas Fever Exodus. These "exodusters" and other African Americans leaving the South prized education and sought educational opportunities as well as land in Kansas, in the West, and in northern cities (Painter, 1977).

During the 1940s and 1950s, African Americans continued to struggle for equality. In some respects and on some issues, their voices were heard. One important change was President Harry Truman's integration of the armed forces in 1948 and 1949. Many members of minority groups capitalized on their opportunities to go to college with expenses paid by the G.I. Bill.

Other important changes occurred when Thurgood Marshall of the NAACP argued constitutional cases, including the landmark *Brown v. Board of Education of Topeka, Kansas* in 1954. In this case, the Supreme Court ruled that segregation of students by race is unconstitutional. The Court also held that education is a right that must be available to all people on equal terms. These events marked the beginnings of the nationwide civil rights movement that Martin Luther King, Jr., and others led into the 1960s.

On the fiftieth anniversary of *Brown v. Board of Education*, the NAACP noted that the right of all students to the best possible education is still under continuous challenge in the courts. Although segregation is still illegal, the NAACP contends that the *Brown* decision is not powerful enough to eradicate segregation in educational quality based on poverty (NAACP Legal Defense Fund, 2005).

Hispanic Americans

Hispanic Americans are the fastest growing ethnic group in America. People from Puerto Rico, Cuba, Central and South America, and Mexico have come to the United States to work and, in some cases, to escape war and political repression.

Most Cubans arrived in the United States as political refugees after Fidel Castro overthrew the Cuban dictatorship in 1959. Puerto Ricans have migrated freely between the United States and Puerto Rico since 1917. In that year, Puerto Rico became a possession of the United States with commonwealth status, and its citizens became U.S. citizens. In the past, Mexican Americans came to the United States through conquest and later through annexation of their lands. For the past several decades, Mexican nationals have attempted border crossings to the United States in search of economic opportunities. Today Hispanic peoples constitute the majority of the migrant workforce, which is made up mainly of farm workers.

Like other immigrant groups, Hispanic Americans struggle to overcome prejudice and discriminatory practices directed against them. Their struggles for civil rights and political representation during the 1960s resulted in four Mexican Americans winning election to Congress. By the 1980s Hispanic Americans were an emerging political force as they elected several members of Congress, a governor in New Mexico, and mayors in Denver, San Antonio, Miami, Tampa, and Santa Fe.

Voices Pro and Con

ILLEGAL IMMIGRANTS

It is a mistake to assume that one person's thoughts and feelings apply to a whole group of people. Nonetheless, Jim, who works on the Iron Range in Minnesota, shares the sentiments of many others who fear the loss of jobs to cheap labor from outside the United States. On the other hand, Bruce, who works for the University of Minnesota, considers himself one of the "last liberals left standing." Both men have children in the public schools.

Jim:

This is the best nation on earth, and it is being overrun with illegal immigrants. Aliens come here from third-world countries and take our jobs and take advantage of educational and social services. They don't contribute—they only take.

Bruce:

Illegal immigrants work here and pay taxes here. That is good for everyone.

Jim:

Corporations like cheap labor. They encourage illegal immigration by hiring people who do not have proper documentation. Because of corporate greed, the average citizen ends up paying for education, medical care, and housing assistance for people who do not belong here.

Bruce:

Americans refuse to do the work that illegal aliens do. They cut our grass, work in meatpacking plants, watch our children, clean our homes, and more. Sure they want a chance for a better life. Who doesn't?

Jim:

Most aliens, legal or illegal, do not adopt the values of this nation. They come here and cling to their language and their customs. They keep to themselves; they do not fit in. They may not vote, but they are counted in the census, and politicians represent their interests. They exert unfair influence on our system of government.

Bruce:

Illegal immigrants eventually become assimilated into American culture. They work long and hard for their families. Parents sometimes may be slow to assimilate, but their children become fully integrated into society much more quickly and easily. The children speak English. They make public education richer, more diverse, and more fully representative of the work world all students will eventually enter.

Jim:

We can't afford to educate children who do not belong here. Policies of "don't ask, don't tell" with regard to determining whether children are here legally only attract students to our public schools. These kids are a drain on the system.

Bruce:

It is a well-documented fact that preventing illiteracy in the young is cheaper than trying to remediate it in adults. Our own self-interest argues for educating the children of illegal immigrants. Besides, the kids aren't to blame for being here illegally. It makes no sense to punish them by withholding education, particularly when they hold the potential for making this land of immigrants even stronger than it is now.

Question for Reflection: What are your thoughts about the place of illegal immigrants in society?

In California, Texas, and Florida, Hispanic American students are the majority in public schools. Yet educational levels of Hispanic Americans rank somewhat lower than those of other groups. To discover why so many Hispanic American students are having academic problems, researchers studied profiles of one hundred at-risk students over a four-year period (Romo & Falbo, 1996). They followed students' grades, use of standards, gang involvement, teen motherhood, the special needs of immigrant families, and schools' administrative punitive policies. The results contend that the students' problems came from having to navigate the boundaries of three cultures in order to graduate: the culture of the home, the adult culture of the school system, and the student culture of the school. They also suggested that some schools failed to respond to the students' problems and simply placed them in low-level classes, without providing any special support. **Do you think more or less emphasis should be placed on helping immigrants learn English?**

Asian Americans

Chinese immigrants entered the United States in large numbers during the 1850s. Many settled in the West, where they could get jobs. They worked in gold mines and helped build the first transcontinental railway. Most lived in Chinatowns, where they continued their traditional customs and cultural practices. Attempts by Protestant and Catholic missionaries to Americanize the Chinese failed. Other settlers used force—burning Chinatowns and cutting off the customary long braids of Chinese men—to try to destroy their "clannish" ways (Carlson, 1975).

Chinese immigrants comprised less than 1 percent of the total population in 1870. Yet Americans grew increasingly distrustful of them, particularly as union leaders began to paint the Chinese as "part of a diabolical plot to deprive white Americans of their rightful jobs and bleed the West of its wealth" (Brown & Pannell, 1985, p. 203). The **Chinese Exclusion Act** was passed in 1882, aimed at stopping immigration.

By 1924 the flow of Japanese into this country was halted with the passage of the Oriental Exclusion Act. With the onset of World War II, Asian immigrants, particularly those of Japanese descent, suffered intense racism. More than one hundred thousand Japanese Americans were placed in temporary assembly centers, relocation centers, and internment camps, and their property was confiscated. The federal government did not officially apologize and offer Japanese Americans restitution for these actions until 1990.

In the 1950s the U.S. government began to lift restrictions on immigration according to race guidelines. In 1965 Congress abolished the quota system that based the annual number of people allowed to enter the United States on a proportion of their relatives who were already here.

Following these loosened immigration restrictions and the Korean and Vietnam wars, many immigrants from Southeast Asia made the United States their home. The first Korean immigrants came to Hawaii and then the United States in the early 1900s. Most Korean Americans, however, came to the United States after 1970. Like many other immigrants, Koreans typically come to the United States for greater economic opportunities.

Vietnamese Americans are the fourth largest Asian ethnic group in the United States, after Filipina/o Americans, Chinese Americans, and Asian Indian Americans. The most significant concentrations of Vietnamese Americans are in California, Texas, Washington, and Virginia (U.S. Census Bureau, 2002). Coming in the early 1970s, the first arrivals "were generals and peasants, schoolteachers and spies, physicians and fishermen,...[who] became in America a poignant symbol of the refugees' will to succeed" (Efron, 1990). These early Vietnamese immigrants have generally done well by American standards and so have their children. Vietnamese who have been immigrating since the fall of Saigon in 1975, however, have not fared so well. Most live in poverty and are poorly educated.

Cambodians, Laotians, and Thais have also immigrated to the United States, but not in such high numbers as the Vietnamese. These tribal peoples were deeply affected by the war in Vietnam and have had a long, hard recovery. They also have had to adjust to a society in the United States that relies on the power of science and technology to solve human and educational problems. This society is truly different from those they left behind.

By the late 1980s and early 1990s, Asian American students were being called the new "whiz kids." Asian American students as a group have the highest SAT scores in the nation. If racial and ethnic quotas had not influenced college admissions during these years, Asian American students would have become a majority at some universities. How might your knowledge of history influence your expectations for the performance of Asian American students in your classroom?

Exceptional Learners in America

In the 1800s physicians, clergymen, educators, and social reformers led efforts to educate children with disabilities. Between 1817 and the Civil War, they established residential schools for people who were deaf, blind, mentally retarded, or orphaned. By the end of the Civil War, many of these schools were overcrowded, impersonal, and inhumane. A new generation of reformers wanted to close these institutions because of the conditions. Around this same time, several states began to add special classes for students with disabilities in their public schools. So as not to produce the inhumane conditions present in previous schools, professional organizations formed to help improve the care and treatment of children with disabilities.

The early twentieth century brought many changes in the ways scientists measured and classified types of disabilities. At the same time, more and more public schools included classes and programs for exceptional learners. Professional organizations tried to help improve the situation by offering specialized training programs for teachers. In spite of all these improvements, however, the majority of people with disabilities were placed in special-care facilities where social isolation and abuse occurred.

It was not until the 1960s that civil rights reform began to affect institutionalized people. Federal involvement at that point also helped create a Bureau for the Handicapped within the U.S. Office of Education. The bureau is now known as the Office of Special Education and Rehabilitative Services in the U.S. Department of Education.

The last two decades of the twentieth century brought dramatic changes to the field of special education (Hallahan 2006). Increasingly, people with disabilities are being integrated with the larger, nondisabled society. Educators encourage early intervention, and schools offer all levels of specialized and integrated classroom programs. In 2005 U.S. Secretary of Education Margaret Spellings announced the details of a new No Child Left Behind policy designed to better assist students with disabilities. New guidelines allow identified students to take alternative assessments based on modified achievement standards (U.S. Department of Education, 2005). **Do you know teachers who work with exceptional learners? Have they done anything special to prepare themselves?**

American Women

Women fought for and won an amendment to the U.S. Constitution in 1920 that granted them the right to vote. The suffragettes, as the women who fought for the amendment were called, included Susan B. Anthony, a teacher; Elizabeth Blackwell, the first woman in the United States to qualify as a physician; Margaret Fuller, a teacher and foreign correspondent for the *New York Tribune;* and Elizabeth Cady Stanton, one of the organizers of the 1848 Seneca Falls Women's Rights Convention. These courageous leaders and others after them also advocated women's education.

Even after they received the right to vote, women did not participate fully in society for many years. During the Depression of the 1930s, they were laid off from their jobs before men were, had greater difficulty finding jobs, and rarely received supervisory positions. When World War II created a labor shortage, women took over many jobs that had previously been male dominated. When the men returned after the war, they took back the jobs, and women were again discouraged from having careers.

Government intervention in cases of discrimination occurred often in the 1950s and 1960s, mainly in response to the increasingly powerful civil rights movement. In 1964 the Equal Employment Act helped eliminate many types of job discrimination, including discrimination on the basis of gender. Women gradually moved out of the traditionally female dominated jobs of teaching and nursing and into nearly all professional and occupational roles, including firefighting, law enforcement, and military combat. In 1970 women accounted for approximately 5 percent of law school graduates; in the late 1980s they constituted about 40 percent (Blum et al., 1993).

In addition, Title IX of the Education Amendments Act, passed in 1972, guaranteed that "no person in the United States shall, on the basis of sex, be excluded from participation in, be denied the benefits of, or be subjected to discrimination under any education program or activity receiving federal financial assistance" (Title IX, Education Amendments of 1972). The greatest impact of Title IX has been on school athletic programs. Girls cannot be excluded from any sport and must be given equal access to coaching and equipment.

The women's rights movement of the 1960s and 1970s also helped bring about legislation that affected education. The **Women's Educational Equity Act (WEEA)** of 1974 attacked sex discrimination in education and affected curriculum and instruction in the nation's schools. The law expanded programs for females in mathematics, science, technology, and athletics.

It mandated nonsexist curriculum materials and implemented programs for increasing the number of female administrators in education. The law also extended educational and career opportunities to minority, disabled, and rural women. **Do you see discrimination against women in K–12 schools today?**

Women have always comprised a large portion of the population living in poverty, and the battle continues. Between 2002 and 2003 the percentage of single mothers living below the poverty line jumped 1.9 percent, to 3.9 million (U.S. Census Bureau, 2004).

How Did Teaching Change after the Civil War?

People who believe teaching is an undesirable job have not kept pace with the evolution of the role. Indeed, perceptions of the job have evolved just as the job itself has changed. At the time of the Civil War, teaching was thought of as an unattractive job. But, by 1900, teaching was perceived as a skilled vocation. As expectations for teachers' and students' performances increased in the twentieth century, so too did the status of teaching increase—use of the term *profession* became commonplace. In modern schools, teachers are essentially ambassadors to multicultural communities and promoters of democracy. Teachers transmit content knowledge and build academic skills, but they do much more. American teachers educate the whole child—cognitively, physically, emotionally, and socially.

Status of Women in Teaching Changes

By 1920, 86 percent of teachers were women, but men controlled public education because they held most of the administrative positions. Leaders of the Chicago Teachers Federation (CTF), an all-female teacher organization founded in 1897, drew attention to discrepancies in salaries between administrators and teachers. They also challenged the old male guard in the NEA and tried to force the association to focus on the concerns of women teachers. The NEA responded with some symbolic gains, such as appointing a female president every other year. Ella Flagg Young, a scholar and leader in the women's movement, spoke against the psychological control that the male management had over female teachers (Tyack & Hansot, 1982, p. 181).

One way that women teachers were controlled was with regard to marital status. That is, marriage typically was a liability for women in education but an asset for men. Even by 1940, only 22 percent of female teachers were married. In 1928 the NEA found that about three-fifths of urban districts prohibited hiring married teachers. In addition, about half of the districts prohibited teachers from keeping their jobs if they got married. During the Depression, thousands of districts passed new bans against employing married women.

The Progressive Movement Begins

From 1920 until U.S. involvement in World War II, the Progressive movement called for increased human and material resources to improve Americans' quality of life. With regard to education, **progressivism** argued that the needs and interests of students, rather than of teachers, should be the focus of schools. Progressive teachers relied on class discussions, debates, and demonstrations, not on direct instruction and rote learning from textbooks. Teachers also experimented with individualized instruction, and the curricula encouraged practical experiences and learning outside the classroom. The teacher's role was that of a helper and guide.

People also were beginning to experiment with the structure of schools and the school day itself. In 1921 Helen Parkhurst implemented the Dalton Laboratory Plan in Dalton, Massachusetts. The Dalton Plan relied on students' own interests to promote learning. Officials turned off the bells and disbanded traditional classrooms. The school day was organized into subject labs, and students from fifth through twelfth grades set their own daily schedules (Edwards, 1991; Parkhurst, 1922).

Helen Parkhurst
(1886–1973)

John Dewey ran the Laboratory School at the University of Chicago. A strong progressive, Dewey wanted to avoid teaching subjects in isolation. Instead, he favored the idea of integrating subjects with social activities, such as cooking, sewing, or building a playhouse, so that students might learn about cooperation among human beings (Kliebard, 1986).

After 1945 and until about 1960, people criticized progressive education because it lacked a common set of principles. Some said that progressivism pandered to individual happiness at the expense of intellectual rigor. Nevertheless, the concept of child-centered education prevailed in various forms. What does the term *child-centered education* mean to you?

Trying to Educate the Nation

World War II caused a teacher shortage. Although the prestige of the teaching profession had increased, the increased money of the wartime economy tempted many teachers to take other jobs. In fact, by 1945 more than one-third of the teachers employed in 1941 had left for better-paying jobs in business, industry, and government. Approximately 109,000 individuals employed on emergency teaching certificates assumed some of those positions.

From 1940 to 1960, many critics expressed dissatisfaction with American education by focusing on progressive education techniques that generally attempted to make education "practical" and relevant to daily life. In 1957 the Soviet Union's launch of the first satellite, *Sputnik,* was seen as evidence of our intellectual and moral flabbiness. Schools, critics charged, had not been teaching students to think. They wanted greater emphasis placed on mathematics, science, and foreign languages.

In the **National Defense Education Act (NDEA)**, passed in 1958, the federal government took the lead in improving schools. The NDEA provided funds for upgrading the teaching of mathematics, science, and foreign languages, as well as for the establishment of guidance services. It also provided low-interest loans to college students. The passage of the NDEA marked the beginning of a pattern of federal leadership, rather than just involvement, in education.

The 1970s through the 1990s saw the responsibility for national education change back and forth between the federal government and state governments. In 1979 President Jimmy Carter and Congress split the Department of Health, Education, and Welfare into two federal departments: Health and Human Services and the Department of Education. But President George Bush's 1989 Education Summit, planned and carried out in cooperation with the National Governors' Association, signaled that public education was to be largely a state, not a federal, matter.

Beginning in 1992 President Clinton tried to expand the federal role in education. He created a new agency called the National Education School Improvement Council (NESIC). He made it responsible for distributing and certifying curricular content, student performance standards, and opportunity-to-learn standards. Education was a key issue for both Republicans and Democrats in the 1996 and 2000 presidential campaigns. In 2002 President George W. Bush kept education in the public eye with the No Child Left Behind legislation. For now, federal involvement in national education remains strong.

How Have Schools Changed during the Modern Era?

The number of schools rose dramatically after World War I, but resources for funding schools rose and fell with the economy. The early Depression years had a profoundly negative effect on funding for schools and colleges. By 1933–1934, school expenditures had dropped by more than 30 percent in many states. This meant that some rural schools' budgets were reduced by one-fifth to one-half. Teachers' salaries were cut, and some teachers were even paid in state bonds rather than in cash or by check. Changes in recent years have aimed to make schools more efficient and cost effective while extending public education further and creating educational alternatives.

Consolidation and Bureaucratization

Most schools were small and rural until a program of consolidation began after World War II. Typically, one teacher taught all ages of students in the same room, and each student progressed at his or her own pace. Rural one-room schools were ungraded until about the 1920s, when they began to fall by the wayside as school districts were combined to increase resources and centralize administration. The number of separate school districts was reduced from about 130,000 in 1930 to fewer than 15,000 in 1997 (U.S. Department of Education, 1999). This consolidation meant that students had to be bused to central locations, such as huge regional high schools, often over long distances.

As consolidation increased in rural areas, bureaucratization became the hallmark of urban schooling. Boston, Massachusetts, and New York City developed complex networks of schools with distinct roles and rules. These urban districts have standardized curricula and procedures for each grade level, as well as administrations geared toward efficiency, rationality, precision, and impartiality. In fact, large cities patterned their school systems on the factory model: the single superintendent with a few foremen (principals) to supervise hundreds of operatives (teachers) (Tyack & Hansot, 1982).

New Links between Schools and Communities

As technological progress accelerated, people perceived more links between schools and society, specifically, the world of work. In 1986 the Carnegie Forum on Education and the Economy argued that weak schools threatened America's ability to compete in world markets. Carnegie depicted large numbers of American children ignorant of the past and unprepared for the future.

Schools that did work well were thought to be alike in several ways (Bossert, 1985):

- They had climates that were safe and free of disciplinary problems.
- Teachers expected that students could achieve and communicated these expectations publicly.
- Schools emphasized basic skills with plenty of time for students to work.
- School personnel monitored and evaluated student progress.
- Successful schools had strong principals who served as program leaders.

Rise of Preschools

The preschool movement began anew in the United States in the 1920s. The people behind the American version of the nursery school saw the possibility of educating the whole child instead of functioning simply as a babysitting service. In this way, nursery schools could give children a jump start on their education and help them be better prepared for their later school careers.

By the depths of the Depression, the country needed good child care, and unemployed teachers needed jobs. The ideas of the nursery school movement had found a practical application. Financial support from the federal government in the early 1930s stimulated the formation of many more nursery schools throughout the nation. By 1937 the Works Progress Administration (WPA) was responsible for 1,472 nursery schools with an enrollment of 39,873 children. At the same time, the WPA sponsored 3,270 parent education classes with an enrollment of 51,093 (Cremin, 1988).

By 1946 the majority of these child care centers closed when federal funds were withdrawn. As women continued to enter the workforce, the need for child care prompted the establishment of many private preschools. Today it is quite common for children to attend some sort of nursery school program prior to entering kindergarten.

When President Lyndon Johnson launched his War on Poverty during the 1960s, education programs such as **Head Start** were the weapons he chose. Since its creation, Head Start has had a dual focus: to stimulate the development and academic achievement of four- and five-year-olds from low-income families and to involve parents in the education of their children. Head Start remains one of the most popular preschool programs.

The Middle School Movement

For many years, the most common pattern of school organization was kindergarten through grade eight in elementary school and grades nine through twelve in high school. During the early 1900s, however, some school systems began to experiment with other ways of grouping students. The 6–3–3 pattern, which put grades seven through nine in a junior high school, proved to be popular in the years following World War I. By the 1950s and 1960s, many school districts began moving ninth-graders back into high schools and replacing junior high schools with intermediate or middle schools (Cremin, 1988). Today many school systems continue to group ninth-graders with high school students in a 4–4–4 pattern. But their middle groups of students (fifth- through eighth-graders) are clustered in a variety of ways with both the primary and high school grades.

Comprehensive High Schools

After the 1870s private academies declined in number and were replaced by public high schools supported by tax monies paid to school districts. By 1890 about 203,000 students were enrolled in public high schools and 95,000 were enrolled in private academies. Together, these two groups accounted for less than 6 percent of the population of high school–age Americans, because attendance was not yet mandatory. Not surprisingly, though, this number was the entire pool of potential college students. By 2012 some 14 million fourteen- to seventeen-year-olds will be enrolled in secondary schools (U.S. Department of Education, 2002).

Although every high school is unique, all share a common feature: many course offerings for students with diverse needs, interests, and abilities. Arthur Powell, Eleanor Farrar, and David Cohen (1985) likened the comprehensive high school to a shopping mall "governed by consumer choice" (p. 309). In this metaphor, teachers are salespeople, classrooms are stores, and students are customers. In marketing terms, they see high schools wanting to "maximize their holding power" (keep students from dropping out) by satisfying consumers. This outlook has led to a variety of course offerings, or "specialty shops," for high achievers, students with special needs, troublemakers, students with vocational and technical interests, athletes, and others.

Homeschooling

Homeschooling is an alternative to on-site public education. Most states allow children to be taught at home, but such arrangements are regulated in various ways. Typically, parents have to show that their children receive an education equivalent to what they would receive in public schools—comparable books, tests, and time spent on studies.

Like private schools, home schools have grown in number for both pedagogical and ideological reasons. Estimates of the numbers of students being homeschooled range from two hundred thousand to three hundred thousand. The majority of these students tend to be from middle-class European American families located in the western and southern parts of the United States. The curriculum services used by homeschoolers suggest that the majority of families homeschooling children do so for religious reasons. Not surprisingly, homeschooling appears to have gotten a boost from the modern telecommunications industry. A quick tour on the Web will reveal hundreds of sites related to homeschooling.

Adult Education

Adult education took many forms in industrial America. Factories taught safety, while lyceums offered reading circles. Settlement houses taught immigrants and their children English and the skills needed to survive in a foreign culture. Beyond the cities, agricultural programs helped farmers improve their methods of growing crops and raising livestock.

The **Chautauqua movement** was the best adult education movement of its time. What began as a Methodist Sunday School Institute in 1874 at Lake Chautauqua, New York, became a secular educational institution through World War I. During those years, the Chautauqua movement pioneered the establishment of music associations, correspondence courses, lecture–study groups, youth groups, and reading circles.

More important than introducing progressive philosophy, the hard times of the 1930s forced people to use every resource they had to help young and old alike work their way out of the Depression. Many programs made it appropriate for adults and children to congregate at schools. The federally funded community education project associated with the Tennessee Valley Authority (TVA) in the mid-1930s, for example, provided educational opportunities that directly related to community needs, not just its youth. These projects taught adults basic literacy and job skills to help people in the tough economy.

Adult education continues to be important in the twenty-first century. Corporations offer incentives for job-related education and for postsecondary adult education. The Chautauqua Institution in New York still offers a wide range of intellectual and spiritual activities at its residential location. Other residential Chautauqua organizations provide individuals and families with alternative learning vacations. Volunteer efforts such as Literacy Volunteers of America and AmeriCorps also underscore the importance of adult education. Whether it be for a degree, job training, or general self-improvement, education is being seen as a lifelong process.

Opportunities for Higher Education

Industrialization, the need for postwar development in the South, and the Morrill Act of 1862 combined to stimulate higher education in America. Technical training produced graduates for occupations and trades. Colleges and universities educated people for the professions, research, business and industry, and virtually every other field. Although higher education remained largely a man's world, by 1890 about 2,500 women a year were graduating from college, many from schools established exclusively for women. Once women's colleges took root in American society, they would develop their own rich tradition of education.

The growing middle class desired upward mobility, so colleges and universities produced experts, specialists, and managers. Technological advances called for more specialized workers, so new professional schools—in dentistry, architecture, business administration, engineering, mining, forestry, education, and social work—emerged alongside the older professions of law, medicine, and theology.

The formation of the Association of American Universities in 1900 helped raise academic standards in postsecondary (after high school) education. Slightly fewer than 1,000 colleges and universities existed in 1900, with a combined enrollment of 238,000 students. By 1920 there were 1,041 institutions of higher education, but enrollment had more than doubled to nearly 600,000 students. The prosperity of the 1920s saw increases in state aid to public universities, colleges, and junior colleges (Link & Catton, 1963).

The years 1940 to 1960 yielded phenomenal growth in higher education. Enrollment increased from 1.5 million students to about 3.5 million. After World War II, with the passage of the Servicemen's Readjustment Act of 1944 (G.I. Bill of Rights), enrollment increased even further. As illustrated in Figure 5.3, young adults with at least a bachelor's degree have higher median earnings than their peers with less education. College education remains a good investment. **Some people worry about "degree creep"—the granting of more and higher degrees, for no particular purpose other than to give and receive them. Do you imagine you will seek more degrees? Why or why not?**

Why Was Curriculum So Important?

After the Civil War, advocates for common schools tried to encourage citizens to send their children to public schools. But deep divisions along class, religious, and ethnic lines made the task difficult. No single philosophy seemed broad enough to permit the integration of all Americans into the same schools. Social changes in the late nineteenth century—the growth of cities, popular journalism, and railroads—forced previously isolated, self-contained communities to live in a bigger world. Whether they wanted it or not, the world was coming into their towns and neighborhoods. These conditions stimulated the struggle for control of American curricula.

Figure 5.3
Annual Earnings
Median annual income
of persons 25 years old
and over, by highest
level of education and
sex: 2002

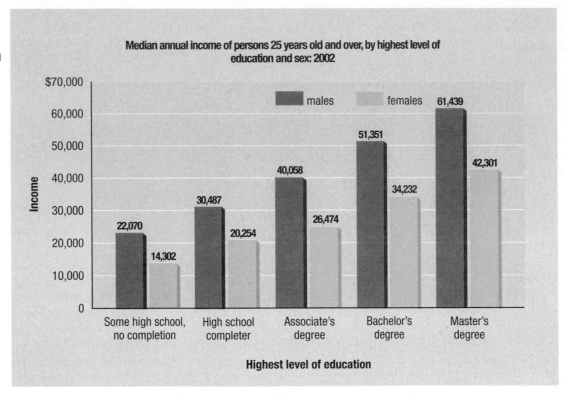

Median annual income of persons 25 years old and over, by highest level of education and sex: 2002

Source: U.S. Department of Education, National Center for Education Statistics (2006). *Digest of Education Statistics, 2005.* Figure 2.4. Available online (http://www.nces.ed.gov/pubsearch/pubsinfo.asp?pubid=2006030).

Standardized Curriculum

In 1893 the **Committee of Ten on Secondary School Studies** (established by the National Education Association in 1892) tried to standardize high school curricula across the country. Chaired by Charles Eliot, president of Harvard University, the Committee of Ten prescribed four different academic courses of study for high school students: classical, modern languages, English, and Latin–scientific. The committee urged high schools to provide four years of English and three years each of history, science, mathematics, and a foreign language. Although the goal of the curriculum was to put modern academic subjects and classical ones on an equal plane, critics viewed it as a program useful only for college-bound students.

In 1895 the **Committee of Fifteen** addressed the curriculum of elementary schools. The chairman of the committee was William Torrey Harris, U.S. Commissioner of Education. Harris advocated a curriculum that focused on "the five windows of the soul"—grammar, literature and art, mathematics, geography, and history. Harris recommended that knowledge of Western cultural heritage be passed on to students through standard literature. He believed the school's role was to be an efficient transmitter of cultural heritage through a curriculum that was graded, structured, and cumulative.

Diversified Curriculum

The purpose of schools and the content of their curriculum, as we have seen, were the subject of much debate during the nineteenth and twentieth centuries. Although some educators were out to safeguard tradition, others wanted to make the curriculum fit the stages of human development and the process of learning. Social efficiency experts advocated training for specialized skills, much like industrial training. In contrast, others viewed the curriculum as an instrument for producing social change.

Progressives, such as John Dewey, diversified curricula or individualized school programs. Dewey also wanted schools to address social problems of race, ethnicity, class, and gender. He believed the standard curricula did not fit the needs of increasingly diverse classrooms. Dewey and others called for pluralism in curricula, meaning that all students were to learn a common culture, but other cultural views were to be both accepted and encouraged. By the late 1880s eight states permitted bilingual instruction in German and English in public schools. In 1872 Oregon legalized monolingual German schools (Tyack & Hansot, 1982).

Americanization efforts in schools began to intensify in 1914 at the start of World War I and continued into the early 1920s. Schools treated southern and eastern European immigrants as a special group requiring a special, nonacademic education. The curriculum for these students emphasized American government, home economics, and vocational training. During World War I, German was eliminated from the curriculum. Schools began to give report card grades not just for academic achievements but also for students' behavior. Citizenship grades were thought to be a "measure of [students] dedication to the creation of a happy harmonious America" (Carlson, 1975, p. 123).

The NEA's Commission on the Reorganization of Secondary Education in 1918 set a new direction for high schools. Its Cardinal Principles of Secondary Education called for comprehensive institutions that served all social groups and trained for many occupations (Commission on the Reorganization of Secondary Education, 1918). High schools were no longer to serve only the college bound. As the curriculum diversified, students took different courses and different programs depending on their abilities and interests, and schools assumed more responsibilities for student welfare and vocational training. **Do you think the curricula of high schools are likely to become more or less diverse in the twenty-first century?**

Censorship and Core Curricula

Was God or Charles Darwin to be part of the common core curriculum? The 1920s saw an ideological fight between science and religion for control of the classroom. It was also one of the most widely supported cases of censorship in education. William Jennings Bryan was concerned about the possibility of atheists posing as teachers in public schools and undermining the Christian faith of American schoolchildren by teaching evolution (Link & Catton, 1963). He led his antievolution crusade to the 1925 Scopes trial in Dayton, Tennessee. The court upheld states' rights to ban the teaching of evolution. In the years after the Scopes trial, the scientific case for presenting Darwinism in schools eventually won out. To this day, however, the teaching of evolution in the public schools remains a heated issue.

> More than 1,000 people turned out last week for a biology lesson in Columbus, Ohio. . . . Advocates of intelligent design—a small proportion of the scientific community—say that scientists still debate many of the key assumptions of Darwin's theories. Too many changes happened too quickly in fossil records, they say, for natural selection to explain them. Therefore, their argument goes, teachers should be free to discuss the possibility that an intelligent designer, such as God, intervened to shape humans and other animals. (Hoff, 2002)

Whether science classes taught Darwinism, creationism, or intelligent design, some reformers in the 1930s believed the core curriculum of high schools was geared too heavily toward traditional academic subjects. In other words, they believed schools were more focused on college-bound students, offering little to students not going on to college. So the Progressive Education Association launched the Eight-Year Study to examine just what was being taught in high schools. They also wanted to see whether students who learned from a core curriculum of traditional subjects performed better than students who did not. The results, published in 1942 and 1943, suggested that students in experimental secondary schools achieved as well in college as did students from traditional high schools. The Eight-Year Study caused educators to modify the core curriculum to include more practical subject matter.

Innovative Curriculum

The argument that the national curriculum is too academic or not academic enough has existed since about the 1850s. In the 1950s critics once again harshly attacked education in America for not being academic enough. Many people believed Russian's launch of *Sputnik* was an embarrassment to the United States. At the same time, feelings of anti-intellectualism, in which practical training is preferred to high-level academics, were fairly strong. Arthur Bestor's *Educational Wastelands* (1953) described the anti-intellectualism he associated with education that emphasized "life adjustment," another term for a practical education. To counter this, he advocated intellectual training for the masses, not just for college-bound students (Kliebard, 1986).

The 1960s and 1970s brought many innovative curricula and instruction methods: School Math Study Group (SMSG), Man: A Course of Study (MACOS), Physical Science Study Committee (PSSC), Harvard Project Physics, Biological Science Curriculum Study (BSCS), Chemical Education Materials Study (CHEM Study), Project English, audiolingual language laboratories, and many more. Most of these efforts tried to involve students actively in their own learning. These programs often de-emphasized teacher-centered instruction while concentrating on methods of inquiry.

Although the curricula became innovative, some students, particularly low-income and minority students, seemed to be learning less in school every year, and the dropout rate climbed. The National Commission on Excellence in Education (1983) warned of a "rising tide of mediocrity." Many reform reports and proposals offered to fix public education. And, often, the proposed remedies come in the form of tests. President George W. Bush's No Child Left Behind legislation in 2002 called for regular testing in grades three through eight. But as opponents of these tests have pointed out, tests often report only part of the picture. Tests themselves are not a solution to educational crises. How do you define educational excellence?

How Do We Typically Judge Educational Success and Failure?

American education has improved dramatically during the modern era. Schools today educate and serve millions of children every year. Progress has been uneven across regions of the country and across time, but schools are dramatically better today than they were at the turn of the twentieth century.

We normally judge schools based on three levels: what goes in, what goes on, and what comes out. The inputs, processes, and products or outcomes of education are the factors people examine when making up their minds about educational success and failure.

Inputs consist of people and material resources devoted to schooling. For example, we might ask ourselves the following questions: Are our teachers well prepared? Do we have the latest textbooks and equipment? Is our per-pupil expenditure higher than our neighbor's?

The processes of education often are described in terms of the programs and curricula offered. Variety, rigor, appropriateness for students' needs and abilities, and so on, all figure into people's assessment of schooling. Educational processes also are described in terms of what teachers do in classrooms—the strategies they use and the skills they demonstrate in their interactions with students. In addition, the amount of time spent on various activities is closely and strongly related to how students learn

The products or outcomes of education can be measured in various ways. Today, test scores often are relied on as concise indications of educational quality. Many respected educational leaders, however, have warned against placing too much emphasis on test scores as either outcomes or predictors of potential to succeed in higher education. Richard Atkinson, president of the University of California, pitched a plan to end the use of SAT I scores for college admissions. He contended that the test was an inadequate measure of what students can do in college or of how much they learned from their K–12 education. In 2001 he proposed that California scrap the test requirement for admissions to the university. Instead, he wanted the university to rely on standardized tests that assess mastery of specific subject areas. As journalist Nicholas Lemann (2000) argued, the SAT was never really "just a test." It has always been a method for sorting people and defining individuals' educational and economic opportunities. Not getting a certain number on the test can prevent a student from entering college or qualifying for financial aid, which can have a lifelong effect on the individual.

Case Perspectives

Think back to the case that opened this chapter. The following comments—a response from Ginny's father, and a historian's look at how events can shape relationships—are designed to provide some context for this case.

A HISTORIAN CONSIDERS THE INFLUENCE OF HISTORY AND "PLACE" ON THE EVOLUTION OF RELATIONSHIPS. History shapes who we are, how we behave, and how we think about our lives. This reality is dawning on Ginny much as it does for other young people. A new generation is born, and a period of disequilibrium ensues. Our familiar roles change. We are forced to move forward even though we do not fully comprehend where we have been. Even contortionists have trouble accomplishing this feat!

Every place has its own unique history, but you do not have to study it very long to discover the large, encompassing themes that cut across locales and time periods. Historians speak of the influences of "local history" or "nearby history" when they describe this idea. If Ginny's school happens to be in Detroit, for example, the history of race relations in that city would inevitably impinge on her outlook.

In his account of one horrible "racial event" in Detroit in 1925, historian Kevin Boyle demonstrated how community life can be swamped by social–historical forces.

> In 1925 Detroit, the auto industry was flourishing. The city served as a Mecca for black Americans escaping Jim Crow in the South and for immigrants fleeing postwar Europe. Some 80,000-plus African Americans lived in Detroit, in close proximity to 35,000 members of the Detroit branch of the Ku Klux Klan.
>
> Dr. Ossian Sweet moved his family out of a black ghetto into a bungalow in a white, working-class neighborhood. When he did so he brought along nine friends and a bagful of guns. Hundreds of the neighbors rioted, throwing rocks at the Sweets' house. The police made no move to stop the mob. And then suddenly, someone inside the house fired shots into the street. The bullets wounded one white man and killed another. The ten black men and Sweet's wife were jailed and charged with first-degree murder. The event and the trial shaped views of race and tolerance for years to come, not only in Detroit but across the nation. (Boyle, 2004)

Admittedly, the events in Detroit in 1925 may be worlds away from Ginny and Sarah and the school they teach and learn in. But few would doubt that other Sarahs and their mothers, and other historical events, help define how we teach and how we learn.

GINNY'S FATHER RESPONDS.
Dear Ginny,

It was great to hear from you. I'm really sorry you're so troubled by what happened at school. In case you didn't realize it, you come by these feelings honestly. Not to diminish your concerns, but your ancestors were all worriers. Your grandfather used to say that the day he didn't worry would be the day they buried him. Not to diminish the importance of the situation you described to me, but let me share one little nugget of wisdom your grandfather extracted from his experience. He said that he often couldn't remember today what he had worried about yesterday. In other words, he believed most of our troubles were minor in the scheme of things. This "Walking-the-walk-talking-the-talk" stuff is a cliché, not unlike the ones that used to roll off Grandpa's tongue. Let me give you a couple of others that strike me as more appropriate in this situation.

Of course you didn't come from the neighborhood where you're student teaching. If that were a requirement for getting a job, we'd all still be digging potatoes out of the Irish countryside. Your family history is one of an up-by-the-bootstraps mentality. Our family has been scratching to build a better life for itself since long before I was born. Ever since you were a baby you've watched your mother and me move, go to school, try new jobs, fail, try again, succeed, and so on. Whether you realize it or not, you've been on the same road. Things have never been easy for you. But you've had the capacity to smile and keep trying.

I have always been so terribly impressed by your warmth and generosity of spirit. You have not blamed others when things didn't turn out the way you wanted. You simply kept trying to make things better. My hunch is that the woman you described may be tired and overworked. No doubt she loves her children and is simply frustrated. The Lord only knows how difficult her life has been.

Take a deep breath and try not to worry too much. Just be your own lovely self, and bear in mind a different cliché. I think Harry Truman may have said it, but if not, he could have. It sounds like him: There are two kinds of people: Those who write about history, and those who make it. You get out there and keep on making history. I am absolutely certain that in the end, history will judge you kindly. Why? Because I'm the person who is going to write it!
Love, Dad

Questions for Reflection: If you were in Ginny's position, what actions might you take, if any, to repair your relationship with Sarah's mother? How important do you think it is to be "like" the students you teach? To understand their backgrounds and community? How important is it to involve parents in the educational process? ▪

Summary

Once the Civil War ended, the nation seemed to rise up, look around, and gather itself for the headlong rush into the twentieth century. Industrialization and urbanization created the need to both care for and educate children. The end of slavery, the "reeducation" of Native Americans, and the political emergence of women all put demands on education systems. The rising tide of immigration greatly intensified the pressure.

Public schools served to assimilate people into the cultural mainstream. Education was supposed to help people fit in as productive, tax-paying contributors to society—but they had to fit in in the right place, in the right way. In addition, shifting demographics and cultural changes influenced education. In some ways, communities got the kinds of schools that circumstances dictated.

As people learned to read, write, speak, and calculate, they shaped their own lives. Demand for education soared. Educational leaders with strong personalities and well-defined beliefs— and millions of students and their parents—defined schooling across the nation. Despite the philosophical wars over the aims, content, and processes of teaching and learning, we have seen that U.S. public schools are remarkably resistant to change. And yet, many people ask: Why should they change? As challenged as some of these schools may be, they are part of the largest and arguably most successful universal education system in the world.

TERMS AND CONCEPTS

black codes
Brown v. *Board of Education of Topeka, Kansas*
Bureau of Indian Affairs (BIA)
Chautauqua movement
Chinese Exclusion Act
Committee of Fifteen
Committee of Ten on Secondary School Studies
Elementary and Secondary Education Act (ESEA) of 1965

Freedman's Bureau
Head Start
Indian Self-Determination and Educational Assistance Act
National Association for the Advancement of Colored People (NAACP)
National Defense Education Act (NDEA)
Plessy v. *Ferguson*
progressivism
Women's Educational Equity Act (WEEA)

REFLECTIVE ACTIVITY: CYCLES OF EDUCATION

Reflective practice is an essential part of good teaching. Reflection is a process that includes making thoughtful decisions, understanding and articulating value structures, acting from knowledge, evaluating your actions and their effects, and sharing your reflections with colleagues. After reading the following scenario, respond to the questions below. The scenario reflects the INTASC Principle and Disposition at the end of this activity.

Change is a constant in education. Like the historical changes occurring in the larger society, educational change often occurs in cycles. Recent changes—magnet and charter schools, school voucher systems, homeschooling (parents teaching their children at home)—in the educational landscape have prompted historians to draw comparisons to the pluralism that characterized education during colonial times.

The variety of educational institutions available during the colonial period made it difficult to classify schools as either public or private. Schools that served a public purpose, such as "education for nationhood," were considered public, regardless of the percentage of public funding they received or their degree of private control. Sources of funding support, like the school structure itself, varied widely among schools. Public sources of funding, such as taxation and land grants, often were supplemented by tuition, church support, private subscriptions, donations, lotteries, and other sources of income.

Studies suggest that a similar type of pluralism has returned to education. Enrollment in Catholic schools is approximately 2.5 million, with enrollment in other religiously affiliated schools estimated at 1.8 million. In addition, the parents of more than 1 million American children have chosen homeschooling. Charter schools also are experiencing tremendous growth in many parts of the country, with the current student enrollment at about four hundred thousand.

Decide   1. School reform has traditionally resulted from efforts to meet the changing needs of society. Does movement toward increased pluralism in education reflect an increasing fragmentation of society? What is the responsibility of schools to address such a trend?

Perceive and Value   2. In our modern return to educational pluralism, what makes a public school public?

Know and Act   3. Competition is a commonly named reason for increasing school options. What are some of the criticisms of attempting to apply this market metaphor to education?

Evaluate   4. What responsibility does our society have to support the education of all our youth, independent of the educational choices they make?

Discuss   5. What are all the kinds of schools that serve your community? How does each serve the larger community?

INTASC Principle 10

The teacher fosters relationships with school colleagues, parents, and agencies in the larger community to support students' learning and well-being.

Disposition

The teacher understands schools as organizations within the larger community context and understands the operations of the relevant aspects of the system(s) within which s/he works. (Interstate New Teacher Assessment and Support Consortium, 1992)

ADDITIONAL READINGS

Adams, D. W. (1995). *Education for extinction: American Indians and the boarding school experience, 1875–1928.* Lawrence, KS: University Press of Kansas.

Angus, D. L., & Mirel, J. E. (1999). *The failed promise of the American high school, 1890–1995.* New York: Teachers College Press, Columbia University.

Callahan, R. (1962). *Education and the cult of efficiency: A study of the social forces that have shaped the administration of the public schools.* Chicago: University of Chicago Press.

Dewey, J. (1938). *Experience and education.* New York: Macmillan.

DuBois, W. E. B. (1903). *The souls of black folk: Essays and sketches.* Chicago: A. G. McClurg.

Vinyard, J. M. (1998). *For faith and fortune: The education of Catholic immigrants in Detroit, 1805–1925.* Urbana: University of Illinois Press.

WEB RESOURCES

www.cedu.niu.edu/blackwell/
The Blackwell History of Education Museum at Northern Illinois University in DeKalb, Illinois, is a nonprofit organization dedicated to promoting interest in the history of American education. The website includes a variety of free materials for teachers and students.

www.si.edu/
The Smithsonian Institution website is a rich resource for teachers and students. Explore the section on "History and Culture" to learn more about people and events that shaped U.S. history.

www.ciweb.org/
Visit the Chautauqua Institution's website to learn about educational opportunities for people of all ages.

www.oah.org/
The website for the Organization of American Historians promotes the study and teaching of the American past through a number of online activities.

CHAPTER 6

Why Teachers Behave As They Do

Case Study: *Developing Civic Attitudes*

As she waved goodbye to the last of her students, Tracy headed for her classroom. She had about fifteen minutes before the schoolwide faculty meeting, just enough time to add one more objective to her six-week plans for social studies. Tracy and her colleagues would be finalizing their plans on Friday, and she wanted to be ready. Before she could pick up her pencil, Brian popped in the door. "Hey, Tracy. Want to grab some coffee before the meeting?"

Tracy laughed. Brian was a great teammate, and she enjoyed talking school with him. "Let's go!" she responded. "While we're walking, let me tell you about an idea I want to propose to our team on Friday. It has to do with civic education. The more I work with our students, the more I believe we need to expand our curriculum to deal with real issues. Like the importance of voting. Did you know that fewer than one-third of eighteen- to twenty-nine-year-olds voted in the 2000 presidential election and that less than one-fifth voted in congressional elections? That's appalling!"

"Hey, calm down," said Brian. "I agree that lack of political engagement is problematic. But our students aren't completely disengaged. I mean, there's plenty of evidence they're patriotic and tolerant. And the volunteerism stats for our school are awesome! So, let's not be so full of gloom and doom, my friend."

"You're right," said Tracy. "Unfortunately, there's no evidence that volunteerism leads to wider civic engagement. Also, our immigrant population gets bigger and bigger every year. I love the diversity, but I worry we aren't working as a team to produce good citizens. Isn't that our responsibility?"

What you believe, what philosophy you hold, can help you make sense out of confusion and guide you in the classroom. This chapter contains some prevalent educational philosophies that are useful to both teachers and students.

What Does Philosophy Have to Do with You As a Teacher?

Philosophy can be defined as a set of ideas that answers questions about the nature of reality and about the meaning of life. What is basic human nature? What is real and true about life and the world? What is knowledge? What is worth knowing or striving for? What is just, good, right, or beautiful? Everyone asks these kinds of philosophical questions, and they are especially important questions in teachers' lives.

There are some practical reasons why philosophy is important. If we know a teacher's or a student's philosophy, then we have some clue about how that person will behave and why. John Dewey (1916) argued, "Whenever philosophy has been taken seriously, it has always been assumed that it signified achieving a wisdom which would influence the conduct of life" (p. 378). It is important for teachers and students to understand one another's philosophies in order for learning to occur.

Philosophy Influences Education

As you begin to develop your own philosophy of teaching, can you identify examples of educational practices you believe are worthwhile? Parents may choose or reject a school for their children because of how they believe the school's philosophy will be translated into educational experiences. Indeed, various philosophies are at work in schools, and they can be found on many different levels. For instance, principals run schools in keeping with their thoughts about managing people and administering programs. Some schools operate like businesses or factories, whereas others are like churches, or colleges, or football teams. Teachers plan lessons, interact with students, and judge students' performances according to their own personal views of knowledge. Sometimes their views depend heavily on their idealized conceptions of the role of teacher. In turn, prospective teachers learn a particular set of instructional methods based on their teachers' educational philosophies. Philosophy shapes the writing of curricula, the preparation and scoring of tests, and even the architecture of school buildings.

Educators disagree routinely and sometimes aggressively about philosophies. One problem with clinging to philosophies is we often forget to reexamine our views in light of changing conditions. Our actions become habitual, out of touch with the present. When this happens, philosophies limit our visions of the future more than they shape them.

It is possible, for instance, to construct educational systems with a view of the "typical" or "average" person in mind when the system is full of "extraordinary" people. When this happens, the systems do not work, because they do not fit the people they are supposed to serve.

Philosophies different from our own can be useful because they stretch our thinking. Someone who calls herself an "idealist," for example, cannot help but grow from a serious consideration of a "realist" view and vice versa. There is almost always some room to change one's mind, but change is unlikely if people are unaware of the options. Big minds have room to consider more than one point of view.

What Are the Roots of American Educational Philosophies?

Western philosophies originated with the ancient Greeks, who systematically addressed life's questions. Figure 6.1 shows how Greek thinkers divided philosophy into three branches:

1. **Metaphysics** and its two corollaries address reality. **Ontology** explores issues related to nature, existence, or being. **Cosmology** deals with the nature and origin of the universe (the cosmos).

Figure 6.1
Summary of Branches
of Philosophy
How might you have to deal
with each branch of philosophy
in your role as a teacher?

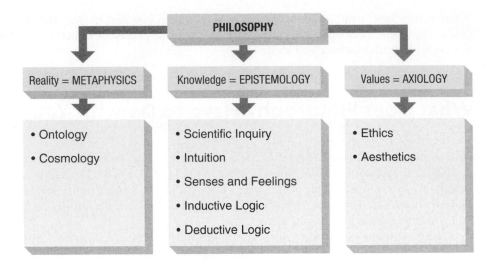

PHILOSOPHY

Reality = METAPHYSICS

Knowledge = EPISTEMOLOGY

Values = AXIOLOGY

- Ontology
- Cosmology

- Scientific Inquiry
- Intuition
- Senses and Feelings
- Inductive Logic
- Deductive Logic

- Ethics
- Aesthetics

2. **Epistemology** addresses the nature of knowledge; that is, it questions how we come to know things. We develop knowledge of truth through observation and logic—by reasoning deductively from a general principle to a particular case and by reasoning inductively from a set of particular cases to a general principle. We also develop knowledge from scientific inquiry, intuition, and our senses.

3. **Axiology** and its corollaries seek to determine what is of value. **Ethics** explores issues of morality and conduct. **Aesthetics** is concerned with beauty.

Our education system remains rooted in the Western philosophies described in the following sections. We also describe a number of non-Western philosophies that affect education in the United States as more non-Western people enter our schools and communities.

Idealism

Do you believe, as Plato did, that the best and brightest people among us should lead our government? **Idealism** says reality lies in our consciousness or our intellect (see Figure 6.2). The father of idealism is Plato (427?–347 BC), who was a student of Socrates and a citizen of Athens. Plato imagined a society driven by the pursuit of knowledge. To search for truth, justice, and beauty in the world, one needed to find meaning in one's own life and in the collective life of the community. Plato believed this search for knowledge would lead us away from the physical world of what we can see, feel, smell, hear, and taste and toward a world of ideas. The job of philosophy and philosophers was to help people think clearly about these important ideas. He further believed this search for ideas would help people govern themselves justly. According to idealism, perfect knowledge of the ideal resided outside humans as an absolute, or as God. By pursuing ideas, however, Plato believed we could move closer to living in a perfect world.

Plato explained his vision of the ideal world through imaginary conversations between Socrates and his students. These conversations, or dialogues, were written as poetry, science, and philosophy. In the dialogues, Socrates asks questions that force his students to examine their thinking about life, truth, beauty, and justice. As they interact with Socrates, students discover the errors in their thinking and form clearer, more accurate ideas about life's important questions. The **Socratic method**, then, is teaching through inquiry and dialogues that help students discover and clarify knowledge. These dialogues have guided thought and action in Western civilizations since their writing, and they continue to guide people today.

Plato's most famous dialogue is *The Republic*, in which he described his ideal society. He outlined how people should think, value, behave, teach, and organize and govern society. Plato knew that this utopia was unattainable. Yet for him, and for the idealists who followed, such visions of perfection are goals we should strive to achieve in our own lifetimes. They are benchmarks against which we should judge human progress over many lifetimes.

Plato
(427?–347 BC)

	IDEALISM	REALISM	HUMANISM
Philosophers	**Plato**	**Aristotle**	**Erasmus**
Metaphysics	Reality is an unchanging world of perfect ideas and universal truths.	Reality is observable events, objects, and matter independent of human knowing.	Reality is also humanity's creation. People strive for personal meaning in their experience and interpretation of life on Earth.
Epistemology	Knowledge is obtained when ideas are brought into consciousness through self-examination and discourse.	Knowledge is obtained when students are taught ideas that can be verified and skills that enable them to know objects they encounter.	Exploration, questioning, and critical thinking enable students to discover or construct and use knowledge.
Axiology	Wisdom of goodness; discipline, order, self-control; preservation of cultural heritage of the past.	Self-control; clear judgment and rational thought; personal excellence; balance and moderation.	Knowing and loving God; serving humanity.

Figure 6.2
Philosophies That Undergird Western Education
How might teachers who are idealists, realists, and humanists differ in their relationships with students and their teaching approaches?

In terms of education, Plato promoted the idea of an aristocracy based on wisdom and goodness rather than wealth and power. Although he believed all men and women should have opportunities to learn, he thought few would demonstrate the wisdom and goodness necessary to govern. In Plato's utopia people who had proved themselves worthy, remained healthy, thought clearly, and were of high moral character would govern. Rulers could come from any segment of society, but only the most talented among them would serve as philosopher kings. An intermediate class of well-trained soldiers would protect the community. And a broad base of farmers, traders, and manufacturers would support the society. Plato's curriculum for this idealized society was straightforward, rigorous, and lifelong: moral education that would make citizens realize they had responsibilities to one another. **What is your ideal classroom?**

Realism

Aristotle advised people to seek balance in their lives. How might it be possible to find balance in a life of teaching? Aristotle (384–322 BC) was a student of Plato, but he saw the world differently. Instead of searching for truth in the world of ideals, as Plato prescribed, Aristotle sought truth by investigating the real world around him. His work, called **realism,** forms the basis for the scientific method. At its core, realism suggests that the objects we sense or perceive exist independently of the mind. In other words, whether or not we perceive these objects, they exist in the world.

Aristotle established a vast library of manuscripts, a collection of zoological and botanical specimens, and a lyceum in Athens, where he taught many young scholars. Despite the lack of scientific equipment and basic knowledge of the laws of nature, Aristotle did much to advance science. Specifically, Aristotle acted on his belief that the study of matter would lead to a better understanding of ideas. In fact, Aristotle and his students provided much of the intellectual groundwork for Mendel's genetic theory, Darwin's theory of evolution, and the disciplines of biology and psychology.

Aristotle believed humans learn through their senses. As individuals experience the world, they develop and refine concepts about objects. Whereas idealists believe

Aristotle
(384–322 BC)

truth and knowledge can be found in the mind of the individual, realists believe knowledge exists independent of human comprehension. Therefore, realists believe the purpose of education is to teach students about the world in which they live.

Aristotle believed that happiness is the ultimate goal in humans' lives. People travel the path to true happiness by stretching their minds to the fullest of their capabilities. "Virtue, or rather excellence, will depend on clear judgment, self-control, symmetry of desire, artistry of means" (Durant, 1961, p. 60). In other words, people develop virtue by accumulating experience and not by having intent or maintaining innocence.

If excellence is desirable, excess is taboo. Aristotle counseled people to seek the middle ground, or Golden Mean, in matters of life: "between cowardice and rashness is courage; between stinginess and extravagance is liberality; between sloth and greed is ambition" (Durant, 1961, p. 60). To Aristotle, the middle ground was where training could make excellence flourish. As people practiced thinking and behaving in productive ways, they developed habits that would lead them to excellence.

Like Plato, Aristotle believed that an aristocracy of talented people should run the government. He envisioned a government-run education system that would emphasize balance in assigning people to the work of society. It also would teach responsibility to the state. **What do you believe is the ultimate goal of education?**

Humanism

When, if ever, do teachers need to step aside and let students learn on their own? Humanism advocates respect and kindness toward all people. As it relates to education, humanism says that students should receive developmentally appropriate instruction in liberal arts, social conduct, and moral principles. These beliefs are grounded in the writings of Erasmus (1466?–1536), Martin Luther (1483–1546), and Jean-Jacques Rousseau (1712–1778), some of the first humanists.

The Renaissance was a time of rebirth in Europe between the fourteenth and sixteenth centuries. After many years of war and death, the arts, literature, and classical interests experienced a revival. In some respects, humanism was the result of a renewed hopefulness for humankind after a long period of suffering. Writing during the Renaissance, Erasmus extended this rebirth to education. He said that the young should be taught with kindness and gentleness. Children were to be nurtured, not scolded and abused.

The Protestant Reformation occurred around the same time as the Renaissance, and education was an essential ingredient in both movements. The Reformation inspired the idea of public-supported education to help people take responsibility for their own lives. Specifically, the goal was to help people read and interpret the Bible for themselves. As people discovered their own ways to worship God, they also began to define how they would educate for character. For people living during the Reformation and the Renaissance, education empowered them to make their own decisions, thereby determining their destiny both on Earth and in the afterlife.

Rousseau enriched Erasmus's humanistic perspective on the needs of children and the goals of education. He suggested children not be viewed as blank slates or as miniature adults, but as individuals possessing natural goodness and needing continual support.

Humanistic psychologists in the twentieth century, including Alfred Adler, Carl Rogers, Paul Goodman, and Abraham Maslow, continued to apply humanist philosophy to schooling. They wrote and spoke often about the assumptions on which a humanistic education should be based. Humanists believe students should not be forced to learn; they will learn what they need and want to know when they are ready. The process of learning is at least as important as the acquisition of facts and skills. Students can evaluate themselves; they do not need to be judged by teachers or other adults. Students' emotional well-being is of critical importance for learning. Schools have to be fear-free places if students are to take responsibility for their learning and to enjoy what they do. Most of all, humanists believe self-fulfillment is the principal aim of education.

Paulo Freire was a humanistic Brazilian educator who encouraged the teaching of illiterate, indigent workers in the developing world. With the abilities to read and write, Freire argued, people will become aware of their own essential humanness and be able to improve their social situation. **Do you believe students should be given more or less responsibility for evaluating themselves?**

What Modern Philosophies Influence Western Education?

Modern philosophies, such as existentialism, Marxism, behaviorism, and cognitivism, have influenced education in the United States. These and other modern philosophical orientations are summarized in Figure 6.3.

Existentialism

"I don't care who my teacher is. The only thing that matters is what my teacher does." Do you agree or disagree? Experts consider Sören Kierkegaard (1813–1855) to be the originator of existentialism, a philosophy that emphasizes the subjectivity of human experience. Here is another way to think of existentialism: every individual is the subject of his or her own reality, and no two realities are the same. Therefore, the importance of both individual creativity and personal choice in a nonrational world is key to existentialism. Friedrich Wilhelm Nietzsche (1844–1900), Martin Heidegger (1889–1976), Jean-Paul Sartre (1905–1980), Albert Camus (1913–1960), Paul Tillich (1886–1965), Martin Buber (1878–1965), and others developed existentialist thought by describing reality not as something beyond the comprehension of humans, but as the result of individual passion and life experience.

Existentialists believe the physical universe has no meaning apart from human experience. The world and forces of nature exist, but they are not ordered in some grand scheme in which humans play their appropriate part. Human life exists, but we are only what we make of ourselves. Sartre's often-quoted phrase is "Existence precedes essence" (1947, p. 28). By this statement, he means we owe our existence to nature, but we define ourselves through our actions.

Nietzsche (1924, 1961) revealed the dark side of this view (Banville, 1998). He characterized life as a grim battle requiring strength, pride, and intelligence merely to survive. Sensitivity, kindness, and consideration were signs of weakness. He did not believe in God or an eternal afterlife. Nietzsche believed we should not strive to better the majority of people, who were mostly worthless. Instead, he argued that we should promote genius and develop superior personalities through restraint and discipline.

Choice is a critical concept for existentialists. People choose who they will be. Some allow others to decide for them, but even this is a choice. Although existentialists do not reject morals or norms of behavior, they do reject unthinking adherence to them. When we make decisions based on what is right for us, we take responsibility for our actions. In other words, we should not do something simply because we are told to do it. Existentialists also believe that when we are free to choose our directions we value that freedom and want it for others.

Martin Buber, existentialist and Hasidic Jew, criticized theologians' talk of God and their pretensions about knowing God. In *I and Thou* (1970), Buber did not try to support religion or to argue that God was present in all things. Instead, he raised the possibility that life without religion lacked an important dimension. Buber proclaimed that the secular is sacred and that God is present when people engage in honest dialogue. Human relationships create meaning in our lives. Buber and other existentialists have influenced the development of humanistic psychology, in which relationships, free thinking, and action lead to self-actualization, or personal fulfillment. Of the values you hold most strongly, which one will be the most important in helping you define yourself as a teacher?

Marxism

How might education be used to promote social revolution? Marxism promotes the belief that forces in history prevent people from achieving economic freedom and social and political equality. Marxism is a philosophy most closely associated with communism and Russia. Despite the collapse of the U.S.S.R. in the late 1980s and early 1990s, Marxist theory remains a powerful philosophical force.

Karl Marx (1818–1883) was a historian, philosopher, and social theorist born to Jewish parents in Germany. Marx learned from the writings of the idealist Georg Wilhelm Friedrich Hegel (1770–1831). Although Marx grew to reject Hegel's political philosophy, he was influenced

	Goal of Education	Role of Students	Role of Teachers	Teaching Methods	Subjects Studied
Existentialism	Develop authentic individuals who exercise freedom of choice and take responsibility for their actions.	Develop independence, self-discipline; set challenges and solve problems.	Encourage students to philosophize about life and to recognize and fulfill personal freedom.	Discussion and analysis, examination of choice-making in own and others' lives.	Drama Art Literature Social Sciences History
Marxism	Shape people and institutions; change material conditions of society, producing classless society.	Live and work harmoniously with others, acquire and use knowledge that will enable them to transform natural and social world.	Lead and advocate change.	Scientific methodology, practical activity (problem solving).	Emphasis on science and history.
Behaviorism	Engineer environments that efficiently maximize learning.	Respond to environmental and behavioral stimuli; become self-regulated.	Manipulate the learning environment and present stimuli, using conditioning and social learning to shape student behavior.	Programmed instruction that provides feedback on performance, behavioral contracts, reinforcement.	Learning tasks in which behavior can be directly observed, measured, and evaluated.
Cognitivism	Develop thinking skills for lifelong self-directed learning.	Construct meaningful knowledge through experience and interaction.	Stimulate cognitive development; mediate student learning and monitor thought processes.	Use of manipulatives and real-life learning opportunities relevant to students' prior experiences.	Integrated curricula; emphasis on thinking and critical thinking skills, study skills, and problem-solving skills.
Pragmatism	Develop and apply practical knowledge and skills for life in a progressive democratic society.	Active learning and participation.	Teach inductive and deductive reasoning, the scientific method, and the powers of observation and practice.	Hands-on curricula, group work, experimentation.	Emphasis on citizenship, knowledge and skills applicable to daily life, and career or job preparation.
Perennialism	Acquisition of timeless principles of reality, truth, and value; learning for the sake of learning.	Receive knowledge and academic skills.	Guide to the classics; teach basic skills.	Teacher-centered direct instruction.	Emphasis on Great Books and core curricula in the arts and sciences.
Essentialism	Acquisition of culture; cultural literacy for personal benefit.	Receive knowledge; demonstrate minimum competencies.	Deliver a standard curriculum.	Subject-centered direct instruction.	Uniform curriculum for all students that emphasizes the essence of traditional American culture.
Social Reconstructionism	Solve social problems and create a better world.	Inquire, apply critical thinking skills, and take action.	Ask questions; present social issues and problem-solving challenges; serve as organizer and information resource.	Stimulate divergent thinking and group investigation.	Emphasis on social studies, social problems, global education, and environmental issues.

Figure 6.3
Today's Philosophical Orientations
What combination of philosophical orientations best matches your own beliefs and values?

greatly by Hegel's thought. He was particularly interested in Hegel's concept of the *dialectic*, or the process by which human thought and human history progress.

The dialectic is a constant intellectual movement from thesis, to antithesis, and finally to synthesis. Movement in thought occurs, for example, when one puts a thesis (idea) against its antithesis (opposite). Hegel believed this type of devil's advocacy was the reality of nature. Synthesis is the new idea that develops from the interplay between thesis and antithesis. The synthesized idea, then, generally is a more evolved or well developed idea. Hegel believed that ultimately this process would reach the Absolute Idea, similar to the idealists' conceptions of truth. He rejected the realist view that truth exists independently of our minds. People become and remain alienated, he thought, until they understand that they are thinking beings. For him, truth is a function of this self-realization.

Hegel argued that the dialectic process also works for history. Civilization progresses along a continuum toward richer, more complex syntheses. In other words, culture moves forward by building on what has come before.

Marx saw progress as a mixed blessing. He believed the dialectic of history to be a clash of economic forces in which the capitalist system exploits the worker. The ruling class seized workers' labor and offered money in return, making workers servants of the system. Capitalists, Marx contended, accumulate great wealth, but they create inequalities and dehumanize people in the process. Marx believed workers would eventually rise up and overthrow the ruling class.

Marx recognized the value of science as a way to acquire knowledge and, ultimately, power. For Marx, perception comes from experiencing the material world through one's senses, and this experience shapes one's knowledge. Therefore, human nature is malleable, meaning people and social institutions can be formed and reformed. A person's social class is a matter of education and circumstance. The aim of Marxism, then, is to change the material conditions of society so everyone shares them equally. When these conditions change, consciousness changes; when consciousness changes, ideology changes. And this is when the perfect, classless society will emerge.

Marxism has been advanced most notably by people referred to as the Frankfurt School— a school of thought based on Marxist assumptions about the social world. Some of the main voices in the school include Max Horkheimer (1895–1973), Theodor Adorno (1903–1969), Herbert Marcuse (1898–1979), and Jürgen Habermas (born 1929). Critical theorists such as Habermas try to reveal the hidden values of the upper class in schooling and society. They claim that schools alienate students and "de-skill" them by establishing the goals of education instead of encouraging students to set their own goals (Apple, 1995). **What implicit or unspoken values influence schooling in the United States?**

Behaviorism and Cognitivism

If teachers can shape students' behaviors, how might students shape teachers' behaviors? **Behaviorism** says that human behavior is determined by forces in the environment beyond our control and not by the exercise of free will. Behaviorism stands in stark contrast to **cognitivism**, a philosophy based on the belief that people actively construct their knowledge of the world through experience. Several names are associated with the development of behaviorism— Ivan Pavlov (1849–1936), John Watson (1878–1958), E. L. Thorndike (1874–1949), and B. F. Skinner (1904–1990).

Skinner was a psychologist who concentrated on scientific experimentation and empirical observation. Although he made his reputation with tightly controlled laboratory experimentation, he could let his mind roam freely over complex social problems. Our failure to solve social problems, he believed, was because of our failure to understand human behavior: "We have made immense strides in controlling the physical and biological worlds, but our practices in government, education, and much of economics, though adapted to very different conditions, have not greatly improved" (1971, pp. 5–6).

Skinner wanted scientists to work for a peaceful and just world by helping us understand human nature. To behaviorists, education conditions people to behave in more and less civilized ways. What is learned about human nature through scientific experiments could help develop more effective teaching and learning methods. In this way, science could be used to shape morality.

Behaviorists, like realists, rely on knowledge derived from the physical world. They examine how people develop behavior patterns in response to environmental influences. The most famous example of this type of conditioning is Pavlov and his dogs. Another example is John Watson, who conditioned and then unconditioned his young son to fear animals. For some behaviorists, including Watson, free will does not exist because it cannot be measured. In other words, all our behaviors are simply learned responses to specific stimuli.

In terms of education, behaviorists believe students are conditioned to learn. So when students are not learning, something is wrong with the educational program. The way to solve the problem is to break down the program into its separate parts and fix the pieces that are broken. If too much is wrong, the program should be scrapped altogether, and a new one should be used. The challenge to educators, then, is to engineer programs that produce desired results.

The educational applications of behaviorism are many and varied. One application is the use of programmed instruction to teach mathematics, reading, and other subject matter. The subjects are organized into ordered units of study, accompanied by unit tests, opportunities for feedback on performance, and chances to practice skills. Educators also use behavioral contracts to influence student behavior. These are organized as "if . . ., then . . ." agreements between teachers and students: For example, a teacher might say, "If you do your homework correctly, then you can spend the end of the class period reading whatever you wish in the library."

The language of education is full of behavioral terminology—*reward, punishment, contingency, reinforcer, shaping, fading.* Teachers speak of "reinforcing desirable behavior." They try to "ignore inappropriate behavior." People want student motivation to become "intrinsic" rather than "extrinsic," and so forth (Cohen & Hearn, 1988). These behavioral terms reflect the scientific nature of the philosophy.

Alternatives to the behaviorist outlook take a variety of forms, loosely grouped under the heading of cognitivism. The word comes from *cognition,* meaning the process of thinking and knowing. Cognitive psychologists assert that people are not passively conditioned by the environment but rather are active learners. They mentally construct their knowledge of the world and beliefs about reality through their own direct experiences and interactions. They then act on those constructs out of free will. To summarize, cognitivists focus on thought, which cannot be observed directly, where behaviorists focus on behavior that is observable and measurable.

Cognitivism, like behaviorism, is a philosophy with implications for education. Educators who favor cognitive teaching models often use student-centered learning experiences. They assist students by teaching them study skills, thinking skills, and problem-solving skills. They try to provide conceptual foundations or **scaffolding** on which students make sense of information for themselves. In education, the movement to modify curriculum and instruction to reflect the cognitivist outlook is called **constructivism.** The Swiss developmental psychologist Jean Piaget is among those associated with cognitivism and constructivism. Can you think of an experience in which a teacher helped you construct your own knowledge?

Many modern constructivist teachers see themselves as action researchers seeking to understand how and why students construct knowledge as they do. They encourage students to experiment and ask lots of open-ended questions. In a constructivist classroom, learning is student centered, not teacher centered.

Pragmatism

Pragmatism defines the truth and meaning of ideas according to their physical consequences and practical value. Charles Sanders Peirce (1839–1914) is acknowledged as the originator of modern pragmatism. Pragmatism is so often equated with "common sense" that many people would claim it as the unofficial American philosophy. William James (1842–1910), John Dewey (1859–1952), and, most recently, Richard Rorty (1931–2007) have used pragmatism to try to balance the realism of the natural sciences and the beliefs of idealists as expressed in art, religion, and politics (Rorty, 1991).

Like other philosophers, early pragmatists wrestled with the dualism of mind and matter: A subjective reality exists in our minds, an objective reality exists in the physical world around us. They agreed with the realists that a world does, in fact, exist and is not merely a figment of our imagination. However, much of the meaning we assign to objective reality comes from our subjective knowledge of the effects that objects have and the consequences that actions have. For instance, you may have been raised to believe that over time a person gets from life what he or she deserves; that is, "appropriate behavior" is rewarded, just as "inappropriate behavior" is punished. If so, you may grow to think that your present state of being, "objectively speaking," is a direct indication of what is right and just, because you have behaved in ways

Technology in Practice

PRAGMATISM AT WORK

Aviation High, a career and technical education school in Queens, New York, is a modern-day example of pragmatism in action. The school has been recognized as one of several promising school-to-work programs. Besides taking the usual courses in math, English, science, and foreign language, students at Aviation High enroll in airframe and power plant shop classes. The 1,600 students can specialize in aviation mechanics and engineering while obtaining a strong academic education. An on-site hangar housing twenty airplanes and various aviation equipment provides intensive exposure to the aviation industry and hands-on experience for students. One of the first topics teacher George Zanetis addresses with students is a history lesson about Nikolaus Otto's 1876 invention of the piston engine, a discovery that took many years of painstaking research:

> After the discussion meanders everywhere, Zanetis begins to recap. His first question: "What

was Dr. Otto's first name?" The answer from a voice in the last row: "Lonely." It is high school after all . . . But in [George] Zanetis' power plant class, it seems as if the students, who wear not-too-stylish mechanics coveralls over their Sean John jeans and Diesel sneakers, are hitting out-dated books. A lesson about a 127-year-old technology? Unbelievably significant, as it turns out. Otto's invention is still used in every kind of aviation today, and the kids need to understand it well because about 300 of them will earn FAA certificates this year, and many will become airline mechanics, engineers, or pilots. (Ernst, 2004 p.25)

Questions for Reflection: Can you think of examples of pragmatic curricula you experienced as a student? What are the pros and cons of such approaches in the classroom?

Source: Ernst, H. (2004). Flight path. *Teacher Magazine, 15*(4), 25–29.

that make it so. The goal of pragmatists has been to seek wisdom, or truth, by thinking about the consequences of having particular beliefs and acting on them.

William James emphasized the right of individuals to create their own reality. He viewed the pragmatic method as a way to settle metaphysical disputes: "Whenever a dispute is serious, we ought to be able to show some practical difference that must follow from one side or the other's being right" (1907, p. 42).

Other pragmatists have argued that the correspondence between human beliefs and physical objects is unimportant. If we believe that something is true, and there is some gap between our beliefs and truth, we can always change our beliefs as new evidence becomes available. For pragmatists, truth is what is good for us to believe (Rorty, 1991). For all practical purposes, if something works, it is true.

John Dewey linked pragmatism to educational preparation for life in a democracy in which many different viewpoints are represented. When people are educated pragmatically, Dewey argued, they are prepared for life. And when education concentrates on real-life problems, people are prepared to live fully and effectively in a democracy. Dewey believed that ordinary people possess the intelligence to govern themselves and to direct their own actions. The function of education, he argued, was to enhance human potential. Dewey believed American public education was indoctrination—mindless and practically irrelevant. **Do you think people need to be taught how to behave democratically, or would they do so naturally if left alone?**

Pragmatists believe that children should learn how to make difficult decisions by considering the consequences their actions might have on others. Because democracy permits people to consider multiple points of view, pragmatic action and democracy complement each other. Education never ends—it is a process that continues throughout one's lifetime. People are instruments of change, capable of experiencing, experimenting, and testing their beliefs (Westbrook, 1991).

Perennialism and Essentialism

Perennialism looks backward through history and forward in time to shape understanding of the goals and processes of education. Perennialists celebrate the great ideas and accomplishments of Western civilization for their own sake and also for what these classical writings can offer to future generations. The purpose of schools, in their minds, is to develop students' intellectual capabilities.

Perennialists contend there are principles of education so important and central to the development of culture that they cannot be ignored. These include the universality of truth, the importance of rationality, and the power of aesthetics and religion to encourage ethical behavior. Like realists, perennialists believe that these enduring principles demand the attention of teachers and students. Culture is not relative to a time or a place, perennialists argue. Rationality and intellectual self-discipline are the traits most desirable in people.

Robert Maynard Hutchins (1899–1977) and Mortimer Adler (1902–2001) are noted supporters of this view. In every important way, they argue, people are basically the same, regardless of where they live and who they are. Therefore, all people need the same basic education. This education should consist of the fundamentals, including history, language, mathematics, science, literature, and humanities.

Hutchins and Adler introduced perennialism in the 1930s in response to progressive educational approaches. They argued that people are rational animals who learn to exercise self-control when their minds are disciplined by knowledge. The logic of their argument suggests that education implies teaching, teaching implies knowledge, knowledge is truth, and truth is the same everywhere. Therefore, education should be the same everywhere (Hutchins, 1936).

Perennialists believe contemporary curriculum that disregards the classics does a disservice to students and society. One must know the past to participate fully in the present and to contribute in the future; think of the old adage, "Those who don't know history are doomed to repeat it." This view led to the development of the Great Books program at the University of Chicago in the 1950s. It also led to Mortimer Adler's *Paideia Proposal* (1982), a more recent expression of perennialism that calls for a one-track system of public schooling that is the same everywhere.

The practical implications of perennialism for schooling are numerous. Perennialists prefer teacher-centered education. The teacher is the authority who must possess the knowledge and responsibility necessary to teach a core curriculum to young people. Moral education, including Bible study, is important for what it teaches about self-control and social responsibility. Concepts of academic tracking and gifted education are acceptable to perennialists, but both should emphasize the classics.

Essentialism claims the existence of a body of knowledge that all people must learn to function effectively in society. Like perennialists, essentialists acknowledge the timeless quality of great works. Unlike perennialists, essentialists do not base their views on realist principles. Nor do they agree on what constitutes the "essentials" that educated people should know. Essentialists simply agree that such essentials exist and that they ought to be represented in the curriculum.

One criticism shared by both perennialists and essentialists is that they define the essentials in terms of Western history and culture. But, unlike perennialists, essentialists want students to study great works not for their own sake but to become better prepared to solve contemporary problems. The sciences, too, are useful and central to the process of knowing and improving one's world.

William Bagley (1874–1946) founded the Essentialistic Education Society as a reaction against progressive, pragmatic trends in education. Bagley and his colleagues feared what they saw as an erosion of moral and intellectual standards in the young. To remedy this situation, they advocated that schools transmit a common essential core of knowledge to all students.

Essentialist curricula are rarely as specific as the recommendations of E. D. Hirsch (1987; Hirsch, Rowland, & Stanford, 1989), professor emeritus at the University of Virginia. Hirsch argues that society cannot function properly without communication among its members, and communication cannot occur in the absence of literacy. But true literacy, Hirsch (1996) contends, is more than the mechanical performance of reading and writing. True literacy depends on a body of information or common knowledge that everyone shares. Hirsch called this shared common knowledge **cultural literacy.**

Hirsch prescribed a curriculum for students in terms of what he believes children need to know by the end of sixth grade. Included in his curriculum are the subjects of literature, religion and philosophy, history, geography, mathematics, science, and technology. Based on the content of this curriculum, people criticize Hirsch's work for being **Eurocentric.** That is, some people believe his curriculum is centered on the history and cultures of Europe and represents works only by "dead white males." His supporters argue that the Core Knowledge Foundation correctly acknowledges valuable contributions from all cultures woven into the American fabric.

Defenders of essentialism, such as Allan Bloom in his book *The Closing of the American Mind* (1987), say that curricula should be exclusionary: "One should conclude from the study of non-Western cultures that not only to prefer one's own way but to believe it best, superior to all others, is primary and even natural—exactly the opposite of what is intended by requiring students to study these cultures" (p. 36). Michelle Fine (1987) and Henry Giroux (1984), on the other hand, believe the essentialist approach silences talk about instances of social, economic, and educational discrimination experienced by minority, female, and low-income students. **If we assume all students should learn the same curriculum, what is the single most important area of content for the curriculum to include?**

Social Reconstructionism

Social reconstructionism says that people are responsible for social conditions, whether good or bad. Theodore Brameld (1904–1987) and George Counts (1889–1974) advocated education as a means of preparing people to create a new society. Influenced by progressivism, Brameld, Counts, and others pushed for rapid, sweeping changes throughout society. The progressives and pragmatists of Dewey's day were politically moderate, urging gradual change, but the social reconstructionists were provocative in advocating immediate change from top to bottom.

The optimism of early social reconstructionists was based on faith in the power of science to solve human problems:

> Unless the profession can develop a superior type of social leadership, a leadership at least equal in intelligence, courage, and power to the leadership in other fields of interest with which it must contend, the profession will find itself unable to incorporate in the systems of public education the findings of educational science. (Counts, 1928, p. 361)

The same kinds of arguments made by early social reconstructionists are still used today to restructure schools and redesign professional education for teachers.

From the 1930s to the 1960s, social reconstructionists saw a world in which confusion and crisis reigned. The Great Depression, World War II, the Nuclear Age, and the Cold War era raised long-running concerns about world order. Social reconstructionists wanted to build a good and just society. They believed people could not sit comfortably in their safe homes enjoying the good life while others less fortunate sat on the outside looking in. People were to bring the have-nots into a better society.

Brameld and others like him thought that the future could be bleak or promising: the choice belonged to us. They believed people had the power to take control of their lives and behave in ways that improved the human condition. But the education system itself needed to be reconstructed as a tool for transforming individuals' lives and shaping a new society.

The spirit of social reconstructionism has been nurtured in the United States by individuals and groups wanting to create change through social activism. Social reconstructionists press for schools to address ignorance, poverty, and the lack of educational and employment opportunities. Education, then, cannot be a simple response to a particular need. It must address an interdependent set of students' intellectual, emotional, personal, and social needs. Complex problems demand complex solutions. Social reconstructionists believe educators should prepare students to meet these demands. **If you could immediately change one aspect of schools, what would it be?**

What Non-Western Philosophies Influence American Education?

Across the country, many foreign and first-, second-, and third-generation American public school students have Asian and Middle Eastern backgrounds. Buddhist Vietnamese Americans in Los Angeles, Islamic Arab Americans in Detroit, Hindu Indian Americans in New York, and others, maintain private schools and educate children and adults through cultural festivals and religious celebrations.

The influence of these many cultures and their philosophies can be found in schools across the country. Classes on world religions are commonplace in many schools. Teachers encourage students to develop secular spirituality, a personal ethical system, and inner peace. Multicultural curriculum materials provide access to past and present ideas and expressions of spirituality. And in some alternative private schools, non-Western philosophies play a significant role.

Western ways often encourage people to concentrate on personal and professional hopes for the future. In these traditions, one's sense of progress is rooted in work and one's place in society. Attendance at church or temple, the latest self-help book, or some traumatic event often prompts people to think about "meaning" in their lives. Non-Western philosophies can remind people that introspection, often undertaken with the help of a spiritual guide or teacher, is an ongoing process that leads to a fulfilling life.

Hinduism

Hinduism is more than a religion; it is a philosophy and a way of life. To use the term *Hindu* as though it represents a single philosophy is misleading. Many kinds of Hindus exist, and their beliefs and lifestyles vary dramatically. Members of some Hindu sects are Stone Age worshippers of trees, snakes, and other objects and phenomena in nature. Other Hindus are sophisticated urban intellectuals who contribute to virtually all aspects of modern life.

Major Hindu writings began to appear in the form of hymns and chants, or mantras, about 1200 BC to AD 200. The three basic Hindu texts—the Vedas, the Upanishads, and the Epics—reveal a way of life that guides believers. The Vedas describe a vision of the universe consisting of Earth, the atmosphere, and heaven. Vedic believers worship many gods and assign human characteristics to nonhuman things. The god Varuna, for example, is thought to control the changes in seasons.

The Upanishads, or secret teachings, recognize a single god, Brahman. They also provide laws to govern personal conduct. These laws established the caste system, which is a social hierarchy that has since been outlawed. In the caste system, the Brahmins, or priests, teachers, and other thinkers, were at the top; the Sudras, or untouchables, were at the bottom.

The Epics were written between 200 BC and AD 200. One of the writings included in the Epics is the Bhagavad-Gita, a poem of more than seven hundred verses that depicts a compassionate god who opens salvation to all devoted, dutiful souls. The Bhagavad-Gita also describes yoga as a means of uniting one's soul with the Absolute. Through yoga's teaching of proper posture, correct breathing, and control of the senses, one learns to free the mind and attain enlightenment.

Mohandas Gandhi, a member of the Jain sect of Hinduism, was known as the Mahatma (the Great). His influence on Western thought included his strong belief in nonviolence as a means to social reform. Martin Luther King, Jr., (1964) wrote about the use of nonviolent political action during the bus boycott in Montgomery, Alabama: "For Gandhi love was a potent instrument for social and collective transformation. It was in this Gandhian emphasis on love and nonviolence that I discovered the method for social reform that I had been seeking for many months" (p. 79).

One example of Hindu education in practice is the Shishu Bharati School of Languages and Cultures of India established in Massachusetts and New Hampshire. The nonprofit school was founded by a group of parents who had immigrated to the United States from India. They wanted to teach their languages and cultural heritages to their children. The school offers language programs in Bengali, Gujarati, Hindi, Marathi, Sanskrit, Sindhi, and Tamil. In addition to language classes, education programs address Indian arts, customs, religion, history, geography, and current events. The curriculum also includes field trips to Indian cultural events, yoga, and advanced culture classes (Shishu Bharati, 2005).

Buddhism

Buddhism is not a fundamentalist religion. It is more a way of thinking about the world, part philosophy and part religion. Its basic aim is to help people gain direct insight into the truth for themselves.

Buddhists think of life as a flowing stream. They believe in reincarnation, that is, rebirth in which people assume a new physical form and status depending on the quality of their deeds (karma). They also believe progress with Buddha's eight steps will allow them to reach *nirvana,* a state of serenity and wisdom in which they can escape the cycle of endless rebirth. Although Buddha did not believe in an Absolute or God, after his death he became revered as a god.

Zen, a sect of Buddhism, took root in Japan in the twelfth century. Shinto was the traditional religion of Japan prior to the introduction of Buddhism and Confucianism from China. Shinto focused on worshipping nature and family ancestors (Holtom, 1984). The Shinto philosophy encourages feelings of reverence toward all life, past and present; thus it mirrored, quite closely, the beliefs of Buddhists. In feudal, patriarchal Japanese society, Zen Buddhist monks stressed the dignity of physical labor, the arts, swordsmanship, and the tea ceremony. They emphasized stern discipline, selflessness, and spontaneity. Zen beliefs and rituals became integral to Japanese culture.

The first Buddhist high school in the United States opened in September 2003 in Honolulu. Funded by a $1.5 million contribution from headquarters in Kyoto, Japan, the Pacific Buddhist Academy is associated with Pure Land Buddhism—a school of thought that advocates "abandoning all need to rely on self-power . . . [relying instead] on faith" (Furukawa, 2005). The school is open to Buddhists of all sects. The nearby Hongwanji Mission School for elementary children up to eighth grade has existed for more than seven years; two-thirds of the students are non-Buddhists.

Islam

Islamic philosophy is based on the writings of the Koran (Quran), the holy or sacred book of Muslims. Muslims believe the word of God, or Allah, was revealed to Muhammad by the angel Gabriel. Abu-Bakr, Muhammad's father-in-law, collected Allah's words (delivered by Muhammad) in the Koran. Muhammad (570–632), then, was a prophet, like Christ, who described Allah's will. Muhammad foretold of a day when Allah would pass the Last Judgment to judge all souls by how well they lived according to Allah's will. Eternal reward is paradise and would be granted to those who succeeded. Those who failed would suffer the pain of eternal fire. The religion of Islam is rooted in both Judaism and Christianity and was strongly influenced by the Old and New Testaments (Corbin, 1993; Fakhry, 1983).

Al-Kindī (died after 870) expressed Islam's view of God as an absolute, transcendent being. God revealed truth through philosophy and religion. Al-Fārābī (875–950) expressed the Islamic view that the goal of life is to attain immortality through education or the development of one's intellect.

In the ancient world, Muslims made important advances in science and medicine. The physician ibn-Sina (980–1037) described concepts of matter, form, and existence in a way that allowed for a Necessary Being, or God. To ibn-Sina, the prophets were teachers who used religion as philosophy for the masses. Their teachings revealed symbolic truths that helped people approach absolute truth, or God.

In the 1960s Islam gained many African American believers in the United States, particularly among urban African American males. The Koran expressly forbids discrimination on the basis of race. Submission to Allah and strict adherence to Islam guarantee automatic brotherhood and equality. In 1965 Malcolm X, an influential Black Muslim, wrote bitterly about the need for Islam at a time when many African Americans felt disappointed that the civil rights acts of the late 1950s and early 1960s had not yet made much of a difference in people's lives:

> I am in agreement one hundred per cent with those racists who say that no government laws ever can force brotherhood. The only true world solution today is governments guided by true religion—of the spirit. Here in race-torn America, I am convinced that the Islam religion is desperately needed, particularly by the American black man. (pp. 368–369)

African and Native American Philosophies

Western thought is rational (I think, therefore I am), whereas African thought is based on feeling and sociality (I feel, and I relate to others, therefore I am) (Asante, 1987).

It is important for educators to have an understanding of African American philosophy and its bearing on educational life in America. Asante (1992) advocated a curriculum that acknowledges African history and culture:

> The African American children in your classrooms are not a black version of white people. They have different cultural and historical experiences that must be looked at and examined in a different way. To give an obvious example, African Americans did not come to America on the Mayflower. We recognize the Mayflower as part of the American experience, but our experience was different: We crossed the ocean packed in boats with as many as 1,000 other people, with only 18 inches of space between us and the deck above, and chained from neck to ankle. (p. 21)

Traditional Native American thought also emphasizes holistic (natural), nonrational existence and social relations. Reason and logic, for example, are not seen as superior methods of explaining events. Like African traditions, Native American traditions encourage spiritualism based on animism—belief in the presence of active supernatural forces in the natural world. Both traditions also prize humans' harmonious coexistence with nature. In these cultures, truth does not come from great books or scientific inquiry. Instead, truth is the result of personal introspection, oral traditions, and the values and knowledge handed down from ancestors.

Native American philosophies stress personal dignity, moral responsibility, and the mutual interdependence of all the people in a society or group. Group identity and well-being take precedence over individual needs and abilities. Traditional social values encourage silent reflection over verbalizing, cooperation over competition, stability over change, and continuity over progress (Banks, 1994).

African American and Native American thought, like the religious and secular philosophies of the Middle East, India, and Asia, influence the development of educational philosophies in the United States. They broaden people's minds, and they enlighten changes in curriculum and instruction that are designed to meet the needs of all students in our culturally diverse society. These curricular influences take many forms. History teachers concentrate on the contributions of different cultural groups to the building of America. Literature teachers focus students on writings of authors with different ethnic backgrounds. Art teachers encourage student expression using various media in genres endemic to certain cultures.

What Shapes Teachers' Personal Philosophies of Education?

Teachers are role models of responsible adult behavior, attitudes, and values. A teacher constructs the social system of the classroom, with its rules, norms, sanctions, and rewards. This system governs behavior for an entire school year, sometimes longer. The personality and values of the teacher reflect her or his philosophy and set the tone for how classroom life is lived. The teacher's philosophy can even find its way into students' lives outside the classroom, lasting well beyond their years in school.

Learning from Teaching: Reflection

Teachers shape their own philosophies—by what they do and by what they think about what they do. Dewey and others have given the name *reflection* to this process of thinking about what you do. Donald Schön (1987) described two types of reflection. The first, reflection-in-action, is a process that helps teachers reshape what they do as they do it. For instance, a teacher launches into a lecture and perceives that students are not listening. She stops, asks a question, takes several volunteers' responses, reinforces those who make positive contributions, and moves on with the lesson. In the thick of activity, she thinks about what is happening and learns from her own actions and those of her students. Over time, these reflections-in-action inform her more general beliefs about teaching.

The second type, reflection-on-action, is a look back at what happened previously. A teacher remembers what happened in particular circumstances and thinks about the lessons he

Case Perspectives

Think back to the case that opened this chapter. The following comments from experienced educators about the responsibility of schools to create engaged citizens—and the possibility of doing this—are designed to provide some context for this case.

CHESTER. E. FINN, JR., HAS WRITTEN WIDELY ABOUT EDUCATION AND CONTENDS THAT THE DIVERSITY OF THE AMERICAN POPULATION MAKES IT IMPOSSIBLE FOR SCHOOLS TO PRODUCE ENGAGED CITIZENS. Because Americans insist that government is the creature of its citizens, we are loath to rely on state decisions and institutions to instruct our children in how to think, how to conduct themselves, and what to believe. After all, civic education may sound like a good idea in theory, but in practice public schools could even do harm in this realm. Some educators harbor worrisome values: moral relativism, atheism, doubts about the superiority of democracy, undue deference to the "*pluribus*" at the expense of the "*unum*," discomfort with patriotism, cynicism toward established cultural conventions and civic institutions. Transmitting those values to children will gradually erode the foundations of a free society. Perhaps society would be better off if schools stuck to the three Rs and did a solid job in domains where they enjoy both competence and wide public support. (Finn, 2005)

STEPHEN MACEDO, A PRINCETON POLITICAL SCIENCE PROFESSOR, BELIEVES AMERICANS SHOULD TURN IN PART TO THE SCHOOLS TO COUNTER THE TREND OF DECLINING CIVIC ENGAGEMENT. Strangely, at a moment when the schools seem capable of becoming a bulwark against civic *dis*engagement among the young, a rising chorus of skeptics is casting doubt on the whole enterprise of civic education. In practice, they charge, civic education is ineffective and potentially harmful. The materials used in social studies courses, where most schooling about the political process occurs, are too often built on a foundation of moral relativism, cynicism toward received traditions. . . .

Critics also question the very idea of government-sponsored civic education, arguing that it threatens basic principles of intellectual freedom. It would be far better, they say, to leave the teaching of values to parents, churches, and private schools. Thus we would avoid the sorry spectacle of government's promoting some values at the expense of others. . . .

So how should we assess civic education as public policy? Let's consider three fundamental questions:

- Is it true that civic education makes no difference or even undermines students' interest and participation in civic life?
- Have the efforts to promote civic engagement been sufficient to conclude that the experiment has failed?
- Are the differences in values among Americans truly so vast that it will be impossible to develop a reasonable public consensus on the goals of civic education?

The answers to each of these questions, I . . . argue, give us substantial reasons to doubt the skeptical position on civic education. However, I am not at all sure that those who wish to eliminate civics from the public schools care much about finding out the facts. Their interest in maligning civic education may stem from a desire not to improve the content of public schooling but to undermine public institutions altogether. (Macedo, 2004)

Questions for Reflection: Do you think schools have a responsibility to provide civic education? In what ways might this responsibility be carried out? Does citizenship need to be an explicit part of the curriculum? Why or why not? ■

---

learned from the experience. The experiences he recollects might be the most vivid, but not necessarily the most successful or most satisfying. The teacher might ask himself: What did I do? Why? What might I have done differently? What might have happened if I had done something else? The people who can truly learn from what they do develop personal philosophies that help them move toward higher levels of professionalism.

Developing a personal philosophy of education and enriching that philosophy over time requires a certain amount of risk-taking behavior. A teacher who relies only on comfortable, familiar methods has nothing new to think about and very little opportunity to learn. What did the principal mean when she said, "I want to hire a teacher with ten years of experience, not a teacher with one year of experience, ten times"?

Summary

Educational philosophies are important for teachers because they both reflect and influence what happens in schools. Our educational roots go back to the Greeks and other ancient Western thinkers. Modern philosophies with quite different views of the nature of reality and the meaning of life have had dramatic effects on curricula, teaching, and learning. Some of these philosophies are associated with mainstream Western thinking, and others have evolved from Eastern and Middle Eastern religions and from African American and Native American life.

Teachers' own philosophies about the way the educational world works develop over time. As they perform their tasks and think about what they do, teachers learn more about what professional practice means to them. The more they stretch themselves to think and behave in new ways, the richer their philosophies become.

TERMS AND CONCEPTS

aesthetics	humanism
axiology	idealism
behaviorism	Marxism
cognitivism	metaphysics
constructivism	ontology
cosmology	perennialism
cultural literacy	philosophy
epistemology	pragmatism
essentialism	realism
ethics	scaffolding
Eurocentric	social reconstructionism
existentialism	Socratic method

REFLECTIVE ACTIVITY: PHILOSOPHICAL DIFFERENCES

Reflective practice is an essential part of good teaching. Reflection is a process that includes making thoughtful decisions, understanding and articulating value structures, acting from knowledge, evaluating your actions and their effects, and sharing your reflections with colleagues. After reading the following scenario, respond to the questions below. The scenario reflects the INTASC Principle and Disposition at the end of this activity.

Stuart Hastings was reluctant to let his high school students in his team-taught class discuss their beliefs about being ethnic minorities in a predominantly white world. Even though they were studying social borders and barriers, he worried that the discussion might turn ugly. Nonetheless, he could not dissuade them. According to his colleague, Suzanne MacCormack, he even seemed to approve of the idea.

"I tell you, it was uncomfortable in there second period. How are we going to address these students' issues?" Stuart asked.

Suzanne had been shifting uneasily in her chair for several minutes. She could keep quiet no longer. "Well, what about our schedule? Your impromptu therapy session has set the whole team plan back." Suzanne could really be a pain in the neck.

"Whoa! Calm down!" Stuart blurted defensively. "What's a bigger border or barrier than the attitudes and stereotypes these kids face in the real world? We barely had time to dive in today. Now we really need more time to discuss positive ways of dealing with these problems."

Suzanne was not soothed. "Fine. Wonderful. We are all social workers. But what happened to our curriculum? These kids need to learn some basic skills and to understand that when we set deadlines they must be met. Let's talk about real-world expectations for a change. And, who do you think gets to clean up the mess after you stir these kids up? I spent the better part of my day tackling crisis after crisis. Some of these kids are just time bombs waiting to go off."

"Suzanne, I really do see your point, but it seemed like the right thing to do at the time," said Stuart.

Decide   1. What issues arose in Stuart's and Suzanne's discussion about the class session?

Perceive and Value   2. Can you describe, in your own words, the main differences between Stuart's and Suzanne's beliefs?

Know and Act 3. If you were the team leader, what might you do to encourage greater cooperation between Suzanne and Stuart, and why?

Evaluate 4. Why might team teaching be advantageous and disadvantageous from a philosophical point of view? How would you know if more or less cooperation between the teachers made a difference in student learning?

Discuss 5. How might Stuart foster culturally sensitive communication among his students when they meet the next day?

INTASC Principle 6

The teacher uses knowledge of effective verbal, nonverbal, and media communication techniques to foster active inquiry, collaboration, and supportive interaction in the classroom.

Disposition

The teacher appreciates the cultural dimensions of communication, responds appropriately, and seeks to foster culturally sensitive communication by and among all students in the class. (Interstate New Teacher Assessment and Support Consortium, 1992)

ADDITIONAL READINGS

Alinsky, Saul David. (1971). *Rules for radicals: A practical primer for realistic radicals*. New York: Random House.

Freire, Paulo. (1993). *Pedagogy of the oppressed*. New York: Continuum.

Gutek, Gerald L. (1997). *Historical and philosophical foundations of education: A biographical introduction* (2nd ed.). Upper Saddle River, NJ: Prentice Hall/Merrill.

Illich, Ivan. (1971). *Deschooling society*. New York: Harper & Row.

Kneller, George. (1971). *Introduction to the philosophy of education* [by] *George Kneller*. New York: Wiley.

McGrath, Alister E. (2001). *In the beginning: The story of the King James Bible and how it changed a nation, a language, and a culture*. New York: Doubleday.

WEB RESOURCES

www.cie.org/
The Council on Islamic Education provides resources for teachers in the handbook Teaching about Islam and Muslims.

www.tolerance.org/
The Southern Poverty Law Center provides materials for teaching tolerance toward people of all philosophies and religions.

www.shishubharati.org/
The Shishu Bharati Schools in Burlington, Massachusetts, and Nashua, New Hampshire, offer programs in the languages and cultures of India for all ages.

www.christianhomeschoolers.com
Christian philosophy and curricula abound on the Web, and much of it is designed to school children at home.

www.edutopia.org/aboutus
The George Lucas Education Foundation promotes modern educational idealism through the use of technology.

http://johndeweysociety.org
The John Dewey Society advocates the use of reflection in the search for solutions to educational and cultural problems.

*Developing a
Professional
Portfolio*

YOUR OWN PHILOSOPHY OF TEACHING

Regardless of our levels of experience as educators, each of us has our own way of thinking about teaching and learning. Our ideas are shaped over time through human interactions and through such influences as reading and coursework. To explore your philosophy of teaching, try to respond to the following questions. Then write a two- or three-paragraph statement that summarizes your philosophy.

- How do you define learning, and how would you determine whether learning has occurred?
- What do you need to know about students to be able to teach them?
- How do you describe good teaching?

Next, find an experienced teacher who is willing to answer the same questions. (You might want to ask her permission to audiotape her responses.) How do your responses compare to hers? Why do you think your answers are the same or different?

Online Activity

Exploring the Library of Congress

No teacher should miss the opportunity to explore our nation's history via the Library of Congress online (www.loc.gov), an amazing resource for teaching and learning. Click on the Site Map link to find America's Library. You will find five links that connect to different ways to use online resources for the teaching of history and American culture. These links are described below.

First, explore the links, then rate each one for its potential motivational value for students. When you finish, compare your ratings to those of your classmates and discuss why you agree or disagree.

1. Meet Amazing Americans— discover the inventors, politicians, performers, activists, and everyday people who shaped our country's history.

   Low   Medium   High

2. Jump Back in Time—travel to an era in American history.

   Low   Medium   High

3. Explore the States—click on a state you wish to investigate.

   Low   Medium   High

4. Join America at Play—explore America's favorite pastimes, sports, and hobbies.

   Low   Medium   High

5. See, Hear and Sing—watch a movie, hear a song, or play a tune from America's past.

   Low   Medium   High

CHAPTER 7

Where Teachers Work: Schools

Case Study: A Rose by Any Other Name

An effective school helps students succeed. Yet some students, even in effective schools, continue to fail—often miserably so—no matter what accommodations are made. It seems that even the most optimistic of teachers must sometimes ask: At what point, if any, does retention become a viable option?

Arthur Ewing, a fourth-grade teacher at Franklin Junior High School, had never thought about recommending retention in four years of teaching. He had made suggestions about special services for some students, and he had requested testing for others to determine specific needs. But Greta Philips was a challenge.

Greta was failing. She had been tested several times over the years but did not qualify for special services. Nevertheless, Greta had been the subject of three conferences during the year—the first to design an individualized education program for her despite her lack of a special needs classification, and two more to monitor her progress. During the first part of the year, Greta really appeared to try, bless her heart, and she had met with some success. But after the December break, her academic year had been characterized by failure. She knew it. Her parents knew it. And Arthur Ewing knew it better than anyone else.

Arthur realized that, despite all the time, effort, and energy he had expended on Greta's behalf (and he had pulled out all the stops in the early part of the year), he felt oddly disconnected from her. Unlike other struggling students he had encountered, Greta often appeared to sort of float through the classroom in a different world. She cried easily when a task was too difficult or when she didn't get a response from another student that she expected. She constantly sought approval from both teachers and peers, to the point that her neediness was annoying. She did seem to learn when she focused, and when material was repeated over and over, but she was easily distracted. Overall, she was not ready to encounter fifth-grade content.

Arthur's feelings about Greta were complicated by his interactions with her parents. He found Greta's mother aggressive and almost bullying. But he had been charmed from the start by Greta's father. Mr. Philips had bent over backwards to help his daughter, and he never even hinted that Arthur might share some blame for Greta's difficulties. Mr. Philips was what Arthur's own father used to call a "real nice guy."

Arthur realized, of course, that his emotional responses to Greta and her family were irrelevant to the decisions and recommendations he needed to make about Greta's future. But he was well aware that emotions would come into play when and if he recommended retaining Greta in the fourth grade for a second year.

He also knew that he could dress up this recommendation in any language he chose, but finally, Greta and her peers would say that she had flunked, pure and simple. It was that fact more than any other that gave Arthur pause. He forced himself to couch his own dilemma in similarly harsh terms: Was it right or wrong to "flunk" Greta Philips?

Today, as in the past, Americans pin their hopes for a better world on schools. As each call for change is debated, the focus of discussion is often on ways to increase learning. Opinions as to how we can accomplish that goal, however, vary greatly.

This chapter provides an overview of the different types of schools that exist in the United States, from public elementary schools and four-year universities to magnet schools and home schools. As prospective teachers you should be aware of all these schooling options so you can consider the full range of teaching options.

How Is Schooling Organized in the United States?

One of the important decisions prospective teachers must make is what level or grade of school they want to teach. Each level has its own set of pros and cons, so if you choose to work in public schooling, you should be familiar with its organization.

Many children attend preschool, but enrollment rates vary according to family income and race or ethnicity, because preschool programs can be costly. By age five, when students are required by law to begin schooling, most children are enrolled in public schools. This begins their involvement with public schooling, where student organization is based primarily on students' ages. Elementary schools often classify students as primary (kindergarten through second grade) and intermediate (third through sixth grade) students. In some school districts, students in grades four through six, five through seven, or six through eight attend middle schools. In other districts students in grades seven through eight or seven through nine are enrolled in junior high schools.

High schools, or secondary schools, usually include grades nine through twelve or ten through twelve. Because parents and school leaders want high school students to continue their education, high schools try to prepare students to move up the academic ladder. When students graduate from high school, their education options include technical or vocational institutions, two-year colleges, and four-year colleges and universities. However, students' access to higher education is influenced in large part by the cost of these programs.

School Districts

In terms of public education, the common method of organization is the **school district.** A school district is a state-defined geographical area responsible for providing public instruction to students living within that area. Grouping schools this way is efficient for administrative and financial purposes. School districts are also useful for creating uniformity in what students in different schools are learning.

There are about seventeen thousand school districts in the United States. Within those districts are approximately ninety-five thousand schools and 48 million students in prekindergarten through twelfth grade.

Because school districts are determined by geography and population, they range in size from quite small to quite large. New York City school district—the largest in the country—has some 1 million students enrolled in 1,200 schools. In contrast, Tecumseh Public Schools in Tecumseh, Nebraska, have 300 students in two schools.

Types of Schools

What types of public and private schools are available to children in the United States? (See Figure 7.1.) Schools are designed for students of many different ages, from preschool to college. Depending on the students they serve, schools can differ in structure (organization) and function (programs and services). Although the most common type of school is the public school, many alternatives are available. Within the boundaries of most public school districts, for example, you also can find magnet schools, charter schools, alternative schools, and vocational or trade schools. These public school alternatives are discussed later in this chapter.

PUBLIC SCHOOLS	PUBLIC ALTERNATIVE SCHOOLS	PRIVATE SCHOOLS
Kindergarten (K)	Head Start	Nursery Schools and Preschools
Elementary School (K/1–6 or K/1–8)	Prekindergarten Programs	"Concept School" Alternatives
• Primary (K–2)	Laboratory Schools	• Montessori Schools
• Intermediate (3–6)	Nongraded Schools	• Waldorf Schools
Middle School (5–8)	Magnet Schools	"Ethnic School" Alternatives
Secondary Schools	Charter Schools	• Afrocentric Schools (Black Academies)
• Junior High School (7–8 or 7–9)	Accelerated Schools	• Reservation Schools
• High School (7–12, 9–12, or 10–12)	Cluster Schools	Parochial/Religious Schools
Post-Secondary Schools	Vocational–Technical Schools	• Catholic Schools
• Community Colleges	Professional Development Schools	• Christian Academies
• State Colleges	Government-Run Schools	• Hebrew Schools
• State Universities	• Department of Defense Dependents Schools	• Islamic Schools
	• Native American Schools	College Preparatory Schools
	• Career Academies	Trade Schools
	• Job Corps	Military Academies
	Home Schooling	Junior Colleges
		Colleges and Universities
		Adult Education Centers

Figure 7.1
Some Types of Schools in America
It is difficult in many cases to draw solid lines between the three columns in this chart. Can you develop a hypothesis that you think might explain this difficulty?

Other ways that schools can be categorized include elementary, middle, junior high, and senior high. In these schools, age is the determining factor. The geographical categories of rural schools, suburban schools, and urban schools each have their own set of issues and concerns, but they also share many of the same goals and purposes. Chief among these goals is providing a positive educational environment for students.

Early Childhood Education

Many of the first early childhood education programs in the United States were day nurseries funded by philanthropic organizations associated with settlement houses. Today, both public and private sponsors support many more kinds of preschool programs. Examples of such sponsors are Project Head Start, infant intervention and enrichment programs, nursery schools, public and private prekindergartens and kindergartens, college and university laboratory schools, church-sponsored preschools, and parent cooperatives, which all offer a variety of educational programs for young children.

Although enrollment in such programs has gradually increased over time, not all children have access to preschool. **Which groups of three- to five-year olds in Figure 7.2 participate in preschool at the highest rates?**

Figure 7.2
Preschool Participation By
Ethnicity and Poverty

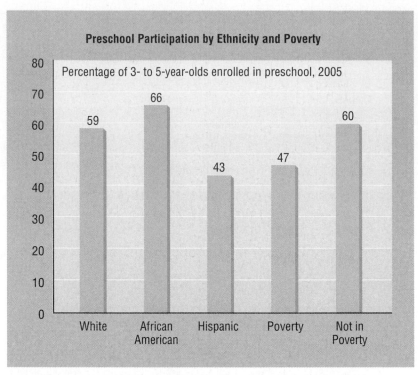

Source: U.S. Department of Education, National Center for Education Statistics (2007). *The Condition of Education 2007* (NCES 2007–064), Indicator 2. Available online: http://nces.ed.gov/fastfacts/display.asp?id=78.

With so many agencies sponsoring preschool programs, many types of services are offered and many families are served. While some preschools offer full-day educational care, others offer only half-day programs. Certain preschools serve only children from low-income families, children of adolescent parents, or children with disabilities.

Program goals and philosophies about teaching and learning vary considerably among various preschools. The professional preparation of early childhood education staff and the quality of programs also differ greatly. In response to these concerns, some states now require preschool programs to earn accreditation from the **National Association for the Education of Young Children (NAEYC),** the largest professional association for early childhood educators.

Some advocates believe such accreditation efforts will improve the quality of preschool programs, but others argue that it is funding for public preschool programs that must be increased. In 2004 the national average wage for an early childhood teacher was reported to be about $11.50 per hour. Such low wages make it difficult to attract and retain qualified staff—and staff ultimately make the difference in what children experience at school (U.S. Department of Labor, 2005). Why are preschool staff paid so poorly?

Kindergarten

Half-day kindergarten programs have existed for most children since the 1930s. In the past twenty years, increasing numbers of full-day programs have sprung up across the country as one strategy for narrowing the academic achievement gaps between middle-class and disadvantaged children. How do the data in Figure 7.3 reflect this trend?

Findings from a study of 17,600 Philadelphia schoolchildren suggest full-time kindergarten programs may have both academic and financial benefits. By the time children in the study reached third and fourth grades, former full-day kindergartners were twice as likely as children without kindergarten experience and 26 percent more likely than children from half-day programs to have succeeded in school without repeating a grade. Researchers estimated the lower retention rates reduced the cost of full-day kindergarten education by 19 percent; that is,

Family Income	Full-Day	Part-Day	
$19,999 or less	58%	42%	100%
$20,000 to $49,999	65%	35%	100%
$50,000 +	58%	42%	100%
All incomes	62%	38%	100%

	Full-Day	Part-Day	
Black	77%	23%	100%
Asian/Pacific Islander	58%	42%	100%
White (non-Hispanic)	63%	37%	100%
Hispanic (any race)	56%	44%	100%
All races	**63%**	**37%**	**100%**

Figure 7.3
Children Enrolled in Kindergarten in 2002

Source: U.S. Department of Education, National Center for Education Statistics (2007). Percentage of pre-kindergarten children ages 3–5 who were enrolled in center-based early childhood care and education programs: selected years, 1991–2005. The Condition of Education 2007 (NCES 2007–064). Available online (http://nces.ed.gov/fastfacts/display.asp?id=78.)

moving children through schools with a lower incidence of failure reduced the cost of providing full-day kindergarten. In 1999 that savings worked out to about $2 million for every one thousand kindergartners (Viadero, 2002).

Despite these and other findings, a 2005 analysis of kindergarten statutes in all fifty states revealed that guidelines for kindergarten are not aligned with the policies and practices that ensure educational quality in the grades that follow. The report recommended that state policies guarantee universal access to kindergarten, provide adequate funding, and establish specific standards pertaining to instructional and teacher quality (Kauerz, 2005).

Elementary Schools

Elementary schools exhibit many variations in curricula and instructional methods. Often, students are grouped homogeneously by ability or achievement for instructional purposes. Such grouping can occur within a single classroom or across many classrooms. In other settings, students work in **nongraded classrooms.** Such classrooms may include students of heterogeneous abilities and sometimes students of different ages. Nongraded programs, also referred to as multiage, multigrade, or family grouping programs, are most prevalent in primary schools.

Nongraded programs try to provide curriculum tailored to students' stages of intellectual, emotional, physical, or social development. They allow for individualized, continuous progress for young children. Although there are standards for students' performance, the time and methods taken to reach these standards vary from student to student. Grouping for instruction is flexible and based on the abilities, interests, and needs of students. In these programs there is no formal promotion from one grade to the next. Instead, a student stays with a group of students until he or she has mastered necessary skills.

Research on elementary schools suggests that nongrading can be quite effective as a grouping method. The positive effects are greatest in situations in which students are grouped across age lines in only one subject (usually reading) or in multiple subjects, with students receiving direct instruction for the majority of a class session. Experts agree that groupings should not be unchanging, however. They should be reassessed frequently and changed when student performance indicates a mismatch in instruction and achievement (Good & Brophy, 2003). **Should schools use multiage rather than graded groupings?**

Junior High Schools and Middle Schools

The first junior high school opened in 1909 as a three-year intermediate school in Columbus, Ohio. Since then, junior high schools have been an important part of the U.S. education system. Most junior high schools include students who are in grades seven through nine. As in elementary schools, instruction occurs mainly in self-contained classrooms. Curriculum at the junior high school level, however, is usually more diversified; that is, more types of courses are offered. Like their colleagues at the senior high school level, junior high school teachers generally specialize in the content and teaching of a particular subject area.

Middle schools, which emerged in the 1960s, aim to provide an educational environment less imitative of high school and better suited to the developmental needs of ten- to fourteen-year-olds. Unfortunately, middle schools have been criticized for a variety of reasons. Often teachers operate in teams, so they can get to know their students. Within these teams, middle-grade teachers generally teach more than one subject. A problem with this arrangement is that school leaders in urban and rural middle schools have difficulty staffing their schools with teachers who meet subject mastery requirements under the No Child Left Behind law.

A 2004 report by the RAND Corporation also questioned the wisdom of separate middle schools for students at the onset of puberty. Although the scores of thirteen-year-olds on national reading, science, and mathematics tests have improved since the late 1970s, statistics show that, compared with their peers in eleven other developed nations, U.S. students have negative perceptions of their learning conditions. They also rank highest in terms of reported levels of emotional and physical problems and view the climate of their schools and the peer culture more negatively than do students in other countries (RAND Corporation, 2004).

Cultural Awareness: Lessons Learned

There is no shortage of praise for Benjamin N. Cardozo High School in Queens—a place where students entering from middle schools and junior high schools are likely to meet with success. The *New York Times* calls Cardozo "one of the city's most prestigious and competitive schools." *Newsweek* recognizes Cardozo as one of the "top 100 schools in the nation." Cardozo students rank high on nearly all academic measures, including Regents diplomas, AP exams, SAT scores, and graduation rates.

And, yet, hundreds of Cardozo students with diverse cultural backgrounds struggle each year to find their place and to earn enough credits for graduation. Principal Rick Hallman has worked with Assistant Principal Sheila Clark and the rest of the faculty to understand why junior high students entering Cardozo lost the urge to succeed in school. They have employed both data collection and personal touches to create a learning community of the heart and of the mind.

Principal Hallman and his staff began by asking sociological questions: Why are these students skipping classes and being truant? What is happening in students' lives that stops them from achieving academically? School leaders' frustrations might easily have led them to adopt rigorous disciplinary solutions. Instead, they have tried to understand why students behave in self-defeating ways in the short term, only to find themselves over-age and under-credited in the long term. Hallman and his colleagues have concluded that to do so teachers must seek the reasons from students.

To almost no one's surprise, teachers have found that these students want to succeed academically, but are faced with issues in their lives that simply but surely overwhelm them. Confronted by this reality, Cardozo leaders have acted decisively by placing students in small learning environments and by creating the focus and momentum necessary for academic success. A student's past academic failure has become a ticket to a second chance.

Mr. Hallman helps teachers do their jobs by allowing them to be human – to care for students and to give them positive reinforcement. Teachers consciously value their abilities to "come down to the level of the students" in order to encourage students to exert the effort necessary to set their own goals. The principal and teachers chant a mantra that is simple but powerful: "Don't give up on the students, and they won't give up on themselves."

Source: http://www.casenex.com (Downloaded March 5, 2008)

The RAND report pointed to a number of promising programs highlighted by the National Forum to Accelerate Middle Grades reform that might "fix" the middle school problem. One is the Talent Development Middle School Model (TDMS) developed at Johns Hopkins University. The program is designed to develop both basic and higher-level skills using hands-on, investigative teaching strategies. The TDMS also provides technical support for teachers before and during classroom instruction.

High Schools

High schools vary greatly in size. The total enrollment in alternative schools may be as low as two hundred. On the other end of the spectrum, one out of four students attends a school with an enrollment of over one thousand. In fact, enrollments of two or three thousand are not uncommon.

Large high schools can offer a wide variety of curricula fairly economically. They typically provide courses to prepare students for vocational or technical areas and for college. To graduate, students must complete a certain number of credit hours in core courses. But high schools offer many other kinds of experiences. Some schools, such as Missouri's Pattonville High School, require students to spend fifty hours performing community service.

Tom Vander Ark, director of education for the Bill and Melinda Gates Foundation, is critical of large, comprehensive schools:

> "If a school is relatively small, it's easier to create a coherent curriculum, easier to create a high-performance culture, to create a personalized environment," says Vander Ark. "All those things get exponentially more difficult the bigger the school gets." (Vail, 2004)

Whether a student attends a small or a comprehensive high school, studies indicate the importance of a challenging high school curriculum. These studies show that students who take rigorous coursework in high school are more likely to receive a bachelor's degree. The American Diploma Project (2004) also suggested the importance of strengthening the connection between requirements for graduation and real-world demands graduates confront in higher education and the workplace. Figure 7.4 reveals seniors' perceptions of the relevance and meaningfulness of schoolwork. **What trends do you see in students' thinking? What can teachers do to alter these trends?**

Figure 7.4
Twelfth-Graders
Increasingly See
Schoolwork as
Irrelevant

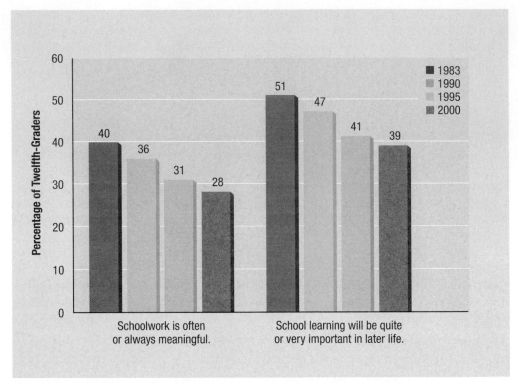

Source: National Center for Education Statistics, 2002. Student effort and educational progress. Available online: http://nces.gov/programs/coe/2002/sect3/tables/t18_1a.asD

Higher Education

A variety of higher education opportunities are available to students once they finish high school, including two-year and four-year colleges, technical training schools, and nondegree courses. Today more than ever students are taking advantage of these opportunities. The number of high school graduates enrolling in college immediately after graduation is an important indication of our national well-being.

Entering a two- or four-year college is the typical choice for many recent high school graduates. The missions of two- and four-year colleges are somewhat different. Two-year colleges typically offer basic undergraduate liberal arts and sciences courses, while providing a wide range of vocational, technical, and adult education programs. They also offer a variety of professional and preprofessional programs, including programs for nursing and education. Four-year colleges and universities generally provide a full undergraduate program, leading to a bachelor's degree. Many four-year institutions offer advanced graduate and professional degree programs as well.

Adult education programs are yet another option for increasing numbers of younger and older adults. Classes offer opportunities for everyone to pursue interests, develop talents, and increase literacy skills, no matter how old they are. Adults with higher literacy skills are more likely to work full time, earn high wages, and maintain better health.

What Are Some Schooling Alternatives?

What do you know about alternative schools? How are they different from "regular" schools?
Some people believe alternative schools provide specialized or "nonconforming" programs for "at-risk" or "bad" students. In reality, alternative schools are for all types of learners. The schools operate within the public school system, and they address the needs or interests of specific student groups.

Issues in School Reform

SCHOOL CONSOLIDATION

Over the past several decades, one trend in the United States has been to consolidate small schools. In 1930 there were more than 247,000 public schools, compared to over 95,000 today.

Rural communities have tried to meet fiscal shortfalls by consolidating schools. As a response to a century-old pattern of rural decline, school consolidation has been one of American education's longest-lasting reform efforts. By combining schools, proponents argue it is possible to cut administrative and facilities expenses while still offering students a broad curriculum.

In recent years, many communities have resisted consolidation, because they like knowing and working closely with a small number of administrators and teachers. Moving their children to a larger, more distant school means parents will have less say in the day-to-day running of schools. Parents also contend that, although money may be saved by closing school buildings, additional transportation expenses may more than offset savings. Furthermore, the prospect of having their children spend excessive amounts of time riding buses to and from school has encouraged many parents to speak out against consolidation.

Another factor contributing to resistance to consolidation is the "small school advantage." A growing body of research suggests that small schools help students develop strong relationships with teachers and colleagues, promote greater student and parent involvement, and foster a positive school culture.

Question for Reflection: If you were a teacher in a small school, what are some of the factors that might prompt you to support or resist school consolidation?

Some **alternative schools** are self-contained programs that exist outside the general public schools. Others are organized as schools within schools. Although many models of alternative schooling can be found in the United States, they share many of the following attributes: small school size, small class size, voluntary membership, lack of ability grouping and other forms of labeling, school-based management, student involvement in governance, and extended roles for teachers that include counseling and guidance.

Magnet Schools

Magnet schools are alternative schools within a public school system that accept students from the whole district, instead of only from the local neighborhood. Magnet schools emerged in the 1970s, primarily as a way to desegregate schools. At that time, many people thought schools were integrated only because of mandatory busing. The goal of magnet schools was to offer an environment so appealing that a racial cross section of students would attend voluntarily. The appeal of magnet programs today is strong enough that they often have waiting lists for enrollment.

The characteristics of magnet schools are (1) an enrollment policy that opens the school to children beyond a particular geographic area, (2) a student body that is present by choice and that meets inclusion criteria, and (3) a curriculum based on a special theme or instructional method. Magnet schools are available at any level, from preschool to senior high school. They may organize their curricula around a specific area, such as mathematics and computers, the arts, or the sciences, or around general academics, such as college preparation and honors courses.

Vocational–Technical Schools

Vocational–technical schools help students prepare to get a job by training them for specific trades and technical employment. In many states, education officials are revamping vocational and technical programs to ensure that they meet the requirements of the No Child Left Behind law. In Connecticut, for example, officials have made admissions and course requirements more stringent. They have also eliminated the process of grouping students in classes based on their performance. In addition, the board has dropped "vocational" from the system's name, which is now the Connecticut Technical High School system. The message they are sending to prospective students?

Slackers need not apply. . . . "What we really want is that when our students graduate, they have mastery in a trade technology, and they have a college preparation program, so they can make some choices," said Abigail L. Hughes, the state official who oversees the schools. Business leaders hope the changes can alter the image of the system as a place for students who can't meet the academic expectations of regular high schools. "It's been treated as an alternative high school system instead of a technical high school or technical training system," said Lauren Weisberg Kaufman, vice president of the Connecticut Business and Industry Association, based in Hartford. (Archer, 2004)

Some believe that raising requirements for vocational and technical programs will result in increased enrollment. Others caution against losing schools' identities as trade-oriented institutions. If that happens, they worry that technical schools will begin to look too much like regular schools. Should that occur, students will have no reason to enroll. **Do public schools put enough emphasis on vocational education?**

Montessori and Waldorf Schools

Both public and private alternative schools often have broad educational philosophies. Montessori and Waldorf schools are examples of philosophies in action. These two alternative schools focus specifically on young students and the best ways for them to learn. Montessori preschools encourage the development of children's perceptual, motor, intellectual, and social skills. These programs are based on the ideas of Maria Montessori (1870–1952), a physician who developed preschool teaching methods in the early 1900s. She focused on students' rates of maturity and their readiness to learn particular skills at certain ages. Teachers trained in Montessori methods use materials specifically designed to help children discover the physical properties of objects. For example, as students interact with the "pink tower" (blocks of graduated size), teachers act as observers. They assist students indirectly by asking questions or providing additional materials to help students learn. Most Montessori instructional materials are graded and self-correcting, so students experience personal freedom within the structure of the classroom. Montessori schools are typically limited to early education and preschools.

At the other end of the philosophical spectrum, Waldorf education opposes the structured acquisition of specific skills. Waldorf education has its roots in the spiritual–scientific research of Rudolf Steiner (1861–1925). Steiner was an Austrian scientist and educator who believed that young children learn primarily through their senses. He also believed that children's most active method of learning is imitation. In Waldorf preschools, therefore, creative play is viewed as the critical element in a child's development. With creative play, children learn at their own pace and from one another. Waldorf teachers argue that premature intellectual demands weaken the very powers of judgment and practical intelligence they are trying to build.

There are over one hundred Waldorf schools in the United States and Canada, and most of them are private. Although the majority are elementary schools, a few secondary schools follow the Waldorf model. All Waldorf schools have a strong spiritual component, though they are not affiliated with a specific religious group. Ideally, teachers remain with the same group of students from first through eighth grades.

Private and Independent Schools

Private schools—sometimes called independent schools—are nonprofit, tax-exempt institutions governed by boards of trustees. They are financed through private funds, such as tuition, endowments, and grants. Some are religiously affiliated, whereas others are secular. All private schools are accredited by state departments of education, must meet state and local health and safety rules, and must observe mandatory school attendance laws.

There are more than twenty-seven thousand private elementary and secondary schools in the United States. Nonreligious private schools vary in focus, structure, social organization, and size. Military schools, for example, emphasize self-discipline and encourage academic study.

Elite college preparatory schools place a high premium on academic achievement. Some private schools are less easily classified and develop their own unique personalities.

Some people support private and semiprivate alternatives because they believe competition will force public schools to improve. Other people like private schools because they may offer smaller classes or more rigorous academics. In some cases, people support private schools because they serve a special interest or set of beliefs. For these reasons and more, private schools are an attractive alternative to public schools for some teachers, parents, and students.

Despite many similarities, private schools differ from public schools in several ways:

- Public schools are tax supported; private schools are not.
- Private schools can set their own admissions requirements; public schools must accept all those who come for an education.
- Private school students are enrolled by parental or student choice; public schools typically serve only students in their districts.
- Private schools are free to follow philosophies that appeal to specific groups of people; public schools must advance philosophies that serve everyone.

Traditionally, the lines separating public from private schools have been the source of funds and the prohibition of religious activity in public schools. Those lines, however, have been continually challenged. In particular, distinctions between public and private education are obscured by (1) state loans of secular textbooks to church schools, (2) state reimbursement of funds for transportation to church schools, and (3) public funding for private and parochial schools' required standardized tests and other services. In 1999 Florida was the first state to enact legislation to permit the use of public funds for private schools. **Do you think distinctions between public and private schooling should be clarified?**

For-Profit Schools

Since the late 1980s, concepts of **for-profit schools** have gained attention as alternatives to public schools. For-profit schools do not claim tax-exempt status because they are run by private companies as businesses. Their goal is to make money. For-profit schools claim that for the same amount of money or less they can deliver better education to children than can public schools. In short, advocates of for-profit schools want to privatize education—move it out of the public realm and into the control of private enterprises.

For-profit schools must meet the same requirements as public schools. Their students must take and pass tests required by the states in which they reside. They cannot discriminate on the basis of ethnic origin, race, or gender.

One of the most visible efforts to create and sustain for-profit schools is Edison Schools. Edison opened its first four schools in August 1995. By 2005 Edison was responsible for teaching approximately 250,000 students in 137 schools. The demand for Edison schools has decreased dramatically. It now manages services for schools and no longer takes them over. **What are the pros and cons of running a school as a business?**

Charter Schools

Charter schools are independent public schools supported by state funds but exempt from many regulations. They are based on a contract, or charter, between school organizers (parents, teachers, or others) and a sponsor (usually a local or state board of education or, in some cases, universities). Organizers generally have the power to hire and fire staff and to budget money as they see fit. In turn, they guarantee the sponsor certain academic outcomes; that is, students will meet or exceed the levels of academic performance expected of their counterparts in public schools. Charter schools developed in the 1990s and have been described as the "upstart reform idea of the decade." To some people, charter schools offer a way to promote school accountability and excellence in educational outcomes. They also permit parents and teachers to have more say in what goes on within the school.

Figure 7.5
Who Attends Charter Schools?
Charter schools are public schools of choice. They serve as alternatives to the regular public schools to which students are assigned. While there are many similarities between charter and other public schools, they do differ in some important ways—including the makeup of the student population and their location.

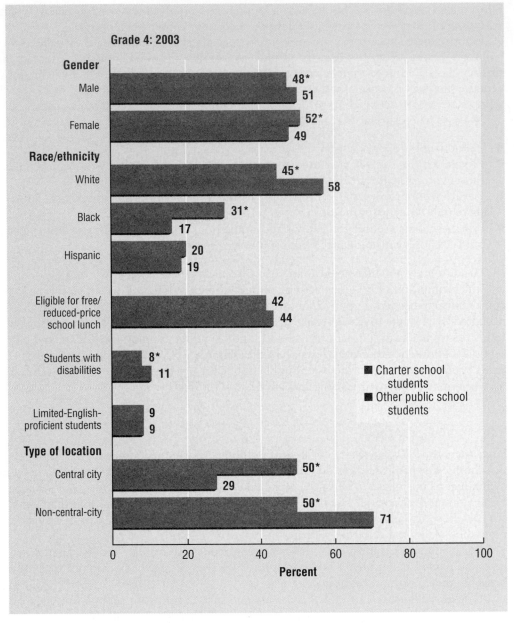

*Significantly different from other public schools

Source: U.S. Department of Education, Institute of Education Sciences, National Center for Education Statistics, National Assessment of Educational Progress (NAEP), 2003 Mathematics Charter School Pilot Study.

Like other reform initiatives, charter schools are meant to be innovative—to reach out to those students who are not being served well by the public schools. Some charter schools offer a rigorous classical education, whereas others integrate academics and counseling with technical and experiential training. Researchers suggest the effectiveness of charter schools varies (WestEd, 2007). Figure 7.5 provides a snapshot of who attends charter schools. **What similarities and differences do you notice between students in public schools and those in charter schools?**

Parochial Schools

Private schools operated by religious organizations, referred to as parochial schools, have long been an alternative to public schools in the United States. Although they receive funding from public schools for student transportation and testing, most parochial schools charge a tuition fee.

Interestingly, more than a few students attending parochial schools are not from particularly religious families. These types of schools often are believed to offer a better education than public schools for less money than private schools.

Catholic schools account for the largest number of parochial school students. The majority of these students attend schools in New York, Pennsylvania, California, Illinois, and Ohio. Other areas of the country where Catholic schools are prominent include New Orleans, Louisiana, and Detroit, Michigan.

In St. Louis, Missouri, and other cities around the country, charter schools are competing with Catholic schools. Some parents who believe inner-city public schools provide a low-quality education view charter schools as attractive alternatives to parochial schools. The movement of students from Catholic schools to charter schools has not gone unnoticed by Catholic educators, but it has not caused alarm. Instead, it has underscored for Catholic educators the importance of marketing.

Although Catholic schools are the most popular parochial schools, some two hundred thousand children attend approximately seven hundred Jewish day schools in North America. The majority of them are Orthodox Jewish schools. In the past twenty years, however, many schools have been founded by groups that once opposed the idea of separate schools for Jewish children. Jewish day schools are springing up not only in large Jewish population centers in the Northeast and Southern California, but also in Atlanta, for example. There, eight Jewish schools operate, representing every major movement. Each of the schools welcomes Jewish children regardless of their family's sect.

Fundamentalist Christian schools are growing in number more quickly than are other private schools. This growth is due primarily to the popular appeal of their philosophies and curricula. Observers suggest that conservative Christians try to "create" an ideal culture to serve as a "crucible of change" for fixing the inadequacies and evils in existing culture. Building their own schools to educate children certainly helps meet this goal.

Home Schools

Some parents choose to take on the role of teacher themselves and educate their children at home. The U.S. Department of Education estimates that more than one million primary and secondary students in the United States study in "home schools." Other estimates go as high as 2.1 million. Reliable numbers are hard to come by for several reasons. First, many states define and track homeschoolers differently. Second, some parents do not comply with state rules requiring them to register their homeschooled children. In addition, some parents do not join home school support groups, another way of counting heads.

Parents homeschool for various reasons: better education, religious concerns, and avoiding a poor public school environment. (See Chapter 9 for a discussion of some legal issues involving homeschooling.) **From your perspective, what are the pros and cons of homeschooling?**

How Are Schools Administered?

When people think about schools, they often picture a school building, teachers, and students. Missing from this picture are the people who administer the schools, who take care of the daily business of running schools so teachers and students can concentrate on learning. From the **superintendent of schools** to the general office staff, the administration of schools has changed over time. Increased demands and constraints from both inside and outside schools have greatly affected the way they operate. For one, today's school administrators have much less flexibility in making decisions than their predecessors had. As you will read in Chapter 8, they must contend with state-aid formulas, government mandates, external standards for educators' and students' performances, and a host of political interests intent on getting power. As a result, many administrators now feel caught between the need to make everyone happy and the need to make effective policy.

In the United States, superintendents and their associates and assistants form the **central office staff.** They, along with school principals, all tend to view their worlds in a remarkably similar way. The demands of their jobs and their training probably contribute to their common outlook. Nevertheless, it is interesting to note that administrators of schools as diverse as those we find in the United States all share some of the same issues, goals, concerns, and characteristics.

The School Superintendent

A superintendent can be thought of the chief executive officer, or CEO, of a school system, usually a school district. Superintendents are appointed by the **school board,** which is the legislative policy-making body responsible for making sure that competent individuals perform the work of schools. The school board functions like a board of directors that sets policies and then hires employees to carry them out. Because the board is made up of people with no particular expertise in school affairs, it delegates much of its power to the superintendent and his or her staff. For a better picture of the typical staff organization of public school systems, see Figure 7.6.

Being a superintendent can be an incredibly demanding job. Superintendents worry about financing schools, planning and goal setting, assessing educational outcomes, improving accountability and credibility, evaluating staff and administrators, developing relations with a school board, administering special education services, negotiating labor contracts, dealing with changing enrollments, and so on.

Superintendents must be able to mediate and compromise without losing the trust of people with opposing goals. They often are the go-betweens for school employees and the school board, as well as for the school and the public. With increased public and media interest in

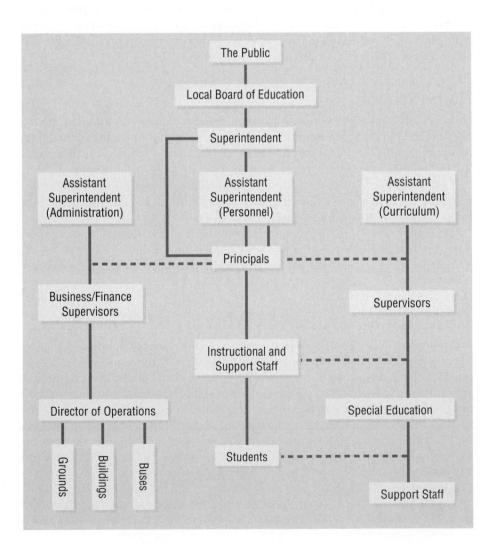

Figure 7.6
Typical Line and Staff Organization of Public School Systems
Why might the term *middle management* be used to describe principals?

schools, the job has become especially challenging. The rapid turnover rate of superintendents reflects this trend.

The leader of the New York City public schools, a sort of super-superintendent, presides over community school-district superintendents and about 1,200 schools, 110,000 employees, and one million students. Believed to have the largest and toughest urban education challenge in the country, the chancellor is expected to be (1) an educator well versed in instruction, supervision, and administration; (2) a leader who exhibits decisiveness, shrewdness, powers of consensus building, and a commitment to children; (3) a manager having skills to run a bureaucracy with more than one hundred thousand employees; and (4) a strategist, good at overcoming institutional barriers.

On a smaller level, the responsibilities of the New York City school chancellor are the responsibilities of superintendents everywhere. Indeed, many more superintendents work in small communities than in large ones. One problem that faces small-town superintendents in particular is declining student enrollments, which make opportunities to offer a diverse and intellectually rich curriculum virtually impossible. Simply staffing the courses to meet minimal requirements can be a major challenge. Another challenge for rural school administrators' success is that they must be a good "fit" with their communities. In small towns, educational leaders are not nameless, faceless bureaucrats. People know where to go and whom to see if they are unhappy about educational policies and practices.

Principals and Assistant Principals

Schools generally have a single administrative officer, a **principal,** responsible for the everyday operation and tone of a school. Large schools often have one or more assistant principals to help complete all the work. Although the job requires formal training, one truly becomes a principal by learning on the job.

Principals typically administer discipline and give guidance to students, deal with staff and faculty on simple to complex issues, locate substitute teachers, implement rules, conduct surveillance of halls, balance the school's budget, and maintain the building and equipment.

Principals in all schools also perform similar everyday duties, such as observing classrooms, circulating through the building, and monitoring hallways. The ways principals interpret these activities, however, can make a big difference in their effectiveness as leaders. As indicated in Figure 7.7, effective principals share several characteristics.

Which of the behaviors of principals have you observed in schools? Can you think of other characteristics of effective principals?

- Lead schools in a way that emphasizes student and adult (teacher, principal, staff members) learning.

- Set high expectations and standards for the academic and social development of all students and the performance of adults.

- Demand content and instruction that ensure student achievement of agreed-upon academic standards.

- Create a culture of continuous learning for adults tied to student learning and other school goals.

- Use multiple sources of data as diagnostic tools to assess, identify, and apply instructional improvement.

- Actively engage the community to create shared responsibility for student and school success.

Source: National Association of Elementary School Principals. (2001). Leading learning communities: Standards for what principals should know and be able to do (p. 2). Washington, DC: Author.

Figure 7.7
Behaviors of Effective Principals

One of the most important characteristics of a principal is the ability to maintain the administrative team's relationship with teachers. In the overall organization, the principal is in a position of middle management—between the superintendent and the teachers and school staff. As such, she must be able to follow and to lead. Ultimately, she must follow the policies of the school administration. But to lead the teachers and the support staff (guidance counselors, special education teachers, media specialists, librarians, custodians, bus drivers, and others), the principal must involve others in formulating and implementing ideas without sacrificing authority. Finding this balance between leading and following is one of the most crucial abilities principals learn on the job.

What Organizational and Policy Issues Do Schools Face?

Schools have been organized in different ways to try to meet the needs of today's students. Decisions about whether to establish separate grades, to implement multiage groupings, or to separate students by abilities shape the unique character of each school. School policies about issues, from retention and tracking to class schedules and class size, also affect life in classrooms. Regardless of school setting, policies are regularly reviewed or revised. Changes can originate with teachers, administrators, parents, and students.

Retention

Flunking, the scornful term for failing a course or repeating a grade, has taken on new significance as education reformers promote high standards. In recent years reformers have urged educators to practice **retention,** or holding students back until they have mastered a grade level. This idea runs counter to the idea of **social promotion,** or passing children to successive grades to keep them with other children of their age.

Schools must set policies regarding retention that are fair to students. Many critics claim that students are graduating from high school without knowing how to read or how to do simple math. At the same time, other students may not have the chance to advance because other classmates need more time to learn a skill or topic.

Research suggests, however, that retention alone does not help students adjust or learn. The social stigma of being held back is painful for many students; it often seems like a punishment. At the same time, administrators need to consider the possibility that students are not learning because of a particular teaching method or because of outside influences.

Class Schedule and Class Size

One effort to restructure schools involves class schedule and class size policies. Recently, the trends have been longer class periods, fewer classes a semester, and smaller classrooms. Experimentation with class schedules and class sizes is done in hopes of providing students with better-quality learning experiences.

Block scheduling is a method of organizing classes that typically provides longer instructional periods during the school day. It is used in roughly 30 percent of the nation's secondary schools. Instead of the traditional seven- to eight-period school day, various block schedules include four periods a day, each lasting eighty-five to one hundred minutes. One model, the 4 × 4 schedule, allows students to complete four year-long courses each semester. Among the benefits of using the 4 × 4 schedule are declining failure rates, improvement in students grades, an increase in the number of students on the honor roll, and greater instructional flexibility for teachers (Rettig & Canady, 1999).

Indiana educators have divided their school year into three parts (trimesters) with five periods a day. This novel approach to block scheduling means that Westfield High School students can earn fifteen credits instead of the usual twelve during an academic year. This 3 × 5 plan is a way for Westfield to offer more joint courses with nearby universities. Students can take off up to three trimesters for travel, work, or illness and still graduate on schedule. Specific subjects, such as calculus, physics, and chemistry, can be enhanced by requiring an additional trimester. And students can take these extra courses without losing out on electives. In addition, this schedule allows students to attend school part-time, work part-time, and still graduate with their class (Keen, 1999).

Class size has always been a controversial issue in schools. How many children should be placed in a single room with one teacher? What happens to teaching and learning when a group becomes larger or smaller? Should the inclusion of one or more students with disabilities or students at risk affect class size?

There is value in having twenty or fewer students, particularly in the early grades. Younger students, especially those economically disadvantaged, learn more in smaller reading and mathematics classes. Their attitudes and behavior improve too. Critics are quick to observe, however, that simply lowering class size does not automatically lead to increases in learning. How teachers organize instruction continues to be critical to student success.

School districts report their average class size in different ways. Surprisingly, just measuring class size can cause problems. Dividing the total number of students by the total number of staff (including noninstructional staff members) yields a more favorable **student–teacher ratio** than do calculations based on the number of actual classroom teachers. The obvious answer—hiring more teachers—is impossible on most schools' budgets, even if the extra teachers are available.

Tracking

Should students be grouped homogeneously or heterogeneously based on estimates of their abilities? Assigning students believed to have similar abilities to certain instructional groups, class sections, and programs of study is a practice known as **tracking**. It has been the focus of bitter debate for almost a century.

Critics of tracking argue that students are tracked on flimsy, often biased evidence. Many assigned to "lower," or nonacademic, tracks may be there as much for behavior problems as for academic reasons. The students hurt most severely and often are disadvantaged, minority-group students. In general, these students are the most at risk and have more needs than average students. These students often get by in lower-track classrooms because the teachers may expect

---

Technology in Practice

RECOGNIZING AND PROMOTING SCHOOL QUALITY

Educators need to understand what constitutes school quality. Quality is defined increasingly in quantitative terms. The data generated in response to No Child Left Behind are so plentiful that making sense of them has been challenging, particularly for those who must guide school improvement. Fortunately, numerous technological innovations are designed to help people see both the forest and the trees. One is called the Quality School Portfolio (QSP), a web-based decision-making tool for schools and school districts.

The QSP was developed at the National Center for Research on Evaluation, Standards, and Student Testing at UCLA (CRESST). It enables educators to collect, analyze, and make sense of data in ways that are consistent with No Child Left Behind. QSP is being used in all fifty states, more than one thousand schools, and eighty school districts.

QSP is divided into the following sections. Each performs key functions required to describe school quality.

- **Groups.** Disaggregate student, teacher, and parent data into custom-designed groups for analysis and reporting.
- **Goals.** Determine goals and set targets to monitor student progress toward meeting standards.
- **Reports.** Create understandable charts and graphs as a basis for decision making.
- **Gradebook.** Track student performance at the classroom level.
- **Students.** Input and organize student work samples and view a history of each student.

Questions for Reflection: Go to the CRESST website (http://cresst96.cse.ucla.edu/resources/justfor teachers_set.htm) and click on the QSP link to take a closer look at this online tool. As a teacher, what might be the benefits of using the QSP? Is there a potential downside to using the QSP?

Source: Heritage, M., & Chen, E. (2005, May). Why data skills matter in school improvement. *Phi Delta Kappan, 86*(9), 707–710.

little of them. Students, in turn, develop a negative self-concept, low self-esteem, poor motivation, and loss of interest in learning. Perhaps the most damning charge against tracking is the static nature of the assignments: once a student falls into the lower tracks, he or she seems caught in an academic tailspin from which few recover (Pool & Page, 1995).

Supporters of tracking believe it is a way to group students with like abilities in the same classes. More advanced students can proceed at a faster pace without leaving classmates behind. Likewise, students requiring more time and instruction can proceed through material together at an appropriate pace. Advocates think these settings provide better learning experiences for students than they receive in mixed-abilities classrooms. They contend that tracking allows teachers to focus on the whole class, rather than on a few individual students who are bored or who need more help. In this sense, as long as teachers do not write off lower-achieving students, tracking can offer a positive learning experience. Until that balance is reached, however, school policies continue to change.

What Makes Some Schools More Effective Than Others?

Effective schools—schools that can demonstrate student learning—allow substantial staff development time. In these schools, improvement goals are sharply focused, attainable, and valued by staff members. School needs guide staff, rather than standardized forms and checklists. Methods for reaching goals are often based on proven successful strategies. A blend of teacher independence and central office control characterizes improvement programs in effective schools. Effective schools also have respectful and supportive relationships among administrators, teachers, support staffs, and students. Figure 7.8 contains some of the elements that contribute to school effectiveness.

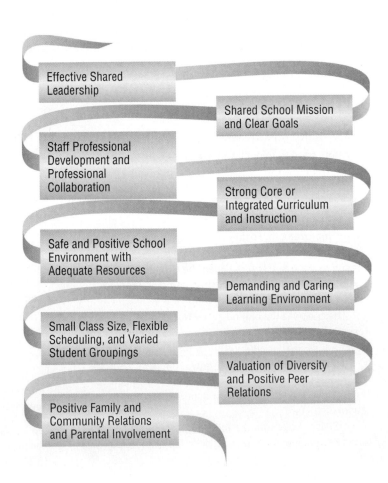

Figure 7.8
Elements That Contribute
to School Effectiveness
What other characteristics of
effective schools might you add?

Effective schools are managed by effective leaders. These individuals provide the leadership necessary to create a strong curriculum and safe environments where students can succeed. Effective leaders care about faculty needs, teacher recognition, and professional development. Good leaders also encourage parental, family, and community involvement in school activities. Many school leaders help parents and teachers assume new and powerful leadership roles.

For example, today over one hundred elementary schools have become part of the Basic School Network—another conception of effective schools. The network was created by an alliance of education foundations and groups, which based its plan on Boyer's (1995) ideas about effective schools. The alliance's goals are to help students communicate effectively, acquire a core of knowledge, and become lifelong learners. Four key components distinguish these schools:

1. *The School as a community.* Separate classrooms are connected through a clear and vital mission. Teachers serve as leaders, and the principal acts as lead teacher. Parents are viewed as partners in the learning process.
2. *A Curriculum with coherence.* There is an emphasis on language and on core subjects, which are organized around common themes.
3. *A Climate for learning.* Class sizes are small, teaching schedules are flexible, and student grouping arrangements are varied. Students are provided with resources ranging from building blocks to electronic tools. They also have access to basic health and counseling services and afternoon and summer enrichment programs.
4. *Character development.* The Basic School focuses on seven core values: honesty, respect, responsibility, compassion, self-discipline, perseverance, and giving.

If you were to guess, which of the preceding four factors might be most influential in helping students demonstrate higher achievement test scores? Why?

Positive School Environments

Educational researchers and practitioners frequently mention the importance of school climate to student achievement and consumer satisfaction. Marzano (2000; 2007) defined school climate in terms of the characteristics of schools that relate to students' perceptions of order and support. A climate that students perceive as positive has these attributes:

- Rules and procedures are clearly articulated and enforced.
- There is an orderly atmosphere.
- The school is characterized by positive interactions among staff and students.
- People recognize and enforce implicit norms of civility.

Despite what adults sometimes think, students themselves are often the chief proponents of school order. Students want to be part of a community that values what they value—in a nutshell, respect for human dignity.

How do teachers demonstrate concern for the four attributes that students value in a school? What specific examples of such teacher behaviors can you recall seeing in your own life as a student? How might teachers themselves detract from a positive school climate?

Relations between Home and School

Evidence suggests that connections between home and school help students adjust and learn. Parents boost their children's academic achievement by exposing them to intellectually stimulating experiences, teaching them directly, monitoring homework, and communicating with the school. Parents also strengthen ties by volunteering at the school, attending school conferences, requesting information, and participating in school governance.

Large schools are often less likely than small schools to provide effective teaching and learning environments. The larger and more diverse the schools are, the less likely parents are to be involved. Teaching large classes means that teachers do not get to know their students

Case Perspectives

Think back to the case that opened this chapter. The following comments are intended to provide a context for your own thinking about this case.

AN EDUCATION PROFESSOR REFLECTS ON ARTHUR EWING'S THOUGHTS ABOUT RETAINING GRETA PHILIPS There are almost never defensible grounds for retaining, or "flunking," a student. The only possible exception—short of a severe medical problem that might require retention—might be when a child is very young—say, in kindergarten—and the parents are fully supportive of the idea. Even then careful thought must be given to how the educational environment will change to encourage success.

The literature is overwhelmingly against retention for several reasons. Once a student is retained, he or she is likely to demonstrate a continual pattern of failure; that is, usually the situation continues to deteriorate. Repeating a grade simply doesn't help a student experience success. In fact, retention is more likely to result in more failure and dropping out of school altogether.

If Arthur Ewing makes this recommendation, and the school entertains it, Greta's parents should be quick to inquire what will be different the second time around. How will Greta's instructional program differ from the experience she has just had? Will she have the same teacher? Will she get special help, and if so, in what form? Should she be tested again as a possible candidate for special education services? How will her placement be monitored? How will success be measured? Answers to these questions are likely to suggest why such a move would be ill-advised.

It would be a mistake to discount the potentially devastating effect that retention can have on a student's self-concept. In the classic style of a self-fulfilling prophecy, the student who fails in a dramatic way—and make no mistake, flunking is high drama—may easily think of himself or herself as a failure. It is only a very short step from thinking about failure to behaving in ways that make it likely. Despite our recent fixation on achievement tests, school is still about a lot more than test scores. We must do everything we can to invite and ensure participation, not discourage it through the practice of retention.

I believe some of the most caustic and damaging criticism of schools comes from those who complain about "social promotion," or the practice of moving children forward through school, even when they have academic difficulties. It typically makes much more sense to keep students together with their classmates and work to improve the educational services for students experiencing difficulty than it does to flunk them. I am not ready to concede that Arthur Ewing has done everything possible to help Greta. He may have exhibited heroic effort, but it is unlikely that all possibilities for strengthening her academic performance have been exhausted. It is time to move Greta forward and redouble the efforts to help her succeed.

A DEVELOPMENTAL PSYCHOLOGIST REFLECTS ON THE POSSIBLE RETENTION OF GRETA PHILIPS. From what little we know about the Greta Philips case, I am inclined to think that retention is a possibility that ought not be discarded too quickly. It is possible that Greta is developmentally unready to be in the fourth grade. Another year with the same or similar academic expectations and a new group of peers might be just what she needs.

Let me say just a bit about psychosocial development. People think or process information in different ways, but all pass through particular stages of development. In general, people are moving toward greater complexity of thought and greater reliance on their own sense of what is good and right. That is not to say that people necessarily reject society's values, only that they become more sure of themselves and more able to interact successfully in the world. Once a person has attained a certain level of development, she or he can operate at previous levels of development if conditions warrant.

Being developmentally complex in psychosocial terms is not the same as being intelligent, although there is a low positive correlation between measures of both. To be well developed in psychosocial terms is to process information effectively and to relate to others in appropriate ways. Deficits in such development can put people, especially young children, at risk for academic and social failure.

Everyone involved—parents, teachers, extended family, and others—must be extremely careful to see that retention is not communicated as something that is punitive, something that should be feared, or something to be embarrassed about. A student who is retained may well experience a period of disequilibrium, but that is to be expected as a precursor to a developmental stage change. In other words, when Greta is retained, she may be upset, even angry for a while, but these reactions often precede genuine growth in psychosocial development.

Questions for Reflection: Do you think retention is ever a viable educational option? Under what circumstances might retaining a child be appropriate? Are those circumstances present in this case? Given Arthur's description of Greta's behavior, and of her parents, might you consider ways to involve her parents more aggressively in her education? What would you do, in Arthur's place? ■

well. Teachers also are unlikely to encourage parental involvement, because they find the idea impractical. The danger is that teachers may focus on the strongest and weakest students, because they seem to require the most attention. The parents of the students of average achievement, then, may be among those least likely to be linked closely to schools.

Some parents who live in dangerous or resource-poor neighborhoods have less time, energy, and resources available for parenting and for getting involved with schools. In these neighborhoods, "family" involvement is probably a more appropriate term than "parent" involvement, because children often are raised by people who are not their parents (Decker, Gregg, & Decker, 1995).

Children from single-parent families and stepfamilies are more likely than are children from two-parent families to experience problems in school. Strong home–school ties are especially important for these students' success.

Connections between home and school may be influenced by social networks and social class. Middle- and upper-class parents may think of education as a joint responsibility of school and home, whereas parents of lower socioeconomic status might view education as the teacher's job (Lareau, 1996). As poorer children grow older, their parents become less likely to be involved in school activities. The gap that exists between socioeconomic status and children's academic achievement also widens with age.

Language barriers and differing cultural practices may halt schools' attempts to reach the parents of students needing the most help. First-year teacher Mary Ann Pacheco tried to overcome some common obstacles to communication:

> Generally, Latino parents hesitate to approach or question teachers because teaching is a highly respected position. I made myself very accessible and expressed my interest in their understanding bilingual education, student learning, and their voice in public education. I also built personal relationships, made phone calls, and made home visits. I reinforced their cultural beliefs but made them aware of certain characteristics that they might want to help their children develop. For example, during parent conferences, some parents were openly concerned with their child's tendency to talk excessively. Many times, I reminded them that in higher education, the willingness to initiate conversations, participate in group projects, and dialogue was required of students and highly valued. (Oakes & Lipton, 1999, pp. 354–355)

Summary

Schools come in all shapes and sizes and with widely varying philosophies. They address school objectives in almost every conceivable way. Administrators use a range of management strategies to deal with organizational and policy issues. Yet, troubling issues remain.

Why do schools look so much alike? Why do young people succeed in some settings and not in others? Do differences among school philosophies represent variations in only their written descriptions? What, if any, more radical approaches to schooling should we explore to help young people succeed?

When you attend your own school reunions, look around you. What was it about your school that made you and your peers want to stay in touch—to remain loyal to your conceptions of what school was all about? Why did the "no-shows" stay away?

TERMS AND CONCEPTS

alternative school	principal
block scheduling	private school
central office staff	retention
charter school	school board
for-profit school	school district
magnet school	social promotion
National Association for the Education of Young Children (NAEYC)	student–teacher ratio
	superintendent of schools
nongraded classroom	tracking

REFLECTIVE ACTIVITY: A NEW PARADIGM FOR SCHOOL GOALS

Reflective practice is an essential part of good teaching. Reflection is a process that includes making thoughtful decisions, understanding and articulating value structures, acting from knowledge, evaluating your actions and their effects, and sharing your reflections with colleagues. After reading the following scenario, respond to the questions below. The scenario reflects the INTASC Principle and Disposition at the end of this activity.

The current emphasis on education standards has fueled much philosophical debate about school goals. Many sectors of society question how well a standards-based educational system is meeting these goals. Among the educators who believe that standards have diverted education from its primary purposes is Peter W. Cookson, Jr., of Columbia University. Cookson (2001) writes that society should worry less that students clear some imaginary age-graded hurdle and worry more that by high school graduation students have internalized values of personal integrity and community responsibility. Cookson proposes an innovative curricular design to foster such an internalization of values.

The early years of the child's schooling would focus on literacy and math skills within a setting emphasizing students' security. Children would develop their appreciation of the world's diversity through exposure to world languages. The cornerstones of environmental ethics would also be laid during these K–3 years by opening the classroom to nature and to ecological concerns. Testing in these early grades would be limited to only diagnostic assessment that would allow teachers to create individualized learning plans that match students' unique abilities.

In grades four to six, Cookson's curriculum shifts to mastery, inquiry, and membership. The active development of analytical skills through the study of science and mathematics that will form the foundation for further learning occurs during this stage. As children proceed through the middle school years, the curriculum must support students as they undergo the transition from childhood to early adulthood. Socially relevant questions about sexuality, tolerance, and ethics would be examined. The curriculum would focus heavily on history and the humanities. By this point in the child's education, Cookson argues, the roots of democratic citizenship have been firmly set and the development of self has been nurtured.

In the high school years, Cookson's proposal veers most dramatically from the tradition of public education. Cookson wants a two-year secondary program that provides opportunities for a wider variety of students to make connections to society through internships and academic programs related to chosen professions. He criticizes the current system as unjustly reproducing social inequalities by emphasizing college preparation.

Decide 1. What are some of the social forces that work against innovation in educational design such as that advocated by Cookson?

Perceive and Value 2. Do you agree with Cookson that public schools provide advantages to already advantaged students?

Know and Act 3. How does the curriculum in Cookson's model compare to the curriculum you experienced as a student? If you worked in a school using Cookson's approach, how would you organize students for instruction? How would your strategies compare to those used by your teachers?

Evaluate 4. Cookson argues that no student should graduate from high school without a specific plan for the next five years of his or her life. What can schools do to increase the likelihood that this occurs?

Discuss 5. Some might argue that Cookson's emphasis on participation in internships and academic programs related to chosen professions is at the expense of excelling in traditional academic subjects necessary for admission to college. How would you respond to that argument?

INTASC Principle 5

The teacher uses an understanding of individual and group motivation and behavior to create a learning environment that encourages positive social interaction, active engagement in learning, and self-motivation.

Disposition

The teacher understands how participation supports commitment, and encourages the expression and use of democratic values in the classroom. (Interstate New Teacher Assessment and Support Consortium, 1992)

ADDITIONAL READINGS

Education Week. (April–May 2001). High School: The Shifting Mission (Special Reports). Available online: www.edweek.org/sreports/special_reports_article.cfm?slug=highschool.htm.

Gary, M., & Nelson, C. (2002). *What's public about charter schools? Lessons learned about choice and accountability.* Thousand Oaks, CA: Corwin Press.

National Association of Elementary School Principals and National Middle School Association. (2002). Supporting students in their transition to middle school: A position paper jointly adopted by the National Middle School Association and the National Association of Elementary School Principals. Ohio: National Middle School Association. Available online: www.nmsa.org.

Reynolds, D., Creemers, B., Stringfield, S., Teddlie, C., & Schaffer, G. (2002). *World class schools: International perspectives on school effectiveness.* New York: RoutledgeFalmer.

Walsh, M. (2002, May 22). Businesses flock to charter frontier. *Education Week.* Available online: www.edweek.org/ew/newstory.cfm?slug=37chartbiz.h21

Walsley, P., Fine, M., Gladden, M., Holland, N., King, S., Mosak, E., & Powell, L. C. (2000). *Small schools: Great strides: A study of new small schools in Chicago.* New York: Bank Street College of Education.

WEB RESOURCES

http://nces.ed.gov/
The National Center for Education Statistics fulfills a congressional mandate to collect, analyze, and report complete statistics on the condition of American education.

www.edweek.org/
Education Week *is an online newspaper that provides daily news and special reports that help educators stay up to date on happenings in schools.*

http://cssrs.ou.edu/
The Center for the Study of Small/Rural Schools is a cooperative effort between the University of Oklahoma's colleges of education and continuing education. The center is endorsed by the National Rural Education Association as one of its five recognized rural education research centers.

http://p12.osu.edu/about.php
This website describes collaborative efforts between Ohio State University and urban school districts in Central Ohio to promote research and programs to improve K–12 education.

www.aasa.org/
The American Association of School Administrators, founded in 1865, is the professional organization for over fourteen thousand educational leaders across America and in many other countries. The AASA's mission is to support and develop effective school system leaders who are dedicated to the highest-quality public education for all children.

CHAPTER 8

Leading, Governing, and Funding Schools

Case Study: Scopes Revisited

"I never would've guessed that we'd be discussing the place of evolution in the school curriculum in this day and age," sighed Bill Calhoun, chairman of the science department at Pinckney High School. He was sitting in the office of the district's curriculum coordinator, Lorna Kim. He put his cup of coffee on Lorna's desk. "These Intelligent Design Coalition folks have forced us to leap headlong into 1925, when William Jennings Bryan beat Clarence Darrow out in the Scopes trial, and the jury decided against evolution. But what that trial really did was show everyone that evolution was *real* science, and it's been the centerpiece of our curriculum ever since. Frankly, I can't believe that we're spending time on this issue when there are so many more important issues on our agenda."

"I know what you mean, Bill," responded Lorna. "I've been so fixated on our primary-level reading scores that I didn't see this coming. But I should have—the whole creationism and intelligent design movement has certainly been getting enough publicity lately. I guess because I don't see this community as particularly religious, I just didn't pay enough attention. But the trigger should have been when that senator from Pennsylvania, Santorum, actually sponsored an amendment to No Child Left Behind based on arguments about intelligent design. I think that lit the fire under the intelligent design proponents. The amendment didn't pass, but Santorum did get a statement inserted into the Conference Report."

Lorna picked up a paper from her desk and read:

The Conferees recognize that a quality science education should prepare students to distinguish the data and testable theories of science from religious or philosophical claims that are made in the name of science. Where topics are taught that may generate controversy (such as biological evolution), the curriculum should help students to understand the full range of scientific views that exist, why such topics may generate controversy, and how scientific discoveries can profoundly affect society.

Bill sat back and folded his arms. "I can't teach something that just makes no scientific sense. It's against everything I believe. And I can't ask the other science teachers in my department to do that either."

Lorna shook her head as she responded. "But I'm not sure that's the issue on the table. What they're saying is, basically, you have to teach students how to analyze arguments and think critically—that students need to understand other ways of thinking and be able to make up their own minds. The push isn't to teach creationism outright—just to acknowledge that the universe is very complex, and that it makes some sense to believe that some kind of intelligent force was at work in creating it. But it appears to be a slippery slope. This is such dicey stuff, Bill. And feelings are running high on both sides."

Lorna folded her hands on her desk. "This is going to come up at the next school board meeting. As chair of the science department, you're going to be at the center of it. You'd better make sure you understand what the Intelligent Design Coalition believes, and what they want to accomplish. You also need to know what your teachers think about evolution and creationism. I'd hate to see us get into a political bind with them."

"OK, Lorna." Bill nodded slowly. "I appreciate the heads-up. Any resources you could suggest for getting more information about this?"

Source: Congressional conferees language on controversies such as evolution (Revised "Santorum Amendment"), 107th Cong., 1st Sess. (2001). House of Representatives Report 107 334, *No Child Left Behind Act of 2001* (Conference Report to accompany H.R. 1).

This chapter explains how leaders organize schools and generate money to advance the public's education agenda. It presents the role of the federal government in public education and the power of state influence and localities on schools. It also illustrates the link between money and educational success, both of which influence the profession of teaching.

What Are School Governance and Education Finance?

The Tenth Amendment to the U.S. Constitution gives people the power to establish and operate public schools. Specifically, the amendment states that any powers and duties not in the domain of the federal government reside with state governments. Because the Constitution does not discuss federal responsibility for public education, the power to educate resides at the state level. That is, the states are ultimately responsible for **school governance,** or for establishing and managing public education. As the processes of public education became more complex, states delegated many educational responsibilities to local education agencies. Over time, a complex network of formal organizations at the federal, state, and local levels has made public education what it is today.

School governance controls finance, and finance shapes practice. Educators who want to have some influence on educational policy and practice must learn how the system works. They need to understand how public education is funded, where the money is allocated, and how it is eventually spent and accounted for. Some knowledge can be gained from examining the formal processes of governance and finance. But it is important to study informal processes, too.

How Schools Are Run

Many people argue that the most important factor in educational success is the school leader. Educational leaders—school board members, superintendents, principals, department heads, and teachers—are responsible for the governance of schools. They control and direct the conduct of schooling within a system of institutions, laws, regulations, policies, politics, and customs.

Even people in the same profession can have different ideas about what makes a good leader. Some characteristics of leadership that people might identify include vision and the ability to articulate it, an understanding of the group's wants or needs, a good personality, thoughtfulness and truthfulness, the ability to inspire others, knowing the right thing to say and the right time to say it, and setting a good example. These diverse characteristics suggest that there is no single model of effective leadership. Like beauty, leadership may be in the eye of the beholder. What do you think it takes to be a good leader? See Figure 8.1 for a questionnaire about what makes a good leader. Complete the questionnaire and discuss your results with your classmates.

How Schools Are Funded

Tax money collected at the local, state, and federal levels provides most of the funding for public schools, as illustrated in Figure 8.2. More than three-quarters of the school boards in the United States have taxing authority. Many reformers believe more funding for public schools is necessary to increase the quality of education offered. In economically troubled times, however, few political leaders at any governmental level are willing to risk angering voters by raising taxes to support public schools.

The chances of school boards successfully raising taxes are further reduced by the fact that an increasing number of voters no longer have children in the public schools. In addition, people who are retired and on fixed incomes often are less willing and less able to support public education.

Connections between Education and the Economy

Money and education are closely linked in many ways, as policymakers will attest. For them, balancing educational funding and educational values is a way of life. The following four values continually compete for attention in many school systems and communities (Guthrie, Garms, & Pierce, 1988). Sometimes one value is at the top of a system's priorities, only to be replaced when another value becomes more urgent.

Figure 8.1
What Makes A Good
Leader?

A Good Leader:

Takes responsibility

1	2	3	4
Strongly Disagree	Disagree	Agree	Strongly Agree

Develops relationships

1	2	3	4
Strongly Disagree	Disagree	Agree	Strongly Agree

Establishes goals

1	2	3	4
Strongly Disagree	Disagree	Agree	Strongly Agree

Is politically minded

1	2	3	4
Strongly Disagree	Disagree	Agree	Strongly Agree

Delegates authority

1	2	3	4
Strongly Disagree	Disagree	Agree	Strongly Agree

Encourages innovation

1	2	3	4
Strongly Disagree	Disagree	Agree	Strongly Agree

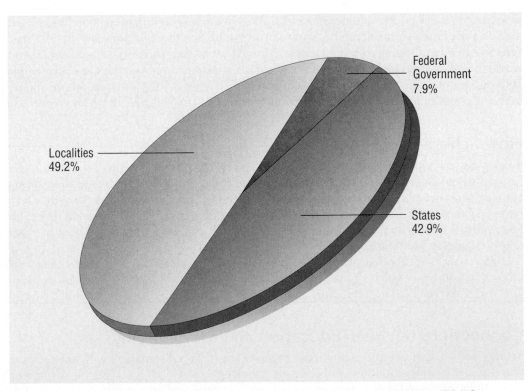

Figure 8.2
**Sources of Revenue
for School Funding**
What factors might alter
the proportion of financial
support that each level of
government provides?

Source: From *Digest of education statistics, 2005,* by U.S. Department of Education, 2005. Washington, DC: U.S. Government Printing Office.

1. *Equality,* or equal educational opportunity, has been defined most often in terms of equal access to schooling. This means public school teachers, administrators, and staff try to offer education tailored to all students' strengths and needs, while ensuring that all students acquire at least minimum or basic skills. Does providing equal educational opportunities mean every school has to receive the same amount of funding?
2. *Adequacy* refers to the minimum resources needed to achieve an educational outcome. Is there a minimum level beneath which funding cannot sink in order to provide basic education?
3. *Efficiency* refers to getting the maximum educational benefit for the dollar spent. How can we recognize efficient and inefficient or wasteful spending on education?
4. *Liberty,* or choice, is about control over where, how, and for what purposes students are educated. Should parents be allowed to choose where and how they spend tax dollars to educate their children?

When thinking about spending money on education, it is important to remember that the connections between education and financial success in life are strong. In general, the more schooling a person has, the greater his or her potential earning power. Education, then, is seen as a way of developing "human capital" (Becker, 1964; Schultz, 1981). Students have reason to expect that the time, effort, and money they invest in their education will yield some personal benefit. Society, too, benefits because education develops productive, tax-paying citizens. Society also benefits from an educated citizenry in terms of reduced crime rates and the spread of moral values—both of which accompany education.

Political Influences on Public Education

Individuals and organizations shape public education both formally and informally. Elected and appointed officials hire, reassign, fire, and reward their staffs. But informal sources of power outside the school system are important as well. This is where politics can become a factor in public education governance. Elected lawmakers have to answer to their constituents, who often voice strong opinions about public schools. In addition, citizens work on their own or in groups to create change in schools based on their political beliefs. Sometimes these informal political powers working outside the system achieve sweeping changes within the system. Figure 8.3 shows some of the influences on education at the national, federal, regional, state, and local levels, which are discussed throughout this chapter.

EDUCATION LOBBIES AND SPECIAL-INTEREST GROUPS How do special-interest groups have a positive effect on education? Public education is everyone's business, but some people are more powerful in influencing its direction than are others. People often gather around specific interests and try to change policy to advance their cause, hence the terms **special-interest group** and *pressure group*. These terms can have a negative meaning by suggesting that group members promote their own narrow points of view. But special-interest groups also educate the public about important issues and offer alternative solutions to problems.

Although authorities at the state level have initiated many education reforms in recent years, special interests have contributed informally to the reforms. Their members have worked publicly and behind the scenes to shape policy at the local, state, and national levels. For example, the largest volunteer education organization in the United States, the **National Parent–Teacher Association (PTA),** has long supported legislation at all levels designed to benefit children. Professional organizations such as the National School Boards Association, the National Association of State Boards of Education, and the American Association of Colleges for Teacher Education also support many education policy initiatives with work and funds.

Special-interest groups often try to influence schools on ideological issues. Such groups are sustained by their beliefs about school curricula and issues of social justice. The Council for Basic Education, for example, advocates curriculum in the liberal arts. Hispanic Americans have tried to establish *unidos,* or unity, among Spanish-speaking peoples for the purpose of changing public schools.

Interest groups concerned with education want to influence curricula, instruction, and governance in public schools. For example, the Americans with Disabilities Association, Inc., provides a political voice for the community of individuals with disabilities. The ADA educates

Figure 8.3
Influences on Public Education
How might this figure change if you ranked the levels in terms of their power? Explain your reasoning.

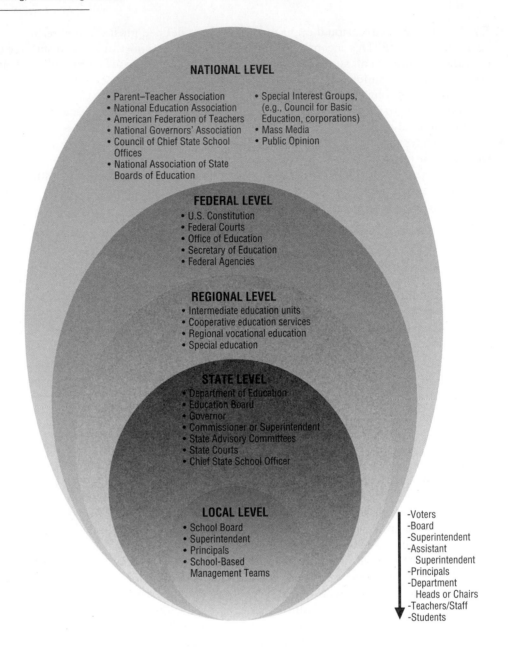

NATIONAL LEVEL
- Parent–Teacher Association
- National Education Association
- American Federation of Teachers
- National Governors' Association
- Council of Chief State School Offices
- National Association of State Boards of Education
- Special Interest Groups, (e.g., Council for Basic Education, corporations)
- Mass Media
- Public Opinion

FEDERAL LEVEL
- U.S. Constitution
- Federal Courts
- Office of Education
- Secretary of Education
- Federal Agencies

REGIONAL LEVEL
- Intermediate education units
- Cooperative education services
- Regional vocational education
- Special education

STATE LEVEL
- Department of Education
- Education Board
- Governor
- Commissioner or Superintendent
- State Advisory Committees
- State Courts
- Chief State School Officer

LOCAL LEVEL
- School Board
- Superintendent
- Principals
- School-Based Management Teams

-Voters
-Board
-Superintendent
-Assistant Superintendent
-Principals
-Department Heads or Chairs
-Teachers/Staff
-Students

the public and works to influence political elections and legislative initiatives. This political action committee, or PAC, seeks to block threats from other groups working against the interests of people with disabilities. The ADA conducts voter registration drives, promotes get-out-the-vote programs, and raises money for candidates who support policies favorable to people with disabilities. In terms of education, their work includes fostering the development of new and useful resources for people with disabilities.

The American Civil Liberties Union (ACLU) is another PAC that has taken public positions on educational issues. Specifically, the ACLU is a legal organization that defends people against what it believes are attacks on their civil liberties. One of its most notable actions was in the Scopes trial of 1925. Tennessee law at the time forbade public school teachers from teaching any theory that denied the theory of creation described in the Bible. The ACLU offered legal representation to any Tennessee teacher who would test this law. John T. Scopes took them up on the offer and was defended by Clarence Darrow against famous orator and politician William Jennings Bryan. Their trial was the beginning of the end for antievolution forces.

Other actions of the ACLU include filing briefs on legal issues as a "friend of the court" for the purpose of educating judges and lawyers. They have endorsed exempting students from the

Issues in School Reform

LEADERSHIP IN AN AGE OF REFORM

For the past ten years or more, James Harvey and Robert Koff have led a Danforth Foundation project on school superintendents. They offer lessons learned from their experience, the first and most important of which is that trying to impose simple solutions on complex problems is a mistake. The classic example of such a top-down approach, according to Harvey and Koff, is the No Child Left Behind (NCLB) Act. There are simply too many interacting influences to believe that single-mindedness of accountability as it reveals itself in NCLB could possibly cure all of the ills of schools.

Instead, Harvey and Koff offer a kind of jigsaw puzzle notion of school reform. They describe the importance of the interactive influences of the "reform puzzle pieces"—pieces that include accountability standards, leadership, governance, standards and assessment, race and class, school principals, out-of-school support for learning, and community engagement.

Let's be clear. The great benefit of the No Child Left Behind Act is that it brought accountability to the top of the nation's education agenda. Its great drawback was to push to the sidelines virtually everything else. Worried about student learning? Accountability is our response. Concerned about teacher adequacy? Annual testing of every child is our ace in the hole. What about educational equity? Accountability, assessment, and adequate annual progress provide both answer and alliteration. The conviction that an assessment system of this sort applied in this way will improve learning in America is so egregiously sophomoric that it gives accountability a bad name. (p. 42)

Questions for Reflection: Do you believe that Harvey and Koff are too negative about the possible power of accountability, or do they have it right? Do we need more or less accountability in American public education?

Source: Harvey, J., & Koff, R. H. (2004, September 1). The tales we tell ourselves. *Education Week, 24*(1), 42–43.

---

flag salute when it is against their religion. They have also opposed the use of public funds for private education.

The Anti-Defamation League (ADL) wants to end discrimination against and ridicule of any religion or group of citizens. It has four hundred staff members in thirty U.S. field offices. In terms of education, the ADL offers a comprehensive educational program for elementary and secondary teachers and students. The program encourages tolerance through teacher awareness training, youth training, classroom discussion guides, student after-school programs, and weekend awareness retreats. According to ADL figures, it has trained more than one hundred thousand teachers and 10 million public, private, and parochial school students.

The Legal Defense and Education Fund (LDEF), part of the National Organization for Women (NOW), works to advance women's rights in education systems across the country. In St. Louis, Missouri, for example, the board of education's policy was to transfer pregnant elementary and junior high school girls to a less desirable school when their pregnancies became obvious. The LDEF stepped in and took up the fight. As a result, the board changed its policy, allowing girls to choose to remain in regular classes or to transfer.

Since its founding in 1909, the National Association for the Advancement of Colored People (NAACP) has worked to achieve racial justice for all people and to improve the living conditions of low-income people. The association is the largest and most influential civil rights organization in the country. Over the years, the NAACP has been a major force behind open housing, job opportunities, prison reform, school desegregation, and education programs for youth and adults.

PUBLIC MEDIA How do the mass media affect education? Public opinion on processes of governing and managing public education is a powerful influence on policy making. When it comes to public opinion, the press has two roles. First, they report what the public opinion is on various matters. Second, the press suggests what people ought to think. Both roles are important, but sometimes the line between the two gets blurred.

One view, expressed by Juan Williams, is that the job of the press is to watch governmental and educational leaders so they do not cheat the public. This time-honored role of journalism is central to our democracy. Williams (1992) described the job of the journalist on the education beat in a way that is truly timeless:

> The truth is, reporters and editors and, most important, readers are interested in education only as a function of political power. A major proportion of any jurisdiction's tax dollars goes into schools. Politicians have to make up those school budgets and defend them. The school or university budget has to be both sufficient to the task of educating young people and simultaneously able to withstand charges that it is really a pork-barrel project, wasting the taxpayers' money. Education budgets pay not only for teachers and books but also for construction workers, maintenance people, teachers' aides, administrators, union chiefs, and cooks. In other words, the tax dollars assigned to educate children are a major source of patronage and power in our society. Newspaper editors, as the public's watchdogs, want to know if the taxpayers are being cheated out of their money. (p. 179)

But too often, critics argue, the press goes out of its way to criticize schools. Negative events seem more newsworthy than positive ones, and many stories about schools focus on something bad—school violence, low test scores, and so on. Critics say that too frequently a story is found interesting to reporters only if it is critical of the schools, if it has some scent of blood about it. Using the news lingo, if it bleeds, it leads.

The media perform not only an informational function in society but an educational function as well. Television, newspapers, radio, and magazines touch more people today than at any time in our history. And they will reach more tomorrow than they do today. Some might raise this question: Are children learning more from the media than they are from their parents and schools?

How Does the Federal Government Influence Education?

Although the wording of the Tenth Amendment to the Constitution leaves control of school governance to the states, the federal government has always had a hand in shaping education. Various court cases have defined education as a property right or a civil right under the Constitution. This interpretation makes education subject to the Fourteenth Amendment, which allows the federal government to intervene in state government matters when necessary. (Section 1: "No State shall make or enforce any law which shall abridge the privileges or immunities of citizens of the United States; nor shall any State deprive any person of life, liberty, or property, without due process of law; nor deny to any person within its jurisdiction the equal protection of the laws.") The Fourteenth Amendment therefore allows the federal government to influence the education of children at the local level.

Some experts suggest that the federal agenda for education is set by the "Iron Triangle"—the combination of education interests in the executive branch, congressional committees, and interest groups outside government (Guthrie, Garms, & Pierce, 1988).

The executive branch combines beliefs and programs to influence public education. Presidential staffs and cabinets speak publicly about education issues, encourage states' attention to education reform, and designate federal funds for education initiatives. In addition, the president is responsible for many departments, agencies, and programs devoted to education.

Congress's role in public education involves passing laws and appropriating funds. Although not part of the Iron Triangle, federal courts also influence public education through their decisions. For instance, the courts set policy when they rule on civil rights cases and other controversial issues, such as prayer in public schools and the use of public funds for private schools.

Federal Funding for Education

Figure 8.4 illustrates trends in total federal funding for education between 1965 and 2005. For elementary and secondary schools, for example, support increased by 144 percent between 1965 and 1975, but rose only 2 percent between 1975 and 1980. Between 1980 and 1985, funding declined 22 percent, and then rose 38.5 percent between 2000 and 2005 (U.S. Department of Education, 2006).

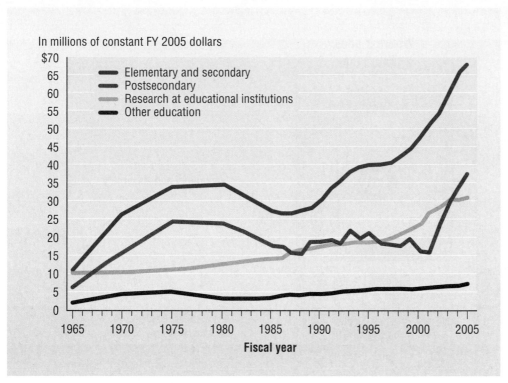

In millions of constant FY 2005 dollars

- Elementary and secondary
- Postsecondary
- Research at educational institutions
- Other education

Fiscal year

Figure 8.4
Federal On-Budget Funds for Education by Level or Other Educational Purpose, Selected Years, 1965 to 2005
Why might support for elementary, secondary, and postsecondary education have declined in the 1980s?

Snyder, T.D., Tan, A.G, & Hoffman, C.M. (2006) *Digest of Education Statistics 2005*. Table 356. Washington, D.C.: U.S. Department of Education. Available online: http://www.nces.ed.gov/pubs2006/2006030 4.pdf.

Many of these statistics on education in the United States are collected and analyzed by the **National Center for Education Statistics (NCES),** an agency in the executive branch. The center reported that the total federal support for education in fiscal year (FY) 2005 was $141.8 billion. As illustrated in Figure 8.5, 48 percent went to elementary and secondary education, 26 percent to postsecondary expenses, and 21 percent to university research. The final 5 percent funded "other" education programs, including libraries, museums, cultural activities, and miscellaneous research. Funds were distributed through the Departments of Education, Health and Human Services, Agriculture, Defense, Energy, and Labor and the National Science Foundation.

Within these federal departments and foundations, funding for education is distributed in many ways. One way is major grant programs that are established through legislation, such as the Vocational Act and the Education for All Handicapped Children Act of 1975 (renamed the Individuals with Disabilities Education Act of 2004). Another method is to provide aid to communities where there are large federal installations, such as military bases. **Categorical grants** support education programs designed for particular groups and specific purposes, including bilingual education and programs for low-income children, such as Project Head Start and Title I.

Sometimes funds for several education programs are grouped together and given as a **block grant** to localities. Chapter Two of the 1981 **Education Consolidation and Improvement Act (ECIA),** for instance, combined thirty-two existing education programs under one block grant. This block grant was then made available to state and local education agencies for general education purposes. The amount of money states receive in this block grant is based on a student population formula. States then prepare a plan for using federal funds based on district enrollment or on measures of student need. Once states receive the federal funding, they give money to local school districts for use in whichever programs need additional services.

Regardless of what type of federal funding a school district receives, the district must comply with federal guidelines when spending grant money. If a school district either does not spend the federal money or misspends it, one of several things can happen: the school system can be forced to return the money, it can be fined, and/or it can be prevented from receiving any federal funds in the future. States and school districts with educational programs or practices that are found to be in violation of federal laws also lose funding.

Figure 8.5
Estimated Federal
Education Dollar,
2005
What proportion of the
federal budget goes
to elementary and
secondary education?

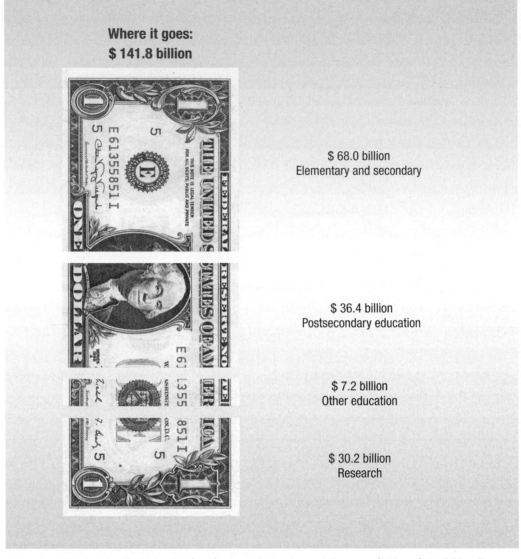

Where it goes:
$ 141.8 billion

$ 68.0 billion
Elementary and secondary

$ 36.4 billion
Postsecondary education

$ 7.2 billion
Other education

$ 30.2 billion
Research

Source: From U.S. Department of Education (2006). *Digest of education statistics, 2005,* (Table 358). Available online: http://nces.ed.gov/programs/digest/d05/tables/dt05_358.asp

How Is Education Financed and Controlled by the States?

According to the Constitution, states are responsible for public education. State governments therefore exercise more influence on public education than does the federal government—and they do so in a variety of ways. Figure 8.6 shows a typical organization of public education at the state level.

The methods of influence state governments use include taxation and distribution of revenues. States also set standards for building schools, educating teachers and school administrators, and licensing school personnel. States establish the curriculum, the minimum length of the school term, attendance requirements, and requirements for school accreditation. In addition, states provide many of the other special services school districts use. Although the structure of state bureaucracies and the influence of key state officers vary, the role of state government in public education has grown through the years.

State Funding

Most of the funding for public education comes from either state or local taxes. The percentage of support the state provides to school districts, however, can vary from year to year. Of federal,

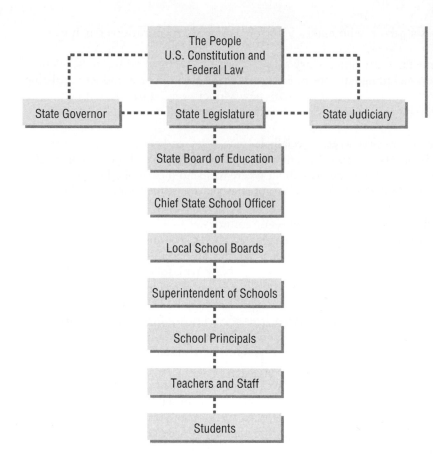

Figure 8.6
Typical Organization of Public Education at the State Level
Why are "The People" shown at the top of this figure? In what sense are the top and the bottom of this figure the same?

state, and local support, states typically provide the most funding. Localities usually provide an amount close to the state level of support, whereas federal funding supplies well under 10 percent of a school budget.

STATE SALES TAXES Most states, excluding Alaska, Delaware, Montana, New Hampshire, and Oregon, have state sales taxes. The money collected from these sales taxes provides a large portion of the funding for public schools. The five exception states receive most of their educational funds from income or property taxes. In addition to the state sales tax, some states allow localities to add their own sales taxes to items. Oneida County (outside Syracuse, New York), for example, charges 5.5 percent in addition to the New York state sales tax of 4 percent, for a total rate of 9.5 percent.

Sales taxes have great appeal because they are relatively easy and inexpensive to administer—retailers collect sales taxes at the point of sale. The state then deals directly with retailers instead of collecting money from individuals, as in the case of personal income taxes. Sales taxes are also attractive because they raise large sums of money. The more money people earn, the more they spend, and the more tax revenue collected for the state. To ease the burden on the poor and the elderly, some items, such as food and drugs, can be exempt from sales taxes. On the other hand, sales taxes on luxury items and so-called sin taxes—taxes on cigarettes and alcohol—are relatively easy to raise because most people do not object.

Sales taxes also have drawbacks, the main one being their dependence on the economy. When the economy is healthy, people buy more things and therefore pay more sales taxes. State programs that depend on sales tax revenue are well funded during these economic uptimes. When retail sales decline during an economic downtime, however, there is less money for all public services, including education. In addition, as more items become subject to taxation, people with limited incomes spend a greater percentage of their income on taxes than do wealthy people. This is referred to as **regressive taxation** (Burrup, Brimley, & Garfield, 1999).

Why do states need different ways to raise money for education?

STATE INCOME TAXES State income taxes, both personal and corporate, are another source of revenue for education. Unlike sales taxes, income taxes are a form of **progressive taxation.** That means people pay more as they earn more. For example, a person who makes $100,000 pays more income tax than does a person who makes $30,000. Likewise, corporations pay much higher taxes than do private citizens.

For most states, income taxes are a necessary source of revenue for providing the services people demand from states, including education. Every state tries to balance a budget consisting of projects that cost money and projects that make money. Money coming in rarely if ever matches money going out. The only options are raising taxes or cutting programs, and neither option satisfies everyone.

In the 1990s the battle over raising taxes, especially income taxes, and cutting services was common to most states. The problem of too much money going out and too little coming in forced state leaders everywhere to make difficult choices about where to spend their limited revenues.

STATE LOTTERIES AND OTHER SOURCES Other sources of state aid for education include estate and inheritance taxes, miscellaneous user fees, licenses, severance taxes—fees for the privilege of extracting natural resources from land or water—and lotteries.

Early attempts to establish state lotteries were complicated and largely unsuccessful. New Hampshire, a state that had neither a sales tax nor an income tax, established a state lottery in 1964 to support public education and to hold down property taxes. New York followed in 1967. Neither state raised as much money as it had expected, because the lotteries cost too much to operate. Tickets cost several dollars each, buyers had to register, and drawings were held only twice a year.

In the 1970s other states created lotteries having streamlined procedures and more frequent payoffs. Now more than three-fourths of the states and the District of Columbia have lotteries that, combined, put billions of dollars into state pockets. Only a small percentage of this money, however, goes for state aid to education.

STATE AID PLANS **Flat grants** are a type of financial aid provided by states to local communities; these grants are classified as either uniform or variable. Uniform flat grants give school districts equal amounts of money on a per student basis, regardless of district needs or financial standing. Variable flat grants try to compensate for differing classroom needs, typically giving more money to schools having more expensive services. For example, high schools with vocational programs can require more money than can elementary schools. Districts having high demands for bilingual or special education classes may also receive more aid.

In **foundation programs,** the state guarantees a certain amount of money for educational expenditures (by pupil or by classroom). In other words, the state says that a certain dollar amount will be spent on public education in a school district. It then determines what proportion of that cost should be paid for by localities. The proportion is based on the total property value of the particular locality, and it is usually expressed in terms of *mills.* (A mill is one-tenth of a cent.) If the locality cannot raise the level of funds required, the state supplies the rest of the money. In poorer communities, for example, where property taxes are low, the state contributes more money than it does in affluent communities, where taxes are high.

Per pupil expenditures are the funds allocated for education services divided by the number of pupils to be served. Think of a $1 million dollar budget that serves one thousand students. In this case, the per pupil expenditure would be $1,000. In practice, the dollar amount of per pupil expenditures can vary from state to state, as shown in Figure 8.7. Variations in the way states distribute funds to localities depend mainly on money available, demand for services, and cost of living.

Results from the 38th Annual Phi Delta Kappa/Gallup Poll indicate that lack of proper financial support for schools is the greatest problem facing schools today (Rose & Gallup, 2006). One plan for putting money to better use in schools is the **district power equalization** plan. Under this plan, localities set the tax rate to collect money for educational spending. The state guarantees an amount of money proportional to the money collected from that local tax. As in the foundation program, the state supplies the rest of the funding if the local tax revenue comes up short of the amount needed. This program does not equalize education expenditures among school districts; it merely equalizes access to funds for expenditures.

Hawaii operates as a one-school-district state and provides **full state funding** for its schools. This type of funding means the state pays all educational expenses through a statewide tax. In this plan, then, all funding is equal and all taxation is equal. In other states the desire for independence causes many districts to reject the idea of full state funding. **Why might states allocate funds in different ways?**

WA
8,297

OR
8,933

ID
6,794

MT
8,833

ND
7,700

MN
8,884

WI
10,040

MI
10,365

NY
13,906

VT
11,476

NH
9,368

ME
10,646

MA
11,749

RI
11,976

CT
11,897

NJ
13,782

DE
10,797

MD
10,317

D.C.
15,511

NV
6,838

UT
5,524

WY
10,428

SD
7,571

IA
8,361

NE
9,000

CO
8,238

KS
8,814

IL
9,798

IN
9,034

OH
9,642

WV
9,500

PA
10,155

VA
8,737

KY
8,135

MO
8,423

TN
7,025

NC
7,429

SC
8,168

CA
8,002

AZ
7,140

NM
7,501

OK
6,884

AR
7,348

MS
6,512

AL
6,992

GA
8,745

TX
8,120

LA
7,886

FL
7,286

AK
11,336

HI
9,231

*Unadjusted U.S. dollars.

Source: From Digest of education statistics, 2005, by U.S. Department of Education, 2005. Washington, DC: U.S. Government Printing Office. Available online: http://nces.ed.gov/pubsearch.

State Education Oversight

State government has the responsibility to ensure that public education truly serves its citizens. The quantity and quality of educational services vary across communities within a state, sometimes significantly. State government, therefore, oversees educational operations so that all communities receive at least the minimal level of services required to educate state residents. State government fulfills this mission by designing and implementing educational programs, monitoring resources for public education, and evaluating the results of programs.

STATE BOARDS OF EDUCATION The state board of education regulates educational practices and advises governors and state legislators about educational business. All states except Wisconsin have state boards of education. The majority of states allow governors to appoint some or all board members. Some states have two boards, one for elementary and secondary education and the other for higher education.

State board members also make decisions about textbook adoption. Adoption procedures vary from state to state, but generally a state board approves a list of textbooks from which local school districts may select. In order to receive state funds to purchase textbooks, local districts must buy from the approved list. State board members in densely populated states can influence school curricula significantly by approving some books and banning others.

Furthermore, state board members in the populous states of Texas, California, New York, and Florida shape the content of textbooks sold across the nation. States with many school students buy a lot of books, so publishers listen closely to their requests. For example, when California state board members voice concerns about the lack of multiculturalism in textbooks, textbooks soon focus more attention on multicultural life. As a result, children in less populous

Figure 8.7
Expenditure per Pupil in Average Daily Attendance in Public Elementary and Secondary Schools, by State: 2002–03
What regional trends do you identify in per pupil expenditures? What factors might account for differences?

states, such as Montana, Kansas, and Vermont, for better or worse, use textbooks designed for other states.

STATE EDUCATION DEPARTMENTS A **state education department (SED)** is an organization that carries out a state's education business. An SED may administer programs directly, for instance, schools for the deaf or blind. SEDs are directed by a state superintendent, a commissioner, or a **chief state school officer.** SEDs oversee a variety of matters, such as how well elementary and secondary schools meet curriculum guidelines and how colleges conduct teacher preparation programs.

An SED also advises the executive and legislative branches of state government on a variety of issues, including school finance. It conducts staff development programs and public relations work for itself and for other governmental and nongovernmental agencies with a stake in education. Over the years, SEDs have taken on more and more tasks. As more laws are passed and regulations established, SEDs are expected to monitor schools' compliance.

Some states are trying to alter the way their state education departments are organized and the way they do their work. Michigan and Iowa, for instance, have reduced the level of services provided at the state level and the number of employees in their state education departments.

STATE STANDARDS BOARDS Should teachers control the state standards board? States have **state standards boards,** which are commissions that regulate professional practices in education In thirteen states these boards have the final authority. In the rest of the states, they serve only in an advisory capacity to policymakers. In Alabama, for example, the State Advisory Committee on Teacher Education and Certification has about thirty members appointed by the state superintendent. As its name suggests, this committee advises state policymakers on such topics as teacher certification requirements. In contrast, standards boards in Minnesota, Nevada, Kentucky, West Virginia, and North Dakota have final authority concerning certification, entry, and exit standards for teachers. In these states teachers themselves make up a majority of the standards board members.

The National Education Association and other teachers groups have encouraged the creation of state standards boards. They believe standards boards help create and promote a concept of professionalism for teachers. Advocates also believe teachers should be the ones who serve on standards boards. Not until teachers control the state policy-making system, it is argued, will they be able to control their own professional destiny. State standards boards are likely to help shape definitions of the "highly qualified teacher" as called for in No Child Left Behind.

GOVERNORS' INFLUENCE Historically, governors have relied on their appointees to formulate and implement educational policy. Only in the past fifteen to twenty years have governors themselves become personally involved in state education issues.

The **Council of Chief State School Officers** is an informal organization for the leaders of state departments of elementary and secondary education across the United States and its jurisdictions. The council provides a forum for education leaders to discuss their mutual ideas and concerns. The council also sponsors a series of special programs (international education, technology, national teacher of the year, etc.), a resource center on educational equity, and a state education assessment center. These programs and activities, plus an electronic network, provide opportunities for communication among leaders of state systems of public education.

In recent years governors themselves have become major participants in education reform through the **National Governors' Association (NGA).** Founded in 1908, the NGA is a coalition of state chief executives. Many governors have come to believe that good education makes good politics. The problems in education are so challenging and so related to other areas of society that real reform demands strong, visible leadership from the very top of state government. The NGA offers governors the opportunity to influence education not only in their respective states but nationwide.

Cooperation among School Districts

Some educational services are so expensive, and both human and material resources so limited, that districts must band together to provide them. These cooperative efforts are run by facilities most often called **intermediate educational units (IEUs),** educational service agencies (ESAs), or boards of cooperative educational services (BOCESs). For example, every high school in a state cannot provide the kind of vocational training that students need to be competitive in the job market. To meet their students' needs, several districts may join together to construct and maintain a technical training center.

About three-fourths of all states mandate and provide support for special cooperative facilities, or units, between the state and local levels. These units further concentrate resources and support to provide high-level care that many schools could not supply on their own. Special education services, particularly for children with severe and multiple disabilities, represent opportunities for such interdistrict cooperation or even for statewide cooperation.

Sometimes school districts cooperate with organizational units besides other school districts. They do so to increase their power, to reduce uncertainty, to increase performance by ensuring a steady flow of resources, and to protect themselves. On a day-to-day level, they share information, people, funds, and equipment. For example, some schools contract with state and federal governments, universities, and private corporations to conduct research and to operate innovative educational projects. Head Start and Follow Through projects are examples of such cooperative arrangements. **Why might vocational programs and advanced placement courses be located in IEUs?**

How Are Schools Financed and Managed at the Local Level?

Schools' personalities reflect the characters of the communities they serve. Some are dull and complacent; others are full of energy and hopefulness. Citizen participation in educational matters is apparent at a variety of events—school board meetings, gatherings of parent–teacher organizations, and high school sporting events. People affect the schools, and the schools, in turn, influence citizens both inside and outside their walls.

The local level is often the best place to observe how money and personalities interact to produce a unique mix of educational practices. In some communities the balance of power rests with a small number of people. At other times in other places, several groups compete to influence the focus and flow of educational policy. Power struggles on the local level can be particularly intense, because the people involved are concerned with the very schools where they teach and send their children. It is public education on the most personal level.

Property Taxes

In most states **local property taxes** on property almost exclusively provide the portion of school funding that localities must supply. There are two kinds of property, real and personal. **Real property** is not readily movable; it includes land, buildings, and improvements. **Personal property** is movable; it consists of machinery, livestock, crops, and automobiles, as well as money, stocks, and bonds. A community's ability to pay for education depends on the assessed value of its property. The local tax rate is a calculation of a community's total property value and the amount of money needed to fund the community budget. The citizens who own property within the community are then responsible for paying local taxes.

Using property taxes as a source of support for public schools is a widely criticized procedure (Burrup, Brimley, & Garfield, 1999). One criticism is homeowners pay an unfairly large amount of the cost for funding education. A homeowner not only pays tax on the land he owns, but on the house as well. Residents living in apartments, on the other hand, pay no taxes of this kind. Another criticism is property assessment procedures are not uniform among communities, thereby creating taxpayer inequities. These and other problems create differences in property tax revenue that ultimately lead to educational inequalities among schools.

Although property taxes often are referred to as "school taxes," in truth the money is used to meet needs other than educational ones. Property taxes also pay for community road maintenance, ambulance and police services, and libraries. This fact may be more problematic in some areas than in others. It can be especially problematic in cities where tax-exempt property (e.g., public buildings, churches, government property, and parks) is a large portion of the total city property. Cities, particularly those in high-crime areas, face many expenses that suburbs either do not face or face on a more modest scale. The result is less money is available to fund city schools.

Cities often provide services paid for with property taxes to people who work in the city but live in the suburbs. When it snows, for example, the city must plow the streets so people can get to work. Workers who live in the suburbs benefit from the plowing of city streets, even though they do not support this activity with their own property taxes. Although snow removal benefits many people, it uses up money that could be earmarked for inner-city schools.

Rural districts, too, may face considerable financial hardship by depending on property taxes to fund schools as well as other services. The main cause of rural hardship is higher per pupil costs. When a rural district builds a new school, for instance, relatively few taxpayers share the cost of the building. To ease such inequities and the burden on property taxes, the trend in recent years has been to replace declining local revenues with state aid. **Should property taxes be abandoned as a way to fund education?**

Local School Boards

Would you ever consider running for a seat on a local school board? The **local school board** is one of the most common, visible examples of democracy in action. School boards are bodies of elected or appointed public servants responsible for providing advice and consent on the operation of public schools. Because overseeing education is a power reserved to the states, local school boards are agents of the states.

The local school board is generally recognized as the policy-making body for public schools. In action, this means school board members have the right to establish schools, select the board's executive officer (the local superintendent of schools), set rules to ensure the smooth running of schools, and spend tax dollars as they see fit.

Like all public representatives, school board members try to interpret the public will, as well as exercise their own personal judgment, in governing the public education system. On some issues, board members and the people they represent are out of tune with one another. A poll conducted for the National School Boards Foundation revealed some points of tension between school boards and their constituents:

> While more than two-thirds of school board members gave their local schools an A or B for overall performance, less than half the general public did so. Three-quarters of school board members said their teachers and principals were doing a good or excellent job. Among the public at large, just 43 percent rated principals that highly, while 54 percent gave teachers similar votes of confidence. More than eight in ten board members said their districts were doing a good or excellent job in combating violence and drugs, but only a third of the public agreed. (Hendrie, 1999, p. 9)

When there is tension between school board members and their constituents, dissatisfaction can result in the limitation of the board's power. In some instances, the concept of local school boards has been abandoned altogether. In Chicago, advocacy groups lobbied successfully for the establishment of popularly elected councils of citizens, parents, and teachers for each school. These councils were given the right to select principals and to decide how discretionary funds should be spent. In New Jersey, community dissatisfaction with the quality of public school education took a different route. In this case, the state took over control of the Jersey City and Paterson school districts.

School District Budgets

The best way to understand local finance of public schools is to study a school district budget. Most school boards control both the staffing of local schools and the types of programs offered to students. In this sense, the budget represents a concrete statement of local values.

Technology in Practice

HOW DO SCHOOLS' EXPENDITURES AND REVENUES COMPARE?

To understand if schools have too much money, not enough, or just about what they need to educate students, school administrators often try to "balance" their budgets with expenditures of other similar districts. In other words, many believe that it is politically wise to propose budgets that are similar to their peers' budgets.

The availability of online databases makes the task of comparing one's own educational spending to the spending of one's neighbors a simple process. Go to the Education Finance Statistics Center online at the National Center for Education Statistics http://nces.ed.gov/edfin/). There you will find a link called "Public School District Finance Peer Search." When you click on the link, you will be asked to supply a district name. The site supplies a peer group for this district according to the total number of students, student–teacher ratio, median household income, and other factors. You might supply the name of the district where you went to high school. (No need to enter the state name; the program gives you a choice if there are multiple districts with the same name.)

When you choose to do a "standard" search, you will see your district compared to its peers by per pupil expenditures. You will also find comparisons of student–teacher ratio, administrative expenditures, sources of revenue, and other information. The screen capture on the right is an example of what you can expect to see.

This exercise is especially useful if you are thinking as school leaders must think. But if you are thinking like a teacher looking for a job, you might also use this website to sharpen your search techniques. For instance, once you identify your target district and its peers, it is

possible to find the starting salaries of these educational systems.

Questions for Reflection: Imagine for a moment that you value a certain type of community as a good place to teach, but the starting salaries are quite different among many communities. How will you decide which place is best for you? What other factors will you consider? Will the diversity of the community be an issue? Will the geographical location of the job matter? Will your access to further higher education be important?

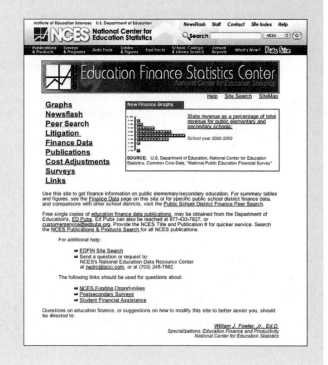

School districts develop long-term financial plans that represent predictions about the future. They predict such things as the cost of new textbooks, money needed for building maintenance, transportation costs, and so on. District employees craft a new budget for each **fiscal year**—a twelve-month period covered by the annual budget, often corresponding with the state's fiscal year (e.g., July 1 to June 30). Once an annual budget is adopted by local officials or approved by the voters, it guides school administrators' actions. Budgets also help administrators know how much money they will need and receive from various sources, including state money and local taxes. These factors, of course, are key to determining how the school will operate in the coming year. In short, the school budget outlines where funding is coming from, what it will be used for, and what services will be provided.

So who creates school budgets, and how are they set in place? In most localities the budget-adoption process involves a number of steps (U.S. Department of Education, 2001):

1. District administrators led by the superintendent analyze needs and costs, set policies for the coming year, and plan an initial draft of the budget.
2. District administrators discuss this draft with the school board in one or more meetings.

3. District administrators make the proposed budget available for public study.
4. The school board holds one or more public hearings, at which they receive comments from citizens about the proposed budget.
5. The school board adopts an official budget based on the proposed budget, but with any amendments it believes necessary.
6. In some districts the school board vote is the final decision. In other districts the budget must then be approved by elected officials or by voter referendum.
7. A budget that has received final approval takes effect in the district.

In areas where site-based management (discussed later in this chapter) is the norm, people are experimenting with **school-based budgeting** or site-based budgeting. This concept puts the responsibility for budgeting resources at the level of the individual building, rather than at the level of central administration. In other words, each school's teachers, parents, and principals make decisions about how money is spent on hiring staff, professional development, and goods and services. To be effective, school-based budgeting requires that the principal and other staff members know students well enough to match available resources to students' needs (Burrup et al., 1999).

Negotiation is key to crafting and adopting school budgets that are acceptable to everyone. Many people (taxpayers, teachers, administrators, and special-interest groups) have a stake in where the money to run schools comes from and where it goes. A school budget, then, is a political document formed from compromise. At its core it should provide adequately for the educational needs of the school district's constituents. Whose values and needs should a school budget represent?

When presenting their next year's budgets, school officials sometimes justify only the increase over the previous year's request. In these cases, the amount the school district is spending is usually accepted as necessary. Some schools, however, must make a case for their entire financial request each year. This is referred to as **zero-base budgeting** because each year program budgets start at zero, rather than at the amount they received the previous year (Pyhrr, 1973).

Whether they are starting from scratch or building on the previous year's budget, most school districts use line-item budgets to explain their financial plans. These budgets include a beginning balance for the year, estimates of revenue by source, planned expenditures, and a projected balance at the end of the year. Sources of revenue may include moneys from federal, state, county or parish, and city government levels; income from local taxes or from the sale of bonds; payments of fees for meals and for use of sports facilities; and private donations expected during the year. Income often is set aside for use with specific groups of students (e.g., students with disabilities) or special programs (e.g., library support or school nurse).

Planned expenditures represent the most detailed portion of a school budget. As illustrated in Table 8.1, a school system can have a number of educational expenditures. Generally, districts categorize expenses in one of two ways. *Functions* are broad categories of purposes, such as instruction and support; *objects* are specific things to be paid for, such as personnel salaries and benefits.

Salaries and benefits for both instructional and noninstructional staff claim the largest portion of any school budget. For this reason, and because they are visible in the budget, salaries often become sources of irritation in communities across the country.

Even with all the work and careful planning administrators put into building a budget, the fact that one has been approved does not mean the numbers are firmly established. In reality, spending can change for a number of reasons: enrollment figures may be higher or lower than projected, unexpected weather may affect utility bills, and unforeseen events (e.g., flooding of a school gymnasium during a heavy rain) can require emergency maintenance. School administrators sometimes have the authority to transfer dollars from one line item to another to take care of unforeseen needs. In other districts, administrators must consult with the school board before making changes. When budget changes are made, however, federal regulations prohibit the removal of money from federal grants designed to benefit specific groups of students or programs.

Table 8.1

HYPOTHETICAL, ACTUAL, AND PROPOSED SCHOOL BUDGET ITEMS

	Fiscal Year 2008, Proposed Budget	Fiscal Year 2007, Actual Budget
Instruction		
Salaries	3,466,867.8	3,194,956.6
Benefits	271,911.2	271,911.2
Purchased services	67,977.8	67,977.8
Supplies	135,955.6	203,933.4
Property	407,866.8	407,866.8
Total Instruction	4,350,579.2	4,146,645.8
Support		
Salaries	1,495,511.6	1,223,600.4
Benefits	135,955.6	135,955.6
Purchased services	203,993.4	67,977.8
Supplies	135,955.6	203,993.4
Property	203,993.4	135,955.6
Total support	2,175,289.6	1,767,422.8
Noninstructional services		
Salaries	67,977.8	135,955.6
Benefits	6,797.78	13,595.56
Supplies	20,393.34	40,786.68
Property	54,382.24	67,977.8
Total noninstructional	149,551.16	258,315.64
Facilities		
Salaries	203,933.4	163,146.72
Benefits	20,393.34	16,314.46
Supplies	271,911.2	163,146.72
Property	183,540.06	65,258.9
Total facilities	679,778	407,866.8
Total expenditures	7,355,197.9	658,025.1

Source: Adapted from *Making sense of school budgets* (p. 15) by U.S. Department of Education, 2001, Washington, DC: Office of Educational Research and Improvement.

How Are Governance and Funding Related to Educational Success?

Public education uses public funds to provide educational opportunities for all children, regardless of their home circumstances. Funds relate directly to educational opportunities; that is, money can buy equipment, materials, and experiences. But the relationship between funds and learning that is measured by standardized achievement tests resists simple explanation.

Two separate researchers set out to prove just what the relationship is between how much money a school has and test scores. Eric Hanushek (1989) reviewed thirty-eight research studies and concluded there is no systematic relationship or direct connection between school expenditures and student performance. In contrast, Larry Hedges and his colleagues (Hedges, Laine, & Greenvals, 1994) reviewed the same studies using a different method and found that higher expenditures do improve school outcomes. Who is right? According to Michael Sadowski (1995), given the methods they used, both Hanushek and Hedges are right.

So perhaps the more important question is: What do schools do with the money they have? When schools use money to reduce class size so educators can change how they offer instruction, there are remarkable gains in student learning. In contrast, when decision makers simply reduce class size but fail to adopt new curricula and methods, more money has little effect on student performance.

How might this community support its schools? Why might this community have less money for education than other nearby communities or municipalities? Would funding relate to how well the students do? What measures might work to reduce disparities in funding from one school district to the next?

Unfortunately, more money is not always available. Debt and economic blues during the 1990s and into the new century have halted much of the educational reform begun in the 1980s. Many states have experimented with a wide range of programs and organizational setups in hopes of getting the most out of the money they spent on public education. These programs include site-based management, high-tech classrooms, career ladders for teachers, professional development schools, better and longer educational programs for teachers, innovative curricula, restructured school calendars, and new testing of both students and teachers.

But innovations can be expensive too. Sometimes the political courage to stick with these new ideas long enough to determine their worth is difficult to come by. Many policymakers got nervous in the 1990s, as states faced budget problems and the public demanded results. They wanted "hard evidence"—test scores—that demonstrated that the money spent on education was not being wasted. If teachers and students did not produce, why spend more money on people and systems that were failing?

Some critics, however, take issue with the belief that schools are failing and that funding for education is not connected to success. They argue that people interpret test results incorrectly to suggest that student performance and educational quality are declining. Moreover, they argue that test results fail to represent the real accomplishments of schools (Berliner & Biddle, 1995; Bracey, 1991; Johnson, 2008; Verstegen & McGuire, 1991).

Furthermore, statistics show that states spending the most on education consistently have many more students seeking college admission than states spending less money. Given the mission of public education in America—to accept and educate any and all students who desire an education—schools do a remarkable job.

The Issue of Funding Equity

People make trade-offs when education dollars are limited. Sometimes the trade-offs exist as choices between educational fairness, or equity, and educational excellence. Some people believe that efforts to promote educational excellence will leave behind poor and minority-group students. Others argue that money spent on equalizing programs and opportunities for all students would be put to better use capitalizing on the strengths of outstanding students. Allan Odden (1984) contended that such choices are ill-conceived, however, because there are more connections between excellence and equity than many realize:

> On economic grounds, the simultaneous pursuit of excellence and equity is mandatory. If our national strategy for maintaining a competitive edge in the international market is to increase the per capita productivity of the U.S. work force, then all U.S. workers must have better-developed skills than their counterparts in other countries. (p. 316)

Although the various state funding formulas are intended to provide some standardization of educational quality among communities, they are unable to do so completely. For example, more affluent school districts can support high levels of education without much assistance from the state. Quite often, these districts are reluctant to support increased state taxes that would benefit other districts. Nor do such communities want to give up control of their ability to collect local taxes. Doing so would potentially reduce their ability to maintain a position of privilege (Ward, 1992).

In some parts of the country, inequalities in available funds are so great that districts poor in property have had to tax themselves three or four times as heavily as rich districts to raise revenue for their schools. On the average, however, high-poverty districts receive much more of their revenue from state and federal sources than do low-poverty districts.

Adding to the general expenses of running schools, expensive items—school buildings and their repair—can be incredible financial burdens. This is especially true in urban and rural districts where the properties and buildings (infrastructure) suffer from years of neglect. Incidentally, these are the same schools that may have less money available for such expenses.

Educational revenue inequities are not a new development; the issue goes back many years. In the 1960s people thought that inequities in school finance might be corrected by taking the issue to the courts. The landmark 1971 case of *Serrano* v. *Priest* was the first case filed in state court (California) to declare unconstitutional a state public school finance system based on taxable wealth. By focusing on the link between educational expenditures and district property wealth, this case challenged school district spending inequities across the nation.

In *San Antonio Independent School District* v. *Rodriguez* (1973), a federal district court ruled that the school finance system of San Antonio, Texas, violated the equal protection clause of the Fourteenth Amendment. The amendment applied because large disparities in school district expenditures existed across the state. The U.S. Supreme Court, however, ruled that education was not a fundamental right under the Constitution and was therefore not protected by the Fourteenth Amendment. This decision was a major setback for those who sought to reform school finance.

In 1989 three landmark school finance reform cases—in Montana, Kentucky, and Texas—invalidated school finance systems because funding disparities had grown dramatically. In part, these cases say that the right to education is fundamental or of extreme importance under state constitutions. This assertion could mean that states have a responsibility to ensure some measure of financial equality for public schools within their borders. These cases may eventually serve as the basis for a revolution in school finance reform. **How might funding equity be achieved?**

The No Child Left Behind Act has focused people on data-driven decision making and provided the means to compare school districts on productivity. New data on pupil learning are revealing where children have adequate and inadequate resources for learning—that is, where children's performance scores do and do not suffer as a result of funding. In half of the states, the highest-poverty school districts received less money from states per student than the lowest-poverty districts (see Figure 8.8).

The Issue of School Choice

Will school choice weaken or strengthen public schools? School choice is the right of parents to choose the schools their children attend. Instead of being limited to the local public school, some parents prefer to send their children to parochial, vocational, or other types of alternative schools, as discussed in Chapter 7. Some people believe school choice should be common practice and argue that competition among schools would improve the overall public school system (Cooper & Randall, 2008). Opponents say school choice would destroy the concept of a public education system in which children of diverse backgrounds live and learn together.

Parents who choose the schools their children attend do so for several reasons, the primary one being academics. The second most important reason that parents list is convenience. Among those who select a private school, the second most important reason is religious preferences.

People who oppose concepts of school choice cite many reasons for their position. They believe that, if citizens can choose where to send their children to school, schools will become

Figure 8.8
Top Five Funding Gaps in
2001–2002
Gap between revenues available
per student in the highest- and
lowest-poverty districts within
states

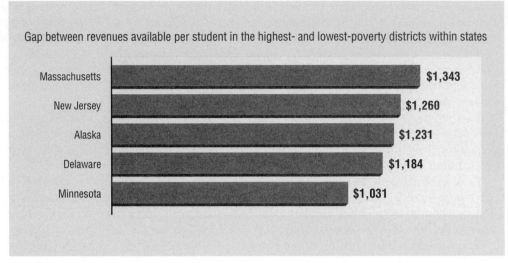

Gap between revenues available per student in the highest- and lowest-poverty districts within states

Massachusetts	$1,343
New Jersey	$1,260
Alaska	$1,231
Delaware	$1,184
Minnesota	$1,031

Source: National Household Education Survey (cited in *Education Vital Signs 2005,* © 2005 NSBA). Arlington, VA. National School Boards Association, p. 25.

racially segregated. At the very least, gains made by students who attend private schools will exacerbate class distinctions. A central purpose of public education is to prepare people to participate in our democracy, they argue, and school choice will prevent this from happening. Also, children who most need their parents' involvement in order to make wise choices will be least likely to get it. Others point out that the money available for most "choice" schools is far below what they actually cost. Therefore, the only people who will benefit are children of wealthy individuals who can pay the extra costs.

Historically, paying for private schooling has been a private matter. If parents wanted their children to be educated in a certain manner, to be taught particular values, and to associate with certain other children, they paid for these privileges out of their own pockets. Those who could afford to send their children to private schools continued to pay their taxes, which in turn supported public schools.

While some private schools have developed and maintained their reputations by appealing to wealthy families, others have attracted people from across the socioeconomic spectrum. The largest alternative school system in the United States, the Catholic schools, teaches high- and low-income students. Catholic schools may offer scholarships and tuition breaks to encourage students from low-income families to attend. Other types of private schools, both religious and secular, may offer similar enticements. Many parents, even those who could least afford to do so, have been willing to sacrifice economically to send their children to private schools.

Recently the debate about public support for private elementary and secondary schools has reenergized. Now part of the debate focuses on possible methods of enacting school choice plans. One of the most widely explored methods is the school **voucher,** an idea first offered in 1955 by economist Milton Friedman. He argued that local governments ought to create vouchers, or certificates, that provided parents with a sum of money to pay for each of their children's education. Parents would be free to spend this money at any school they chose, as long as it met minimum governmental standards.

Another way to set up and pay for school choice programs involves a **tuition tax credit.** This method allows taxpayers to subtract educational costs from the amount of taxes they owe. Similarly, a **tuition tax deduction** allows taxpayers to subtract educational costs from their incomes before taxes are calculated. Tax credits and tax deductions resemble vouchers in that they all are designed to give parents at least part of the money they will spend on private schooling for their children. Opponents contend that tax credits and deductions may encourage people to abandon public schools. They fear the public school system will serve only low-income families, who cannot afford to pay up front for the cost of education and wait to receive a deduction later. In addition, public schools would receive less taxpayer support, and the quality of education would decrease considerably.

The use of tuition tax credits, deductions, and vouchers must meet with state approval. When states adopt new funding mechanisms, they cannot conflict with federal law. For example, if a proposed plan denied certain people their civil rights, federal courts would rule the plan unconstitutional. Issues of the separation of church and state have been particularly confusing when it comes to school choice. In short, there is debate about whether allowing public funds to be spent on private schools violates the separation of church and state. For example, if a family decides to use its vouchers to send its children to Catholic school, is that line of separation crossed? This issue will continue to make private schools a focus of public interest and court scrutiny.

In June 2002 the U.S. Supreme Court ruled that the state-enacted school voucher program in Cleveland, Ohio, does not violate the U.S. Constitution. The program provides benefits to people defined only by financial need and residence in a particular school district. It allows individuals to exercise choice among public and private schools that are either secular or religious. The ruling ensures that some 3,700 students can continue attending private, mostly religiously affiliated schools at taxpayer expense (Walsh, 2002). It remains to be seen whether this is a one-time decision or an indication of how courts will rule on this topic in the years to come.

The Issue of Site-Based Management

Principals lead **site-based** or school-based **management teams** composed of teachers and parents—and sometimes students. The belief is that people closest to a school best understand the school culture and have the biggest stake in its outcomes. Therefore, these are the people who should share responsibility for student learning and school decision making (Darling-Hammond & McLaughlin, 1995).

Who could argue with the idea of involving in the formation of educational policies those affected by such policies? The nation's historical commitment to the common school has meant that public education should serve all the people by involving all the people. Site-based management, then, has historical precedent and seems to make sense. But what appears reasonable in theory does not necessarily translate smoothly into practice (Holloway, 2000). Moreover, certain reform efforts, such as those aimed at professionalizing education, tend to conflict with group or team decision making. Some educators believe that people working outside the public education system do not have enough training to make decisions that will affect children's educational experiences. **Why might teachers not want to participate in site-based management?**

Like other educational innovations, site-based management must overcome a number of obstacles to succeed. One of the biggest obstacles is inertia. When people are used to behaving in certain ways, it is difficult to change these patterns. For instance, teachers often resist decisions that require them to make drastic changes in the way they teach. Moreover, teachers must be convinced that reform is permanent and real, and not simply this year's trend. They need to be convinced that they can exert power over events and decisions if they are to participate enthusiastically.

Summary

A layer of control and oversight exists in public education that is not readily apparent to the untrained eye. Government at the federal, state, and local levels shapes the activities of schooling, the behaviors of leaders, and ultimately the lives of teachers and their students.

Federal funding to elementary and secondary schools, small in relation to state and local funding, comes with requirements. Increasingly, these have been translated into a national agenda for public schooling. Both incentives and sanctions exist that can be used to enhance educational performance.

Case Perspectives

Think back to the case that opened this chapter. The following comments are designed to provide a context for your thinking about that case.

A LOCAL SCIENTIST TRIES TO HELP BILL UNDERSTAND THE DEBATE ON INTELLIGENT DESIGN   I do not know a reputable scientist who denies the validity of evolution. There is no question that recent events such as the Santorum Amendment have stirred the philosophical pot, but evolution is a well-regarded scientific theory. You might say that Darwin took an evolutionary leap forward when he promulgated the theory.

The scientific community is not concerned about attacks on the science of evolution, but it is gravely concerned about the effect that the Santorum Amendment and other like-minded efforts may have on science curriculum in schools. They believe that intelligent design advocates weaken curricula by suggesting that evolution is questionable. Evolution does not have all the answers. No science claims all knowledge. But that is not to say that the scientific community is willing to fill in the gaps with supernatural explanation. Quite the contrary. Scientists condemn efforts to attack evolution theory as a means to affirm the reality of God. Simply because evolution theory leaves room for doubt does not mean that the unexplained can be attributed to God. Intelligent design, scientists argue, is a misguided attempt to insert creationism into the curriculum. The notion of countering our ignorance of the universe with faith instead of relying on scientific method is unacceptable to a scientist.

A MEMBER OF THE INTELLIGENT DESIGN COALITION STATES THE ORGANIZATION'S BELIEFS   There is more evidence for intelligent design than there is for evolution. I am not arguing that we know who the intelligent designer is, just that such design is prevalent in nature.

It is a complex world out there. Somebody or something has had a hand in it. There are bacteria, for instance, that contain various components to function. It is incredibly unlikely that these bacteria could have evolved gradually as neo-Darwinian theory suggests.

The existence of patterns in the universe such as nonrandom radio waves in space also suggest the presence of a designer. William A. Dembski, noted expert on intelligent design, suggests that scientists seeking extraterrestrial intelligence have sophisticated techniques for eliminating chance in the search for complex, sequenced patterns of radio waves from outer space. These patterns exhibit intelligence in their design. See what Dembski said in a piece he wrote that appears on the World Wide Web:

> For instance, how do the radio astronomers in *Contact* (the Jodie Foster movie based on Carl Sagan's novel of the same name) infer the presence of extraterrestrial intelligence in the beeps and pauses they monitor from space? The researchers run signals through computers that are programmed to recognize many preset patterns. Signals that do not match any of the patterns pass through the "sieve" and are classified as random. After years of receiving apparently meaningless "radom" signals, the researchers discover a pattern of beats and pauses that corresponds to the sequence of all the prime numbers between 2 and 101. (Prime numbers, of course, are those that are divisible only by themselves and by one.) When a sequence begins with 2 beats, then a pause, 3 beats, then a pause . . . and continues all the way to 101 beats, the researchers must infer the presence of an extraterrestrial intelligence. (Dembski, undated)

You should also know that the president of the United States agrees with me. Please don't misunderstand. I'm not arguing that President George W. Bush is a scientist, but he has the best scientists at his disposal, and he advocates the inclusion of intelligent design in school curricula. When he was questioned by reporters, President Bush said he thought schools should discuss intelligent design as one approach to advancing students' knowledge. On various occasions he has advocated exposing students to different schools of thought about the creation of life.

Questions for Reflection: What do you think Bill's role should be in negotiating the potential situation described here? What are his obligations to his training as a scientist? To the feelings of his community and the decisions of his school board? To the members of his department? What might he do to help his district and school board better understand the underlying issues? What questions should he be asking? ◼

States and localities, too, have increased expectations for teacher and student performance. They also have multiple ways to raise money in support of public education. What individual schools and school districts cannot do alone, they often try to accomplish by sharing resources and collaborating on services.

School leaders must contend with these disparate forces and conflicting demands. Who are the pressure groups that want to influence education policy and practice? Who will decide what is best for all the people in a community, and how will those decisions be made? Teachers, by the nature of their jobs, have an important say in these matters. The more they know about governance, finance, and leadership, the more likely they are to maximize their abilities to work successfully within the system they inhabit.

TERMS AND CONCEPTS

block grant
categorical grant
chief state school officer
Council of Chief State School Officers
district power equalization
Education Consolidation and Improvement Act (ECIA)
fiscal year
flat grant
foundation program
full state funding
intermediate educational unit (IEU)
local property taxes
local school board
National Center for Education Statistics (NCES)
National Governors Association (NGA)
National Parent–Teacher Association (PTA)

per pupil expenditure
personal property
progressive taxation
real property
regressive taxation
school-based budgeting
school choice
school governance
site-based management teams
special-interest group
state board of education
state education department (SED)
state standards board
tuition tax credit
tuition tax deduction
voucher
zero-base budgeting

REFLECTIVE ACTIVITY: SCHOOL BOARD MEMBERSHIP

Reflective practice is an essential part of good teaching. Reflection is a process that includes making thoughtful decisions, understanding and articulating value structures, acting from knowledge, evaluating your actions and their effects, and sharing your reflections with colleagues. After reading the following scenario, respond to the questions below. The scenario reflects the INTASC Principle and Disposition at the end of this activity.

There is nothing quite like a school board election to focus public attention, especially when the most pressing issue is money. That is just what Eileen Bracey learned when she ran and won a seat on her local board. Eileen's children were grown and out of school—a school system she, her husband, and her children loved dearly. She felt just as passionately about the schools as she did when her daughter and son were there. Now that she had more time to devote to public service, she looked forward to helping the community protect educational quality.

However, Eileen also believed the schools wasted money, and she ran for office on that premise. School enrollment had declined while the staff had increased. The administration poured incredible resources into remodeling old buildings that really were not needed. She realized that her neighbors had grown older and were worried about educational costs. They watched young parents speak convincingly about the need to "invest in youth," while they witnessed a steady decline in the stock market that depressed the value of their savings.

Would Eileen have to resist all efforts to raise funds for education—increasing property taxes, lobbying for a sales tax hike, fighting for a larger share of the lottery proceeds, reassessing property values (which would automatically raise taxes), and any other plan that came down the pike—or could she possibly find some way to balance the need for material support with the need to hold the line on spending? Eileen's reelection and the political fate of her colleagues on the board depended on charting a course of reason and sticking to it.

Decide 1. What problems and opportunities do Eileen Bracey and her fellow board members face?

Perceive and Value 2. If you were a young parent in this district, why might you be willing to support any attempt to raise additional funds for the schools? If you were a retired person, why might you oppose any such attempt? If you were a beginning teacher in this school system and Eileen Bracey asked you what to do, what kind of advice might you give her?

Know and Act   3. What kinds of ideas might the board explore for saving money? What are the pros and cons of these strategies? How might they build public support for "smarter education," that is, education that protected or enhanced the quality of teaching and learning while holding down costs?

Evaluate   4. How might Eileen know if she were successful in her attempt to be a good board member?

Discuss   5. What more would you like to know about the school and the community to better understand the district's issues related to quality and funding?

INTASC Principle 10

The teacher fosters relationships with school colleagues, parents, and agencies in the larger community to support students' learning and well-being.

Disposition

The teacher understands schools as organizations within the larger community context and understands the operations of the relevant aspects of the system(s) within which she or he works. (Interstate New Teacher Assessment and Support Consortium, 1992)

ADDITIONAL READINGS

Hanushek, E., & D. W. Jorgenson (Eds.). (1996). *Improving America's schools: The role of incentives.* Washington, DC: National Academy Press.

Hess, F. (2004). *Common sense school reform.* New York: Palgrave Macmillan.

Hoy, W. K., & Miskel, C. G. (2004). *Educational administration: Theory, research, and practice* (7th ed.). New York: McGraw-Hill.

King, R. A., Swanson, A. D., & Sweetland, S. R. (2003). *School finance: Achieving high standards* (3rd ed.). Boston: Allyn & Bacon.

LeLoup, L., & Schull, S. A. (2003). *The President and Congress: Collaboration and combat in national policymaking* (2nd ed.). Boston: Allyn & Bacon.

Sharp, W. L, & Walter, J. K. (2004). *The school superintendent: The profession and the person* (2nd ed.). Lanham, MD: Rowman and Littlefield Education.

WEB RESOURCES

www.aclu.org/
Visit the website for the American Civil Liberties Union to learn more about the educational issues they believe are important.

www.naacp.org/
The website for the National Association for the Advancement of Colored People provides information about efforts to ensure quality education for all people.

www.aasa.org/
See the website of the American Association of School Administrators to learn more about educational issues through the eyes of school leaders.

www.pta.org/
Learn about what the 6.5 million members of the National Parent–Teacher Association are doing to support children and teachers.

www.census.gov/govs/www/school.html
The U.S. Census Bureau provides education finance data for elementary and secondary public schools in all states and the District of Columbia.

www.ccsso.org/
The council of Chief State School Officers view schools from a state perspective.

The Influence of the Law

Case Study: To Catch a Thief

"In hindsight, I may have gotten a bit carried away," said Richard Brautigan, first-year teacher and football coach, to Jackson Wellingham, his principal. "But when Matt Wiggins told me somebody stole $1,200 from his locker, I was dumbfounded. I couldn't imagine Matt having $1,200 in the first place. What is he, a drug dealer? And there was only one real possibility. It had to be one of three guys on the team—Phillip, Mahool, or Mike. They were the only people around when Matt's locker was open. So I made those guys strip and prove they didn't have the money. I figured if they didn't have it, they were off the hook, and it was no sweat. They'd be glad to help catch the guy who did it. Heck, they'd even get some credit for it. How was I to know that none of those guys would have it?"

Principal Wellingham listened intently to Brautigan. As he restrained himself from yelling "You fool!" he had to admit to himself that the young teacher actually made some sense—$1,200 was a lot of money, and if the search had found it, Brautigan would have been a hero. "But a *strip*-search?" Wellingham said out loud. As the words echoed, both men realized how ridiculous—and offensive—the whole idea sounded. Even if Brautigan were right, there was bound to be trouble.

Wellingham continued, "I know there are times when we can take extreme measures, but I'm just not sure this was one of them. I think we'd better check with central office fast and get some advice. There's already a message on my desk saying Mahool's parents want to meet with me this afternoon, and I'll bet Phillip's and Mike's won't be far behind. Both you and I had better have some sense of what the law says about these things—and we'd better be clear on why this happened."

Schools work, in part, because we agree collectively there must be rules that govern educational life. These rules or laws help people find answers to educational problems. This chapter explores such problems and suggests how court cases have evolved into our present legal system in which people share rights and responsibilities for schooling.

How Does Government Influence Education?

How does government influence education? Choose your answer to this question from one of the following responses: (1) slowly, (2) with haste, (3) minimally if at all, (4) profoundly, or (5) all the above. The astute observer will probably argue that the correct answer depends on the definitions of government, influence, and maybe education, too. To best answer this question, then, one must consider exactly what these terms mean.

Government is organized into federal, state, and local units. The constitutional authority for making educational decisions belongs to the states. They, in turn, encourage localities to assume much responsibility for operating schools. The federal government, however, can and does exert powerful influence on schooling. The U.S. Congress and state legislatures pass laws meant to stop inappropriate behavior in schools and to encourage all that is good about teaching and learning. The chief executives (the president and the governors) must enforce these laws. And both federal and state courts interpret the laws when disagreements arise.

In one of its many functions, government decides who should go to school, how a school building is constructed, how children travel to and from school, what subjects they take, what they eat for lunch and when they eat it, who teaches the children, how, if, and when they progress, and so forth. *Government*, then, can be defined by its organizational structure and by the functions it performs. (See the Democracy Project at http://pbskids.org/democracy/mygovt/school.html/.)

The term *influence* is probably best measured on a scale from little or none to strong or profound. Legislation that concerns funding for educational programs may be the easiest way to think about governmental influence. Here, influence can be defined in terms of dollars and power. That is, the more dollars, the more likely the influence will be strong. Furthermore, those who supply the money have the power. In truth, however, more money buys more *potential* influence, but not necessarily actual educational power. Real influence depends on how the money is spent.

Governmental influence on education can also be defined in other ways. For instance, the president of the United States and the governors of the fifty states support a set of national standards for education. They encourage local schools to adopt these standards, because they believe these standards for world-class education will benefit the economy. The cycle continues with Congress and state legislatures. They regulate the development and use of tests meant to assess teachers' and students' success in meeting these standards. City and town councils and local school boards then look to school employees to deliver satisfactory test results. In this example, influence might be defined in terms of the resources that go into the activities of these governmental officials, the activities in which they engage, and the results of their work. All are difficult and costly to measure with any precision.

The term *education* seems simple enough. When used in relation to public policy and governmental control, education often refers to public schooling. It is education supported by public money and governmental institutions. Public schools currently serve slightly less than 90 percent of the K through twelve population, and they have been institutions in our society for many years. Public money usually is thought of in terms of tax dollars, and the source of funding for most public education is in fact tax dollars. But the issue is not that simple. Although it is true that the majority of funding schools receive comes from various government levels, public schools may also receive support from private sources. Individuals buy jerseys for the football team, and local businesses and service organizations raise money for computers; large corporations give discounts and grants for facilities, programs, equipment, training, and scholarships.

Private schools may also receive public funds for their programs. In some communities children who attend private religious schools ride public school buses paid for by public funds. The renewed interest in a voucher system, as we discussed in Chapter 8, would allow children to attend private schools of their choice at taxpayer expense.

So the lines between public and private education are not as black and white as some might believe. If the definition of education is further stretched to include educational activities that occur outside school walls, such as online access to public educational services, the definition of what constitutes education becomes even murkier.

The roles of the legislative and executive branches of the government differ at various levels. But what is the influence of the third branch of government, the judiciary? How and to what degree do the courts influence education?

The courts remain the one governmental authority through which individuals or groups of people, often from outside the political mainstream, can have real influence on educational policy. The courts exercise their influence by settling disputes between parties—interpreting the law in the process. As you will see, court decisions have been the basis for some of the most relevant and far-reaching policies and practices in education.

What Legal Principles Affect Public Education?

The U.S. Constitution does not specifically mention education. States' legal control over education is authorized by the Tenth Amendment's provision that gives states powers not claimed by the federal government. The Constitution is very clear, however, that such state control cannot violate the Constitution's provisions for the basic rights of individuals.

When disputes arise over educational practices or policies, the parties involved try to settle differences at the local level of governance. Depending on the type of case it is, either state courts or the federal judiciary system hears unresolved cases. As Figure 9.1 illustrates, the Supreme Court of the United States is the highest court in the land, beyond which there is no appeal.

Courts frequently consider several statutory and constitutional provisions when ruling on educational matters. One is the First Amendment to the Constitution, which contains two clauses often cited in lawsuits. The **establishment clause** prohibits favoritism toward a particular religion, and the **free exercise clause** ensures religious freedom. Here are some key legal provisions that courts rely on and reasons why they are important:

- The First Amendment states that "Congress shall make no law respecting an establishment of religion, or prohibiting the free exercise thereof; or abridging the freedom of speech, or of the press; or the right of the people peaceably to assemble, and to petition the government for a redress of grievances."

This amendment is the basis for many lawsuits challenging aid to and regulation of non-public schools, public school policies that advance or inhibit religion, and actions that restrict expression by teachers and students.

- The Fourth Amendment guarantees citizens that the right "to be secure in their persons, houses, papers, and effects, against unreasonable searches and seizures, shall not be violated, and no warrants shall issue, but upon probable cause, supported by oath or affirmation, and particularly describing the place to be searched, and the persons or things to be seized."

When a student's bookbag, locker, or person is searched for illegal or dangerous items, this amendment usually serves as the basis for judgments about the legality of such actions.

- The Fourteenth Amendment is the most widely invoked constitutional provision in school-related cases (McCarthy, Cambron-McCabe, & Thomas, 2004). Section 1 states that "[N]o State shall make or enforce any law which shall abridge the privileges or immunities of citizens of the United States; nor shall any State deprive any person of life, liberty, or property, without due process of law; nor deny to any person within its jurisdiction the equal protection of the laws."

This clause, the **equal protection clause**, is significant in legal cases related to school finance, the expulsion and suspension of students, the dismissal of teachers, and discrimination on the basis of race, gender, and disability.

Figure 9.1
Levels at Which Disputes
Are Heard
In settling disputes, why is it
important for the extra-legal
grievance system to function
effectively?

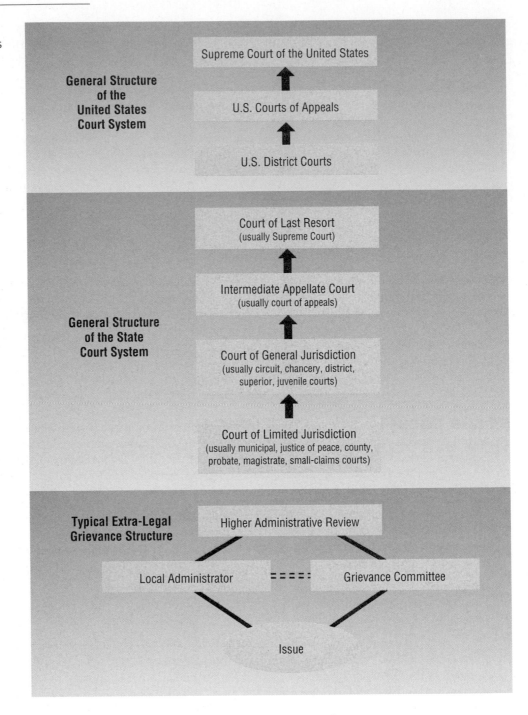

When disputes arise in contractual situations, Article I, Section 10 of the Constitution typically is consulted. This article states in part that "no State shall . . . pass any . . . ex post facto law, or law impairing the obligation of contracts." Courts' interpretations of this article are key to decisions about the validity of contracts and possible breaches of contracts. Figure 9.2 suggests why these disputes may arise.

In the scenarios that follow, note that the courts use constitutional provisions, state and federal legislation, rules and regulations of state and local boards, and case law (common law) to settle disputes. Note also that Supreme Court decisions have brought some uniformity to educational practices and policies across the country.

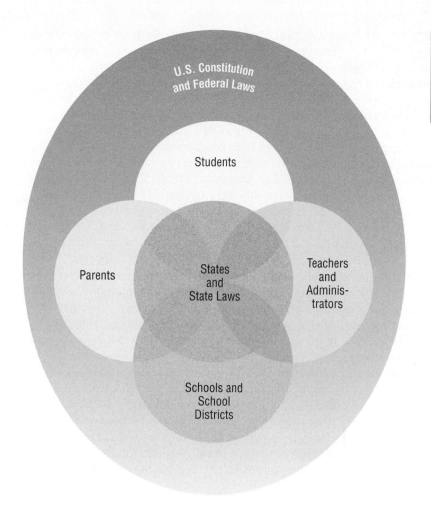

Figure 9.2
Groups with Rights and Responsibilities under the U.S. Constitution and Federal Laws
What do overlapping areas in this diagram represent?

What Are Parents' Rights and Responsibilities?

A number of cases decided by the courts have dealt directly with parents' rights and responsibilities as guardians of their children. As the following scenarios suggest, knowledge of such rulings is just as important for teachers as it is for parents.

A Question of Religious Principle

At the end of the school day, Betty Anne Mason fell into stride with three of her ninth-grade students weaving their way to the locker room. The students—James, Lashanta, and Miranda—were so engrossed in conversation that they didn't notice Betty Anne until they reached the locker room. Normally friendly and outgoing in class, the students seemed suddenly fidgety and nervous when Betty Anne asked good-naturedly if they planned to attend the ninth-grade dance Friday night. Miranda muttered something about having to stay home to "do some stuff," then rushed for the front door. As Betty Anne turned toward the other two students, James blushed and whispered something to Lashanta, who bobbed her head in agreement. "Hey, what's with you guys today?" asked Betty Anne.

"Mrs. Mason," said Lashanta, "I don't know if you heard or not, but there is a meeting tonight after the Bible study session at Miranda's house. Some parents who don't like what is going on here at Walden High are getting together to talk about taking their kids out of school and teaching them at home. Miranda's parents have already told her this is her last week at Walden. Can you believe it?"

As she headed for the principal's office, Betty Anne was upset. Miranda was one of her most promising students. Surely her parents wouldn't try to pull something like this. If they did,

What are the rights and responsibilities of parents who claim that public school curricula or the public school experience violates their religious principles?

wouldn't they be violating the compulsory attendance law? By the time she reached the office, Betty Anne's mind was racing. She headed straight for the principal, hoping to get some answers to her questions.

ANALYSIS OF "A QUESTION OF RELIGIOUS PRINCIPLE" If parents have religious or philosophical objections to a public school program, can they exempt their children from school? The Supreme Court's 1972 decision in *Wisconsin* v. *Yoder* said members of the Old Order Amish religious community were not obligated to send their children to school beyond eighth grade, even though subsequent home instruction was not equivalent to instruction in public schools. (The Amish had argued that compulsory attendance in the upper grades would have a negative effect on the established way of life in their farm-based, traditional community.) The Court's decision was based on the religious freedom clause of the First Amendment and on evidence that the Amish way of life was an acceptable alternative to formal education (Dewalt, 2006; Zirkel, Richardson, & Goldberg, 1995).

Litigation since *Wisconsin* v. *Yoder* suggests that the "Amish exception" cannot be used by parents who wish to exempt their children from schools for philosophical or religious reasons unless evidence suggests that such schooling might destroy their own religion. For those dissatisfied with the public schools, however, compulsory attendance requirements may be fulfilled in private, alternative, or parochial schools. In all states and the District of Columbia, homeschooling is yet another option.

An examination of data collected by the Home School Legal Defense Association indicates, however, that the way states regulate homeschooling varies widely. Only forty states specifically regulate home schooling, and the vast majority do not require parents to have specific qualifications to teach. Only twenty-five states require students to have regular evaluations or take standardized tests. In Kentucky, for example, state law specifies that homeschooled students must spend 185 days per year focusing on seven areas: reading, writing, spelling, grammar, history, civics, and math. There are no teacher qualifications for parents. Parents are expected to maintain an attendance register and progress reports, but no student testing is required (Home School Legal Defense Association, 2005).

In contrast, North Dakota law requires homeschooled students to study a prescribed curriculum 175 days per year, four hours per day. The elementary curriculum in North Dakota stretches beyond the Kentucky curriculum to include English grammar, geography, U.S. history, government, the U.S. Constitution, nature, effects of drugs (alcohol, tobacco, and narcotics), disease control, and elements of agriculture, physiology, and hygiene. Curriculum at the secondary level is equally specific. To continue studying at home, North Dakota students must meet cutoff scores on standardized tests. Parents serving as teachers must also meet standards. Those who do not possess a teaching certificate or a baccalaureate degree are required to meet or exceed the cutoff score for a national teacher exam. Alternatively, they could have a high school diploma or GED and be monitored by a certified teacher during the first two years of home instruction. Monitoring must continue thereafter if the child scores below the fiftieth percentile on standardized achievement tests (Home School Legal Defense Association, 2005).

Several states, including Arizona, Colorado, Florida, Maine, Washington, and Wyoming, have passed laws requiring public schools to open sports and other extracurricular activities to homeschooled students. Other states are considering such policies, but most states leave decisions on whether to open activities to homeschoolers to local districts. It is important to note that most of the activity in support of homeschooling has come about as a result of legislative, not judicial, action. The courts have "overwhelming upheld the constitutionality of restrictions on home instruction" (LaMorte, 2005, p. 27).

You Can't Spank My Child!

Can teachers use physical punishment on a child? Steve Donovan's face was flushed as he escorted Brian's parents to the door. As the principal, he suspected there might be some backlash from his actions the day before. But, as he had explained to Brian's parents, he had warned Brian several times that if he kept spitting on other students he was going to be spanked. When

Brian repeated the offense yesterday, Steve made good on his promise. Brian's parents were furious. "We know Brian has some behavior problems," they said, "but we sent a note to Brian's teacher telling her that spanking was not to be used as a disciplinary measure. Your behavior was an infringement on our rights as parents, and we're going to see that you don't get away with something like this again!"

ANALYSIS OF "YOU CAN'T SPANK MY CHILD!" Given that Brian's parents requested formally that their child not be spanked, would a court of law support Steve's actions? In *Ingraham* v. *Wright* (1977), the Supreme Court ruled that the Constitution does not prohibit the use of corporal punishment in schools. In so ruling, the Court concluded that cases dealing with corporal punishment should be handled at the state rather than the federal level. Whether Brian's parents have a legitimate complaint, then, depends on state and local school board policies.

In states that allow corporal punishment, parental objection to the practice does not necessarily take precedence. In *Baker* v. *Owen* (1975), a case challenging a North Carolina state law permitting reasonable corporal punishment, the federal district court recognized parents' basic right to supervise the upbringing of their children. The court also recognized the importance of maintaining order in the schools. Ultimately, the court said that parents' wishes should not interfere with methods chosen by school officials for maintaining discipline.

To head off problems down the line, some states and localities have laws requiring written permission from parents that spanking their children in school is acceptable. If there is no state or local regulation to the contrary, however, schools are not required to seek parental permission before administering corporal punishment. Educators must be aware of state laws and board policies banning or restricting the use of corporal punishment in the classroom.

Another common restriction in some states is that principals are the only ones who can use corporal punishment, doing so only in the presence of an adult witness. Educators who violate such policies may face monetary fines, dismissal, and even imprisonment (McCarthy, Cambron-McCabe, & Thomas, 2004).

Furthermore, many states restrict the methods and intensity with which corporal punishment may be used. Though often equated with paddling, corporal punishment is more broadly defined as "reasonable physical force used by school authorities to restrain unruly students, to correct unacceptable behavior, and to maintain the order necessary to conduct an educational program" (Data Research, Inc., 2002, p. 139). Sometimes teachers who have demonstrated excessive force when disciplining a student (e.g., throwing a student against a chalkboard and then pulling him upright by his hair) have been dismissed for cruelty or charged with criminal assault and battery.

Teachers working in school systems in which corporal punishment is allowed must avoid excessive force and follow local guidelines when administering such punishment. Overall, corporal punishment is unacceptable in most states. Those that allow it do so only as a last resort, to be avoided if at all possible.

Do Some Parents Have Special Rights?

Kenneth and Karen Rothschild, deaf parents of non-hearing-impaired students, used American Sign Language as their primary means of communication. When the school system denied their request to hire a sign language interpreter for school-sponsored functions, the Rothschilds were forced to obtain their own interpreter at great personal expense. Subsequently, they brought action against the school district and the superintendent for violating section 504 of the Rehabilitation Act of 1973, which prohibits discrimination on the basis of a disability. School officials denied the charge, arguing that they had made good-faith efforts to accommodate the Rothschilds's needs by providing special seating arrangements at all school-sponsored functions.

ANALYSIS OF "DO SOME PARENTS HAVE SPECIAL RIGHTS?" Must a school system provide special services, such as sign language interpreters, to parents who are disabled? In *Rothschild* v. *Grottenthaler* (1990), the U.S. Court of Appeals ruled that a public school system receiving federal financial assistance is obligated to provide a sign language interpreter, at school district expense, to deaf parents attending school-initiated events. In explaining its decision, the court said that, without an interpreter, people like the Rothschilds do not have equal opportunity to participate in activities related to their children's education. The court also noted that the Rehabilitation Act specifies that access to necessary accommodations for individuals with disabilities should not impose undue financial or administrative burdens on them. Accordingly, the school system was ordered to (1) reimburse the Rothschilds for money spent on interpreters and (2) hire an interpreter to assist the Rothschilds at school-initiated activities directly involving their children's academic or disciplinary progress. Dillon (2007) explains how the Rowley case in 1977 complicated and enriched the meaning of a free and appropriate education (FAPE) for students under IDEA.

What Are Students' Rights and Responsibilities?

In *Tinker* v. *Des Moines Independent Community School District* (1969), the Supreme Court emphasized that students do not lose their rights when they pass through the schoolhouse door. Under the Constitution they continue to be persons "possessed of fundamental rights which the state must respect." Although school authorities have broad powers for the development and implementation of an educational program, they must avoid unreasonable, vague, arbitrary actions or actions in direct conflict with students' constitutional rights and freedoms.

In God Somebody Trusts

Can students conduct religious practices in school? Jack Mills sat at his desk grading papers late one afternoon. He heard singing coming from the direction of the principal's office. He recognized the strains of "Onward Christian Soldiers" being sung by what sounded like a fairly large group of students. Students often sang in the building after the final bell; Omega High had many afterschool activities. But they did not usually sing hymns. When Ellie Ferro, the sophomore English teacher, stormed into his room, Jack was surprised by her anger.

"Jack, the Young Crusaders for Christ are holding a prayer meeting in the gymnasium again. Apparently the principal said they could meet there whenever the basketball team was not practicing. It really ticks me off that they get to stay here when nobody else gets to use the building for church meetings. The principal has been cuddling up to those fundamentalists every chance she gets. It isn't fair. I want you to come with me to her office. I think we need to call her on this one."

ANALYSIS OF "IN GOD SOMEBODY TRUSTS" Jack feels nervous about Ellie's anger, largely because the law on prayer clubs in schools is a mystery to him. Given the number of court cases focusing on the separation of church and state since the mid-twentieth century, Jack's confusion is understandable. In the tug of war over where the lines of separation should be drawn, some argue that the First Amendment's establishment clause prohibits religious observance of any type in public schools. Others contend that the Amendment's provisions for free speech, free exercise, and association rights prohibit schools from practicing religious discrimination.

In *Widmar* v. *Vincent* (1981), the Supreme Court ruled that refusing to give religious groups access to facilities while allowing other groups to use the same facilities was a violation of students' rights of free speech. Furthermore, the Court deemed college students less impressionable than high school students. As adults, college students could be expected to understand that the university was neutral in granting permission to a prayer club to meet on public property. With passage of the **Equal Access Act (EAA)** in 1984, Congress indicated that secondary school students were also mature enough to understand that a school does not condone religion merely by allowing prayer clubs on public property.

The EAA states that secondary public schools accepting federal aid must treat student religious groups in the same way as other extracurricular clubs. That is, if a school allows noncurriculum student groups (e.g., the computer game club or the chess club) to meet on school property during noninstructional time, other student-initiated groups, regardless of their religious, philosophical, or political views, must have equal access to school premises. In *Board of Education of the Westside Community Schools* v. *Mergens* (1990), the Supreme Court upheld the constitutionality of the EAA.

Given the Supreme Court's ruling, approving any single student club not directly tied to the curriculum prohibits schools from discriminating against other student organizations, such as the Young Crusaders for Christ. This even applies to groups having little community support, such as religious cults or white supremacists. If schools do permit noncurriculum student group meetings during noninstructional time, teachers or other school employees may be present only in a nonparticipatory capacity. Furthermore, meetings may not be coordinated or led by people other than school students (LaMorte, 2005).

Following are rulings on other major cases dealing with separation of church and state that contain implications for educators:

- *School District of Abington Township* v. *Schempp* (1963). Prayer and Bible reading in public school classrooms are unconstitutional. However, study of the Bible as part of a secular program of education focusing on its literary and historic value is allowed.
- *Wallace* v. *Jaffree* (1985). Educators cannot require students to pause for a moment of silence for meditation or voluntary prayer.
- *Lee* v. *Weisman* (1992). Prayers at a high school graduation ceremony are unconstitutional. Yet recent and sometimes contradictory rulings by circuit courts have complicated the situation. Until the U.S. Supreme Court settles matters, school systems in some states have skirted the ban on prayer at graduation services by allowing students to initiate, plan, and lead invocations.
- *Guyer* v. *School Board of Alachua County* (1994). The court ruled that the depiction of witches, cauldrons, and brooms did not constitute an establishment of religion, and that Halloween signified nothing more than the secular celebration of a traditional cultural event.

Since 1971, Supreme Court justices have often applied the three-part **Lemon test**, developed from the *Lemon* v. *Kurtzman* case (1971), when deciding whether specific practices or policies constitute an establishment of religion. Under the Lemon test, each of the following questions must be answered affirmatively to satisfy the Constitution:

1. Does the challenged practice or policy have a secular purpose?
2. Does it neither advance nor inhibit religious practices?
3. Does practice or policy avoid an excessive entanglement between government and religion?

How much longer the Lemon test will survive as the yardstick for settling establishment clause disputes is uncertain. As Justice Antonin Scalia noted, there are several problems with the Lemon test: "For my part, I agree with the long list of constitutional scholars who have criticized *Lemon* and bemoaned the strange Establishment Clause geometry of crooked lines and wavering shapes its intermittent use has produced" (Bureau of National Affairs, 1993). **Does the Lemon test really work?**

Playing Fairly

At the end of the school day, Mary Ellen, Joe, and David went to the principal's office. Anne Jeffrey, the assistant principal, handed each of them a sealed envelope addressed to their parents. "As I understand it," she said, "each of you is suspended for three days. This notice of suspension should be given to your parents."

"Are you kidding?" said Joe. "Nobody said anything to me about this. What are the charges against us?"

"Wait a minute," interrupted Mary Ellen. "Does this have anything to do with what happened during lunch today? If it does, this is a bunch of crap. We weren't the ones who started that fight."

"Yeah," said David. "It was that bunch of rednecks. They're always mouthing off and getting in your face. How come they aren't getting suspended? They cause trouble every day! You guys just never see them!"

"Look, I don't want to hear it," said Anne. "The principal asked me to give you these forms and that's it. Now go get on the bus before you get into any more trouble."

Voices Pro and Con

ZERO TOLERANCE

School safety is on the minds of school leaders across the nation. The violence in public schools in Colorado, Tennessee, Oregon, and elsewhere has raised awareness to new levels, even though schools remain one of the safest places where young people and adults can spend their time.

One response to the fear has been the implementation of *zero-tolerance* policies with regard to student violence—the "one-strike-and-you're-out" approach to school management means that students who threaten others or bring weapons to school are suspended or expelled. These policies raise questions about what is reasonable and legally defensible administrative behavior. They also divide people by philosophical orientation.

Zero tolerance has led to the following actions:

- A sixteen-year-old female student in Washington was met by police and expelled for using her finger to make a gun and jokingly saying, "Bang." She has since been reinstated.
- A thirteen-year-old male student in Texas was arrested and spent five days in jail awaiting a hearing for writing a spooky story about killing classmates. He is currently receiving homeschooling.
- An eighteen-year-old male student in Georgia wrote a story in his journal about a deranged student who goes on a rampage at school, which resulted in expulsion and arrest with no opportunity to graduate.
- A seven-year-old was suspended for bringing nail clippers to school in Illinois, and a fifteen-year-old in Virginia was suspended for dyeing his hair blue (Essex, 2005, p. 60).

The only case to reach the courts was the one involving the account of the deranged student. The judge ruled that the student's journal did not constitute a threat. Nonetheless, the student had to change schools. Prosecutors are still considering pressing charges against him. Educators think about zero-tolerance policies in different ways.

Con   Robert Frank, a special education teacher at a middle school in Boston, argues that there must be some compassion for "offbeat" behavior—some room to bend zero-tolerance policies to acknowledge the special plight of children with disabilities. To do otherwise, he contends, is to behave unfairly.

Pro   Sarah Compton, an elementary school principal in Michigan, believes we should hold all children accountable, regardless of who they are, for strict and certain rules pertaining to violence. According to Compton, to do otherwise creates a sliding scale that cannot be administered fairly and that encourages disrespect for the community.

Michael LaMorte, author of school law textbooks, suggests the following: "There is little doubt that school systems would decrease antagonism toward zero-tolerance policies if they adopt policies that are clearly written, adequately communicated to both students and parents, fairly enforced, and, perhaps most important, show that there is a need for such a policy by demonstrating the serious threat which exists to the school environment" (2005, p. 146).

Questions for Reflection: With which educator do you agree? Why?

"You mean we don't even get to tell our side of the story?" asked Joe. "Man, this is really wrong!"

If you were these students' teacher, how would you respond to their complaints about the way their suspension was handled? Can students ever be denied the right to due process of law?

ANALYSIS OF "PLAYING FAIRLY" In *Goss* v. *Lopez* (1975), the Supreme Court addressed the grievances of Dwight Lopez and several of his peers. They had been suspended by the principal for ten days without being given a hearing, a practice forbidden by Ohio law. Because the principal did not follow mandated legal procedures, the Court ruled the students were denied **due process of law.** Specifically, the Court noted that the principal's actions were in violation of the Fourteenth Amendment. The Court subsequently ordered school officials to remove references to the students' suspensions from school records.

The Court held that students facing temporary suspension from school must be given oral or written notice of the charges, an explanation of evidence if they disagree with the charges, and an opportunity to present their side of the story. Whenever possible, the notice and hearing are to precede suspension from school (LaMorte, 2002).

When student behavior is serious enough to warrant long-term suspension or expulsion, prudent educators provide students with a written notice stating the charges, time and place of a hearing, and procedures to be followed in the hearing. Students have the right to know what evidence will be presented and who will testify, as well as the substance of such testimony. They also have the right to cross-examine witnesses and to present witnesses to testify on their behalf. Written or taped records of proceedings and the decision of the group conducting the hearing are to be made available to students. Students are also to be informed of the right to appeal (Essex, 2005).

Show Me What's in There!

When Assistant Principal David Adams stepped outside, his attention was drawn to three students walking across the school courtyard. As he moved toward them, he noticed the boys were looking at a small black bag held by William, one of the students. The bag, a vinyl calculator case, had a suspicious bulge in its side.

When he questioned the boys about where they were going and why they were late to class, William, palming the leather case and hiding it behind his back, responded that his classes had ended and he was on his way home. Curious about what William was hiding, the assistant principal insisted, to no avail, that William show him the object in his hand. "It's nothing," said William. "Leave me alone. You have a search warrant or something?"

After sending the other two boys back to class, David took William to the office and asked an aide to witness his efforts to look at the calculator case. When William refused to let him see it, David pried it out of William's hand, unzipped it, and found marijuana and other drug paraphernalia. David called the police, and William was arrested. As he was being escorted out of the office, William turned to David and said, "You haven't seen the end of this. I know my rights. You can't be searching me or anybody else without a warrant!"

ANALYSIS OF "SHOW ME WHAT'S IN THERE!" **Does a school official have the right to search students?** The scenario of William follows closely the events that occurred in a California public school. After being convicted in juvenile court, William appealed the decision, saying the evidence against him came from an illegal search and should have been excluded from the hearing. In *In re William G.* (1985), the Supreme Court of California agreed, basing its decision on the reasonable suspicion standard set forth in *New Jersey* v. *T.L.O.* (1985).

In *New Jersey* v. *T.L.O.* (1985), the Supreme Court stated that school officials are acting not **in loco parentis** (in place of the parents) but as agents of the state when they search students under their authority. This should mean that school officials are subject to the Fourth Amendment. The Court ruled, though, that schools are special settings and thus there should be some "easing of the restrictions" normally placed on public authorities when conducting searches. Accordingly, school officials do not need to obtain a warrant or show "probable cause" when searching a student suspected of violating school rules or the law. Instead, when determining the legality of school searches, school officials can rely on "reason" and "common sense." Tests for determining reasonable-ness are whether (1) at the inception of the search there are reasonable grounds for suspecting that evidence will be found to prove a student is in violation of the law or school rules, and (2) the scope of the search is reasonably related to the objectives of the search, the age and sex of the student, and the nature of the infraction.

Such guidelines allow for much latitude among courts when interpreting Fourth Amendment rights (McCarthy, Cambron-McCabe, & Thomas, 1998). In the case of William, the court decided that the assistant principal had insufficient grounds for conducting a search. First, the assistant principal had no prior knowledge of William using or selling illegal drugs. Second, suspicion that William was late to class and William's attempt to hide the leather object provided no reasonable basis for a search. Third, William's demand for a warrant merely indicated that he wanted to preserve his constitutional rights; it was not an admission of guilt (National Organization on Legal Problems of Education, 1988).

The *New Jersey* v. *T.L.O.* case itself was a markedly different situation. In this case a student claimed that her Fourth Amendment rights were violated when a school official searched her purse. The student (T.L.O.) was one of two girls sent to the office for smoking in the girl's restroom (a violation of school rules). When questioned by the assistant vice principal, T.L.O.

denied having smoked at all. However, when T.L.O. complied with the request to open her purse, the assistant vice principal found marijuana and drug paraphernalia, $40.98 in single dollar bills and change, plus a handwritten note to a friend, requesting that she sell marijuana at school. Subsequently, the school official notified T.L.O.'s mother and the police. After being advised of her rights, T.L.O. admitted to selling marijuana at the high school.

When the state brought delinquency charges against T.L.O., she claimed that the assistant vice principal had violated her Fourth Amendment rights, and thus evidence from her purse and her confession should be suppressed. The Supreme Court disagreed, saying that the search met the criteria for reasonableness. That is, a teacher had witnessed T.L.O. smoking and had a duty to investigate whether a school code had been broken (LaMorte, 2005).

More recently, the Supreme Court's ruling in *Veronia School Dist. 47J* v. *Acton* (1995) gave school officials the right to screen student athletes for drug use. In explaining its decision, the Court said random urinalysis drug testing is not a violation of students' protection against unreasonable search and seizure, because schoolchildren have fewer rights than adults. The Court further held that students who participate voluntarily in sports have low expectations for privacy, because teammates undress together and shower in communal locker rooms. Furthermore, privacy rights compromised by urine samples are considered negligible, because conditions of collection are similar to public restrooms and the results are viewed only by limited authorities. Finally, the Court emphasized that governmental concern over the safety of minors under their supervision overrides the minimal, if any, intrusion in student athletes' privacy. In 1999 more than one hundred districts in at least twenty states required students to submit to urine tests if they wanted to play sports (Portner, 1999).

In 2002 the Supreme Court expanded its view of authorized drug testing. The Court ruled five to four that drug testing all students in extracurricular activities, not only those in athletics, does not violate the Fourth Amendment's prohibition against unreasonable searches. In the 2005–2006 school year 373 high schools got federal funds for testing up from 79 schools two years earlier (Leinwand, 2006).

Are There Limits on Student Expression?

Students at Kirkwood High School in suburban St. Louis, Missouri, had enjoyed much freedom in the production of the school newspaper. When the students agreed to run an ad for Planned Parenthood, Birthright (an organization concerned with reproductive issues) requested that students run an antiabortion ad to counteract Planned Parenthood's message. Several parents and local citizens considered such advertisements inappropriate and insisted that principal Franklin McCallie ban the ads from the student newspaper (Conkling, 1991). **Can school administrators censor student publications?**

ANALYSIS OF "ARE THERE LIMITS ON STUDENT EXPRESSION?" Students had reason to cheer in 1969 when the Supreme Court ruled on *Tinker* v. *Des Moines Independent Community School District,* a case in which three public school students were suspended for wearing armbands to protest the Vietnam War. Deciding in favor of the students, the Court declared that public school authorities do not have the right to silence students' political or ideological viewpoints simply because they disagree with students' ideas. Under *Tinker,* students' verbal or symbolic expression may be restricted only in instances when student behavior could result in disorder or interfere with the rights of others (Imber & van Geel, 2005).

In 1988, the Supreme Court restricted students' First Amendment rights (*Hazelwood School District* v. *Kuhlmeier*) when it ruled that principals could censor school-sponsored publications. The basis for the Court's decision was a case involving students in a high school journalism class. Those students had claimed their First Amendment rights were violated when the principal reviewed their material and removed two stories—one on divorce, the other on three students' experiences with pregnancy—from the school-sponsored newspaper. According to the Supreme Court, a student newspaper does not represent a forum for public expression when it is part of the school curriculum. Thus, school officials can censor material considered inconsistent with the educational mission of the school. This includes material that is ungrammatical, poorly researched, biased or prejudiced, vulgar, or inappropriate for an immature audience.

On the other hand, if schools have clearly established, either through practice or policy, students' rights to control editorial content, the publication is considered an open forum and restrictions under *Hazelwood* do not apply. At Kirkwood High School, Principal Franklin McCallie firmly believed the newspaper should be an open forum for student expression. Thus he allowed student journalists to decide what to do about the controversial ads.

Treating Different Students Differently—Illegal Discrimination?

As Sam Miller's fifth-grade class lined up to leave the gymnasium, Tyrone grabbed Tony's hat and ran to the end of the line. Tony, a mainstreamed student with emotional disturbance, raced after Tyrone, knocked him to the gym floor, and punched Tyrone hard enough to bloody his nose. When Sam pulled Tony away from Tyrone, Tony swung his fist and hit another child in the stomach. Sam wrapped his arms around Tony's waist and carried him to the back of the gym before he could do any more damage. He sent one of his students to get the principal. This wasn't the first time Tony had exploded, but it was the most serious and dangerous incident.

Sam was nearing his wit's end. He had talked with the resource teacher about ways to defuse Tony's anger, but it was sometimes impossible to intervene before Tony's quick temper caused incidents like the one in the gym. In Sam's mind, Tony threatened other students and needed to be disciplined for his misbehavior. Sam decided to ask the principal either to expel Tony or to give him a long-term suspension so Tony's individualized education program (IEP) team could have sufficient time to rethink Tony's placement. **Can students with disabilities be expelled for dangerous conduct?**

ANALYSIS OF "TREATING DIFFERENT STUDENTS DIFFERENTLY—ILLEGAL DISCRIMINATION?" Disciplining students with disabilities has been a controversial and confusing issue for educators and parents. Under the 1975 Education for All Handicapped Children Act (EAHCA), now called the Individuals with Disabilities Education Act (IDEA), students with disabilities are guaranteed a "free and appropriate public education (FAPE)." In 1988 the Supreme Court ruled in *Honig* v. *Doe* that expulsion of students with disabilities for behavior attributable to their disabilities would be a violation of EAHCA provisions (Data Research, Inc., 2002). The Court did agree, however, that students with disabilities who exhibit behavior dangerous to themselves or others could be temporarily suspended for up to ten days. But this suspension would be acceptable only if such punishment were the same as would be used for a nondisabled student. The 1997 IDEA amendments altered this ruling by allowing school officials to establish a forty-five-day interim educational placement. This interim placement would remove students carrying weapons, using drugs, or demonstrating behavior that might result in injury to themselves or others from the classroom while a solution was found.

IDEA regulations established in 1999 offer schools even more leeway in disciplining disruptive students with disabilities. School officials are allowed to suspend a student for up to ten days at a time for each separate act of misconduct, as long as the removals do not constitute a pattern. Special education services do not need to be provided during the first ten days of suspension. However, if a child is subsequently removed for up to ten school days for other violations of school conduct codes, services must be provided. Administrators and the special education teacher determine which services are needed. Furthermore, decisions as to whether a student's behavior is related to his or her disability are now required only for a suspension that results in a change of placement (U.S. Department of Education, 1999).

Would You Check These Papers for Me?

The terse phone call from Amy Aller's mother, a local lawyer, should have alerted Charles Armstrong to the possibility of an unpleasant parent conference. Amy was a good student, though, and, as far as Charles knew, she had been quite happy in school. Amy had left school that afternoon a little upset by the low score on her math quiz, but her grades in general were so good that he couldn't imagine one assignment prompting a parent conference. It had to be something else.

As Charles sat facing Mrs. Aller that afternoon, she explained the reason for her conference. Amy was in fact upset—not so much because of her low math score but because of the "unkind" comments about her paper made by classmates. "How did anyone else know Amy's grade on this quiz?" asked Mrs. Aller.

Charles shifted uncomfortably in his chair. "I have student helpers who grade papers for me when they finish their work," said Charles. "I guess one of them must have told the others about Amy's paper today. I'm sorry. This has never been a problem before. I'll be sure to say something to my students tomorrow so this type of thing doesn't happen again."

As she stood to leave, Mrs. Aller said, "I like you, Mr. Armstrong, but I want to tell you I don't think you should use this system anymore. I believe it violates the Buckley Amendment. No student should have knowledge of another student's progress in school."

Later that night Charles pulled out his college textbook, read about the Buckley Amendment, and reflected on his conference with Mrs. Aller. If Mrs. Aller was right, did he also violate students' rights of privacy when he displayed some students' papers as examples of good work? What about when he asked students to raise their hands to indicate whether they got something right or wrong on written assignments? Was he in violation of the law when he had students work problems at the board in front of their peers? Charles made a mental note to call the legal advisor to the teachers' organization the next day to get some answers to these questions. **Is posting grades an invasion of students' privacy?**

ANALYSIS OF "WOULD YOU CHECK THESE PAPERS FOR ME?" Before 2002 Charles might very well have been in violation of the **Buckley Amendment** when he allowed students to grade each other's papers. Part of the Family Educational Rights and Privacy Act (commonly referred to as the Buckley Amendment) prohibits schools from releasing information about a student to third parties without parental or student permission. In 2002's *Owasso Independent School District v. Falvo (No. 00-1073)* case, however, the Supreme Court ruled unanimously that the classroom practice of allowing students to grade each others' papers does not violate the law.

What Are Teachers' Rights and Responsibilities?

Teachers enjoy a number of rights also extended to students. For example, they may be excused from saluting or pledging allegiance to the flag if such actions violate their beliefs and commitments. However, as with students, there are times when teachers' constitutional rights must be considered in light of important educational goals. Because of the nature of their jobs, teachers usually are held to higher standards of behavior than are ordinary citizens (Imber & van Geel, 2004). The scenarios that follow examine some of the issues decided by the courts in this delicate balance between teachers' rights as citizens and their rights as state employees. The scenarios also suggest some of the responsibilities inherent in teachers' jobs, particularly with regard to student safety.

There's Got to Be a Way to Keep This Job!

Sandra Allen, a second-year teacher, loved her teaching job. With the exception of two or three students who had difficulty controlling their actions, her class was well behaved and motivated to learn. Most students consistently completed assignments on time, and their work was accurate and neat. Sandra knew that parents had been ambivalent about their children having the "new" teacher at school, but their comments during parent conferences indicated that they, too, were pleased with their children's academic progress.

When Sandra received notice in May that she would not be rehired for the upcoming academic year, she was shocked and angry. Because her principal's midyear evaluation rated Sandra as "above average" or "outstanding" in all categories, Sandra had assumed her contract would be renewed. She needed only one more year of teaching in the system to earn tenure. Surely the school board could not force her out of the system without giving her reasons for doing so, or could it?

ANALYSIS OF "THERE'S GOT TO BE A WAY TO KEEP THIS JOB!" Sandra's story is much like that of David Roth, an assistant professor of political science at Wisconsin State University–Oshkosh, who was hired for a fixed term of one academic year. When Roth was notified at the end of the academic term that he would not be rehired for the following year, he went to court, claiming that the decision infringed on his Fourteenth Amendment rights. In ruling on *Board of Regents of State Colleges* v. *Roth* (1972), the Supreme Court disagreed with Roth's charge, explaining that a probationary teacher does not have the same rights as a tenured teacher.

According to the Court, tenured teachers may not be removed from their positions without specific or good cause, nor may they be dismissed for arbitrary reasons (e.g., political beliefs and activities). Thus, tenured teachers have a "property interest" that merits due process protection. In most states, however, the contract of a teacher with probationary status can be terminated at the end of the year without cause (state statutes generally specify a date by which teachers must be notified of such action). This means that a probationary teacher maintains property interest only for the duration of a one-year term. In other words, the teacher is protected by due process during that term, but not afterward. However, if the probationary teacher can present evidence to suggest that nonrenewal is in retaliation for exercise of constitutional rights (e.g., freedom of speech), the employer must follow due process (Essex, 2005).

If the school board resorts to **dismissal** (removing a probationary or tenured teacher before the completion of his or her contract), the board must provide a notice, hearing, or notification of reasons for dismissal. State statutes typically list broad causes for dismissal, such as incompetency, immorality, unprofessional conduct, and neglect of duty. Lack of funding and a decline in student enrollment may also be just cause for the midyear dismissal of both tenured and nontenured teachers (LaMorte, 2005). Many state laws also stipulate that nontenured teachers must be dismissed before tenured teachers, and, among tenured teachers, the least experienced must be dismissed first.

A Line between Personhood and Professionalism

Can a teacher be dismissed for private conduct? Jason O'Hara enjoyed his most-popular-teacher status at Baker Middle School. Students, parents, and colleagues respected him for his innovative ideas, sharp wit, and ability to interest students in learning. Now in his fourth year of teaching, Jason had tenure in the school system and was chair of the English department.

When Jason received a note from John Wright, the principal, requesting that he come to the office that afternoon, Jason thought nothing of it. Mr. Wright had been very supportive of Jason and his efforts to upgrade the English curriculum. As he stepped through the office door, however, Jason knew that something was wrong. Mr. Wright, a grim look on his face, handed Jason a two-page letter addressed to the superintendent. The letter, written by a teacher with whom Jason had had a brief homosexual relationship the year before, made explicit the nature of their relationship. Jason read it in stunned silence.

"Jason," said Mr. Wright, "this letter was also mailed to members of the school board. Several of them are really uptight about this. They want to dismiss you for immoral behavior. I think this is going to be an ugly battle. I'll do everything I can to help you, but I think you also need legal assistance. Do you have a good lawyer?"

ANALYSIS OF "A LINE BETWEEN PERSONHOOD AND PROFESSIONALISM" Teachers in earlier times were held to rigid codes of conduct. Those who crossed the line between moral and immoral behavior resigned or were dismissed immediately from their teaching duties. In recent times, however, the line has blurred because it is often difficult to get community consensus about what constitutes immoral conduct. Actions that were believed immoral during colonial times are not given a second thought today. Moreover, many educators believe that when the school day ends, what occurs in the privacy of their homes is their own business and should not affect negatively their status as professionals. Those who disagree argue that being a private person does not relieve educators of their duty to serve as role models for children (Castro, 2006).

Ambiguity about what constitutes moral and immoral behavior is reflected by court decisions in different states. In making employment decisions based on a teacher's sexual orientation, courts usually consider "the adverse effect on students or fellow teachers, adversity anticipated within the school system, surrounding circumstances, and possible chilling effects on discipline" (Alexander & Alexander, 2005, p. 696). Therefore, much of the decision is left to the local school board, because it is in closer touch with the beliefs of both the community and the school.

Depending on public reaction to Jason's case, then, he may or may not be dismissed from his teaching position. In 1969 the California Supreme Court heard a case (*Morrison v. State Board of Education*) involving a teacher, Marc Morrison, whose circumstances were much like those of Jason. When the superintendent received a letter from a male teacher who had been involved sexually with Morrison the year before, the school board voted to dismiss Morrison on grounds of immoral and unprofessional behavior. The court disagreed with the school board's actions, saying that the board's definition of immoral behavior was dangerously vague and could implicate many educators. Ruling in favor of Morrison, the court also stated that disapproval of an educator's private conduct was insufficient reason for dismissal, particularly when there was no proof that the educator's professional work was affected negatively by the conduct.

However, eight years later in *Gaylord* v. *Tacoma School District No. 10* (1977), a case heard by the state supreme court of Washington, the court upheld the dismissal of a teacher who admitted his homosexuality to the vice principal of the school. Based on the fact that at least one student and several teachers and parents had challenged the individual's fitness to teach, the court held that the teacher's continued employment would likely disrupt the educational process. In another such example, an untenured guidance counselor told several colleagues that she was bisexual and had a female lover (*Connick* v. *Myers*). She was released, and a federal appellate court in 1983 ultimately upheld her nonrenewal.

Such cases end differently in different localities because the U.S. Supreme Court has not yet recognized a constitutional privacy right to engage in homosexual behavior. Based on the 1984 ruling in *National Gay Task Force* v. *Board of Education of Oklahoma City*, however, teachers have the right to advocate publicly for legalization of homosexuality, as long as such activity is not disruptive to the educational process.

As indicated in the 1984 ruling in *Rowland* v. *Mad River Local School District*, advocacy does not include talking with coworkers about personal sexual preferences or those of students. In this case, an Ohio guidance counselor who had been dismissed by the school board for admitting her bisexuality to several members of the staff argued that her First and Fourteenth Amendment rights had been violated. The Court disagreed, saying that the First Amendment did not protect the guidance counselor's statements because they were not made as a citizen on matters of public concern. Rather, the counselor's statements were a matter of private concern. Furthermore, the court held that, without evidence that heterosexual employees had been or would be treated differently for discussing sexual preferences, nonrenewal of the counselor's contract did not violate the Fourteenth Amendment (Essex, 2005).

What Do You Mean I'm Violating Copyright Laws?

During summer vacation, Robert Wells, the newly appointed chair of the mathematics department at Central High, videotaped a two-part series titled "Mathematics in Today's Workplace" and added it to his growing collection of tapes. Robert's students had responded well to his occasional use of a videotape to illustrate concepts being taught in class. He believed that these newest tapes would be especially effective in the spring, when math analysis students planned projects showing real-life applications of mathematics.

As he thought about the upcoming in-service program he would conduct for department members, Robert also realized that his videotapes might be an excellent tool for helping others think about ways to vary their own instruction. Excited by the prospect, Robert contacted Dorothy James at the media center to see if she would make copies of his videotapes and place them on reserve in the school library. When Dorothy asked Robert if he had permission to videotape the copyrighted television programs, he was caught off guard. "What do you mean?" Robert said. "I'm using these tapes for teaching purposes. Lots of people do that. What's the big deal?"

"I used to think it was okay myself," said Dorothy, "but now I'm not so sure. I'll call central office and see what I can find out. Until we know, we'd better not copy any of those videotapes." Can teachers videotape television programs and use them for educational purposes?

ANALYSIS OF "WHAT DO YOU MEAN I'M VIOLATING COPYRIGHT LAWS?" What constitutes fair use?
The Supreme Court has not decided whether it is illegal for teachers to tape television broadcasts on home video recorders for later classroom use. Congressional guidelines from 1981 for off-the-air taping, however, suggest that such activities may in fact constitute copyright

infringement. Guidelines specify that copyrighted television programs may be videotaped by nonprofit educational organizations. But the videotapes must be destroyed or erased after forty-five calendar days if the institution has not obtained a license for such videotaping. Teachers may use the videotapes with students at school or with students receiving homebound instruction one time during the first ten school days after recording occurs. One additional showing is allowed during the ten-day period, but only for instructional reinforcement. Additional use is limited to evaluation of the videotape's usefulness as an instructional tool (McCarthy, Cambron-McCabe, & Thomas, 2004).

In *Encyclopedia Britannica Educational Corporation v. Crooks* (1982), a New York federal district court found a school system guilty of violating fair use standards by engaging in extensive off-the-air taping and replaying of public television programs. The court found that such taping interfered with the marketability of producers' films. In 1984, in *Sony Corporation of America v. Universal City Studios,* the Supreme Court ruled that personal video recording for the purpose of "time shifting" (recording of a program for later one-time viewing), however, did not harm the television market (McCarthy, Cambron-McCabe, & Thomas, 2004).

Until the Supreme Court decides whether home taping for broader viewing by students in classrooms constitutes fair use of copyrighted materials, teachers are advised to follow congressional guidelines. Another option, of course, is to seek written permission from copyright owners to videotape their programs for classroom use.

A new question of fair use arose in the 1990s with the explosion of the World Wide Web. The Internet offers an exciting array of motion media, music, text material, graphics, illustrations, and photographs for educational purposes. When incorporating others' electronic materials in multimedia projects, however, teachers and students are obligated to act responsibly. The same level of care is expected when using print materials from textbooks, magazines, and other sources.

Maybe She Is Just a Sickly Child

Theresa chose a desk near the back of the room, not near anyone in particular. She was quiet and somewhat plain in her dress, but her long brown hair was striking. Joan Mason didn't know much about eight-year-old Theresa, because Theresa had just moved to town in August. Her permanent records indicated that she was above average in ability. Although Theresa had missed a lot of school last year, her grades were about average, maybe a little low in math.

Another parent told Joan that Theresa's mother had been divorced last year and had moved here, at least in part, to get away from her former husband. The family—Theresa's mother and her younger sister; a man she called Jim, whom she described as the mother's friend; and Jim's seventeen-year-old son—lived in a small ranch house in a nice neighborhood on the outskirts of town.

As Joan worked with Theresa the first few weeks of school, Theresa seldom missed a day of school and kept up with daily assignments. By mid-October, however, things had changed. Theresa's attendance became sporadic, and Joan noticed that Theresa often was passive and uncommunicative, both with Joan and with classmates. During seatwork, Theresa chewed her fingernails, her constant gnawing sometimes drawing blood. When Joan talked with Theresa's mother during a parent–teacher conference, she did not seem overly concerned by Joan's observations. Her mom indicated that Theresa's behavior at home had not changed. She attributed Theresa's recent absences and withdrawn manner to her tendency to be a "sickly child." After the conference, Joan still worried about Theresa, but she didn't know what to do. **What about this situation concerns you? What, if anything, would you do if you were Theresa's teacher?**

ANALYSIS OF "MAYBE SHE IS JUST A SICKLY CHILD" Educators, unlike physicians, social workers, and law enforcement officers, have a unique opportunity to monitor students' social behaviors, academic progress, and attitudes over time. Some patterns of behavior, especially sudden, dramatic changes, can be a warning sign of something gone awry in a child's life. Teachers need to be particularly alert to patterns of behavior that could indicate a child is the victim of abuse or neglect.

As defined by the Child Abuse Prevention and Treatment Act, child abuse and neglect include physical or mental injury, sexual abuse or exploitation, negligent treatment, or maltreatment (1) of a child younger than eighteen years of age (unless state law specifies a younger age), (2) by any person responsible for a child's welfare, (3) under circumstances that harm or threaten a child's health or welfare. Sexual abuse is defined as

> [(1)] the employment, use, persuasion, inducement, enticement or coercion of any child to engage in, or assist any other person to engage in, any sexually explicit conduct (or any simulation of such conduct) for the purpose of producing any visual depiction of such conduct, or (2) rape, molestation, prostitution, or other form of sexual exploitation of children, or incest with children. (U.S. Department of Health and Human Services, 1999)

Abuse can occur at any socioeconomic level to both males and females. In every state, educators must report cases of abuse or neglect resulting in physical injury to a child. In the majority of states, educators also must report instances of emotional, mental, or sexual abuse. Failure to report suspected abuse and neglect constitutes a misdemeanor in most states and, with a few exceptions, teachers are identified among the professionals required to make such reports. Certain behaviors or signs occurring repeatedly or in combination may cue an educator that child abuse is present in a family (see Table 9.1).

Once a teacher suspects that a student is being abused or neglected, the teacher should consult state statutes that specify procedures for reporting it. Many localities also have school board policies and procedures to encourage effective reporting of suspected child abuse. Under the Child Abuse and Neglect Act, educators are assured immunity from civil liability if reports of abuse and neglect that are made in good faith later turn out to be inaccurate.

Table 9.1

RECOGNIZING CHILD ABUSE

The following signs may signal the presence of child abuse or neglect.

The Child:
- Shows sudden changes in behavior or school performance.
- Has not received help for physical or medical problems brought to the parents' attention.
- Has learning problems (or difficulty concentrating) that cannot be attributed to specific physical or psychological causes.
- Is always watchful, as though preparing for something bad to happen.
- Lacks adult supervision.
- Is overly compliant, passive, or withdrawn.
- Comes to school or other activities early, stays late, and does not want to go home.

The Parent:
- Shows little concern for the child.
- Denies the existence of—or blames the child for—the child's problems in school or at home.
- Asks teachers or other caretakers to use harsh physical discipline if the child misbehaves.
- Sees the child as entirely bad, worthless, or burdensome.
- Demands a level of physical or academic performance the child cannot achieve.
- Looks primarily to the child for care, attention, and satisfaction of emotional needs.

The Parent and Child:
- Rarely touch or look at each other.
- Consider their relationship entirely negative.
- State that they do not like each other.

Source: National Clearinghouse on Child Abuse and Neglect Information (2003). Recognizing child abuse and neglect. Available online: http://www.childwelfare.gov/pubs/factsheets/signs.cfm

You Should Have Known Better

Two teachers organized a trip to a museum of natural history for a group of about fifty students ranging in age from twelve to fifteen years. When they arrived at the museum, students divided into small groups to tour the museum without supervision. One student, Roberto Mancha, of his own volition joined a group and proceeded with them to the various exhibits. While out of his teacher's sight, Roberto alleged that he was accosted by a group of youths not connected with the school, was beaten by them, and as a result suffered serious injuries. In *Mancha* v. *Field Museum of Natural History* (1972), Roberto's father initiated action against the school district, the two teachers, and the museum for the injuries his son suffered while at the museum. **When can a teacher be sued for negligence?**

ANALYSIS OF "YOU SHOULD HAVE KNOWN BETTER" Lawsuits brought by students injured during school-related activities are the most common type of litigation in education. A teacher who demonstrates **negligence** (failure to exercise reasonable care to protect students from injury) may be held liable for damages if an injured student can prove the following:

1. The teacher had a legal duty to offer a standard of care that would have prevented the injury from occurring.
2. The teacher did not live up to the standard of care.
3. The teacher's carelessness resulted in harm to the student.
4. The student sustained an actual injury that could be measured in monetary terms. (Imber & van Geel, 2004)

When accused of negligence, a teacher can try to prove that a student's injury was a mere accident, that her action or inaction was not the cause of such injury, or that some other act intervened and was the cause of the injury. Other responses to claims of negligence include contributory negligence, comparative negligence, and assumption of risk (Alexander & Alexander, 2005).

Contributory negligence occurs when the student who was injured failed to exercise the required standard of care for his or her own safety. When this condition exists, depending on such things as a child's age and mental maturity, the teacher may be absolved from liability. A high school student, for example, who has been taught how to use a power saw and observed to determine that she can operate the machine safely may be guilty of contributory negligence if injured while removing a piece of wood from the machine with her hands—a violation of safety practices the students have been taught.

In situations in which teacher and student are both held liable for an injury, there may be a charge of **comparative negligence**. Generally, this means that a teacher is held accountable for a proportion of damages in line with the degree to which he contributed to the injury. **Assumption of risk**, rarely applicable except in cases of competitive athletics, means that people who are aware of possible risks involved in an activity voluntarily participate, thus agreeing to take their chances.

In *Mancha* v. *Field Museum of Natural History* (1972), an Illinois court dismissed charges of negligence brought against the school, museum, and teachers. The lower courts did state that the teachers' action of letting students tour the museum in an unsupervised group was an intentional act. But given the nature of the environment (a museum), it was not an act that teachers should have anticipated would result in harm to a student. In explaining their verdict, the court argued that a museum is very different from a factory, a stone quarry, or a place where there might be dangerous machinery, or a place where there might be a shooting or an assault:

> The Museum in question is itself a great educational enterprise which enables teachers, parents, and children to learn much that could be learned at school. . . . To say that the teachers had a duty to supervise and discipline all students during the entire Museum trip would be to ignore the realities of the situation and to make such trips impossible. (*Mancha* v. *Field Museum of Natural History*, 1972, p. 902)

Technology in Practice

ONLINE TRAINING FOR RECOGNIZING CHILD NEGLECT AND ABUSE

The U.S. Department of Health and Human Services (2003) reports that each week fifty thousand claims of suspected child abuse or neglect are received by Child Protective Services agencies.

In the period of one year in the state of Virginia, for example, nearly nine thousand cases of neglect and abuse were documented. These fell into four categories:

- 57 percent neglect
- 28 percent physical abuse
- 11 percent sexual abuse
- 4 percent emotional and medical maltreatment

Teachers are required by law to report suspected child abuse and neglect. Because teachers have regular contact with students, they are in an opportune position to recognize indicators of child maltreatment. The first challenge is recognizing abuse and neglect when you see indications that either has occurred—an incredibly difficult challenge. For instance, what is the difference between neglect and abuse? How do you differentiate

neglect from poverty? Is corporal punishment different from outright abuse? When, where, and how would you report abuse or neglect? How do you support a child who is subjected to abuse or neglect?

In Virginia, all teachers seeking licensure must complete an online module—Recognizing, Reporting, and Responding for Educators—created by Virginia Commonwealth University's Institute for Social Services Training Activities. In addition to excellent written information, this website provides some of the best videos available on troubling problems. After working through the module, check your knowledge by responding to the true/false questions in the Summary at www.vcu.edu/vissta/training/va_teachers/faq.html.

Question for Reflection: On which issues related to child abuse and neglect do you still need additional information or guidance?

Source: Virginia Commonwealth University, Institute for Social Services Training Activities. (2005). Child abuse and neglect: Recognizing, reporting, and responding for educators. Available online: www.vcu.edu/vissta/training/va_teachers/

However, there have been several cases in which students were injured and educators were found to have breached duty of care:

- A group of students with mental retardation was left unattended for a half-hour, and a student received an eye injury when another pupil threw a wooden pointer (*Gonzalez* v. *Mackler*, 1963).
- A student who was permitted to wear mittens fell while climbing on a jungle gym (*Ward* v. *Newfield Central School District No. 1*, 1978).
- A student was burned when she and her peers were working on a project for the science fair. The accident occurred when the students tried to light a defective burner that had gone out and alcohol exploded. Although the teacher had set up the experiment and checked to see that it worked properly, the teacher was not in the room when the students lit the burner. Because the students were not advised to wait until the teacher's return to light the fire and were not personally supervised, the teacher was held liable for negligence (*Station* v. *Travelers Insurance Co.*, 1974).

What Are School Districts' Rights and Responsibilities?

Although the courts have consistently asserted that the authority for public education resides in the state legislature, schools for the most part are administered locally. Local school boards deal with a variety of educational issues and problems. A number of court cases, in conjunction with federal and state statutes, have clarified the special responsibilities and rights of local school districts. **Do school boards have the power to ban textbooks?**

Balancing Academic Freedom

The school board meeting raged on for several hours. Three English teachers from the high school and a number of parents voiced their opinions about the list of texts used in elective high school literature courses. When the board voted to eliminate ten texts from the diverse list of 1,285 books, the teachers were enraged. They believed all the books were necessary components of a curriculum designed to encourage debate and broaden student knowledge. Viewing the board's action as an invasion of their First Amendment right to academic freedom, the three English teachers decided to seek legal counsel. They could not believe that a local school board had ultimate authority to determine what textbooks would be used in schools.

ANALYSIS OF "BALANCING ACADEMIC FREEDOM" Since the U.S. Supreme Court ruling in *Hazelwood School District* v. *Kuhlmeier* (1988), the Court indicated a willingness to give local school boards the final decision regarding the curriculum and the availability of books, films, and materials in elementary and secondary classrooms. However, if school boards' actions narrow rather than expand knowledge, judicial intervention is not uncommon (Alexander & Alexander, 2005). When deciding individual cases, the courts usually consider the educational relevance of controversial material, teaching objectives, and the age and maturity of the intended audience.

In *Virgil* v. *School Board of Columbia County, Florida* (1989), the Supreme Court upheld a local school board's right to remove two readings from the curriculum because of objections to the material's vulgarity and sexual explicitness. Although the Court did not endorse the decision, stating that they seriously questioned how reading the masterpieces of Western literature could harm young people, the Court acknowledged that the school board's decision was reasonably related to "legitimate pedagogical concerns." That is, as in *Hazelwood,* school officials considered the emotional maturity of the intended audience when determining the appropriateness of readings dealing with potentially sensitive topics (Alexander & Alexander, 2005).

How much freedom does a teacher have in the selection of material for her students? In 1989 a Fifth Circuit Court of Appeals ruling held that teachers cannot assert a First Amendment right to replace an official supplementary reading list with their own list of books without first getting administrative approval. Nor may teachers delete parts of the curriculum that conflict with their personal beliefs. A kindergarten teacher, for example, who refuses to teach a unit on patriotic topics may be dismissed by the school board for not covering prescribed material (LaMorte, 2005).

Teachers do have freedom in selecting teaching strategies, however. Teachers who want to assign controversial materials usually may do so, as long as the selected materials are relevant to the topic of study, appropriate to the age and maturity of the students, and unlikely to cause disruption. When a high school psychology teacher in a conservative Texas community was fired for having her students read a masculinity survey from *Psychology Today,* the court ruled that the school violated the teacher's constitutional rights. In the eyes of the court, there was no evidence that the material caused substantial disruption, and there was no clear, prior prohibition against the use of such materials (Fischer, Schimmel, Stellman, & Kelly, 2003).

Equal Treatment

Fifteen African American preschool and elementary students living in a low-income housing project in Ann Arbor, Michigan, brought suit against the board of education for practices they claimed denied them equal educational opportunities. According to the students, their language (African American English) differed from the standard English spoken by teachers and used in written materials of the school. The students claimed a violation of Title 20 of the U.S. Code, which says that no state can deny individuals educational opportunities due to their race, gender, or national origin by failing to overcome language barriers that might inhibit learning (*Martin Luther King, Jr., Elementary School Children* v. *Michigan Board of Education,* 1979).

ANALYSIS OF "EQUAL TREATMENT" Are school boards legally obligated to make special provisions for students who speak "black English"? In its 1954 landmark decision *Brown* v. *Board of Education of Topeka, Kansas,* the Supreme Court addressed for the first time issues of educational inequality when it rejected the "separate but equal doctrine." Their decision was an attempt to put an end to racial segregation in schools. As the courts worked, and continue to work, to create united school systems, many have questioned the quality of educational opportunities for minority-group students in such settings.

One area of concern about equality has been classification of minority-group students for special services. Sometimes courts and legislatures have directed attention to discriminatory classifications of minority-group students. In other situations, such as those involving linguistic minority-group students, the courts have addressed the absence of student classifications.

In *Lau* v. *Nichols* (1974), the Supreme Court held that a school district receiving federal aid must provide special instruction for non-English-speaking students whose opportunities to learn are restricted because of language barriers. This particular case centered on the plight of about 1,800 Chinese American students in San Francisco public schools. They spoke little or no English, yet were offered no remedial English language instruction or other special compensatory program by the school system. According to the Court, such treatment of students violated Title VI of the **Civil Rights Act of 1964,** which specifies that no one, regardless of race, color, or origin, can be discriminated against or denied participation in programs receiving federal assistance.

Following *Lau,* Congress offered further protection to students when it passed the **Bilingual Act of 1974,** amended in 1988. This act calls for parental involvement in the planning of appropriate educational programs for children with limited English-speaking ability. Neither the Bilingual Act nor Title VI, however, specifies what types of programs are appropriate for addressing the needs of students with limited English-speaking abilities. Types of assistance offered to students who have difficulty understanding standard English vary greatly from state to state.

Since the *Lau* ruling, the courts have heard many cases, one of which was *Martin Luther King, Jr., Elementary School Children* v. *Michigan Board of Education* (1979). As described earlier, African American students who protested the use of standard English as the sole medium of instruction brought this suit before the court.

In ruling on the case, the Court acknowledged that Michigan schools had provided special assistance to these and other students through learning consultants, a speech therapist, a psychologist, a language consultant, tutors, and parent helpers. Evidence existed of good-faith efforts to meet the needs of students who spoke black English. The Court noted, however, that teachers seemed to lack knowledge about black English and thus were restricted in their ability to educate African American students. To remedy this, the Court did not order the establishment of a bilingual program, as was done in the *Lau* case. Instead, the Court required the school board to develop a plan whereby teachers would learn to recognize the home language of students. That knowledge would then be used to teach reading skills and standard English more effectively.

How Could You Let This Happen to a Student?

Are schools liable for educational malpractice? When Peter graduated from high school, he sought $500,000 in damages from the San Francisco Unified Schools for failing to provide him with an adequate education. According to Peter, the school system was at fault for his poor skills because it had (1) failed to understand his reading disabilities; (2) assigned him to classes in which curricular materials were not geared to his reading level; (3) allowed him to pass from grade to grade without seeing that he mastered basic skills necessary for succeeding levels; (4) assigned him to teachers who did not know how to meet his learning needs; and (5) allowed him to graduate without being able to read at the eighth-grade level, as required by the Education Code. Moreover, Peter said that his mother had been told that his reading ability was not much below the school's average.

ANALYSIS OF "HOW COULD YOU LET THIS HAPPEN TO A STUDENT?" Historically, teachers and educational institutions have been exempt from legal responsibility and accountability. Increasing numbers of educational malpractice claims, however, have forced the courts to deal frequently with issues of academic negligence. A precedent-setting case occurred in California in 1976, when Peter W., the high school graduate just described, accused the school system of negligently and intentionally depriving him of basic skills.

The state appellate court dismissed Peter W.'s suit, contending that there were no explicit "standards of care" by which schools or classroom teachers could be judged negligent in their duties. Besides conflicting ideas about the best way to educate students, the court noted that a variety of physical, neurological, emotional, cultural, and environmental factors influence learning but were beyond a classroom teacher's control. In addition, the court reasoned that attempts to hold school districts to a "duty of care" in academic matters would likely result in a flood of malpractice suits that would only inhibit schools' abilities to fulfill their academic functions (*Peter W.* v. *San Francisco Unified School District*, 1976).

For the most part, the California court's decision has been followed in educational malpractice litigation. However, in instances in which educators have maliciously or intentionally caused injury to children, courts have allowed parents to bring action against school officials (LaMorte, 2005). Such instances include cases in which educators furnish false information about a child's learning problems and alter information to cover their actions (*Hunter* v. *Board of Education of Montgomery County*, 1982) or when they place a child in a program despite scores showing the placement to be inappropriate (*B.M. by Berger* v. *State of Montana*, 1982).

Somebody Will Pay!

Can students who are victims of sexual harassment sue for damages? Christine Franklin, a tenth-grade student, felt uncomfortable around Andrew Hill, a sports coach and economics teacher at her high school in suburban Atlanta. According to Christine, Hill sexually harassed her by doing such things as asking if she would be willing to have sex with an older man, calling her at home to ask her out, and forcibly kissing her on the mouth in the school parking lot. During Christine's junior year, things got much worse; on at least three occasions, Hill allegedly pressured her into having sex. When Christine reported Hill's actions to school officials, they took no immediate steps to curtail Hill's behavior. By the time Christine had lodged a complaint with the U.S. Education Department's office for civil rights, however, Hill had resigned and the school had adopted a grievance procedure to avoid future violations.

Still angry about the abuse she had suffered at the high school, Christine decided to sue the school district for monetary damages. She argued that Hill's behavior toward her violated Title IX—a law prohibiting schools supported with federal monies from discriminating on the basis of gender (Darden, 2007). In school officials' eyes, Christine didn't stand a chance in court; they had resolved the problem and it was unlikely to occur again.

ANALYSIS OF "SOMEBODY WILL PAY!" In 1992, when the Supreme Court heard Christine Franklin's case (*Franklin* v. *Gwinnett County Public Schools*), the Court ruled unanimously that Christine had suffered sexual harassment. Furthermore, the Court stated for the first time that schools supported by federal funds were susceptible to lawsuits and, in instances of sexual harassment and other forms of sex discrimination, liable under Title IX for monetary damages to the victims of such mistreatment.

Because *Franklin* was about a teacher's harassment of a student, some lower courts concluded that the Supreme Court's decision did not apply to student-on-student harassment. The Supreme Court's ruling in *Davis* v. *Monroe County Board of Education* (1999), however, proved this assumption about harassment erroneous. LaShonda Davis, on whose behalf the case was filed, was only ten years old when a classmate, G. W., sexually harassed her by touching her breasts and genitals, telling her he wanted to have sex with her, and rubbing up against her. Despite LaShonda's complaints to teachers, no one intervened on her behalf. One teacher even refused for more than three months to let LaShonda change seats so that she could distance herself from G. W. in the classroom. Only after LaShonda's mother filed a criminal complaint against G. W., alleging sexual battery, did the harassment stop. Concerned by her daughter's declining grades and a suicide note, LaShonda's mother next filed a lawsuit against the district, alleging that Title IX had been violated. The Supreme Court's decision in this case reversed the decision of the U.S. Court of Appeals for the 11th Circuit, which in 1998 ruled that institutions have no obligation to address complaints of student-on-student harassment. This time, the Supreme Court held that schools can be held liable for monetary damages if they are deliberately indifferent to known sexual harassment (Williams, 1999).

What Kind of Choice Is This?

When the special education teacher and Anita Leopold met at the end of second grade to construct Miranda Leopold's IEP, they agreed that Miranda was at a point where she could benefit academically and socially from interactions with regular education students. Accordingly, they created a plan that would allow Miranda to be mainstreamed into a regular third-grade classroom. With the exception of daily tutorial sessions with a resource teacher, Miranda would experience the regular curriculum for third-grade students.

Anita liked her daughter's new placement. When she learned, however, that Miranda also qualified for the Milwaukee Parental Choice Program, she didn't know what to think. One of the private schools on the choice list focused on art and music, both of which Miranda loved. The idea of sending Miranda to such a school appealed to Anita. When she phoned the school for information about the program, however, Anita learned that the choice school had no resource teacher to help Miranda with her reading skills. Anita was perplexed. Didn't choice schools have to offer the same services to students with disabilities as did the public schools? How could state taxes be used for educational programs that, in a sense, discriminate against certain students? **Are choice schools held to the same standards as public schools?**

ANALYSIS OF "WHAT KIND OF CHOICE IS THIS?" On March 3, 1992, the Wisconsin Supreme Court voted four to three to overturn a court of appeals ruling that the Milwaukee Parental Choice Plan (MPCP) was unconstitutional. Established in March 1990, the Choice Plan allowed up to one thousand low-income students in Milwaukee to receive a voucher worth $2,500 each year to attend certain private, nonsectarian schools in the city. According to Shirley S. Abrahamson, one of the dissenting justices, the majority opinion on this issue "permits the legislature to subvert the unifying, democratizing purpose of public education by using public funds to substitute private education for public education without the concomitant controls exerted over public education" (*Davis* v. *Grover*, 1992).

Participating private schools do not have to meet the same standards as public schools in the Milwaukee Parental Choice Plan. Julie Underwood (1991) noted that "quality assurances" in the Choice Plan ensure that participating schools be operating as private schools and that one of the following occur: at least 70% of the student body should advance one grade level per year, average attendance rate should be at least 90%, at least 80% of the pupils should show "significant" educational progress; or at least 70% of the pupils' parents should meet school criteria for active involvement in the program.

In 1995 the legislature approved a budget proposal that would expand the program to include religious schools and 15 percent of the public school population, or roughly fifteen thousand students. The Milwaukee Teachers' Education Association and the American Civil Liberties Union immediately challenged the proposal. In 1998 the Wisconsin Supreme Court upheld the constitutionality of the revised proposal, which at the time provided vouchers of $4,400 to some 1,500 children (Walsh, 1998). By 2005 some fifteen thousand children were enrolled in Milwaukee's choice program (School Choice Wisconsin, 2005).

The *Zelman* v. *Simmons-Harris* case, argued before the Supreme Court on February 20, 2002, may have permanently changed the legal landscape of support for the voucher system and school choice. In a five-to-four opinion delivered by then-Chief Justice William H. Rehnquist, the Court held that Ohio's voucher plan, which allowed students to attend both religious and nonreligious schools, did not offend the Constitution's Establishment Clause.

Case Perspectives

Think back to the case that opened this chapter. The following comments are designed to provide a context for your thinking about that case.

A SCHOOL BOARD MEMBER WHO IS ALSO AN ATTORNEY-AT-LAW COMMENTS   There is little doubt in my mind that this strip search would be ruled as "highly intrusive" by a court of law. It may or may not have been unreasonable—which is another important factor considered by the courts. The adults who run schools are bound by law to keep their charges safe. As a school board member I understand full well that the community expects teachers and school administrators to do what is necessary to protect the children in their care. If this particular situation had involved a search for drugs or weapons, then it might have been a reasonable action. After all, there is an immediate threat of danger in those situations. But even then, Brautigan's actions are questionable. A search for money instead of guns or drugs, however, is quite different. There was no immediate threat of danger in a student concealing money. The federal courts have been quite clear about forbidding strip searches for money. The courts have issued mixed messages on strip searches for other purposes, so I would never expect a teacher to know what is an acceptable strip search and what is unreasonable. It's best not to get involved in such things under any circumstances.

A HIGH SCHOOL PRINCIPAL REFLECTS ON THE PROBLEMS WITH SUCH ACTION   Right off the top I would tell Richard Brautigan not to even think about taking on the responsibility of conducting a strip search—not under any circumstances. A lone teacher or coach should never put himself or herself in such a position. School administrators have much more experience handling troubling situations than do teachers. They know the school and district policies with regard to students' rights. Administrators have also taken college course work on school law. They may not be attorneys themselves, but they are smart enough to know when they are skating on thin ice. For example, school administrators would never conduct a strip search even to find weapons without having more than one adult present.

I wonder why Brautigan didn't detain the boys and get some additional help before taking the extreme step of a strip search. He might even have called the boys' parents and waited until they showed up. There was so much money involved that school authorities might even have called the police. They could have handled the situation.

Questions for Reflection: What steps should the coach and the principal take at this point? Do you think extreme actions by teachers—strip searches, physical restraint—are ever justified in a school setting? What other choices do you think the coach might have had in this situation? ■

Summary

Government at all levels influences schools by passing, enforcing, and interpreting laws and by funding educational programs. The locus of power resides at the state level, as authorized by the Tenth Amendment to the Constitution.

Public education works in the United States because we maintain a balance between our rights and our responsibilities to the communities of which we are a part. Parents have the right to expect that their children will receive an adequate basic education from school authorities. But parents must also make certain their children are cared for and that they come to school ready to learn. Students themselves must be afforded real opportunities to learn and be subjected to rules that are fair and fairly administered. They, in turn, must behave reasonably and with respect toward others.

Teachers do not have to surrender their personhood when they go to work; they can expect to exercise their professional judgment in the performance of their duties. Teachers are responsible for teaching their students and for protecting their students' physical, intellectual, emotional, and social well-being. School systems and their leaders must provide the infrastructure to support teaching and learning and govern fairly and openly. They have the right to expect the people to provide support for public education.

Sometimes teachers must face situations that are gray or ill defined, legally speaking. Seeking advice is always wise. It also makes sense for teachers to ask themselves what a reasonable person would do if faced with the same situation and take their cues accordingly.

TERMS AND CONCEPTS

assumption of risk
Bilingual Act of 1974
Buckley Amendment
Civil Rights Act of 1964
comparative negligence
contributory negligence
dismissal
due process of law

Equal Access Act (EAA)
equal protection clause
establishment clause
free exercise clause
in loco parentis
Lemon test
negligence

REFLECTIVE ACTIVITY: SEXUAL HARASSMENT

Reflective practice is an essential part of good teaching. Reflection is a process that includes making thoughtful decisions, understanding and articulating value structures, acting from knowledge, evaluating your actions and their effects, and sharing your reflections with colleagues. After reading the following scenario, respond to the questions below. The scenario reflects the INTASC Principle and Disposition at the end of this activity.

Lexington, North Carolina. First-grader Johnathan Prevette is accused of sexual harassment of a classmate. Johnathan kissed a female classmate on the cheek, and the girl's mother charged sexual harassment. The superintendent suspended Johnathan from school.

If Jane Ottinger, a teacher at Lincoln Middle School, had read this headline in her Sunday paper a year ago, she would have believed that it was some kind of cruel joke. Since when did a little boy kissing a little girl become sexual harassment?

But that was before she had lived through what was to become known as the Amy Christopher Incident. Amy was a bright, pretty girl in Jane's sixth-grade class. Mr. and Mrs. Christopher argued that the boys in Amy's class had treated her so badly that she had become an emotional wreck. When the Christophers complained to Jane about the behavior, Jane went immediately to the principal and recounted her conversation with them. The principal said that he would handle the matter and that Jane should be alert to signs of inappropriate behavior but not to worry too much. As nearly as Jane could remember, he said something like, "The hormones begin to rage about this time in kids' lives. Sometimes the boys, and the girls too, get carried away. This is natural. Although the school does not want and would never condone such behavior, you need to understand that some parents are fanatics who blow everything out of proportion. Flirting and teasing are part of life in the sixth grade."

Six months later the Christophers moved to another school district. Their move was accompanied by a front-page story in the local paper, in which they were quoted as saying that they had complained repeatedly to the teacher and school officials about the sexual harassment of their daughter and other children, but gotten no results.

Now, some four months later, when Jane read the story about little Johnny she felt sad. Had times changed so much since she was a child? Where would all these claims and counterclaims end?

Decide   1. How do issues such as the Amy Christopher Incident offer opportunities for teaching and learning? How do incidents of possible sexual harassment impede learning?

Perceive and Value   2. If you were Amy's parents, what might you say to your daughter's teacher and principal if you suspected other children of sexual harassment? If you were Amy's teacher, what would you think of the principal's response?

Know and Act   3. If you were a teacher faced with a situation like that presented by Amy Christopher, what more would you want to know? Assuming that you reported incidents between students and told your principal about parents' concerns, what more if anything might you do? Rank the following activities in the order in which you might undertake them. Explain your reasoning.

- Weave prevention of sexual harassment throughout the curriculum.
- Train peer leaders in awareness and prevention, and use them to teach workshops for other children.
- Provide students with safe avenues to report harassment.
- Involve parents in lessons and homework on sexual harassment (LRP Publications, 1996, p. 3).

Evaluate   4. Examine your own perceptions about sexual harassment. What standards guide your assessment of acceptable and unacceptable behaviors among young people? Examine a school's faculty handbook. Does it mention sexual harassment among students? If so, what does it communicate?

Discuss   5. The Johnathan Prevette incident involves a single incident between two first-grade students. The Amy Christopher incident involves several events involving a sixth-grade girl and several sixth-grade boys. How would knowledge about development at each of these ages help you to understand these two incidents? Are these incidents examples of typical development, inappropriate behavior, or both?

INTASC Principle 2

The teacher understands how children learn and develop, and can provide learning opportunities that support their intellectual, social, and personal development.

Disposition

The teacher understands that students' physical, social, emotional, moral, and cognitive development influences learning and knows how to address these factors when making instructional decisions. (Interstate New Teacher Assessment and Support Consortium, 1992)

ADDITIONAL READINGS

American Civil Liberties Union. (1999). *Freedom is why we are here.* New York: Author. Available online: www.aclu.org.

Crockett, J. B., & Kauffman, J. M. (1999). *The least restrictive environment: Its origins and interpretations in special education.* Mahwah, NJ: Erlbaum.

Essex, N. L. (2005). *School law and the public schools: A practical guide for educational leaders* (2nd ed.). Boston: Allyn and Bacon.

Imber, M., & van Geel, T. (2005). *A teacher's guide to education law* (8th ed.). Mahwah, NJ: Erlbaum.

LaMorte, M. W. (2005). *School law: Cases and concepts* (8th ed.). Boston: Allyn & Bacon.

Zirkel, P. A. (2001). *A digest of Supreme Court decisions affecting education* (4th ed.). Bloomington, IN: Phi Delta Kappa Educational Foundation.

WEB RESOURCES

www.nps.gov/brvb/
This site commemorates the landmark Supreme Court decision (Brown v. Board of Education) *aimed at ending segregation in public schools.*

www.nytimes.com/learning/index.html
Go to the New York Times *Learning Network and search on "law" to find lesson plans on hot topics.*

www.aclu.org/
The American Civil Liberties Union works to protect individual rights and liberties.

www.freedomforum.org/
The Freedom Forum is a nonpartisan foundation dedicated to free press, free speech, and free spirit for all people.

www.educationlaw.org
Information about legal issues affecting schools, colleges and universities.

www.tolerance.org/teach/
Supported by the Southern Poverty Law Center.

Developing a Professional Portfolio

PLANNING YOUR PROFESSIONAL DEVELOPMENT

Being a professional means, in part, knowing how to strengthen your knowledge and skills. Teachers make *professional development plans* and include them in their portfolios to guide their own work and to demonstrate to others that they have clear, attainable professional goals. As you think about becoming a teacher, what is your plan for developing as a professional? Use the following questions to guide your planning, specifying the materials that you will include in your portfolio:

- What courses will you take in your program of studies?
- How will these courses enhance your knowledge of the content you plan to teach?
- Which courses have field placements?
- What types of activities will you be doing in these field placements?
- What options are there to work through school- or community-based organizations with both children and their parents? How might these options help you stretch beyond the required program of studies to make you a better professional?
- What credentials do you need to work as a substitute teacher in the schools?
- How might substitute teaching help you think about your own eventual work as a full-time teacher in schools? At what point in your college career might you be able to serve as a substitute teacher?

Next, talk with someone in your college or university career services office about paid and volunteer work you can do to enhance your employability as an educator. Many organizations rely heavily on volunteers to support young people. They provide opportunities for you to demonstrate your abilities and your commitment to worthy causes. These include secular organizations (e.g., Big Brothers, Big Sisters, computer clubs, and after-school programs), as well as religiously affiliated organizations (e.g., Hillel, Catholic Youth Organization, Sunday school, and summer camps).

Online Activity

Oyez Project

Go to the Oyez Project, a U.S. Supreme Court Multimedia Database (http://oyez.org). Search on *Santa Fe Independent School District* v. *Doe* (06/19/2000).

This case addressed the question of whether a school system's policy permitting student-led, student-initiated prayer at football games violated the Establishment Clause of the First Amendment. Click on Abstract to examine the facts of the case and the decision made by the Court. Listen to the oral argument and access the written opinion on the website.

What did the Supreme Court decide? How was the Court's ruling affected by principles endorsed in *Lee* v. *Weisman* (1992)? How do you think this decision might affect your job as a teaching professional?

CHAPTER 10

Curriculum and Instruction

Case Study: Reaching Every Student

It was Thursday evening, and John Sampson was feeling particularly energetic. The first few weeks of school had flown by, and he was itching to sketch out his plans for the next teaching quarter. As the new math hire at Gainesville High School, John had been assigned two basic- and three higher-level classes of students. John loved math—a subject that had always come easily to him. He couldn't explain why, but it was as if he were born understanding the subject. His classmates, and at least one of his teachers, used to jokingly refer to him as the class "egghead."

Now as he planned for instruction, however, he did not feel so smart. Although most students had done well on his first quiz, there were at least seven or eight who had not. John was stumped by their poor performance. Each day he had started classes with a review of previous material before introducing new information. And because he wanted students to understand math concepts, not simply memorize material, John followed the review session with problems that illustrated a new concept. Students were to work individually or in pairs to figure out what the problems had in common. They were to then determine how those problems were different from examples presented in earlier classes. This approach had worked well for John as a student, and he believed it would benefit Gainesville High students as well.

Although most students engaged eagerly in discussion, others had to be prodded to get involved in the lesson. On at least one occasion, John had been challenged by a couple of students who said they would never get the math lesson if John didn't start teaching. John took the comments with good humor and assured the students that they would soon catch on. In fact, he predicted, they would soon become math stars. As John looked at students' papers, however, he saw that many—not just the lowest performers—had a long way to go before they reached stardom. Was he being impatient, expecting too much too soon from his students? What might he do to "hook" the reluctant students and get them involved in instruction?

This chapter presents some of the more prevalent ways curriculum has been defined through educational practice. It explores the forces influencing curriculum content and the goals underlying the curriculum. The ways educators design curriculum and models of instruction also are described. Finally, this chapter considers factors that determine effective classroom instruction.

What Is Curriculum?

The term **curriculum** refers to what is taught in school. (*Curricula* is the plural form.) In practice, curriculum can cover a wide variety of ideas. A good working definition of curriculum is the knowledge and skills that schools are supposed to help students master. Books and study guides are curriculum. Movies, newspapers, computer programs, board games, animals, and songs can be curriculum as well.

For some people, the word *curriculum* can mean a set of subjects, subject content, a program of studies, a set of materials, a sequence of courses, a set of performance objectives, and a course of study. Curriculum can be regarded as everything that goes on within the school, including after-school activities, guidance, and interpersonal relationships, as well as everything taught both inside and outside school that is directed by the school or planned by school personnel. Curriculum is a series of student experiences in schools.

Because curriculum can have so many interpretations, Americans often disagree about what children should or should not be taught in classrooms (Kliebard, 2002). Politics, economics, and religious beliefs differ among the population, and they are all elements that can change rapidly. Because states and localities control education, they are left to define curriculum. Therefore, shifts in politics, economics, and religious beliefs within the community and the state can influence schools' curricula to a large degree. If you examine battles over curriculum, you often will find political, economical, and religious beliefs at the root. To prevent some of these battles over curriculum, states have recently made efforts to establish common educational standards and assessments. Their efforts have done much to build consensus on the practical meaning of education. Because we are such a diverse nation, we do not have—nor is it likely we ever will have—a national curriculum, or one comprehensive curriculum that all children must master.

As noted, curriculum exists outside school as well as inside. Educational opportunities are not limited to only schools and universities. Business, industry, churches, prisons, and other organizations provide out-of-school training on topics as diverse as dog obedience, home sales, and natural childbirth. Curriculum is at issue when children watch *Sesame Street* and attend Scout meetings, when people study for a real estate license, and when people participate in a local library's reading program. **Who should define the curriculum in schools?**

Explicit and Implicit Curricula

Explicit curriculum is the official description of programs, courses, and objectives of study that explain specific educational expectations for both teachers and students. Explicit curriculum exists in policy statements, manuals of school procedures, instructional materials, and textbooks that stipulate what and how students should learn. Teachers are expected to teach the explicit curriculum; students are supposed to learn it. Explicit curriculum might, for example, outline what specific subject matter or skills should be taught in each grade. This is the type of curriculum for which schools are held publicly accountable.

Explicit curriculum dominates the public view, but another side of the curriculum is unvoiced, often unintended, and equally as powerful. This side reveals itself in the way teachers present subject matter and in the classroom atmosphere they establish. Philip Jackson (1990, p. 33) called this curriculum the "hidden curriculum," and Elliot Eisner (1985, p. 89) used the term **implicit curriculum.**

Students learn many implicit lessons while they attend school, and some of them might stay with students longer than the explicit curriculum. "Trying" is one such lesson taught implicitly, rather than explicitly, through school experiences. If a student "does his homework (though incorrectly), he raises his hand (though he usually comes up with the wrong answer), [and] he keeps his nose in the book during free study period (though he doesn't turn the page very often)," he will likely gain the teacher's approval and be labeled a "model" student (Jackson, 1990, p. 34). Students may also implicitly learn that participating in class puts them in the teacher's good favor. In these ways, students discover implicitly that mastery of content is not the only road to success in the classroom.

School routines and rituals also are part of the implicit curriculum. Teacher behavior, such as calling on students whose hands are raised while ignoring those who speak without permission, is one of the subtle ways that teachers convey values. Other implicit classroom examples teach students to cooperate with others, to have patience, and to demonstrate group skills.

Another type of implicit curriculum relates to teachers' values and to the subject matter they teach. In other words, how a teacher presents the material can be as important as the content itself. In case studies of four high school teachers, Sigrun Gudmundsdottir (1991) found that teachers' values seeped into the curriculum through personal interpretations of subject matter and through teaching methods. For example, when English teachers were presenting *Huckleberry Finn*, one teacher viewed the book as an illustration of "an individual rebelling against conventions." The other considered it "a book about relationships [between Huck and Jim]" (p. 48). Each teacher selected passages for discussion that represented her interpretation of the book, thereby creating different "texts" for their students. **What lessons did you learn from the implicit curriculum in the high school you attended?**

What aspects of the explicit curriculum are evident in this photograph? What aspects of the implicit curriculum might you infer?

Null Curriculum

Should schools be concerned about aspects of the curriculum that are not taught? If so, which ones? The **null curriculum** is the curriculum that is *not* taught (Eisner, 1985, 1994). When educators develop curriculum, they select the skills and subject matter they believe students should learn. This process necessarily means that some skills and topics will not be taught. Sometimes the decisions about what not to include in curriculum are conscious and sometimes they are not. For instance, some critics believe many textbooks portray U.S. history and contemporary life experiences in unrealistic ways, glossing over controversial issues and avoiding discussion of discrimination and prejudice. They suggest that such texts produce citizens with a narrow sense of reality.

That is to say, almost 50 percent of all marriages end in divorce. One-third of all children will live with a single parent during part of their lives. Yet many textbooks portray the typical U.S. family as one having two adults and two children in suburbia (Banks & Banks, 2005).

Time schedules for different classes and locations for instruction can also be part of the null curriculum because they communicate to students "what counts" in schools (Eisner, 1992, 1994). Time devoted to the arts, for example, is substantially less than time devoted to such courses as science and math. Moreover, the fact that art teachers are often "floaters"—moving from classroom to classroom—suggests to students that the arts are less permanent and perhaps less important than other courses. **What curriculum was absent from your high school's program of study—curriculum you might reasonably have expected to encounter?**

Extracurriculum

By definition, **extracurriculum** refers to activities that do not earn credits—it is extra, or over and above the required curriculum. Yet it can be a significant part of students' lives. Students' feelings about themselves, their desire to come to school, their need to belong or be part of a group, and even their performance in academic areas can be influenced greatly by extracurricular activities. In addition, extracurriculum can help students develop skills in leadership and cooperation, as well as in the particular activity they pursue.

Sports, band, clubs, study groups, school plays, cheerleading, dance, and so on, may fall under the heading of extracurriculum. In some schools these activities may be considered *cocurricular* and weighted equally with other academic classes. Most of the time, though, these activities are viewed as being outside the typical curriculum.

Nevertheless, people frequently make conceptual and policy ties between the curriculum and the extracurriculum. If a student performs poorly on the required curriculum, someone is sure to argue the student should not be allowed to participate in the extracurriculum, at least until his or her grades improve. Others will argue the opposite—were it not for the appeal of extracurricular activities, a student with academic problems might be a dropout.

Researchers at the U.S. Department of Education's Office of Educational Research and Improvement (OERI) found a strong connection between extracurricular activities and academic performance. Generally, extracurricular participation rates rose with students' socioeconomic levels, enrollment in an academic curriculum, and attainment of a B+ or better average. **Should extracurricular activities be part of every student's life or only those who are mastering the explicit curriculum?**

Integrated Curriculum

Many traditional practices compartmentalize subject matter in the curriculum, with separate classes for math, English, science, and so on. Educational critics have challenged these methods of teaching and learning, however, by arguing that they bear little resemblance to life outside schools. These critics favor an **integrated curriculum,** or a curriculum that combines concepts and skills from different subject areas (Drake & Burns, 2004). They believe an integrated curriculum will better prepare students for life beyond school, where subject matter is not so segregated.

In one real example of integrated curriculum, the teachers of primary grade students in a California school plan and teach science, social studies, and foreign languages to support the connections between the subjects. The teaching team helps students learn concepts, skills, and values by exploring themes that cut across subject matter. They resist separating the disciplines by class period and by the classrooms students occupy.

Another example of integrated curriculum is found with middle-school teachers in North Carolina, who take the study of science, social studies, language arts, and mathematics beyond school walls to their community. The teachers' goal is to forge connections in students minds between acquired content and using that content to solve problems. High school teachers and administrators in Illinois have restructured blocks of time in their conventional eight-period day into four periods. They assign staff to interdisciplinary teams, change student entrance and exit requirements for courses, and incorporate an entirely new set of instructional models. Students can spend longer periods of time on a topic and examine all the related subjects. All these programs are attempts to tear down walls that separate subject matter.

The development of integrated or interdisciplinary curriculum is made easier by emerging technologies. For example, teachers from across the United States and other countries work together on the Web to solve real-life problems by analyzing cases of interdisciplinary teaching and learning. The Web itself has brought a world of ideas into schools, making it even easier for students to see the relationships that exist among all topics, skills, and values.

What Forces for Change Affect Curriculum Content?

Many interests shape the curriculum of public schools. Historically, some interests operate within or close to the school itself. Others' interests exercise power indirectly and from a distance, both conceptually and physically. As Figure 10.1 indicates, some of the powerful forces shaping the curriculum include national interests, social issues and public opinion, and mass media.

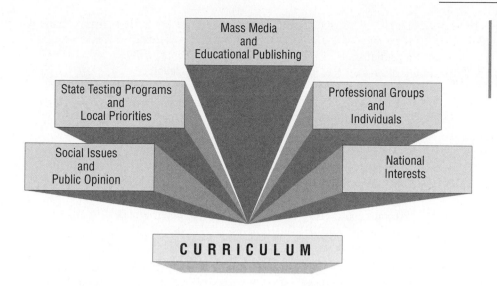

The National Interest

What kind of curriculum is in the national interest? The influence of national government on public school curriculum has a long and rich history. Much of its work is said to be on behalf of the "national interest," which can be thought of those ideas, skills, and values that build a strong democratic nation—the things that are best for the country as a whole. Passage of the Environmental Education Act (Public Law 91-516), for example, stimulated the modern environmental education movement (DeBoer, 1991). The U.S. Congress influenced vocational education (Smith–Hughes Act of 1917) and preschool education (Economic Opportunity Act of 1964), in addition to expanding school access for students with disabilities (Education for All Handicapped Children Act of 1975 and final regulations in the Individuals with Disabilities Education Act, 1997). These laws reflect values about education that are in the national interest.

Federal influence on curriculum development also occurs through funding and advisement. In the 1990s, for example, the federal government funded states to help students meet national learning and testing standards. In 2008 President George W. Bush spoke often about his education agenda as expressed in the No Child Left Behind legislation. He continually emphasized the place of standards and the importance of testing students to provide evidence of progress. The combination of formal actions (offering a legislative agenda with funding implications) and informal efforts (urging educators to rely more heavily on testing) affected the curriculum in schools across the nation, as educators worked to align the content of instruction with the standards to be assessed.

State and Local Priorities

State laws and local policies, many promoted by special-interest groups, influence everything in public schools from textbooks to discipline. Concerns about violence in schools, for example, caused the Georgia legislature to sign into law the Improved Student Learning and Discipline Act of 1999. The law requires school districts to teach character education to students at all grade levels. The twenty-seven traits listed in Figure 10.2 are the main focus of the "character curriculum." Many states have advanced programs to discourage bullying and violent acts against fellow students.

Other ways states are forcing curriculum revisions include dictating graduation requirements, adopting state achievement tests, and, in many instances, requiring new textbooks to match recommended instructional approaches. One particularly strong motivation for changing a school's curriculum is the results of student achievement tests. In response to students' poor scores on state and national reading tests, California education officials redesigned their

Figure 10.2
Georgia's Character-
Building Traits
Which, if any, of these character
traits might be controversial to
special-interest groups? Why?

courage	generosity
patriotism	punctuality
citizenship	cleanliness
honesty	respect for the environment
fairness	school pride
respect for others	respect for the creator
kindness	cheerfulness
cooperation	patience
self-respect	creativity
self-control	sportsmanship
courtesy	loyalty
compassion	perseverance
tolerance	virtue
diligence	

Source: Georgia Department of Education. (1999–2003). Character education: History and development of the concept. Available online: www.glc.k12.ga.us/pandp/chared/implmnt.htm.

language arts program. Officials have also revised their mathematics programs to teach basic skills. They want to move attention away from real-life application of mathematics and instead focus on students' abilities to calculate.

Curricula also can be influenced by local history and geography. In the Midwest, for example, memories of the Dust Bowl days of the Great Depression still linger. So schools in Nebraska farming communities teach students about the threats of soil erosion. On the Atlantic shores, students and their families do not have to own oceanfront property to be affected adversely by harsh storms. Schools on the New Jersey coast instruct students about the evils of beach erosion. **Did the community where you grew up emphasize any particular local issue in the curriculum?**

Social Issues and Public Opinion

To what extent should the curriculum reflect local interests and values? Public schools exist to serve the community and are responsible, to some degree, for providing curricula the public supports. Funding from public tax dollars causes school officials to consider public opinion and social issues when they develop curricula. Some social issues in which public opinion is often heard include teaching sex education, creationism, and multiculturalism.

In society's view perhaps the most controversial curriculum reform is *family life education,* which is now an integral part of most school programs. Family life education focuses on topics such as personal health and safety, substance abuse prevention, mental health education, human growth and development (including sex education), and sexually transmitted disease (STD) prevention. It is probably the area of the curriculum most closely scrutinized by the public. Parents often must sign a permission form for their children to participate in family life education.

Family life education programs around the country acknowledge the central role of parents in educating their children. School curricula on the topic try to help parents and fill in some of the gaps. What the curriculum covers, however, varies from place to place. In some localities, contraceptives are discussed in sex education classes; in other school systems, educators are prohibited from mentioning condoms or other contraceptives.

Professional Groups and Individuals

Professional organizations offer advice on material that should be taught, methods of teaching, and forms of evaluation. They also promote teacher involvement in school policy-making activities. Some organizations, such as the National Council of Teachers of Mathematics (NCTM), have developed standards intended to guide curricular reform in schools. The NCTM's *Curriculum and Evaluation Standards for School Mathematics* (1989) comprises fifty-four value statements. Each consists of three parts that address (1) what mathematics the curriculum should include, (2) a description of student activities associated with that mathematics, and (3) instructional examples. The NCTM standards make computation serve a more important goal—the development of mathematical thinking.

The NCTM standards offer guidelines for core knowledge, or that knowledge common to all students, as well as special requirements for college-bound students. In a companion volume, entitled *Professional Standards for Teaching Mathematics* (National Council of Teachers of Mathematics, 1991), NCTM recognizes teachers as central to changing mathematics education in schools. They emphasize the need to shift instruction toward the use of logic and mathematical evidence and away from a reliance on teachers as sources of right answers. The standards also promote responsive teaching practices. Standard 5, which follows, addresses how teachers should engage in ongoing analysis of teaching and learning:

Standard 5: Learning Environment

The teacher of mathematics should create a learning environment that fosters the development of each student's mathematical power by

- providing and structuring the time necessary to explore sound mathematics and grapple with significant ideas and problems;
- using the physical space and materials in ways that facilitate students' learning of mathematics;
- providing a context that encourages the development of mathematical skill and proficiency;
- respecting and valuing students' ideas, ways of thinking, and mathematical dispositions, and by consistently expecting and encouraging students to work independently or collaboratively to make sense of mathematics, take intellectual risks by raising questions and formulating conjectures, and display a sense of mathematical competence by validating and supporting ideas with mathematical argument. (NCTM, 1991, p. 57)

Figure 10.3 illustrates two teaching activities, one of which the NCTM might consider more "worthwhile" than the other. **To what extent should teachers and professional associations determine the curriculum?**

As individuals leading a classroom, teachers' habits, dispositions, and areas of professional expertise influence what is taught and learned. When teachers stick to familiar tools, content, and activities, they operate as conservative—and some believe negative—forces on curriculum (Cuban, 1992). In the 1970s criticisms of ill-prepared teachers led designers to create what are often called "teacher-proof" curricula, or curricula from which students can learn, regardless of the teacher's level of experience, interest, or skill (Grobman, 1970). Today, attitudes toward teachers as professionals are much more positive. Teachers' esteem is increasing in the public eye. Teachers are routinely characterized as a powerful force in children's lives. A Harris poll shows that teachers rank behind only scientists, doctors, and firefighters in terms of prestige (see Table 10.1).

Creative teachers make curricula come alive. In language arts or literature-based instruction, for example, teachers with a constructivist philosophy guide students to define knowledge for themselves, using curricula as the groundwork for innovative thinking. Teaching in these instances is not a matter of transmitting knowledge; it is more a matter of helping students construct and interpret knowledge for themselves.

At times it seems as though everyone, from the president to the person on the street, has an idea for curriculum. Students' needs, however, can and must dictate the nature of some curricula. As students' problems increase in number and/or severity, the standard curriculum may have to be reduced or modified. Curricula, and the programs used to deliver them, can be organized to fit the students instead of the other way around.

When a curriculum stimulates and holds student attention, it is likely to be copied, extended, promoted, adapted, and used with other students. Also, students influence teachers to behave in certain ways in the classroom. That is, students encourage teachers, or "pull" them,

Figure 10.3
Structuring Worthwhile Mathematics Tasks
What skills are required to solve Tasks 1 and 2? Why might the National Council for Teachers of Mathematics consider Task 2 the more "worthwhile" assignment?

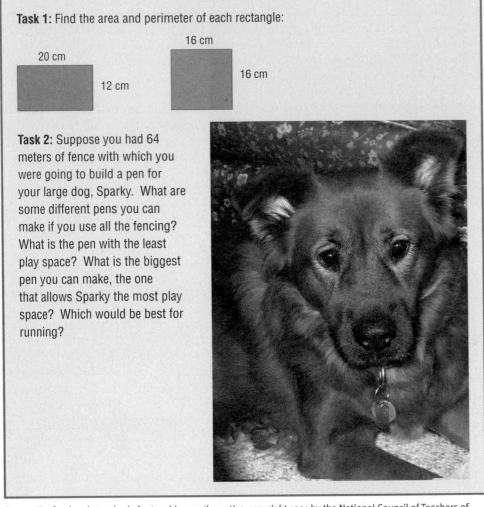

Task 1: Find the area and perimeter of each rectangle:

20 cm

12 cm

16 cm

16 cm

Task 2: Suppose you had 64 meters of fence with which you were going to build a pen for your large dog, Sparky. What are some different pens you can make if you use all the fencing? What is the pen with the least play space? What is the biggest pen you can make, the one that allows Sparky the most play space? Which would be best for running?

Source: Professional standards for teaching mathematics, copyright 1991 by the National Council of Teachers of Mathematics. Reprinted with permission. All rights reserved.

to emphasize or de-emphasize various aspects of the curriculum. The act of asking students to voice their own ideas on curriculum can be enlightening.

Educational Publishing and Mass Media

Textbooks play an important role in student learning, and the people who select them play an important role in shaping the curriculum. Deciding which textbooks a school should buy is not always an easy process. One outspoken critic of the $4.3 billion textbook market put it this way:

> Textbooks are a core part of the curriculum, as crucial to the teacher as a blueprint is to a carpenter, so one might assume they are conceived, researched, written, and published as unique contributions to advancing knowledge. In fact, most of these books fall far short of their important role in the educational scheme of things. They are processed into existence using the pulp of what already exits, rising like swamp things from the compost of the past. The mulch is turned and tended by many layers of editors who scrub it of anything possibly objectionable before it is fed into a government-run "adoption" system that provides mediocre material to students of all ages. (Ansary, 2004, p. 31)

Both conservative and liberal organizations urge people to get involved in textbook selection in their states and communities. About half the states have official state-level processes by

Table 10.1

OCCUPATIONS WITH THE MOST PRESTIGE

Occupation	Percentage Who Rate This the Most Prestigious
Scientist	52%
Doctor	52%
Firefighter	48%
Teacher	48%
Military officer	47%
Nurse	44%
Police officer	40%
Priest/minister/clergy	32%
Member of Congress	31%
Engineer	29%
Athlete	21%
Architect	20%
Business executive	19%
Lawyer	17%
Entertainer	16%
Union leader	16%
Actor	16%
Banker	15%
Journalist	14%
Accountant	10%
Stockbroker	10%
Real estate broker/agent	5%

Source: Harris Poll of 1,012 adults conducted August 10–15, 2004. Available online: www.usatoday.com3/money/economy/employment/2005-05-23-prestige-usat_x.htm.

which curricula are evaluated and endorsed. A state-level endorsement in populous states that tightly control textbook selection, such as Florida, Texas, and California, can be the difference between success and failure for a particular text and for its publisher.

State-level textbook adoption policies shape curricula in public schools across the entire state. These policies exist for several reasons. First, textbooks can be purchased at a lower cost when large orders are placed (a group of school districts as opposed to a single school district). Second, the state wants to protect children from being exposed to poor-quality textbooks, so they rely on experts to make selections. Third, a minimum standard curriculum for the entire state can be more easily established if schools are using the same books. **To what extent does the textbook publishing industry determine the curriculum?**

Textbooks often are the first thing people think of when they think about curriculum. Textbooks may constitute as much as 70 percent of the curriculum. People worry, however, that the drive to produce textbooks suitable for all students has instead led to textbooks that teach to the "lowest common denominator" or "dumb down" the curriculum. Critics believe textbook publishers avoid controversial subjects in trying to appeal to schools that may be urban or rural, liberal or conservative, wealthy or poor, and so on. In addition, some textbooks teach inaccurate and erroneous information.

Educators also worry about texts in all subject areas that are structured in pedagogically poor ways. A frequent criticism of math textbooks, for example, is curriculum coverage that is "a mile wide and an inch deep." As they customize lesson plans to meet the needs of students of varying ability levels, teachers need a focused, coherent curriculum that gives them more time to teach key concepts (American School Board Journal, 2007).

Textbook publishers influence the curriculum through the authors they hire and the books and materials they produce. Publishers argue that they do not influence the curriculum as much as do the people who buy the books. Publishers say they simply provide what they believe people will buy. And buy they do—elementary and secondary textbooks net nearly $492.9 million a year (Association of American Publishers, 2005).

In addition to news coverage of school policies, school funding, and testing scores, media also provide a wealth of information through television, film, radio, publications, and the Internet. In this sense, the media are involved directly in producing their own curricula.

One example of this direct curriculum production is Channel One Network, the leading provider of television news and educational programs for students. Channel One delivers programs by satellite to some twelve thousand middle schools and high schools in the United States. Participating schools receive a satellite dish and classroom television monitors in exchange for showing the programming. In turn, schools agree by contract to make Channel One available to their students on 90 percent of school days. Channel One has nearly 6 million students as regular viewers. Liberals and conservatives have differing views on Channel One. Some worry about Channel One's effects on students, criticizing in particular Channel One's introduction of commercials into the classroom. Others praise this public/private partnership for bringing quality content and technology to schools free of charge. Some believe that Channel One may have peaked. The company now faces the cost of having to replace outmoded technology with no new subscribers in sight (Borja, 2005). Figure 10.4 shows the Channel One homepage.

Another example of media-produced curriculum is the *New York Times* Learning Network on the Web. This website contains daily lesson plans that match each day's edition of the newspaper, an archive of previous plans, a special section on education news, education product reviews, science quizzes, special news packages on current events and historic events, and many more curricular materials. *New York Times* employees also conduct professional development sessions for teachers (see www.nytimes.com/learning/).

How Are Curriculum and Instruction Planned and Organized?

Ralph Waldo Emerson captured the essence of curriculum and instruction when he stated "the things taught in schools are not an education but the means for education" (Emerson, undated). In other words, teachers attempt to prepare students for life beyond school walls. They do so by considering their audience (students) and the aims of education.

Decisions about what is taught in schools are made by many levels of government and by many organizations. When it comes to the day-to-day business of education, however, teachers play a crucial role in developing and using curriculum. For all the decisions, ideas, and values others put into curriculum, teachers ultimately are responsible for making curriculum work.

Aims of Education

Through the years, educators have had different ideas about what and how students should learn. As illustrated in Figure 10.5, some approaches put students at the center of learning, encouraging them to work with teachers to structure and evaluate their own educational experiences. Other approaches rely more on the teacher to establish goals, to present academic tasks relevant to the goals, and to determine whether students are successful. **Which of the aims of education listed in Figure 10.5 have you experienced as a student?**

Teacher Planning for Instruction

Teacher planning weaves the curriculum or the content of teaching with the processes of teaching (Marsh & Willis, 2007). When planning instruction, teachers consider the curriculum, state and local goals for student learning, instructional strategies for meeting those goals, and

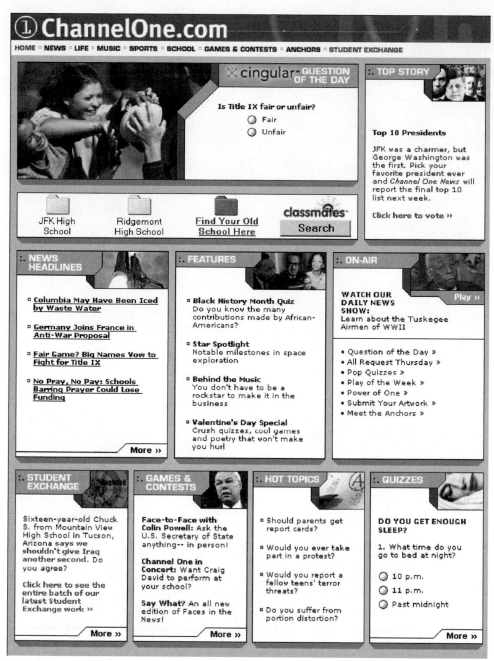

Source: www.channelone.com/

means of assessing students' understanding. Teachers should never underestimate the importance of planning how to evaluate student learning and the effectiveness of a lesson.

When identifying goals and objectives, teachers determine what students should learn or be able to do as a result of instruction (e.g., students should be able to solve nine out of ten math problems correctly). Deciding what the intended results of learning should be helps teachers clarify their thinking about the methods and materials they should use. Although educational objectives are influenced by state and local mandates, they also are shaped by teachers' perceptions of students' needs and abilities before, during, and after instruction (Wiles & Bondi, 2007).

To maximize students' opportunities to learn, teachers plan on their own and in teams. Sometimes team planning occurs across grade levels and even across schools. As teachers consider goals and objectives, they may create time lines indicating approximate dates when concepts and skills will be introduced. The resulting documents, sometimes referred to as **curriculum maps,** help

Aims of Education	Curriculum Orientation	Roles of Students and Teachers	Examples of Curriculum Content	Examples of Instructional Approaches
Teach students how to learn	Development of cognitive processes	Student centered: Students think about academic tasks and construct meaningful knowledge in relationship to prior experiences. Teachers mediate and facilitate students' learning.	Thinking skills; study skills; problem-solving skills	Scaffolding; inquiry learning
Impart culture to students	Academic rationalism	Teacher centered: Students receive instruction and demonstrate competencies.	Great ideas; great works of art; literary classics; basic skills	Direct instruction
Help students find self-fulfillment, develop effective learning styles	Personal relevance	Student centered: Students and teachers collaborate to create or match curricula to individual and group interests and needs. Teachers provide opportunities for student reflection and self-evaluation.	Opportunities for personal expression; clarification of personal values	Individualized instruction; nondirective teaching
Help students become productive citizens capable of changing the social order	Social adaptation, change, and outcomes-based views	Teacher centered: Teachers present facts, issues, problems, and learning challenges for students to act upon or apply in life.	Citizenship; communication skills; environmental, social issues, and job-related skills	Questioning; cooperative learning; project-based learning; internships
Give students the tools they need to master subjects; deliver instruction efficiently	Curriculum as technology	Subject centered: Teachers preestablish developmentally appropriate learning goals, outcomes, objectives, and criteria for assessment for a subject area. Students demonstrate minimum competencies.	Traditional subjects; basic skills	Direct instruction; mastery learning

Figure 10.5
Five Aims of Education and Corresponding Curricular Orientations
Which aims of education and curricular orientations interest you the most at this time?

teachers identify gaps and repetitions in the curriculum. They also are helpful for pointing out occasions when different subjects can be integrated.

When planning for instruction, teachers also think about classroom management. By establishing clear rules and routines, teachers minimize confusion and maximize instructional time. This aspect of planning is particularly important at the beginning of the year, when teachers establish patterns, limits, and expectations that set the tone for the rest of the year.

Methods for motivating students also should be part of teachers' instructional planning. According to Thomas Good and Jere Brophy (2003), teachers can motivate students by (1) establishing a supportive classroom environment in which students feel comfortable taking intellectual risks and (2) selecting activities at an appropriate level of difficulty "that teach things that are worth learning" (p. 223). Other motivational strategies include beginning the lesson by explaining how the subject matter relates to students' personal lives and to what they have already learned. Teachers should also let students know what they will need to do to demonstrate understanding of the lesson.

Grant Wiggins and Jay McTighe (1998) coined the term "backward design" to describe the idea of using desired end results to determine the curriculum needed to produce such results. The idea is simple: Ask yourself what a student needs to accomplish, then determine the kinds of lessons and practices needed to help students get there. This approach to curricular design encourages teachers to think about where and how assessment fits into teaching.

What Are Four General Models of Instruction?

No single best way exists to teach all things to all people. Different learners and different objectives often require different **instructional models,** or systematic approaches to teaching. Successful teachers have a variety of teaching instructional models they can use when they need them. When a teacher uses the same model of instruction over and over, only those students who learn well with that particular model will succeed. A teacher who uses different models will reach more students and will encourage them to learn in multiple ways.

As Bruce Joyce and his colleagues have found (Joyce, Weil, & Calhoun, 2004), models of teaching can be placed in four groups according to the models' purposes (see Figure 10.6) The Behavioral Systems Family models use ideas about manipulating the environment to modify students' behaviors. The Social Family capitalizes on people's social instinct to learn from and relate to one another. The Information-Processing Family focuses on increasing students' abilities to think—to seek, organize, interpret, and apply information both inductively and deductively. The Personal Family encourages self-exploration and the development of personal identity. As you read the following descriptions, see if you can determine which philosophies described in Chapter 6 influence each teaching model group. How should decisions be made about what teaching models to use?

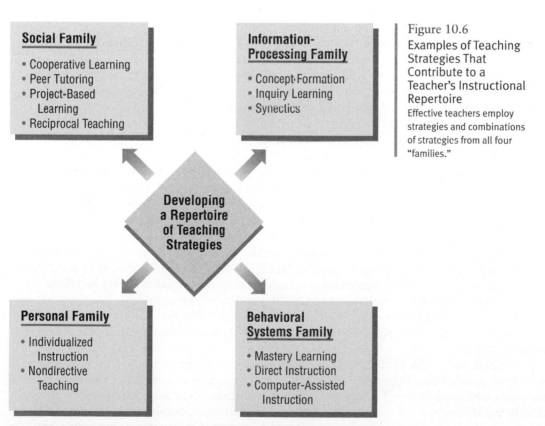

Figure 10.6

Examples of Teaching Strategies That Contribute to a Teacher's Instructional Repertoire

Effective teachers employ strategies and combinations of strategies from all four "families."

Social Family

- Cooperative Learning
- Peer Tutoring
- Project-Based Learning
- Reciprocal Teaching

Information-Processing Family

- Concept Formation
- Inquiry Learning
- Synectics

Developing a Repertoire of Teaching Strategies

Personal Family

- Individualized Instruction
- Nondirective Teaching

Behavioral Systems Family

- Mastery Learning
- Direct Instruction
- Computer-Assisted Instruction

Source: Adapted from *Models of teaching* (7th ed.) by B. R. Joyce, M. Weil, & E. Calhoun, 2004. Boston: Allyn & Bacon.

Issues in School Reform

IMPROVING ACHIEVEMENT

The key to improving student achievement is to pay attention to child and adolescent development. So says James P. Comer, the Yale professor of psychiatry and the mind behind the Comer School Development Program— a highly successful model for transforming urban schools. In an age in which educators worry about the consequences of failing to make adequate yearly progress under the No Child Left Behind Act, Comer's insight seems particularly relevant:

> Many improved practices in education that have been developed over the past two decades have been less successful than they might have been because they have focused primarily on curriculum, instruction, assessment, and modes of service delivery. Insufficient attention has been paid to child and adolescent development. When these matters are addressed at all, the focus is often on the student—on a problem behavior—and not on how to create a school culture that promotes growth. . . . We often forget that, for many children, academic learning is not a primary, natural, or valued task. It is the positive relationships and sense of belonging that a good school culture provides that give these children the comfort, confidence, competence, and motivation to learn. . . . Based on our experience, we believe that the framework that improves the school culture must be in place first, or the relationships needed to engage students in a powerful way won't be created. (Comer, 2005 p. 758)

Questions for Reflection: How might the needs of students whose focus is on survival be different from those who have experienced academic success? How can teachers show that they care while still holding high expectations for student performance?

Source: Comer, J. P. (2005). Child and adolescent development: The critical missing focus in school reform. *Phi Delta Kappan, 86*(10), 757–763.

Behavioral Systems Strategies

Mastery learning is based on the idea that student learning is a function of a student's aptitude, his or her motivation, and the amount and quality of instruction received. Supporters of mastery learning define aptitude as the amount of time a student requires to master an objective and not as the student's natural ability. Students are thought to be capable of mastering almost any subject matter, given enough time, the inclination to learn, and instruction fitted to their needs. The teacher's role in mastery learning is to organize instruction into manageable units, identify students' needs with respect to the material, teach in ways that meet those needs, and evaluate progress regularly. Developed by Benjamin Bloom (1971), John Carroll (1971), and their colleagues, mastery learning has proved to be a popular behavioral system model.

Teachers following the mastery learning model select learning objectives from a list of simple to complex thought processes (recall, comprehension, application, analysis, synthesis, and evaluation). Bloom's guide to learning objectives has aided the development of many curricula. Table 10.2 shows Bloom's guide and the tasks teachers must address to help students accomplish the objectives.

Like mastery learning, **direct instruction** is a highly structured, teacher-centered strategy. It relies on behavioral techniques such as modeling, feedback, and reinforcement to teach basic skills, primarily in reading and mathematics. Teachers using this model must set high but attainable goals for students. Activities and teaching environments should be structured so students succeed at a high rate. Direct instruction focuses on basic mathematics and reading objectives, not complex objectives. For this reason, and because it works, direct instruction is popular with policymakers.

BEHAVIORAL OBJECTIVES In the 1960s and 1970s, Robert Mager (1962) encouraged educators to write instructional **behavioral objectives.** They are goal statements that specify conditions under which learning will occur and criteria for success. Since then, teaching objectives and learning objectives have become the backbone of curriculum development, particularly in subject areas that can measure learning in quantifiable terms. These statements about what students should know or be able to do after completing a unit of study form the basis of what is

Table 10.2

BLOOM'S TAXONOMY OF EDUCATIONAL OBJECTIVES

Level	Learner Objectives	Teacher Tasks
1.00 Knowledge	To define, distinguish, acquire, identify, recall, or recognize various forms of information.	To present and/or elicit facts, conventions, categories in ways that enable learners to demonstrate knowledge.
2.00 Comprehension	To translate, transform, give in own words, illustrate, prepare, read, represent, change, rephrase, or restate various forms of information.	To present and/or elicit definitions, words, phrases, relationships, principles in ways that enable learners to demonstrate comprehension.
3.00 Application	To apply, generalize, relate, choose, develop, organize, use, transfer, restructure, or classify various forms of information.	To present and/or elicit principles, laws, conclusions in ways that enable learners to apply what they have learned.
4.00 Analysis	To distinguish, detect, identify, classify, discriminate, recognize, categorize, or deduce various forms of information.	To present and/or elicit elements, hypotheses, assumptions, statements of intent or fact in ways that encourage learners to critically analyze information.
5.00 Synthesis	To write, tell, relate, produce, originate, modify, or document various forms of information.	To present and/or elicit structures, patterns, designs, relationships in ways that encourage learners to form new structures of knowledge.
6.00 Evaluation	To judge, argue, validate, assess, appraise various forms of information.	To present and/or elicit from learners different qualitative judgments.

Source: Teacher development (p. 57) by R. F. McNergney and C. A. Carrier, 1981, New York: Macmillan.

taught and how success is judged. As the following example illustrates, behavioral objectives should specify the intended result or product of instruction.

An Instructional Behavioral Objective in Mager's Terms

Conditions of performance:	Given ten story problems,
Behavior:	students will show their work using basic algebra
Criteria for performance:	to solve at least 90 percent correctly.

Although behavioral objectives are widely used in curriculum development, when schools overemphasize them, teaching becomes simplistic and mechanized (Henderson & Gornik, 2007). By necessity, the objectives must be specific and structured, which can lead to staleness. Many educators resist strict adherence to behavioral approaches so they can remain open to spontaneous opportunities for learning.

Social Strategies

Instructional models in the social family help students work together to attain both academic and social goals. Teachers serve as guides, encouraging students to express their ideas and to consider others' perspectives as they deal with a variety of issues. Cooperative learning and project-based learning are two examples of strategies for classroom teaching and learning in the social family.

COOPERATIVE LEARNING **Cooperative learning** is more social in nature than behavioral systems models. Cooperative learning promotes the careful, purposeful formation of mixed groups of students within classrooms to accomplish social, personal, and academic objectives.

Cooperative learning is popular because it influences student self-esteem, intergroup relations, acceptance of students with academic and physical limitations, attitudes toward school, and ability to work cooperatively.

One cooperative learning technique, Students Teams–Achievement Divisions (STAD), has the teacher use direct instruction to teach students concepts or skills. Students then work in four-member, heterogeneous learning teams to help each other master the content by using study guides, worksheets, and other materials. Following group work, students take quizzes on which they may not help one another. Teams earn recognition or privileges based on the improvement made by each team member over his or her past record (Slavin & Fashola, 1998). The success of groups depends on what each individual in the group has learned, not on a single group product (Slavin, 1995).

The jigsaw strategy is a cooperative learning strategy that has been used to reduce racial conflict among schoolchildren, while promoting learning and student motivation. As the name suggests, the strategy resembles a jigsaw puzzle—each piece, or in this case each student, is essential to the creation of the full, complete product. Every student needs every other student to succeed.

Here is how the jigsaw strategy works. Assume an English class is studying *Huckleberry Finn*. The teacher assigns all the students in the class to small groups of five. The teacher then assigns one student in each group a particular task. For instance, student #1 researches life on the Mississippi River in the nineteenth century. Student #2 examines Mark Twain's life as a boy. Student #3 studies Twain's life as an adult. Student #4 investigates the law pertinent to slavery in Missouri. Student #5 studies the representation of slavery in other authors' works produced when *Huckleberry Finn* was published.

All #1 students form an expert group and work together to assemble the best collective research on life on the Mississippi in the nineteenth century. Other expert groups are formed the same way—that is, students with identical assignments become "experts" on their topic. Eventually each expert returns to his or her jigsaw group and presents a report to the group on her or his area of study. Students are then tested on what they have learned about *Huckleberry Finn* from their fellow group members. Sometimes teachers give both individual grades and group grades. Did you ever participate in a jigsaw exercise when you were in high school? How would you judge its success? How might the exercise have been improved?

OTHER FORMS OF PEER-MEDIATED INSTRUCTION Is peer-mediated instruction as effective as teacher-mediated instruction? **Project-based learning,** sometimes called case-based learning (www.casenex.com), helps students pursue solutions to important problems raised by students, teachers, or curriculum developers. Students approach the problems by "asking and refining questions, debating ideas, making predictions, designing plans and/or experiments, collecting and analyzing data, drawing conclusions, communicating ideas and findings to others, asking new questions, and creating artifacts" (Blumenfeld, Soloway, Marx, Krajcik, Guzdial, & Palcinsar, 1991, p. 371). Artifacts are models, reports, videotapes, and computer programs representing students' problem solutions. Feedback on their artifacts helps students revise their solutions. New York students in a middle school economics unit constructed a barter economy and calculated the most and least valued services. A group of high school students in Arizona constructed a wind-driven generator to power lightbulbs. The principal benefit of project-based learning may be that students learn to draw on many curricular areas to make connections among subject matter areas. In this respect students learn to function much as they might be expected to in later life.

Information-Processing Strategies

Models in the information-processing family stimulate the development of thinking skills such as observing, comparing, finding patterns, and generalizing. Simultaneously, students learn specific concepts or generalizations (Eggen & Kauchak, 2005). These models are built on the ideas of information-processing theorists and modern constructivists. Information-processing models take their cues for instruction from theory that explains how people think.

FORMING CONCEPTS AND GENERALIZATIONS Teachers using the **concept formation** method of instruction want students to analyze and synthesize data to construct knowledge about a specific idea. A science teacher using concept formation during a unit on plants would likely ask students to (1) examine a variety of plant specimens, (2) place the plants into groups based on

Jigsaw Classroom

Jigsaw learning, as developed by Elliot Aronson, is a cooperative learning strategy designed to increase collaboration. For more information, visit www.jigsaw.org.

Welcome to the official web site of the jigsaw classroom, a cooperative learning technique that reduces racial conflict among school children, promotes better learning, improves student motivation, and increases enjoyment of the learning experience. The jigsaw technique was first developed in the early 1970s by Elliot Aronson and his students at the University of Texas and the University of California. Since then, hundreds of schools have used the jigsaw classroom with great success. The jigsaw approach is considered to be a particularly valuable tool in averting tragic events such as the Columbine massacre.

Explore the *Jigsaw Classroom:*

▶ **Overview of the Technique**

▶ **History of the Jigsaw Classroom**

▶ **Jigsaw in 10 Easy Steps**

▶ **Tips on Implementation**

▶ **Books and Articles Related to the Jigsaw Technique**

▶ **Chapter 1 of Aronson's Book "Nobody Left to Hate: Teaching Compassion After Columbine"**

▶ **Links on Cooperative Learning and School Violence**

▶ **About Elliot Aronson and This Web Site**

Content © 2000-2005, Elliot Aronson
Web Site © 2000-2005, Social Psychology Network

Read in: Español | Français | Deutsch | Italiano
Site Statistics

Source: Content © 2000–2005. Elliot Aronson. Website © 2000–2008, Social Psychology Network. Reproduced with permission.

structural characteristics, and (3) create labels for each of the plant groups. The teacher might then provide additional specimens for students to classify. Although most of these plants would probably fit existing groups, students might have to create new categories for some of the plants. In a lesson of this type, students are active "creators" or "inventors" of knowledge.

THINKING AND CREATIVITY Can creativity be taught? **Synectics** is a teaching model that seeks to increase students' problem-solving abilities, creative expression, empathy, and insight into social relations. Developed by William Gordon, a businessman from Cambridge, Massachusetts, synectics is designed to "make the familiar strange." The key teaching strategy is to force distance between the student and the object or subject matter being investigated. Through a series of exercises, students work as a team to experiment with traditional ways of thinking to discover new perspectives on topics from a wide range of fields.

Synectics activities begin with a statement of a problem or a topic. A series of *stretching exercises,* familiarizes students with using analogies in new ways. A teacher might use *personal analogies* to encourage students to identify with animate or inanimate objects. For instance, the teacher might say, "I want you to close your eyes and be a rock. Don't imagine yourself looking at a rock; actually be that rock. Tell me how you feel." A *direct analogy* might fuel a fresh view of how ideas, events, or objects are alike and different: "How is a desk drawer like your mother's ear?" And *symbolic analogies* or a *compressed conflict* might trigger the creative juices: "Think about the term *nourishing flame.* Can you give me an example of something, someone, or some idea that is both nourishing and destructive at the same time?"

INQUIRY LEARNING When students engage in **inquiry learning,** they try to answer questions and solve problems based on facts and observations. They think as scientists do while analyzing data and testing theories and hypotheses. The Suchman Inquiry Model, one of several ways to structure inquiry lessons, lets students see that knowledge is tentative. That is, as new information is discovered and new theories evolve, old ideas are modified or discarded.

A history teacher might use the Suchman model to teach about the generational change within families:

> Grandmother and Grandfather Farley were born and raised on farms in the Midwest. They loved the rural countryside and the simplicity of life, because they believed it was the best of all places to raise a family. Their five children grew up on a farm, went to church together, and all went to college at the nearby state university. After graduation they married and moved to both the East and West Coasts of the nation. They live in different cities, and they rarely return to the Midwest. The Farleys have never seen two of their grandchildren. The other four grandchildren never write or call their grandparents. Why might this formerly close family, and other families like them, be so out of touch with one another?

The teacher would then guide students through five steps:

1. Define the problem
2. Formulate hypotheses
3. Gather data
4. Organize data and modify hypotheses accordingly
5. Generalize from findings.

Personal Sources Strategies

Personal sources models of instruction try to involve students actively in deciding what and how they will learn. The goal is for students to develop lifelong character traits, rather than to focus on short-term educational goals (Joyce, Weil, & Calhoun, 2004). Specifically, teachers use personal models to help students develop effective learning styles and healthy self-concepts. The nondirective teaching model, based on the work of Carl Rogers (1971), is one approach to attaining these goals.

In the **nondirective model,** teachers facilitate students' learning based on students' own interests and concerns. In this sense, teachers are more like guides than instructors. Instead of lecturing on a topic, teachers encourage students to identify problems and feelings, to take responsibility for solving problems, and to determine how personal goals might be reached. Students' problems may relate to personal, social, or academic issues. When focusing on personal problems, students generally explore their own feelings. When considering social issues, students investigate their feelings about others and how their thoughts can influence relationships. Academic concerns generally center on students' feelings about their competence and interests in certain areas (Joyce, Weil, & Calhoun, 2004).

As this lesson structure suggests, students determine classroom activities. Acting as a facilitator, the teacher follows five steps when using the nondirective model:

1. The teacher describes the learning situation, and teacher and student agree on procedures for meeting and interacting with one another. The student may also identify a problem.
2. The teacher, using strategies such as paraphrasing and asking open questions ("Can you say more about that?"), encourages the student to express positive and negative feelings and to clarify the problem.
3. The teacher uses supportive language ("Yes, it is difficult to be alone") to encourage the student to explore the problem and to develop new insight.
4. The teacher clarifies a student's plan for dealing with the problem.
5. The teacher listens as the student explains the actions she has taken. The teacher may also help the student to consider other things that might be done to solve the problem.

The five phases of the nondirective model might occur in one day or across a longer period of time. Meetings between teacher and student typically are one on one, allowing for privacy and time to explore problems and issues important to the student (Joyce, Weil, & Calhoun, 2004).

What Is Effective Instruction?

Teachers are students, too. They are always learning and applying skills in new ways to be effective in their unique situations. Even the best among them do not always know how or why they are successful. With experience, though, they grow accustomed to not having all the

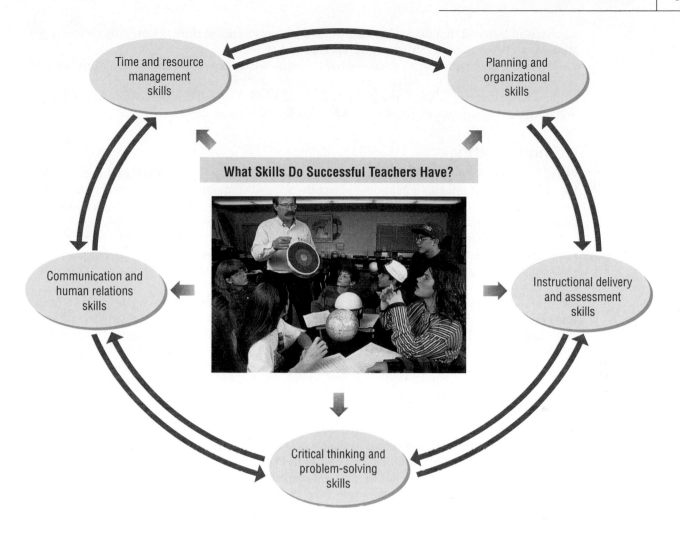

Figure 10.7
Teachers' Skills
These skills underlie teachers' abilities to understand students, set goals, create learning environments, evaluate student learning, and communicate.

answers. They learn to combine the best information available about teaching and learning with their prior teaching experiences. In addition, teachers cannot rely exclusively on either creativity or technical expertise. Instead, they must build a stockpile of knowledge, methods, and practices they can call on at a moment's notice. Good teachers, like good students, push all their capabilities to the limits.

Much time is spent debating the surefire way to be an effective teacher. The literature on educating teachers is brimming with lists of skills that one expert or another claims are essential. Yet it is hard to imagine a single method that could accommodate the variety of students and material that teachers encounter during their careers. As knowledge grows and as philosophies change, programs require that teacher education students demonstrate far fewer yet more complex skills. Instead of relying on specific methods and structures, teacher education is now likely to promote some basic skills and concepts that can be adapted to a number of situations. Some of these skills and concepts are described in the sections that follow and are also listed in Figure 10.7.

Understanding Students

Good teachers learn about their students so they can challenge and support them (Holmes, 2007). Teachers try to understand what students know, what they can and cannot do, how they think, what they value, and what gets in the way of their learning. Teachers learn about students formally by reading and studying student artifacts, such as tests and projects. They can also informally observe, talk with, and listen to students and their parents.

The most frequent, the most critical, and the most generous evaluators of teaching are the students themselves. Students watch what teachers do and listen to what teachers say. Good teachers understand that when they help students become critical thinkers they also encourage students to become good evaluators of teachers and teaching.

We remember the great students—what they did, what they said—and like to think we had something to do with their success. But too often we overlook the bored, the tired, the restless student who may be "telling" us a great deal about what does and does not work in teaching. **What might we learn about our own teaching by listening to students?**

Communicating

Good teachers are good communicators. They communicate clearly, both verbally and in writing. They transmit information about subject matter and communicate with parents, administrators, and other teachers. Good teachers also use their skills to communicate expectations for student performance, as well as empathy, positive regard, and willingness to help.

Skillful teachers know how to establish, negotiate, and help students set reasonable goals for learning. Sometimes goals are established within a curriculum, and teachers must help all students accomplish the same goals. At other times, teachers must help students set and reach their own goals.

Communicating expectations for success and reinforcing success when it occurs are two of the most important skills a teacher exhibits. Teachers must state their expectations clearly so that students understand. They also must recognize students' successes and acknowledge their failures. If feedback is infrequent or unclear, students may not know if they have met or exceeded their teachers' or their own expectations. Furthermore, teachers must help students judge their own progress.

Creating Learning Environments

A great teacher is part artist, part scientist. Successful teachers adapt general principles of effective teaching to help students get involved in their work and stay that way. Successful teachers also have many ways to help students succeed and to feel good about themselves.

Years ago from her experience of teaching mathematics, Marilyn Burns offered a set of practical lessons for teachers that are relevant to the creation of learning environments in all subject areas yet today:

1. Whatever you do, create a clear structure at the beginning of the year. (Spend the first month helping children learn how to be effective learners.)
2. For sane planning, organize your year into units (whole-class lessons; a menu of independent activities for partners, individuals, or groups to work on).
3. Give students choices; this helps to motivate them.
4. Remember that children can often do more than you think they can.
5. Focus on basic facts and emphasize reasoning; these are not mutually exclusive activities.
6. Talk less in class; have children talk more.
7. Want to know what children are learning? Ask them to write about it.
8. Use homework as a vehicle to inform parents about children's learning. (Burns, 1995, pp. 87–88).

Adapting Instruction for Students with Special Needs

Every child is special in some particular way. Students' needs, abilities, and interests can be helpful guides for determining how best to plan for and teach them. For example, kindergarten teachers give their students books with more pictures than words, because the children are only beginning to read and are easily overwhelmed. Chemistry teachers teach high school students about molecular bonding before they teach cell signaling, because students could not understand the latter without the former. The challenge in most teaching circumstances is to find out what students know and can do and move them forward, sometimes each in his or her own way.

Three general approaches exist for adapting instruction to differences among learners. Each has its own potential strengths and weaknesses.

The first approach is to remediate students' learning problems. If students cannot organize their thoughts to write a paper, for instance, teachers show them how to use outlining or concept-mapping techniques. In truth, teachers spend their lives, often with the assistance of parents, helping students overcome deficiencies. The appeal of remediation is obvious. It's also a matter of common sense: If students knew everything, why would they go to school? The basic idea behind teaching is to help students acquire and apply new knowledge. It can be fun to explore new intellectual territory and learn to behave in ways that are new and different.

However, this strategy has the potential to spiral downward. When everything is remediated, students may feel like they are too dumb to learn anything. Instead of being excited to learn, they may come to believe their teacher has little confidence in their abilities. In turn, students play their roles by living down to their teacher's low expectations.

The second approach is to compensate for student deficiencies that no one will ever be able to correct. Such deficiencies include poor eyesight, small stature, or any other physical or mental setback a student may have. To compensate, teachers can say things like "If you can't see the chalkboard, take a seat closer to the front of the room," "If you can't do long division in your head, use a calculator," and "Too small for football, try wrestling." Good teachers encourage students to try new things, but they do not encourage them to pursue the impossible. And they must never make students feel bad for things beyond their control.

But what if a teacher misreads a student's capabilities and expects too little? The downside of compensating for students' weaknesses may be failing to challenge them or denying them the opportunity to learn to cope with failure. Educational history has many examples of people conquering adversity, triumphing over weakness, and doing the impossible. Knowing when and how far to push students—and when to back off—can be a hard decision.

The third approach is to capitalize on what students do well and prefer to do. Teachers know that students cannot spend all their time doing what they like to do and do well. They need to be challenged to think and behave in new ways. Yet the really great teachers learn to

Cultural Awareness: Lessons Learned

The beginning of the school year is an important time for teachers and students. Like any human being in a new social setting, each is trying to learn more about the other. As elementary teachers "size up" their students, they often think about the academic capabilities and general classroom behavior of children. High school teachers tend to focus on academic characteristics, work habits, behavior, subject matter interest, and attitudes. If "sizing-up" assessments are done poorly, teachers' impressions can have a negative effect on the classroom environment (Airasian, 2004).

Students with disabilities—particularly those with physical disabilities—may be perceived as less able than their peers. Colleen Willard-Holt, an educator in Pennsylvania, recalled her interactions with Ian, a six-year-old child with cerebral palsy. Ian was confined to a wheelchair and his speech was difficult to understand. Although it was physically exhausting for him to complete his schoolwork, Ian refused to accept special treatment in the form of extended due dates, multiple-choice versus essay tests, and the like. He was a bright and witty student who seemed to want to prove that he could do as well as or better than his colleagues:

I can see the wicked gleam in his eye when he played a joke on someone by purposely giving a wrong answer or inventing some clever word play.

I can hear his friends arguing over who got to push him out to recess. Ian's life demonstrates nothing less than the triumph of the human spirit over tremendous obstacles.

As I have reflected on it over the years, I realize the lessons I learned from Ian have changed me . . . . I remember him as I work with a student who despairs of ever "getting it," and I assure the student that I believe he or she will succeed. I remember him when I'm a little tired or don't feel like teaching, and that memory shames me into getting out of bed and doing my best, just as he did every day. Remembering Ian keeps me humble. . . . When I hear someone comment that students with disabilities have no business being in regular classrooms, my temper flares. . . . I am one reformed ostrich who will always try to keep Ian's spirit alive. (Willard-Holt, 2005, p. 516)

Question for Reflection: What are some additional factors, other than disabilities, that might affect a teacher's perceptions of students?

Source: Willard-Holt, C. (2005). And the children shall teach us—A tribute. *Phi Delta Kappan,* 86 (7), 515–516.

look for student success and build on it, so they can help students gain power over their own educational lives. "You like to read mysteries? Great, try *The Hound of the Baskervilles*." "You are an amazing piano player. You should apply for summer music camp at the university." "You are one of the few students in class who speaks two languages. Would you please write your next paper on what it is like to live in a multilingual home?" These are examples of ways teachers can use students' existing interests and abilities to further pursue learning experiences. Such occasions can also make students feel proud of what they already know, making them more willing to pursue something new.

Evaluating Student Learning

Teachers must be able to decide what works in teaching and what does not. They have access to a variety of information about students that can help them make such decisions. They can use formal measures, such as tests and quizzes, and informal measures, such as questionnaires, interviews, and observations of in-class behaviors.

Teachers make judgments daily about students' academic performance, their attitudes and interests, and their ability to work with others. Such information enables teachers to (1) determine what students already know and want to know about topics, (2) plan instruction that is appropriately challenging, (3) motivate student performance, (4) assess progress toward affective and cognitive goals, and (5) communicate progress to others.

Typically, the best indicator of students' performance is their classwork. Two types of assessment are used for classwork: formative and summative. Formative assessment is conducted while a lesson is in progress to discover information about students' errors, misunderstandings, understandings, and progress. Teachers can use this information to shape new plans that will improve student performance. Summative assessment is conducted at the end of a lesson, unit, or course to allow students to demonstrate what they have learned.

Teachers have a responsibility to use the best information available about students before making evaluative decisions. This means assessing students frequently and using procedures that allow students to demonstrate what they can do. After collecting information, teachers are obligated to protect its privacy, recognize the limits of its use in decision making, and not use it to demean or ridicule a student (Airasian, 2004).

How Do Teachers Manage Students Effectively?

What is the key to effective classroom management? Classrooms are often "crowded, competitive, contradictory, multidimensional, simultaneous, unpredictable, public . . . [places where] teachers work with captive groups of students on academic agendas that students have not helped to set" (Weinstein & Mignano, 2003, p. 56). Teachers who understand the complexity of classrooms realize the importance of finding ways to gain students' cooperation. Through careful planning with many other people, these teachers can prevent problems from occurring. **Classroom management,** then, is the collective ability of teachers, students, administrators, school boards, and even police and the courts to establish a common framework for social and academic interactions (Doyle, 1986; Wolfgang, Bennett, & Irvin, 1999).

Classroom management does not concern only discipline. Successful teachers create total systems of management that address various aspects of behavior. As Jere Brophy (1988, 1996) argued, a classroom management system is designed to maximize student engagement, not merely to minimize misconduct. Teachers who create and maintain classrooms as caring communities are more successful than teachers who assert their roles as authority figures and disciplinarians.

Research Informs Teacher Management Behavior

Jacob Kounin's (1970) book on classroom management and discipline is a classic. He filmed hundreds of hours of teacher–student classroom interactions, preschool through college levels. From his research he learned that teachers often created problems for themselves. Many teachers behaved in ways that actually encouraged students to become uninvolved in classroom activities and to misbehave.

Kounin suggested that good classroom managers motivate students to get involved in learning. They prevent student boredom by varying tasks and by maintaining momentum. They avoid giving too many directions or lengthy explanations. They stop activities when students become restless and make smooth transitions from one activity to the next. The intent is to maximize student involvement and to minimize disruptions.

When disruptions occur, Kounin suggested tactics teachers can use to stop problems from escalating—tactics such as "with-it-ness" and "overlapping" behaviors. A teacher who is "with it" seems to have eyes in the back of her head. Aware of what is going on, this teacher stops students who are misbehaving and gets them back on task. Overlapping, which is a teacher's ability to handle more than one thing at a time, can occur when a teacher working with a small group of students also manages a disruption in another part of the room.

Ed Emmer and his colleagues (Emmer, Evertson, & Anderson, 1980) found that the tone teachers set in the beginning of the year affects the entire year. When teachers are organized and prepared at the start of the school year, they give students the impression that things will run smoothly. In most cases that initial impression becomes reality. In addition, when teachers teach and reteach desirable behaviors, they reinforce a classroom community where people respect each other.

Here are a few dos and don'ts from research on classroom management and discipline:

- Be motivated yourself, and communicate why—students are likely to catch the bug.
- Never demean or embarrass students.
- Help students learn to manage themselves.
- Look for ways to reduce students' confusion and increase their involvement in activities.
- Make sure students understand what you expect from them.
- Build on what students already know—it helps them succeed and keeps them involved.
- Reinforce success! Reinforce success! Reinforce success!

Relationships between Teachers and Students

Personal relationships help shape how people behave and get along with one another. Educational research is full of examples of counseling and personal development approaches that are useful for defining and managing how classroom relationships should function. As any guidance counselor would tell you, a classroom management system must be based on respectful relationships between teachers and students if it has any hope of being effective (Henderson & Gysbers, 1998).

What teachers expect from students is a powerful prediction of what they will get. Robert Rosenthal and Leonore Jacobson (1968) were among the first researchers to speak of students' "self-fulfilling prophecies," or students' tendencies to behave in ways they believe teachers expect. Other researchers have further explained the influence of teacher expectations not only on teacher–student relationships and student classroom behavior, but on student achievement as well (Brophy & Good, 1971, 1974; Good & Brophy, 2003). Like Kounin before them, Good and Brophy suggested that teachers create problems for themselves and for students by communicating their expectations differently—sometimes inappropriately—to high and low achievers. In this sense, if teachers expect little from students, students will pick up on it and behave accordingly. If teachers don't expect low-achieving students to try as hard as everyone else, why would they try at all? Good and Brophy called the teacher behaviors listed in Figure 10.8 "danger signals" if they occur often and on many levels. **Are you aware of other teacher behaviors that might be danger signals?**

Classroom Management: An Environment of Self-Control

Teachers demonstrate many techniques to encourage student self-control. For one, teachers use nonverbal signals to alert students that they recognize inappropriate behavior. Teachers use physical proximity—they move closer to students—to communicate disapproval. They show

1. Waiting less time for lows to answer a question before giving the answer or calling on someone else

2. Giving lows answers or calling on someone else, rather than trying to improve their responses by giving clues or repeating or rephrasing questions

3. Inappropriate reinforcement: rewarding inappropriate behavior or incorrect answers by lows

4. Criticizing lows more often for failure

5. Praising lows less often for success

6. Failing to give feedback to the public responses of lows

7. Generally paying less attention to lows or interacting with them less frequently

8. Calling on lows less often to respond to questions or asking them only easier, nonanalytic questions

9. Seating lows farther away from the teacher

10. Demanding less from lows

11. Interacting with lows more privately than publicly, and monitoring and structuring their activities more closely

12. Differential administration or grading of tests or assignments, in which highs but not lows are given the benefit of the doubt in borderline cases

13. Less friendly interactions with lows, including less smiling and fewer other nonverbal indicators of support

14. Briefer and less informative feedback to questions of lows

15. Less eye contact and other nonverbal communication of attention and responsiveness

16. Less use of effective but time-consuming instructional methods with lows when time is limited

17. Less acceptance and use of lows' ideas

18. Exposing lows to an impoverished curriculum

Figure 10.8

How Teachers May Treat High and Low Achievers Differently

Source: Good, T. L., & Brophy, J. E. (2000). *Looking in classrooms* (8th ed.). New York: Addison Wesley Longman, Inc., pp. 85–86.

interest in students' appropriate behavior, and they ignore inappropriate student behavior. Teachers help students who need it, thus helping students help themselves, while decreasing the odds of student misbehavior. Teachers often help students by restructuring or rescheduling activities, removing distractions, or removing students from troubling situations. Teachers set routines and help students know what to expect. All these tactics teach students how to control themselves in a classroom environment by communicating what is acceptable behavior and what is not.

Building a classroom community where people manage themselves in appropriate, productive, and respectful ways is a bit like looking for the secret of life. Once, when the Dalai Lama was at a gathering in New York City's Central Park, a young woman asked him, with the proper respect due the leader of Tibetan Buddhism, what he believed was the secret of life. He wrinkled his brow in thought for a moment and then said with a large smile, "Be nice."

In teaching, as in life, to be nice can be a sign of strength, not a sign of weakness. To smile costs nothing. To enjoy being around others is to make oneself enjoyable to be around. These simple acts may have more to do with building productive, self-regulating classrooms than we typically acknowledge.

Case Perspectives

Think back to the case that opened this chapter. The following comments are designed to provide a context for your own analysis of John Sampson's situation.

MARTA JONES IS CURRICULUM COORDINATOR AT GAINESVILLE HIGH SCHOOL.   John sounds like a bright, hardworking young man. What he is learning firsthand is that each student is unique. In other words, what works for one student (or John himself) may not work for another.

Besides using an inductive approach, John might also use direct instruction—a strategy that can be used to teach both concepts and skills. With direct instruction, the teacher reviews and describes the goals for a lesson, explains a new concept (perhaps modeling how to solve a problem related to the concept), provides students with opportunities to practice solving similar problems (guided practice), and then gives students feedback about their performance. While modeling instruction, John can "think out loud" (sometimes referred to as cognitive modeling), verbalizing his thinking as he solves a problem. In doing so, he is teaching thinking strategies—a goal that seems foremost in his mind.

As the research on teaching illustrates, teachers do make a difference. By using alternate strategies, John will have greater opportunities to help all students succeed.

JORGE MATEO IS AN EXPERIENCED FELLOW MATH TEACHER.   I agree with Marta's ideas about varying teaching strategies. Besides the approach she suggests, I encourage John to continue to think of ways to allow students to work together during instruction. Cooperative learning and other social interaction models can maximize students' involvement in instruction and help improve their thinking skills. Such strategies can also be used to

supplement many other models of instruction. Think-pair-share, for example, is a group-work strategy which requires students to first work alone to answer a question and then to share the answer with a partner. This strategy might be used during the third step of direct instruction (guided practice) to help students reach both low- and higher-level goals.

Before organizing his students for group work, John needs to teach them skills of how to work together effectively—how to criticize ideas and not people, for example. He also needs to think carefully about how students will be grouped. Will they work in pairs or larger groups? Will he try to maximize the variation in the groups to ensure there are multiple perspectives? When dividing students for group work, he must also give students a specific task to accomplish, specify the amount of time they have to accomplish the task, require that each student in the group participate in the activity, and monitor groups as they work.

While trying out these and other models of instruction, John might want to ask the curriculum coordinator or one of his colleagues to observe a lesson or two. All of us, no matter how experienced, can benefit from the perspectives of others.

Questions for Reflection: How do you prefer to learn, and how do you learn best? What instructional strategies seemed to work best in your own education? Do you have friends or colleagues whose approaches to learning are different from yours? How important do you think it is to be aware of how your own students learn? Can you think of other strategies that John could use that might help his students learn? Are there universal characteristics of good teaching—that is, factors that characterize effective teaching regardless of differences in how students learn? ■

Summary

Curriculum takes many forms. You can see and touch it in books, study materials, and other physical artifacts. The expectations that teachers communicate to their students also constitute a kind of curriculum. Some curriculum is "extra" or outside normal academic requirements. And sometimes curricula are integrated around themes or particular issues.

Curriculum represents various conceptions of the knowledge, skills, and values considered critical to success in later life. Most all curriculum has been shaped by powerful forces, both inside and outside the educational world. Our elected and appointed leaders use their visibility to advance ideas that influence curriculum. Public opinion, professional education groups, and vocal individuals all work to influence the curriculum in its many forms. Influential interests in publishing and the mass media also play important roles in what is taught and learned in schools across the nation.

Teachers deliver curriculum through instruction. The forms of instruction they use depend largely on what is to be taught and on the students' needs and abilities. Clearly identifiable models of teaching are based on both theory and research. These models or strategies enable teachers to help students to develop personally, socially, cognitively, behaviorally, and academically.

Effective teaching—teaching that helps students learn—depends on teachers' abilities to understand what students know and can do. Effective teachers create environments that complement and supplement students' abilities. They assess student progress and give feedback on student performance that reinforces desirable behavior. Effective teachers are good communicators and good managers, helping students take control of their own learning.

TERMS AND CONCEPTS

behavioral objectives

classroom management

concept formation

cooperative learning

curriculum

curriculum map

direct instruction

explicit curriculum

extracurriculum

implicit curriculum

inquiry learning

instructional model

integrated curriculum

mastery learning

nondirective model

null curriculum

project-based learning

synectics

teacher planning

REFLECTIVE ACTIVITY: MAKING REAL-LIFE CONNECTIONS

Reflective practice is an essential part of good teaching. Reflection is a process that includes making thoughtful decisions, understanding and articulating value structures, acting from knowledge, evaluating your actions and their effects, and sharing your reflections with colleagues. After reading the following scenario, respond to the questions below. The scenario reflects the INTASC Principle and Disposition at the end of this activity.

Bob Dunleavy approached the kickoff of his geography unit with unbridled enthusiasm. He had loved history as a kid, but geography was his favorite subject. Just as his mentor had done for him, he wanted to excite students about a subject that is too often minimized in the curriculum.

He was determined to wrap important concepts from classical geography study in a captivating story about the students' hometown, Greenville, South Carolina. He would use this story to encourage students to do their own research on a community they knew on the surface but probably did not appreciate fully. Only then, he thought, would his students engage in geography with the enthusiasm that the discipline deserved.

Bob knew that from the time of the earliest European settlers the natural advantages of Greenville County propelled the area toward prosperity. The cultural background of the settlers was one of hard work and attention to quality. From the beginning, they had exhibited the desire to capitalize on the industrial potential of the area. The people foresaw opportunities for economic development that they had dreamed of in the old country.

Rivers and waterfalls provided abundant natural power. By the 1920s, Greenville was the textile center of the world because of a nearby supply of cotton. Transportation facilities and a booming economy made Greenville one of the most successful industrial centers in the world.

The textile industry waned in modern times, to be replaced by new business and industry. Much of the new development was fueled by international investment. Open land, low taxes, a reasonable cost of living, and a forward-thinking government have made Greenville not only a good place to work and live, but a modern case study of the relevance of geography to everyday life.

Decide 1. What will Bob want to know about local and state educational standards before planning his unit on the importance of Greenville geography?

Perceive and Value 2. Why might Bob want to make certain that his students think about Greenville from the points of view of foreign investors? How might he use examples of German investment in a local BMW plant to teach curricular issues of international cooperation and competition?

Know and Act 3. What might Bob want his students to know about the importance of "connections" and community development? How might he introduce and reinforce concepts of "connections" using links between resources and manufacturing, suppliers and producers, marketing and consumption?

Evaluate 4. If you were Bob, how might you judge your students' understanding of the importance of place, or physical geography, in modern civic decision making?

Discuss 5. What should Bob do to learn more about the experiences, needs, and aptitudes of his students that might affect the success of this unit?

INTASC Principle 7

The teacher plans instruction based upon knowledge of subject matter, students, the community, and curriculum goals.

Disposition

The teacher knows how to take contextual considerations (instructional materials; individual student interests, needs, and aptitudes; and community resources) into account in planning instruction that creates an effective bridge between curriculum goals and students' experiences. (Interstate New Teacher Assessment and Support Consortium, 1992)

ADDITIONAL READINGS

Bloom, B. S. (Ed.). (1956). *Taxonomy of educational objectives; the classification of educational goals, by a committee of college and university examiners.* New York: Longman, Green.

Eisner, E. (1982). *Cognition and curriculum: A basis for deciding what to teach.* New York: Longman.

Good, T. L., & Brophy, J. E. (2007). *Looking in classrooms* (10th ed.) New York: Longman.

Joyce, B. R., Weil, M., & Calhoun, E. (2004). *Models of teaching* (7th ed.). Boston: Allyn & Bacon.

Tyler, R. W. (1950). *Basic principles of curriculum and instruction.* Chicago: University of Chicago Press.

WEB RESOURCES

www.ncte.org
The website for the National Council of Teachers of English offers a variety of resources for teaching reading, writing, and English language arts to elementary, middle, and high school teachers.

www.nctm.org/
Visit the National Council of Teachers of Mathematics to learn more about mathematics standards, grant opportunities, and online resources for teachers.

www.aahperd.org/naspe/template.cfm
The website for the National Association for Sport and Physical Education describes quality physical education programs.

www.socialstudies.org
The National Council for Social Studies provides online publications, teaching resources, and curriculum information for educators.

http://nap.edu/html/nses/html/
This website describes the National Science Education Standards. You can read the teaching, content, and program standards before focusing on the professional development, assessment, and systems standards.

www.menc.org/
The National Association for Music Education encourages the use of music to celebrate our cultural heritages and to provide students with opportunities to develop new knowledge through expression, imagination, and creation.

CHAPTER 11

Recognizing Educational Success: Standards and Assessment

Case Study: Dodging Academic Disaster

During the fall of 2008, Nemaha County Public Schools faced what many described as a "crisis of confidence." Ellsworth Elementary School had failed to make "adequate yearly progress" for the second year in a row. According to No Child Left Behind, the school was obligated to take corrective actions to improve student performance. If they failed to raise students' scores by the end of the upcoming year, the school would have to allow children and parents to choose another school to attend.

Dan Davis, the Nemaha superintendent, was both embarrassed and determined to turn the Ellsworth situation around before school choice became a reality. He contended publicly and privately that there was every reason to believe that all the Ellsworth students could score above the state averages in math and reading/language arts. The problem, according to Davis, was twofold: existing resources had to be concentrated on the children most in need, and teachers had to exert extra effort to help these children succeed.

Davis took his case to the school board and to the parents of Ellsworth in a series of public meetings. He pressed his plan, which consisted of several staff development projects and after-school tutoring. He also advocated the formation of a Parents as Partners program to encourage better communication between home and school. Davis made a habit of inviting criticism at or near the end of every public presentation. "If you can think of a better plan," he would say, "please speak up. Share the details."

Laura, a first-year teacher at Ellsworth, had student taught there the year before. As part of her work for the student teaching seminar she attended every week, she had conducted an action research study to explore how best to help the weak readers in her classroom. While doing the project, Laura had identified several promising strategies—ideas about testing, designing instruction, evaluating the children's progress, working with parents, and involving community members in school activities.

Now Laura wanted to share her ideas with the district as a whole but was at a loss about how to do so. She did not want to speak up in a public forum, fearing she would sound like a naïve know-it-all. But she also remembered her university supervisor's admonition: "Young turks who do not speak up, who do not share what they know, who do not take chances to help children succeed, grow into old turkeys." Laura talked with her university supervisor, suggesting that she might redraft the conclusions from the action research project as a set of recommendations for teaching and learning at Ellsworth. "I'd like to share them with the superintendent," Laura said, "and maybe the school board as well."

She was excited about being able to contribute to her new district. But where to start?

The purpose of this chapter is to explore the place of standards in modern public education and to describe teachers' responsibilities for assessing students fully and fairly.

How Do We Know What Works in Education?

How can we convince others and ourselves that what teachers do makes a difference in students' lives? Deciding whether an educational program or activity is valuable is always a matter of answering this question: Compared to what? **Standards** in education are the necessary or required levels of knowledge and ability a student should possess—they are the benchmarks against which we can compare programs, teaching, and learning. Standards are determined in various ways and from multiple sources. Some are defined by the school or by the teachers themselves. Other standards of educational quality are set by outside sources, such as professional education associations and state education departments.

Standards can also vary in what they measure. Some, such as **content standards,** represent the knowledge, skills, and attitudes students must attain to master a subject matter. For example, a fifth-grade student might be expected to use whole numbers, fractions, and decimals to solve math problems. **Performance standards,** on the other hand, indicate the level at which students should be able to use the knowledge they possess to solve problems. Thus a fifth-grader might be expected to correctly solve nine out of ten word problems requiring the use of whole numbers, fractions, and decimals.

Assessment and **measurement** are synonyms for formal attempts to determine students' knowledge, skills, and attitudes. **Evaluation** is the process of examining student performance to determine whether students have met or exceeded standards of performance set by the teacher. Although the topic of standards and assessment can be rather controversial, most people would agree they are necessary parts of the educational process. We can predict how students will respond to certain teaching methods, what they will learn from various curriculum designs, and how teacher training will influence students' acquisition of knowledge. In truth, though, these are all predictions and educated guesses. Until and unless students are evaluated according to educational standards, we do not know for certain whether our planning is effective or how well students are learning anything at all. It is important to remember that students' performance on assessment or evaluation measures is a direct indication of how well they are being taught. We cannot expect students to know what they have not been taught. In this way, assessment is as important for educators as it is for students.

Personal Standards

How do personal standards influence one's judgment of educational quality? In terms of education most of us judge quality by comparing it to what we value. The comparisons might be simple and casually made. For instance, a student might say, "I like Mr. Jackson's class. I am learning the material, and he treats me like what I have to say is important. I think it is valuable for students to learn and to feel good about themselves. Mr. Jackson cares about me. Mr. Jackson is a good teacher." From her statements, this student appears to use her conceptions of caring and learning as standards for judging a teacher's effectiveness.

Other personal assessments of educational quality can be elaborate and carefully made. For example, your own personal philosophy might suggest that good teachers do not behave the same way with all students. Instead, they take their lead from students' differing needs and abilities, and they tailor teaching to fit students' present conditions. You might think, "If students change for the better as a result of working with a teacher who behaves in this fashion, then I judge that teacher to be good."

To gather information for your judgments or standards, you would probably make several observations and ask many questions of different people. You would be seeking evidence of students' needs and abilities, of students' differences, of "tailored instruction," of changes in both students and teaching over time, and so forth. The answers to the questions in addition to your observations would help you decide whether a teacher measured up to your personal standards for effective teaching.

If you are a supporter of equal opportunity in education, you might judge programs and curricula by how well they meet the needs of all the students in the classroom. If you value competitiveness, you might believe a cooperative classroom environment is ineffective. Traditionalists might label a school unsuccessful if it offered bilingual classes but did not offer Latin. All these judgments are based on people's personal standards for effective teaching and valuable education.

National Goals and Standards

Where is the nation headed, educationally speaking? Every major parent, education, and business group across the country endorsed the **National Education Goals** as soon as they were announced. (See Figure 11.1.) People realized that many of the goals would remain unmet for years to come, but the goals themselves raised nationwide concern for quality education. Although no longer funded by Congress, the National Education Goals continue to offer direction for educational change.

Other groups have created similar national standards, including the National Council of Teachers of English, the Center for Civic Education, and the National Academy of Sciences. The National Council of Teachers of Mathematics (NCTM) stands as an excellent example of how one national organization designed and explained mathematics standards. Their standards specifically outline what material should be covered and what methods should be used to teach students from prekindergarten through high school. As shown in Figure 11.2, NCTM teaching standards are complemented by general expectations for student performance. These standards and expectations are strengthened through the use of elaborate explanations and graphics meant to help teachers guide their students to perform appropriately (National Council of Teachers of Mathematics, 2000). Standards such as these help teachers prepare lesson plans for specific topics. They also help teachers stay on course with a national curriculum for a subject.

Goal 1:   Ready to Learn   All children in America will start school ready to learn.

Goal 2:   School Completion   The high school graduation rate will increase to at least 90 percent.

Goal 3:   Student Achievement and Citizenship   All students will leave grades 4, 8, and 12 having demonstrated competency over challenging subject matter including English, mathematics, science, foreign languages, civics and government, economics, the arts, history, and geography, and every school in America will ensure that all students learn to use their minds well, so they may be prepared for responsible citizenship, further learning, and productive employment in our Nation's modern economy.

Goal 4:   Teacher Education and Professional Development   The Nation's teaching force will have access to programs for the continued improvement of their professional skills and the opportunity to acquire the knowledge and skills needed to instruct and prepare all American students for the next century.

Goal 5:   Mathematics and Science   United States students will be first in the world in mathematics and science achievement.

Goal 6:   Adult Literacy and Lifelong Learning   Every adult American will be literate and will possess the knowledge and skills necessary to compete in a global economy and exercise the rights and responsibilities of citizenship.

Goal 7:   Safe and Disciplined Alcohol- and Drug-Free Schools   Every school in the United States will be free of drugs, violence, and the unauthorized presence of firearms and alcohol and will offer a disciplined environment conducive to learning.

Goal 8:   Parent Participation   Every school will promote partnerships that will increase parental involvement and participation in promoting the social, emotional, and academic growth of children.

Source: From National Education Goals Panel. (1998). *National education goals: Building a nation of learners.* Available online: http://govinfo.library.unt.edu/negp/page3.htm.

Figure 11.1
National
Education Goals

4.3 Learning Geometry and Measurement Concepts by Creating Paths and Navigating Mazes: Hiding Ladybug

Figure 11.2
Geometry Standard for Prekindergarten to Grade 2

Hiding Ladybug

Making Rectangles

Ladybug Mazes

The three-part ladybug example presents a rich computer environment in which young students can use their knowledge of numbers, measurement, and geometry to solve interesting problems. Planning and visualizing, estimating and measuring, and testing and revising are components of the ladybug activities. These interactive figures can help students build ideas about navigation and location, as described in the Geometry Standard, and use these ideas to solve problems, as described in the Problem Solving Standard. In the first part, Hiding Ladybug, students create a path that enables the ladybug to hide under a leaf. In the second part, Making Rectangles, students plan the steps necessary for the ladybug to draw rectangles of different sizes. In the last part, Ladybug Mazes, students plan a series of moves that will take the ladybug through a maze.

Source: Reprinted with permission from *Learning geometry and measurement concepts by creating paths and navigating mazes: Hiding ladybug. Principles and standards for school mathematics.* Copyright 2000 by the National Council of Teachers of Mathematics. Available online: http://standards.nctm.org/. All rights reserved.

The Nation's Report Card

How are we to know if the nation is reaching its goals? The National Assessment of Educational Progress (NAEP) is a survey designed to give policymakers and the general public information about the academic achievement of students across the United States. It serves as one kind of benchmark against which specific educational programs can be compared. The U.S. Department of Education refers to the NAEP as the Nation's Report Card—one specific set of assessment results on which we can judge progress toward some of our National Education Goals.

Since 1969 the NAEP has been administered annually to samples of students in grades four, eight, and twelve. The survey is not based on any particular curriculum. Instead, the NAEP uses broad assessment frameworks that describe the knowledge and skills being evaluated in each subject area. In other words, the NAEP is a general survey of students' knowledge in particular subject areas at various points in their educational careers, no matter what type of school they attend.

Education reformers view the NAEP as a stimulus to change teaching. Results from the survey indicate areas where U.S. students in general are strong and weak. The results are also useful because they offer a comparative view over time. For instance, the results might show that on average fourth- and eighth-grade students meet reading standards for their age, but by the twelfth grade the average student is below the standard level. As a result, the NAEP can indicate subjects that need to be emphasized more than they presently are. These surveys therefore can inform teachers' decisions about lesson plans, teaching methods, and classroom management. For example, a teacher might reconsider the effectiveness of group work on science projects if NAEP results are low for science.

Although many believe the current NAEP surveys are useful, some assessment experts recommend that NAEP begin to assess broader definitions of school achievement than it currently measures (National Research Council, 2001). These new, broader concepts might include students' thinking about how problems can be represented, their use of problem-solving strategies and self-regulatory skills, and their explanations and interpretations.

The accountability provisions in No Child Left Behind for failing to meet **adequate yearly progress** (AYP), or a collective measure of the numbers of children succeeding in a particular school, have largely forced attention at the state and local levels away from the National Education Goals and toward other measures of school and district success. All public school campuses, school districts, and states are evaluated for AYP, which means they must meet AYP criteria on three measures: reading/language arts, mathematics, and either graduation rate (for high schools and districts) or attendance rate (for elementary and middle/junior high schools). If a campus, district, or state that is receiving money from the federal government fails to meet AYP for two consecutive years, the relevant unit must offer supplemental education services, offer school choice, and/or take some corrective actions. (Examine the Issues in School Reform feature to see what determines whether a school, district, or state is making adequate yearly progress.)

State Standards

Why are state education standards so important for teachers to understand? Teachers are most likely to be held accountable for state standards. State school boards and other state-level organizations determine the state standards that all schools must meet. Teachers shape instruction to match the standards, assessing student performance through both teacher-made tests and standardized tests. Because states provide much of the funding for public education, the consequences of meeting or not meeting state standards may ultimately determine the financial support for schools. At the classroom level, students who do not perform to standard may be denied entry to special programs or prevented from graduating. When tests are used in this manner, they are often referred to as **high-stakes tests.**

Although most states have their own sets of standards and tests for determining whether the standards are being met, Maryland has been a leader in the development and use of state standards. They are a good example of what can be done to encourage the teaching and testing of both lower- and higher-level thinking in students. The Maryland Learner Outcomes are state standards developed by Maryland educators that were approved by the State Board of Education in 1990. They specify what students should know and be able to do as a result of their educational experiences. The Maryland State Performance Assessment Program (MSPAP) is designed to evaluate how well schools are teaching the basic and complex skills outlined in the standards. The MSPAP consists of **performance tests**—assessments that produce observable indications of how well students can apply what they have learned—in reading, mathematics, writing, language usage, science, and social studies for students in grades three, five, and eight.

The MSPAP measures a broad range of knowledge and skill competencies. Tasks require students to respond to questions or directions that lead to a solution for a problem. They also might be asked to make a recommendation or decision or to explain the reasons for their responses. Some tasks assess one content area; others assess multiple content areas. For instance, a mathematics task may be explained in the form of a long, detailed paragraph that would test both students' math and reading comprehension skills. Tasks may encompass group or individual activities; hands-on, observation, or reading activities; and activities that require extended written responses, limited written responses, lists, charts, graphs, diagrams, and/or drawings.

MSPAP tasks assess basic as well as higher-level skills and knowledge. In terms of basic knowledge, they measure reading for general understanding, writing to communicate clearly, making accurate arithmetic calculations, understanding key scientific concepts, and identifying historical and geographic information. For higher-level knowledge, the tests include tasks such as supporting an answer with information, predicting an outcome and comparing results to the prediction, and comparing and contrasting information (Maryland State Department of Education, 2000). See Figure 11.3 for an example of an MSPAP question for eighth-graders.

Opportunity Standards

How might standards spread educational accountability to those in charge? Opportunity standards (sometimes called opportunity-to-learn standards) are meant to hold school leaders—school board members and administrators—accountable for giving students a fair chance to succeed. The point of opportunity standards is simple: those in charge must provide students with appropriate support, in terms of books, materials, machines, highly prepared teachers, time to learn, and other tools, for students to do their work.

Issues in School Reform

MEASURING PROGRESS UNDER NCLB

What Determines Whether Your School, District, or State Is Making Adequate Yearly Progress (AYP) Under No Child Left Behind?

If the answer is "yes" to all of the following questions, then the criteria have been satisfied.

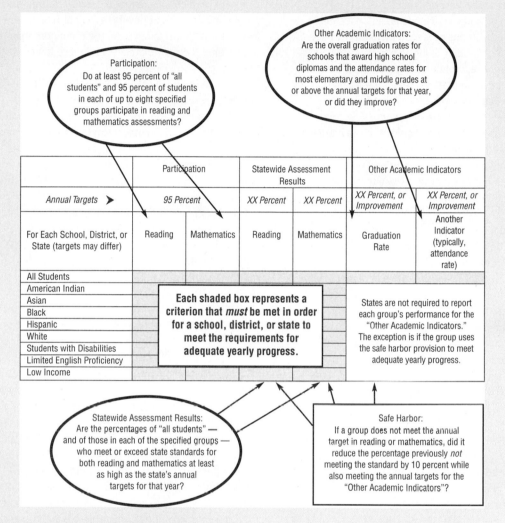

Question for Reflection: How might you find the annual targets for your own state?

Source: Southern Regional Educational Board. (2005). Focusing on student performance through accountability. Atlanta, GA: Southern Regional Education Board, p. 16. www.sreb.org. Used with permission.

To meet an opportunity standard, a school must provide the required quantity and quality of resources, practices, and conditions necessary for student success. Supporters of these standards argue that the responsibility to meet such standards lies with the states and the districts, as well as with individual schools.

These standards are largely symbolic, however, because all schools are supposed to be meeting them already. In addition, they are not enforced by any specific organization. Any influence these standards have on actual school policy comes from persuading board members and administrators to abide by them. The intent is clear, however: leaders ought to be as accountable for their behaviors as are teachers and students.

Here is how an eighth-grade student might describe an assessment task that requires test takers to think about planetary patterns.

1. Today, my teacher asked us to imagine that we were scientists working at the Goddard Space Flight Center in Greenbelt, Maryland. The *Voyager* spacecraft has been sending back data on a newly discovered solar system. There are four planets in this new system, and they have nearly circular orbits that do not overlap. A chart tells us the surface temperature, number of moons, tilt of axis, and chemical composition of each planet. Based on this data and an orbit diagram, we have to identify similarities between patterns present in this new solar system and our own solar system. Looking at the model provided, I see that the planets in the new solar system orbit around a sun which is at the center of the system, just like ours. I also notice that the surface temperature of any planet in the system decreases as its distance from the sun increases.

2. Next we are asked to come up with at least three questions about the new solar system which are not answered by the chart. I have quite a few questions about the system, including the size of each planet, each planet's distance from the sun, the atmospheric pressure of each planet, and the age of the planet. Next, I am asked to identify and write about three repeating patterns of astronomical change that occur in the sky. I remember that the moon goes through phases regularly, the sun rises and sets each day, and there is a difference in the position of the stars in the sky as the seasons change.

3. My classmates and I are given a chart listing the position of the four planets in the new solar system for the months of January, February, March and April. Working with three other students, we must complete the orbit data logs, also provided in our packet, to show in a picture form where each planet is at each of these times. Working carefully, we pinpoint the position of each planet in each of the four months using the data given.

Then, on our own, we use what we have learned about the rate of the orbit of each planet to predict the position of all four planets in the month of May. We are allowed to use pennies on our chart to represent planets and move them around the diagram to help make our predictions. Once our predictions are made, we write about our methods. I figured out how far each planet moved around its orbit in a month and moved the penny representing each planet the right distance, and there it was, at the right spot.

4. The next instructions I read ask me to imagine that *Space and Telescope Magazine* wants to record the next planetary alignment of this new solar system. To do this, I need to figure out when the planets will be aligned so I can reserve time on the orbiting space telescope. This takes a little more doing than the last task, and I find that using the pennies on my diagram helps me keep track of the motion of the planets. Carefully keeping track of which month I am in, I move each planet around its orbit the right number of spaces. Finally, after moving all the planets around their orbits several times, I come to a month when they are all in a row, or aligned. This is the month I predict should be reserved for the use of the orbiting space telescope.

5. Next, I write about how predicting the alignment of the planets was different from predicting their position in the month of May, one month after our data ended. It was a little more difficult to predict the alignment, but I found that by moving the pennies around the diagram one at a time and keeping track of the month, I was able to find the answer. In the space on our worksheet I write a paragraph for a younger student describing how the model of the solar system using orbit diagrams and pennies helped with my predictions. Finally, I write about how working with others in a group influenced or changed our beginning ideas about the position of the planets. My group basically agreed on how to go about predicting the positions of the planets, and our idea worked.

Source: Maryland Standards © 1995 Maryland State Department of Education. Available online: www.mdk12.org/. Reprinted with permission from MSDE.

Figure 11.3
The MSPAP in Action

What Types of Classroom Assessments Do Teachers Use?

Judging students is never easy. Everybody seems to have an opinion about what it means to be a successful student, as evidenced by the multiple standards and assessments established at various levels. In addition to national and state standardized tests, classroom assessment is an important part of the overall assessment of teaching practices and students' knowledge. Because classroom assessment occurs over long periods of time and takes many different forms, some believe it is the most accurate measure of what students are learning, how well they are progressing, and how effective teaching methods and curricula are.

Furthermore, classroom assessments also can say the most about teacher performance, because in measuring what students have learned, we measure what we have taught them. Student assessment should be part of an ongoing process in which teachers develop and revise their teaching plans and methods based on what does or does not work for students.

Assessing students, however, can be one of the most difficult parts of a teacher's job. The process of evaluating students—determining what they should be learning, how that will be tested, and what the results mean—can be particularly nerve wracking for new teachers. The best advice for professionals trying to meet the challenge of student assessment is to specify the goals and objectives of education, determine learners' needs and abilities, and take action to close the gap between where learners are and where they need to be (National Research Council, 2001). Successful teachers strive for high levels of student intellectual engagement that foster the acquisition of new knowledge and skills (American School Board Journal, 2007).

Classroom Assessment Triad

What do new teachers need to know and be able to do regarding assessment to meet their job responsibilities? Teachers have three responsibilities for classroom assessment. First, teachers need to know what is expected of students. They need a clear view of the learning goals that drive the local educational program. Teachers and students can only move forward together if they know which way to proceed. Second, teachers need to be able to determine what students presently know or can do in relation to these learning goals. This baseline information defines the starting point from which progress can be measured. Third, teachers need instructional strategies and methods to narrow the gap between where students are and where they are expected to be. This third challenge means teachers need to teach based on their readings of students' needs and abilities as identified by classroom assessments.

How do you know whether a teacher has properly assessed student progress? One simple way to answer this question is to examine how well students are learning. We can look at students' projects and grades, their classroom participation, and their ability to move on to more difficult material. If students are progressing, we may assume the teacher has properly used assessment results to guide instruction.

We might also ask and try to answer the following questions: Did the teacher provide practical information to meet the needs of his primary audiences—students, parents, colleagues, and administrators? Was his evaluation realistic? Did he behave legally and diplomatically? Was his evaluation accurate—did it gather correct information about student performance? Answers to these questions can help establish whether the teacher correctly understood students' needs and abilities.

Cognition and Learning

How might assessing student thinking help teachers develop successful lessons? The ways students think about their educational tasks can greatly influence their performances. A teacher who understands student thinking—who watches and assesses students' work and asks questions about how students think—can organize instruction to fit students' needs and abilities. Being in tune with students' feelings and attitudes is one sure way to know what appeals to them and what does not. From there, it becomes easier to develop lesson plans that will engage students.

Here is how this strategy can work in a math class. Given the math problem $2 + 4 = ?$, most students use the strategy of counting on from the first addend (e.g., the student thinks 2 plus 1 is 3, plus another 1 is 4, plus another 1 is 5, plus another 1 is 6). Only later do students learn to count on from the larger addend (e.g., the student thinks 4 plus 1 is 5, plus another 1 is 6). If a teacher carefully assesses a student's approach to this math problem, she might modify her instruction in several ways. She might pose a more difficult or an easier problem. She might change the size of the numbers in the set. Or she might compare and contrast different students' strategies to help them learn new ones (National Research Council, 2001).

If a teacher knows more than a student's answer—if she understands how a student works toward a solution—she can use that information to improve her instruction. She can pull, push, stretch, and inspire the student to think in new ways. The teacher who assesses student thinking and not just student results in any content area is likely to increase the chances for student success.

Educators Shea, Murray, and Harline (2005) argued that the evidence teachers require to understand how students think permeates classroom activities.

> Teachers anecdotally note significant thinking, knowing, and problem solving displayed during classroom performances that require learners to apply knowledge and skills in situations similar to those they'll encounter outside school. These performances might include taking part in formal and informal discussions, writing personal pieces, participating in problem-solving activities, conducting experiments, playing on a team, working in a group, and giving presentations. (2005, p. xiv)

Standardized Testing

Tests are attempts to make standards apply directly to life. If you have a standard for student learning, it is argued, you ought to have a test to see if students meet that standard. When people make this argument, they usually have in mind tests that are said to be *standardized*. In common usage, **standardized tests** are commercially prepared examinations designed to obtain samples of students' knowledge or aptitudes. They are standardized in that the same type of test is given to all students, no matter where they are, using the same directions for classroom administration and the same procedures for scoring and interpreting the results. Standardized tests are given to students at all points in their academic careers in the form of IQ tests, national standards tests, state standards tests, and so on. In addition, standardized tests often are a main factor in deciding whether a student can proceed to a higher level of education, for example, the Scholastic Aptitude Test (SAT) for entrance to college and the Law School Aptitude Test (LSAT) for entrance to law school.

How do standardized tests both help and hinder teachers' efforts to judge their students' needs and abilities? Academic progress is assessed formally most often by standardized tests. The tests are usually, but not always, multiple-choice, paper-and-pencil assessments. The items do not necessarily reflect the knowledge that students are supposed to learn in their classes; that is, sometimes the tests and curricula are not aligned. In some cases, standardized tests measure students' potential or aptitude, rather than their actual knowledge.

Standardized tests help equalize opportunities for students to demonstrate the knowledge they have and the skills they possess. Comparing students' scores on these tests is easy, because they are standardized in terms of administration and interpretation, and they are widely applied. In other words, students are starting from the same place; they take the same type of test that is scored in the same way. Therefore, standardized tests enable nationwide comparisons of students at the same grade level or age. These comparisons can be very instructive for teachers and parents. For example, a particular student might score at the ninety-seventh percentile in reading (97 percent of the students in the norm group had lower scores), but only at the fifty-seventh percentile in mathematics (57 percent of the students in the norm group had lower scores). This information might stimulate teachers and parents to arrange for more instruction or a different kind of assistance in mathematics for this student.

Some people do not have a lot of faith in standardized tests, however, because students' scores represent estimates of their capabilities based on samples of their performance. The tests are not complete measures of students' knowledge or talents. The amount of knowledge and the number of skills that a student might be expected to command at any point in time are immense. By necessity, standardized tests must be fairly short, so the samples must be restricted in size. Thus, the items might not deliver a full representation of what a student knows and can do.

Another criticism of standardized tests is that scores are derived from student performance on paper-and-pencil tasks, not from performance on real-life situations. Some students simply do not do well on tests for any number of reasons, including anxiety and pressure to do well. They might not perform well on a standardized test question that would be easy for them to solve in a classroom discussion. Furthermore, many circumstances beyond students' capabilities can affect their scores: the temperature of the room in which the test is given, lucky guesses, illness, and problems at home (Airasian, 2004).

Another set of issues arises when discussing standardized test scores, specifically their reliability, validity, and utility. To be useful, test scores must be **reliable**—a student's score today must be the same as or close to the score he would get tomorrow. A reliable test does not yield erratic results. Many standardized tests are scored by machines and therefore have black and white answers. This helps eliminate scoring disagreements—an answer is either correct or wrong. When humans score tests with variable answers, they must be able to agree on their estimates of student performance. This becomes an especially difficult and expensive requirement in the case of essay tests.

Standardized tests also must be **valid;** that is, they must measure what they are supposed to measure. For instance, if a test claims to assess students' understanding of the workings of an internal combustion engine, it should not be a test of students' reading abilities.

Also in terms of scoring, standardized tests must demonstrate a high degree of **utility.** The results need to be reported in ways that people can easily understand and apply to help students improve their performance.

When it comes to interpreting what standardized test scores mean, people usually look at them in one of two ways. On a **norm-referenced test,** students' test scores are compared to the scores of other similar students. The comparison group students are usually from the same age or grade level, with half of the scores above the average or mean score and the other half below the mean. In norm-referenced tests, then, a student's test score acquires value in relation to every other student's score. For example, if the comparison group scored particularly high on a test, a score of 340 might put a student in the fifty-fifth percentile. However, if that same score were achieved in a comparison group in which the scores were particularly low, the student might be in the eighty-fifth percentile. Norm-referenced test are useful for determining where a student is in terms of other students of her age or at her level.

Cultural Awareness: Lessons Learned

The Golden Apple Awards: The Way It Spozed to Be James Herndon Memorial Award goes to Bill Cosby, Barack Obama, and Henry Louis Gates, Jr. Cosby started it, Obama legitimized it, and Gates expanded on it—it being a dialogue within the African American community about the causes of the black/white achievement gap. Cosby's comments caused a stir. Some thought them the demeaning remarks of a rich man—and maybe an old man—who had forgotten what it was like to be young, black, and poor. Aaron McGruder appeared to mock these famous African Americans in his comic strip *The Boondocks*. Others thanked Cosby for injecting honest commentary into a bad situation. Gates asked, "Why the huge flack over Bill Cosby's insistence that black teenagers do their homework, stay in school, master standard English, and stop having babies? Any black person who frequents a barber shop or beauty parlor in the inner city knows that Mr. Cosby was only echoing sentiments widely shared in the black community."

Obama, the Democratic senator from Illinois, galvanized the Democratic National Convention with a speech of remarkable beauty and eloquence. About education he said, "Go into any inner-city neighborhood, and folks will tell you that government alone can't teach kids to learn. They know that parents have to parent, that children can't achieve unless we raise expectations and eradicate the slander that says a black youth with a book is acting white."

Gates, quoting his father, averred that too many black youths now think it is easier to become a professional athlete than a doctor or lawyer: "If our people studied calculus like we studied basketball, we'd be running M.I.T." Gates admired the "marvelously rich and inventive tongue" that is black vernacular, but he observed that "there's a language of the marketplace, too, and learning to speak that language has generally been a precondition of success, whoever you are. . . . These issues can be ticklish, no question, but they're badly served by silence and squeamishness."

Question for Reflection: Cosby, Gates, and Obama have learned that being quiet about the difficult challenges of educating and evaluating inner-city youth does not help. Why are people, regardless of their race or position, wary of discussing these issues?

Source: Bracey, G. W. (2004, October). The 14th Bracey report on the conditions of public education. *Phi Delta Kappan, 86*(2), 149–168.

The other type of standardized test scores comes from a criterion-referenced test. In contrast to a norm-referenced test, a **criterion-referenced test** assesses a student's performance against a clear, external standard. Returning to the previous example, on a criterion-referenced test a student who scored a 340 would always be in, say, the seventy-fifth percentile. By comparing a student's score to some clearly defined benchmark, a teacher can interpret student performance in terms of instructional objectives, instead of comparing students to one another.

Minimum Competency Testing

Is there a common body of knowledge and minimal level of learning that all public school students should be expected to master? People who think so support minimum competency programs, curriculum, and instruction geared toward the successful completion of **minimum competency tests.** These tests are meant to assess the lowest acceptable levels of student performance in various subject areas, including reading, writing, math, and science.

The minimum competency movement, sometimes called **outcome-centered learning** because it focuses on "results," began in the 1970s. Advocates worried about what they perceived as a declining emphasis on content and academic rigor in schools. Some wanted to end the practice of social promotion—promoting children through the grades to keep them with their peers even if they could not keep pace academically. Others wanted to make sure public funds were spent on **literacy,** which was defined most often as students' scores on tests of reading, writing, and calculation. The purpose of the movement was to return curricula to the basics and to make sure all students learned at least that much. The minimum competency movement defined "minimum" in terms of the knowledge and skills adults believe children need to possess to maintain employment in their adult lives.

Critics contend that the minimum competency movement has led to an overemphasis on high-stakes tests, which determine students' grade promotion, graduation, and access to specific fields of study. Some critics argue that high-stakes tests limit the curriculum to simplistic ideas and punish students who do not score well.

Asking Questions

Why is the ability to ask good questions one of the most important assessment skills a teacher can have? Teachers cannot—nor do they want to—test students at every possible turn of the curriculum. They do, however, ask questions while they teach. A main purpose of these questions is to assess student thinking. Students' responses can inform teachers about what students understand, as well as indicate areas where students need more time or help. Teacher questions also let students know what is important. If a teacher asks several questions about the latter portion of a history chapter, for example, students can infer that they should focus on this part of the text when studying for the upcoming test. Teachers who ask the right questions at the right time and respond appropriately to student answers are conducting effective evaluations.

What kinds of questions do teachers ask? Many strategies can be used to classify the types of questions teachers ask: closed questions (a single answer) versus open questions (many answers); divergent questions (request elaboration) versus convergent questions (narrow responses); higher-level questions (requiring respondents to analyze, apply, evaluate, or synthesize) versus lower-level questions (requiring recognition and recall). One simple but useful guide organizes teachers' questions into four categories. Students' answers to these questions can provide valuable evaluative information that will guide instruction. The four categories are:

1. Questions that elicit information from students (e.g., "Why do you think John Kerry was defeated for the presidency?").
2. Questions that establish or put information into students' minds (e.g., "If you were a newly freed slave in Alabama, what problems would you face?").
3. Questions that expand students' thinking about particular topics (e.g., "Because students are required to attend school, what subjects do you think should be required?").

4. Questions that extinguish or close down student thinking (e.g., "What kind of evidence would convince you that the statement you just made is erroneous?") (Mackey & Appleman, 1988).

How might teaching or learning conditions or settings dictate teachers' questions? Teachers ask students questions about subject matter in a variety of ways. In addition to questions on written examinations, teachers often ask questions during the common give-and-take lectures and discussions that occur in the classroom. Sometimes teachers direct these questions toward selected individuals, sometimes toward volunteers, and sometimes toward the class as a whole, in search of a united group response (e.g., OK, class, what is 6 times 6?'). Teachers also provide questions in written study guides or as comprehension checks to be answered after students complete assigned readings. Sometimes teachers give written questions to small groups of students and ask for either group or individual responses in oral or written form. One-on-one tutoring sessions provide opportunities for individualized questions that yield an in-depth account of a student's attitudes, beliefs, or understanding.

Questions in the classroom, however, should flow in both directions. Astute teachers know there is great value in soliciting students' questions. Students' questions can be a useful tool when teachers are trying to determine where the class is in terms of understanding the subject or skill. In fact, student questions may be a better indication of the class's level of understanding than are the teacher's questions.

Authentic Assessment

Authentic assessment is an alternative to traditional standardized tests, because it assesses student performance on real-life tasks in many forms. The idea behind authentic assessment is to encourage the application of knowledge to problems that students can expect to encounter in real life. We all know that in many real-life problems there are rarely right and wrong answers. Instead, there are more and less acceptable courses of action. Rather than ask students to perform limited tasks that are rarely seen outside standardized tests, authentic assessments ask students to synthesize ideas to find answers to real-life problems. Such assessments are increasingly driven by technology (Hardy, 2007).

Many advocates support authentic assessment as a more reliable and accurate way to measure what students have learned and, perhaps more important, how well they can apply this knowledge. In assessment terms, however, this means that judging a student's performance becomes a complicated, time-consuming, and often expensive venture. It is also more difficult to compare the results of students' authentic assessment in terms of state and national standards. **What are some forms of authentic assessment that teachers use?** Authentic assessment takes place over a period of time (weeks, semesters, etc.) during which students' work is measured in terms of the progress made and material mastered. Various means are available for observing and collecting student work for purposes of authentic assessment.

JOURNALS Teachers can use a student's **journal** or log—written collections of students' reflections on learning—to increase their knowledge of students' needs and abilities. Journals may be hard-copy notebooks or online files that contain graphs, notes, charts, pictures, and any artifacts that students choose to include. Students can use their journals to record their feelings about a particular assignment, to describe what they learned from a project, to explain why they did or did not think a test was fair, and so on.

Typically, teachers generate questions that guide students' written reflections in their journals. Teachers usually have access to the journals, but not always. Sometimes students are encouraged to designate their entries as "shared" or "private." Teachers set the ground rules for journal use up front, often cooperatively with students, and respect these rules throughout the school year.

PORTFOLIOS A **portfolio** is a collection of a student's work, often selected by the student himself, that represents the best of his learning efforts. Portfolios might include test papers, essays, diagrams, art projects, audiotapes of musical performances, videotapes of drama productions, computer programs, and the like. Portfolios can exist as physical collections of work or as electronic files. The work that students include in a portfolio may be accompanied by their own or their peers' critiques. Sometimes students share their portfolios with would-be employers to demonstrate their accomplishments and to show their potential value as employees.

Portfolios are alternatives to traditional tests because they document student performance in outcomes not typically measured by tests that take place over an hour or two. For example, a writing portfolio may include writing assignments that a student has completed over the course of a marking period or an entire school year. As a result, portfolios may offer some of the best available evidence of student learning and progress. Teachers and parents can use portfolios to enrich their understanding of student learning and to better plan how to encourage student progress.

RUBRICS A **rubric** is a scoring key. Teachers create and use rubrics to help assess how well students have grasped important aspects of learning activities. Rubrics are sometimes as simple as checklists that help teachers note the presence or absence of specific attributes in students' performances or products. For example, a teacher may have a checklist for a group math activity that includes such items as "mastered the computational skill," "arrived at the correct answer," "worked cooperatively with rest of group," "applied previous lessons to current work," and so on.

Rubrics can also be used to note the strength of various aspects of students' work. These sliding-scale judgments replace the all-or-nothing characteristic of a checklist. For instance, a teacher might use a 3-point scale with the following descriptors of student work: 3 = excellent, 2 = satisfactory, 1 = unsatisfactory.

TEACHER-MADE TESTS Teachers often build their own tests to measure students' grasp of material taught in their classrooms. One useful tool for building tests is a test **blueprint,** which is a set of specifications for the content and objectives to be assessed. Designing a blueprint is an excellent way for teachers to plan ahead—they can make sure their lesson plans cover the content that will be assessed on the test, and vice versa.

A sample test blueprint is shown in Table 11.1. It outlines ten areas of content and four types of exercises (requiring two lower-level and two higher-level types of thinking) that students will face. The higher-level exercises (application and analysis) are weighted more heavily in the teacher's test than are the lower-level exercises (knowledge and comprehension). In other words, the test will have more exercises (a total of sixty-five items) that require students to apply and analyze ideas, much as they might have to do in real-life settings. After looking at the sample blueprint in Table 11.1, do you see how the teacher might have an easier time developing a lesson plan with the blueprint in place?

CURRICULUM-BASED ASSESSMENT Curriculum-based assessment measures students' competence in various areas using the materials (books, readings, etc.) students encounter in the classroom. This type of assessment assumes that academic success is heavily dependent on read-

Table 11.1

BLUEPRINT FOR A TEST ON BODIES OF WATER

Course Content	Knowledge	Comprehension	Application	Analysis	Total
Salt water	2	3	2	3	10
Fresh water	2	2	3	3	10
Plants	1	2	4	3	10
Currents	1	1	3	5	10
Animals	1	2	4	3	10
Tides	2	3	3	2	10
Temperature	2	2	4	2	10
Maritime law	1	2	4	3	10
Commercial	2	2	4	2	10
Recreation	1	1	4	4	10
Total	15	20	35	30	100

ing and writing skills and that such skills are most fairly and accurately measured using material somewhat familiar to students (Jones, Southern, & Brigham, 1998).

One example of a curriculum-based assessment is a timed oral reading assessment. In such an assessment the teacher might identify a previously unread passage from a class text and ask the student to read aloud from it for one minute. The teacher would then count the words the student reads correctly as a percentage of the total words read. (Reading fluency is highly related to reading comprehension.) A similar strategy is for the teacher to read one sentence that is the beginning of a story. The student listens, thinks for one minute, and then writes for three minutes. Scoring is based on the student's number of correct words, correct word sequences, and so forth.

SELF-ASSESSMENT **Why not ask students to evaluate themselves?** Too often, teachers overlook the obvious source of information about what does and does not work in the classroom: students themselves. They know what they like and dislike. They often know what they can and cannot do. They also know the consequences of taking and not taking risks in their learning experiences.

Good teachers take advantage of this plentiful resource in classroom assessment and ask students to evaluate themselves. The process of **self-assessment** requires students to evaluate their own participation and their own products. In practice, this means teachers should ask students such questions as these:

- How hard did you try?
- How difficult was the assignment for you?
- If you were to do this assignment again, what might you do differently?
- What did you learn?
- How well did you like this work?

Students are most likely to respond to these kinds of questions in honest, useful ways when they believe they are in a nonthreatening environment. Therefore, their responses should never be used against them. When done properly, student self-assessment can provide a wealth of information to both teachers and students about classroom learning experiences. It can also involve students more closely with their education and help build strong relationships between teachers and students.

Grading and Recommendations

Why is grading such a difficult issue for teachers? Grades are more than letters or numerals on a report card; they are used to reward students, to give feedback to students and parents on performance, and to provide estimates of students' potential for postsecondary study. In reality, grades determine a student's future. For example, grades often are a key factor in a student being assigned to a particular course of study (college prep or remedial), winning awards and scholarships, and being admitted to various colleges and training programs. Grades play an influential role in how students feel about themselves and about their academic careers because they count for so much.

Grades result from student assessments. Assessments can take many forms. Some school systems use collections of students' work to report students' progress instead of using traditional grades. But using such methods to replace grades is rare. Most schools continue to use traditional assessment methods—unit tests, quizzes, midterms, final exams, classroom participation, homework—to determine grades.

The only people who probably dislike grading more than students are teachers. Good teachers would probably do anything in their power to help make grading fair and not punitive. To that end, teachers try to state grading procedures clearly and explain them in class. They set policies on late work. They try to be consistent, avoiding in particular any modification in grading policies during the grading period. They give students lots of chances to demonstrate what they know and can do. Teachers often consider letting students choose among alternative assignments. They encourage students who are doing poorly, often providing extra help to improve their grades. Teachers keep good records of student performance.

Concentrating on good grades is wise, but it is critically important for teachers to recognize the negative power of giving zeros. Mathematically speaking, zeros overrepresent failure (Reeves, 2004).

Recommendations are another way teachers convey information about student performance. Letters teachers write in support of their students may be some of the most important writing teachers ever do. These letters of recommendation and character references can be used by students seeking awards, honors, and loans. A character reference, as the phrase suggests, is a reflection on the personal qualities and traits of a student. The strongest letters are usually those that explain general sentiments with specific examples of a student's behavior. (For instance, Jack Smith is one of the top two students I have ever taught. Jack's personal diligence and creativity were never more evident than in his senior thesis. . . .) Because teachers often know their students better than most other adults know them, and because teachers write well, these letters can carry a lot of weight with readers.

Teachers also write letters of recommendation for student admission to college and training programs, scholarships, and jobs. These letters often take the form of reflections on a student's past performances, with an eye toward his or her aptitude for future success. A letter says as much about the writer as it does about the person for whom it is written. Wise writers follow principles of composition and share a draft with an editor before mailing.

Student's Role

Why is it so important for teachers to understand what students can do and want to do?
Researchers have found that about 50 percent of a student's success with learning new topics can be explained by his or her attitudes and prior knowledge (Bloom, 1982). In other words, what students already know and their feelings toward particular educational tasks can greatly affect their classroom experiences and their grades. In these same studies, researchers found that teachers can account for as much as 30 percent of students' learning. Another way to think about this point is that for some students teachers could be the difference between a grade of 70 and a grade of 100!

Stanford professor Nate Gage argued that if a medical treatment had about one-tenth the power that teachers do, it would be declared a miracle cure (Gage, 1985). Teachers can have dramatic effects on their students, as evidenced by students' scores on tests. The key to maximizing teacher effects is understanding students' present needs and abilities. The more a teacher knows about her students' knowledge and attitudes and how her students think, the better prepared she will be to help them succeed.

Still, students can and must help themselves. Peer feedback and self-monitoring can yield valuable information for self-guidance. When students understand how they reason and how they can collaborate with their peers, they can often improve their learning and their grades.

How Can Teachers Know Whether They Are Assessing Students Fairly?

With the increasing use of high-stakes and standardized tests comes heightened concern for fairness in testing. Most commercial producers of standardized tests review test items with great care and try to guard against built-in flaws that make tests unfair. The individual teacher who creates her own tests must also guard against a variety of threats to fairness in her own assessments. Grades and assessments count for so much in education; they are a determining factor in things such as school funding and students' admission to college, and training programs. Educators need to do all they can to ensure fair and accurate evaluations of all students.

Bias in Assessment

What is assessment bias, and how can a teacher avoid it? According to educational researchers, "assessment bias refers to qualities of an assessment instrument that offend or unfairly penalize a group of students because of students' gender, ethnicity, socioeconomic status, religion, or other such group-defining characteristics" (Popham, 2005). Assessments can offend people when they depict negative stereotypes of certain subgroups. Test items that show African

Technology in Practice

RUBRICS

You will find it useful to explore the concept of rubrics—a scoring guide used in subjective assessments. A rubric suggests a rule defining the criteria of an assessment system to be used in evaluation. A rubric can be a description of performance characteristics corresponding to a point on a rating scale. Kathy Schrock's website provides a lot of good examples that will help you answer the question: Does a particular rubric provide a full and fair assessment of a student's performance?

Source: http://school.discoveryeducation.com/schrockguide.

Americans in stereotypical roles such as service work or sports, for example, may offend African American students. If you take a test when you are offended or angry, the result probably will not be a fair or accurate representation of what you know or can do.

Students are also unfairly penalized when their test scores are distorted because the test content puts the student at a disadvantage. The content need not be offensive, merely out of reach, for one reason or another. Young women may be penalized if test questions revolve around football or other sports with which they are unfamiliar. Students from lower socioeconomic backgrounds may be penalized by questions that require familiarity with dining out or attending high-priced entertainment events.

Sometimes students claim they have been victims of unfair tests when they simply have not studied or did not pay attention in class. In these cases, the penalty for poor test performances is low grades, but a low grade is not automatically an indication that an assessment is unfair.

Teaching to the Test

Is it wrong to teach to the test? Although it is not wrong to *teach to the test,* the phrase is confusing. Teachers are supposed to create classroom opportunities for students to learn the material for which they are held accountable. Typically, this means that teachers teach domains of knowledge, which are large, inclusive bodies of subject matter. Test items, if they are constructed appropriately, sample fully and fairly the knowledge contained in these domains. Good teaching covers the material students are supposed to learn. When this material appears on the test, students are prepared, and teachers receive an accurate assessment of students' knowledge.

Beware, though, sometimes people use the phrase *teaching to the test* to mean teaching specific items on the test or teaching the test itself. This is wrong and doing so is poor teaching. Although teachers are held accountable for students' standardized test scores—and the pressure to produce satisfactory scores can be intense—it is never acceptable to teach in this manner. There is much less educational value for students in learning answers to specific test items than in learning domains of knowledge.

Multiple Measures

What is the best way to protect against unfairness in assessment? One of the best ways to ensure fairness in testing is to use different measures of success by creating multiple opportunities for students to demonstrate what they know and can do. When multiple ways for students to demonstrate their knowledge and skills are offered, definitions of success are expanded. Pressure for high scores and the best letter grades is lessened, and focus is returned to the processes of learning. For example, creating a portfolio of a student's creative writing can showcase his success in ways that standardized tests do not offer.

The state of Nebraska has a creative strategy for multiple assessment measures in its Student-based, Teacher-led Assessment and Reporting System (STARS). STARS is based on the assumption that no single assessment can meet all needs. Instead, educators need to use multiple measures to provide a full, round representation of educational success.

STARS requires school systems to develop local assessment plans that are aligned with state (or district) learning standards. These plans combine norm- and criterion-referenced assessments for students in grades four, eight, and eleven in mathematics, reading and writing, science, and social studies. The norm-referenced tests must be selected from a state-approved list. Districts can develop their own criterion-referenced assessments, including observations, portfolios, or rubrics. They can also purchase assessment tests from commercial publishers. If they develop their own, the assessments must meet certain criteria for the absence of bias (e.g., appropriate content and consistency in scoring). In addition, all students in grades four, eight, and eleven participate in a statewide writing assessment.

Every year Nebraska school districts must issue a report to local residents containing data on student performance, district demographics, and financial information. Every two years, the report must describe what is being done instructionally to help students demonstrate successful performance. And every three years, the report must contain the results of a follow-up survey of graduated students (Nebraska Department of Education, 2005).

Case Perspectives

Think back to the case that opened this chapter. The following comments are intended to provide some context for your reflections on this case.

KATHERINE SMITH, AN EXPERIENCED TEACHER AT ELLSWORTH, IS NOT AT ALL SURE ABOUT THE WISDOM OF LAURA SENDING HER STUDENT TEACHING ACTION RESEARCH CONCLUSIONS TO THE SUPERINTENDENT. SHE IS, HOWEVER, FAIRLY SURE WHAT SHE WOULD TELL ANYONE WHO WOULD LISTEN IF SHE HAD THE OPPORTUNITY. I've been reading a book that makes a tremendous amount of sense to me called *Drowning in Data*. The authors argue that we teachers too often overlook important information we have about children, believing instead that we do not possess enough relevant evidence to inform our teaching. Not so.

Criminal investigators, as the authors observe, work wonders with seemingly trivial evidence—a strand of hair, a drop of blood, a tire track. Ask the right questions in the right ways, and this seemingly "trivial evidence" can scream back at you. Effective teaching—teaching that yields student learning—is all about gathering and interpreting evidence that is abundant both inside and outside classrooms.

This is how the authors see it:

> Every gesture, utterance, or performance offers evidence of a child's progress toward developmental standards. With their posture, facial expressions, and gesticulations, learners unconsciously as well as consciously insist that we read their motions. Their body language is generally at high pitch and could easily fill volumes. Any parent can tell you all about it. When we say, "Let's talk about it," kids sometimes answer, "But I didn't say anything!" "You didn't have to," we tell them, "your face said a paragraph." This sensitive barometer is too easily ignored in the rush to teach and assess our way through a curriculum.

This statement rings incredibly true to me. We don't need to work harder to help our students at Ellsworth. We need to work smarter. We have too much data on students from our testing program that is marginally helpful in terms of designing instruction. But we have some of the best evidence anyone could ever want right before our eyes every day. If only we teachers had opportunities to talk with each other about our students. I am absolutely certain that we could design individually tailored programs for all our students—programs that would go a long way toward boosting their test scores and toward making them and their parents happy campers. Mr. Davis needs to provide more time for teachers to work together and give us the power to make instructional decisions. We are the professionals who are closest to the problems, and we have more evidence than anyone else.

LAURA'S UNIVERSITY SUPERVISOR THINKS ABOUT LAURA'S INTENT TO SHARE HER ACTION RESEARCH PROJECT WITH OTHERS WHO HAVE A STAKE IN ELLSWORTH SCHOOL. Superintendent Davis impresses me as a well-meaning man. I like the way he puts himself on the line when he meets with people. He appears to be making every effort to turn a bad situation around at Ellsworth School.

But I am concerned about Mr. Davis's statement that all the children at Ellsworth are capable of beating the state testing averages in reading/language arts and mathematics. This is either (1) a purely political statement meant to placate the school board, (2) a long-shot bet, or (3) the statement of a man who doesn't understand standardized testing. I'm not qualified to address 1 and 2, but Mr. Davis might well remember that good standardized achievement tests are designed to separate the test takers from one another. A norm-referenced test is no good if it fails to yield results that spread children's scores along a continuum. To accomplish this goal, test makers create a small number of easy items, a larger number of moderately challenging items, and a small number of difficult items in an attempt to ferret out what all students know and can do. A good test is overall neither too hard nor too easy. The test produces a bell curve. If a school has lots of students who do not score well on standardized achievement tests, and then they start scoring well for whatever reason, the test makers would begin to add more difficult items in an effort to separate test takers from each other or to reproduce the bell curve. Over time, of course, as the tests become more difficult, one might assume that schools are improving. But the horse race philosophy that drives norm-referenced testing will produce losers in the process. I would encourage Mr. Davis to look for a variety of measures of student success.

Questions for Reflection: There are at least two different issues in this case. One involves professional judgment: What role should a new, inexperienced teacher play in formulating educational policy? If you were Laura, how might you think about presenting your research findings to the superintendent or to others? Or would you choose not to do so?

A second issue in the case focuses on assessment: How can standardized test scores inform instructional decisions? What other sources of information might be used to judge the success of teachers and schools? What role should or do standardized tests play in instruction? What kind of evidence do you think should be used to make instructional decisions? What kind of evidence do you think should be used to judge how well a school is doing its job? How ought test results be used as a measure of student progress?

Source: Shea, M., Murray, R., & Harlin, R. (2005). *Drowning in data? How to collect, organize, and document student performance* (p. xiv). Portsmouth, NH: Heinemann. ■

Summary

Standards provide benchmarks against which we can judge educational success and failure. These benchmarks may come from many sources, including personal, national, and state sources. Standards are so important because they help clarify the term *accountable* when trying to determine the performances of students, teachers, school leaders, and elected and appointed governmental representatives who bear responsibility for public education.

Standards help teachers understand what is expected of their students. They also help teachers communicate expectations and support students' continuous learning. Teachers who understand the technical characteristics of classroom assessment can use them to shape teaching plans and practices. Teaching, learning, and assessment do not exist in isolation; they are processes that inform one another.

Regardless of the particular assessment used, ideas of *fairness* permeate all activities directed toward judging student performance. Efforts to develop and use *authentic* measures to assess student performance are driven by such concerns. Good teachers want to give their students every opportunity to "show what they can do" when faced with tasks that mirror the challenges they will face in real life—tasks that are real or authentic. They give students opportunities to demonstrate their abilities by using multiple measures, both standardized and nonstandardized or teacher-made. The more perspectives a teacher has on a student's performance, the more likely she is to provide a complete, fair representation of that student's achievement.

TERMS AND CONCEPTS

adequate yearly progress
assessment
assessment bias
blueprint
content standards
criterion-referenced test
curriculum-based assessment
evaluation
high-stakes test
journal
literacy
measurement
minimum competency tests
National Education Goals

norm-referenced test
opportunity standards
outcome-centered learning
performance standards
performance tests
portfolio
reliable
rubric
self-assessment
standardized tests
standards
utility
valid

REFLECTIVE ACTIVITY: ARITHMETIC TEST

Reflective practice is an essential part of good teaching. Reflection is a process that includes making thoughtful decisions, understanding and articulating value structures, acting from knowledge, evaluating your actions and their effects, and sharing your reflections with colleagues. After reading the following scenario, respond to the questions below. The scenario reflects the INTASC Principle and Disposition at the end of this activity.

Do this activity with a group of five to fifty peers.

Following is a problem that appeared on a sixth-grade arithmetic test taken by Freddie. How many points would you award Freddie for this problem? _____ Assume that Freddie gets the same number of points on the other nine questions. Compute Freddie's score on the test. _____ Assign a test grade (A, B, C, D, F) to Freddie. _____

Directions

Take your time and work all the problems below. Be sure to show the steps in your work:

1. If 5 bananas cost 84¢, how much would 7 bananas cost? Show your calculations.

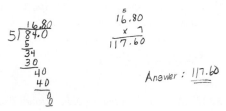

Decide 1. Mathematics is an exact science—a closed system in which there are right and wrong answers. Do you agree or disagree with your peers on the assignment of points and the giving of a grade? How might a disagreement about grading result in problems for a group of teachers?

Perceive and Value 2. Why might the awarding of points and grades on this simple exercise differ considerably from teacher to teacher? Can you state, in relatively few words, your own value position with regard to giving grades? Can you summarize the value positions of some of the people in your group who hold positions different from your own?

Know and Act 3. How might having teachers discuss their disagreement in scores and grades on Freddie's test be used to develop a common and comprehensive set of expectations for grading across a grade level or a school?

Evaluate 4. What does being fair mean in grading? How might you determine whether you were being fair in awarding points and grades to Freddie?

Discuss 5. How else might you assess Freddie's understanding of this math concept?

INTASC Principle 8

The teacher understands and uses formal and informal assessment strategies to evaluate and ensure the continuous intellectual, social, and physical development of the learner.

Disposition

The teacher understands the characteristics, uses, advantages, and limitations of different types of assessments (e.g., criterion-referenced and norm-referenced instruments, traditional standardized and performance-based tests, observation systems, and assessments of student work) for evaluating how students learn, what they know and are able to do, and what kinds of experiences will support their further growth and development. (Interstate New Teacher Assessment and Support Consortium, 1992)

ADDITIONAL READINGS

Airasian, P. (2004). *Classroom assessment* (4th ed.). New York: McGraw-Hill.

Joint Committee on Standards for Education Evaluation. (2003). *The student evaluation standards: How to judge evaluations of students.* Thousand Oaks, CA: Corwin Press.

Loveless, T. (2004). *The 2004 Brown Center report on American education: How well are American students learning?* Available online: www.brookings.edu/gs/brown/bc_report/2004/2004report.htm.

Popham, W. J. (2005). *Classroom assessment: What teachers need to know* (4th ed.). Boston: Allyn & Bacon.

WEB RESOURCES

www.fairtest.org
The National Center for Fair & Open Testing works to end what they perceive as the abuses, misuses, and flaws of standardized testing.

http://nces.ed.gov/
The National Center for Education Statistics has information that can inform both the design and conduct of educational program assessments.

www.ncte.org/
This site contains Standards for the English Language Arts and is sponsored by the National Council of Teachers of English and the International Reading Association.

www.nctm.org/
Find mathematics standards and teaching resources here.

http://nces.ed.gov/nationsreportcard/
This is the place to learn about the National Assessment of Educational Progress (NAEP), also referred to as the Nation's Report Card.

www.teachervision.com/lesson-plans
Teachervision.com provides an overview of authentic assessment methods.

Developing a Professional Portfolio

ASSESSING STUDENTS THROUGH OBSERVATION

One type of information that is potentially useful for your portfolio and likely to arise in job interviews is your opinion about student assessment. A large part of teachers' professional lives revolves around making judgments about students. Today, much of the assessment or evaluation work done to render such judgments is formal or based on standardized testing. But just as certainly, teachers gather much of the information on which they base their judgments on an informal basis—they observe the ways students behave and listen to what students say. The key to collecting good data and making sound judgments is to learn to use a variety of methods of observing a variety of activities and to use these strategies consistently and accurately. Student work samples and data on performance tasks can be used to demonstrate student academic growth over time.

Observe a teacher and her students as they interact during a lesson. Take notes on students' reactions to the lesson and list activities they work on during class. How do students demonstrate understanding of what they are supposed to learn? For example, does the teacher ask questions? Does she ask students to recite, do seatwork, and work in teams to create a product? What other activities do you see? Observe one student you think may not understand the lesson and someone else whom you believe does understand. Verify your assumptions by observing their performance in class and by talking after class with the teacher about the students. How did your perceptions fit with those of the teacher? Ask what types of assessments the teacher typically uses to inform her teaching.

Save this exercise and try it again later when you student teach. Determine how your knowledge of informal assessment has changed over time. How you judge students is a tremendously important part of your life as a teacher. Be sure to leave yourself room to grow. Changing your view of what is "fair," what is "right," and what is "wrong" are not indications of sacrificing your values. Quite the contrary. Your view of student assessment should mature over time—both you and your students will benefit in the long run if you possess a rich, robust sense of what constitutes student success.

Online Activity

Teaching with Census Information

When you go to the U.S. Census Bureau website (www.census.gov), click on For Teachers under Special Topics. You can download lesson plans for making sense of data from the 2000 census and from earlier years. These lessons help students recognize historical trends and contemporary issues by using real numbers about real people. Here is one exercise high school students can use to project future trends based on historical data. Read over this portion of the Forecasting the Future activity. As you do so, think about how you might incorporate this type of activity in a social studies or math lesson. What skills would a student need to be successful at this task?

Lesson 6 Activity Worksheet | **Estimating/Projecting Rates**

Forecasting the **Future**

Grades 11 and 12

Population Projections

To make population projections for the United States or for individual states, demographers make assumptions about future trends in the components of population change. These assumptions, which reflect professional judgment and take into account past trends, are made in terms of rates for births and deaths, and in terms of rates or numbers for migration.

For simplicity, the population projections discussed below are based on assumptions about past trends in total population, not on assumptions about each component of population change. Table 1 shows the 1970 and 1990 census populations for four states, all with populations that increased between 1970 and 1990. Calculate numerical growth (1990 population minus 1970 population) and percent growth (population growth as a percent of 1970 population, with percent change rounded to one decimal place).

Table 1. Population of Selected States: 1970 and 1990

State	1970	1990	Population growth, 1970–1990	
			Numerical	Percent
2. Connecticut	3,032,217	3,287,116		
3. Minnesota	3,806,103	4,375,099		
4. South Carolina	2,590,713	3,486,703		
5. Arizona	1,775,399	3,665,228		
6. Your State				

Calculate population projections for each state for the year 2010 assuming a continuation of trends for the 1970–1990 period: first based on numerical change (an arithmetic rate of change), then based on percent change (a geometric rate of change) with the results rounded to the nearest integer.

Table 2. Population Projections for Selected States: 2010

State	Based on numerical change	Based on percent change
7. Connecticut		
8. Minnesota		
9. South Carolina		
10. Arizona		
11. Your State		

Questions about population projections

Why are the population projections for the year 2010 larger when based on percent change than when based on numerical change for the 1970–1990 period? _____

_____

_____

Source: U.S. Census Bureau (14 February 2002). Chapter 6: Forecasting the future, grades 11–12. Available online: www.census.gov/dmd/www/ schtm03.html.

A Global Educational Context

Case Study: The USA as International Magnet

"Becca! Wait up," hollered Jim Baker, principal of Johnson Elementary School, as he ran across the parking lot to meet Becca Twyman. "Slow down, Jim," she called back. "I'm only on my way to the grocery store. The cottage cheese will still be there when I arrive."

Becca Twyman was in her second year of teaching fourth grade at Johnson Elementary School in a Washington, DC suburb. It was Friday afternoon, and she felt lighthearted. The week was over, things had gone well, and she had the whole weekend to do whatever she wanted—once she did her shopping and laundry, cleaned her apartment, got the oil changed in her car, and talked to her folks.

As Baker caught up with her, he breathlessly explained his haste. "I hate to have to tell you this way, but you're going to get three new students on Monday—refugees from Somalia. They'll be at the school sometime before lunch, along with a representative from the county's Welcome to the USA Committee."

"Do you want to run that by me again?" muttered Becca. "Monday? Somalia? Three? Jim, please tell me you're kidding."

"I wish I were, Becca. I just found out thirty minutes ago myself. You know how the committee works. Since they started doing this work ten years ago, they've never known for certain how many refugees would come to our community until just before their arrival. They do a lot of last-minute scurrying to arrange housing, school placements, and all the other social services these families need to get over the hump. This time is no different—except that this time there are three kids about the same age, and you're the teacher of choice."

"Why me?" asked Becca. Jim Baker looked her in the eye. "Frankly, I think your reputation is starting to get around. Your efforts to give your classroom an international flavor have been noticed by people in our central office. The flags around your room, your integration of foreign languages into the curriculum, and your ability to work with ESL students have drawn attention."

"Well, I guess I should be flattered," said Becca. "But I have to be honest. I don't really know where to begin. How should I get ready to accept these children into my classroom?"

This chapter explores why it so critical to learn about educational life outside the United States, how this life unfolds in schools around the world, and where teachers and students fit in the global, interdependent community.

Why Learn about Educational Life Outside the United States?

People around the world live with increasing cultural, economic, political, and social diversity. Progress in transportation and communication systems is enabling people within and between nations to interact with one another in new ways. One outcome of these technological innovations is that people are able to travel and live far from where they were born. Millions of "guest workers" or migrant laborers around the world live in a country they do not call home. In 2003, slightly more than one in ten residents of the United States was foreign born (Larsen, 2004). Governors Granholm of Michigan and Schwarzenegger of California are merely two of the more visible.

Schools around the globe both shape and reflect this diversity, teaching multicultural education, cross-cultural education, international education, comparative education, and global studies. These programs assume that human life is interdependent, and such mutual dependence has important implications for how we teach and learn.

Diversity and innovation, however, can make it hard to maintain relevant and current educational programs and experiences. Educators plan curriculum, instruction, and assessment for the "typical" student in their systems. When the populations of these schools change by the addition of even a few students from other nations and cultures, however, what worked in the past may not work in the future. **What problems and opportunities might you anticipate in classrooms where students are from different cultures and countries?**

Preparing for the Future

Anticipating the future with any sense of confidence requires knowledge. We need to understand what others value, how they think, what they are likely to do and not do. Knowledge also improves our chances to teach with sensitivity and intelligence. To learn about today's diversity of life and to imagine what it might be like tomorrow, we have only to look in schools around the world. There we find the future leaders and followers who will affect our own lives. The future of politics, business, art, science, and much more depends on today's students knowing the world in which they live.

The International Baccalaureate Organization (IBO) is one unusually creative way to shape international citizens of the future. Founded in 1968, the IBO is a nonprofit educational foundation based in Geneva, Switzerland. It emerged from efforts by international schools to establish a common curriculum and university entry requirements for geographically mobile students, such as children of diplomats and military personnel. International educators also believed a shared academic experience that exposed students to a variety of viewpoints would foster tolerance and intercultural understanding among young people.

The IBO offers three programs: the diploma program for students in their last two years of high school, the middle years program for students eleven to sixteen years old, and the primary years program for ages three through twelve. Classes at all levels are offered in English, French, and Spanish. All the programs promote international understanding and academic excellence.

The IBO mission statement emphasizes teaching skills beyond the academic classroom:

Education for Life

The International Baccalaureate Organization aims to develop inquiring, knowledgeable and caring young people who help to create a better and more peaceful world through intercultural understanding and respect.

To this end the IBO works with schools, governments and international organizations to develop challenging programmes of international education and rigorous assessment.

Figure 12.1
International
Baccalaureate
Program
Launches
Rebuilding
Effort

The International Baccalaureate Organization . . . is launching its own campaign to help schools in the devastated tsunami zone.

"In Indonesia, it's just a catastrophe. A whole sort of swath of teachers has been wiped out," said George Walker, the director-general of the organization, which reaches about 200,000 students a year around the world, including in the United States. . . . The money that is being raised will support travel expenses for the volunteers, according to Peter Kenny, the head of its Asia-Pacific operations. Providing teachers on a temporary basis can help get schools back on their feet, he said, and the organization also hopes to train Indonesian college students to replace the educators who were killed. Undamaged International Baccalaureate schools in Indonesia will also be lending their support, he said.

Inquiries can be addressed to tsunami@ibo.org.

Source: Samuels, C. A. (2005, January 19). *Education Week, 24*(19), 10.

These programmes encourage students across the world to become active, compassionate and lifelong learners who understand that other people, with their differences, can also be right. (International Baccalaureate Organization, undated)

Some two thousand and two hundred schools in 126 countries participate in the IBO. The IBO provides these schools with curriculum and assessment development, teacher preparation and information seminars, and electronic networking. With these materials, teachers can help students understand ideas and events around the world as they occur (Smith, 2006). Figure 12.1, for example, shows how one IBO school reacted to the events of the tsunami that struck Indonesia and other countries in 2004.

Becoming Globally Aware

Why is global awareness important? **Global awareness** refers to students' abilities to recognize their connections to other people and other nations around the world. Being aware of countries beyond our own is important, because the welfare of the United States depends on the welfare of other countries. We are tied to others by economics, the environment, politics, culture, technology, and personal and familial connections. Events in distant parts of the globe—war in Iraq, the discovery of fossils in Sudan, drug production in South America, and so on—create waves and ripples in the United States.

It works the other way around, too. What happens in the United States can affect the rest of the world in major and minor ways. Terrorism in the United States results in war in Afghanistan. A drop on the New York Stock Exchange forces the loss of jobs in Thailand. An American bicycle rider wins the Tour de France, and sports training programs around the world mimic his methods.

The daily news offers much evidence that actions in one nation affect life in many far-flung parts of the world. In addition, the past twenty years have witnessed incredible advances in technology and science with far-reaching effects. For instance, more people traveling and working outside their home countries means more intercultural contact. Dramatic advances in communications technology give ordinary people around the world new opportunities for learning from others. In some instances increased contact leads to competition and conflict. In other cases, familiarity breeds cooperation, for different people realize that they must work together if they are to survive and prosper.

To help negotiate all these effects and exchanges, people everywhere call on schools. Schools are asked to teach technical and communication skills in the hope of promoting mutual understanding. Their curricula must continually evolve to incorporate ever-changing politics and cultures. Schools around the globe must help tomorrow's adults learn languages, understand world history, and use a host of electronic communication systems. A global society is no longer the pipe dream of the futurist. It is an idea that people define each day as they reach around the world with their computers, telephones, and fax machines.

Many books have been written for young audiences to help them understand the importance of stability and interdependence in the world. *A Middle East Primer for Students* by

Joseph Wilcox (2004), for example, tries to provide students with a basic understanding of the Middle East in terms of history, geography, economics, and the challenges the region faces. Wilcox also demonstrates how the region's history continues to fascinate so many people and why America would want to fight wars in the region in the early 1990s and again at the turn of this century. Wilcox's intent is to help students understand where the Middle East fits into the modern world and how important the region is to world stability and prosperity. **Are you familiar with other books, poetry, music, or art works with an international flavor that exert influences on curriculum in the United States?**

How might joining schools and classrooms from around the world on the World Wide Web affect teaching and learning? Some education professionals believe that a global perspective, aided by technology, forces people to consider problems that cut across national boundaries (Wallace & Steptoe, 2006). Educators who think about the world also develop students' abilities to view the world from other perspectives. This process of exposing students to international perspectives has occurred for many years through associations referred to as *nongovernmental organizations,* or **NGOs.** These transnational associations—churches, scouts, farmers, chambers of commerce, physicians, athletes, educators, and so on—have grown in number to more than 40,000. The popularity of the Web is largely responsible for the growth of NGOs and cooperative efforts that focus on problems of common interest across national borders.

Global Education Motivators (GEM) is one NGO that focuses on developing global education programs for schools and communities. Educators founded GEM in 1981 to "bring the world into the classroom." Such notables as the late Fred Rogers, of television's *Mr. Rogers' Neighborhood,* and former U.N. Secretary General Kofi Annan have endorsed the work of the organization.

- GEMNET promotes video and e-mail exchanges among schools around the world.
- GEMRIM provides online instructional materials that concentrate on human rights, conflict resolution, and environmental protection.
- GEMQUEST organizes international travel to advance human rights efforts.

The emergence of a global community means that educators must prepare students for a world quite different from the one in which the educators themselves grew up. For teachers to enlarge their views of the world or to think globally and encourage their students to do the same, the basic curriculum and instruction in most schools must change to keep up with the times. To make these changes occur, however, a number of obstacles or competing demands must be overcome. Historically, school leaders have not considered global education to be a high priority. Teachers' limited time is already devoted to existing curricula, standardized testing, and accreditation demands. To a certain degree, the events of September 11, 2001, changed this situation. Educators are working to bring global information and perspectives into U.S. classrooms.

Understanding and responding to crises, however, is not the only reason for globally educating students. Money and jobs also fuel interest in international and worldwide issues. Business leaders have been among the more vocal proponents of global and comparative education. They view schools as vital to the production and maintenance of a workforce able to compete in a wider world.

Located in the Cincinnati suburb of Erlanger, Kentucky, Toyota Motor Manufacturing North America, Inc. (TMMNA) was founded in 1996 to manage Toyota's growing manufacturing operations in North America. Today, these include eleven plants in six states, two Canadian provinces, and one in Baja California, Mexico. These plants create many jobs in a variety of areas—purchasing, production control, production engineering, quality control, and administration. American public schools prepare people to assume such jobs.

German auto manufacturer BMW located in South Carolina offers internships, a cooperative education program, and training programs to move local people into career paths in the company. Interns study engineering, human resources, management, finance, and other areas of expertise. Corporate-sponsored education programs have great value to the public schools in the area. Students have opportunities to work in state-of-the-art facilities that the schools could never afford to provide. Their efforts often lead directly to good jobs after graduation.

One of the biggest challenges facing American public education is preparing students today for careers they will have tomorrow in a world that is growing smaller and faster by the day. *Edutopia* Magazine (sponsored by the George Lucas Educational Foundation) put it this way:

> Children today are growing up in a global age. The role of our nation in the international community, the face of American neighborhoods, the sources of everyday consumer products, the challenges confronting science, health, and law enforcement experts—these must all be understood and managed by a new generation of citizens, workers, and leaders. Are our schools equipping young Americans with the necessary international knowledge and skills to navigate today's interconnected world? ("Schools for a Global Age," 2005)

Why Study Educational Policy in Other Countries?

International comparative education teaches that problems of educational development are common in many societies. By studying education in societies different from their own, educators learn to see these commonalities. They also develop new insights into other cultures that can lead to new and innovative ways of looking at their own societies (Tanner & Tanner, 2007). For instance, the United States is not the only country that is home to a wide variety of cultural groups. Nor is the United States the only country addressing problems that arise from clashing cultures. People in other countries face these problems too, often with considerable success. Their experiences can help us learn to behave in new ways. Likewise, when we look at the education systems of other cultures, we may find they are successfully using techniques, curricula, and classroom experiences that we never considered.

As communication systems bring people closer together, multicultural understanding becomes more important for all people and all nations. The ancient Greeks were among the first to recognize the importance of learning about and from others. For Plutarch, people who studied life's lessons wherever they found them demonstrated their strength of character. Thucydides suggested that people who learn from others may be more prepared to avoid some of life's pitfalls and to capitalize on success. What makes the transmission of culture through schooling a problem in any country?

Education in Canada

When the 1995 rebellion of French-speaking Canadians nearly split the country in two with a secession vote, we Americans paid little attention. Yet Canada remains our best trading partner and most trusted military ally—a friend we cannot afford to ignore. How Canada educates its citizens bears directly on how Canadians think about the United States and their relationship with us. It is important to know how our neighbor's educational system works.

Canada's landmass makes it the second largest country in the world. Its economy is diverse and successful. Nearly two-thirds of the population live in metropolitan areas along the border with the United States. Some 60 percent of Canada's population live in two of its twelve provinces and territories, English-speaking Ontario and French-speaking Quebec. Canada has also been a home for immigrants from around the world.

Canada is a federal state, meaning provincial governments control education, just as our individual states are responsible for U.S. education. Canada has neither a national system of education nor a central office of education. Instead, each province has its own Ministry of Education headed by an elected minister. In all provinces, schools are operated by local boards of education; the extent of their power varies across provinces. Both provincial governments and local governmental units fund schools.

Typically, children start school at age six or seven. They must attend for at least ten years, or until the age of sixteen or seventeen. The organization of school levels (elementary, middle, and high) varies by province, with some using a system of seven years in elementary, two in middle, and three in high school. Others use a 7–5, 8–4, or, as in Quebec, a 6–5–2 system. The school year runs between 180 and 200 days.

Promotion through the elementary grades is more or less automatic. At the secondary level, systems of promotion vary among the provinces, but most use the credit system. Under a credit system, students take varying levels of courses to accumulate credits for graduation. In addition, students in the provinces of British Columbia, Alberta, and Quebec must pass a graduation diploma examination. Many schools offer general and advanced levels of diplomas. Most high school graduates go on to some form of postsecondary education.

The Canadian educational system, like many others in modern economic states, faces the challenges of the information age and an increasingly competitive global economy. The Canadian Broadcasting Corporation demonstrates, through its online archives, not only the richness of Canadian culture but also the power of technology to sustain and extend this culture via education (http://www.cblearning.ca/further).

Canada, much like the United States, relies heavily on testing in schools. Increasingly, tests drive educational decision making with regard to student placement and advancement. Educators are keenly aware of the possible positive and negative consequences of testing students. For instance, they fear that testing can promote tracking—or streaming students into classes and programs designed for a particular achievement level that typecasts students and limits their opportunities for learning. The seemingly precise or scientific nature of standardized achievement tests, critics argue, encourages unfounded consumer confidence in test results. Proponents of the use of testing in Canadian schools contend that the development and use of standardized assessments have opened new opportunities for students to demonstrate what they know and can do. Movements for teacher accountability, strengthening basic skills education, accommodating increasing cultural diversity, and addressing gender inequality characterize current Canadian education reform.

Canadian schools reflect the cultural similarities among Canadians, as well as the deep division that exists between French speakers and English speakers in Quebec. There has always been a strong belief among the French Canadians of Quebec that they should split off from Canada and form their own nation. Bill 101, passed in 1977, established French as the only official language in the province and imposed many restrictions on the use of English or any other language in business and education. The bill was an attempt by the government of Quebec to preserve French culture in the face of the increasing number of immigrants entering the province, the majority of whom spoke no French. In the years since the bill was passed, the Supreme Court of Canada has eased these restrictions. Again on March 31, 2005, the Supreme Court of Canada upheld Quebec's language law but ruled that the province must allow greater access to English schools. The tension, however, remains, and every so often the move to secede reemerges.

Bill 101 has had a profound effect on education in Quebec, because immigrants to Quebec had to attend French-only schools. The Montreal Catholic School Commission, which operates more than three hundred schools in Montreal, has considered an outright ban on any language but French in its schools in recent years. (Public schools in Quebec are designated as either Protestant or Catholic and are supported financially by the government.) This ban would include all school-sponsored activities, as well as speech in the halls and on schoolyards. Offenders would be transferred to other schools, and repeat offenders would be expelled.

Many educators in the United States, particularly those in the West and Southwest, probably can identify with teachers in Quebec and the movement for single-language schools. California, for instance, has an English-only contingent that wants Spanish offerings removed completely from classrooms. **How are the positions of students with English as their primary language similar to and different from one another in the two countries? How do the positions of the language-minority students compare in both countries?**

Although they are interesting, if we relied on only the sensational events in Quebec, we would have a distorted view of life in the majority of Canadian schools. Most school jurisdictions have developed and now use multicultural curricula, particularly in social studies. The ministries of education, teachers, university professors, and publishers have cooperated to develop learning resources and instruction appropriate for the richness of ethnicity and culture that characterizes all Canadian schools.

Mexico

Education in Mexico

What effects does the United States have on education in Mexico? Movies, television, and the popular press portray Mexico at the extremes: culturally rich, socially warm, and humanly inviting or stunningly poor, socially archaic, and openly hostile to outsiders. These images tell only part of the story. The reality, as it usually does, lies somewhere in the middle.

The United States of Mexico is a country of thirty-one states that shares its borders with the United States of America, Guatemala, and Belize. The nation has one of the highest population growth rates in the world. Population density varies greatly among the states. The capital, Mexico City, and one of its neighboring states account for more than 22 percent of the country's total population. Mexico City is recorded as being the second largest city in the world, with 25 million people. Although it has not been documented, some people believe that Mexico City is actually the largest city in the world with closer to 30 million inhabitants. Overall the Mexican population is becoming more urbanized: the percentage of the population living in urban areas increased from 42 percent in 1950 to 76 percent in 2005.

The Mexican economy has been hit by a series of economic crises in the past several decades that has resulted in a continued and radically uneven distribution of wealth. A devaluation of the peso in late 1994 threw Mexico into economic disarray, triggering the worst recession in more than fifty years. The nation continues to make an impressive recovery. Economic and social concerns include low wages, underemployment for a large part of the population, inequitable income distribution, and few advancement opportunities for the mostly Amerindian population in the impoverished southern states. Elections held in July 2000 marked the first time since the 1910 Mexican Revolution that the opposition defeated the party in government, the Institutional Revolutionary Party (PRI).

Technology in Practice

LET THE MACHINE DO THE TRANSLATION?

Teachers with students and parents who do not speak English have some online options that may prove to be extremely useful. Royal Van Horn writes of the challenge of translating foreign languages into English via the use of computer translation programs.

> Since I am a monoglot, I was surprised to learn recently that my [computer] is a polyglot. A monoglot, of course, is a person who knows only one language. . . . When I started exploring the topic of machine translation of languages, most of [my] colleagues told me that machine translation worked so poorly that it was essentially useless. Because I wanted to find out for myself how well machine translation worked, I began to explore the capabilities.

> The quickest and easiest way to see what computer language translation programs can do is to visit some of the free sites. These include the Systran website (www.systransoft.com/index.html) and the Babelfish website (http://babelfish.altavista.com). When you arrive at these sites you can translate up to 150 words into a host of languages.

> "Teaching is a great profession," becomes "Teaching är ett viktigt yrke," in Swedish. The Italians would say: "L'insegnamento è una professione grande."

> Bear in mind, however, that it would be unwise to rely on these machine translators for important communications. Letters home to parents, for instance, should never go out without seeking verification from another source. But then, letters home written by English speakers to other English speakers should not be sent without verification either. There is nothing quite so embarrassing as a mizspelled word!

Question for Reflection: Have you asked teachers what their school does to communicate in writing with parents who do not speak or read English?

Source: Van Horn, R. (2004, January). English learners and machine translation. *Phi Delta Kappan, 85*(7), 409–410.

Spanish is the official language of Mexico, although more than ninety-three languages and dialects are present. Nearly 1 million Mexican citizens do not speak Spanish, and 10 percent are illiterate.

Since 1993 the state governments have controlled the running of preschools, primary and secondary schools, and teacher-training institutes, except in the Federal District. This decentralization of power represents a major shift in education policy from a tightly controlled, centralized authority.

The Mexican education system is structured in a 6–3–3 configuration. The first six years are spent in primary school, and the next three years are for lower secondary school. For the final three years, students either pass an entrance examination to gain entry to upper secondary school (*bachillerato*), which leads to higher education, or they transfer to a three- or four-year technical school.

Mexican schools have many overage students in each grade because students repeat grades and/or drop out and then reenroll. Overage students account for up to 30 percent of the enrollment in some grades, particularly in the fifth and sixth grades. Because overage students inflate enrollment numbers in elementary schools, pupil–teacher ratios are high, generally around thirty to one. Many Mexican students do not attend the upper secondary school level. The average educational attainment of the population over fifteen years of age is eight grades.

The most serious problem at the basic level of education may be the high and persistent dropout rate, a consequence of family poverty. Only about 50 percent of entering students at any level complete their studies. In rural areas of the country, approximately 75 percent of schoolchildren do not finish the first six years of primary education.

The growing number of school-age children places a heavy burden on the Mexican educational system. Overall, national basic education programs have emphasized access to education rather than its relevance or quality. The expansion of the educational system has not been equal in all regions of Mexico. Larger cities have more residents and therefore more students, and the northern part of Mexico and Mexico City generally have the highest enrollment numbers. States in the southeast regions, which are more rural and less populated, logically have lower enrollment rates (Reyes, 1995). About 23 percent of Mexican elementary schools are one-teacher schools, and 15 percent do not offer all six grades. Although some sort of accommodations are made for students with special needs, only about 10 percent of such students use them.

The immigration, both legal and not, of Mexican people into the United States along the southern border has been well publicized. In the late 1990s there were about 15 million Mexican Americans, between 2 and 3 million of whom were illegal workers. By 2004, there were 25.9 million residents of Mexican origin (U.S. Census 2006). What happens in Mexico, of course, can be directly linked to the United States.

Latino children will soon comprise the majority of students in the California public schools. On average, Latino students score much lower on standardized achievement tests than do white and non-Latino students. About 53 percent of Latino teenagers in California do not graduate. One-third drop out in the tenth grade. Across the state, the dropout rate for Latinos is double that for whites and non-Latinos.

How might teachers in U.S. schools help Latino children succeed? There are a variety of often competing answers to this question: Provide more bilingual programs. Provide fewer bilingual programs, thus forcing children to learn English sooner. Raise academic standards—low standards for students mean low expectations leading to poor performance. Provide extra help for children enabling them to progress. And so on. As the Latino population grows throughout the United States, more locales will grapple with challenges of helping Latino children succeed in environments where cultures do not always easily mix.

One interesting example of bringing cultures together can be found in Austin, Texas. The Austin School District signed an agreement with the northern Mexican state of Nuevo Leon that allows Texan and Mexican student athletic teams to compete in baseball, basketball, golf, soccer, tennis, track and field, softball, and wrestling in Austin or Nuevo Leon. Austin School Board President Doyle Valdez was quoted as saying, "The international language of sports provides student athletes and their parents with an informal, friendly and safe environment to meet each other, and learn new customs." Valdez wants to begin academic competitions too (Keating, 2005).

Japan

Education in Japan

Critics of American education often hail Japan as an example we should be following. The Japanese, they argue, demand educational excellence and get it. Others argue that Japan's schools foster conformity and reward obedience.

Japan is a country of more than three thousand islands in East Asia, with a population of more than 127 million. This densely populated country of city dwellers is ethnically homogeneous (with only a 1 percent minority population). Tokyo, the capital, is the largest city in the world, with more than 28 million inhabitants.

From the time of its defeat in World War II until 1990, Japan enjoyed extraordinary economic success. Between 1990 and 1994, however, land values fell dramatically and industrial giants, such as Nissan, closed factories when car production fell about 22 percent. While Japanese citizens struggle with the realities of increasing unemployment and the social problems accompanying it, they continue to place a high priority on the development of a well-educated and skilled populace.

How does Japan's educational system compare to the U.S. system? The Japanese education system closely resembles the U.S. system. Most Japanese students attend public schools in mixed-ability classrooms. Unlike the United States, there is no external examination scheme in Japan—no public or private testing service that creates, distributes, and scores a set of examinations common to students across the country. Instead only internal, school-system assessments determine students' promotion and certification of completion.

Japanese students begin school at age six, attending elementary schools (grades one to six) with an average pupil–teacher ratio of twenty to one. After completing elementary school, students attend a three-year lower-secondary school, with fifty-minute class periods and an average pupil–teacher ratio of 17.4 to 1. Nearly all lower-secondary school students study English as a foreign language. Students at all levels wear uniforms.

Upper-secondary school is not compulsory, but 94 percent of the children who complete lower-secondary school proceed to the next level. Some 90 percent of these students attend public school, while the remainder pay to attend private schools. In upper-secondary schools, 75 percent of the students pursue a general, academic course of study, and the rest enroll in specialized (streamed) tracks, such as technology, foreign languages, and computers. Students with special needs can complete secondary school by correspondence. Since 1988 some students with special needs have been able to attend credit-system upper-secondary schools. These schools award diplomas for courses taken, instead of requiring students to pass a graduation examination. About one-third of Japanese upper-secondary school graduates continue their higher education after passing a competitive entrance examination.

In addition to the regular public school system, many young people in Japan attend private after-school classes. Classes may be of two types: *okeiko-goto* (enrichment classes in areas such as music, the arts, and physical education) and *juku* (supplementary classes in academic subjects). Together, *juku* and *okeiko-goto* are a multimillion-dollar industry. *Okeiko-goto* often begin during children's elementary years and may continue throughout their lives. *Juku,* however, are taken exclusively during children's elementary and secondary years. *Juku* classes help young people keep up with the demanding school curriculum, provide remedial instruction in areas of weakness, and prepare students for various entrance exams.

Juku range from classes of one to three students meeting in a teacher's home to multiple schools all over the country, with dozens of classes offered at each site. Classes meet two or three times a week and may last two to three hours or more. Unlike teachers in the public schools, *juku* teachers often group their students by ability, rather than by grade level. *Juku* teachers often rotate common drill exercises with individual assistance.

Some people contend that the instruction young people receive in *juku* and *okeiko-goto* settings closes the gap between what is learned in public schools and what students must know to move up the educational ladder (Rosegaard, 2006). Presumably, as in other cultures, this gap represents the difference between the explicit curriculum (what is set forth for public consumption) and the implicit curriculum (the more subtle but quite powerful adult expectations of student performance).

Japan has a rigorous curriculum, and some reports suggest that Japanese public schools demand intense rote learning and conformity from their students. Other studies suggest that teachers in the public schools generally function more as facilitators and "knowledge guides" than as givers of information. Instead of lecturing, for example, math teachers may ask individual students to present their solutions to the class and then ask members of the class to evaluate the solutions. They use other strategies to involve students actively in instruction (Wieczorek, 2008).

In whole-class instruction, Japanese teachers go beyond simple conceptual learning by purposely withholding the correct answer to a problem and asking the class to think of as many ways to solve the problem as possible. Presenting the material as a sort of puzzle sparks their curiosity in the subject matter and encourages them to participate (Wu, 1999).

According to some critics, the mass media frequently compare American public education to Japanese education in ways that produce a distorted view of both systems. Many news reports proclaim the Japanese system superior in producing higher achievement among its students (Berliner & Biddle, 1995). These reports often suggest that Japanese students attend school more days per year than do American students and earn higher mathematics and science test scores. Much emphasis also has been placed on Japanese schools' adherence to national standards that are enforced through nationwide examinations.

But this is not the whole story. When eighth-grade American students' mathematics abilities were compared to those of their Japanese counterparts, who had been exposed to similar curricula that was coherent and rigorous, American students' scores were found to match or exceed those of the Japanese students (Westbury, 1992). Although Japanese students spend more days in school than do American students (240 days and 180 days, respectively), the difference in the amount of academic instruction is not profound. A typical school year in Japan includes sixty-five to seventy afternoons of either free time or nonacademic activities. Three or four days a year also are devoted to cleaning the school. Japanese students enjoy longer lunch periods and longer breaks between classes than do American students. Furthermore, although Japanese students must pass an entrance exam to enter upper secondary school, it is a test of elimination. For example, if 300 freshman slots are available and 304 students apply, the test is given to eliminate four students. Passing scores can be as low as 5 percent (Goya, 1994).

In contrast to others who have found fault with Japan's system, Wieckorek (2008) argues that Japan's education system helps teachers encourage student learning through a well-rounded coherent curriculum—curriculum that is integrated through all subjects and across the grades. With a narrower curricular focus than many western countries, Japan fosters deeper understanding in its students. Teachers emphasize effort over ability, engaging students, and builds strong classroom relationships. While Americans are relying more and more on standards and benchmarks, the Japanese are moving in a different direction. They are deemphasizing and deconstructing national standards, easing the pressure of national exams, and concentrating more on individual students. Increasingly, Japanese teachers have also relied on "lesson study" to interact with one another as professionals who are intent on building their professional expertise by learning from their own failures and successes in the classroom (Rock & Wilson, 2005).

Education in India

India is a nation of more than 1 billion people. In addition to being the world's largest democracy, it may be the most culturally and ethnically diverse country in the world. It is a country known historically for its tolerance of diversity; nonetheless, regional and ethnic tensions continue. The language of commerce and of instruction in India is English, although more than a dozen regional languages (such as Hindi, Urdu, and Tamil) and local dialects are used in everyday speech in all but the major cities. In India bilingualism is the norm, and trilingualism is common.

The Indian Constitution set forth in 1950 directs the government to provide free and compulsory education for all children up to age fourteen. It also provides for equal educational opportunity and the protection of religious and linguistic minority groups. The school system, which varies from state to state, is generally organized as two to three years of private kinder-

garten (beginning at about age three), followed by ten years of private or public basic education. This is perhaps followed by two years of private or public higher secondary education, which also may be followed by three years of tuition-free higher education. School holidays include twenty religious festivals from Hindu, Muslim, Christian, Sikh, Parsi, and Jain traditions.

In 1986 the federal parliament adopted its National Policy for Education and Policy of Action, which formed the foundation for the National Curriculum for Elementary and Secondary Education. The intent of the common core is to cut across subject areas and to encourage attention to similarities among Indians, not to exploit their differences.

The realities of schooling in India often vary considerably from the official intent and formal proclamations. The literacy rate has more than tripled since India's independence was attained in 1947, rising from 15 to 61 percent (CIA, 2008). Enrollment rates are greater in the cities than in the rural areas. They also are greater for boys than for girls, especially girls from disadvantaged groups (people of low castes, tribal people, and religious minorities). These numbers suggest that, similar to other countries around the globe, the desire for equality is still unfulfilled.

Despite government claims that education is open to all, caste discrimination prevents millions of children from attending school. The caste definition of "untouchable" was abolished in 1950, but the country's 200 million Dalits—now referred to as "scheduled castes" or "scheduled tribes"—routinely suffer discrimination. Dalits are at the bottom of the economic scale, often performing the most menial and degrading jobs. At least 40.5 percent of Dalit children in rural areas and 24 percent in urban areas drop out of school. At least 11 million Dalit girls between the ages of six and eleven are not enrolled in any type of school.

According to a report by the National Institute of Educational Planning and Administration, Dalit children are victims of a hidden agenda of discrimination in the classroom. They are made to sit and eat separately, and the higher-caste teachers do not touch their exercise books. In rural Karnataka, teachers refer to children from the lower castes as *kadujana* (forest people). They claim the children cannot learn unless they are beaten. Often the children are denied the right to free textbooks, uniforms, and a midday meal (Behal, 2002).

Programs run by nongovernmental organizations (NGOs) provide education programs for India's poor children. One nonprofit organization, Udbhas, promotes literacy among children living in the slums of Calcutta. Classes, which have at least forty students, are held in the open air every day from 6:30 to 10:30 A.M. There are no tuition fees, and books and pencils are distributed for free. Udbhas also provides students with free breakfasts each day and with new clothing once a year. Used clothing is provided at least three times per year. Many of the children they help live in environments in which they are exposed to violence, alcohol, drugs, and abuse; to them, Udbhas is like an "oasis" (Guha, 2002, p. 207).

Four Udbhas teachers hold classes every day for a monthly salary of one hundred rupees (about $2.10), and volunteers assist with classes. The founder, Mrs. Kundu, describes the challenges of providing education services:

> It is really hard carrying on classes during the rains. We had requested . . . a raised platform with some sort of a covering over our heads, but all our efforts [to acquire this] are . . . in vain. . . . It is hard work. Many members have not been able to devote time and have left. We survive on donations and try to make the best of what we have. (Guha, 2002, p. 209)

Indian schools, like schools in the United States and elsewhere, are subject to many outside political pressures. Since the Hindu nationalist Bharatiya Janata Party (BJP) came to power in 1998, a radical Hindu-revivalist movement has promoted the "Hinduization" of education in India (Lloyd, 1999). In part the movement is an effort to counter the influence of Christian missionaries, who Hindu fundamentalists believe tricked people into conversion. Christians comprise 2.5 percent of India's nearly 1 billion people; Hindus account for 80 percent and Muslims for 12 percent. **How do struggles over the influence of religion on curriculum play themselves out in public schools in the United States?**

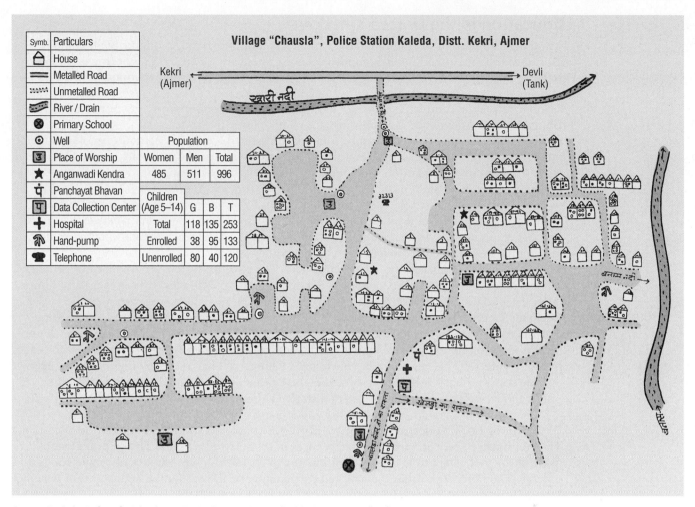

Symb.	Particulars			
⌂	House			
═	Metalled Road			
⋯	Unmetalled Road			
≈	River / Drain			
✪	Primary School			
⊙	Well	**Population**		
③	Place of Worship	Women	Men	Total
★	Anganwadi Kendra	485	511	996
ч	Panchayat Bhavan	**Children**		
ᄝ	Data Collection Center	(Age 5–14)	G	B	T
✝	Hospital	Total	118	135	253
🚶	Hand-pump	Enrolled	38	95	133
☎	Telephone	Unenrolled	80	40	120

Village "Chausla", Police Station Kaleda, Distt. Kekri, Ajmer

Kekri (Ajmer)   Devli (Tank)

खारी नदी

Source: Govinda, R. (2002). School mapping in the LJ Project, *India Education Report*. (p. 5). Oxford: University Press. Reprinted by permission of Oxford University Press India, New Delhi.

Indian researchers estimate that about 95 percent of the rural population live in about 826,000 villages, towns, and cities across the country. On average, a primary school is within a radius of one kilometer. They also indicate that 85 percent of the population has an upper-level primary school within three kilometers. About 11 percent of rural and 8 percent of urban children do not attend school. Of the total enrollment in primary schools, about 38 percent has been in schools with a student-classroom ratio of 60 and above (Mehta, 2007).

One of the greatest challenges facing education planners in India is simply describing the current state of schooling in the country. See Figure 12.2 for a sample from the school mapping project of Lok Jumbish. The purpose of the project is to map where people are located so officials can better determine where services are needed. Project workers receive minimal training on mapping and then fan out across neighborhoods to depict households, schools, hospitals, and other buildings. The maps, or community surveys, become the basis for educational planning. Even the nonreading villagers can make proposals for improving education, thus building support for schools in the community.

India correctly sees education as the way toward economic prosperity.

Most economists agree that first India, and then China, will surpass [the United States] in overall economic output in the foreseeable future. And the quality of the Chinese, Indian, and Eastern European workforces has already grown to the point where those countries have become havens for outsourcing even our most skilled jobs. (Carnevale, 2005)

Figure 12.2
School Mapping in the LJ Project
The technique of "school mapping" is Lok Jumbish's special contribution to the task of mobilizing people for education.

Education in the United Kingdom

More than 90 percent of children in the United Kingdom (England, Scotland, Wales, and Northern Ireland) attend publicly funded schools. These are called *state schools, government schools, maintained schools,* or *council schools* (run by local government councils). The remainder of students attend privately funded schools, called *public schools* or *independent schools.* (Note the completely opposite meaning of the term *public* from how it is used in the United States.) Attendance is compulsory for children ages five to sixteen.

Four other types of schools can be found in the United Kingdom. *Foundation schools* are publicly funded, but the properties on which they are constructed are usually owned by a religious or charitable foundation. The foundation may influence the appointment of teachers, governors, and other staff, as well as the selection of students. *Special schools* teach children with physical, educational, or behavioral disabilities. *Comprehensive schools* are state-funded secondary schools that take all local children, regardless of talent or ability. *Specialist schools* and *city technology colleges* are also state-funded schools. They teach the national curriculum but emphasize a particular subject, such as technology or the arts.

Schools are organized into two or three tiers. The two-tier system is composed of primary schools (ages five to eleven), occasionally subdivided into infant (ages five to seven) and junior (ages seven to eleven), and secondary schools (ages eleven to sixteen or eighteen), which resemble American comprehensive high schools. The three-tier system, used only in England, consists of first schools (ages five to eight or nine), middle schools (ages eight to twelve or nine to thirteen), and upper schools, which usually are nonselective (ages twelve or thirteen to sixteen or eighteen). The state church, which is the Church of England, and other churches help operate some primary and secondary schools, even though these schools are supported by public funds. **How does the existence of a state religion affect education in any country?**

Every school is run by a head teacher and a board of governors who represent parents, staff, and the Local Education Authority (LEA). LEAs are part of the local government system. They own school property and provide services to schools and parents. The central government, through its Department for Education and Skills (DfES), sets school policy and funds schools. The DfES establishes the national curriculum and the evaluation or inspection system. Schools' test results and attendance figures are published annually.

Because the United Kingdom has an official state church, religious education (RE) is a core subject in British schools. With the diversity of cultures and religions students and teachers bring to schools, the practice of emphasizing Christian education has not been without its critics. In January 1996 more than 1,500 junior school students in forty schools were withdrawn from RE courses by their Muslim parents who were worried that their children would receive inaccurate information about Islam and be confused by other faiths introduced in religious classes. In 2001 race riots in northern England again raised questions about imposing Christian values on multifaith students. Today, daily worship sessions are to be of a "broadly Christian character," half of which can be devoted to "other faiths and interests." Furthermore, if a Christian emphasis is deemed inappropriate to students' backgrounds, educators can apply to the local Standing Advisory Council For Religious Education to have the RE requirement lifted. Parents also have the right to withdraw their children from RE (The TES, 2008).

United Kingdom

In addition to its inclusion of religion in the national curriculum, the British educational system had a long tradition of local control. In 1988, however, the Education Reform Act emphasized two themes in the education of all students in the British system: back to the basics and the link between education and the economy. The act was followed by pressure for a national curriculum and teacher accountability. It also promoted the idea of giving parents a greater voice in managing schools. The result was the creation of a new system of national compulsory and universal examinations.

As is the case in many other parts of the world, the United Kingdom is intent on making technology a part of teachers' lives. Education leaders had estimated that 60 percent of teachers made little or no use of computer technology. So in January 2002, the British government gave one hundred thousand free laptop computers to schools for teachers' use—twice the number they had planned to provide. Program originators wanted to give teachers better access to technology so they could begin to catch up with professionals in the private sector.

In addition to bringing technological advances into the classroom for teachers and students, educators are exploring other ways UK schools can participate in the developing global community. One of these ways can be experienced by visiting the Eden Project in Cornwall, England. It represents British aspirations for the integration of art, science, and technology in a single educational project focused on global interdependence. Described as a kind of "living theatre of plants and people," the Eden Project is designed to help people understand the world we live in and inspire us to action (ICONS, undated). Students who are unable to travel to the large covered conservatories, or biomes, in Cornwall can visit online the living replicas of rainforests and environments in the Mediterranean, South Africa, and California to understand how plants affect people, and vice versa. (See Figure 12.3.)

No program similar to the Eden Project exists in Wales, although every head of Welsh secondary schools was given a laptop in 2000. Over one hundred other school leaders received

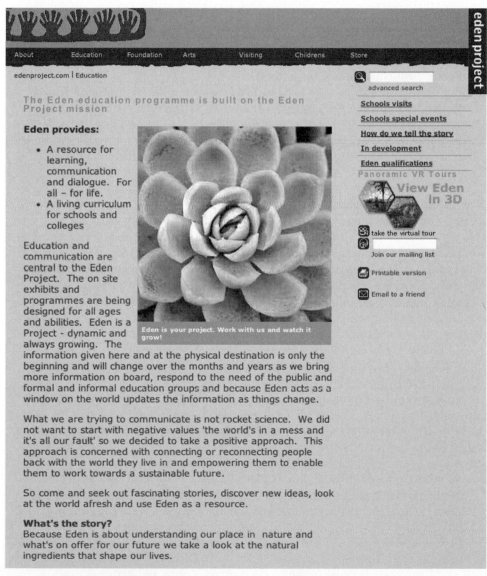

Source: www.edenproject.com/3679.htm.

Figure 12.3
The Eden Project
How do larger-scale projects such as Eden help stimulate curriculum development for young people?

Singapore

them in the second stage of the program. During this same time, nine thousand Scottish teachers received small grants to help them buy home computers. Clearly then, all members of the United Kingdom recognize the benefits technology can offer teachers and students in their quest to learn about and connect with the rest of the world.

It is too soon to know how the UK's education system might be affected by its participation in the European Union (EU). EU membership could revolutionize education and employment.

Education in Singapore

The Republic of Singapore, a city-state on the southern tip of continental Southeast Asia, is considered the world's laboratory for experiments in social engineering. It is a multicultural society, including people of Chinese (77 percent), Malay (14 percent), Indian (8 percent), and Eurasian (1 percent) ancestries. More than 3 million people inhabit the 231 square miles of Singapore (Singapore Department of Statistics, 2001). The city-state, with one of the highest standards of living in Asia, bills itself as the Switzerland of Asia, the Gateway to the Future. Singapore is a city of business opportunity and a hub of high-tech development. The government tries to assure all citizens that, no matter what their ethnic or cultural background, they are first and foremost Singaporean, even though most are immigrants and their descendants.

While Singapore was a British colony, English was the required language of government and advanced schooling. The system also fostered ethnic segregation and had separate schools that taught in Chinese, Tamil, and Malay languages.

Since Singapore's establishment as a republic in 1965, however, life has changed. Today, most tourists to Singapore know that it is illegal to chew gum (actually, it is illegal to import chewing gum) and that extinguishing a cigarette on the sidewalk can draw a large fine. But few realize that the Singaporean educational system has developed innovative approaches to multicultural education. For example, even though Singapore maintains four official languages, the government has unified the English- and non-English-speaking schools (Chinese, Malay, and Tamil) into a single educational system. Leaders viewed the unification of schools, undertaken in the late 1950s, as an essential ingredient in their strategy to build a nation with its own unique identity. **Would other countries' solutions for multilingual education work for the United States?**

The government's vigorous efforts to blend competing cultures into a unified Singaporean culture sometimes take a tough approach. For instance, the government suspended four six-year-old Muslim girls whose parents dressed them in traditional headscarves (Wood, 2002). Their suspension is an especially strong symbolic statement, because Singapore lies between Malaysia and Indonesia, both of which are Muslim countries.

Despite the government's efforts, tensions in Singapore can sometimes heighten around issues of religion, ethnicity, and race. Islam is the second largest religion among Singapore's citizens; the Buddhist Chinese community is the largest. In addition, Singapore experienced race riots in the 1950s and 1960s, the memory of which is still alive.

Overall, the government tries to balance religious freedom and social cohesion, whenever and however possible. Singaporeans celebrate their religions in private, with the blessing of the government, but the schools are supposed to be secular places. Students wear uniforms to stress the commonalities among people. Schools and apartment houses have racial quotas to ensure that racial ghettos do not emerge. Nonetheless, minorities sometimes feel left out.

Singapore has invested a lot of effort and money in education in the last forty years or so. As a result of a strong family planning program and a large investment in school facilities and teacher education, by 1968 all primary-school-age children in Singapore were enrolled in school. In 1973 educational authorities required all students to know English as either their first or second language and to know one other major language of the community. In the 1980s authorities backed off this overly ambitious goal. Still, most students try to become bilingual, and many seek the English track as a first choice because of the access it offers to jobs and higher education.

The current education system of Singapore is comprehensive, and children begin school at age six. During their six years of primary education, they focus on English, mathematics, their mother tongue (Chinese, Malay, Tamil), music, art and crafts, and physical education. In Primary Six, all students take the Primary School Leaving Examination (PSLE) and then move on to the next stage of secondary education.

Students spend four to five years in secondary school. They take curricula based on their aptitudes and interests. In general, the subjects studied in secondary schools include English, the mother language, mathematics, science, literature, history, geography, art, technical studies, home economics, civics and moral education, music, and physical education. At the end of secondary school, students take examinations that screen them for either postsecondary education or training.

Unlike the United States, Singapore has developed close relationships among government, industry, and secondary and postsecondary education. Annual surveys estimate workforce needs, and the schools and informal educational organizations respond with programs to fill those needs. These connections are especially important to a country that must depend on the talents of its people for its place in the world.

Singapore's students must leave school with strong technology skills, because people are the nation's primary resource. In 1997 the government committed 750 million pounds (about $400 million US) to build a rich technological environment by 2002—a goal that was largely achieved. Schools have about one computer for every five students, and every teacher has a laptop. The nation itself is served by one high-speed Internet system. Schools have digital cameras, data projectors, and CD burners in most classrooms. Nonetheless, teaching methods remain largely didactic, not student-centered or constructivist.

Singaporean students' math scores, traditionally among the highest in the world, ranked first among all nations, and well above the United States', on the Trends in International Mathematics and Science Study (released January 5, 2005). Some believe that part of the reason may be Singapore's mandatory national curriculum.

Also, Singapore provides its academically "at-risk" students with the best teachers. Singapore's textbooks stress composition and decomposition of numbers, a way that leads students to complex lessons on grouping of numbers. Teachers' lessons also put a much stronger emphasis on using illustrations and diagrams in mathematics than do those of U.S. teachers to foster problem-solving skills. (Cavanaugh, 2005).

Education in South Africa

What educational challenges does South Africa face? South Africa is one of the most multicultural societies in the world. From 1949 to 1991, the structure of its society was shaped by an official policy of **apartheid** (pronounced "a-pár-tate" or "a-pár-tite"), or separation of the races. Under apartheid blacks lived in *homelands, black states,* and segregated *townships* outside the major cities. Whites were not allowed to enter the townships without permission, and nonwhites were not permitted to stay overnight in white urban areas without special permission. People had to carry passes at all times. Schools for white students received money, facilities, and teachers, whereas black schools were neglected.

Although the United States is marked by a history of slavery, it is difficult for most Westerners to imagine how apartheid could be justified in recent history anywhere in the world. The former language of apartheid in South Africa, however, must sound hauntingly familiar to Western ears. The ultimate goal of apartheid was to create "a mosaic of peoples, each with a separate national identity. They will be politically independent but economically interdependent" (King, 1988, p. 600).

The open challenge to segregated education began in 1976 to 1977 with riots in Soweto, a black township outside Johannesburg (Lemmer, 1993). This revolt was triggered by an attempt to have instruction be carried out in Afrikaans (an amalgam of Dutch, French, German, African, and Malay) instead of English. The apartheid legislation was repealed in 1991, initiating a dramatic restructuring of South African society, including a restructuring of the segregated education system that supported it. A new constitution was adopted in 1993, opening the door to free elections in which all South Africans may participate. In daily life, however, segregation continues to be reinforced by great disparities in wealth, personal attitudes, and historically separate and unequal education systems.

South Africa

In general, South African schools have adopted the British view of a liberal education. Students are to be well grounded in history, languages, mathematics, the sciences, and the arts. Teaching is teacher centered, and learning is passive, with a heavy emphasis on rote and academics. Also like its Western counterparts, almost all South African school systems are organized into four years of junior primary, three of senior primary, three of junior secondary, and two of senior secondary instruction.

The white, so-called coloured, and Indian schools use either English or Afrikaans as the primary language of instruction. Many black students at these schools have a mother tongue that is not English or Afrikaans. Consequently, they often do not have a sufficient command of either language (particularly in secondary schools) to cope with the academic demands made on them. The school system is made up of 82 percent blacks, 8.5 percent whites, 7.5 percent coloureds (multiracial), and 2 percent Indians. Even though apartheid is over, these percentages, in light of most schools' use of English and Afrikaans for instruction, suggest that the current situation is still not equal.

Indeed, the battle for quality education for all of South Africa's people continues. For the blacks of South Africa the rallying cry "liberation before education" used to guide their actions. They boycotted schools and thus sacrificed their education. Now the township schools are full, but the conditions of schooling vary greatly.

Zola Senior Primary School is in one of the poorest districts in the township of Soweto. The long brick school building is on a dusty piece of shrub-covered land bordered by rubbish and rusty barbed wire. Classrooms house about fifty-five students.

Three or four pupils often have to share a small desk and bench meant for two in classrooms that are otherwise virtually bare of furniture. . . . Three pupils have to share each textbook, but one classroom has six 10-year-old computers and the children sit in queues waiting for their five-minute slot. For some subjects there are no books, no equipment, nothing but the educator and the pupils' enthusiasm.

What is lacking in terms of resources is being compensated for by everyone's determination that these pupils succeed as much as possible. Even after school there is a formidable range of activities—sporting, artistic and social—to allow the children to develop their skills.

The children are proud, happy and glad to show off their talents. At one point a class of fifty-six pupils breaks into spontaneous song, moving and clapping in perfect rhythm to the amazing sound.

Almost every pupil wears the school's uniform. Their parents are so proud of their child's education that, no matter what their level of poverty, they do everything possible to ensure that every day their child walks to school properly dressed. (Burns, 2002)

Hundreds of miles to the west, in a remote area on the banks of the Orange River, lies Oriana—a community of seven hundred established in 1994 by white Afrikaaners. To avoid confrontation with the government, the community calls itself a "limited company." High fencing surrounds Oriana, and there is a Strictly Private sign at its only entrance. A committee decides who can live here; there are no blacks and no coloureds, only those who believe that an all-white Afrikaaner independent state is possible.

Children in Oriana are educated in one of three ways: at home by their parents, at a traditional school, or at the community's model school. Only thirty-seven students attend the model school. To enroll, a student is required to have his or her own computer.

Oriana students, who range in age from nine to seventeen, are housed in one large classroom. The youngest children spend most of their time learning to read and write. The rest of the students sit at individual stations and work on weekly computer-based assignments in all subject areas. Computer programs allow students to assess their own learning. If they achieve 80 percent or more, students move on in the curriculum. Those completing the curriculum ahead of schedule can begin the next level of assignments or take time off from school. Slower students must stay behind at the end of each school day.

The classroom walls are covered in shelves of reference books. The two teachers are there more as facilitators and evaluators because most of the information needed for the pupils' programmes [sic] is found on the Internet. The pupils also support each other when necessary.

There is an entrepreneurial aspect to school life, with the children being encouraged to set up their own after-school businesses. These range from selling sweets to hiring out a film projector that a group of them had saved up to buy. (Burns, 2002)

Oriana's computer programs are being marketed all over South Africa. The income from sales ensures that the school is always well funded. Although the curriculum encourages independent learning, critics worry that it does not promote social interaction or creativity. And at Oriana in particular, computing seems to have created another apartheid—an "educational apartheid" (Burns, 2002).

Fiske and Ladd (2005) noted that during the last ten years, the South African government has worked to dismantle racist structures of apartheid-era education and create a race-blind state education system. Yet the goal of promoting equal educational opportunity for black learners who are not part of the growing black middle class remains elusive.

Many factors account for this limited progress, including the lack of additional public funding for redress of structural inequities that linger from the apartheid era. Even had additional public funding been available, however, limitations in human capacity throughout the system—from officials in the national ministry to provincial education officials, to principals and teachers in the schools—would have made it difficult for the country to have brought about major improvements in educational outcomes for disadvantaged black learners within such a short period of time. . . . The South African experience teaches us that the struggle for educational equity requires much more than a commitment to race-blind policies. The historical legacy of past racial inequities means that providing equal educational opportunity to all students requires substantial investments over a long period of time (Fiske & Ladd, 2005, p. 38).

How Might We Enhance Understanding of Global Interdependence?

The events of September 11, 2001, may have changed forever how Americans think about people in other nations. It shocked many of us into believing that, like it or not, we are connected to people around the globe, in ways we never imagined. In terms of economics, technology, communications, and politics, we are increasingly becoming a global community. We cannot afford to look at the world and see only ourselves and our own neighborhoods. We must work to understand others and ourselves in relation to people around the world.

On one level the Trends in International Mathematics and Science Study, or TIMSS (originally named the Third International Mathematics Science Study), makes possible simple comparisons of students' test scores from different countries. By focusing narrowly on scores, these comparisons often invite simplistic arguments about who is better at educating their young. At the same time, the existence of TIMSS also encourages nations to focus on shared objectives and on methods of attaining them. As is true in most cases, test scores can provide insight, but they should not be used as the only evidence of educational achievement.

Trends in International Mathematics and Science Study

Given in 1995, 1999, and again in 2003, TIMSS is the largest, most comprehensive, and most rigorous international study of schools and students ever conducted. Researchers examined students' mathematics and science achievements by studying schools, curricula, instruction, textbooks, policy issues, and the lives of teachers and students to understand the educational contexts in which mathematics and science learning occur. The 1995 study included twenty-six countries, and the 2003 study polled forty-six.

Issues in School Reform

WILL JORDAN LEAD THE WAY IN EDUCATIONAL REFORM IN THE MIDDLE EAST?

Ultimately, education may prove to be the only answer to lasting peace in the Middle East. As Mary Ann Zehr noted, the Jordanian Ministry of Education has initiated reforms aimed at changing teaching and learning in government-sponsored schools:

Amal Hawamdeh teaches a physics lesson at the Al-Khansa'a Comprehensive Secondary School for Girls in Jerash, about 30 miles north of Jordan's capital city, that veers away from the "chalk and talk" teaching methods that are the staples of an education in the Middle East.

On a day in April, Hawamdeh divides her class of 28 11th graders into small groups to learn about the properties of concave and convex lenses.

Several girls, all wearing the green tunics that are part of their school uniforms and the white or cream-colored headscarves that signify their Islamic faith, head out to the school's concrete schoolyard to experiment with how lenses capture sun rays. Another group goes to the school's computer lab to see what the students can find about lenses on the Internet. A third experiments with candlelight and lenses.

Soon, in authoritative tones, the girls take turns telling their classmates what they've learned (2005, p. 24).

This teaching is designed to encourage students to think for themselves. The new methods are the core of a five-year plan to improve public or government-supported schools. The plan is called Education Reform for the Knowledge Economy. The idea is to prepare young people to be competitive in the Middle East's job market.

With modernization taking place in a country where most of the people are Muslim, says John Middleton, the director of the Center for Global Education at the Washington-based Academy for Educational Development, Jordan's leaders will have to be attentive to the tension between traditional and modern Islamists. "The Jordanians, as near as I can tell," said Middleton, "are walking a careful line between being Islamic and Arabic-based while modernizing in other ways."

Question for Reflection: The United States Agency for International Development has provided a $14.2 million grant to support Jordan's school improvement agenda. What might be gained and lost by U.S. involvement in this project?

Source: Zehr, M. A. (2005, June 15). Will Jordan become the educational model for the Middle East? *Education Week, 24*(40), 24–29.

In 2003, U.S. fourth-grade students scored 518, on average, in mathematics, exceeding the international average of 495. U.S. fourth-graders outperformed their peers in 13 of the other 24 participating countries, and performed lower than their peers in 11 countries..

In 2003, U.S. eighth-graders scored 504, on average, in mathematics. This average score exceeded the international average as well as the average scores of their peers in 25 of the 44 other participating countries. U.S. eighth-graders were outperformed by students in five Asian countries—Chinese Taipei, Hong Kong SAR, Japan, Korea, and Singapore—and four European countries—Belgium-Flemish, Estonia, Hungary, and the Netherlands.

In 2003, fourth-graders in the United States scored 536, on average, on the TIMSS science assessment, which was higher than the international average of 489. Of the 24 other participating countries, fourth-graders in 16 countries demonstrated lower science scores, on average, than fourth-graders in the United States, while students in three countries—Chinese Taipei, Japan, and Singapore—outperformed their peers in the United States.

In science, U.S. eighth-graders exceeded the international average and outperformed their peers in 32 of the 44 other participating countries. U.S. eighth-graders performed lower, on average, than their peers in seven countries and were not found to perform measurably different from students in five countries (National Center for Education Statistics, 2004).

Researchers found that U.S. math teachers focus on drill and practice, whereas other countries also focus on application. Ninety-four percent of students said their teachers "almost always" or "pretty often" showed them how to solve math problems when they were having difficulty. Only 86 percent of the total students polled in the thirty-eight-nation survey said this happened. Nearly 80 percent of the U.S. students said they "almost always" or "pretty

Table 12.1

AVERAGE MATHEMATICS SCALE SCORES OF FOURTH-GRADE STUDENTS, BY COUNTRY: 2003

Country	Average score	Country	Average score
International average	495	Cyprus	510
Singapore	594	Moldove, Republic of	504
Hong Kong SAR	575	Italy	503
Japan	565	Australia	499
Chinese Taipei	564	New Zealand	493
Belgium-Flemish	551	Scotland	490
Netherlands	540	Slovenia	479
Latvia	536	Armenia	456
Lithuania	534	Norway	451
Russian Federation	537	Iran, Islamic Republic of	389
England	531	Philippines	358
Hungary	528	Morocco	347
United States	518	Tunisia	339

Source: International Association for the Evaluation of Educational Achievement (IEA), Trends in international mathematics and science study (TIMSS), 2003. Available online: http://nces.ed.gov/timss/TIMSS03Tables.asp.

often" were given time to do homework in class. Only 55 percent of students in the overall survey made the same claim. Students in the United States also indicated that they did worksheets and textbook exercises, whereas students abroad said they engaged in projects where they discovered mathematical or scientific concepts by applying them in real-life simulations. **How do your education experiences in math and science compare to those of student respondents?**

The 2003 TIMSS mathematics scores for U.S. fourth-graders indicate that we still have a long way to go. (See Table 12.1)

International Comparisons: Smoke and Mirrors?

The Program for International Student Assessment (PISA) provides international comparisons of student achievement on a standardized test for fifteen-year-olds. The TIMSS tests (Trends in International Mathematics and Science Study) provide similar information for a different set of countries and student age groups. Both assessments provide benchmarks against which participating national education systems are judged. Eric Hanushek of Stanford University contended that we in the United States do not take them as seriously as we should.

> The United States, which has participated in each of the 15 international assessments conducted over the past four decades, has typically ignored the results. Perhaps it reflects a desire to ignore bad news. Indeed, U.S. students have never performed very well—invariably falling in the bottom half of the distribution of participating countries. The latest PISA performance placed U.S. 15-year-olds tied for 27th out of 39 participating countries. . . . The most recent TIMSS results placed our students higher in the rankings than on PISA, but there is little reason to believe that this represents any real turnaround in performance. . . . Improving on the system that has had stagnant results for as long as we have measured results will not come by doing more of the same. Improvements are vital to our national well-being. Delay in moving on them will have real and important effects, albeit ones that are difficult to see in the short run. (Hanushek, 2005, p. 41)

What long-term and short-term effects might you expect to see if Hanushek is correct?

Some critics believe that, although international comparisons of schooling are commonly used to rank educational systems, they are just as routinely abused. Gerald Bracey, for example, contended that students from the United States are often found wanting when there are no real differences between them and students in other nations. Other critics charge that international comparisons distract schools from the real issue: how to prepare our students for the future.

On the topic of the legitimacy of international comparison tests, Bracey (2002) argued that TIMSS and other such tests obscure the fact that the United States does not really have a *public school system*. Instead, he said, we have two systems: "One is for poor and minority students; the other is for the rest of us" (2002, p. 2). To support his contention, Bracey cited the rankings of American ethnic groups in reading, mathematics, and science from the Program for International Student Assessment (PISA). Bracey contended that politicians' attention to international comparisons too often distracts us from the real work of dismantling what he calls the "Poor People's Education System." **Do you agree or disagree with Bracey that the real threat to public education in the United States comes from within and not from outside the system?**

Whatever the results of international comparisons of achievement are used for, they must account for students' opportunities to learn the material on which they are tested. If students in different countries do not have opportunities to learn the same things at the same time or by the same age, the value of comparing these students in terms of academic achievement is questionable. Although money is often cited as the best way to improve education, one could make the argument that wisely spending money is a more important factor in improving educational systems. When this is the case, money can create many opportunities for students to learn. Figure 12.4 contains comparative information on national spending on education. **How closely do you think a nation's spending on education is linked to its students' performance on international comparison tests?**

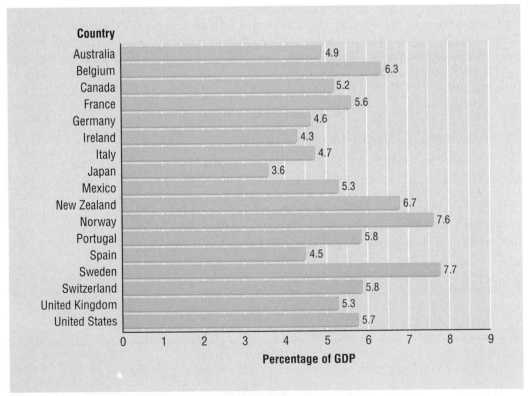

Figure 12.4
Public Direct Expenditures for Education as a Percentage of the Gross Domestic Product: Selected Countries, 2002–2003

Note: Includes all government expenditures for education institutions.

Source: UNESCO.org

Comparisons That Foster a Global View

Concepts of global and comparative education can stretch to address commonalities among people, regardless of where they live. People are naturally curious about what we share as a result of our humanness. **Are there activities in which we all engage that make us more alike than different from one another? How and what can we learn about ourselves by learning about others who live in markedly different cultures?**

Studies of teaching and learning across cultures suggest how much educators share, regardless of where they live and work. For example, the educational construct of *wait-time* has been investigated in many settings in many international contexts and with different kinds of students. Mary Budd Rowe (1986) originated the concept of wait-time as a way to describe the pauses in a classroom teacher's verbal activity. One type of wait-time occurs when a teacher asks a question and then waits for a student to respond. The other type occurs after the student responds. If a teacher can learn to wait for at least three seconds before filling the void with her talk, then the quantity and quality of students' responses increase dramatically, regardless of where in the world these events take place.

Classroom interaction studies point out common concerns among educators around the globe and highlight culture-based differences in their responses to those concerns. Research on Asian teachers, for example, suggests that they, like their U.S. counterparts, learn much by watching their students. Their learning differs in important ways, however, particularly when interpreting students' mistakes.

> For Americans, errors tend to be interpreted as an indication of failure in learning the lesson. For Chinese and Japanese, they are an index of what still needs to be learned. These divergent interpretations result in very different reactions to the display of errors—embarrassment on the part of American children, calm acceptance by Asian children. They also result in differences in the manner in which teachers utilize errors as effective means of instruction. (Stevenson & Stigler, 1992, p. 27)

Regardless of where teachers and students are scattered around the globe, we are united with one another by some common characteristics or forces that influence our lives (Boyer, 1992). These make us more like one another than different. Figure 12.5 suggests that human dignity is shaped by some of the same kinds of forces in all cultures. Imagine how teachers might use these ideas to stimulate learners to search for common ground.

The following are some of the things that we as humans share, no matter where we live. They are important ideas to keep in mind as you continue to explore the occupation of teaching, and they are ideas you should share with your students.

Figure 12.5
Some Forces That Shape the Lives of All Teachers and Students
What other factors operate either inside or outside people to make them like one another? What, for instance, might all teachers believe about teaching and learning?

Case Perspectives

Think back to the case that opened this chapter. The following comments are designed to provide a context for your own thinking about Becca Twyman's situation.

A VETERAN TEACHER OF ESL STUDENTS REFLECTS ON THE CASE. Becca Twyman faces an interesting and potentially exciting challenge with three refugee children about to join her class and little time to prepare for their arrival. There is no indication in the case, but I suspect these children do not speak English, or if so, only slightly. Let me say a few things about what I might do immediately and in the near future.

These children are likely to be frightened, even though they may not reveal their fear in typical ways. I would be on the telephone right away with the Welcome to USA Committee representatives in an effort to get as much information as possible before they arrive on Monday. Are the children brothers and sisters? Cousins? Are they accompanied by their parents, and if not, why not? If they are not related, do the children know one another? How much time have they spent together?

And thank our lucky stars for the Internet! As soon as I got off the telephone I would be on the Web learning everything I could about Somalia—history, people, culture, customs, religions, economy, schools, foods, and so on. How soon can I get to the library and see what the librarian can do to help me find pictures from that part of the world? I would call every friend I have to locate pictures and artifacts from East Africa. It would be wonderful to have some materials already in place when they arrived on Monday. I noticed in the case that Becca has displayed flags of other countries in her room. I would avoid trying to determine which flag is appropriate for Somalia. The land has been war torn for years, and there is probably no way of knowing what meaning the children may attach to different national symbols.

I would also spend some time first thing Monday morning explaining the situation to my class. I have always found it useful to assign buddies to new students, and I would do so in this situation too, even though the new students may have limited or no English proficiency. My own students have never failed to rise to the occasion of welcoming new students into their midst. There is so much to be learned about the new students and about ourselves as we encounter such challenges that I am certain Becca and her students will be thrilled by the opportunity.

Once we caught our breath, I would be moving quickly to learn as much as possible about the support network for the children. They may or may not be the only Somalis in the community. I would call the local college immediately and see if they had resources that that might help all of the children work together to make the transition efficacious.

A PRINCIPAL WITH CONSIDERABLE INTERNATIONAL EXPERIENCE CONSIDERS THE SITUATION IN WHICH BECCA TWYMAN FINDS HERSELF. My children were educated abroad in American schools founded and supported by the U.S. government. They also attended both private and government-sponsored schools in South America. My wife and I were in the Foreign Service for some twenty years, working in a half dozen countries in Central and South America. We spent three years in Africa. I can tell Becca Twyman what mattered to us, or how we judged whether our children's educational experiences were valuable.

When the teachers treated our children as individuals with their own needs and interests, we were satisfied—happy even. We were initially apprehensive about putting them in local government schools because we thought they might be categorized as "the Americans' children" and treated in accordance with the locals' views of Americans. Often their views were about as accurate as Americans' views of people in other nations. Our children were real people with parents and grandparents and well-established family values. Two of the children loved to read. For the other two, reading was like pulling teeth. Some liked sports; others didn't. They were normal children. They just happened to be in a culture that was quite different from the one their parents grew up in. When the teachers were warm and understanding and eager to help our children learn a new language and experience a new culture, without denigrating them as people, we knew we had made the right decision.

My advice to Becca Twyman would be simple. The most important way to judge whether the integration of the Somalian children is successful is to ask the children and their parents how they are feeling and what they are thinking. Be a good listener. You will know if you have done your best to help the children and the families when you find out what they think.

Questions for Reflection: Have you ever traveled to another country? Have you spent any extended period of time in another country or had any international educational experience? Have you known students from other countries who have attended school in the United States? What are some of the problems that you or others encountered? What special efforts did teachers make to include outsiders in their classrooms? Have the classes in your teacher education curriculum encouraged you to think about international education issues? If so, has this been helpful to you in defining what you believe about American education? If not, would you like to learn more? ■

- Human beings share the mysteries of the life cycle—birth, growth, and death. **What milestone events do you celebrate in your culture? How do these events and celebrations resemble such events in another culture that is distant geographically (or philosophically) from your culture?**
- We all use languages to express feelings and ideas. **Do you speak, write, or read a language other than English? How many of your friends and family are bilingual or multilingual? What encourages or discourages you from learning other languages?**
- We connect with others through music, dance, painting, sculpture, and the many visual arts. **Is there a particular form of artistic expression that is especially important to you? How do artists from other nations and various cultures affect you?**
- We believe we are unique among living creatures in our abilities to recall the past and to anticipate the future. **What do you imagine your future might hold? Personally or professionally, how is your future likely to be similar to and different from that of an aspiring teacher in another nation?**
- Every person belongs to groups. Some memberships are brief; others last a lifetime. **To what groups do you belong? To what groups have you been assigned? Do you share membership in any of these groups with people from different nations or cultures?**
- We are all connected to planet Earth. We all depend on the natural world for our survival. **What environmental issues are important to you in your own locale? What environmental events in your immediate locale affect people who are distant from you? How might environmental events in other places be felt in your own neighborhood?**
- Work occupies our lives. Taking is key to our survival, but we all must give back if people are not only to survive but to prosper. **What do you take and give back?**
- In every corner of the globe, we can find people searching for a larger purpose in life. **Sometimes educators describe their desire to make a difference or to be part of something bigger than themselves. Do you have these thoughts?**

Summary

The United States of America has always been a part of the world community. Recent events and increased interaction with more people from different nations make the need to learn about the rest of the world more important than ever. The revolution in communications technology only makes our connections to others faster, stronger, and more numerous. Therefore, this land of immigrants has many reasons for taking a global educational perspective that outweigh any inclinations to narrow our sights.

As we learn about education in other countries, we shape and verify our perceptions of the physical, intellectual, emotional, and social life in schools around the world. In many instances our knowledge helps us work more effectively with our close neighbors. We also learn how to support those who emigrate from distant nations to the United States. Almost without fail, when we study educational life in other places we learn more about ourselves—why we teach and learn as we do.

Learning about education often means making comparisons between ourselves and others in the global community. Some sources of information upon which we base these comparisons, such as international performance tests, provide useful information. Comparison test results, however, should not be the extent of our interest in other countries' educational systems. When we look beyond the competition to be the best, we allow ourselves to learn new skills, ideas, and techniques that can improve education for all students. The forces that define teachers and students as citizens of the world impel us to minimize our differences and look for what we have in common.

TERMS AND CONCEPTS

apartheid

global awareness

international comparative education

juku

NGO

okeiko-goto

REFLECTIVE ACTIVITY: PROJECT CUBA

Reflective practice is an essential part of good teaching. Reflection is a process that includes making thoughtful decisions, understanding and articulating value structures, acting from knowledge, evaluating your actions and their effects, and sharing your reflections with colleagues. After reading the following scenario, respond to the questions below. The scenario reflects the INTASC Principle and Disposition at the end of this activity.

To most outsiders, Cuba is an enigma. North Americans often know the nation only as a well-developed set of images crafted during the past forty years by governments, the movie industry, and the popular press. The romantic image of this mysterious island in the Caribbean, located only ninety miles from Florida, has had remarkable staying power—so strong that tourists' appetite for Cuban music, beaches, rum, and cigars is an emerging force in the dollar economy.

But the vivid image of life under communism also looms large over Cuba. North Americans have been taught to imagine communism as a police state that leaves its citizens powerless. In so many ways, Cubans and non-Cubans alike seem trapped by the history represented in these stereotypical images that rarely reveal much about life in Cuba.

Young Cubans do as well as most other children in the world on educational tests. Virtually all children who do not have serious disabilities advance to secondary schools, which start at grade seven. The overwhelming majority of students, about 95 percent, graduate from ninth grade.

Decide 1. What do young people everywhere, regardless of nationality, care about? What do they need to grow up with a sense of hope? How do they think about themselves, and how do they want others to view them? How might the goals and expectations of education in Cuba differ from those in the United States? How might they be the same?

Perceive and Value 2. How do you think teachers are regarded in Cuba? What might a Cuban perceive as the benefits and shortcomings of public schools in the United States?

Know and Act 3. What would you like to know about educational standards in Cuba? How do test scores of Cuban students compare to those of U.S. students? What percentage of Cuban students do you think attend college? How might adults help young people, regardless of where they live, stake out common ground or find common interests?

Evaluate 4. In Cuba, both undergraduate and graduate education are free. How might you judge the advantages and disadvantages of providing students with a free education, from start to finish?

Discuss 5. Find someone who has moved from another country to the United States. What were the biggest language, cultural, family, and community challenges he or she faced while adjusting to life and learning in the United States?

INTASC Principle 3

The teacher understands how students differ in their approaches to learning and creates instructional opportunities that are adapted to diverse learners.

Disposition

The teacher understands how students' learning is influenced by individual experiences, talents, and prior learning, as well as language, culture, family, and community values. (Interstate New Teacher Assessment and Support Consortium, 1992)

ADDITIONAL READINGS

Brown, S. C., & Kysilka, M. L. (2002). *Applying multicultural and global concepts in the classroom and beyond.* Boston: Allyn & Bacon.

Davidman, L. (2001). *Teaching with a multicultural perspective: A practical guide* (3rd ed.). New York: Longman.

Martorella, P. H. (2002). *Social studies for elementary school classrooms: Preparing children to be global citizens.* Upper Saddle River, NJ: Prentice Hall.

National Research Council. (1999). *Global perspectives for local action: Using TIMSS to improve U.S. mathematics and science education / A joint project of the Committee on Science Education K–12 and the Mathematical Sciences Education Board.* Washington, DC: National Academy Press.

Spring, J. H. (2004). *How educational ideologies are shaping global society: Intergovernmental organizations, NGOs, and the decline of the nation-state.* Mahwah, NJ: Erlbaum.

WEB RESOURCES

www.gsn.org/
The Global SchoolNet site creates opportunities for teachers worldwide to collaborate online.

www.ibo.org/
Learn more about the International Baccalaureate Organization's educational programs.

www.ngo.org/
Explore nongovernmental organizations associated with the United Nations.

www.aaie.org/
The Association for the Advancement of International Schools promotes connections among educators in American schools abroad (e.g., military, diplomatic, etc).

www.globalization101.org/
Student-centered site with excellent teacher resources relevant to many issues that accompany globalization.

www.un.org/cyberschoolbus
Lesson plans and project ideas that emphasize social responsibility on global issues—brought to you by the United Nations.

www.cie.org/
Council on Islamic education offers services, teaching resources, and materials.

www.askasia.org/
Interdisciplinary classroom resources for elementary, middle, and high schools.

What Lies Ahead

Case Study: Looking to the Future

Janeeta Morris looked at the paper in her hand. She knew that the next fifteen minutes would mean the difference between getting this teaching appointment—one that she really wanted—and continuing to make the rounds looking for her first job. She had just been in an interview room with the elementary school's principal, Yolanda Sanborne, and a committee of teachers.

"Thank you for spending time with the selection committee and with me," Ms. Sanborne had said after they had all talked for half an hour or so. "I've been the principal here for nine years, and interviewing potential teachers remains one of the best parts of my job. To have a hand in interviewing and selecting new faculty for our school is both a weighty responsibility and a special honor. A young teacher like you has the potential to affect so many young lives—and some old ones, too!"

Janeeta heard the mature teachers sitting around the table chuckle. Clearly everyone in the room liked Ms. Sanborne.

"Before you leave today, we'd like to invite you to reflect on one ground rule for working together in this building. It goes like this: You are among friends and colleagues here. It's OK to make mistakes. It's OK to ask questions. We are a team. Just give it your best at all times.

"For us, Eleanor Roosevelt expressed well the spirit with which we approach our work." Ms. Sanborne looked down at a paper on the table in front of her and read: *You gain strength, courage, and confidence by every experience in which you really stop to look fear in the face. You must do the thing which you think you cannot do.*

"Janeeta, we'd like you to take fifteen minutes to gather your thoughts. When we return, we'd like you to speak to the points listed on this paper."

The principal handed Janeeta the sheet of paper, and then she and the teachers left the room. Janeeta read over the paper one more time.

Real teachers start to build their legacy from the moment they begin to teach. What scares you most about being a teacher? How do you want to be remembered?

This chapter discusses the unusual opportunities that now exist for teachers to make a difference in people's lives, including trends in standards development, curriculum formation, student assessment, diversity, and character development. The chapter also examines how technology is changing the landscape of teaching and what you can expect from participation in collaborative networks of people devoted to common educational goals. The chapter concludes with suggestions on how teachers develop productive, satisfying careers in education.

How Are Teachers' Professional Roles Changing?

Why is now a good time to be a teacher? There has never been a better time to be a teacher. Technological advances, innovative curricula, access to more information, highly diverse students, and the developing global community are only a few of the reasons being a teacher today is so exciting. Many people outside the system have much to say about how teaching and learning should be improved. But teachers are there at the center of activity every day, working to inspire, inform, and support young people. They know that, in spite of negative opinions in the public and in the press, an abundance of good work is being done in classrooms. Teachers will be there, advancing civilization, when everybody else has gone home.

The history and ideology of education in the United States are marked by change and evolution. From how schools are funded to what students are taught and how they are assessed, the rules and standards are constantly changing. Changes in teaching, learning, and public education can be described in terms of trends—trends toward the use of common goals and standards, toward comprehensive curriculum development and performance assessment, and toward the development of human talent in inclusive settings. As we prepare ourselves and future generations for life in a faster, smaller, and more high-tech world, it is more important than ever that teachers help shape these educational trends.

Trends toward Common Educational Expectations

Critics of American Public Education worry that students are not learning the information and skills they need, that teachers are not fully trained before entering the classroom, and that a dangerous rift is forming between rich and poor schools. Implementing common educational expectations for all schools, teachers, and students is one way to address these issues. Common expectations will provide educators with guidelines and ways to evaluate how well schools are doing compared to one another.

One of the most important moves toward common education expectations is the No Child Left Behind Act passed in 2001. A revision of the Elementary and Secondary Education Act of 1965, the No Child Left Behind Act is the most comprehensive federal legislation covering K–12 education. It affects every public school in the United States in the following ways:

- **Annual testing.** By the 2005–2006 academic year, all states had to begin testing pupils in grades three to eight every year in reading and mathematics. The tests must be aligned with state standards, and fourth and eighth graders in every state also have to take the **National Assessment of Educational Progress (NAEP)**.
- **Academic progress.** States must demonstrate that all students reach at least a level of proficiency on their exams by the 2013–2014 academic year. In the meantime, all schools must make "adequate yearly progress." If they fall short two years in a row, they must offer students the option of attending other public schools at no cost. If the schools fall short three years in a row, they must offer supplemental services to pupils, including tutoring. The clock started ticking on failing schools in 2002.
- **Report cards.** In 2002–2003, states had to begin documenting student achievement by subgroup and by district. Districts must produce similar report cards for each school.
- **Teacher qualifications.** By 2002–2003, all newly hired teachers had to be "highly qualified," which means licensed (or certified) and teaching in content areas for which they are endorsed. By 2005–2006, all teachers had to meet this requirement. Also, all newly hired

Cultural Awareness: Lessons Learned

"This is a world in which a very high level of preparation in reading, writing, speaking, mathematics, science, literature, history and the arts will be an indispensable foundation for everything that comes after for most members of the workforce.

The best employers the world over will be looking for the most competent, most creative and most innovative people on the face of the earth and will be willing to pay them top dollar for their services. This will be true not just for the top professionals and managers, but up and down the length and breadth of the workforce. Those countries that produce the most important new products and services can capture a premium in world markets that will enable them to pay high wages to their citizens." (NCEE, 2007, p.7)

How might teachers encourage the development of a workforce that exhibits a global, multicultural view of the world? The answer, Alexander Russo (2007) argues, is simple: take advantage of resources close at hand and partner with others that have international components in their educational programs.

Local resources can include teachers, students, and community members from other nations, businesses that work with overseas partners, and cultural organizations such as churches.

Communities are chock full of assets. Russo notes that a high school class on international business in a rural farming community in Texas discovered that a local company was selling cattle guards to India. The owner explained to the class how the relationship with an overseas buyer worked and drew attention to important logistical and cultural issues. Other schools have immigrant students help non-native speakers practice language skills.

Question for Reflection: Can you think of any resources in your own community which might be useful for promoting a global, multicultural perspective?

Sources: National Center on Education and the Economy (2007). *Tough Choices or Tough Times: The report of the new commission on the skills of the American workforce,* Available online (www.skillscommission.org), p.7. Russo A. (2007). *Global education on a dime: A low-cost way to connect.* Edutopia.org (Available online: http://www.edutopia.org/print/4976.

---

paraprofessionals or aides had to have at least two years of college preparation, possess an associate's degree, or meet standards of quality. By 2005–2006, this had to hold true for all paraprofessionals.

- **Reading first.** The federal government began investing $900 million in reading programs in 2002.
- **Funding changes.** More money will flow to poorer school districts, and they will have greater flexibility on how to spend it.

How do you think these new expectations influence life in schools? Some people worry that the mandates of the act will never be implemented and enforced effectively. Others see the discrepancies in funding between rich and poor schools and argue that the proposed changes in funding are not enough to help those who need it most.

Utah wants to use its own state testing and accountability program, instead of No Child Left Behind (NCLB). But federal officials have rejected the idea. Utah does not report test results by individual student groups, as required under NCLB. At least fifteen other states are also considering legislative challenges. Texas, Virginia, and North Dakota are quarreling with the U.S. Department of Education over various provisions of the law (Dillon, 2005).

Trends toward Comprehensive Curriculum and Assessment

Policymakers at all levels of government, parents, philosophers, educational practitioners, citizens, and would-be citizens want to influence what is taught and learned in schools. The public's evolving expectations for educational standards are stimulating reform in curriculum, methods of teaching and learning, and processes of assessment. These reforms will occur slowly in some places and rapidly in others. When viewed together, these reforms constitute noticeable changes in the way teachers perform their jobs.

Real curricular reform requires integration: blending old and new material, forming links between concepts within and across content areas, structuring content so students can make connections in their minds, organizing people and ideas by themes, and teaming students with teachers. As the curriculum reforms are enacted, teachers will become increasingly responsible for creating opportunities for students to demonstrate what they know and can do in real-life settings. For instance, teachers will charge their students to study concepts of time, rate, and distance by packing them off to football fields and amusement parks with maps and stop-watches in hand. Students will be running races, timing roller coasters, and calculating the values of missing variables. In all likelihood, however, they will be doing so in virtual space, using the technological tools of the twenty-first century to solve timeless problems. And their teachers will be at their sides, helping them learn from their mistakes.

Assessment will continue to be a major part of teachers' lives in the foreseeable future—but not only in the form of standardized achievement tests. In the future, tests that yield information on students' abilities to pick "right" and "wrong" answers will diminish in importance. In their place, educators will develop a **comprehensive assessment** of student progress. These assessments will tap students' capacities to reason, think divergently, solve problems creatively, and express themselves clearly. Comprehensive assessments will contain challenges students will face in real life. They will provide estimates of students' abilities to live and work successfully.

Changes in curriculum development and in assessment will greatly affect what teachers need to know and do. Teachers need well-honed *clinical* skills to help students grow into independent, successful adults. That is, teachers need to base their judgments and actions on the best information available. Getting and using such information effectively is what skilled clinicians do. Teachers of the future, like physicians, will take their instructional cues from the people they serve. They will work with students to identify outcomes that are logical and attainable, and they will help students work toward these outcomes. How will teachers know when they succeed? They will judge their success by studying their own teaching and by examining the learning of their own students.

School districts are also undergoing reform to help prepare both teachers and students for the demands of the future. Successful school districts can be identified by the following characteristics:

- *Strong leadership.* The superintendent, central office staff, and school board members are committed to collecting and using data for decision making.
- *Supportive culture for using data for continual improvement.* Data are readily available to teachers, students, and parents to guide school improvement. Teachers who do not agree with this view are encouraged to look elsewhere for a job.
- *Strong service orientation toward principals and teachers.* The district makes curriculum specialists available to schools and offers help in getting and using data to inform practice.
- *Partnerships with other organizations.* Districts join with universities, businesses, and non-profit organizations to obtain expertise and technology to support school activities.
- *Mechanisms to support and train personnel to use data.* Most districts assign a person to be in charge of data collection, analysis, and reporting. In addition, the time of others in the central office and resources from outside groups are made available.
- *Monitoring every student's performance on academic standards.* The system gives tests often and sets performance targets for students to meet between the tests.
- *Flexible time use.* Grouping and instructional patterns are changed to address students' needs and to allow teachers to plan together. Vertical integration—teachers meeting from all the grade levels—to coordinate curricula and instruction occurs in some districts.
- *Defined improvement process.* Data help these schools identify needs. The school personnel, in turn, behave systematically to address them.

Trends toward Education for Diversity

Standards are uniform, but children are different. If they are to achieve the same or similar outcomes, children need different levels and kinds of support. Increasingly, in the years ahead, teachers will make informed decisions about students' needs and abilities in order to deliver appropriate support. This means, among other things, that educators will develop curricula and instruction for students from different cultures and subcultures and for students with special learning needs.

GENDER SENSITIVITY TRAINING Gender-fair education provides **gender sensitivity training** to all students. Curricula are designed to avoid sex-role stereotyping and to promote equal educational opportunities for girls and women. Standard textbooks draw attention to women's relevant contributions and routinely encourage girls to take and master mathematics and science courses throughout their educational careers. In addition, education texts and classroom activities should avoid the generic use of male terms and examples.

The Appalachia Educational Laboratory (AEL) promotes gender-fair curricula by suggesting how materials and programs can be adapted to diverse situations. They offer assessment checklists to help identify curricular areas that would benefit from modification. In keeping with recent research, AEL staff argue that special actions must be taken to encourage girls to learn mathematics and science (2005). These include, but are not limited to, the use of cooperative learning, patterns of rewards, and career guidance.

Equity between males and females might be realized as people adopt a more caring attitude toward others.

> The concept of gender sensitivity has been developed as a way to reduce barriers to personal and economic development created by sexism. Gender sensitivity helps to generate respect for the individual regardless of sex.
>
> Gender sensitivity is not about pitting women against men. On the contrary, education that is gender sensitive benefits members of both sexes. It helps them determine which assumptions in matters of gender are valid and which are stereotyped generalizations. Gender awareness requires not only intellectual effort but also sensitivity and open-mindedness. It opens up the widest possible range of life options for both women and men (UNESCO, 2002, pl vi).

How do you think schools might encourage a culture of caring?

TEACHING ALL STUDENTS IN INCLUSIVE CLASSROOMS The inclusion movement in special education has encouraged the teaching of children with disabilities in general education classrooms, instead of teaching them in self-contained classrooms or separate facilities. Inclusion carries the force of the law and considerable public support. At the same time, disagreement exists about which settings are most appropriate for which students and how to provide instruction for students with disabilities in inclusive classrooms.

As a classroom teacher, you will be expected to understand the needs and abilities of all students as fully as possible so you can set tasks or objectives that students with disabilities can accomplish. As you fit instruction to individuals' goals, needs, and strengths, you may need to structure teaching and assignments for students in different ways. You also will have to assess students in ways that allow them to demonstrate what they know and can do. This will mean focusing less on standard measures of learning and more on alternative assessments of what they have learned.

Trends toward Defining Diversity in Economic Terms

U.S. public schools are showing signs of economic segregation. While two-thirds of the nation's student population is middle class (not eligible for federal subsidized lunches), one-quarter of all schools have a majority of students from low-income households. To avoid becoming two United States—one rich, the other poor—policymakers must encourage the integration of students of different socioeconomic levels. Race should be a factor in integration only if economic criteria do not work. Because children perform best in middle class schools, the idea is to bring children of different races and economic classes together. Doing so should provide all students with opportunities for educational success.

To accomplish this goal, the Century Foundation (2002) recommended a policy of public school choice, accompanied by fairness guidelines:

> Within given geographic regions, parents can rank preferences among a variety of schools, each of which has a distinctive curricular theme or teaching approach. School officials then

honor those choices with an eye to promoting integrated schools, a system now successfully employed in Cambridge, Massachusetts, Montclair, New Jersey, and elsewhere. Alternatively, communities might promote integration using a system of public school choice that provides substantially greater funding to low-income children, with dollars traveling with students, thereby making low-income students more attractive to middle-class communities. (2002)

Do you believe using incentives to accomplish economic integration would or would not be more effective than using coercion?

Trends toward Character Education

Teaching or clarifying values, sometimes referred to as **character education,** is one way educators try to shape young people's lives. In the past decade or more, schools have been under increased pressure to provide students with character education in addition to the normal skill- and information-building curriculum. Karen Bohlin, Deborah Farmer, and Kevin Ryan (2001) described three approaches to character education that currently dominate school activities: views, virtues, and values. Each approach, although somewhat unique, is meant to stimulate moral and intellectual development.

The *views approach* is meant to help students develop and explicitly state their intellectual positions on controversial issues related to laws, politics, wealth, poverty, religion, and the like. Classroom discussion is the typical method used by teachers when attempting to help students strengthen their views.

The *virtues approach* attempts to develop good habits and dispositions (virtues) that help students develop into responsible adults. Virtues such as diligence, sincerity, personal accountability, courage, and perseverance are the things that help us develop better relationships and do our work better, thereby attaining human excellence. For instance, a virtue lesson might teach that it is not enough to value the Bible; one must also act out the Bible's rules for living with one's neighbors. Thus, "education in virtues—those good dispositions of the heart and mind that are regularly put into action—is the foundation of solid character development" (p. 12).

The *values approach* is the most popular one used in schools. This approach teaches students that values are what people want, desire, or assign worth to; the things valued can be morally good, bad, or neutral. It also teaches that, besides being a matter of personal choice, values are a personal right. Thus, teachers using the values-driven approach to character education are not supposed to indoctrinate or impose their views on students. Instead, teachers are supposed to provide students with opportunities to sort out their own values, so they can make wise choices in their lives. **How far should schools go in teaching moral values?**

Schools also provide students with character education by encouraging them to participate in the responsibilities of community, state, and nation. Many schools encourage volunteerism, or **service learning** even with ESL students (Russell, 2007). Some service learning programs encourage students to adopt a moral stance of caring, a political view of the value of reconstructing society, and an intellectual stance on the importance of engaging in experiences that transform the way people think. Other charity programs are organized around the moral principle of giving and the intellectual value of gaining experience by participating in service activities.

Volunteer projects take a variety of forms and provide a variety of services for the school and the community. In many instances, volunteer groups perform their services outside school hours and receive no credit, awards, or certificates of appreciation from their school. Individual service projects, such as tutoring peers or younger children or working with residents in nursing homes, foster communication and intergenerational understanding. Group service projects, such as repairing bleachers or cleaning up the local park, help students learn to plan and cooperate with others to get a job done. Students who volunteer also become more responsible and develop more favorable attitudes toward the people they work with than do students who do not volunteer.

Some parents and teachers will tell you that one of the best ways to encourage character development is to encourage participation in Americorps immediately after high school graduation. AmeriCorps comprises national service programs that engage more than 40,000 Americans each year in service to meet critical needs in education, public safety, health, and the environment. AmeriCorps members tutor and mentor youth, build affordable housing, teach computer skills, clean waterways, run after-school programs, and help communities respond to disasters. In doing so, Corps members learn teamwork, communication, responsibility, and other essential skills that can help them the rest of their lives. Those who successfully complete service in AmeriCorps earn nearly $5,000 that can be used for postsecondary education expenses.

How Are Links to Technology Changing the Foundations of Education?

It is impossible to discuss the subject of education, even at the elementary level, without referring to the power of technology. As schools develop capacities to deliver video, audio, data, and text to classrooms through electronic media, teachers will have opportunities to use technology in two ways. First, they can use it as a means of direct instruction that focuses on basic skills; second, they can use it to help students construct their own knowledge and develop a deep understanding of subject matter. Educators will also teach students to use technology for themselves.

The challenge educators face is to use technology in ways that help students to think and learn. To address the challenge, both teachers and students must become "media literate."

> Media literacy means various things to different people, encompassing everything from the basics of graphic design to critical analysis of advertising images and news broadcasts. "One of the radical ideas behind media education is to make school more student centered," says Robert Kubey, director of Rutgers University's Center for Media Studies. "That isn't to say that we pander to whatever students are interested in so that the whole curriculum is about video games and rap music. But we want to understand a little better about the pleasures and interests that students have and use that as an avenue to have intellectual and analytic discourse about these products. Could they be better? What makes this one good? Are there moral values being taught? In other words, reach kids where they live." (Ellis, 2005).

Most experts agree that some basic conditions must exist if computers are going to be used effectively to link students with information and people in the larger world. Computers must be available in sufficient number so that workstations can be provided for every two or three students. Teachers need training and opportunities to use computers for themselves if they are going to help students use them. Teachers also need time to restructure their curricula around computers if the machines are going to be used for anything other than drill and practice work. Finally, computers must be made available in individual classrooms, because teachers will have difficulty integrating technology with classroom instruction if students have to go to a lab to access a computer.

Educational technologists have been studying the topic of computers in classrooms to help define ways technology is being used effectively. Mark and Cindy Grabe (2000) identified five themes that describe the different uses of technology in classrooms. The first theme is found when students use technology to study a particular content area; at this point, the technology has been *integrated into content-area instruction*. As teachers encourage students to learn to use general-purpose software, such as word-processing programs, they are employing a *tools approach* to technology instruction, the second theme. The Grabes identified the third theme as using technology to promote *an active role for students*. By active, they mean the mental behavior of students as they use technology to construct meaning for themselves or to solve complex problems. The fourth theme occurs when technology is used to facilitate *an integrated or multidisciplinary approach* to teaching and learning involving a broad range of skills. Finally, technology can enhance interactions among students, providing the benefits of *cooperative learning*. See the technology skills students will need to master to be competitive in Table 13.1.

Students' access to **Internet** technology, the electronic network that links computers, has steadily increased in public schools. Now there is almost no difference in Internet access between poor schools and wealthy schools.

Table 13.1

TECHNOLOGY SKILLS FOR THE 21ST CENTURY (INTERNATIONAL SOCIETY FOR TECHNOLOGY EDUCATION):

- Creativity and Innovation
- Communication and Collaboration
- Research and Information Fluency
- Critical Thinking, Problem Solving, and Decision Making
- Digital Citizenship
- Technology Operations and Concepts

"Leadership in technology is best illustrated by ISTE's creation of the National Educational Technology Standards (NETS), first published in 1998. ISTE is now leading the creation of the next generation of NETS. In 1998, it was enough to define what students needed to know about and be able to do with technology. Now, we're defining what students need to know and be able to do with technology to learn effectively and live productively in a rapidly changing digital world."

—Don Knezek, ISTE CEO, 2007

Source: http://www.iste.org/AM/Template.cfm?Section=NETS

The NCES also reports that schools are using their Internet access more frequently to build school websites. This means they can offer everything from lunch menus to online practice tests and daily homework assignments. During the 2001–2002 school year, 75 percent of all public schools had websites. That figure had increased to 88 percent for the 2003–2004 school year. About 80 percent of high-minority schools and 72 percent of high-poverty schools had websites (Fox, 2005).

Teachers and students use the Internet in a variety of ways and for a variety of tasks. People's access to information and services is defined by *protocols,* or programs, that specify how information moves online. These include the following:

- **Chat.** A form of real-time or **synchronous communication** on the Internet, meaning that the parties involved must be online simultaneously for communication to occur. The chat program allows people to send and receive typed messages almost instantaneously.
- **Electronic mail (e-mail).** The most popular application of the Internet, in which messages are sent, received, stored, and forwarded to others. Teachers often establish a mailing list, or **listserv,** that allows them to send messages to all their students in a class at the same time with a single keystroke. Mailing lists are a good way to continue a class discussion outside the classroom, offering an immediacy that benefits the exchange of ideas.
- **World Wide Web.** A system of Internet servers that supports specially formatted documents that often have text and still images, as well as audio and video. These documents are called **hypermedia.**
- **Websites.** Individual locations on the Web owned and managed by a person, group, company, or organization. They may contain a single Web page or many files, graphics, and other information, usually on the same or related topics.
- **Web browser.** Computer applications that allow users to access and view Web materials. Examples of Web browsers include Internet Explorer, Netscape, and Safari.
- **Home page.** The first page of a website or document. A home page is usually organized much like the table of contents in a textbook. Besides indicating who or what organization has posted the document, the page suggests what might be found within the site. It may also list the most recent articles or news related to the website's topic.
- **Newsgroups.** Electronic message services that post to local, regional, national, and international Web servers. People subscribe to a newsgroup to gain access to these messages and to post their own messages. Newsgroups are widely used in education. They, like e-mail, are a form of **asynchronous communication,** meaning that the parties involved in the communication do not have to be present online at the same time. Instead, e-mail can be sent and messages posted to newsgroups and viewed at a later time.

■ **Videoconferencing.** A form of synchronous communication that allows people to see and hear one another over computers. This is a useful technology for online instruction courses and meetings, as it helps people communicate across the miles.

With appropriate software and an Internet connection, one can access virtually any of the Web's documents. The range of information accessible on the Web is vast. One can travel to points all around the world, as well as find a rich repository of educational resources. Getting information from the Web requires no permission (although some of the information may be copyrighted or password protected to restrict its redistribution). Users can share what they have with the rest of the world.

Distance Learning

Televised instruction has been a fact of life for several decades, but new technology designed to promote **distance learning** is transforming how and what students learn—and where they learn it. In its most advanced form, which usually involves Internet connections, video equipment, and special computer software, distance learning allows people to interact with one another as if they were in the same room. Students can see and hear teachers, and teachers can answer students' questions and react to students' comments instantaneously. These features are especially useful when students are located in geographically remote areas.

The Star Schools Program, established by the U.S. Department of Education in 1988 has been instrumental in promoting distance education. The purpose of the Star Schools Program is to encourage improved instruction in mathematics, science, and foreign languages, as well as improved literacy skills and vocational education. The program uses telecommunications equipment to teach underserved populations, including low-income and nonliterate students, students with limited English proficiency, and students with disabilities.

Students in one-third of the nation's public school districts took distance education courses in the 2002–2003 school year. The National Center for Education Statistics (NCES) interprets this fact as evidence of the increasing popularity of distance education. The NCES study revealed thousands of students enrolled in courses taught on the Internet or through video- or audio-conferencing, with the teacher and student in separate places. About one in ten public schools in the nation had students enrolled in such distance education courses (Honawar, 2005).

There were an estimated 328,000 enrollments in distance education courses among students regularly attending public schools. Schools surveyed reported that they typically offer courses online that are otherwise not available to their students, such as Advanced Placement courses. Distance education courses also reduce the scheduling conflicts students might have with other courses or school activities.

As opposed to the traditional model of offering instruction in particular buildings according to standard calendars and schedules, online programs allow for "any time, any pace, any place" learning. NASBE representative Michael David Warren, Jr., from the Michigan State Board of Education, described an information age education system that would be enabled by a technology-rich learning environment. The system would include

■ a focus on learning, not schools;
■ learning organizations defined by mission, not by geography and facilities;
■ student-focused, customized learning, not mass-produced, one-size-fits-all instruction;
■ self-directed and holistic learning, not regimented recitation;
■ learning on a 24/7 basis and throughout the year, not artificial schedules and calendars;
■ empowerment of families and educators, not bureaucracies; and
■ a number of options and educational providers for each student, not a standard model for all (2001, p. 13).

Distance learning projects are especially important for many small, isolated school districts that have had to exclude all but basic-level courses from their curriculum because of budget constraints. Distance learning offers attractive possibilities for making connections with people and ideas. Efforts must be made, however, to make sure financial constraints do not limit computer resources and access to distance learning options for the schools that need them the most.

Technology in Practice

BLOGGING, VLOGING, AND PODCASTING

Teachers finding their voice on blogs: More educators are using the online publishing forum to vent, or to instruct kids

By Associated Press
Published July 10, 2005

WEST PALM BEACH—It's a digital teachers lounge, missing only the coffee-stained sofas.

It's what a teacher mentions when she wants students to look up from their iPod playlists and take an interest in class.

It's the blog—an online publishing forum. An intrepid group of educators in Florida and nationwide are starting to use it to kvetch about their day or as a teaching tool.

—St. Petersburg Times
(www.sptimes.com/2005/07/10/State/
Teachers_finding_thei.shtml)

What is a blog? The word *blog* is a short form for weblog, a personal journal published on the Web. Blogs often include philosophical reflections and opinions on the Internet and social issues. They frequently provide a "log" of the author's favorite Web links. Blogs are usually presented in journal style with a new entry each day.

Teachers are increasingly creating their own blogs to share their thoughts and observations and to let off steam. You can find many examples of teacher blogs on the Web (for instance, see www.teachervision.fen.com/page/33550.html).

Blogs are big, but *vlogs*—video weblogs—may eventually surpass them as tools for enabling teachers and students to conquer the barriers to publishing and broadcasting. People are creating their own videos and posting them for anyone to see on the Web. News, commentary, documentary, or art? Vlogs can take many forms, serve many purposes. Teachers will help define how these new methods of communication shape the future.

Don't look now, but the teacher down the hall may be podcasting or publishing audio files via the Internet. Podcasting allows users to subscribe to particular feeds or shows that are automatically downloaded to a computer or portable listening device. The approach takes its name from the iPod, or digital portable music player from Apple Computer. Sounds a lot like radio, doesn't it?

Question for Reflection: What are the pros and cons of allowing students to use teacher's blogs to post their work or to reflect on schoolwork?

The gap between those who have access to technology and those who do not is often referred to as the **digital divide.**

Telecommunications Capabilities in the Schools

To understand how technology is changing the foundations of education, we need to know how and where technology is being made available. **Do educators and their students enter the "information age" when they enter schools? Or do they step back in time, technologically speaking?** As illustrated in Figure 13.1, states' expenditures on educational technology can vary considerably. For example, California has 10.2 students per Internet connection in the classroom, while allocating $15.3 million specifically for educational technology (Metzger, 2005a). In contrast, Texas has 7.0 students per Internet connection, and it allocates $117.8 million specifically for educational technology (Metzger, 2005b). As states' economies vary from year to year, so do their expenditures on educational technology.

It is always difficult to know, relatively speaking, what constitutes appropriate and sufficient use of technology. Interest in the topic can be found in a variety of places, from private enterprise to the federal government. The business sector, for instance, showed their interest at the CEO Forum on Education and Technology (2000). The Forum created a STaR Chart to help people gauge School Technology and Readiness (hence the acronym STaR) to use technology. The chart can serve as both an evaluation and a planning device for technology use in schools. Six areas are described in the chart: hardware and connectivity, content, professional development, student achievement and assessment, integration and use, and educational benefits. It is possible to classify a school as low-tech, mid-tech, or high-tech in each of the six

California		Texas	
State Education Agency **Technology Contact:**		**State Education Agency** **Technology Contact:**	
Name: Barbara Thalacker; E-mail: bthalack@cde.ca.gov		Name: Anita G. Givens; E-mail: anita.givens@tea.state.tx.us	
Phone: (916) 323-5072		Phone: (512) 463-9400	
Website: www.cde.ca.gov		Website: www.tea.state.tx.us	
Vital Statistics:		**Vital Statistics:**	
Number of public schools:	9,087	Number of public schools:	7,757
Pre-K–12 enrollment:	6,356,348	Pre-K–12 enrollment:	4,259,823
Number of public school teachers:	307,672	Number of public school teachers:	288,655
Average annual E-rate funding:	$292,213,482	Average annual E-rate funding:	$217,589,938
State funding allocated specifically for educational technology:	$15.3 million	State funding allocated specifically for educational technology:	$117.8 million
Internet Use:		**Internet Use:**	
Students per Internet-connected computer:	5.8	Students per Internet-connected computer:	3.7
Students per Internet-connected computer in classrooms:	10.2	Students per Internet-connected computer in classrooms:	7.0
Percent of instructional computers with high-speed Internet access:	83.0	Percent of instructional computers with high-speed Internet access:	88.5

Source: Technology Counts, 2005. Editorial projects in education. Reprinted with permission.

Figure 13.1 Technology Counts: Spending in California and Texas

categories and to set targets for improvement. Figure 13.2 contains the STaR Chart standards for hardware and connectivity.

The federal government has also done much to stimulate the use of technology in schools, particularly those schools with financial needs. The Universal Service program for schools and libraries, better known as the **E-rate,** is a federal program that provides discounts on telecommunications and Internet technologies to elementary and secondary schools and public libraries. Congress authorized the E-rate discount program as part of the Telecommunications Act of 1996 and created a fund of some $2 billion (Palchick & Stewart, 2005). The idea was to provide schoolchildren and library users with affordable access to the Internet, distance learning, and other telecommunications-based learning technologies. The program provides discounts ranging between 20 and 90 percent, with the poorest schools and libraries receiving the highest discounts. The discounts apply to Internet, telecommunications, and internal connections services. Thousands of libraries and schools, from every state in the nation, have participated in this program.

Much of schooling is controlled and funded by state education authorities. They make many of the decisions regarding the availability and use of technology in classrooms. States are spending more and more on powerful new data-management systems to help them keep up with the reporting requirements and student achievement goals of No Child Left Behind. Consequently, they are de-emphasizing the purchase of personal computers and learning software for classroom use.

"States are betting the farm on new data-management systems in hopes of keeping up with No Child Left Behind," said Virginia B. Edwards, the editor and publisher of *Education Week* and of the technology report. "But it remains to be seen whether these investments will have a greater effect on student achievement than investments in instructional software and hardware." (Bushweller, 2005, p. 11)

States may have specific criteria for evaluating computer software, audiovisual materials, CD-ROM-based reference databases, websites, and print materials. States and school districts may also help teachers with the challenging task of selecting appropriate online resources by

STaR Indicators	Students per Computer Connected to the Internet	Technical Support	Percent of Instructional Rooms and Administrative Offices Connected to the Internet	Quality of School's Connection to the Internet	Use and Availability of Other Forms of Hardware and Technology
EARLY Tech	More than 10	Takes several days	More than 25%	Dial-up access on some computers	VCRs, cable TV, projection devices, calculators
DEVELOPING Tech	10 or less	Takes place next day	50% or more	Direct connectivity of campus and in some classrooms	VCRs, cable TV, telephones, voicemail, projection devices, digital cameras, calculators
ADVANCED Tech	5 or less	Takes place same day	75% or more	Direct connectivity in most classrooms Adequate bandwidth	Wide variety of VCRs, cable TV, telephones, voicemail, random-access video, projection devices, digital cameras, scanners, portals, personal digital assistants, two-way video conferencing, calculators
TARGET Tech	1 student per instructional computer connected to the Internet	Tech support available 24/7	100% or more of all instructional rooms and administrative offices are connected	Direct connectivity in all classrooms with adequate bandwidth to prevent delays	There is broad use of a wide variety of other technologies, such as VCRs, cable TV, telephones, voicemail, random-access video, personal digital assistants, two-way video conferencing, projection devices, digital cameras, scanners, portals, calculators, thin clients, and servers.

Source: CEO Forum on Educational Technology. (June 2001). *StaR Chart: A tool for assessing school technology and readiness,* p. 18. Key building blocks for student achievement in the 21st century: Assessment, alignment, accountability, access, analysis. Washington, DC: Author.

providing one-stop access to a variety of resources, such as a statewide *digital library.* Having access to such gateway sites can save teachers much time and energy.

The combined efforts of government and business to improve U.S. students' access to technology seem to be working. Since first measured, the ratio of students to instructional computers with access to the Internet (connectivity) has improved (12.1 to 1 in 1998 as opposed to 5.1 to 1 in 2005).

Current trends in technology availability and use suggest that technology in the hands of ordinary people is democratizing the foundations of education. Technology brings opportunities for a person anywhere with a computer and a telephone line to make, acquire, interpret, and apply knowledge. But is there a price to be paid for this new freedom—besides the economical one? With increasing opportunities for people to make themselves public electronically comes the necessity of sorting the good information from the poor. The kind of quality control

Figure 13.2
School Technology and Readiness (STaR)

exercised in traditional publishing does not exist in electronic communication and publication, except in a few instances. Issues of censorship that have been settled legally and practically in traditional publishing also must be reexamined with regard to the new communication technologies. Should the creators and managers of the Internet censor materials? Should school leaders control what is appropriate and inappropriate for young people to read, see, and hear online? Who will decide? Could the Internet have a negative effect on education?

Technology will be a key aspect of the educational system in years to come. By its very nature, technology forces people to look forward, to anticipate not only what is important at the moment but also what is likely to be important later. When teachers consider how technology might be used to collaborate on their own professional development, they can get a sense of what their students will need to know and be able to do if they are to live successfully in the future.

How Are Small Schools Transforming Teaching and Learning?

The Bill & Melinda Gates Foundation has made $2.2 billion grants to education in the past five years, about $650 million of which has gone to create smaller, more personalized high schools. Bill Gates is driven by the idea that today's large high schools simply cannot educate young people for life in today's and tomorrow's world. What we need, he argues, are smaller schools where individual young people do not disappear from view.

The Gates Foundation grants have gone to both cities and states from New York to California and many places in between. The foundation has also supported other foundations and nonprofit groups who themselves have programs aimed at creating smaller, more personally responsive schools ("Major Gates Foundation Grants," 2005).

There is a good deal of logical appeal to the idea of creating smaller schools. Such schools should facilitate greater personalization, more adult accountability, and better connections among schools, families, community organizations, and colleges and universities, than do larger schools. As the movement toward smaller schools has advanced, however, a new set of challenges has emerged.

Myatt (2005) observed that to start a new small school from scratch is not the same as converting a large school into smaller units. He described nine "friction points" that inhibit the movement of large schools toward smaller learning communities.

1. *Facilitating teacher talk.* As schools are converted to smaller learning communities, teachers will be asked to make more complicated decisions. They will need time to talk to each other.
2. *Challenging the cultural glue.* Large schools have identities—the winning athletic team, the school that performs Broadway musicals, and so forth. Change does not happen easily when community schools have strong identities.
3. *Horizontal structures, short-lived relationships.* The energy and goodwill expended in helping students learn to function in smaller, more challenging high school environments can be wasted when we repeatedly introduce them to unconnected sequences of teachers, schedules, subject matter, and fellow students.
4. *Reprogramming our special populations.* Advocates of small schools must take special care not to segregate limited-English-speakers and students with special needs in efforts to create smaller communities.
5. *Reconsidering the guidance model.* With smaller high schools taking greater responsibility for the social and emotional lives of their students, the traditional "guidance counselor" model may not work—the load may be too great.
6. *Prisoners of the infrastructure.* Old structures may not lend themselves to smaller learning communities. Negotiating schedules for the science classrooms, technology labs, or the nine-hundred-seat auditorium can be a challenge when you have three hundred students.
7. *Too much curriculum, too little time.* Can small schools offer a broad curriculum? Is it reasonable, for example, to expect a math department of four teachers to offer a dozen levels of math courses to fit the needs of students?

8. *Cohort thinking versus human nature.* The developmental continuum for high school students is at least as great as it is for young children. Can teachers take high school students wherever they find them and move them forward developmentally and academically?
9. *Public engagement cannot be an add-on.* Timing is important. Advocates of small schools must capture the hearts and minds of people involved before those people become resisters or bystanders.

Targeting Students at Risk

Collaborative networks have been especially helpful for at-risk students. Many programs operate across the country and sometimes around the world; they offer specially designed curricula, innovative teaching methods, and specific ways to get parents and the community involved in schools and students' lives.

Since the 1970s, James B. Comer, professor of child psychiatry at Yale University, and his colleagues have been working with teachers, principals, parents, and community members to help children at risk beat the odds and succeed. Comer uses a collaborative process to create programs that foster child development. He calls the process the School Development Program. His approach is a form of site-based management, in which teams of professionals engage in "no-fault problem solving" and "consensual or collaborative decision making." In other words, people do not blame one another for problems; they work together to solve them.

Comer's School Development Program has transformed some of the toughest schools in the nation. His recipe for success contains curricular, organizational, and interpersonal ingredients.

> The Comer schools require new structures, new procedures, new curriculums and new responsibilities. But these new arrangements are installed primarily to facilitate new relationships between children and the adults responsible for them.
>
> Curriculum reform, new governance models, stiffer tests for students and teachers may be fine, but there's no magic in them. The magic is in a culture that supports child and adolescent development, and that can happen only through relationships. (Raspberry, 2005, A15)

Collaborative networks also are transforming teaching and learning for at-risk students in U.S. high schools. In 1984 Theodore Sizer of Brown University organized the **Coalition of Essential Schools** (CES) with nine member schools. Sizer's intent was to build and maintain

Collaborative networks such as the School Development Program are effective in some of the country's toughest inner-city schools.

Figure 13.3
Principles of Essential Schools
If you were asked to rank by importance the attributes of an Essential School listed here, what would be your top two or three?

The Essential School should

✓ focus on helping young people learn to use their minds;

✓ have a simple mission requiring students to master essential skills and knowledge;

✓ help all students strive for the same goals, but vary means according to students' needs;

✓ personalize teaching and learning;

✓ be guided by the metaphor of student as worker, not teacher as deliverer of instruction;

✓ prepare students to meet education standards and assess teaching and learning using multiple forms of evidence;

✓ set a tone that communicates expectations, trust, and decency; use incentives; and encourage parents to collaborate;

✓ help staff think of themselves first as generalists and next as specialists;

✓ provide for teaching loads of no more than 80 students at the high school and middle school levels and 20 or fewer on the elementary level; planning time, competitive salaries, and per pupil costs of no more than 10 percent above traditional schools; and

✓ demonstrate nondiscriminatory and inclusive policies, practices, and pedagogy.

Source: The CES Benchmarks (2000). Available online at http://www.essentialschools.org/.

viable networks of parents, students, and educators who could transform high schools into better places to teach and learn. Each school defines for itself what constitutes a good school, but participating schools abide by the nine common principles shown in Figure 13.3.

One challenge for Essential Schools is to link or integrate everything from curricula to people, and cross-discipline curriculum is a strong theme of the program. Their motto is "less is more." Therefore, high school teachers in the Essential Schools program are encouraged to think about reducing lessons from their own discipline specialties to the essentials and linking instruction among the disciplines. Coalition members try to adopt common themes or align similar classes and then combine the content of two or more classes into a single course of study. For instance, a theme such as "The Growth of Capitalism in Nineteenth-Century America" would be explored by studying history, literature, government, and the arts from the time period in a single class.

Being a collaborative network, the involvement of parents and community members is a key factor in the success of Essential Schools. Strategies for encouraging their involvement include sponsoring evening study groups in which adults explore the same educational issues that the students explore, holding public exhibitions of student work, paying parents to be classroom aides, organizing parent advisory groups, holding small-group sessions with the principal, publishing a newsletter, encouraging the local newspaper to cover educational issues, and so forth.

Success for All is another type of collaborative network for schools. Founded by Robert Slavin and Nancy Madden at Johns Hopkins University, the Success for All Foundation seeks to help all students achieve at the highest levels. The foundation's number one priority is the education of disadvantaged and at-risk students in pre-K through grade eight.

The credo of Success for All is that all children can learn, but not necessarily in the same way. Teachers must be prepared to implement a range of strategies to reach individual students. The school is a key unit. It must be committed to providing services to help children meet expectations. Schools' effects on students can be magnified by families. The intent is to create and maintain a web of services for young people at school and at home. Education must be guided by research. The educational products and practices that will be of greatest value will be those that have withstood rigorous evaluation.

A carefully conducted study of thirty-eight schools that use the Success for All improvement program found that students read better after two years in the program and outperformed students in regular classrooms by up to half a school year (Viadero, 2005).

After one year, the researchers found, kindergartners and first-graders in Success for All were scoring two months ahead of their peers in the comparison group on tests measuring their ability to decode words. The two groups were still evenly matched, though, on other reading skill measures.

At the end of two years, the Success for All students' advantage had increased and spread. In word decoding, the Success for All pupils outperformed their peers by 4.7 additional months of schooling. They scored 1.3 months ahead of the control students on tests measuring their understanding of written passages and 1.7 months ahead on word identification.

Increasing Parental Involvement

Children's futures are linked to their parents. It is essential that teachers look for opportunities to involve parents in schooling. When parents take an interest in their children's progress— holding high but reasonable expectations for their children's performance and meeting their basic needs—good things happen: Students' school attendance, self-esteem, achievement, and prospects for living successful, productive lives all increase. It would be hard to overestimate the significance of the role parents play in their children's chances for success in school and in life.

Too often, however, it is difficult to meet and work with the parents and guardians of the children most in need of a strong home–school support network—single parents, those working at more than one job, those pulled in so many directions by so many problems that they are struggling merely to survive. In reality, many single and overly stressed parents are children themselves. Despite the small number of glowing exceptions, far too many of these young parents fail in school, relegating themselves and their children to a bleak future. The majority of teens who start families before they reach the age of eighteen do not complete high school. Children of teenage parents often perform more poorly in school than other students and are half again as likely to repeat a grade.

Involving immigrant parents can be an especially challenging task. Schools and districts in high-immigration areas of the country, including Arizona, Texas, Illinois, Virginia, and Idaho, are beginning to offer outreach programs to help immigrant parents understand what their children are learning. The efforts range from simple orientation packets to full-fledged learning centers. All are based on the assumption that involved parents make for better students.

> When Eun Young Lee emigrated from Korea a little more than two years ago, she landed on a foreign planet. Along with all the other strangeness she found in the United States, her son's new school—St. John's Lane Elementary, in Ellicott City, Maryland—practiced odd customs. Not only did teachers speak an unfamiliar language and let her son play between lessons; they also invited and even expected her to openly question them about his education. Lee says she felt isolated and afraid whenever she had to set foot on school grounds.
>
> But that feeling changed this past fall, when she attended an eight-week program at St. John's called Parent and Child Adult ESOL. PACE helped her understand what and how her son learns in his 4th grade class and encouraged her to learn English . . . through an interpreter. (Moawa, 2005, p. 13)

Figure 13.4 illustrates some of the ways teachers might overcome barriers that can inhibit parent involvement.

Enhancing Relationships among Educators

One of the most important benefits of collaborative networks is that they bring educators into contact with one another for purposes of professional development and exchange of ideas. Working in cooperative settings helps both students and educators themselves. Educators are

- If parents do not speak English, arrange for an interpreter at meetings and conferences. Have printed materials sent home to parents translated—English on one side, the parents' language on the back.
- For parents who lack the ability to read, communicate information by way of phone calls or home visits. One-on-one meetings and other personal contacts are important. Check to see if your school system has a home–school coordinator who can assist you in efforts to connect with parents who are hard to reach.
- Learn about the backgrounds of students and find out about ways to communicate with diverse people.
- To build parent's trust in schools, encourage them to get involved in special activities like PTA and school outings. Also encourage them to visit the school, observe classes, and provide feedback. Make them feel welcome in your classroom.
- Plan one or more social events that allow teachers, administrators, and parents to interact on a social basis.
- Conduct conferences focusing on student performance at least twice a year, with follow-up as needed. Make meeting times flexible, perhaps scheduling conferences in the evenings or early mornings before school.
- Hold parent–teacher conferences at community centers or other off-campus locations that are near parents' homes.
- Make your first communication with parents a positive one. Let them know what their child is doing well or how much you are enjoying working with their child before calling to talk about misbehavior or poor performance.
- Seek out opportunities for professional development and training in parent involvement.

Sources: National PTA. (1998). National standards for parent/family involvement programs—Standard 1: Communication. Available online: www.pta.org/.

Figure 13.4 Overcoming Barriers to Parent Involvement

able to ask questions, receive answers, discuss current issues, exchange personal experiences, and otherwise support one another. The benefits of these networks are then taken back to the classroom.

One visible attempt to encourage education professionals to work together on relevant tasks has been the concept of the **professional development school,** or PDS. A PDS is a college–school partnership that stimulates cooperation among professors, teachers, student teachers, and pupils. A professional development school is a place where theory, research, and practice mix at the precollege and in-service levels. Thus, reform is cultivated in colleges as well as schools.

Collaborative networks for teachers also focus on content areas and mutual professional development through collegial activities. Many teachers enter the profession and stay because of their intellectual interest in the subject matter. For instance, the allure of the stage and the power of theater have attracted and sustained more than a few English teachers through the years. The National Council of Teachers of English (NCTE) serves as a professional touchstone for many of them. The NCTE's programs and publications help unite English teachers by providing opportunities for professional involvement and outlets for the expression of creative energies. Science and social studies teachers, math and physical education teachers, technologists and school counselors, and teachers in other fields connect to one another through their professional associations.

Without support, of course, even the best ideas rarely take hold. The give and take of colleagues who share a commitment to deal openly with difficult issues contributes to a climate that is hospitable to educational growth and development. As concern for education increases around the world, more and more collaborative networks for purposes of education that involve educators, parents, and students are forming all the time. Fortunately, through the power of the Internet and other new and evolving technologies, these networks can reach, involve, and help more people than ever imagined.

For example, CaseNEX (www.casenex.com) offers opportunities for teachers to work collaboratively on common problems of teaching and learning. Like lawyers, business people, and physicians, teachers analyze cases that describe real-life situations in classrooms. The cases they examine are multimedia representations of classrooms in schools around the world. Using both synchronous (real time) and asynchronous (any time) tools, teachers work collaboratively to identify problems and opportunities for intervention. They also examine research on teaching, forecast actions they might take if they were in a similar situation, and speculate on the possible consequences of actions by explaining how they and others might judge the effectiveness of their proposed actions.

How Can Professional Educators Prepare for the Future?

So much to know, so much to do. It is natural for educators to feel overwhelmed by the complexity and pace of our rapidly changing world, knowing that they have to make sense of it for themselves as well as prepare future generations. Faced with the diversity of interests that contend for attention in public education, it would be easy to either leap headfirst or be paralyzed with indecision. As professionals, educators distinguish themselves from nonprofessionals in two important ways: by what they know and by what they know how to do. To help prepare for the future, teachers use technology and participate in collaborative networks. By doing so, they build their store of knowledge and refine their repertoire of skills (see Figure 13.5). **Can collaborative networks contribute to the professionalization of teaching?**

Using Professional Knowledge

Both informal and formal sources of knowledge inform the practice of teaching. The formal knowledge base of a profession exists in books, periodicals, and other writings. This type of knowledge serves as a foundation for teacher education programs, as a basis for licensure and certification examinations, and as a benchmark by which teachers assess their own practices. The informal knowledge base exists in the minds and hearts of those who practice the profession and is derived from their experiences on the job, as well as their beliefs, values, and personal standards. For many teachers this personal source of knowledge is rich and immediately applicable to classroom life.

The formal knowledge base for teaching consists of theories about what constitutes effective teaching and the results of empirical research. Educational theories attempt to explain how teaching and learning occur, while research provides the results of observations or experiments that help to explain relationships between teaching and learning. These two kinds of knowledge often complement each other. The most useful theories and research for educators explain what teachers should do and why.

Why is formal research so important to educators? Researcher Harold Mitzel (1960) gave educators a way to think and talk about the knowledge underlying our field so we could apply it and participate in its development. Mitzel depicted a set of four instructional variables we can use to discuss teaching and learning as interrelated activities. Those variables are teacher characteristics, teaching processes, student products, and instructional contexts. By breaking down the idea of education into these four variables, we are able to see how they interact and affect one another to produce an educational experience.

Teachers' characteristics precede their teaching acts; for example, teachers' personalities and background knowledge influence how they approach the learning environment. Teaching process variables are demonstrated by teachers during a lesson—the questions they ask, the feedback they provide, and the like. Student product variables are student outcomes measured by tests, demonstrations, applications of knowledge, and other indications of learning. Instructional context variables are factors both inside and outside the classroom that influence teaching and learning, such as students' characteristics, school leadership, money spent on education, and children's home environments. The relationships among these variables are shown in Figure 13.6.

Jere Brophy (1999), a researcher and professor at Michigan State University, offered the most recent and comprehensive critique of research on effective teaching. In doing so, he

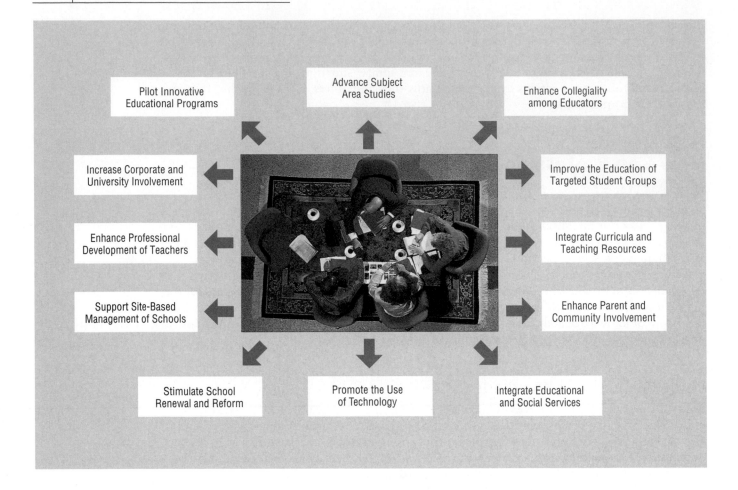

Figure 13.5
Uses of Collaborative Networks

People are more likely to collaborate when they have reasons to do so and opportunities for working together. What barriers, other than time and opportunity, might restrict collaboration among teachers? What other factors might enhance the likelihood of collaboration?

described twelve principles that can guide teachers' work. The research support for these principles comes from studies of relationships between classroom processes and student outcomes (typically gains in standardized achievement tests). Some principles are based on logic. Brophy also relied in part on emerging theories of teaching and learning (e.g., sociocultural, social constructivist) and on standards stated by organizations representing the major school subjects. Brophy's effective teaching principles appear in Figure 13.7.

Current research supports earlier indications of how important teachers are when it comes to stimulating student learning (Good & Brophy, 2003). This new research also focuses on the role of the student in the education process and recognizes that students do not passively receive or copy input from teachers. Instead, they make sense of it and relate it to what they already know (or think they know) about the topic.

The teachers best prepared to face the future, though, possess practical knowledge of teaching, as well as empirical and theoretical knowledge. Practical knowledge is constructed from teachers' own experiences. Teachers have always constructed their own knowledge by learning and experiencing what it takes to work with others to help them learn. In many ways, teachers' practical knowledge is far ahead of theory and research, because it comes from the classroom application of the theory and research we learn. It is through classroom application of theory and research that we learn for ourselves what really works and what does not. For instance, we might learn from theory and research that a specific style of classroom management is effective. We might learn from classroom application, however, that the management style works well for seventh-grade students, but not at all for ninth-graders.

Although some people believe being a teacher is something one can learn wholly on the job, practical knowledge and formal knowledge go hand in hand—one without the other is

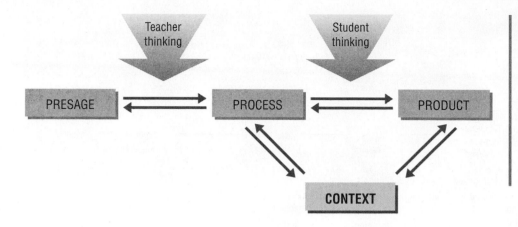

Figure 13.6
Model for Describing Research on Teaching
Research on teaching cannot be conducted without the help and cooperation of lots of people—teachers, students, parents, administrators. What factors might influence your willingness to participate in research studies either as an investigator or as the focus of investigation?

insufficient. The importance of formal knowledge of teaching and learning cannot be overestimated. Empirical investigation helps separate fact from fiction and, in doing so, opens people's minds. Turning that formal knowledge into practical knowledge through classroom application requires testing theories and staying in touch with current situations in education. The process of putting ideas to work in the classroom helps fine-tune theories and suggests new paths for investigation. Knowledge, whether practical or formal, changes, evolves, and advances. As in medical research, research in education advances our knowledge.

Keeping track of progress can be a difficult process. Concept maps can be useful for this endeavor; they are ways of organizing relationships among ideas. For example, when Caroline

1. *A supportive classroom climate.* Students learn best within cohesive and caring learning communities.
2. *Opportunity to learn.* Students learn more when most of the available time is allocated to curriculum-related activities and the classroom management system emphasizes maintaining their engagement in those activities.
3. *Curricular alignment.* All components of the curriculum are aligned to create a cohesive program for accomplishing instructional purposes and goals.
4. *Establishing learning orientations.* Teachers can prepare students for learning by providing an initial structure to clarify intended outcomes and cue desired learning strategies.
5. *Coherent content.* To facilitate meaningful learning and retention, content is explained clearly and developed with emphasis on its structure and connections.
6. *Thoughtful discourse.* Questions are planned to engage students in sustained discourse structured around powerful ideas.
7. *Practice and application activities.* Students need sufficient opportunities to practice and apply what they are learning, and to receive improvement-oriented feedback.
8. *Scaffolding students task engagement.* The teacher provides whatever assistance students need to enable them to engage in learning activities productively.
9. *Strategy teaching.* The teacher models and instructs students in learning and self-regulation strategies.
10. *Cooperative learning.* Students often benefit from working in pairs or small groups to construct understandings or help one another master skills.
11. *Goal-oriented assessment.* The teacher uses a variety of formal and informal assessment methods to monitor progress towards learning goals.
12. *Achievement expectations.* The teacher establishes and follows through on appropriate expectations for learning outcomes.

Source: Brophy, J. (1999). *Teaching.* Geneva, Switzerland: International Academy of Education, International Bureau of Education, UNESCO.

Figure 13.7
Brophy's Effective Teaching Principles

Figure 13.8
Caroline's Concept
Map of Teacher
Planning
What thoughts about
planning seemed
most important to this
teacher?

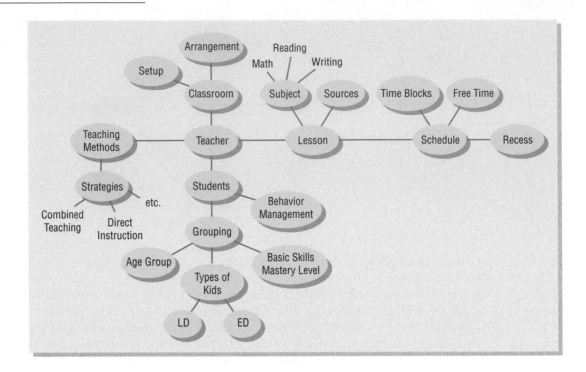

created her own concept maps of "teacher planning" at the beginning and again at the end of a two-semester course, they turned out to be very different, because her thinking had changed over time. Her second concept map of teacher planning appears in Figure 13.8. Caroline said this about her maps and her thinking:

> My initial reflections did not touch on teacher–parent interactions or on teacher–colleague interactions. In my end-of-year map, however, I devoted an entire section to communication with others. I believe the curriculum this past year, along with teacher training courses and student teaching, made me realize how vital these relationships are. I believe effective teachers work at reaching out to colleagues, gaining support from administrators, creating support systems, and communicating with parents from the start, not just after a problem has arisen.
>
> Social skills are also new items on my final map. The extent to which they should be addressed depends on the students, the school, and the community. Over the course of the year, it has become increasingly clear how necessary it is for teachers to explicitly teach what is appropriate behavior, for example, how to show respect or how to respond to aggression. (personal communication, 2004)

With time and experience, good teachers learn how to apply their professional knowledge differently with different students. Jere Brophy and Mary McCaslin (1992) underscored the importance of teaching to individual students' needs in a series of studies they did on teachers with problem students (students exhibiting unsatisfactory achievement, personal adjustment, or classroom behavior). Teachers who had been identified by their principals as less successful in dealing with problem students described those students as underachievers, low achievers, aggressive, defiant, distractible, immature, shy, or rejected by peers. Typically, successful teachers demonstrated more willingness to become personally involved with students, showed more confidence in their own abilities to help the students improve their behaviors, and were better able to describe how to help students change their behavior and increase their learning.

Teachers' need for professional knowledge is also closely connected to their disciplines. It is not enough to possess general teaching knowledge at the expense of content knowledge, any more than it is to know the content and be ignorant of teaching practice. To teach mathematics successfully, for example, teachers must master the subject matter, but they must also possess the teaching knowledge necessary for creating environments in which students can learn mathematics. This blending of content knowledge and teaching knowledge has been called **pedagogical content knowledge** (Shulman, 1986).

The influences of teachers and teaching in children's lives are a matter of national importance. The knowledge teachers acquire is key to determining whether these influences will help or hinder students. Being knowledgeable is one of the best assets a teacher can possess.

Reflecting on Professional Practice

Great teachers become great by continuing to learn while on the job. Those who can reflect intelligently on their own practices can learn from what they do. They have the greatest chance of continuing to progress as teachers. In addition, these teachers are best prepared to help other teachers, especially new ones, become great teachers. The following five steps of professional practice promote such professional behavior:

1. In any field, professionals *perceive* problems and opportunities—they are mentally alert to what is going on around them.
2. Professionals also can articulate their *values* in relation to the values of others they work with and serve. Peoples' values help determine whether professionals' actions will be accepted or rejected.
3. Professionals possess some specialized knowledge that nonprofessionals do not. Professional educators *know* their content, and they know how to communicate in ways that students will understand and accept. Exceptionally talented teachers, both experienced and novice, also know when they need to know more.
4. Professionals *act* on the basis of their perceptions, values, and knowledge. They continually apply their knowledge and demonstrate their skills in ways that nonprofessionals cannot.
5. Professionals *evaluate* their actions to determine their effectiveness and to plan for the future. People who can reflect intelligently on their practice—and who enjoy doing important work as best they can—turn jobs into careers.

Teachers are students, too, and the learning never stops. Even the best among us do not always know how or why we are successful. With experience, we grow accustomed to not having all the answers all the time. We learn to rely on the best information available, as well as information acquired from successful and unsuccessful practice. No matter how professionally capable or personally adept we become, we will never single-handedly teach our students all that they need to know and all they will need to be able to do. Nor can we anticipate all the problems students will face. We must learn to work together with educators, parents, community members, and students to maximize our effects. The most important people with whom we must collaborate are students. By working together we model for students what we hope they in turn will model for others. We also transmit a set of democratic values that form the foundation of our society.

The best teachers stretch themselves time and again to be creative and technically proficient; they know they can call on their abilities when the need arises. They are not afraid to fail, because they have done that too and have lived to teach and learn another day. A good teacher, like a good student, gains power from doing the work.

Case Perspectives

Think back to the case that opened this chapter. Here are Janeeta's thoughts, as well as those of a second candidate faced with the same questions. These comments are designed to provide some context for your own thoughts about these questions.

CANDIDATE JANEETA MORRIS SHARES HER GREATEST FEARS AND HOPES.   I have always been terrified of public speaking. How can a teacher be afraid to speak in front of others? I don't have the slightest idea. It makes no sense. I remind myself of the country-western star Mel Tillis. He sings like an angel, but he stutters so badly when he tries to talk that he is nearly unable to communicate.

I was fine during student teaching. But if I have to stand and deliver even brief comments to an audience of adults, I freeze. When I told my husband about it, he tried to help me imagine the worst-case scenario. "Even if things go badly," he asked, "how bad could it be?"

That prompted me to imagine myself in the auditorium on Parents' Night, jaw locking, eyes rolling back in my head as I fainted while falling sideways cracking the superintendent on top of his head with my jaw, knocking him senseless. How bad could it be, indeed!

I thanked my husband—and then enrolled in a public speaking course. That experience really helped me conquer my fears.

My legacy? I do not have a disability, but I am different from other people in some significant ways—one of the most important being my willingness to take on difficult personal challenges. I want more than anything else to help others do the same.

CANDIDATE LEONA FEDERICK REFLECTS ON HER FEARS AND HER LEGACY.   I'm very excited about being out of school. I can't wait to try the things I have learned. Maybe I shouldn't say so, but I'm excited about getting a real salary too. People say that teaching

does not pay very much, but it seems like a lot to me compared to the kinds of jobs I have always had.

It is difficult to say what frightens me most. I have never been afraid of hard work. My fiancé says that is what worries him most—not the hard work but the fact that I do not shy away from it. I have a tendency to overdo things—work too much, try too hard. My mother says that the definition of a perfectionist is a person who takes pains . . . and gives them to others. I am like her in that regard. We both find it difficult to let go at the end of the day.

When I think about what the new job will require of me, I really am concerned about the demands. I must think about my students, the curriculum, parents, and so forth and so on. Will I still have time in the day to have a life of my own? I want to be a great teacher, but I want to get married, have my own children, and spend time with them. I don't want to be so tired and consumed by teaching that I have no energy to be a good mother. Maybe the fact that I will have the same schedule as my children will help.

I would like to be remembered as someone who did her best and who helped others do the same. The old adage about leaving the world better than you found it really works for me. I also want to be remembered as a fun-loving person, not as a worry-wart. When I have a full-time job, I'm going to try to keep taking classes. I want to learn a new language and travel. Maybe I will learn to row as part of team. I'm going to take Pilates too. There are lots of things I still want to learn.

Questions for Reflection: How would you answer the questions Yolanda Sanborne and her teachers asked? What is your greatest fear about teaching? What might you do now to help conquer it? How would you like to be remembered as a teacher? What might you do now—and in the years to come—to ensure that your legacy is what you'd like it to be? ▪

Summary

Teachers of the twenty-first century will witness the evolution of their professional roles. They will lead their nation's efforts to set common expectations for academic success and to protect and advance the collective character of our increasingly diverse society.

Technology will figure prominently in teaching and learning in the years ahead. Teachers will use technology in many forms to plan, teach, and evaluate their student's work and, by implication, their own work. Technology will reinforce the ideas that more and better things happen when people work together to accomplish a common goal. Collaborative networks—sometimes technologically driven, sometimes not—will be increasingly popular.

The best teachers will be those who have the foundational preparation to continue learning on the job. These same teachers will get out of bed every morning with the anticipation of doing important work and doing it better than it has ever been done before. The great ones will relish the challenge of professional practice and savor the sweet success of a job well done.

TERMS AND CONCEPTS

asynchronous communication
character education
chat
Coalition of Essential Schools
comprehensive assessment
digital divide
distance learning
E-rate
electronic mail (e-mail)
gender sensitivity training
home page
hypermedia
Internet

listserv
National Assessment of Educational Progress (NAEP)
newsgroups
pedagogical content knowledge
professional development school (PDS)
service learning
Success for All
synchronous communication
videoconferencing
Web browser
website
World Wide Web

REFLECTIVE ACTIVITY: TURNING CLASSROOMS OVER TO INTERNS

Reflective practice is an essential part of good teaching. Reflection is a process that includes making thoughtful decisions, understanding and articulating value structures, acting from knowledge, evaluating your actions and their effects, and sharing your reflections with colleagues. After reading the following scenario, respond to the questions below. The scenario reflects the INTASC Principle and Disposition at the end of this activity.

In 2002 the Kansas City, Missouri, public schools offered nine student teachers two-year full-time teaching contracts in an attempt to address the state's worsening teacher shortage. The interns were slated to graduate from state universities in December 2002.

The arrangement had the backing of the Missouri education department, and interns were offered plenty of support inside and outside the classroom. Interns received full-time pay for the two years, and they all lived rent-free the first year in the same apartment building—some even shared apartments.

Experienced teachers worked with pairs of interns, providing advice on such topics as lesson design and delivery, discipline, classroom management, and communication with parents. Faculty members from the interns' universities observed the interns' classrooms at least once a week and provided regular group and individual feedback (Manzo, 2002).

Decide 1. Visit the website for the federal No Child Left Behind Act (www.nochildleftbehind.gov/). How does Kansas City's arrangement square with federal guidelines for teacher preparation?

Perceive and Value 2. What might the student teachers in this program find advantageous and disadvantageous about the intern program? How might parents view the program? How about Missouri's Education Association (the state affiliate of the NEA)?

Know and Act 3. What are some of the strategies other school districts have employed to attract and retain beginning teachers? How do these efforts compare to the intern program in Kansas City? In which of these programs might you like to enroll? Why?

Evaluate 4. What factors should the school system consider when determining whether to expand its intern program?

Discuss 5. How might this program benefit the experienced teachers who act as mentors to the interns?

INTASC Principle 9

The teacher is a reflective practitioner who continually evaluates the effects of his/her choices and actions on others (students, parents, and other professionals in the learning community) and who actively seeks out opportunities to grow professionally.

Disposition

The teacher seeks out professional literature, colleagues, and other resources to support his/her own development as a learner and a teacher. (Interstate New Teacher Assessment and Support Consortium, 1992)

ADDITIONAL READINGS

Egbert, J. (2009). *Supporting learning with technology: Essentials of classroom practice.* Boston: Allyn & Bacon.

Noddings, N. (2006). *Critical lessons: What our schools might teach but do not.* New York, NY: Cambridge University Press.

Rose, L. C., & Gallup, A. M. (2006, September). The 38th annual Phi Delta Kappa/Gallup poll of the public's attitudes toward the public schools. *Phi Delta Kappan, 84*(1), 41–56.

Wallis, C., & Steptoe, S. (2006). How to bring our schools out of the 20th century. *Time, 168*(25), 50–56.

Zucker, A., Kozma, R., & Dede, C. (2004). *The virtual high school: Teaching Generation V.* New York: Teachers College Press.

WEB RESOURCES

www.ed.gov/teachers/how/tech/international/index.html
The Teacher's Guide to International Collaboration on the Internet provides resources for cross-cultural interaction and project work.

http://npin.org/
The National Parent Information Network (NPIN) provides access to research-based information about the process of parenting and about family involvement in education.

http://www.nnerpartnerships.org/
The National Network for Educational Renewal is an independent, nonprofit corporation that conducts professional development programs on a wide range of educational issues. They bring together K–12, college of education, and arts and sciences faculty to advance teaching and learning.

www.pta.org/
The National PTA is the largest volunteer child advocacy organization in the United States. Parents, teachers, and administrators who visit the PTA's website can find information about productive ways they can work together to promote the welfare of children.

http://www.pbs.org/teachers/
The PBS Teachers website provides digital media resources that can be used to enhance instruction.

Developing a Professional Portfolio

PREPARING YOUR RÉSUMÉ

The most important element of your portfolio is your résumé. When writing letters of inquiry or application, it is common practice to include a copy of your résumé, which is a synopsis of your professional life. As such, your résumé reflects your work and educational history. Your résumé is also a plan for your future. You build it through experience with attention to what will make you a more complete professional.

Although you can construct a résumé in a variety of ways in terms of content and design, there are some common expectations. As you can see in the following example, a résumé opens with personal contact information.

Nakisha Barnes
7715 Laredo Avenue
Benzinger, AZ 90220
(508) 475-0912
nbarnes@acme.com

Your contact information is often followed by your educational history.

Education	Major area	Degree
Colorado State Univ.	Elementary Education	Bachelor of Arts, 2008

Next, you can include your past work experience, which is relevant to your future employment.

Work Experience:

2005–2007:	**Cashier, Colorado State University Bookstore; responsible for sales and bookkeeping.**
2004–2005:	**(summers): Lifeguard, Henley Swimming Pool, Greeley, CO; responsible for pool supervision and teaching beginning swimming class.**
2002–2004:	**Wait staff, Donuts and More, Shelby, AZ; responsible for customer orders and shop cleanliness.**

You can also include your volunteer work; it shows interest in and compassion for others.

Volunteer Experience:

2004–2005:	**Leader of Student Guides, Colorado Childrens Museum**
2006–2007:	**Reader, Center for the Visually Impaired**

Your basic certification and add-on endorsements demonstrate your qualifications.

Certification (or License): Elementary teaching (K–6) with endorsements in music and physical education.

List your interests to communicate balance and richness beyond your professional capabilities.

Special Interests: Piano, skiing, swimming, reading, and travel.

Finally, you will need to ask people to serve as references. You need people who can comment on your professional capabilities and your character.

References:

Mrs. Leona Tatum (The supervising teacher with whom I worked in student teaching) Contact information, using her title, school address, telephone number, and e-mail address.

Dr. Irving Shapiro (Director of Colorado Children's Museum) Contact information, including his business address, telephone number, and e-mail address.

Rev. Donald Spooner (minister of my local church) Contact information, including his business address, telephone number, and e-mail address.

You can also include information in the categories of leadership positions, memberships in clubs and honor societies, and supervised field experiences.

Assume for a moment that you are reading Nakisha's résumé to hire her for a teaching position. What patterns do you see in her record? What items do you think are most important and least important? Why?

If your college or university has a career counselor or career services (placement) office, they often give workshops on writing résumés. You should attend these workshops and ask for advice. Be sure to save a digital copy of your résumé. It is an active document that will change with each new experience.

Online Activity
Teaching Overseas

Have you ever considered teaching overseas? The Association for the Advancement of International Education (AAIE) exists for the purpose of encouraging such thinking and supporting those who undertake the challenge. The organization has members teaching all over the world.

Visit the AAIE website (www.aaie.org) to learn about the kinds of services the organization provides. Where is AAIE's next conference? What school-to-school projects does the organization promote that link schools around the world? Who is in the AAIE Hall of Fame, and why are they there? When and where is the next recruitment fair?

Pick a country in which you might like to teach. Why do you want to teach there? Do you have any idea of what it would be like to teach in this country? Check the Regional Associations linked to the AAIE home page. Contact the people listed for more information on your countries of interest.

accreditation: review and approval of education programs by outside experts.

Adoption and Safe Families Act of 1997: act of Congress designed to enhance the services and extend the scope of child welfare agencies.

aesthetics: branch of philosophy concerned with beauty.

alternative licensure: granting of approval to teach to individuals who have not participated in a traditional, state-approved teacher education program.

alternative school: any school operating within the public school system that has programs addressing the specific needs or interests of targeted student groups.

American Federation of Teachers (AFT): political organization of eight hundred thousand members devoted to the advancement of educational issues and affiliated with the American Federation of Labor/Congress of Industrial Organizations (AFL/CIO). The organization has sponsored such projects as Dial-a-Teacher and Learning Line. It has also supported teacher internship programs, adopt-a-school programs, and national conferences for paraprofessionals and other school personnel.

apartheid: separation of the races.

apprenticeship: practical work experience under the supervision of skilled workers in the trades and the arts.

assessment: formal attempt to determine students' knowledge, skills, and attitudes.

assessment bias: qualities of an assessment instrument that offend or unfairly penalize students because of their gender, ethnicity, socioeconomic status, religion, or some other characteristic.

assimilation: process of educating and socializing a group to make it similar to the dominant culture.

assumption of risk: implicit responsibility assumed by people who are aware of the possible risks involved in an activity in which they voluntarily participate, thus agreeing to take their chances.

asynchronous communication: communication on the Internet that occurs at times convenient for any of the parties involved (e.g., news groups, e-mail).

at-risk students: children who are unlikely to complete high school; have failed one or more grades; are enrolled in special education classes; speak a language other than English; and/or are affected adversely by life- and health-threatening factors, such as poverty, disease, abuse and neglect, substance abuse, teenage pregnancy, and physical violence.

authentic assessment: assessment concerned less with students' recognition and recall of facts and more with students' abilities to analyze, apply, evaluate, and synthesize what they know in ways that address real-world concerns.

axiology: a branch of philosophy that seeks to determine what is of value.

behavioral objectives: objectives that describe conditions for teaching and learning, what is to be learned, and criteria for success.

behaviorism: philosophical orientation based on the belief that human behavior is determined by forces in the environment that are beyond human control rather than by the exercise of free will.

Bilingual Act of 1974: law requiring parental involvement in the planning of appropriate educational programs for children with limited English-speaking ability.

bilingual education: instruction in both English and a student's native language.

black codes: conduct codes established by southerners that allowed African Americans to hold property, to sue and be sued, and to marry, but forbade them to carry firearms, to testify in court in cases involving European Americans, or to leave their jobs.

block grant: money provided in a lump sum for several education programs in a locality.

block scheduling: organizing class schedules typically to provide longer instructional periods during the school day.

Blue-Backed Speller: Webster's *American Spelling Book,* first published in 1783.

blueprint: test specifications for the content and objectives to be assessed.

Brown v. Board of Education of Topeka, Kansas: Supreme Court case that determined that segregation of students by race is unconstitutional and that education is a right that must be available to all Americans on equal terms.

Buckley Amendment: part of the Family Educational Rights and Privacy Act that prohibits schools from releasing information about a student to third parties without parental or student permission.

Bureau of Indian Affairs (BIA): governmental agency established to, among other activities, oversee education programs for Native Americans.

career ladder: incentive program designed to acknowledge differences in the skills of teachers.

categorical grant: funding for an education program designed for a particular group and a specific purpose (e.g., bilingual education).

central office staff: superintendents and their associates and assistants.

certification: recognition by the state that a teacher has met minimum standards for competent practice.

character education: curricular approach driven by personal relevance that focuses on clarifying or unifying teaching values.

charter school: independent public school supported by state funds but freed from many regulations and run by individuals who generally have the power to hire and to fire colleagues and to budget money as they see fit.

chat: form of real-time or synchronous communication on the Internet.

Chautauqua movement: adult education movement that began in the late 1800s and led to the establishment of civic music associations, correspondence courses, lecture-study groups, youth groups, and reading circles.

chief state school officer: chief administrator of the state department of education and the head of the state board of education, sometimes referred to as the state superintendent or the commissioner of education.

Child Abuse Prevention and Treatment Act: passed by Congress in 1974 to provide financial support to states that implement programs for identification, prevention, and treatment of instances of child abuse or neglect.

Chinese Exclusion Act: legislation passed in 1882 aimed at stopping immigration.

Civil Rights Act of 1964 (Title VI): law that specifies that no one, regardless of race, color, or origin, can be discriminated against or denied participation in programs receiving federal assistance.

classroom management: collective ability of teachers and students to agree on and implement a common framework for social and academic interactions.

Coalition of Essential Schools: alternative high schools serving targeted students through school-based educational reform initiatives; based on Theodore Sizer's work.

cognitivism: philosophical orientation based on the belief that people actively construct their knowledge of the world through experience and interaction rather than through behavioral conditioning.

collective bargaining: negotiation of the professional rights and responsibilities of workers (e.g., teachers) as a group.

Committee of Fifteen: committee that addressed the curriculum of elementary schools in 1895. Its curriculum focused on "the five windows of the soul"—grammar, literature and art, mathematics, geography, and history. It believed the role of school to be an efficient transmitter of cultural heritage through a curriculum that was graded, structured, and cumulative.

Committee of Ten on Secondary School Studies: committee established by the NEA in 1892 to standardize high school curricula.

common school: tax-supported school established in colonial times to allow all boys and girls to receive three free years of education focused on reading, writing, arithmetic, and history; predecessor of public schools.

comparative negligence: situation in which teacher and student are both held liable for an injury.

compensatory education program: program that provides children from low-income families with education opportunities beyond those offered in a school's standard program to compensate for factors (e.g., teachers, curricula, time, and materials) missing in young people's lives.

comprehensive assessment: assessment that measures students' capacities for reasoning, thinking divergently, and solving problems creatively.

concept formation: method of instruction used by teachers when they want students to analyze and synthesize data to construct knowledge about a specific concept or idea.

conflict mediation: formal efforts to help students solve their differences peaceably.

constructivism: view of knowledge as constructed by individuals acting within a social context that molds knowledge but does not determine absolutely what constitutes knowledge.

content standards: description of content to be mastered.

contributory negligence: failure of a person who is injured to exercise the required standard of care for his or her own safety.

cooperative learning: teaching model that encourages heterogeneous groups of students to work together to achieve such goals as mastery of subject matter and understanding and acceptance of one another.

cosmology: study of nature and origin of the cosmos, or universe.

Council of Chief State School Officers: nonpolicy-making organization composed of leaders of state departments of elementary and secondary education in the fifty states, the District of Columbia, the Department of Defense Dependents Schools, and five U.S. extrastate jurisdictions—Virgin Islands, Puerto Rico, Northern Mariana Islands, Guam, and American Samoa.

criterion-referenced test: test by which a student's performance is judged by comparing it to some clearly defined criterion for mastering a learning task or skill. The quality of a student's performance is measured against an absolute standard.

cultural literacy: shared information or common knowledge of a culture supposedly needed to function fully in that culture.

cultural pluralism: state in which people of diverse ethnic, racial, religious, and social groups maintain autonomous participation within a common civilization.

culture: sum of the learned characteristics of a people (e.g., language, religion, social mores, artistic expression, sexual behavior), which may be tied to geographical region. *Culture* also can be used in a "micro" sense to describe more conceptually discrete groups of people—cultures within cultures, subcultures, or microcultures.

curriculum: what is taught inside and sometimes outside school.

curriculum-based assessment: benchmarks for the knowledge, skills, and attitudes students must attain to master subject matter.

curriculum map: timeline indicating approximate dates when concepts and skills will be introduced.

dame school: educational program for boys and girls run by local women in a colonial community that typically focused on rudimentary reading skills.

digital divide: socioeconomic gap between communities that have access to technology and those that do not.

direct instruction: highly structured, teacher-centered strategy that capitalizes on such behavioral techniques as modeling, feedback, and reinforcement to promote basic skill acquisition, primarily in reading and mathematics.

dismissal: removal of a probationary or tenured teacher before the completion of his or her contract.

distance learning: capacity for teachers to communicate interactively with students or with one another over long distances.

district power equalization: relationship between state and local government in which localities establish the tax rate for educational spending and the state guarantees a set amount of money proportional to local revenue.

due process of law: mandated legal procedures designed to protect the rights of individuals.

early intervention: providing care and support from the prenatal period through the first years of life to enable children to enter school ready to learn.

Education Consolidation and Improvement Act (ECIA): 1981 act of Congress that consolidated many education programs into two major programs.

Education for All Handicapped Children Act (Public Law 94–142): federal law that requires all states to provide a free and appropriate public education to children between the ages of five and eighteen with disabilities. Education is to be planned through an individualized education program (IEP) and carried out in the least restrictive environment.

electronic mail (e-mail): messages sent and received via computers.

Elementary and Secondary Education Act (ESEA) of 1965: single most comprehensive extension of federal involvement in education, which resulted in policy-making power shifting to the federal level. The act provided funds to alleviate the effects of poverty through a variety of programs. It supported school libraries, the purchase of textbooks and other instructional materials, guidance, counseling, health services, and remedial instruction. It also established research centers and laboratories to advance educational practice.

emergency licensure: licensure granted temporarily until requirements and standards required for becoming a practicing teacher are met.

English academy: school established in Philadelphia in 1749 by Benjamin Franklin that emphasized the acquisition and application of knowledge thought to be most useful to the modern man.

English as a Second Language (ESL): instructional program designed to teach English to speakers of other languages.

epistemology: branch of philosophy concerned with the nature of knowledge or how we come to know things.

e pluribus unum: Latin term meaning "one out of many."

Equal Access Act: 1984 law passed by Congress that recognizes that secondary school students are mature enough to understand that a school does not condone religion by merely allowing prayer clubs on public property.

equal educational opportunity: access to the resources, choices, and encouragement each student needs to achieve his or her fullest potential through education, regardless of race, color, national origin, gender, disability, or socioeconomic status.

equal protection clause: Section 1 of the Fourteenth Amendment, which prevents states from making or enforcing laws that abridge the privileges or immunities of citizens of the United States; deprive people of life, liberty, or property without due process of law; or deny equal protection of the laws.

E-rate: federal program that provides discounts on telecommunications and Internet technologies to elementary and secondary schools and public libraries.

essentialism: philosophical orientation that acknowledges the existence of a body of knowledge that all people must learn if they are to function effectively in society.

establishment clause: clause in the First Amendment prohibiting Congress from making laws respecting the establishment of religion or prohibiting the free exercise of religion.

ethnicity: term describing a group of people with a common tradition and a sense of identity that functions as a subgroup within the larger society; membership is largely a matter of self-identification.

Eurocentric: curriculum and/or teaching depicting Europe as the cradle of Western culture.

evaluation: interpreting and attaching value to data relevant to people, programs, teaching, and learning.

exceptional learner: a child who has a special ability or disability that sets him or her apart from other children.

existentialism: a philosophy that emphasizes the subjectivity of human experience and the importance of individual creativity and choice in a nonrational world.

explicit curriculum: curriculum contained in policy statements, manuals of procedure, instructional materials, books, and other printed matter that explicate what and how students are to learn.

extracurriculum: non-credit-bearing activities, such as debate club and cheerleading, that are over and above the required curriculum.

fiscal year: twelve-month period covered by the annual budget, often corresponding to the state's fiscal year (e.g., July 1 to June 30).

flat grant: uniform or variable grant provided by the state to the school districts.

formative assessment: evaluation conducted for the purpose of shaping, forming, and improving knowledge and performance.

for-profit school: school that does not have tax-exempt status because it is run by people to make money.

foundation program: program by which the state guarantees school districts a certain amount of money for educational expenditures and determines what proportion of that cost should be shouldered by localities.

free exercise clause: clause in the First Amendment prohibiting Congress from making laws abridging the freedom of speech or of press or the right to peaceably assemble or to petition the government for a redress of grievances.

Freedman's Bureau: government-sponsored organization established one month before the end of the Civil War to provide food, medicine, and seed to destitute southerners.

full-service school: school that attempts to meet basic needs of students by providing such things as food, clothing, showers, medical care, and family counseling.

full state funding: payment by the state of all educational expenses of school districts through a statewide tax.

gender bias: discriminatory treatment, often subtle or unconscious, that unfairly favors or disfavors individuals because they are females or because they are males.

gender sensitivity training: use of curricula that avoid sex-role stereotyping and the creation of educational opportunities for females to take advantage of all their opportunities for education.

giftedness: potential for high performance due to strengths in one or more of the following areas: general intellectual ability, specific academic aptitude, creative or productive thinking, leadership skill, ability in the visual or performing arts, and psychomotor development.

global awareness: recognition of people's connections to other countries and peoples of the world.

Head Start: first major early childhood program subsidized by the federal government; provides comprehensive services to low-income three- and four-year-olds and their families.

hidden passage: educational activities that provided slaves with the intellectual power to escape bondage and to make lives for themselves after the Civil War.

high-stakes test: test used to evaluate school performance that determines students' grade promotion, graduation, and/or access to specific fields of study.

holding power: ability to keep students in school until they receive a high school diploma or an equivalency certificate.

home page: first page of a Web document.

hornbook: instructional material used during colonial days. Letters, numerals, and other information were affixed to a piece of wood and covered with transparent material made from the horns of cattle that served as a protective layer.

humanism: philosophy that, in terms of education, calls for respect and kindness toward students and developmentally appropriate instruction in liberal arts, social conduct, and moral principles.

hypermedia: documents that consist of text and still images, as well as audio and video.

idealism: philosophy that suggests that ultimate reality lies in consciousness or reason.

implicit curriculum: unvoiced and often unintended lessons influenced by teachers' value orientations.

inclusive education: education designed and offered to all people regardless of their physical, social, emotional, or intellectual characteristics; most often used to refer to education provided in mainstream or general education classrooms to students with disabilities.

Indian Self-Determination and Educational Assistance Act: decision by Congress in 1975 to do away with federal reservations for Native Americans.

individualized education program (IEP): plan approved by parents or guardians that spells out what teachers will do to meet a student's individual needs.

Individuals with Disabilities Education Act (IDEA): 1990 act of Congress that amended the Education for All Handicapped Children Act by changing the term *handicapped* to *with disabilities* and by extending a free and appropriate public education to every individual between three and twenty-one years of age, regardless of the nature or severity of his or her disability.

induction program: program that provides special assistance, monitoring from experienced colleagues, and feedback on teaching performance to beginning teachers in the first one to three years on the job.

in loco parentis: term meaning "in place of the parent" that suggests that educators possess a portion of a parent's rights, duties, and responsibilities.

inquiry learning: answering and solving problems by analyzing data and creating and testing theories and hypotheses to expand the conceptual system with which one processes information.

instructional models: deliberate, explicit, complete plans for teaching that can be fitted to students and objectives.

integrated curriculum: curriculum that combines concepts and skills from different subject areas so that they are mutually reinforcing.

intermediate educational unit (IEU): collaborative organization maintained by separate districts to provide educational services (e.g., joining together to construct and maintain a technical training center for students).

international comparative education: study of education in different societies to develop new insights into these societies and to derive innovative understanding of one's own society.

Internet: electronic network with the capacity to span the globe.

Interstate New Teacher Assessment and Support Consortium Standards (INTASC): standards describing the necessary knowledge, dispositions, and performances for all teachers, regardless of their specialty areas.

journal: written collections of students' reflections on learning.

juku: after-school classes offered to elementary and secondary students in Japan to help them keep up with the demanding school curriculum.

kindergarten: educational program for young children; first established by Friedrich Froebel in 1837.

land grant school: public school established through federal assistance, the first of which was provided by the Northwest Ordinance of 1785.

latchkey child: child who is without adult supervision for several hours each day.

Latin grammar school: first formal type of secondary school in the colonies, established in Boston in 1635 for boys from nine to ten years of age who could read and write English.

Lemon test: tripartite test used to decide whether specific practices or policies are an establishment of religion.

licensure: process of meeting basic requirements and standards for becoming a practicing teacher.

limited English proficient (LEP): categorization of students who are qualified for instruction in English as a Second Language.

listserv: mailing list that allows a person to send a message to a group of individuals with a single keystroke.

literacy: one's ability to read, write, and calculate.

local property taxes: taxes on land and improvements firmly attached to the land (e.g., fences, barns) and on personal property, such as automobiles.

local school board: primary policy-making body for public schools, composed of elected or appointed public servants.

looping: grouping strategy that keeps students together with the same teacher for more than one year.

lyceum: out-of-school program, such as a reading circle or debating club, designed to improve the education of children and adults.

magnet school: alternative school within a public school system that draws students from its whole district instead of drawing only from its own neighborhood and that offers a curriculum based on a special theme or instructional method.

Marxism: philosophy based on Karl Marx's belief that the human condition is determined by forces in history that prevent people from achieving economic freedom and social and political equality.

mastery learning: one of several behavioral models that suggests that, given enough time, the inclination to learn, and instruction fitted to a student's needs, students are capable of mastering a range of subject matter.

McGuffey Reader: book first produced in 1836 by William Holmes McGuffey to teach literacy skills and to advance the Protestant ethic through stories and essays.

measurement: collection of data from individual students from a variety of sources (e.g., tests and quizzes, interviews, questionnaires, observations of in-class behaviors).

mentoring program: support system aimed at enhancing academic success and self-esteem of at-risk students; also, a program to help new teachers.

merit pay: incentive program designed to encourage teachers to strive for outstanding performance by rewarding such practice.

metaphysics: branch of philosophy that focuses on the study of reality.

minimum competency tests: tests designed to assess the lowest acceptable level of student performance.

mission school: school established by priests to convert Native Americans to Catholicism.

monitorial method: method devised by Lancaster for teaching large groups of students, by which a master teacher instructed monitors, and they, in turn, instructed younger children.

National Assessment of Educational Progress (NAEP): congressionally mandated battery of achievement tests operated by the Educational Testing Service to assess the effects of schooling.

National Association for the Advancement of Colored People (NAACP): established in 1934, the first nationwide special-interest group for African Americans.

National Association for the Education of Young Children (NAEYC): one of the largest professional associations for early childhood educators.

National Board for Professional Teaching Standards (NBPTS): nonprofit organization charged with the task of creating a national system of certification to be used to designate truly outstanding teachers.

National Center for Education Statistics (NCES): arm of the executive branch responsible for collecting and analyzing education statistics for the nation.

national certification: recognition for individual teachers, based on a national sample.

National Defense Education Act (NDEA): federal law passed in 1958 to provide funds for upgrading the teaching of mathematics, science, and foreign languages and for establishing guidance services.

National Education Association (NEA): organization with 2 million members guided by the vision of enabling students to develop themselves as people, to practice human relations skills, to learn how to be economically productive citizens, and to be responsible for their community and nation. It was instrumental in creating the National Council for Accreditation of Teacher Education (NCATE), a national organization that monitors the quality of collegiate teacher education programs.

National Education Goals: national goals established by President George Bush and the fifty governors in 1989 to ensure readiness for school; high school completion; student achievement and citizenship; excellence in science and mathematics; adult literacy and lifelong learning; and safe, disciplined, and drug-free schools. Extended by President William Clinton in 1994 to include teacher education and parental involvement.

National Governors Association: coalition of state chief executives.

National Parents–Teacher Association (PTA): largest volunteer education organization in the United States; it has long supported legislation at the state and national levels designed to benefit children.

negligence: failure to exercise reasonable care to protect students from injury.

newsgroups: electronic message services that post to servers locally, regionally, nationally, and/or internationally.

NGO: international nongovernmental organization that advances agendas focused on problems and issues of common interest, regardless of national interest.

nondirective model: teaching strategy in which teachers act as facilitators and reflectors to encourage students to define problems and feelings, to take responsibility for solving problems, and to determine how personal goals might be reached.

nongraded classroom: classroom in which children are grouped heterogeneously by ability, sometimes with students of various ages.

normal school: educational program established in the 1800s dedicated solely to training teachers so that they could perform according to high standards, or "norms."

norm-referenced test: test used to compare the quality of a student's performance to that of other students.

null curriculum: curriculum that is not taught in schools.

okeiko-goto: enrichment classes in areas such as music, the arts, and physical education that people in Japan may continue throughout their lives.

ontology: study of nature, existence, or being.

opportunity standards: standards meant to hold schools accountable for giving students a fair chance to succeed by providing them with appropriate support: books, materials, machines, teachers, time to learn, and other tools.

outcome-centered learning: focuses on results in terms of student achievement.

paraprofessional: unlicensed teacher aide.

parochial school: school established by one of various religious groups to inculcate their beliefs and ideas in children.

pedagogical content knowledge: particular teaching knowledge necessary to impart content knowledge.

perennialism: philosophy that exalts the great thoughts and accomplishments of the past for their own sake and for what they can offer to future generations.

performance standard: the level at which students should be able to use the knowledge they possess to solve problems.

performance tests: assessments that measure how well students can apply what they have learned.

per pupil expenditure: money allocated for educational services divided by the number of pupils to be served.

personal property: property that is movable, either tangibles (e.g., machinery, livestock, crops, automobiles) or intangibles (e.g., money, stocks, bonds).

philosophy: set of ideas about the nature of reality and about the meaning of life.

Plessy v. *Ferguson:* 1896 Supreme Court case that legalized separate but equal public facilities for African Americans and served to legalize school segregation.

pluralism: state of society in which members of a diverse society maintain their unique characteristics.

portfolio: purposeful collection of student work that tells the story of the student's efforts, progress, or achievement in a given area(s).

pragmatism: philosophical method that defines the truth and meaning of ideas according to their physical consequences and practical value.

Praxis Series: examination battery that purports to assess skills and knowledge at each stage of a beginning teacher's career from entry into teacher education to actual classroom performance.

primer: textbook for children designed to impart rudimentary reading skills that also reflected the religious values of the colonies.

principal: person responsible for managing a school at the building level.

private school: nonprofit, tax-exempt institution governed by a board of trustees and financed through private funds, such as tuitions, endowments, and grants; sometimes called a *for-profit school.*

professional development school: school in which university and public school people work together to explore problems of teaching and learning.

progressive taxation: taxes, such as income taxes, that require people who earn more to pay more.

progressivism: movement aimed at using human and material resources to improve the American's quality of life as an individual; in schools this meant focusing on the needs and interests of students rather than on those of teachers. The movement was characterized by a willingness to experiment with methods of teaching and learning.

project-based learning: involvement of students in relatively long-term, problem-based units of instruction that allow students to pursue solutions to problems posed by students, teachers, or curriculum developers.

pull-out program: program in which individual students are removed from regular classes for a period of time each day for special instruction.

race: classification that is not typically chosen but is instead assigned by others; defined most often by physical characteristics.

realism: philosophy that suggests that objects of sense or perception exist independently of the mind.

real property: property that is not readily movable (e.g., land, buildings, improvements).

reciprocity agreement: pact by which professional licensure for educational practice in one state makes one eligible for licensure in another state.

regressive taxation: a method of taxing citizens that requires those with limited incomes to spend a greater percentage of their income on taxes than wealthy people spend.

reliable: consistent.

retention: nonpromotion from one grade to the next at the expected time because of school failure.

rubric: scoring key.

scaffolding: method of teaching in which a teacher provides assistance, guidance, and structure to enhance student learning and self-regulation.

school-based budgeting: allocating resources at the building level rather than at the level of central administration; sometimes referred to as *site-based budgeting.*

school board: legislative policy-making body overseeing the work of educators in schools.

school choice: idea that people should be free to choose schools for their children.

school district: state-defined geographical area assigned responsibility for public instruction within its borders.

school governance: establishment and overseeing of the structure and functions of public education.

self-assessment: evaluating one's own work.

seminary: academy for girls that was the primary means for advancing the educational skills of future teachers.

service learning: learning that results from volunteer work performed outside school hours.

site-based management: involvement of people at the school level in decisions about teaching and learning, budgeting, and hiring personnel.

social promotion: passing of children to successive grades to keep them with others of their age, regardless of their past performance or academic abilities.

social reconstructionism: philosophy based on the belief that people are responsible for social conditions and can improve the quality of human life by changing the social order.

Socratic method: teaching through inquiry and dialogues in which students discover and clarify knowledge.

special-interest group: group of people who coalesce around particular interests and try to exert pressure for the advancement of their causes.

standardized tests: tests, often multiple-choice paper-and-pencil tests, administered and scored under conditions uniform to all students.

standards: benchmarks against which progress can be judged.

state board of education: regulatory agency that controls standards for educational practice in most states and advises governors and legislators about the conduct of educational business.

state education department (SED): bureaucracy that acts as an advisor to the executive and legislative branches of a state government. An SED is organized to carry out a state's education business, including regulating or overseeing elementary and secondary schools' and colleges' and universities' conduct of teacher and administrator preparation.

state standards board: commission established to regulate professional practice in education that either has final authority or serves only in advisory capacity to policymakers.

student–teacher ratio: estimate of average class size, calculated by dividing the total number of students in a school by the total number of staff (often including noninstructional staff).

student teaching: field experience in which preservice teachers plan, organize, and provide instruction to students full time over a period of weeks.

Success for All: school reform model whose main goal is to ensure success in reading, especially for urban students at risk for academic failure.

summative assessment: assessment designed to inform a summary decision, for example, an assessment of a teacher's strengths and weaknesses to be used to make decisions about such matters as tenure and termination of contract.

superintendent of schools: executive officer of the local school board, appointed by the board.

synchronous communication: interactions that take place simultaneously.

synectics: teaching model that seeks to increase students' problem-solving abilities, creative expression, empathy, and insight into social situations.

teacher planning: consideration of such things as curriculum, state and local goals and objectives for student learning, instructional strategies for meeting those goals, and methods for assessing students' understanding.

teacher portfolio: compilation of products displaying a teacher's knowledge and skills, such as teacher-created tests and videotapes of one's own teaching.

teacher union: confederation of educators joined politically to advance their cause.

tenure: continuing contract that guarantees a teacher's employment unless just cause for termination can be demonstrated.

Title I: one of the largest federally funded education programs for at-risk elementary and secondary students; begun in 1965 as the first bill of President Lyndon Johnson's War on Poverty.

Title IX: provision of the 1972 Education Amendments Act that guarantees that individuals may not be excluded on the basis of sex from any education program or activity receiving federal financial assistance.

tracking: process of segregating students by ability.

tuition tax credit: provision that allows a taxpayer to subtract educational costs from taxes owed.

tuition tax deduction: provision that allows a taxpayer to subtract educational costs from taxable income before computing taxes.

universal schooling: educating all citizens for the common good.

Upward Bound: federally funded program to improve academic performance and motivational levels of low-income high school students.

utility: capable of being understood and used easily.

valid: true; measuring what it is supposed to measure.

videoconferencing: form of synchronous communication that involves seeing and hearing one another via computer.

voucher: scrip used to purchase education for a child.

Web browser: software that enables a person to retrieve and see what is on the World Wide Web.

website: individual location on the Web owned and managed by a person, group, company, or organization.

Women's Educational Equity Act (WEEA): 1974 law that expanded programs for females in mathematics, science, technology, and athletics; mandated nonsexist curriculum materials; implemented programs for increasing the number of female administrators in education and raising the career aspirations of female students; and extended educational and career opportunities to minority-group, disabled, and rural women.

World Wide Web: subset of the Internet consisting of multimedia documents.

zero-base budgeting: process of budgeting that requires all expenditures to be justified each fiscal year.

CHAPTER 1

Abood v. Detroit Board of Education, 431 U.S. 209, 97 S. Ct. 1782 (1977).

American Federation of Teachers. (2004). survey and analyis of teacher salary trends 2004. Available online: www.aft.org/salary/index.htm.

Barber, L. W. (1990). Self-assessment. In J. Millman & L. Darling-Hammond (Eds.), *The new handbook of teacher evaluation: Assessing elementary and secondary school teachers* (pp. 216–228). Newbury Park, CA: Sage.

Berg, E. (2004–05). Do clothes make the teacher leader? Teacher Leaders Network. Available online: www.teacherleaders.org/diaries04_05/EB02_04_05.html.

Chicago Teachers Union, Local No. 1 AFL-CIO v. Hudson, 475 U.S. 292, 106 S. Ct. 1066 (1986).

Darling-Hammond, L., Holtzman, D. J., Gatlin, S. J., & Heilig, J. V. (2005). Does teacher preparation matter? Evidence about teacher certification, Teach for America, and teacher effectiveness. Available online: www.schoolredesign.net/srn/server.php?idx=934.

Ellis v. Brotherhood of Railway, Airline, and S.S. Clerks, 466 U.S. 435, 104 S. Ct. 1885 (1984).

Feistritzer, C. E. (2005). Alternative teacher certification: A state-by-state analysis 2005. Washington, DC: National Center for Education Information.

Glickman, J., & Babyak, S. (2002, June 11). Paige releases report to Congress that calls for overhaul of state teacher certification systems. Available online: www.ed.gov/PressReleases/06-2002/061120 02.html.

Henke, R. R., & Zahn, L. (2001). Attrition of new teachers among recent college graduates: Comparing occupational stability among 1992–93 graduates who taught and those who worked in other occupations. National Center for Education Statistics. Available online: http://nces.ed.gov/das/epubs/2001189/results_1.asp.

Hess, F. M. (2002). Tear down this wall: The case for a radical overhaul of teacher certification. Paper delivered at the White House Conference on Preparing Tomorrow's Teachers. Available online: www.ed.gov/inits/preparingteachersconference/hess.html.

Imber, M. & van Geel, T. (2005). *A teacher's guide to education law.* Mahwah, NJ: Erlbaum.

Interstate New Teacher Assessment and Support Consortium. (1992). *Model standards for beginning teacher licensing and development: A resource for state dialogue.* Available online: www.ccsso.org/intascst.html#draft.

Jacobson, L. (2002, June 19). Public wants data on teacher quality. Available online: www.edweek.org/ew/ewstory.cfm?slug=41penpoll.h21&keywords=Public%20Wants%20Data.

Little, J. W. (1990). The mentor phenomenon and the social organization of teaching. In C. Cazden (Ed.), *Review of research in education* (Vol. 16, pp. 297–351). Washington, DC: American Educational Research Association.

Mehlman, N. (2002, June 24). "My brief teaching career." *New York Times.* Available online: www.nytimes.com.

Montgomery County Schools. (2008). WABE guide: FY 2005. Available online: www.fcps.k12.va.us/fs/budget/wabe/.

National Education Association. (1999). *Beginning teacher coaching program.* Available online: www.nea.org/newunion/mtdiablo.html.

Peske, H. G., Liu, E., Johnson, S. M., Kauffman, D., & Kardos, S. M. (2001, December). The next generation of teachers: Changing conceptions of a career in teaching. *Phil Delta Kappan, 83*(4), 304–311.

Public Agenda. (2003). Stand by me: What teachers really think about unions, merit pay and other professional matters. Available online: www.publicagenda.org/specials/standbyme/standbyme.cfm.

Rogers, B. (2005). Teacher of the year. *Teacher Magazine.* Available online: http://blogs.edweek.org/ teachers/brogers/.

U.S. Department of Education. (2003). Projections of education statistics to 2014. Available online: http://nces.ed.gov/programs/projections.

U.S. Department of Education. (2003). Digest of education statistics. Available online: http://nces.ed.gov/.

CHAPTER 2

American Psychological Association & Music Television. (undated). *Warning signs. Fight for your rights: Take a stand against violence.* Washington, DC: American Psychological Association.

Americans for the Arts. (2004). Local and state arts success in Kentucky. Available online: www.americansforthearts.org/public_awareness/pac_article.asp?id=647.

Centers for Disease Control and Prevention. (2005). Youth risk behavior surveillance—United States, 2005. Available online: http://www.cdc.gov/.

Centers for Disease Control and Prevention. (2001). Births to teenagers in the United States, 1940–2000. *National Vital Statistics Reports, 49* (10). Available online: www.cdc.gov.

Children's Defense Fund. (2007). Each day in America. Available online: www.childrensdefense.org/.

Fernandez, M. (2005, March 7). A young father's rare choice: As a single parent, D.C. teen juggles school, adult responsibility. *The Washington Post.* Accessed online (March 21, 2005): www.washingtonpost.com/wp-dyn/articles/A12174-2005Mar6.html/.

Finn, C. E., Jr. (1991). *We must take charge: Our schools and our future.* New York: Free Press.

Hoff, T., & Greene L. (2000). *Sex education in America. A series of national surveys of parents, teachers, and principals* (p. 31). Menlo Park, CA: Henry J. Kaiser Family Foundation.

Hughes, D. R. (2001). Rules of the road: Top 10 things to teach your children to keep them safe online. Available online: www.protectkids.com/parentsafety/rulesoftheroad.htm.

Institute of Medicine of the National Academies. (2005). Focus on childhood obesity. Available online: www.iom.edu/focuson.asp?id=22593.

Interstate New Teacher Assessment and Support Consortium. (1992). *Model standards for beginning teacher licensing and development: A resource for state dialogue.* Available online: www.ccsso.org/intascst.html#draft.

Kominski, R., Jamieson, A., & Martinez, G. (2001). At-risk conditions of U.S. school-age children. U.S. Census Bureau, Population Divided, Education & Social Stratification Branch. Available online: www.census.gov/population/www/documentation/twps0052.html#data.

Kozol, J. (1995). *Amazing grace.* New York: Random House.

Landau, S., Pryor, J. B., & Haefli, K. (1995). Pediatric HIV: School-based sequelae and curricular interventions for infection prevention and social acceptance. *School Psychology Review, 24*(2), 213–229.

National Center for Education Statistics. (2002). The nation's report card: Fourth-grade reading 2000. Available online: http://nces.ed.gov/nationsreportcard/pubs/main2000/2001499.asp.

National School Boards Association. (2005). Education vital signs 2005. Available online: www.asbj.com/ evs/.

Peterson, R. L., & Skiba, R. (2001). Creating school climates that prevent school violence. *Clearing House, 74*(3), 155–163.

Project Alert (2008). Welcome to Project Alert. Available online: http://www.projectalert.com.

Reilly, E. (2008, January). Parental involvement through better communication. *Middle School Journal,* volume 39, number 3, 40–47.

Rural School and Community Trust. (2005). *Maine's smaller schools cut poverty's power over student achievement.* Accessed online (March 22, 2005): www.ruraledu.org/.

Sheras, P., & Tippins, S. (2002). *Your child: Bully or victim. Understanding and ending school yard tyranny.* New York: Skylight Press.

Siris, K., & Osterman, I. K. (2004, December). Interrupting the cycle of bullying and victimization in the elementary classroom. *Phi Delta Kappan, 86*(4), 288–291.

U.S. Census Bureau. (2006). Income, poverty, and health insurance converge in the United States: 2006 report. Available online: http://www.census.gov/.

U.S. Department of Education. (2000, June). The need for after-school programs. Available online: www.ed.gov/pubs/afterschool/intro.html.

U.S. Department of Education. (2004, March 12). Statement by U.S. Secretary of Education Rod Paige on controlling obesity in children and adolescents.

Available online: www.ed.gov/news/pressreleases/2004/03/03122004.html.

U.S. Department of Education (2005). Projections of Education Statistics to 2014, Thirty-third Edition. Washington, DC: National Center for Education Statistics.

U.S. Department of Education. (2007). Digest of education statistics. Youth indicators: 2005. Available online: http://nces.ed.gov/programs/digest/d06.

U.S. Department of Health and Human Services, Administration on Children, Youth and Families. (2005). *Child maltreatment 2003: Reports from the states to the National Child Abuse and Neglect Data Systems: National statistics on child abuse and neglect.* Washington, DC: U.S. Government Printing Office.

U.S. Department of Health and Human Services. (2008). Frequent questions. Available online: http://www.aids.gov/prevention/faq/index.html.

CHAPTER 3

Associated Press. (2004, February 4). Class seeks to rid kids of Appalachian accents. Available online: www.ajc.com/news/content/news/stories/0205/04appalachian.html.

Banks, J. A. (2002). *An introduction to multicultural education* (3rd ed). Boston: Allyn and Bacon.

Banks, J. A. & Banks, C. A. (2004) *Multicultural education: Issues and perspectives* (5th ed). New York: Wiley.

Brown, A. (1994). The advancement of learning. *Educational Researcher, 23*(8), 4–12.

Brown v. Board of Education of Topeka, 347 U.S. 483 (1954).

Education Commission of the States. (2004). State gifted and talented definitions. Available online: www.ecs.org/clearinghouse/52/28/5228.htm.

Hallahan, D. P., & Kauffman, J. M. (2006). *Exceptional children: Introduction to special education* (10th ed.). Boston: Allyn and Bacon.

Interstate New Teacher Assessment and Support Consortium. (1992). *Model standards for beginning teacher licensing and development: A resource for state dialogue.* Available online: www.ccsso.org/intascst.html#draft.

Johnson, D. W., & Johnson, R. T. (2003). Teaching students to be peacemakers. Association for Conflict Resolution. Available online: http://acrnet.org/resources/articles/crejohnson.htm.

Kilbane, C. R. & Milman, M. B. (2003). *The digital teaching portfolio handbook: A how-to guide for educators.* Boston: Allyn and Bacon.

Lehrer, R., & Schauble, L. (1998). Reasoning about structure and function: Children's conceptions of gears. *Journal of Research in Science Teaching, 35,* 3–25.

Louis Harris and Associates, Inc. (1996). *The Metropolitan Life survey of the American teacher, 1996: Students voice their opinions on violence, social tension and equality among teens, part I.* New York: Author.

Marlowe, B. (2001, April 18). The special education conundrum. *Education Week, 20*(31), 43.

McNergney, R., & Keller, C. (1999). Appendix. Some effective teachers' actions. In R. McNergney & C. Keller (Eds.), *Images of mainstreaming: Educating students with disabilities* (pp. 211–212). New York: Garland Publishing.

Metz, K. E. (1995). Reassessment of developmental constraints on children's science instruction. *Review of Educational Research, 65,* 93–127.

National Research Council. (1996). *National science education standards.* Washington, DC: National Academy Press.

NEA Today. (2005, April). Safe schools: Teaching tolerance. Available online: www.nea.org/neatoday/0504/teachtolerance.html.

Oakes, J., & Lipton, M. (1999). *Teaching to change the world.* Boston: McGraw-Hill.

Ogbu, J. U., & Simons, H. D. (1998). Voluntary and involuntary minorities: A cultural–ecological theory of school performance with some implications for education. *Anthropology & Education Quarterly, 29*(2), 155–188.

Ponessa, J. (1995). NEA backing for gay month sparks firestorm. *Education Week, 15*(8), 3.

Rosebery, A. S., & Warren, B. (Eds.). (1998). *Boats, balloons, and classroom video.* Westport, CT: Heinemann.

Sadker, D. (1999). Gender equity: Still knocking at the classroom door. *Educational Leadership 56.* Available online: www.american.edu/sadker/stillknocking.htm.

Sadker, M., & Sadker, D. (1993, March). Fair and square? *Instructor, 102*(7), 45, 46, 67, 68.

Seymour, L. (2001, October 1). Driven by the ignored child within: Fairfax school chief intent on helping all pupils succeed. *Washington Post,* p. A1.

Sleeter, C. E., & Grant, C. A. (2002). *Making choices for multicultural education: Five approaches to race, class, and gender* (4th ed.). New York: Wiley.

Suro, R. (1998, July 19). The next wave: How immigration blurs the race discussion. *Washington Post,* p. C1.

U.S. Department of Education. (2003). Digest of education statistics. Available online: http://nces.ed.gov/programs/digest.

U.S. Department of Education. (2005). Special programs: Inclusion of students with disabilities in regular classrooms, Indicator 27. *Condition of Education.* Washington, DC: U.S. Government Printing Office.

Valdes, G. (1999). Incipient bilingualism and the development of English language writing abilities in the secondary school. In C. J. Faltis & P. Wolfe (Eds.), *So much to say: Adolescents, bilingualism, and ESL in the secondary school* (pp. 138–176). New York: Teachers College Press.

Wainer, A. (2004). *The new Latino south and the challenge to public education: Strategies for educators and policymakers in emerging immigrant communities.* Los Angeles, California: The Tomás Rivera Policy Institute, University of Southern California.

Weil, E. (2008, March 2). Teaching to the testosterone. *The New York Times Magazine,* 38–44, 84–87.

Zehr, M. A. (2005). Newcomers bring change, challenge to region. *Education Week, 24*(34), 1, 18–19, 21.

CHAPTER 4

Ambrose, S. E. (1996). *Undaunted courage: Meriwether Lewis, Thomas Jefferson, and the opening of the American West.* New York: Simon & Schuster.

Barman, J., Hebert, Y., & McCaskill, D. (1986). *Indian education in Canada* (Vol. I). Vancouver: University of British Columbia.

Barnard, H. (1857, March). The public high school. *American Journal of Education,* pp. 185–189.

Berlin, I. (1974). *Slaves without masters: The free negro in the antebellum South.* New York: Vintage.

Blum, J. M., McFeely, W. S., Morgan, E. S., Schlesinger, A. M., Jr., Stampp, K. M., & Woodward, C. V. (1993). *The national experience: A history of the United States* (8th ed.). Belmont; CA: Wadsworth.

Boyd, W. (Ed.). (1962). *The Emile of Jean-Jacques Rousseau.* New York: Bureau of Publications, Teachers College, Columbia University.

Boyer, P. S., Clark, C. E., Kett, J. F., Salisbury, N., Sitkoff, H., & Woloch, N. (2000). *The enduring vision: A history of the American people* (4th ed.). Boston: Houghton Mifflin.

Bullock, H. A. (1967). *A history of Negro education in the South: From 1619 to the present.* Cambridge, MA: Harvard University Press.

Coleman, M. C. (1993). *American Indian children at school, 1850–1930.* Jackson: University Press of Mississippi.

Cremin, L. A. (1970). *American education: The colonial experience, 1607–1783.* New York: Harper & Row.

Cremin, L. A. (1980). *American education: The national experience, 1783–1876.* New York: Harper & Row.

Deighton, L. C. (Ed.). (1971). *The encyclopedia of education* (Vol. 9). New York: Macmillan Company and The Free Press.

Dolan, J. P. (1985). *The American Catholic experience: A history from colonial times to the present.* Garden City, NY: Doubleday.

Downs, R. B. (1978). *Friedrich Froebel.* Boston: Twayne.

Edwards, P. (Ed.). (1972). *Encyclopedia of philosophy* (Vol. 7). New York: Macmillan Company and The Free Press.

Elsbree, W. S. (1939). *The American teacher: Evolution of a profession in a democracy.* New York: American Book.

Emerson, R. W. (1884). *Lectures and biographical sketches.* Cambridge, MA: Riverside.

Flynn, G. (1971). *Sor Juana Ines de la Cruz.* New York: Twayne.

Fogel, D. (1988). *Junipero Serra, the Vatican, and enslavement theology.* San Francisco, CA: Ism.

Ford, P. L. (Ed.). (1899). *The New England primer.* New York: Dodd, Mead.

Froebel Foundation USA. (2005). *The Froebel kinder-garten philosophy.* Accessed online (April 10, 2005): www.froebelfoundation.org/philosophy,html.

Gay, P. (Ed.) (1964). *John Locke on education.* New York: Bureau of Publications, Teachers College, Columbia University.

Gutek, G. L. (1968). *Pestalozzi and education.* New York: Random House.

Hahner, J. (1976). *Women in Latin American history.* Los Angeles: University of California.

Hallahan, D. P., & Kauffman, J. M. (2006). *Exceptional children: Introduction to special education* (10th ed.). Boston: Allyn and Bacon.

Interstate New Teacher Assessment and Support Consortium. (1992). *Model standards for beginning teacher licensing and development: A resource for state dialogue.* Available online: www.ccsso.org/intascst.html#draft.

Kaestle, C. F. (1983). *Pillars of the republic: Common schools and American society, 1780–1860.* New York: Hill and Wang.

Krug, E. A. (1964). *The shaping of the American high school, 1880–1920.* New York: Harper & Row.

Lannie, V. P. (1968). *Public money and parochial education: Bishop Hughes, Governor Seward and the New York school controversy.* Cleveland, OH: Press of Case Western Reserve.

Manuel, H. T. (1965). *Spanish-speaking children of the Southwest: Their education and the public welfare.* Austin: University of Texas Press.

Padover, S. K (1939). *Jefferson: A great American's life and ideas.* New York: D. Appleton-Century Company.

Pestalozzi, J. H. (1898). *How Gertrude teaches her children* (2nd cd.). Syracuse, NY: C. W. Bardeen.

Ronda, B. A (1999) *Elizabeth Palmer Peabody: A reformer on her own terms.* Cambridge, MA: Harvard University Press.

Rury, J. L. (1989). Who became teachers?: The characteristics of teachers in American history. In D. Warren (Ed.), *American teachers: Histories of a profession at work* (pp. 9–48). New York: Macmillan.

Shapira, I. (2005, April 3). Foreign teachers a quick fix: Va. Schools lose language instructors when visas expire. *The Washington Post.* Available online: www.washingtonpost.com/WP-dyn/articles/A21733-2005Apr5.html.

Steinhardt, M. A. (1992). Physical education. In P. W. Jackson (Ed.), *Handbook of research on curriculum* (pp. 964–1001). New York: Macmillan.

The Sun. (1833a, December 19), p. 2.

Ulich, R. (1968). *History of educational thought.* New York: D. Van Nostrand.

Zitkala-Sa. (1921). *American Indian stories.* Washington, DC: Hayworth.

CHAPTER 5

Associated Press. (2005, June 14). Senate sorry for inaction on lynching. *The Daily Progress.*

Blum, J. M., McFeely, W. S., Morgan, E. S., Schlesinger, A. M., Jr., Stampp, K. M., & Woodward, C. V. (1993). *The national experience: A history of the United States* (8th ed.), Belmont, CA: Wadsworth.

Bond, H. M. (1934). *The education of the Negro in the American social order.* Upper Saddle River, NJ: Prentice Hall.

Bossert, S. T. (1985). Effective elementary schools. In R. J. Kyle (Ed.), *Reaching for excellence* (pp. 39–53). Washington, DC: U.S. Government Printing Office.

Boyle, K. (2004). Arc of Justice: A saga of race, civil rights and murder in the Jazz Age. New York: Henry Holt and Company, LLC.

Brown, C. L., & Pannell, C. W. (1985). The Chinese in America. In J. O. McKee (Ed.), *Ethnicity in contemporary America: A geographical appraisal* (pp. 195–216). Dubuque, IA: Kendall/Hunt.

Callahan, R. E. (1962). *Education and the cult of efficiency.* Chicago: University of Chicago Press.

Carlson, R. A. (1975). *The quest for conformity: Americanization through education.* New York: Wiley.

Carr, C. K. (2000, Winter). On writing biography. *Profile: Smithsonian National Portrait Gallery News, 1*(4), 12–13.

Cole, J. Y. (1979). *For Congress and the nation: A chronological history of the Library of Congress.* Washington, DC: Library of Congress.

Commission on the Reorganization of Secondary Education. (1918). *Cardinal principles of secondary education* (Bulletin No. 35). Washington, DC: U.S. Government Printing Office.

Cremin, L. A. (1988). *American education: The metropolitan experience.* New York: Harper & Row.

Dabney, C. W. (1969). *Universal education in the South: Vol. II.* New York: Arno Press & *The New York Times.*

Degler, C. N. (1959). *Out of our past: The forces that shaped modern America.* New York: Harper & Row.

DuBois, W. E. B. (1903). *The souls of black folk: Essays and sketches.* Chicago: A. C. McClurg. Available online: http://etext.lib.virginia.edu/modeng/modeng0.browse.html.

DuBois, W. E. B. (1904). *The souls of black folk.* Chicago: A. C. McClurg.

Edwards, J. (1991). To teach responsibility, bring back the Dalton Plan. *Phi Delta Kappan, 72* (5), 398–401.

Efron, S. (1990, April 29). Few Viet exiles find U.S. riches. *Los Angeles Times,* p. 1.

Franklin, J. H. (1967). *From slavery to freedom* (3rd ed.). New York: Knopf.

Fuchs, L. H. (1990). *The American kaleidoscope: Race, ethnicity, and the civic culture.* Middletown, CT: Wesleyan University Press.

Hallahan, D. P., & Kauffman, J. M. (2006). *Exceptional learners: Introduction to special education* (10th ed.). Boston: Allyn and Bacon.

Hoff, D. J. (2002, March 20). Debate of teaching of evolution theory shifts to Ohio. *Education Week, 21*(27), 14, 16.

Interstate New Teacher Assessment and Support Consortium. (1992). *Model standards for beginning teacher licensing and development: A resource for state dialogue.* Available online: www.ccsso.org/intascst.html#draft.

Kliebard, H. M. (1986). *The struggle for the American curriculum, 1893–1958.* Boston: Routledge & Kegan Paul.

Lemann, N. (2000). *The big test: The secret history of the American meritocracy.* New York: Farrar, Straus and Giroux.

Link, A. S., & Catton, W. B. (1963). *American epoch: A history of the United States since the 1890s.* New York: Knopf.

Mayhew, M. (2005, July 17). Fluvanna teacher awarded for technological insight. *The Daily Progress,* p. A2.

NAACP Legal Defense and Educational Fund. (2005). Brown matters: The 50th anniversary of *Brown* v. *Board.* Available online: www.naacpldf.org/content.aspx?article=572.

National Commission on Excellence in Education. (1983). *A nation at risk: The imperative for education reform.* Washington, DC: U.S. Department of Education.

Painter, N. I. (1977). *Exodusters: Black migration to Kansas after Reconstruction.* New York: Knopf.

Parkhurst, H. (1922). *Education on the Dalton Plan.* New York: Dutton.

Peabody, E. P. (1886). *Sara Winnemucca's practical solution of the Indian problems: A letter to Dr. Lyman Abbot of the "Christian Union."* Cambridge, MA: John Wilson and Son.

Powell, A. G., Farrar, E., & Cohen, D. K. (1985). *The shopping mall high school: Winners and losers in the educational marketplace.* Boston: Houghton Mifflin.

Rice, J. M. (1969). *The public-school system of the United States.* New York: Arno Press.

Rideout, M. A., Roberts, D. F., & Foehr, U. G. (2005). Generation M: Media in the lives of 8–18 year-olds. A Kaiser Family Foundation Study. Available online: www.kff.org/entmedia/entmedia030905pkg.cfm.

Romo, H. D., & Falbo, T. (1996). *Latino high school graduation: Defying the odds.* Austin: University of Texas Press.

Travers, R. M. (1983). *How research has changed American schools: A history from 1840 to the present.* Kalamazoo, MI: Mythes.

Tyack, D., & Hansot, E. (1982). *Managers of virtue.* New York: Basic Books.

U.S. Bureau of Indian Affairs. (1974). Government schools for Indians (1881). In S. Cohen (Ed.), *Education in the United States: A documentary history* (Vol. 3, pp. 1754–1756). New York: Random House.

U.S. Census Bureau. (1975). *Historical statistics of the United States: Colonial times to 1970 (Part 1).* Washington, DC: U.S. Government Printing Office.

U.S. Census Bureau. (1990). *Statistical abstract of the United States* (110th ed.). Washington, DC: U.S. Government Printing Office.

U.S. Census Bureau (2002, May 8). *American community survey.* Available online: www.census.gov/acs/www/.

U.S. Census Bureau. (2002). Census 2000: Chinese largest Asian group in the United States. Available online: www.census.gov.

U.S. Census Bureau. (2003). Educational attainment : 2000. Washington, DC: U.S. Department of Commerce.

U.S. Census Bureau. (2004). Income, poverty, and health insurance coverage in the United States: 2003. Washington, DC: U.S. Department of Commerce.

U.S. Department of Education. (1999). *Digest of education statistics, 1998.* NCES 1999-036, by Thomas D. Snyder, Charlene Hoffman, Claire M. Geddes. Washington, DC: U.S. Government Printing Office.

U.S. Department of Education. (2005). New *No Child Left Behind* provision gives schools increased flexibility while ensuring all children count, including those with disabilities. Available online: www.ed.gov/news/pressreleases/2003/12/12092003.html.

U.S. Department of Education, National Center for Education Statistics. (2002). Enrollment in grades 9–12 in public schools. Projections of Education Statistics to 2012. Available online: http://nces.ed.gov/pubs2002/proj2012/table_08_2.asp.

U.S. Department of Health and Human Services. (2007). The 2007 HHS poverty guidelines. Available online: http://aspe.hhs.gov/poverty/07poverty.shtml.

Washington, B. T. (1907). *The future of the American Negro.* Boston: Small, Maynard.

CHAPTER 6

Adler, M. (1982). *The Paideia proposal: An educational manifesto.* New York: Macmillan.

Apple, M. (1995). *Education and power.* New York: Routledge.

Asante, M. K. (1987). *The Afrocentric idea.* Philadelphia: Temple University Press.

Asante, M. K. (1992). Learning about Africa. *Executive Educator, 14*(9), 21–23.

Banks, J. A. (1994). *Multiethnic education: Theory and practice* (3rd ed.). Boston: Allyn and Bacon.

Banville, J. (1998, August 13). The last days of Nietzsche. *New York Review of Books, 45*(13), 22–25.

Bloom, A. (1987). *The closing of the American mind.* New York: Simon and Schuster.

Buber, M. (1970). *I and thou* (W. Kaufman, Trans.). New York: Charles Scribner's Sons. (Original work published 1937)

Cohen, S., & Hearn, D. (1988). Reinforcement. In R. F. McNergney (Ed.), *Guide to classroom teaching* (pp. 43–66). Boston: Allyn and Bacon.

Corbin, H. (1993). *History of Islamic philosophy.* London: Kegan Paul International.

Counts, G. S. (1928). *School and society in Chicago.* New York: Harcourt, Brace.

Dewey, J. (1916). *Democracy and education: An introduction to the philosophy of education.* New York: Macmillan.

Durant, W. (1961). *The story of philosophy: The lives and opinions of the great philosophers.* New York: Simon and Schuster.

Fakhry, J. (1983). *A history of Islamic philosophy* (2nd ed.). New York: Columbia University Press.

Fine, M. (1987). Silencing in public schools. *Language Arts, 64*(2), 157–174.

Finn, Jr., C. E. (2005). Faulty engineering, *Education Next,* pp. 16, 18–21.

Furukawa, G. (2005). First U.S. Buddhist high school. Associated Content. Available online: www.associatedcontent.com/content.cfm?content_type=article&content_type_id=191.

Giroux, H. A. (1984). Public philosophy and the crisis in education. *Harvard Educational Review, 54*(2), 186–194.

Hirsch, E. D., Jr. (1987). *Cultural literacy: What every American needs to know.* Boston: Houghton Mifflin.

Hirsch, E. D., Jr. (1996). *The schools we need and why we don't have them.* Garden City, NY: Doubleday.

Hirsch, E. D., Jr., Rowland, W. G., Jr., & Stanford, M. (Eds.) (1989). *A first dictionary of cultural literacy: What our children need to know.* Boston: Houghton Mifflin.

Holtom, D. C. (1984). *The political philosophy of modern Shinto: A study of the state religion of Japan.* Chicago: University of Chicago Libraries.

Hutchins, R. M. (1936). *The higher learning in America.* New Haven: Yale University Press.

Interstate New Teacher Assessment and Support Consortium. (1992). *Model standards for beginning teacher licensing and development: A resource for state dialogue.* Available online: www.ccsso.org/intascst.html#draft.

James, W. (1907). *Pragmatism and four essays from The Meaning of Truth.* New York: Longmans, Green and Co.

King, M. L., Jr. (1964). *Stride toward freedom: The Montgomery story.* New York: Harper & Row.

Macedo, S. (2004). Crafting good citizens. *Education Next,* pp. 10, 12–15.

Nietzsche, F. (1924). *On the future of our educational institutions.* New York: Macmillan.

Nietzsche, F. (1961). *Thus spake Zarathustra: A book for everyone and no one* (R. J. Hollingdale, Trans.). New York: Penguin. (Original work published 1883)

Rorty, R. (1991). *Objectivity, relativism, and truth: Philosophical papers: Vol. 1.* Cambridge, MA: Cambridge University Press.

Sartre, J.-P. (1947). *Existentialism.* New York: Philosophical Library.

Schön, D. A. (1987). *Educating the reflective practitioner: Toward a new design for teaching and learning in the professions.* San Francisco: Jossey-Bass.

Shishu Bharati (2005). Shishu Bharati: School of Languages and Cultures of India. Available online: www.shishubharati.org/.

Skinner, B. F. (1971). *Beyond freedom and dignity.* New York: Knopf.

Thirteen/WNET New York. © 2005 Available online: www.thirteen.org/nyvoices/features/schoolremembers.html.

Westbrook, R. B. (1991). *John Dewey and American democracy.* Ithaca, NY: Cornell University Press.

X, Malcolm. (1965). *The autobiography of Malcolm X.* New York: Grove Press.

Zehr, M. (2001). Fearing potential for backlash, Islamic schools step up security. *Education Week.* Available online: www.edweek.org/ew/newstory.cfm?slug= 03dc.h21.

CHAPTER 7

American Diploma Project. (2004). *Creating a high school diploma that counts.* Available online: www.americandiplomaproject.org.

Archer, J. (2004). Conn. polishes image of 'technical' schools. *Education Week, 24*(4), 26.

Boyer, E. L. (1995). *The basic school: A community for learning.* Princeton, NJ: Carnegie Foundation for the Advancement of Teaching.

Decker, L. E., Gregg, G. A., & Decker, V. A. (1995). *Teacher's manual for parent and community involvement.* Fairfax, VA: National Community Education Association.

Good, T. L., & Brophy, J. E. (2003). *Looking in classrooms* (9th ed.). New York: Longman.

Interstate New Teacher Assessment and Support Consortium. (1992). *Model standards for beginning teacher licensing and development: A resource for state dialogue.* Available online: www.ccsso.org/intascst.html#draft.

Kaucrz, K. (2005). Full day kindergarten: A study of state policies in the United States. Denver, CO: Education Commission of the States.

Keen, M. (1999). Three semesters for learning. *School Administrator, 3*(56), 27–30.

Lareau, A. (1996). Assessing parent involvement in schooling: A critical analysis. In A. Booth & J. F. Dunn (Eds.), *Family–school links: How do they affect educational outcomes?* (pp. 57–66). Mahwah, NJ: Erlbaum.

Marzano, R. J. (2000). *A new era of school reform: Going where the research takes us.* Aurora, CO: Mid-Continent Research for Education and Learning.

Marzano, R. J. (2007). *The art and science of teaching: A comprehensive framework for effective instruction.* Alexandria, VA: Association for Supervision and Curriculum Development.

National Association of Elementary School Principals. (2001). *Leading learning communities: Standards for what principals should know and be able to do* (p. 2). Washington, DC: Author.

Oakes, J. (1995). More than meets the eye: Links between tracking and the culture of schools. In H. Pool & J. A. Page (Eds.), *Beyond tracking: Finding success in inclusive schools.* Bloomington, IN: Phi Delta Kappa Educational Foundation.

Pool, H., & Page, J. A. (Eds.). (1995). Introduction. *Beyond tracking: Finding success in inclusive schools.* Bloomington, IN: Phi Delta Kappa Educational Foundation.

RAND Corporation. (2004). *Focus on the wonder years: Challenges facing the American middle school.* Santa Monica, CA: Author.

Rettig, M., & Canady, R. L. (1999). The effects of block scheduling. *School Administrator, 3*(56), 14–20.

U.S. Department of Labor, Bureau of Labor Statistics. (2005). National occupational employment and wage estimates, May 2004. Available online: www.bls.gov/oes/current/oes252011.htm.

Vail, K. (2004). Remaking high school. *American School Board Journal, 191*(11). Available online: www.asbj.com/2004/11/1104coverstory.html.

Viadero, D. (2002, April 17). Study: Full-day kindergarten boosts academic performance. *Education Week.* Available online: www.edweek.org/ew/newstory.cfm?slug=31kinder.h21.

WestEd. (2007). *K–8 charter schools: closing the achievement gap: innovations in education.* Washington, DC: U.S. Department of Education, Office of Innovation and Improvement.

CHAPTER 8

Becker, G. S. (1964). *Human capital: A theoretical and empirical analysis, with special reference to education.* New York: Columbia University Press.

Berliner, D. C., & Biddle, B. J. (1995). *The manufactured crisis: Myths, fraud, and the attack on America's public schools.* Reading, MA: Addison-Wesley.

Bracey, G. W. (1991). Why can't they be like we were? *Phi Delta Kappan, 73*(2), 105–117.

Burrup, P. E., Brimley, V., & Garfield, R. R. (1999). *Financing education in a climate of change.* Boston: Allyn and Bacon.

Cooper, B. S., & Randall, E. V. (2008). Fear and privatization. *Educational Policy, 22*(1), 204–227.

Darling-Hammond, L., & McLaughlin, M. W. (1995). Policies that support professional development in an era of reform. *Phi Delta Kappan, 76*(8), 597–604.

Dembski, W. A. (undated). *Detecting design in the natural sciences. Intelligence leaves behind a characteristic signature.* Available online: www.actionbioscience.org/evolution/nhmag.html.

Friedman, M. (1955). The role of government in education. In R. A. Solo (Ed.), *Economics and the public interest* (pp. 123–144). New Brunswick, NJ: Rutgers University Press.

Guthrie, J. W., Garms, W. I., & Pierce, L. C. (1988). *School finance and education policy: Enhancing educational efficiency, equality, and choice.* Upper Saddle River, NJ: Prentice Hall.

Hanushek, E. (1989). Expenditures, efficiency, and equity in education: The federal government's role. *American Economic Review, 79,* 46–51.

Hedges, L. V., Laine, R. D., & Greenvals, R. (1994). Does money matter? A meta-analysis of studies of the effects of differential school inputs on student outcomes. *Educational Researcher, 23*(3), 5–14.

Hendrie, C. (1999, May 17). Survey finds gap between public, board members on urban schools. *Education Week, 18*(27), 9.

Holloway, J. H. (2000, April). The promise and pitfalls of site-based management. *Educational Leadership,* vol. 57, no. 7, 21–27.

Interstate New Teacher Assessment and Support Consortium. (1992). *Model standards for beginning teacher licensing and development: A resource for state dialogue.* Available online: www.ccsso.org/intascst.html#draft.

Johnson, D. (2008). *Stop high-stakes testing: An appeal to America's conscience.* Lanham, MD: Rowman & Littlefield Publishers.

Odden, A. (1984). Financing educational excellence. *Phi Delta Kappan, 65*(5), 311–318.

Pyhrr, P. A. (1973). *Zero-base budgeting: A practical management tool for evaluating expenses.* New York: Wiley.

Rose, L. C., & Gallup, A. M. (2006). The 38th annual Phi Delta Kappa/Gallup poll of the public's attitudes toward public schools. Available online: www.pdkintl.org/kappan/kpollpdf.htm#k0509pol.htm.

Sadowski, M. (1995, March/April). The numbers game yields simplistic answers on the link between spending and outcomes. *Harvard Education Letter, 11*(2), 1–4.

Schultz, T. W. (1981). *Investing in people: The economics of population quality.* Berkeley: University of California Press.

U.S. Department of Education. (2001). *Making sense of school budgets.* Washington, DC: Office of Educational Research and Improvement.

U.S. Department of Education. (2006). *Digest of education statistics.* Washington, DC: U.S. Government Printing Office.

Verstegen, D., & McGuire, C. K. (1991). The dialectic of reform. *Educational Policy, 5*(4), 386–411.

Walsh, M. (2002, June 27). Supreme Court upholds Cleveland voucher program. *Education Week.* Available online: www.edweek.com/ew/newstory.cfm?slug=42voucher_web.h21.

Ward, J. G. (1992). Schools and the struggle for democracy: Themes for school finance policy. In J. G Ward & P. Anthony (Eds.), *Who pays for student diversity?* (pp. 241–250). Newbury Park, CA: Corwin Press.

Williams, J. (1992). The politics of education news. In R. F. McNergney (Ed.), *Education research, policy, and the press: Research as news* (pp. 177–200). Boston: Allyn and Bacon.

CHAPTER 9

Alexander, K., & Alexander, M. D. (2005). *American public school law* (6th ed.). Belmont, CA: Wadsworth.

Baker v. Owen, 395 F. Supp. 294 M.D.N.C. (1975).

B.M. by Berger v. State of Montana, 649 P. 2d 425 (Mont. 1982).

Board of Education of the Westside Community Schools v. Mergens, 496 U.S. 226 (1990).

Board of Regents of State Colleges v. Roth, 408 U.S. 564 (1972).

Brown v. Board of Education of Topeka, Kansas, 347 U.S. 483 (1954).

Bureau of National Affairs. (1993). *Lamb's Chapel and John Seigerwald, petitioners v. Center Moriches Union Free School District et al. United States Law Week,* 61(46), 4549–4554.

Castro, A. (2006, June 17). Teacher's topless pics may cost job. *The Seattle Times.* Available online: http://seattletimes.nwsource.com/html/nationworld/2003067346_teacher17.html.

Conkling, W. (1991, November/December). The big chill. *Teacher Magazine,* pp. 46–53.

Connick v. Myers, 461 U.S. 138 (1983).

Darden, E. C. (2007, February). Even out the playing field. *American School Board Journal,* vol. 194, no. 2, 41–42.

Data Research, Inc. (2002). *1999 deskbook encyclopedia of American school law.* Rosemount, MN: Author.

Davis v. Grover, 480 N. W. 2d 460 (Wis. 1992).

Davis v. Monroe County Board of Education (1999). 97-843, 526 U.S. 629; 119 S. Ct. 1661.

Denn, R. (2002). Seattle schools consider Native American mascot ban. *Seattle Post Intelligencer.* Available online: http://seattlepi.nwsource.com/local/75354_mascot20.shtml.

Dewalt, M. (2006). Amish education in the United States and Canada. Lanham, MD: Rowman & Littlefield Education.

Dillon, N. (2007, March). Lost in translation. *American School Board Journal,* vol. 194, no. 3, 14–19.

Encyclopedia Britannica Educational Corporation v. Crooks, 542 F. Supp. 1156 (W.D. N.Y. 1982).

Essex, N. L. (2005). *School law and the public schools: A practical guide for educational leaders.* Boston: Allyn and Bacon.

Fischer, L., Schimmel, D., Stellman, L., & Kelly, C. (2003). *Teachers and the law* (6th ed.). Boston: Allyn and Bacon.

Franklin v. Gwinnett County Public Schools, 112 S. Ct. 1028 (1992).

Gaylord v. Tacoma School District No. 10, 88 Wa. 2d 286, 559 P. 2d 1340 (1977).

Gewertz, C. (2002, July 10). A great day, or a dark one, for schools? *Education Week.* Available online: www.edweek.com/ew/newstory.dfm?slug=42voucheract.h21.

Gonzalez v. Mackler, 241 N.Y.S. 2d 254 (N.Y. App. Div. 1963).

Goss v. Lopez, 419 U.S. 565, 95 Ct. 729, 42 L. Ed. 2d 725 (1975).

Guyer v. School Board of Alachua County, 632 So. 2d 806 (Fla. App. 1994). Home School Legal Defense Association. (2002, April 25).

Hazelwood School District v. Kuhlmeier, 484 U.S. 260 (1988).

Home School Legal Defense Association. (2005). State laws. Available online: www.hslda.org/laws/default.asp.

Honig v. Doe, 484 U.S. 305, 108 S. Ct. 592 (1988).

Hunter v. Board of Education of Montgomery County, 425 A. 2d 681 (Md. App. 1981), *aff'd in part and rev'd in part on other grounds,* 439 A. 2d 582 (Md. App. 1982).

Imber, M., & van Geel, T. (2004). *Education law.* (3rd ed.) New York: McGraw-Hill.

Imber, M., & van Geel, T. (2005). *A teacher's guide to education law* (8th ed.). Mahwah, NJ: Erlbaum.

Ingraham v. Wright, 430 U.S. 651, 97 S. Ct 1401, 51 L. Ed. 2d 711 (1977).

Interstate New Teacher Assessment and Support Consortium. (1992). *Model standards for beginning teacher licensing and development: A resource for state dialogue.* Available online: www.ccsso.org/intascst.html#draft.

In re William G., 221 Cal. Rptr. 118 (1985).

Jamieson, Jr., R. L. (2002, July 13). The mascot victory is a triumph to build on. *Seattle Post Intelligencer.* Available online: http://seattlepi.newsource.com/jamieson/78459_robert13.shtml.

LaMorte, M. W. (2005). *School law: Cases and concepts* (8th ed.). Boston: Allyn and Bacon.

Landau, B. (2002). Educating for citizenship. *Education Week,* 21(24), 40, 44.

Lau v. Nichols, 414 U.S. 563 (1974).

Lee v. Weisman, 69 U.S. L.W. 4723 (1992).

Leinwand, D. (2006, July 12). Ore schools test for drugs. *USA Today,* A1.

Lemon v. Kurtzman, 403 U.S. 602, 91 S. Ct. 2105, 29 L. Ed. 2d 745 (1971).

LRP Publications. (1996, May). Five ways to prevent peer sexual harassment. *Your School and the Law,* 26(5), 10.

Mancha v. Field Museum of Natural History, 283 N.E. 2d 899 (Ill. App. 1972).

Martin Luther King, Jr., Elementary School Children v. Michigan Board of Education, 473 F. Suppl., 1371 (1979).

McCarthy, M. M., Cambron-McCabe, N. H., & Thomas, S. B. (2004). *Public school law: Teachers and students' rights* (5th ed.). Boston: Allyn and Bacon.

Morrison v. State Board of Education, 1 Cal. 3d 214, 82 Cal.Rptr. 175, 191, 461 P. 2d. 375, 391 (1969).

National Gay Task Force v. Board of Education of Oklahoma City, 729 F. 2d 1270 (10th Cir. 1984), *aff'd by divided court,* 470 U.S. 903 (1985).

National Organization on Legal Problems of Education. (1988). *Education law update 1987–1988.* Topeka, KS: Author.

New Jersey v. T.L.O., 221 Cal. Rptr. 118 (1985).

Owasso Independent School District v. Falvo, 534 U.S. 426 (2002).

Peter W. v. San Francisco Unified School District, 131 Cal. Rptr. 854 (1976).

Portner, J. (1999, April 7). Drug testing latest tactic in prevention. *Education Week, 18*(30), 1, 16–17.

Rothschild v. *Grottenthaler,* 907 F. 2nd, 286 (1990, June 27).

Rowland v. *Mad River Local School District, Montgomery County, Ohio,* 730 F. 2d 444 (6th Cir. 1984).

School District of Abington Township v. *Schempp,* 374 U.S. 203, 300, 83 S. Ct 1560, 1620 (1963).

Sony Corporation of America v. *Universal City Studios, Inc.,* 464 U.S. 417 (1984) *reh'g denied,* 465 U.S. 1112 (1984).

Station v. *Travelers Insurance Co.,* 292 So. 2d 289 (La. Ct. App. 1974).

Tinker v. *Des Moines Independent Community School District,* 393 U.S. 503, 89 S. Ct. 733, 21 L. Ed. 2d 731 (1969).

U.S. Department of Education. (1999, April 14). IDEA Regulations Published. Available online: www.ed.gov/pubs/EDInitiatives/99/99-03-18.html#4.

U.S. Department of Health and Human Services. (1999). Child Abuse Prevention and Treatment Act. Available online: www.acf.dhhs.gov/programs/cb/policy/capta.htm.

U.S. Department of Health and Human Services, Administration on Children, Youth and Families. (2003). *Child maltreatment 2001.* Washington, DC: U.S. Government Printing Office.

Veronia School Dist. 47J v. *Acton,* 515 U.S. 646 (1995).

Virgil v. *School Board of Columbia County Florida,* 862 F. 2d 1517 (1989).

Wallace v. *Jaffree,* 427 U.S., 38 (1985).

Walsh, M. (1998, June 17). Court allows vouchers in Milwaukee. *Education Week, 17*(40), 1, 16.

Ward v. *Newfield Central School District No. 1,* 412 N.Y.S. 2d 57 (N.Y. App. Div. 1978).

Widmar v. *Vincent,* 454 U.S. 263 (1981).

Williams, V. L. (1999). A new harassment ruling: Implications for colleges. *Chronicle of Higher Education, 65*(41), A56.

Wisconsin v. *Yoder,* 406 U.S. 205 (1972).

Zelman v. *Simmons-Harris,* 536 U.S. No. 00-1751 (2002).

Zirkel, P. A., Richardson, S. N., & Goldberg, S. S. (1995). *A digest of Supreme Court decisions affecting education* (3rd ed.). Bloomington, IN: Phi Delta Kappa Educational Foundation.

CHAPTER 10

Airasian, P. W. (2004). *Assessment in the classroom* (5th ed.). New York: McGraw-Hill.

American School Board Journal. (2007). *Education vital signs: U.S. Schools: The facts & figures.* Alexandria, VA: National School Board Association.

Ansary, T. (2004, November/December). The muddle machine: Confessions of a textbook editor. *Edutopia,* pp. 30–35.

Apple, M. W. (1998). The culture and commerce of the textbook. In *The curriculum: Problems, politics, and possibilities* (2nd ed., pp. 157–166). Albany: State University of New York Press.

Association of American Publishers. (1999). Industry statistics: 1998 preliminary estimated industry net sales. Available online: www.publishers.org/home/stats/index.htm.

Banks, J., & McGee Banks, C. A. (2005). *Multicultural education: Issues and perspectives* (5th ed.). Boston: Allyn and Bacon.

Bloom, B. (1971). Mastery learning. In J. H. Block (Ed.), *Mastery learning: Theory and practice* (pp. 13–28). New York: Holt, Rinehart and Winston.

Blumenfeld, P., Soloway, E., Marx, R., Krajcik, J., Guzdial, M., & Palcinsar, A. (1991). Motivating project-based learning: Sustaining the doing, supporting the learning. *Educational Psychologist, 26*(3 & 4), 369–398.

Borja, R. R. (2005, July 27). Channel One struggling in shifting market. CEO of TV newscast confronts loss of ads and aging. *Education Week, 24*(43), 3, 14.

Brophy, J. (1988). Educating teachers about managing classrooms and students. *Teaching and Teacher Education, 4*(1), 1–18.

Brophy, J. (1996, April). Classroom management as socializing students into clearly articulated roles. Paper presented at the Annual Meeting of the American Educational Research Association, New York.

Brophy, J., & Good, T. (1971). Teacher's communication of differential expectations for children's classroom performance: Some behavior data. *Journal of Educational Psychology, 61,* 365–374.

Brophy, J., & Good, T. (1974). *Teacher–student relationships: Causes and consequences.* New York: Holt, Rinehart and Winston.

Burns, M. (1995). The 8 most important lessons I've learned about organizing my teaching year. *Instructor, 105*(2), 86–88.

Carroll, J. B. (1971). Problems of measurement related to the concept of learning for mastery. In J. H. Block (Ed.), *Mastery learning: Theory and practice* (pp. 29–46). New York: Holt, Rinehart and Winston.

Cuban, L. (1992). Curriculum stability and change. In P. W. Jackson (Ed.), *Handbook of research on curriculum* (pp. 216–217). New York: Macmillan.

DeBoer, G. E. (1991). *A history of ideas in science education: Implications for practice.* New York: Teachers College Press.

Doyle, W. (1986). Classroom organization and management. In M. C. Wittrock (Ed.), *Handbook of research on teaching* (3rd ed., pp. 392–431) New York: Macmillan.

Drake, S. & Burns, R. (2004). *Meeting standards through integrated curriculum.* Alexandria, VA: Association for Supervision and Curriculum Development.

Eggen, P. D., & Kauchak, D. P. (2004). *Strategies for teachers: Teaching content and thinking skills* (5th ed.). Boston: Allyn and Bacon.

Eisner, E. W. (1985). *The educational imagination: On the design and evaluation of school programs* (2nd ed.). New York: Macmillan.

Eisner, E. W. (1992). The misunderstood role of the arts in human development. *Phi Delta Kappan, 73*(8), 591–595.

Eisner, E. (1994). *Cognition and curriculum reconsidered* (2nd ed.). New York: Teachers College Press.

Emerson, R. W. (undated). In R. I. Fitzhenry (Ed.) (1993). *The Harper Book of Quotations* (3rd. ed., p. 136). New York: HarperCollins Publishers.

Emmer, E., Evertson, C. & Anderson, L. (1980). Effective management at the beginning of the school year. *Elementary School Journal, 80,* 221–231.

Frieberg, H. L., & Driscoll, A. (1996). *Universal teaching strategies* (2nd ed.). Boston: Allyn and Bacon.

Goetz v. Ansell, 477 F.2d 636 (2nd Cir. 1973).

Good, T. L., & Brophy, J. E. (2003). *Looking in classrooms* (9th ed.). New York: Addison Wesley Longman.

Grobman, H. (1970). *Developmental curriculum projects: Decision points and processes.* Itasca, IL: Peacock.

Gudmundsdottir, S. (1991). Values in pedagogical content knowledge. *Journal of Teacher Education, 41*(3), 44–52.

Henderson, J. G., & Gornick, R. (2007). *Transformative curriculum leadership* (3rd ed.). Upper Saddle River, NJ: Pearson, Merrill, Prentice Hall.

Henderson, P., & Gysbers, N. C. (1998). *Leading and managing your school guidance program staff.* Alexandria, VA: American Counseling Association.

Holmes, C. S. (2007, April). Putting students first: Winners of ASBJ's Magna Awards work with their communities to help children succeed. *American School Board Journal, 194*(4), 29–32.

Interstate New Teacher Assessment and Support Consortium. (1992). *Model standards for beginning teacher licensing and development: A resource for state dialogue.* Available online: www.ccsso.org/intascst.html#draft.

Jackson, P. W. (1990). *Life in classrooms.* New York: Teachers College Press.

Joyce, B., Weil, M., & Calhoun, E. (2004). *Models of teaching* (7th ed.). Boston: Allyn and Bacon.

Kliebard, H. M. (2002). *Changing course: American curriculum reform in the 20th century.* New York: Teachers College Press.

Kounin, J. S. (1970). *Discipline and group management in classrooms.* New York: Holt, Rinehart and Winston.

Mager, R. F. (1962). *Preparing instructional objectives.* Palo Alto, CA: Fearon.

Marsh, C. J., & Willis, G. (2007). *Curriculum: Alternative approaches, ongoing issues* (4th ed.). Upper Saddle River, NJ: Pearson, Merrill, Prentice Hall.

National Council of Teachers of Mathematics. (1989). *Curriculum and evaluation standards for school mathematics.* Reston, VA: Author.

National Council of Teachers of Mathematics. (1991). *Professional standards for teaching mathematics.* Reston VA: Author.

Rogers, C. (1971). *Client centered therapy.* Boston: Houghton Mifflin.

Rosenthal, R., & Jacobson, L. (1968). *Pygmalion in the classroom: Teacher expectation and pupils' intellectual development.* New York: Holt, Rinehart and Winston.

Slavin, R. E. (1995). *Cooperative learning* (2nd ed.). Boston: Allyn and Bacon.

Slavin, R. E., & Fashola, O. S. (1998). *Show me the evidence! Proven and promising programs for America's schools.* Thousand Oaks, CA: Corwin Press.

Sowell, E. J. (1996). *Curriculum: An integrative introduction.* Upper Saddle River, NJ: Prentice Hall.

Weinstein, C. S., & Mignano, Jr., A. J. (2003). *Elementary classroom management: Lessons from research and practice* (3rd ed.). New York: McGraw-Hill.

West Virginia State Board of Education v. *Barnette,* 319 U.S. 624; 642 (1943).

Wiggins, G., & McTighe, J. (1998). Understanding by design. Alexandria, VA: Association of Supervisors and Curriculum Developers. Available online: www.ascd.org/framebooks.html.

Wiles, J., & Bondi, J. (2007). *Curriculum development: A guide to practice* (7th ed.). Upper Saddle River, NJ: Pearson, Merrill, Prentice Hall.

Wolfgang, C. H., Bennett, B. J., & Irvin, J. L. (1999). *Strategies for teaching self-discipline in the middle grades.* Boston: Allyn and Bacon.

CHAPTER 11

Airasian, P. W. (2004). *Assessment in the classroom: A concise approach* (5th ed.). Boston: McGraw-Hill.

American School Board Journal. (2007). *2007 Education vital signs: U.S. Schools: The facts and figures.* Alexandria, VA: National School Boards Association.

Bloom, B. (1982). *Human characteristics and school learning.* New York: McGraw-Hill.

Gage, N. L. (1985). *Hard gains in the soft sciences: The case of pedagogy.* Bloomington, IN: Phi Delta Kappa's Center on Evaluation, Development and Research.

Hardy, J. (2007, January). Technology and program evaluation. *American School Board Journal, 193*(01) 29–31.

Interstate New Teacher Assessment and Support Consortium. (1992). *Model standards for beginning teacher licensing and development: A resource for state dialogue.* Available online: www.ccsso.org/intascst.html#draft.

Jones, E. D., Southern, W. T., & Brigham, F. J. (1998, March). Curriculum-based assessment: Testing what is taught and teaching what is tested. *Intervention in School and Clinic, 33*(4), 239–249.

Mackey, J., & Appleman, D. (1988). Questioning skill. In R. McNergney (Ed.), *Guide to classroom teaching.* (pp. 145–146). Boston Allyn and Bacon.

Maryland State Department of Education. (2000). The Maryland School Performance Assessment Program

(MSPAP). Available online: www.mdk12.org/mspp/mspap/how-scored/mspap_info/index.html.

National Council of Teachers of Mathematics. (2000). About principles and standards and E-standards. Available online: http://standards.nctm.org/info/about.htm.

National Research Council. (2001). *Knowing what students know: The science and design of educational assessment.* Committee on the Foundations of Assessment. J. Pelligrino, N. Chudowsky, & R. Glaser (Eds.). Board of Testing and Assessment, Center for Education. bibliodiv of Behavioral and Social Sciences and Education. Washington, DC: National Academy Press.

Nebraska Department of Education. (2005). School-based, Teacher-led, Assessment, Reporting System (STARS). Available online: www.nde.state.ne.us/stars/index.html.

Popham, W. J. (2005). *Classroom assessment: What teachers need to know* (4th ed.). Boston: Allyn and Bacon.

Reeves, D. B. (2004, December). The case against the zero. *Phi Delta Kappan, 86*(4) 324–325.

Shea, M., Murray, R., & Harlin, R. (2005). *Drowning in data? How to collect, organize, and document student performance* (p. xiv). Portsmouth, NH: Heinemann.

CHAPTER 12

Behal, S. (2002, April 26). Caste cruelty makes school a nightmare. *Times Educational Supplement,* no. 4478, p. 18.

Berliner, D. C. & Biddle, B. J. (1995). *The manufactured crisis: Myths, fraud, and the attack on America's public schools.* Reading, MA: Addison-Wesley.

Boyer, E. (1992). Educating in a multicultural world. In D. Bragaw & W. S. Thomson (Eds.), *Multicultural education: A global approach* (pp. 48–53). New York: The American Forum for Global Education.

Bracey, G. W. (2002, January 23). International comparisons: An excuse to avoid meaningful educational reform. *Education Week, 21*(19), 30, 32. Available online: www.edweek.com/ew/newstory.cfm?slug=19bracey.h21&keywords=timss.

Burns, J. (2002, July 26). Liberation through education. *TES.* Available online: www.tes.co.uk/search/search_display.asp?section=Archive&sub_section=Scotland&id=366885&Type=0.

Carnevale, A. P. (2005, February 2). Education and the economy: If we're so dumb, why are we so rich? *Education Week, 24*(21), 40–41, 52. Available online: www.edweek.org/ew/articles/2005/02/02/21carnevale.h24.html?querystring=India.

Cavanaugh, S. (2005, February 9). Researchers cite uniform standards in Singapore's success. *Education Week, 24*(22), 10. Available online: www.edweek.org/ew/articles/2005/02/09/22math.h24.html?querystring=singapore/.

CIA (2008). The world factbook: India. Available online: https://www.cia.gov/library/publications/the-world-factbook/print/in.html.

Fiske, E. B. & Ladd, H. F. (2005, March 16). Learning from South Africa. *Education Week 24*(27), 38, 52. Available online: www.edweek.org/ew/articles/2005/03/16/27fiske.h24.html?querystring=south%20africa.

Goya, S. (1994). Japanese education: Hardly known facts. *Education Digest, 59*(8), 8–12.

Guha, S. (2002). In pursuit of learning: Educational programs for at-risk children in India. *Childhood Education, 78*(4), 206–209.

Hanushek, E. A. (2005, February 2). Education and the economy: Our school performance matters. *Education Week, 24*(24), 40–41, 52. Available online: www.edweek.org/ew/articles/2005/02/02/21hanushek.h24.html?querystring=TIMSS.

Huerta, A. E. (1999). *Las Trampas de la identidad en un mundo de mujeres.* Mexico: Editorial Itaca.

ICONS (undated). Eden Project. Available online: http://www.icons.org.uk/theicons/collection/eden-project.

Interstate New Teacher Assessment and Support Consortium. (1992). *Model standards for beginning teacher licensing and development: A resource for state dialogue.* Available online: www.ccsso.org/intascst.html#draft.

Keating, C. (2005, January 2). Austin schools, Mexican state agree to compete in athletics. *The Washington Post,* No. 28, p. A2.

King, E. J. (1988). South Africa. In T. N. Postlethwaite (Ed.), *The encyclopedia of comparative education and national systems of education* (2nd ed., pp. 600–605). Oxford: Pergamon Press.

Lemmer, E. M. (1993). Educational renewal in South Africa: Problems and prospects. *Compare, 23*(1), 53–62.

Lollock, L. (2001, January). The foreign-born population in the United States: Population characteristics. Washington, DC: U.S. Department of Commerce, Economics and Statistics Administration, U.S. Census Bureau. Available online: www.census.gov/prod/2000pubs/p20-534.pdf.

Martin, M. O., Mullis, I. V. S., Gonzalez, E. J., Gregory, K. D., Smith, T. A., Chrostowski, S. J., Garden, R. A., & O'Connor, K. M. (2000, December). *TIMSS 1999 International Science Report Findings from IEA's Repeat of the Third International Science and Science Study at the Eighth Grade.* Boston: Boston College, International Study Center. Available online: http://isc.bc.edu/timss1999i/science_achievement_report.html.

Mehta, A. C. (2007). *Elementary education in India: Analytical report 2005–06.* India: National University of Educational Planning and Administration.

Mullis, I. V. S., Martin, M. O., Gonzalez, E. J., Gregory, K. D., Garden, R. A., O'Connor, K. M., Chrostowski, S. J., & Smith, T. A. (2000, December). *TIMSS 1999 International Mathematics Report Findings from IEA's Repeat of the Third International Mathematics and Science Study.* Available online: http://isc.bc.edu/timss1999benchmark.html.

Reyes, M. E. (1995). Mexico. In T. N. Postlethwaite (Ed.), *International encyclopedia of national systems of education* (2nd ed., pp. 643–652). New York: Elsevier.

Rock, T., & Wilson, C. (2005). Improving teaching through lesson study. *Teacher Education Quarterly.* Available online: http://findarticles.com/p/articles/mi_qa3960/is_200501/ai_n9522068.

Rosegaard, M. H. (2006). *Japanese education and the cram school business: Functions, challenges and perspectives of the juku.* Copenhagen: NIAS.

Rowe, M. B. (1986). Wait time: Slowing down may be a way of speeding up. *Journal of Teacher Education, 37*(1), 43–50.

Schools for a global age: Promising practices in international education. (2005). *Edutopia.* Available online: www.edutopia.org/products/report.php.

Singapore Department of Statistics. (2001). Census of population 2000. Available online: www.singstat.gov.sg/keystats/c2000/topline2.pdf.

Smith, F. (2006). Cool schools: Global superpower. *Edutopia, 2*(8), 24–27.

Stevenson, H. W., & Stigler, J. W. (1992). *The learning gap: Why our schools are failing and what we can learn from Japanese and Chinese education.* New York: Summit.

Tanner, D., & Tanner, L. (2007). *Curriculum development: Theory into practice* (4th ed.). Upper Saddle River, NJ: Pearson, Merrill, & Prentice Hall.

The TES. (2008, Feburary 22). From culture to collective worship: How the latest government initiatives will affect schools. Available online: http://www.tes.co.uk/search/story/?story_id=2583921.

U.S. Census (2006). Facts for features. Available online: http://www.ccnsus.gov/.

Union of International Associations. (2002). International organizations and NGOS Project. Available online: www.uia.org/organizations/.

Westbury, I. (1992). Comparing American and Japanese achievement: Is the United States really a low achiever? *Educational Researcher, 21*(5), 18–24.

Wallace, C., & Steptoe, S. (2006). How to bring our schools out of the 20th century. *Time 168*(25), 50–56.

Wieczorek, C. C. (2008, Winter). Comparative analysis of educational systems of American and Japanese schools: Views and visions. *Educational Horizons, 86*(2), 99–111.

Wilcox, J. D. (2004). *A Middle East primer for students.* Lanham, MD: Scarecrow Press.

Wood, A. (2002, February 15). Suspended aged six for wearing headscarves. *Times Education Supplement.* Available online: www.tes.co.usearch_display.asp?section=Archive&sub_section=News+%26+opinion&id=359809&Type=.

Wu, A. (1999). The Japanese education system: A case study and analysis. National Institute on Student Achievement, Curriculum, and Assessment, Office of Educational Research and Improvement, U.S. Department of Education. Available online: www.ed.gov/pubs/ResearchToday/98-3038.html.

CHAPTER 13

Appalachia Educational Laboratory. (2005, April 13). *A guide to gender fair education in science and mathematics* Available online: www.enc.org/resources/records/0,1240,017094,00.shtm.

Bohlin, K. E., Farmer, D., & Ryan, K. (2001). *Building character in schools resource guide.* San Francisco: Jossey-Bass.

Brophy, J. (1999). *Teaching.* Geneva, Switzerland: International Academy of Education, International Bureau of Education, UNESCO.

Brophy, J., & McCaslin, M. (1992). Teachers' reports of how they perceive and cope with problem students. *Elementary School Journal, 93*(1), 3–68.

Bushweller, K. (2005, May 4). Technology report tracks spending shift. *Education Week, 24*(34), 11.

Century Foundation Task Force on the Common School. (2002). Divided we fail: Coming together through public school choice. New York: Century Foundation Press. Available online: www.tcf.org/Publications/Education/dividedwefail.pdf.

CEO Forum on Education and Technology. (2000). *Teacher preparation StaR Chart: A self-assessment tool for colleges of education.* Washington, DC: Author.

CEO Forum on Educational Technology. (2001, June). *Key building blocks for student achievement in the 21st century: Assessment, alignment, accountability, access, analysis.* Washington, DC: Author.

Clandinin, D. J., & Connelly, F. M. (1996). Teachers' professional knowledge landscapes: Teacher stories—stories of teachers—school stories—stories of schools. *Educational Researcher, 25*(3), 24–30.

Dillon, S. (2005, March 6). Education law finds few fans in Utah. *New York Times,* p. A33. Available online: www.nytimes.com/2005/03/06/national/06Utah.html.

Ellis, K. (2005, July 13). Media smarts. *Edutopia.* Available online: www.edutopia.org/php/article.php?id=Art_1321.

Fox, E. (2005, May 5). Tracking U.S. trends. There is now almost no difference in the availability of Internet access between poor schools and wealthy ones. *Education Week, 24*(35), 40–42.

Good, T. L., & Brophy, J. E. (2003). *Looking in classrooms.* New York: Addison Wesley Longman.

Grabe, M., & Grabe, C. (2000). *Integrating the Internet for meaningful learning.* Boston: Houghton Mifflin.

Honawar, V. (2005, March 9). Education department tracks growth in distance learning. *Education Week, 24*(26), 6.

Interstate New Teacher Assessment and Support Consortium. (1992). *Model standards for beginning teacher licensing and development: A resource for state dialogue.* Available online: www.ccsso.org/intascst.html#draft.

Manzo, K. K. (2002). Kansas City turns classrooms over to interns. *Education Week, 22*(5), 5.

Major Gates Foundation grants to support small high schools. (2005, June 16). *Education Week, 23*(40), 28–29.

Metzger, S. (2005a, May 5). California. *Education Week, 24*(35), 56.

Metzger, S. (5 May 2005b, May 5). Texas. *Education Week, 24*(35), 76.

Mitzel, H. E. (1960). Teacher effectiveness. In C. W. Harris (Ed.), *Encyclopedia of educational research* (3rd ed., pp. 1481–1486). New York: Macmillan.

Moawa, E. (2005, March 1). Up to speed. Many schools are trying to leave no immigrant family behind. *Education Week, 16*(5), 13.

Myatt, L. (2005, April 6). Nine friction points in moving to smaller school units. *Education Week, 24*(30), 34, 36–37.

National Association of State Boards of Education. (2001). *Any time, any place, any path, any pace: Taking the lead on e-learning policy.* Alexandria, VA: Author.

National Center on Education and the Economy. (2007). Tough Choices or Tough Times: The report of the new commission on the skills of the American workforce. Available online: www.skillscommission.org.

Noddings, N. (1984). *Caring: A feminine approach to ethics and moral education.* Berkeley: University of California Press.

Noddings, N. (1992). Gender and the curriculum. In P. W. Jackson (Ed.), *Handbook of research on curriculum* (pp. 659–686). New York: Macmillan.

Palchick, M., & Stewart, J. (2005, January 12). 10 basic rules for E-rate applications. Securing a fair share of $2 billion in federal funds. *Education Week, 24*(18), 30.

Raspberry, W. (2005, July 18). A culture for teaching. *The Washington Post,* p. A15.

Russell, N. M. (2007, June). Teaching more than English: Connecting ESL students to their community through service learning. *Phi Delta Kappan, 88*(10), 770–771.

Shulman, L. S. (1986). Paradigms and research programs in the study of teaching. In M. C. Wittrock (Ed.), *Handbook of research on teaching* (3rd ed., pp. 3–36). New York: Macmillan.

UNESCO (2002). *Gender sensitivity: A training manual for sensitizing educational managers, curriculum and material developers and media professionals to gender concerns.* Paris, France: UNESCO. Available online: http://unesdoc.unesco.org/images/0012/001281/1281 66eb.pdf.

Viadero, D. (2005, May 11). Long-awaited study shows 'success for all' gains. *Education Week, 24*(36), 3, 15.

NOTE: Page references followed by *f* indicate figures; *t*, tables.

Photo Credits:

Chapter 1

p. 5: Frank Siteman

Chapter 2

p. 27: RubberBall RF

Chapter 3

p. 52: Lindfors Photography

Chapter 4

p. 69: Courtesy of the National Library of Medicine

p. 71: Carondelet Historic Center

p. 72: North Wind Picture Archives

p. 74: North Wind Picture Archives

p. 76: North Wind Picture Archives

p. 78: North Wind Picture Archives

p. 80 (top): North Wind Picture Archives

p. 80 (bottom): Lyrl Ahern

p. 81: North Wind Picture Archives

Chapter 5

p. 97: Courtesy of the Library of Congress

p. 99: Messinger/Corbis

p. 100: Courtesy of Joanne McNergney

p. 101 (top): North Wind Picture Archives

p. 101 (middle): Courtesy of the Library of Congress

p. 101 (bottom): Courtesy of the Library of Congress

p. 107: Courtesy of the Daulton Public Library

Chapter 6

p. 120: North Wind Picture Archives

p. 121: North Wind Picture Archives

Chapter 7

p. 143: Frank Siteman

Chapter 8

p. 178: Robert Harbison

Chapter 9

p. 190: Robert Harbison

Chapter 10

p. 215: Ian Shaw/Stone/Getty Images

p. 220: Courtesy of Virginia Blanford

p. 231: Brian Smith

Chapter 13

p. 301: Lindfors Photography;

p. 306: Anthony John Colletti Photography